Thomas Hearne, Charles Edward Doble

Remarks and collections of Thomas Hearne

Thomas Hearne, Charles Edward Doble

Remarks and collections of Thomas Hearne

ISBN/EAN: 9783742858269

Manufactured in Europe, USA, Canada, Australia, Japa

Cover: Foto ©Thomas Meinert / pixelio.de

Manufactured and distributed by brebook publishing software
(www.brebook.com)

Thomas Hearne, Charles Edward Doble

Remarks and collections of Thomas Hearne

REMARKS AND COLLECTIONS

OF

THOMAS HEARNE

𝔖𝔲𝔲𝔪 𝔠𝔲𝔦𝔮𝔲𝔢

VOL. I

(JULY 4, 1705 — MARCH 19, 1707)

EDITED BY

C. E. DOBLE, M.A.

WORCESTER COLLEGE, OXFORD

𝔒𝔵𝔣𝔬𝔯𝔡

PRINTED FOR THE OXFORD HISTORICAL SOCIETY

AT THE CLARENDON PRESS

1885

PREFACE.

IT is but a tardy act of reparation to a scholar who was neglected during life, and has been imperfectly appreciated in the century and a half which has elapsed since his death, for an Oxford Historical Society to select as one of its earliest issues a portion of the writings of THOMAS HEARNE. We should have to go very far back, and to come down to our own day, in order to find many names worthy to be placed beside his on the roll of Oxford *alumni* who have done distinguished service to the cause of historical research. To supersede those numerous editions of the sources of English history which HEARNE gave to the world in a too brief lifetime of fifty-seven years, the resources of the Treasury, with a large staff of learned specialists at its disposal, have been employed for a generation past. HEARNE's *Remarks and Collections,* of which the first instalment is now before us, contain fragments of the materials of which he afterwards made such excellent use, beside memoranda on any subject that attracted his attention at the moment. It may be readily conceded that the words of Bentley—surely as magnificent a eulogy as was ever pronounced on one scholar by another—are not in their full sense applicable to our antiquary :—*The very dust of his writings is gold.* But we certainly claim that with the dust very much gold is mingled. That delightful book *Reliquiae Hearnianae,* originally printed in a small edition by Dr. Philip Bliss (Oxford, 2 vols. 8vo., 1857), and afterwards published with additional matter in 3 vols. (London, 1869), hardly professes to contain more than a series of illustrative selections. It may safely be said that until these Diaries of HEARNE's (to give them a title which he himself rejected), together with his extensive Correspondence, are rendered accessible to students in a more complete form than hitherto, the history of the Nonjurors, and that of the Universities in the earlier portion of the eighteenth century, cannot be finally written. And if it be objected that the history of the Nonjurors is of purely antiquarian interest, we need only point to the numerous questions concerning the relations between the ecclesiastical and civil power which agitate men's minds at the present day, and which Sancroft and Kettlewell, Dodwell and Hickes, Collier and Ken, had thought out and illustrated with various learning, nearly two centuries ago. As a proof of the importance, in the

annals of English and indeed of European scholarship, of the body to
which HEARNE belonged, it is only necessary to recall the words of one
whose singular competence to judge will be universally admitted.   Professor John E. B. Mayor writes, in the Preface to the *Life of Ambrose
Bonwicke* :—*Perhaps* . . *the time has come when one may venture, without
offence or loss of intellectual caste, to challenge the vulgar verdict upon the
Nonjurors ; and may at least call on their censors to name any English sect
as eminent, in proportion to its numbers, alike for solid learning, and for
public as well as private virtues.*   There is yet another subject on which
these Collections must be most carefully consulted, and that is one the
importance and interest of which such a Society as ours is scarcely likely
to underrate—I mean the *personnel* of the Oxford of HEARNE's day.   The
Athenae Oxonienses ends shortly before 1700; this work takes up the
thread a few years later, and, at all events until Dr. Rawlinson's Continuation of Wood's great work appears in print, must remain our chief
authority on Oxford men and manners in the first half of the century.
There is indeed no Laud or Fell dominating the Oxford with which we
are dealing ; but even this first volume brings us into contact with many
men whose names are part of the annals of scholarship,—such as Mill,
Hody, and Potter; Halley, Gregory, and Hudson; Wanley, Gibson,
and Tanner.   There is much original work; the spirit of research, the
newborn spirit of criticism, is abroad.

This is not the place to give a full biography of HEARNE; that must
be done when the ' Collections ' are completely published, and when the
editor who has succeeded to me and my imperfect work has only to
gather up the scattered references in the Diary, and to piece them together
with what we know from HEARNE's Autobiography and from other sources
of the details of this laborious and well-spent life.   It must suffice here
to recapitulate very briefly a few of the leading facts.   The Diarist was the
son of George Hearne, parish-clerk of White Waltham, Berks, and was
born in July 1678, so that when the Diary opens he was just completing
his twenty-seventh year.   On account of his boyish promise, he was sent to
Bray School at the suggestion of Mr. Francis Cherry, of Shottesbrooke,
who in 1695 took him into his own house, and, in concert with Henry
Dodwell, superintended his education.   He was entered in December
1695 a 'Batteler' of Edmund Hall, of which Dr. Mill was then Principal,
and Dr. White Kennett, Rector of Shottesbrooke, Vice-Principal.   While
still an undergraduate, he assisted Mill, Grabe, and other scholars
with collations of MSS., transcripts, &c.; several instances are mentioned in the present volume.   After taking his B.A. degree in 1699 he
was urged to undertake mission work in Maryland, together with the

general supervision of the libraries of that province ; but his inclination to the study of Antiquities was already too strong, and he accepted the office of Assistant Keeper under Dr. Hudson, then Bodley's Librarian. In 1703 he took the degree of Master of Arts, and refused the offer of a chaplaincy at Corpus Christi and at All Souls Colleges. HEARNE'S appointment at the Bodleian was therefore his only official post when he made the first entry in the Diary on July 4, 1705. It should be added that, beside Indexes to L'Estrange's *Translation of Josephus* (1702), to Milles' edition of Cyril (1703), to Dr. Edwards' *Preservative against Socinianism* and to Clarendon's *History of the Rebellion* (1704), he had published the following works :—

(1) *Reliquiae Bodleianae ; or, some Genuine Remains of Sir Thomas Bodley* (London, 1703).

(2) *C. Plinii Caecilii Secundi Epistolae et Panegyricus* (Oxford, 1703).

(3) *Eutropii Breviarium Historiae Romanae* (Oxford, 1703).

(4) *Ductor Historicus.* Vol. I. ed. 2. [part only] (London, 1705).
      ,,   ,,   Vol. II. (Oxford, 1704).

(5) *M. Juniani Justini Historiarum ex Trogo Pompeio Libri XLIV.* (Oxford, 1705).

HEARNE was at this time accumulating materials for his edition of Livy, which was published at Oxford in 1708. With regard to the state of public affairs when the Diary opens, the reader need only be reminded that the great victory of Blenheim in the previous year had consolidated the Whig party; that a General Election took place in the spring of 1705, and that, when the new Parliament met, the Whigs found themselves in possession of a working majority.

I must, in conclusion, indicate in a few words what the reader will find in these pages. They contain the substance of thirteen only out of the 145 MS. volumes in which the *Collections* are comprised. I have sought to include all the matter of the original which seemed to me in any way interesting, and to summarise what was not worth printing in full; but I am conscious of a few omissions which may furnish a portion of the material for a supplementary volume. It is only fair to say that this first volume must be the least interesting of the series. As we proceed, the entries become more elaborate and less of the nature of hasty jottings, while HEARNE is continually advancing in literary repute and enlarging the circle of his literary acquaintance. I have adopted a uniform mode of printing the date of each entry ; but with this exception I have made it a rule to enclose in square brackets every word that is not in the original. To save space, thick dashes (—) have been employed to denote a change of topic or of paragraph. It will of course be understood that the notes which are not bracketed are the author's own. As regards the Correspondence, an abstract of which is printed at the foot of the page, it has not been thought necessary to give the precise reference in each case, as the Letters—with the exception of those of Dr. Thomas Smith to HEARNE (Bodl. MS. Smith 127)—are all bound up in one Series (Bodl. MSS. Rawl. Letters), and any particular letter can be readily found by consulting the excellent Slip Index, arranged in chronological order, which has been provided by the Society for the purposes of this edition.

Finally, I must ask the kind indulgence of my critics, on account of the many difficulties—some personal, some inherent in the nature of the work —with which I have had to contend in its execution. They cannot be more dissatisfied with the result than myself—and this remark applies especially to the Notes, where I have found it necessary to confine myself almost entirely to identifying the persons mentioned, and to indicating the most obvious sources of information. I have not been able, for various reasons, to make by any means an adequate use of the manuscript treasures of the Bodleian, and have been obliged too often to content myself with the books bearing on the subject to be found in my own modest library. But one duty yet remains, and that a wholly pleasant one, viz. to return my warmest acknowledgments to my friends Mr. T. W. Jackson, M.A., Fellow and Tutor of Worcester College, and Mr. F. Madan, M.A., Sub-librarian of the Bodleian, and late Fellow and Lecturer of Brasenose College, who have given me constant help and sympathy, and have supplied me with much valuable information on special points. I wish that I had been able to draw even more freely on the stores of knowledge which they are ever so ready to place at the disposal of other workers. Nor must I forget to express my thanks to Mr. George Parker, of the Bodleian, for his accurate transcription, and for his assistance in the compilation of the temporary Index to this volume.

C. E. D.

OXFORD:
March 25, 1885.

Suum cuique.

THOMAS HEARNE.

VOL. I.

PICTURES in the Gallery of the Publick Library[1]. [1–51.] ...
Vettius Valens collected his *Anthologia* from divers old Authors, now
lost, wch makes it so much the more valuable. D^r. Bernard transcrib'd
part of it for Huetius, who promis'd to print ye whole Work at Paris:
But w^t hinder'd him I know not.

July 4, 1705 (Wed.). M^r. W^m. Joyner told me that M^r. Selden writ
ye Life of Fryer Bacon. But he cannot tell where 'tis now. At ye same
time he gave large Encomiums of M^r. Milton: but denyes that he died a
Papist. — L^d. Wharton and L^d. Godolphin have differ'd very much: so that
the latter has promis'd to come over to the High Church Party. Upon 10
wch Account the L^ds. Rochester and Northumberland have had some
private Discourse with the Queen. — Vettius Valens, p. 153, writes an
Epistle to one Marcus. Quære who this should be? Mr. D. does not
think him to be Marcus Antoninus. The same Marcus is mention'd
again in p. 138. The whole work seems to be writ to him. M^r. D.
thinks he liv'd in Antoninus Pius's time, as being several times mention'd
by him. The last note being the 21st year of his Reign. See p. 146 a.
Scaliger in his Notes upon Eusebius believes he flourish'd in ye Reign of
Adrian. M^r. Dodwell being writing a Book concerning the Immortality
of the Soul may have occasion to mention his Age, and to insert a Frag- 20
ment out of him, there being a Passage to his Purpose. — Salmasius was
a Person who did not consider very accurately what he writ; being more
addicted to Writing and the laborious part of Learning, than true Study,
wch consists in a due consideration of w^t one reads. — The Translation
into English of the first six Books of Euclid, with Annotations upon
them, lately Printed, was done by S^r. Charles Scarburgh, and not M^r.
Edm. Scarburgh his Son, who hath put his name to them. For 'tis well
known that he is not able to do any thing of this kind, or any thing else
relating to Learning. — D^r. Mill's[2] Testam^t one of the best Books of its
kind ever yet done. He has now (July 6th 1705.) been eight years or 30
thereab^ts about his Prolegomena. W^n I first came to settle at Oxon, viz.

---

[1] This List is printed from a Letter I sent to London in 1708.
[2] Yet he was not so accurate in collating the most ancient Copies as could have been
wished.

A⁰ 1696, he was then upon his Appendix, & I help'd him compare several MSSᵗˢ for that end.

    July 6 (Fri.). . . .

    ¹ Ex Anthologia Vettij Valentis in Bibl. Bodl. Arch. Seld. 35, fol. 153. . .

    Sʳ. Gᵉᵒ. Mackenzy p. 8 of his Jus Regium tells us that Buchanan's Book *De jure Regni apud Scotos* was condemn'd by the Parliament of Scotland in Anno 1584, wᶜʰ he says was the very first Parliament yᵗ ever sate after that Book was printed : wᶜʰ is a great Error, there being a Parliament in 1581, & the first Edition was in 1580, if not 1579. — I am told that Dʳ. John Edwards of Cambridge, Author of *The Preacher,* (wᶜʰ some say, tho' I think otherwise, is a very trite, silly Book) has assum'd to himself the Honour of being Author of *The Preservative against Socinianism,* written by Dʳ. Jonathan Edwards, Principal of Jesus College in Oxford. — A. Popma collected Fragmenta Sallustij, printed in a seperate Book from his Fragmenta veterum Historicorum Latinorum. I have not yet seen it. — I am told of a 2ᵈ Edition of Mʳ. Dodwell's Book against Occasional Conformity, wᶜʰ I have not yet observ'd. (nec quidem constat talem prodijs[s]e Editionem.) — Amongst Mʳ. Selden's MSSᵗˢ in the Publick Library is a very old one, (Seld. Supra num. 12.) written above 700 years since, containing several Things of Philo, some pieces whereof being commentaries upon the Commandments, were never yet printed. See there fol. 59, and compare it wᵗʰ the Printed Copies. Mʳ. Grabe has a fair Transcript wᶜʰ he has communicated to Mʳ. Dodwell². — Amongst the Baroccian MSSᵗˢ is a Comment upon Aristides. Mʳ. Bergerus, lately admitted a Student in the Publick Library, (being Professor of Poetry in the University of Wittemberg) is taking a Copy of it wᵗʰ a Design to make it publick in a new Edition of Aristides, wᶜʰ I am inform'd he intends to put forth.

    July 7 (Sat.). Some Corrections of Livy in Pareus's Lexicon Criticum. — Lately found at Wells the Hair of a Woman very fresh and firm, tho' she had been buried above 140 Years, as appears from the Date.

    July 8 (Sun.). Morhofius in his Polyhistor has given but a very indifferent Character of our English Authors, especially such as have written in Latin. He finds several Faults in Milton, tho' it is well known that his Latin is much better yⁿ Salmasius's. — I am inform'd that Morhofius's Discourse³ *De Livij Patavinitate* is judiciously written. I have not yet seen it. Mʳ. Berger has a Discourse upon yᵉ same subject not yet publish'd. — Sⁱʳ James Astrey tells me he was imploy'd by the University of Oxoñ to buy for yᵐ Dʳ. Isaac Vossius's Study of Books, & yᵗ upon their Refusal to give yᵉ Price wᶜʰ was demanded, Grævius procur'd the most considerable.

    Ex MS. Baroc., num. 91, f. 17 a. τοῦ ἁγιωτάτου Πατριάρχου . . . εἴη μετὰ πάντων τῶν τὴν ὀρθοδοξίαν ἀσπαζομένων.

    Germanus was made Patriarch of Constantinople Anno 1222, but

---

    ¹ See Mr. Dodwell's Discourse about the Distinction betw. Soul and Spirit. p. 245. . . . Ad cl. Dodwellum misi hujus exscripti partem, qui et edidit in libro de Animae Immortalitate.

    ² Cl. Dodwellus plura ex hoc codice propria exscripsit manu quae nunc habentur apud chartas ejus ineditas.

    ³ Ex quo hoc scripsi, vidi equidem & perlegi.

resided at Nice, whither the Patriarchate had been translated upon the Taking of Constantinople by the Latins.

July 9 (Mon.). Just publish'd *The Memorial of the Church of England,* a Pamphlet in 4to, wherein divers intrigues of a great Minister of State are discovered, and the Designs of the Whigs for destroying the Church are manifested. — Sr James Astrey tells me that Morhofius's Posthumous Works are lately publish'd, & That his tract *de Livij Patavinitate* is reprinted amongst y^m. — In M^r. Badger's Copy of Aldus's Ed. of Pliny's Epp. is a MS^t Epistle concerning Pliny of P. Beroaldus ad Jo. Vectimbergensem. The Beginning Epistolicam Scriptionem, quæ longe omnium utilissima est—with a Poem. — He has also a curious edition of Phavorinus's Lexicon in a small neat Letter wch I never saw before. There is an Index at the End, wch I think is in ye other Editions. He likewise shew'd me a Lexicon to the Greek Testament done by M^r. W^m. Dugard, much after ye same manner with Smidius's Concordance.

July 10 (Tu.). *Cassiodorus de Reyna* Author of ye Spanish Version of ye Bible. — Remember to consult upon Livy *Fabrettus contra Gronovium & Gronovius contra Fabrettum.* Also *Scheffer de re vehiculari* (where are Emendations) . . . *Boxhornius* . . . & Lucius Florus by Freinshemius. . .— Concerning K. Ælfred's Works relating to Learning see D^r. *Tho. Smith's Bibl. Cot. Hist. & Synopsis,* p. xxxiii. — One of the Græcians of Glocester Hall tells me w^n he came out of his Country he brought with him a Greek MS^t written above a thousand years since in capital Letters, and containing all S^t. Paul's Epistles & Part of ye Old Testament. But that the ship being taken by the French he lost it, with another Gr. Printed Book in Folio, containing Simeon Thessalonicensis de Statu Ecclesiæ Græcæ. — Remember to put Dr. Smith in mind to ask Dr. Lister to send to the Publick Library his new Edition of *Apicius de Opsonijs.*

Literae Christinae Suedorum Reginae Octavio Ferrario Patavium Missae. [96–99.]

— Newent in Gloucestershire.

Mr. Timothy Nourse, who dyed July 21st 1699. gave to ye Bodlejan Library by his last Will and Testament, as followeth, in these Words:

Item, I give to the Bodlejan Library in Oxford All my Collection of Coines and Medalls whether of Gold Silver or Copper, being in all about Five or Six Hundred Pieces in thankful Remembrance of the Obligations I have to that famous University.

This was faithfully transcribed out of the said Will

By me, ABRA. MORSE, Rector de Huntley in Com. Glouc.

Gould peeces 2, White 121, Copper 409, In all 532. A Brass Buckle.

That wch is above Written is a Copy of the Paper sent by Mr. Morse now in the Publick Library. —

Mr. Ant. à Wood in the II^d vol. of *Ath. Oxon.* col. 595, tells us that M^r. Andr. Allam had laid ye Foundation of a *Notitia Ecclesiæ Anglicanæ,* wherein he would have spoke of ye Foundation of all Cathedrals, with a touch of their Statutes and Customs, together with the names of the Present B^p., Dean, Archdeacon, Canons & Officers of each Cathedral.— These Papers I think Dr. Kennett perus'd after his Death, & extracted from them several materials, wch will be of great Service to him in a Book he is now upon conc. the Foundation of Churches in England. — 'Tis said M^r. King, who writ *the History of the Apostles Creed*, is now upon an Ecclesiastical History, wch will commence wth the Birth of Christ.

July 11 (Wed.). Out of a MS^t wch D^r. Hudson borrowed of Sir John Osborn, containing divers curious things relating to the Reigns of Ed. 3^d and Hen. 5th (wch however Mr. Tyrrel says (See below, pag. 133) contains little but w^t we have an Account of in print already).

Te Matrem laudamus, te Dominam confitemur, te aeterni patris præelectam veneramur. | Tibi omnes Angli, tibi coeli & universae potestates, tibi
10 Cherubin & Seraphin humili nobiscum voce proclamant, Ave, Ave, Ave Maria, Virgo Theotecos |. Pleni sunt coeli & terra majestate filij tui, | Te gloriosam Apostoli praedicant | Te gloriosam prophetae pronunciant |. Te pretiosam martires floribus circumdant | Te per orbem terrarum sancta confitetur Ecclesia, matrem immensae majestatis, venerandam Dei sponsam marisque nesciam, sanctam quoque solamque gravidam Spiritu. Tu Regina es coeli, tu Domina es totius mundi, tu ad liberandum hominem perditum vestisti altissimum filium, tu vincendo mortis aculeo protulisti clarissimo vitam ex utero, tu ad dextram nati sedes dignitate matris. Te ergo quaesumus Angligenis subveni, quos pro dote propria defendisti, aeterna fac cum sanctis
20 ejus gloria numerari, salvum fac populum tuum domina, et a mortis peste dotem tuam libera. Et rege eos et extolle illos usque in aeternum. Per singulos dies benedicimus te, et laudamus nomen tuum in saeculum, quae cunctas Haereses sola interemisti. | Dignare domina laude digna in fide firma nos custodire. Miserere nostri Domina mater misericordiae. Fiat misericordia filij tui Domina super nos ope tua qui clamitamus illi. In te Domina speramus, non confundamur in aeternum.

This is the conclusion of the Book, being the last Chapter of an anonymous piece conc. the Acts of Hen. Vth. The contents of this Hymn are thus worded: De Hymno à gente Anglorum cantando ad
30 laudem Dei genitricis mariæ, propter gloriosam expeditionem Regis Henrici quinti, & pro successu Regni Angliae dotis suae, quae cunctas Haereses cum Haeresiarcha Johanne Oldecastel suis precibus interemit. — Tables of the Grecian, Roman & Jewish Measures, Weights & Coins; reduc'd to the English Standard, by Jo. Arbuthnott. *Lond.* 1705, 8°... — M^r. Proast in his 2^d Letter conc. Toleration, p. 37. says That Miracles were continued till Christianity was received for ye Religion of the Empire, not so much to evince the Truth of ye Christian Religion, as to supply the Want of the Magistrates' Assistance, & quotes M^r. Dodwell's Second Dissertation to favour his opinion; but M^r. Lock in his Answer
40 to y^t Letter (viz. in p. 263 of a Third Letter for Toleration) shews that he has misrepresented Mr. Dodwell's meaning. M^r. Dodwell being now in Oxford, I ask'd him wch was in the right, & he was pleas'd to tell me y^t M^r. Lock had fairly explain'd his sense, & that he did not remember that he had said anything wch Mr. Proast ought to insist upon to establish his Hypothesis. — See whether M^r. Arbuthnott in his Tables (above mentioned, p. 106) has not made use of D^r. Hakewell in his Discourse of Providence & D^r. Bernard de Ponderibus & Mensuris.

July 12 (Th.). The Messenger of ye Press is order'd to discover if possible the Author Printer and Publisher of the Memorial of the Church
50 of England, there being several things in it wch give great offence at Court. Whilst those of ye other side are wink'd at, as the History of y^e

Court of Poland, &c. — M^r. Wotton, who wrote *the Essay upon Ancient and modern Learning*, was enter'd at Cambridge in ye 9th year of his Age.

July 13 (Fri.). D^r. Wallis in a spare leafe, before a 4to Book of tracts, w^{ch}, (with another in 8vo,) he gave to the Bodlejan Library, hath inserted, under his own hand, ye following memorandum:

GEORGE KEITH,

A Scotch man, (the Author of those Tracts contained in this volume in 4°, and of those in another volume in 8°,) was, for some time, himself a *Quaker* (and a Preacher amongst them;) induced thereunto by the Quakers great Pretensions to a more than ordinary Degree of Piety and Spirituality, and a 10 *Light within*, wch they pretended to be a sufficient and Infallible Guide. And did distinguish themselves from others, by divers affected Singularities, such as these; not to use the words *you, your*, (with relation to a particular person) but *Thou, Thee, Thine*; not to use the words *yes* and *no*, but *Yea* and *Nay*, not to use the Titles of *Master, Lord*, and the like, as savouring of Pride and Ambition; not to wear in their Apparel, *Laces, Silks, Gold* and *Silver*, as savouring of Vanity; not to salute any, by *pulling off the Hat*, or like Gestures; not to *strike* however wronged or provoked, as pretending to greater Meekness and Patience; not to join in our publick *Worship*, as not spiritual enough, but in seperate Meetings of their own, with other ye like Affections. 20

But when he was better acquainted with them, he found that they did (under divers uncouth and affected Expressions) entertain many gross and erroneous Tenets, inconsistent wth the Fundamentals of Christian Religion, and destructive thereof.

He did thereupon endeavour, for some years, (by Arguments, Persuasions, and Books written for that purpose,) to reduce them from those erroneous Principles, (which by the Craft and Subtiltie of some of their Leaders, with the Ignorance and Simplicity of their Followers, they had entertained,) and did prevail with divers of them, so far as to divide from the rest of the Quakers, to disclaim their gross Opinions, and meet separately from them; and were 30 called (by way of distinction) the *Reformed Quakers*. And, after some time, he, with most of these, did return to the Communion of the Church of England.

These small Tracts, published on several occasions, I thought not amiss (that they be not lost) to gather together, and bind-up in these two Volumes, and put them into the *Bodlejan Library*; that, in future times, such as shall be inquisitive into such Matters, may thence understand, what kind of People they are who are now called *Quakers*.

JOHN WALLIS, D.D.,
April 12, 1701.   Geom. Prof. Oxon.

— Amongst the Testimonies for the Antiquity of Oxford before King 40 Ælfred's time, may be added w^t Thomas Gulielmus says in Chron. Brit. viz. *Pherychtiand ordh yn trigo yn Rhydychen cyn gwneithyr O Alphred yscol yndhi;* i.e. that *Chymists* dwelt at *Oxford* before Ælfred built a school there. See in the Additions to the xth chapter of D^r. Plot's Nat. Hist. of Oxfordshire, 2^d Ed. — Sidonij Opera, cum notis Jac. Sirmondi. *Par.* 1652. 4°. P. 128....

July 14 (Sat.). M^r. Stratford, Chaplain to ye House of Commons, made one of the Canons of X^t C^h. in room of D^r. Ratcliff deceas'd. He took his D^r of Divinity's Degree upon that Account this Act Term. D^r. Ratcliff left all he had, being betw. 2 or 3,000 lib in money, besides 50 other wealth, to ye Col. — Epictetus did not draw up his Enchiridion himself, but Arrian. — Characteres Aegyptij, etc.... per Laurentium Pignorium. *Franc.* 1608. — M^r. Lock in his 3^d Letter for Toleration, p. 266. *Athanasius*, the great Defender of the Catholick orthodoxy, writ ye Life

of his Contemporary S^t. Anthony, full of Miracles; wch though some have
question'd, yet the Learned Dodwell allows to be writ by Athanasius: &
the stile evinces it to be his, wch is also confirmed by other Ecclesiastical
Writers. M^r. Dodwell has this in his Diss. upon Irenæus. — Ibid.
p. 267. S^t. Chrysostom is call'd by M^r. Dodwell the contemner of
Fables. This M^r. D. has also in his Diss. upon Irenæus. — Tis said
the Duke of Buckingham is Author of the Pamphlett call'd *The Memorial
of the Church of England,* and that he has sent to the Ld Treasurer
(Godolphin) to desist from making any further search concerning that
10 particular, being ready at any time to defend w^t he has said in it. —
A Gentleman of New-Colledge tells me there is leather money to be
seen in that College, being some of that wch was put in the Treasury
chest by the Founder himself; and that the like is to be seen at Winchester. This I never heard before, and (I think) is not credible. —
M^r. Dodwell amongst other Discourse at ye Coffe-House was pleas'd
to mention a Silver Coyn of Amyntas, now in the Custody of M^r. Francis
Cherry of Shottesbrook, being found in a Field near his (M^r. Cherry's)
House. This is a great curiosity, especially upon the Account of its being
found here. Quære whether 'twas dug up in a Field call'd *Weycock,*
20 where was formerly a Roman Castle, as M^r. Camden has noted. Examin also whether it be not a counterfeit. M^r. Cherry never yet[1] shew'd
it me, tho' I think he once (at least) ask'd me whether we had any one
in Bodley? When M^r. Dodwell was at Bath, there was a great number
of Roman Coyns dug up, of the lesser sort, very much defaced. Upon
wch Account he believ'd them to be of little use. I am of the same mind,
but upon another reason, viz. because we have no Roman Coyns dug up
in England of good note, but those relating to the Thirty Tyrants, (w^{ch}
it seems are found no where else); & of these we know as much already
as can be discovered by Coyns. — The most considerable Piece of Anti-
30 quity that I have heard of, wch hath been of late found in these Parts, is
a Gold Roman Torques, plow'd up by a Husbandman either in or near
Wales, wch he sold for a little money, being greatly impos'd upon by the
person who procur'd it. S^r. Andrew Fountain, who told me the Story,
mention'd his name to me, in whose Possession it is now; but I have
quite forgot it. — Just publish'd a 2^d Edition of D^r. Plot's *Natural History
of Oxfordshire,* by M^r. J. Burman, Master of Arts of University Coll.,
Son in Law to the D^r. 'Tis four shillings dearer to the subscribers than
ye former Edition, tho' the Additions make but two Sheets more. 'Twas
expected several Particulars, wherein the D^r. was found to be mistaken,
40 should have been left out; but there is hardly any thing omitted that
appears in the former Edition ; & those Improvements wch are made are
very inconsiderable. I believe it might have received great Additions
from M^r. Antony à Wood's Papers in Musaeo Ashmoleano, particularly
from his collections concerning many Towns in Oxfordshire, contain'd
in a folio volume. He has also a volume in folio concerning the Antiquities of the Town and City of Oxon, wch I have look'd into, & judge
it to be very usefull for such a work. — D^r. Hicks communicated to M^r.
Cherry a folio Book in French, fairly written & curiously illuminated,
containing the History of y^e Deposition of Richard the Second. M^r.

---

[1] I have since printed it in Leland's Itin.

Cherry has a Transcript of it, and procur'd as exact a Copy of the several Figures as he could. 'Twas compiled by a Person who liv'd in Rich. II$^{d's}$ Reign, & seems to have been the original Copy. I remember I once saw both M^r. Cherry's Transcript, & the Book whence he took it. I then reckon'd it a Romance; but M^r. Dodwell who has perus'd it assures me there are divers curious pieces of History in it. W^t I value it most upon, is the several Habits of that Age wch are to be known from it. Amongst the rest, there is an Irish King, without Stockings and in a very odd Bonnett upon his Head, & 'tis there said y^t his Horse cost him 400 Cows. Remember to ask M^r. Cherry for a sight of this Book. [10]

July 15 (Sun.). The Master of University Col. shew'd me a Letter from a Non-Juror complaining very much of the Hard usage of the Jacobites from some chief Members of the University, who have presented them to the B^{ps}. M^r. Parker is said to have divers Pupils whom he instructs in Jacobite Principles. The Master seems to be concerned at this, as thinking it will do them more hurt y^n any thing else. — At the end of the Master's Copy of Athenæ-Oxonienses is a testimony in MS^t that M^r. Wood died in ye Communion of the Church of England, and y^t there was no Papist come to him during all the time of his Sickness. He rec'd the Sacrament from M^r. Martin of Hart-Hall for whom he seem'd to have [20] a very good Opinion. — The Character of S^r. Geo. Mackenzy & M^r. Dodwell, in Athen. Oxon. for the most part, drawn up by D^r. Charlett & D^r. Gregory. So D^r. Charlett told me himself. The Acc^t of D^r. Mill there drawn up by D^r. Kennett. — I have heard y^t the reason why M^r. Dodwell[1] would not go into orders was some objection he made relating to the Athanasian creed. Ask him ab^t it. — In Tanaquil Faber's Epistles are some things concerning Livy. — Remember to tell D^r. Hudson that Seguinus in his Coyns corrects *Rhascupolis* in Vellejus Paterculus Lib. 2. cap. 129, by reading *Rhæcuporis*. — A Scotch Gentleman of University College tells me S^r. Geo. Mackenzy's Estate was ab^t 2000 lib^s. — I hear [30] M^r. Blackett a Gentleman Commoner of a vast Estate of University College gave only 20 shillings towards the Relief of ye Scotch Episcopal clergy, w^n D^r. Hudson gave 40^s. — Just publish'd, The Diet of Poland, a Satyr; consider'd Paragraph by Paragraph : To wch is added, A Key to the whole, wth the names of the Authors, & ye Nobility & Gentry, that are scandalously pointed at in it. pr. 1^s. — Hotly discours'd that ye Earl of Kingston will be made Ld Chamberlaine of ye Houshold & ye Earl of Kent created a Duke. —

July 15. Hearne to Dr. T. Smith. 'I heartily thank you for your Readiness to assist me in my design'd edition of Livy. I am very sensible of the ill Temper of the Belgick Critik, who takes all opportunitys of exposing our Theatre Editions. But as I design to use him very civilly, so I believe he will not be much hearken'd to; since his Abuse of so many already has render'd him odious to most Learned men.' Remarks on Mr. Chishull; Selden's Life of Friar Bacon; Vettius Valens; Essay upon Government by Parker; Works of Philo among Selden's MSS.; Berger on Aristides; Morhofius de Livii Patavinitate. Has transcribed for Zacagnius MS. Baroc. 91. Does Smith know anything of it?

---

[1] This is a false Report as I have been well assur'd. Tis nevertheless certain from a Letter or two y^t he writ to D^r. Thomas Smith, y^t he had some scruples upon y^t score.

pag. 8. of the *Oxford Dialogue* (writ, as some say, by D^r. Tyndal of AlSoul's College) :—

Besides the Episcopal Clergy in Scotland, neither desired his (K. William's) Protection, nor would own his Authority; so y^t he could have no great reason to encourage his Enemies to desert his Friends. But after all, had it been the King's own Act (he means the Abolishing Episcopacy in Scotland), it was no worse in him, y^n in K. Charles I. who abolished Episcopacy there much more effectually y^n the other. For he made a grant of the Church-Lands there, wch K. William could never have been prevail'd upon to do; and this
10 you will find mentioned in ye L^d. Clarendon's History, wth a kind of Reflection upon K. Charles for it. —

D^r. Radcliff (ye Physitian) always very gratefull to M^r. Walker Master of University Coll. for the favours rec^d from him whilst he was of that College. — M^r. Badger, the Schoolmaster, tells me he has discover'd some words in C. Nepos not us'd in Augustus's Age. — 'Tis s^{d1} that lately was found at Rewley Abbey in Oxford a Saxon Inscription. W^t it is I cannot tell. I believe 'tis not Saxon, w'ever the Letters may be. Because y^t monastery was built after the Saxon Language was disus'd, namely *An. Dom.* 1281, 9 Ed. I.

20 **July 16 (Mon.).** On Thursday last (Jul. 12) died Titus Oates, the sham Salamanca Doctor. — H. Clapham's Chronological Discourse touching the Church, &c. by H. Clapham. *Lond.* 1609. 4°... Here is a History of the Emperors Lives. — Everardi Feithij Antiquitates Homericæ. *Ludg. Bat.* 1677. 8°... & p. 3711. *Lug. Bat.* 1699... This last Edition amongst Gronovius's Antiquities. 'Tis a Book very much recommended by M^r. Dodwell. — Mr. Tyrrel having further examin'd the Book of Instruments above mention'd[2] of S^r. John Osborn's tells me there are several curious things in it not taken notice of by any Printed Authors. — Will Baldwin's Last part of ye Mirrour for Magistrates. *Lond.* 1574. 4°. . . . Here are
30 several things of note to be consulted by those who write of the English History. — A Commission being granted for Discovery of the King of France's Estate, concealed in this Kingdom, ye same open'd at Guildhall, and afterwards the Commissioners adj^d to Monday next, w^n Monsr. Hugueton, a great French Banker, who lately wthdrew from y^t Kingdom, will appear, & make a discovery of ab^t 110000 lib^s he has of ye French Kings Money in his Hands, wch will be paid to the Queen's use, & he have ye Protection of ye Government. — This Day M^r. Swinfin of New-Inn-Hall, was chosen Lecturer of Grammar for the University, being put in by the Vice-Chancellor, to whose choice it fell by reason one of the
40 Colleges, viz. Oriel, to whom it otherwise belong'd, did not take care of the matter in time.

July 17 (Tu.). In the Master of university col. Lodgings is a Picture of King Ælfred. — He had a Duplicate of Lambin's Tully, wch he has given to New-Inn-Hall. — D^r. Rich. Tillesley's Animadversions upon M^r. Selden's History of Tythes. *Lond.* 1619. 4°. — [Notes on Livy from Ger. Vossius *de vitijs Sermonis* and Richteri Epistolae, &c.] — Is. Casauboni Epistolae cura Graevij, *Magdeb. & Helmst.* 1656. Look it over whether there be anything in it concerning Livy. —

---

[1] Apr. 20, 1710. This Inscription is that concerning Ela Longespee, as I have told afterwards.   [2] See page 102.

M^r. Rich. James (the Antiquary) to his printed pieces wch he gave to the Publick Library has præfix'd these verses in MS^t.

Deere God by whome in dark wombes Shade
I am to feare and wonder made,
Learne me what parte I am to beare
On this world's Stage and Theatre.
Awters & Croziers are no things
That give to my Ambition Wings.
For this I neare did Mammon woe,
Nor flatter one great Lord or two.
But with a simple diet fed,
Scarce cloath'd and friended with a bed,
I was content in middle rancks
Of meaner sorte to view the prancks
And feates of men more active, who
Are better pleas'd in what they doe
Than I, who skeptiklye scarce dare
Of beare, of Lyon, or of Hare,

Or the worse race of Malepar'd
Loud speake what I have seen or heard.
Yet thrice I have bin hal'd before
Our Ephorismes of state full sore
Against my will. And sure I must
Before to tiring roome of duste
I turne, instruct some scene and give
My name to storie whilst I live.   10
Then whether on Italian stage
Or English free or forc'd I rage
Or steale a silent parte, let be
Dear Lord my soul's rest ever free.
As of Calanus let none saye
Truly of me another daye.
That I well seen in Antique lore
Did other Lords then God adore.

Composed by the Author R. James, written with his own Hand, & præsented to me J. Rous Bibli : by him 1633. —   20

M^r. Tyrrell tells me y^t there is a MS^t in Cotton's Library wch has ye same things (besides an Addition of others) wth the MS^t of S^r. John Osborn's above mention'd, see pag. 133. — Yesterday Joan. Hoffman, a Holsteiner, was admitted a Student in the Publick Library. He has been a great Traveller, and is related to Hoffman y^t wrote the Lexicon.

July 18 (Wed.). Duke of Marlborough attack'd ye French in their Lines, near Hillesheym, on the 18th Jul. new Style, wth great Bravery, taking a great Number of Prisoners, (several of wch considerable Officers) besides a good number slain. Since y^t by fresh Letters we have an Account y^t the Duke has forced Louvain to surrender, killing 7000 of the 30 Enemy who oppos'd his March, and taking divers prisoners. — Carry'd wth much Difficulty at Edinburgh that the Parliament there shall first go upon the *Succession* this Sessions. — Philippi Camerarij horae subcisivae, (centuria I^{ma}) *Franc.* 1624. 4°... In pag. 219. is an Excell^t Account of the Virgin brought to Scipio Africanus upon the taking of Carthage. In relation to wch he has discover'd a great Error in Livy & some other Historians. Centuria II^{da}. *Franc.* 1642. 4°... — ... The Mirrour of Golde to ye Sinfull Soule, translated out of French into English by Margaret Countess of Richmond. — Genealogia Illustrissimae Principis Margaretae Richmondiae & Derbiae Comitissae. [143-145.]   40

July 19 (Th.). Sanson's Mapps, corrected by Willm. Berry, the best in their kind, in M^r. Halley's Opinion. D^r. Charlett tells me y^t he is afraid the Antiquities of Middlesex, consisting mostly of Inscriptions, (the 1st Part whereof is already publish'd containing only the Towns of Chelsey and Kensington) will find but small Incouragement. —

The following Extract out of M^r. Seller's Will sent to D^r. Hudson, wth a Letter, whereof here is also the transcript. .

First I bequeath to ye Publick Library of the University of Oxford one Manuscript Folio containing *Willielmi* Malmesburiensis de Gestis Pontificum Anglorum, &c. Together with Chronicon Lichfeldense de Episcopis Cantuariensibus et de Episcopis Lichfeldensibus, all conteyned in one volume. 50

London, 17 July, 1705. S^r,—Mr. Abednego Seller by his will gave the above mentioned Manuscript to ye Publick Library of ye University of Oxford,

& I being one of his Executors am now in Towne on purpose to inspect his Affairs. I have found the Manuscript in his Study, & desire you will be pleased to order some sufficient person to call on me for it that I may have a Receipt upon the delivery thereof. He has also by his will given to Lincoln College in Oxford yᵉ perpetual use of his Byzantine Historians in Folio of yᵉ Par. Edit. I have this post written to yᵉ Rector, and desire you will be pleased to speak to him about it that he will order some one to come to mee for them. I understand you was very well acquainted wᵗʰ Mr. Seller. He desired a Tomb Stone might be put
10 over his Grave and the Inscription theron should be short & in Greek. Now I shall take it kindly if you please to write me what is proper. I am now busie in Catalogueing his Books which he directs shall be sold for the Benefit of his Grandchildren who are under age. I desire you'l let me heare from you per return of the Post. For I must hasten into Devonshire as soon as possible. I subscribe, Sir,   Your most humble Servᵗ,
                                                        Wᴍ. Prowse.

Direct For me at Mrs. Knightly's in Red Lyon Square, London.

ΤΩ ΕΝΔΟΞΟΤΑΤΩ | ΚΑΙ | ΠΟΛΥΜΑΘΕΣΤΑΤΩ | ΑΒΔΕΝΑΓΩ ΣΕΛΛΗΡΩ | ΤΗΣ
ΑΓΓΛΙΚΗΣ | ΕΚΚΛΗΣΙΑΣ | ΠΡΕΣΒΥΤΕΡΩ | ΑΡΕΤΗΣ ΕΝΕΚΑ ΚΑΙ ΚΑΛΟΚΑΓΑΘΙΑΣ |
20 ΑΝΕΘΗΚΕ | ΓΥΛΙΕΛΜΟΣ ΠΡΟΥΣΕΑΣ.

— On Sunday last (Jul. 15) in the Morning preach'd before yᵉ University at Sᵗ. Mary's Mʳ. Bisse of Corpus Xᵗⁱ Col. upon Gal. 4. 18. He shew'd the unreasonableness of Indifferencey in matters of Religion, & apply'd the whole to the present case of Occasional Conformity : much to yᵉ satisfaction of the greatest part of yᵉ Auditors. — To day preach'd at Sᵗ. Mary's before yᵉ Judges Mʳ. Tilly of Corpus Xᵗⁱ Coll. He brought in the same thing of occasional conformity, & his sermon was very much approv'd of. — On Munday last in the Evening, when news came to Town of the Duke of Marlborough's forcing yᵉ French Lines, 'twas observ'd
30 that there were no Illuminations here, but in Dʳ. Mill's Lodgings, wᶜʰ made some think, who pass'd by, that the chief reason of his Hanging out Lights was that the *Memorial of the Church of England* might be read by those who walk'd in the street, believing he had put up that Book upon the wall, but they were otherwise satisfied wⁿ they heard he was for Occasional Conformity.

July 20 (Fri.). I hear that *The Secret History*, (mentioned by Mʳ. Lesley in the IIᵈ Part of *the Association* &) written by Bᵖ. Burnett, is to be printed out of Hand, a Gentleman Commoner of Magd. Hall having procur'd the Intire Copy from Geneva : & he is resolv'd it shall see yᵉ
40 Light, with a Latin Translation for the use of such who do not understand English. I ask'd Dʳ. Mill abᵗ it, who believes yᵗ there is such a Book, & that there is a Copy abroad besides the original. — Several Persons at London taken up on suspicion of being Authors of the Pamphlett called *The Memorial of yᵉ Church of England*. — The Inscription on the Tomb Stone of Mʳ. Trafles, Warden of New College, should have been thus, as he desir'd himself, *Hic situs est Ricardus Trafles Humilis Peccator.* — I heard one of New College say That Dʳ. Busby desired the Inscription over his Grave might be *OBLIVIO*. But Mʳ. Southcombe,

---

July 20. T. Cherry to H. Asks H. to send him his Dictionary, Lexicon, Pomponius Mela, Grk. Test., Patrick's treatises, or anything 'convenient for the better prosecuting my designes here.'

a Nonjuror told me, that he view'd his Monument at Westminster, & that there is a large Inscription, of wch he has a Copy. — D^r. Woodward, of Oriel College, and Register of the Vice-Chancellor's Court, very ill. He is now in the 56th year of his Age. — D^r. Hudson gave to the Publick Library the following Books written & translated by Abraham Woodhead : Two Discourses, one conc. the Spirit of Martin Luther, the other conc. ye Celibacy of ye Clergy. *Oxon.* 1687. 4°.—Church Government, Part V^th. *Oxon.* 1687. 4°.—A Compendious Discourse of the Eucharist, with two Appendixes. *Oxon.* 1688. 4°.—Catholick Theses on several chief Heads of Controversy. 4°.—The Life of Greg. Lopez out of Spanish— 10 1675. 8°.—The Institutions of ye Congregation of ye Oratory of S^t. Maries in Vallicella w^thin ye City of Rome founded by Phil. Nerius; in English. *Oxon.* 1687. 8°. — The Pamphlett call'd *The Rights of the Church of England asserted and proved, in Answer to another intitl'd* The Rights of the Protestant Dissenters, *Oxon.* 1705. 4°. was not all writ by M^r. Sacheverell. He was Author of y^t Part only wch Reflects upon the Dedication of y^t Book. The other part wch is far the larger, & much better written, was done by M^r. Perks of Corpus Christi Colledge. — The Pamphlett call'd, A Letter proving the Occasional Conformists guilty of Schism & Hypocrisy. *Oxon.* 1704. 4°. was writ by M^r. Buckridge of Corpus 20 Christi Colledge. — Some say D^r. Drake is Author of *ye Memorial* &c. — . . . Joannis Bonæ Tractatus de Divina Psalmodia, *Par.* 1663. 4°. In the beginning is Notitia Auctorum qui in hoc opere citantur, notantur, illustrantur. Amongst the rest is this of Livy: Titus Livius Historiæ Latinæ princeps, lactea ubertate fluens, cui tamen Asinius Patavinitatem objecit. Lipsius frigidum aliquando, & supinum agnoscit. — . . . I have look'd into the 1st part of ye Antiquities of Middlesex, & the Author seems to have taken no pains, and to be ignorant both of Latin & Greek ; besides his Observations are trivial, & give no light to the Antiquities of the Places. This is also ye Judgment of others. — Martini Hanckij de 30 Romanarum Rerum Scriptoribus Liber II^dus. *Lips.* 1675. 4°. . . In pag. 235 are Additions to his Life of Livy, wth Testimonies of him. — . . . Christian Religion, substantially, methodicallie, plainlie & profitablie treatised. *Lond.* 1611. 4°. . . In a spare Leaf at the Beginning is this following writ wth S^r. Tho. Bodley's own Hand: *The Gifte of Jo. Man, Master of the Companie of ye Stationers, & ye first y^t was given, after their Indenture was sealed to ye Universitie.* — Jacobi Usserij Historia Dogmatica de Scripturis & Sacris vernaculis. *Lond.* 1690. 4°. In pag. 123 are some remarkable Things of King Alfred. . .

July 21 (Sat.). Mr. Westley a Beneficed Minister in Lincolnshire, 40 (who formerly wrote the Life of Christ, wch he dedicated to Q. Mary,) lately unhappily writing ag^t ye Dissenters, & since y^t giving his vote for the Tacking Interest at the Election in y^t County, and his Reasons in writing for his so doing, was in ye first place removed from being Chaplain to a Regim^t worth about 100^l per Annum, & in the next place, after a thousand Insults in his House & Streets of Jacobite, Perconite, &c. was arrested, and carried to Lincoln Goal in a violent manner for some small Debts contracted by the smallness of his Income, the Numerousness of his Family, & other Providential Accidents; but, it seems, he was pertinacious, & would not Retract his Book (being Fact) 50

otherwise he might have faired better. — The Q. has presented Col.
Durell wth 2000 pounds for bringing the Express of forcing the French
Lines from the D. of Marlborough. — A Bookseller having Reprinted
The Memorial of the Church of England, answ^d *Paragraph by Para-
graph,* the Copies are seized. —

Viro Clarissimo Johanni Hudsono S. P. D. Jac. Perizonius [dated
Lugduni, postridie Eidus Junias MDCCI]. . . — Latini Latinij Epistolæ,
Conjecturæ, &c. *Rom.* 1659. 4⁰ .. Remember to look this over conc.
Livy. In pag. 382 there is an Epistle wth divers matters relating to
10 him. — A short Declaration of ye Mystery of Iniquity by Tho. Helwys.
1612. 8⁰. . . Given, I believe, by the Author himself, who in a spare leafe
at ye beginning has added these words in writing,

Heare of ye King, and despise not the Counsell of the poore, and let their
complaints come before thee.

The King is a mortal man, & not God, therefore hath no power over the
Immortal Soules of his Subjects, to make laws & ordinances for them, &
to set spiritual Lords over them.   If ye King have Authority to make Spiritual
Lords and Laws, then he is an immortal God, and not a mortal Man.

O King be not seduced by Deceivers, to sin so against God, whom thou
20 oughtest to obey, nor against thy poor subjects who ought and will obey thee
in all things with body, Life, and Goods, or else let their lives be taken from
the Earth.

God save the Kinge.

Spittlefeild, neare London.   Tho. Helwys.

— Mr. Peisley tells me M^r. Tilly is going to print his Assize Sermon, not
y^t he has been desired, but because one of the Judges was displeas'd at
it, as were some others, for some particulars wch they thought reflecting. . .

July 22 (Sun.). D^r. Mill shew'd me an Extract in the Paris Edition
of Athanasius by the Benedictines wch he sent them.   They have taken
30 notice of it, but for *Joannes* have put *Jacobus,* & for *Aula S. Edm.* there is
Collegium S. Edm. — Last Week a Committee of Enquiry sate at Guild
Hall and Examin'd witnesses ab^t several French Men residing here who
are suspected of Remitting money from France hence for the Paym^t of
the French Army, & (as 'tis s^d) it appear'd that they have 705000^l
in Bank ready for y^t service, and that they have rec^d goods from hence to
the value of a Million to Enable them to send money from hence. — Not.
ad Gronov. Edit. Livij, l. 2. c. 27. Dionys. lib. 9. ait centum ac sexaginta
milites subesse primipili imperio, si codices non fallunt, quod suspicor.
Glareanus.   Remember to ask D^r. Hudson whether he has taken
40 notice of this.

July 23 (Mon.).   The Manifesto of ye Church of England that was
endeavoured to be supprest, is now againe publickly sold ab^t streets at
London, the Bookseller being resolved to take ye Benefit of his Copy,
& stand the Test of the Law, & ye pretended Remarks that are printed
with it strengthen & not confute the Assertions of ye Author. — Some
Letters from Paris say, y^t a Hermit there dyed of 144 years of Age, who
being asked what his Food used to be, replyed Milk & Honey. — D^r.
Hody in his Book of the Translations of the Bible, has published some
excellent Fragments of Fryer Bacon's from a MS^t amongst those given
50 to the Bodleian Library by S^r. Ken. Digby.   But he has not tr[an]scrib'd

them truly, being done when he was a young Man. I told Dr. Mill of this, who got me to help him collate it, putting the variations &c. wch are considerable in the Margin of his Book. — Whoever continues Athenæ Oxon. must remember in the Account of M^r. Milles's Edition of S^t. Cyrill to acquaint the reader that the greatest part of the notes were taken from Suicerus, & that he had several from M^r. Dodwell & M^r. Grabe. As also that the Text in a great measure was corrected by M^r. Potter. So y^t he did himself but little to ye Book, myself drawing up the 3 Indexes & assisting him in some Collations, and transcribing the things from MSS^{ts} in ye Publick Library which he was not able to read. — The Continuer also 10 must remember to acquaint the world that he (M^r. Milles) writ *Remarks upon the occasional Paper number* 8th in Vindication of the Learned M^r. Dodwell, wch were afterwards answered, wth two or three more pieces of y^t nature. Upon wch M^r. Milles writ a large Reply, never yet printed, & I believe never will by himself, he being now asham'd of both these Papers, as having chang'd his opinion. He like-wise began an Edition of *Aristophanes*, but having compar'd a comedy or two, he gave it over, being not a man of Resolution to go thro' with any thing. — [Notes on Livy from Freinshemii Com. in Quintum Cur-tium, III, ix, 4, and VII, iv, 1.] — D^r. Hudson shew'd me a Coyn, 20 whereof there is the same in the Publick Library, viz. *Drusus Ger-manicus*. 'Tis of the bigger Brass, and the Description is, NERO CLAVDIVS DRVSVS GERMANICVS IMP. Caput Drusi. Rev. TI CLAVDIVS CAESAR AVG PM. TR. P. IMP. S. C. Figura insidens subsellio, dextra ramum lauri, sin. sceptrum, ad pedes plura armorum genera. — I hear D^r. James, Head of Queen's Coll. in Cambridge, & a very Rich Man, is made Prebendary of Canterbury in the room of D^r. Isham deceas'd. — [Notes on Livy from Freinshemii Com. in Q. Curtium, IV, x, 7; III, iii, 11; VIII, v, 6; IV, xiii, 35; VII, vii, 5; VIII, x, 25; X, vi, 14; and Index.] — Joannes Terentius publish'd *Textus Jobi Chaldaice, cum notis*: item, 30 Græce στιχηρῶς cum varijs lectionibus. *Franek.* 1663. 4°... This Greek version was printed from Patrick Junius's (or Young's) Edition; who printed it from the Alexandrian copy, but here are divers notes & collations wth other old Editions, & therefore will be of use to Mr. Grabe in his designed Edition of ye Septuagint. He never knew of it, 'till we shew'd it him in ye Publick Library. Junius's Edition is at ye End of his Edition of Nicetas' Catena Græcor. Patrum in Job, pr. at *Lond.* 1637. fol. — Just publish'd *Otia Votiva*, or Poems upon several occasions, many of wch in memory of ye late King and Queen. Price bound 2s. 6d. — Serious Reflections on ye Scandalous Abuse and 40 Effects of ye Stage, in a sermon preach'd at ye Parish church of S^t. Nicholas in the city of Bristol, on Sunday the 7th day of January, 1705 By Arthur Bedford, M.A., vicar of Temple Church in the s^d city.

July 24 (Tu.). Last Night being wth M^r. Halley, the Savilian Pro-fessor of Geometry, he was pleas'd to tell me, that he had discover'd a Great Error in D^r. Gregory (the Scotch Professor of Astronomy in this University's) Book of Astronomy, notwthstanding it was for the most part taken from S^r. Isaac Newton's Book. Upon wch the D^r. printed the sheet over again, & wthout any acknowledgment to M^r. Halley put them into such Copies as he had left, and he could come at secretly, that ye 50

Matter might not be known. I remember particularly the time when he put in ye Copy of ye Publick Library; tho' he did not let any one of ye Library know of it, wch w^thout doubt he ought to have done according to ye Statute. — M^r. Halley also shew'd me the Inscription of Theophrastus at Westminster as he had taken it, wch is much more correct than 'tis in the Marmora Oxoniensia. For wch reason he says he will print it in ye Philosophical Transactions. — M^r. Hoffman tells me M^r. Foss, a Dane, who design'd a new Edition of Libanius, having procur'd divers things from the Chief Libraries in Europe for that end, is married, and has now laid
10 aside this Work. I told D^r. Hudson of this, but he will not believe it, being satisfied of the contrary. M^r. Hoffman likewise tells me that he saw a MS^t of Livy at Paris, wch I believe is ye same wth that wch Colbert collated, whose Observations are inserted in the Dauphin Edition of this Author. I ask'd him whether he ever heard of any Fragments of him preserv'd at Luca. He answer'd he did, & y^t he thinks they are different from those printed. — The Inscription I have mention'd above to have been corrected by M^r. Halley is . . . printed in Marm. Oxon. p. 301. I do not remember all the differences, but I very well remember that in his copy for τῆς εὐνοίας καὶ καλο . . . is τῆς ἀρετῆς ἕνεκα καὶ
20 καλοκαγ . . . [adds D^r. Prideaux' note.]. — The sheet wch D^r. Gregory has alter'd in his Astronomy is that wch begins with pag. 217. — D^r. John Earle, a very ingenious & learned Man, translated all ye VIII Books of M^r. Hooker's *Ecclesiastical Polity* into Latin. They are in MS^t & were never yet printed. *Quære* where they are. — Sylloge Annotationum &c. in Aur. Prudentium, per Johan. Weitzium. *Hanov.* 1613. 8°. . . Epistolæ xxx. Philologicæ & Historicæ de Fl. Josephi Testimonio quod Jesu Christo exhibuit lib. 18. c. 4. *Norib.* 1661. 8°. . . (Look 'em all over whether there be any thing of Livy.) — S. 4. 15. Art. A Book containing divers Authors, wherein are corrections of Livy. —
30 . . . The Friendly Debate writ by B^p. Patrick. — M^r. Priest of Bisley in Glocestershire has a design of Translating into Latin M^r. Greaves's Books of the Pyramids & the Roman Foot & Denarius. D^r. Smith gave some hopes in his Life of M^r. Greaves of doing it himself. Inquire of him whether he ever perform'd it, or intends it. — B^p. Sanderson began a Translation of M^r. Hooker's Books of *Ecclesiastical Polity* : but never perfected it. See in his Life by M^r. Walton. — S^r. James Astrey is about a new Edition of S^r. Hen. Spelman's Glossary. He should look over all M^r. Junius's MSS^ts upon this subject in the Publick Library. — . . . Denarius S. Petri, Disputatione Historico-theologica expositus per And. Arnoldum.
40 [*Altdorfi Noricorum*]. 1679. 'Twill be of use in the Life of King Ælfred by S^r. John Spelman. — . . . Index librorum prohibitorum & Expurgatorum jussu Bernardi de Sandoval & Roxas editus. *Matriti*, 1614. 4°. . . In a spare Leafe at ye Beginning are these two following memorandums written by M^r. Wanley & D^r. Wallis, viz.

Sept. 2, 1698. Dr. Wallis told me, that once a Popish Priest came to this Library, when Dr. Barlow (afterwards B^p. of Lincoln) was Library-Keeper. They chanced to have some talk together about Religion, & so of ye Indices Expurgatorij, & the said Priest flatly denied that ever any Index Expurgatorius was printed at *Madrid*, but that the Calvinists of *Geneva* had fathered
50 that lye upon them, & had counterfeited such an Edition. Dr. Barlow thereupon shewed him this Book, which was undoubtedly printed at *Madrid*,

& had yᵉ *Names of several of the Inquisitors written in it, who owned it from time to time,* before it *came hither.* Upon which, the Priest, being convicted, would fain have bought this Book of the Doctor, and profered whatever he would ask for it, with an intent to destroy it: but could not corrupt the Doctor.

Dr. Wallis afterwards made suit to the Curators that this Book might be removed into a securer place, for fear of Afterclaps, and the Book was accordingly removed from among the Libri Theol. in fol. where it was chained, to the *Th.* in 4ᵗᵒ where I now found it: but I do not find herein such ample Testimonies of several Inquisitors owning it, tho' I perceive what is written on the back side of the Title-Page; and at the Bottom of the Page, about 24 Leaves from the End, and am therefore afraid that some ill Person has torn them from the End, where they might have been written upon the spare Leaves.

N.B.—The very Letter shews that the Book was printed in Spain. Consider the marks of the Paper.   H. WANLEY.

I do very well remember that Dr. Barlow (since Bᴾ. of Lincoln) when he was Library-Keeper at Oxford, did tell me the story above-mentioned; and that I did advise the Removal of the Book (which I do believe to be this individual Book). There are now the names of two Inquisitors intimated in the Backside of the Title-Page to whom (it seems) it had successively belong'd). But I do well remember, that formerly there were divers others; which I guess to have been in the last Leafe which hath been torn out, as appears by some part of it now remaining.

Sept. 15, 1701.   JOH. WALLIS.

Dʳ. Wallis writ this at the Request of Dʳ. Hudson soon after he had been elected Library Keeper in Room of Dʳ. Hyde. There appears to have been two Leaves torn out at the End, which will answer the spare Leaves at yᵉ Beginning.

VOL. II.

July 25 (Wed.). On Munday last a Proclamation came forth for a General Thanksgiving for our late Victory the 23ᵈ of August next. — Letters from Scotland say yᵗ the Question being put whether they should bring in yᵉ Succession Bill before they treat of a Union 'twas carried in yᵉ Negative. — ... Last week came an Account of a Taylor who died at Northampton 122 years of Age. — This day (being Sᵗ. James's day), Mr. Martin, Vice-Principal of Hart-Hall, preach'd before the University at Sᵗ. Mary's, upon Prov. 13. 5. *But a wicked man is loathsome and cometh to shame.* In wᶜʰ taking occasion to discourse that Sin was the cause of Shame, he laid open the Hainousness of Hypocrisy, Perfidiousness, & Inconstancy, with a great deal of Spirit, sufficiently shewing that those Persons ought to be abominated, who are for occasional Communion, taking up arms against their Sovereign, and for swearing to all Governments, purely out of self Interest. — ...Lucius Florus, cum notis Annae Tanaquilli Fabri filiae. *Par.* 1674. 4°. Look over the Notes and Testimonies for things relating to Livy. — ... Truth advanced in yᵉ Correction of many Gross and hurtfull Errors, &c. by Geo. Keith— 1694. 4°. ... Mʳ. Keith in the Spare leafe at the Beginning has put this Memorandum:

1. I give this Book with the following small treatises to the Bodlejan Library in the University of Oxford, there to remain as a Testimony I have given to the true doctrine and faith of the Christian Religion against the vile

Errors asserted by some of the great Leaders among them called Quakers, directly opposite to the true Christian Faith and Doctrine.
2. The Arraignment of Worldly Philosophies.
3. Heresie and Hatred, &c.
4. New England's Spirit of Resserection.
5. The Causeless ground of Surmises.
6. A Testimony against that false and absurd opinion, &c. (Note, this Book when reprinted in England in my Absence in America had a false Title prefixed to my true Title, which false Title is, *George Keith's Eyes opened.*)
10   7. A seasonable Information.
8. A further Discovery.
[9. Wanting.]
10. The Yearly Meeting of the Quakers their nameless Bull of Excommunication.
11. The true Copy with a short List, &c.
12. A Seasonable Testimony, &c. with a Confession of our sincere Faith, in 8ᵛᵒ.   GEORGE KEITH.

[Book-titles (two to be looked over for Livy, &c.). — Notes on Livy from F. Jureti Notae ad Paulini vitam Martini, pp. 248, 249; Ortelius'
20 Thesaurus Geographiae, Masson's Jani Templum etc. Christo nascente reseratum. — News from the Scottish Parliament, dated Edinburgh, July 17.]

July 26 (Th.). MS. Seld. Supra num. 79. A Collection of several Matters. See whether Dʳ. Dee's *Speculum unitatis sive Apologia pro Rogero Bachone* be there. — In MS. 15. Baroc. is a short treatise called, Κοσμᾶ Ἰνδικοπλεύστου πρόλογος εἰς τοὺς ψαλμούς. 'Tis only a Preface to his Exposition upon the Psalms, concerning wᶜʰ see Dʳ. Cave's IIᵈ vol. of his Historia Lit. Here is nothing in it only an Account of yᵉ Psalms, proving that all the CL Psalms were writ by David, &
30 particularly for this Reason, because our Saviour & the Apostle mentions no other Psalms but those of David. — Mʳ. Joyner says the Life of Fryer Bacon written by Mʳ. Selden was sent to Sʳ Kenelm Digby at Paris to be printed; but what hinder'd it, or wᵗ became of it afterwards he cannot tell. — MS. Seld. supra 79. pag. 142.

De Influentijs Coelestibus; utrum ab aliquo particulari coelo, an à toto aggregato simul, vel ab astro quopiam particulari secundum suam formam: Et quid sit proprie influentia coelestis, et quatenus operatur. Veteres enim ista probe callebant: et istarum influentiarum ope per congruam influentiarum electionem, multa mirabilia praestiterunt: istarum ope sine dubio Rog. Bacon,
40 aeneo capiti loquelam indidit, et quemadmodum accepi à quibusdam fide dignis D. Dr. Godwyn, nunc Episcopus Herefordensis, etiam istam artem optime callet, effecitque saepius ut equinum caput loqueretur; qua etiam de re tractatum quendam, necnon de modo mittendi nuntium per longissimam viam, brevissimo tempore, conscripsisse aiunt. Haec omnia per influentias istas Quaeratur de his ulterius. Vide aliquid hac de re in Bartholomaeo Anglico de proprietatibus; in Paracelso. Consule etiam Camillum in libro de gemmis et lapidibus; ubi agitur de quodam Chrystallo, cujus ope, si lunaribus radijs objiciatur, secreta per longam distantiam revelari possunt. —

Ibid. p. 147. Dʳ. Dee in a certain Treatise of his reporteth that he
50 knew a clock, yᵉ motions of whose wheeles were not to be finished in an C years, no not in a thousand years, nay perpetual; as namely an instrument made by Janollus Turianus Cremonensis, & presented to yᵉ Emperor Charles the 1st, of wᶜʰ there is made some mention lib. 17.

Cardani de subtilitate. — I am told y^t D^r. Sloane has committed the care of Printing the Philosophical Transactions to M^r. Thorp of University College, to whom the several Pieces are to be sent. — ... Remember to tell M^r. Dodwell that M^r. Halley wishes he would write ye Life of Dioclesian, believing no man so capable. — The Continuer of Athenæ Oxon. must look into M^r. Edm. Trench's own Account of his Life printed at *Lond.* 1693. 8⁰....

July 27 (Fri.). The Discourse is reviv'd that the King of Denmark has assur'd his Uncle P^r. George that in case there be an Eruption with Scotland, he will forthwith spare him 20000 Men, & 10 Men of War. — 10 M^r. Hoffman tells me that M^r. Berger, who is publishing *Aristides*, has published nothing as yet. but that his Brother is Professor of Physick at Wirtemberg, & is accounted a very learned Man, wch he has also discovered by the Books he has published, as *Fundamenta Medicinæ*, &c. He likewise tells me that M^r. Fabricius at Hamburg has already published his[1] 4 volumes in 4to. De Græcis Scriptoribus, wch he intitles *Bibliotheca Græca.* He sent a little while since a Specimen (containing several Sheets) of the 1st vol. to D^r. Hudson, as also he did of *Eunapius*, which is to be in 8⁰. He told D^r. Hudson in a Letter that he was preparing a new Edition[2] of his *Bibliotheca Latina*, with large Improvements. 20 — M^r. Hoffman also tells me that *Joh. Mollerus, Flensburgensis* is writing *Historia Cimbrica* in 3 fol. Volumes. 'Tis the same *Moller* that wrote (1) *Bibliotheca Septentrionis Eruditi, sive Syntagma Tractatuum de Scriptoribus illius. Lips.* 1699. 8⁰. (2) *Introductio in Ducatuum Cimbricorum, Slesvicensis & Holsatici Historiam, chorographicam, Naturalem, antiquariam, &c. Partibus IV. Hamb.* 1699. 8⁰. (3) *Homonymoscopia Historico-Philologico-Critica, sive schediasma παρεργικὸν de Scriptoribus Homonymis quadripartitum. Hamb.* 1697. 8⁰. — ... The Quotations in D^r. Hody's Book in folio concerning the Versions of the Bible are for the most part taken at second Hand. So M^r. Grabe insinuated to me, who 30 has had occasion to examin them. — Joannis Henrici Ursini Analecta sacra. *Franc. & Marburgi*, 1668. 8⁰. . . Consult whether there be anything in it relating to Livy. — M^r. Arbuthnott has alter'd his Tables of Measures, &c. — M^r. Wood, in his Athenæ Oxon. Vol. II. in vit. Abr. Woodhead intimates y^t several people did report that M^r. Woodhead was Author of the whole Duty of Man & ye other Pieces writ by him; wch however he wonders at. In the Ladies Calling the Author wishes the Nunneries had not been dissolved.

July 28 (Sat.). Tho' there be a II^d Edition of Psalmanezzer ye Formosan's Book, giving an Account of his Country, &c. come out, 40 wherein he has answered most of ye material objections made against him, yet I am told he is still taken to be a Cheat in London. — On Tuesday last ye Earl of Leycester departed this life, & his Estate and Honour descend to his Brother ye Honble Geo. Sidney. — M^r. Tilny has recover'd 50^libs. Damage of one Croply of Southampton for scandalous words, wherby he lost his Election at ye aforesaid place. — Just publish'd, A Sermon preach'd at ye funeral of M^rs. Catherine Lorrain, lately deceas'd, in the Parish of S^t. Andrew, Holborn, Wednesday, June 27th,

---

[1] False. They are since come out.   [2] This Ed. is since come out.

1705, by Hen. Shute, M.A. Chaplain to ye R^t. Honble Edw. Earl of
Orford, & Lecturer of White Chappel. — Also A new Edition of the
List of the Principal Officers Civil & Military in England, on a Broad
Sheet. — M^r. Milles (Tho.) has declar'd he will not speak anymore in
Behalf of those who are call'd *High-Church*. — This Morning D^r.
Hudson went to London with M^r. Halley. — Just publish'd a Latin
Translation of H. Lukin's Book call'd *The Chief Interest of Man*, or, a
Discourse of Religion &c. by Simon Priest, A.M. of Bisley in Glocester-
shire. Printed at Oxon. 8°.   There are several Recommendatory Verses
10 before it, wch makes some People prejudic'd at the Book, tho' the Trans-
lation is very well perform'd. — Promis'd from Gresham College
Library in June last, by the care of D^r. Hudson, who apply'd himself
to M^r. Halley, 3 old Editions of *Livy*, one at *Rome* An. 1470, a 2^d at
Venice, 1518, 1519, and a 3^d at *Tarvisium* 1482. At the beginning of
this last I find the following Inscription (not in Gruter) in·MS^t, viz.[1] . . .
— This day was admitted into the Publick Library *Baggus Seerup Danus*.
— Just come out in 8°. an Answer to a Book call'd, *An Essay towards
Catholick Communion*. *Quære* who is the Author[2]? I formerly saw in
MS^t some such Book in the Hands of D^r. Hudson; but I am not sure
20 whether 'twas the same, tho' 'tis probable it may, the Bookseller, M^r.
Hartley, having sent him a Copy. — I hear Dr. Woodward of Oriel
College had some hand in citing the Jacobites, who meet at a House in
S^t. Mary's Parish neare that College for the sake of Devotion, into the
Bishop's Court. This makes me think that D^r. Mill, whatever he may
say to the contrary, further'd the matter, it being certain that the Bishop
and he a little while before met at D^r. Woodward's Lodging; which was
in order, without dout, to talk about it. — D^r. Mill, in printing his
Edition of the *New-Testament* from *Rob. Stephens's* Edition, has not
made the best choice, the Complutensian being far better, wch he should
30 have follow'd, as M^r. Grabe has told me, & of which himself is now
sensible.

July 29 (Sun.). Notand. that there is nothing in the Parish Church of
White-Waltham in Berks to shew it's Antiquity. The oldest Book there
concerning the Affairs of the Parish is one of ye Church Wardens &c.
But I think there is nothing in it beyond the time of Queen Eliz. 'Tis
almost worn out. [3] 'Twas formerly call'd *Abbot's-Waltham*, as belonging
to *Waltham-Abbey* in Essex. I am told the Papers belonging to it are at
Winchester. — M^r. Halley's Translation into Latin of *Apollonius Pergæus's* Treatise περὶ λόγου ἀποτομῆς, *sive de rationis divisione* (wch he was
40 forc'd to do from the Arabick, the Greek being lost) is now in the Press.
— D^r. Prideaux (pag. v. of ye Preface to his *Life of Mahomet*) tells us he
design'd to publish *The History of the Eastern Church* (whereof the Life
of Mahomet is only the interspersed Parts of one Chapter) beginning at
the Death of the Emperor *Mauricius* & ending at ye fall of ye Saracen

---

[1] I have since published this Inscription in my Ed. of Livy.
[2] See below, pag. 154.
[3] This a mistake. It belong'd to another Abbey, I think *Chertsey* in *Surrey*. *Quære*.
It certainly so far belong'd to Chertsey, as y^t the Abbat had a Pension out of it.
Otherwise it belong'd to Waltham-Abbey in Essex, as I have noted upon Leland's
Collectanea.

Empire, Anno 936. The whole Design is treated of in the said Preface. The Publication was hinder'd by the unhappy Disputes about ye Trinity. — Yesterday was publish'd *Memoirs of the Marquis de Guiscard*, translated out of French. *Lond.* 8°. price 1s. . . . — D^r. Smith in his Account of y^e *Seven Churches of Asia* mentions Livy upon occasion of an Inscription he found wherein is mention of *Quadratus*. — M^r. *Wood* almost finished a 3^d Vol. of *Athenæ Oxon.* wch he left with other Papers at his Death to M^r. *Tho. Tanner*, now Chancellor of Norwich, to be continued by him ; but whether he will publish it or no I cannot yet tell. He has promis'd an Edition of *Boston* and *Leland* who wrote *de Scriptoribus Britannicis.* 10 But I am afraid he will not make good his promise, tho' in a Letter he sent lately to D^r. *Charlett* he told him he was continually drudging at it, and wonder'd any one should be so uncivil as to take ye work out of his Hands, the D^r. having told him that I had a design of printing *Leland* by itself. — The Account of the Life of D^r. *Wallis* was drawn up by D^r. *Gregory*, that of M^r. *Ashmole* & D^r. *Plot* by M^r. *Llhuyd* (of the *Museum Ashm.*) & that of M^r. *Anton. à Wood* by D^r. *Wood* of *New*-College, his Nephew, all wch are inserted in the Supplement to M^r. *Collier's Dictionary.* If any one desires a farther Account of M^r. *Wood* he must consult the *Vindication* of him, written as 'tis said by D^r. *Wood*, & printed some years 20 since, and another Paper lately printed in answer to some part of D^r. Pope's Life of Bishop Ward. D^r. *Kennett* has also writ an Account of him wch I formerly saw in a Spare Leaf at the Beginning of his Copy of the 1st vol. of *Athenæ Oxon.* wch M^r. *Cherry* then had in his hands. Who 'twas drew up the Account of M^r. *Lock's* Life in the said *Supplement*, I cannot yet tell ; but I believe 'twas done by M^r. *Tyrrel*, who was his great Acquaintance. — Usual in the Hot Countries of *Arabia*, as it is in all *India* over, wch is in ye same *Clime* with *Arabia*, for women to be ripe for Marriage at 8 Years of Age, & also to bear Children the Year following. D^r. *Prideaux Life of Mahomet*, p. 52. — D^r. Charlett shew'd me 30 a Lettr. to day of S^r. *John Packington* to D^r. *Lloyd*, B^p. of *Worcester*, writ in June last, wherein he declares his Resentment of the Aspersions cast upon him by his Lordship, as being a drunken, debauch'd Person ; which he could have the more easily pardon'd provided he had not spoke ill of his Ancestors, who, 'tis well known, deserv'd well of ye Church of England. The D^r. tells me that he spoke with one who had seen the Original Copy of *the whole Duty of Man*, which was my old Lady Packington's own hand writing. — I saw a Gentleman at the Drs Lodgings who told me that M^r. Fr. Willoughby, the Virtuoso, fell sick upon occasion of a Law suit. — D^r. *Charlett* says M^r. *Blackett's* Schoolmaster was one M^r. 40 [1] *Ellis* a *Non-Juror* now living within 4 Miles of *London*. — Those in an Error that say the *Mahometans* expect *Mahomet* to return to them again here on Earth, there being no such Doctrine among 'em. *Prideaux's Life of Mahomet*, p. 133. — *Mahomet* lies buried at *Medina* without *Iron-Coffin* or *Loadstones* to hang him in, as ye stories wch commonly go about of him among *Christians* fabulously relate. *Ibid.*, p. 134.

[Extracts relating to D^r. Pocock from Prideaux's *Life of Mahomet*, pp. 177, 190.]

[1] He teaches young Gentlemen of the best Quality, with very good success & much satisfaction to their Parents & Relations at Thistleworth.

July 30 (Mon.). On Monday night was sennight the Lord Leigh's Lady departed this Life, at his Lordship's seat at *Stonely* in *Warwickshire.*

[News from the Scottish Parliament, dated Edinburgh, July 31.] The Earl of Castlemain, who was Embassadour from King James to ye Pope, is dead at his seat in Wales. —

Out of a Letter wch D^r. Charlett received from M^r. Wanley.

I have taken care to beg two Specimens of our Papers for yourself & for the Publick Library. In them you will find my Translation of Mr. Ostervalds Catechism, wch I should have presented to you, & to ye Library, long since,
10 but that I never had any to dispose of, I being paid for my pains in Money.

I beg to know whether in ye Publick Library there be a Book printed in Quarto, with these words in the Title Page, SACRÆ BIBLIÆ TOMVS PRIMVS, IN QVO CONTINENTUR, Quinque libri Moysi, Libri Josue, & Judicum, Liber Psalmorum, Proverbia Salomonis, Liber Sapientiæ, Et Novum Testamentum JESV CHRISTI; at the end this Inscription, LONDINI. EXCVDEBAT THOMAS BERTHELETVS REGIVS IMPRESSOR. ANNO MDXXXV. MENSE IVL. And if there be this Book, whether there be also the second Tome ? I ask this Question, because I take King Henry VIIIth to have been ye Editor of it, & to have written the Preface at ye Beginning of ye Book, wherein the Remaining parts
20 of Scripture are promis'd to be printed in the second Tome, which 2^d Tome I have not as yet seen. I want also to know, whether Bishop Burnet in the year 1535, or Mr. Strype, do mention any such Book, of that King's *own* Edition, for I have not their Books by me to consult.

About 10 days ago, I bought in More-feilds an odd Tractt, entitled, LE MOYEN DE PARVENIR, which I guess formerly to have belonged to the Publick Library. Upon the Edges is written *Arts* 8°. M. 125. If the Book be wanting i'le send it by some convenient opportunity; if it be there, & this a duplicate, sold by Dr. Hyde or Dr. Hudson, i'le keep it, tho' tis worth little.

The Bible above mention'd is not in ye Publick Library[1].—There is
30 but one of the Books entitled LE MOYEN &c. in the Library, wch is in Selden's Library, 8°. M. 51. Art. Nor are there any more expressed either in our present Catalogue, or ye more ancient one of D^r. James.— Neither B^p. Burnett nor M^r. Stry[p]e mention the Bible abovesaid.—At the Beginning of ye said Letter of M^r. Wanley's—I am glad you are pleas'd to approve my Design, as to a Saxon Bible, wch will be as large a Book as D^r. Hicks's, &, I believe, will be gratefull to ye curious, even to those who do not understand ye Language. — On Saturday last (Jul. 28.) was publish'd *Y^e Life of John Duke of Marlborough, Prince of the Empire, on a large broad Sheet, wth his Grace's Picture, curiously en-*
40 *graven on Copper.* — M^r. Dodwell in the preface to his *Defence of ye Vin-dication of the Deprived B^ps., p. 33. §. 16. Though Bishop Burnet observes that no such form was imposed on B^p. Ridley, nor on B^p. Thirlby, who were consecrated in ye year 1550.*—Ridley was consecrated B^p. of Rochester Sept. 5, 1547. Thirlby was translated indeed to Norwich *An.* 1550, but consecrated B^p. of Westminster Dec. 19, 1540. (Since the writing of this I have received a Letter from M^r. Tho. Cherry satisfying me that M^r. Dodwell acknowledges this to be a Mistake, & giving me liberty to alter the Passage in the copy in the Bodlejan Library.) —

Given by D^r. Hudson to ye Publick Library.

50   (1) Justi Fontanini de usu & præstantia Literarum oratio. *Romæ* 1704. 4°.
    (2) De Ecclesiasticæ Hierarchiæ Originibus Dissertatio, per Bened. Bacchi-

---
[1] [See it 4°. B. 1. Th. BS.—Dr. Bliss.]

nium. (pars 1ma.) *Mutinæ* 1703. 4°. (3) Alexandri de *Burgo* de Ecclesiasticæ Historiæ in Theologia Auctoritate Præfatio. *Perusiæ* 1702. 4°. (4) Antonij *Gatti* Gymnasij Ticinensis Historia & Vindiciæ a sæculo V. ad finem XV. *Mediolani* 1704. 4°. There is a Catalogue of Authors cited and confuted. (5) Petri Marcellini *Corradini* Vetus Latium Profanum & Sacrum. (Tom. 1^{mus}) *Romæ* 1704. fol. (6) Dominici *Quartaironij* Responsiones ad nonnullas Assertiones pro Reformatione Kalendarij Gregoriani de Paschate Anni 1700. fol.

July 31 (Tu.). D^r. *Charlett* shew'd me to day S^r. *Edm. Warcupp's* Relation of *The Treaty of Peace* between King *Charles* I. and y^e *Rebells* in the Isle of *Wight*. At the beginning is S^r. *Edmund's* Letter to the D^r. giving an Account of the Extraordinary Piety and Learning of that King, and of his great Success in touching for the Evil, which is a signal Instance of his being in the Divine Favour. He gives the D^r. Leave to put it into the Publick Library, when he shall think fit. There was some Proposal made to ye Bookseller for Printing it with S^r. *Edw. Walker's* Papers; but S^r. *Edmund* having been formerly of the Wrong side, and there being several considerable variations in his Account from that of S^r. *Edward's* (which is certainly the most to be relied upon) the matter was let drop. — I saw in the Master's Study *Colinæus's* Edition of the New Testament in Greek,—1539. 8°. 'Twas formerly D^r. Bernard's Book, as appears from a note of his at the Beginning testifying that 'tis a much better Edition than that of *Rob. Stephens* in *folio*. — Yesterday came to ye Publick Library the MS. wch M^r. *Seller* bequeath'd to us, containing (1) *Willielmi Malmsburiensis* De Gestis Pontificum Anglorum libros IV. There is a 5th printed in *Anglia Sacra*. (2) *Chronicon Lichfeldense*, libris 3. à mundo condito ad annum Domini 1388. 'Twas done wthout doubt by divers Authors, it being usual with the Monks to continue the *Acts* of their Predecessors. (3) *Thomæ Chesterfeild* Historiam de Episcopis Lichfeld à Diuma an. 656. ad Simon de Borisley an. 1347. 'Tis printed in vol. I. p. 423. of the *Anglia Sacra* published by M^r. Wharton, with several Additions. I believe M^r. *Wharton* borrow'd this copy from M^r. Seller, for in the Preface p. 34. he hath these words:

Historiæ Lichfeldensis ad annum usque 1347. *quinque exemplaria mihi præsto fuerunt. Primum ex Bibliotheca Cottoniana Cleop. D. g. ante* 300. *annos exaratum. Secundum, ejusdem circiter ætatis, ad calcem Chronici insignis Lichfeldensis (quod Amicus quidam possidet) reperitur. In his nullam invenire potui variationem; adeoque Historiæ textum ex ijsdem expressi, &c.* —

M^r. Berger tells me that Gronovius, in some discourse he had wth him, defended the word *concitur* as being used in the time of *Livy*. Quære whether there be any such word in any old Copy of Livy? Answer I have found it in all the MSS^{ts} wch I have consulted.

[Various notes on Livy from C. Neapolis' Anaptyxis ad P. Ovidii Fastorum lib. iv, v. 49, &c.; P. Victorii var. Lectt. viii. 3, x. 2.]

To day was admitted into ye Publick Library these two Gentlemen (1) *Christianus Fredericus Boernerus, Dredensis*. (2) *Balthasar Heinricus de Platen, Pomeranus*.

Aug. 1 (Wed.). On July 27th last ye Queen Knighted D^r. Wm. Read, ye Oculist. — On the 29th of ye same Month She also Knighted D^r. Edw. Hannes the Physitian.

[Notes on Livy from P. Victorii var. Lectt., l. xxi. c. 1; l. xxiv. c. 11.]

This day D^r. Mill resign'd his Prebend of *Excester* to M^r. Humph. Smith, formerly of Queen's Coll.

[News from the Scottish Parliament, dated Edinburgh, July 24.]

Aug. 2 (Th.). . . . We have an Account from ye Assises at Maidstone, y^t ye Soldier belonging to Sheerness Fort, y^t Bastinadoed to death one Mack-lennan, a whiggish & busy Pedlar, was condemned to die for ye same; But that ye Major, who 'tis pretended hired him for ½ a Crown, was cleared by ye Jury, tho' contrary to ye Direction of my L^d. C. J.   The same was made a mighty party cause. — An Indictment of Purjury being brought by a
10 Party at ye Assizes at Northampton against a Clergy Man, who has a Benefice of 100 lib^s. per Annum for swearing himself a Freeholder, & giving his vote for ye Knights of ye Shire, ye Judges who sate there declared against it, & put an End to ye Project. — On Tuesday last (Jul. 31) was published (1) A True & Exact Map of ye Seat of ye war in Brabant & Flanders, &c.   (2) The Life & Character of M^r. John Locke, written in French by M. Le Clerck & done into English by T. F. P. Gent. — . . . *Erasmus's* Epistles . . Amongst which is his Dedicatory Epistle of *Livy*, which must be look'd over when a Preface is written upon this Author to give an Account of Editions of him.
20   [Notes on Livy from V. Contareni Var. Lectt. c. 1. p. 6; C. Verderii Censiones et Correctiones; Cuperi Apotheosis vel Consecratio Homeri, p. 16; and Monumenta Antiqua, p. 208.]

D^r. Hudson tells me y^t D^r. Smith told him that M^r. *Wotton* (Will.) has translated into Latin M^r. Greaves's Discourses of the *Pyramids* & the *Roman Denarius.*

[Notes on Livy from G. Budaeus de Asse, lib. V.]

Aug. 3 (Fri.). Yesterday came to the Library some Gentlemen of *Hamburg*, amongst whom was M^r. *Pritius*, a Superintendent in those Parts, who brought a Letter to D^r. Hudson from M^r. *Fabritius*, with y^e
30 first vol. of his *Bibliotheca Græca*.   Amongst other things in the Letter he mention'd that he had heard that D^r. *Hody* was dead, wch I suppose somebody had related to him, as a jest upon his Book, which is very insipid. — D^r. Mill told me last night that he has brought the History of the New Testament from ye year 110 to 1555.   So that now there is hopes his *Prolegomena* may be finish'd in a little time.

[Notes on Livy from Budaei de Asse, libb. I, II, III.]

The Title of the first Vol. of *Fabricius's* Book which he has sent to D^r. Hudson, Jo. Alberti Fabricij SS. Theologiæ D. & Prof. Publ. Bibliotheca Græca (. . .) *Hamburgi*, 1705. 4°. — . . . D^r. *Hudson* had also
40 sent him *Elogium Funebre in Joan. Wincklerum*, spoken by George Eliezer Edzard, Professor of the Greek Tongue & History at Hamburg. M^r. Hoffman tells me D^r. *Winckler* was a very celebrated Divine, & one

---

Aug. 3. F. Cherry to H. 'Dr Chum, For all y^r friendly advice I met with a fall before I got to Henly which caus'd a great fraction in my nose but did me not much hurt else, tho the effects of that & our happy meeting disabled me from getting home y^t night to the great detriment of my pockett.   I found all ffriends here well.   My Cozen studys as little here as I doe at Ox: when I have money; for I ha'nt seen him look in a Book since I come.'   Messages from and to friends.

of the most pious men he ever knew; that he preach'd with so much Zeal & Affection that few ever went out of the Church wth dry eyes & that he was generally lamented at his Death.

[Notes on Livy from P. Merulae Com. ad. Q. Ennij Fragmenta.—Letter from Fabricius to Dr. Hudson, dated Hamburg, a. Cal. Julij, 1705. Sends Vol. I. of his *Bibliotheca Graeca*. Introduces Dr. Pritius. Fears his letters to Hudson, Dodwell, Grabe, &c., may have miscarried. Reads in A. Van Dale on Aristeas that Hody is dead; is it so? Best wishes to Hudson.]

D^r. *Pritius*, Superintendent of *Sleufens*, has published ye New Testament in Greek with various Readings. So he told D^r. Hudson himself. Ask D^r. Mill about it[1]. — I am satisfied that 'twas a malicious Story wch was raised about M^r. Dodwells making objections[2] against ye Athanasian Creed, & y^t he refus'd going into orders upon y^t Account.

[News from the Scottish Parliament, dated Edinburgh, July 26.]

Aug. 4 (Sat.). ... We have an Account from ye Late Assizes at Horsham in Sussex y^t ye Clergy of y^t County in a full Body making upwards of 150 waited on Arthur Turner Esquire ye High Sheriff & in a solemn manner gave him their thanks for standing up for ye Interest of ye Church in the late Elections & for vindicating ye Rights of y^c Commons & not permitting a great Lord to be present at takeing ye Poll for Knights of y^c Shire. The Grand Jury for ye County returned the High Sheriff ye like thanks & were both magnificently treated by him. — Doctor Wake Dean of Exeter is declared B^p. of Lincoln & Doctor Blackbourne the B^r. of Exeter's favourite is made Dean of Exeter. — Dr. Pritius besides ye Edition of ye New Testament in Greek, has also publish'd Introductio in lectionem Novi Testamenti. D^r. Smith some time since sent me an Extract out of it, giving an Account of D^r. Mill's undertaking. — Out of a Letter Dr. Charlett received from Mr. Wanley dated Aug. 1. 1705[3].

Since the *Moyen* is among Mr. Selden's books, I believe that wch I have was sold, as a Duplicate, about 30 years ago, and shall therefore keep it. I am not surprized that ye Edition of ye Bible I mentioned is not in ye Library, nor mentioned by our Reformation Writers, for 'tis not mentioned [in] any of the Catalogues of our *old* Bookes, wch Catalogues have been thought very comprehensive & Exact. The Preface or dedication (wch is PIO LECTORI, not to any particular man) perswades me that the King was ye Editor : for amongst other passages therein I observe these, Probe nosti quemadmodum Dominus Deus noster, de cujus verbis seu scripturis agitur, imperaverit, ut Rex postquam in Regni sui solio sederit, Legem Dei sibi describeret, & habens secum legeret omnibus diebus vitæ suæ: quo disceret timere Dominum Deum suum, & verba ejus custodire. Nos itaque consyderantes id erga Deum *officij nostri, quo suscepisse cognoscimur, ut in Regno simus sicut Anima in corpore & sol in mundo, utque loco Dei judicium exerceamus in Regno nostro, & omnia in Potestate habentes quoad jurisdictionem, ipsam etiam Ecclesiam vice Dei sedulo regamus ac tueamur :* & Disciplina ejus sive augeatur aut solvatur, *nos ei rationem reddituri simus, qui Nobis eam credidit, in eo Dei vicem agentes, Deique habentes imaginem,* quid aliud vel cogitare vel in animum tam inducere potuimus, quam ut eodem confugeremus, ubi certo discendum esset, ne quid aliud vel ipsi faceremus vel faciendum

---

[1] [8°. 1703. W. 83. Th.—Dr. Bliss.]

[2] 'Tis certainly true that he had some Objections about the Athanasian Creed. What they were I know not, 'twas not for y^t reason that he did not go into Orders.

[3] [MS. Ballard xiii. 70.—Dr. Bliss.]

alijs præscriberemus, quam quod ab hac ipsa Dei lege ne vel transversum quidem digitum aberrare convinci queat? *Et licet sacerdotes bene multos habeamus, profecto* (sit Deo gratia) *nihil inidoneos ad id præstandum ac rite complendum, quod populi nostri necessitas in spirituale sui regimen expetierit: nostra tamen nihilominus interesse judicavimus, ut ipsam Dei legem ipsi tanquam in sinu gestemus, qua continue pervisuri simus uti tam plebs ipsa quam spirituales Patres ejus utrique quod debeant fideliter ac vigilanter adimpleant*—oculi quanquam Dei dono satis adhuc acuti, quia tamen a solito (quod per ætatem assolet) acumine mutare poterunt, literam adaptavimus nostro judicio magis oportunam atque 10 ocellis perviam: licet elegantiores ac plausibiliores alie fortasse judicabuntur, quibus hec ut in una aut altera recedat, ut in ceteris multo magis applaudit. Voluntas enim erat, eas vel Instrumenti Scripturas cum Evangelicis conjungendi, in quibus Hystoria humanæ vitæ cum preceptis, moralibus Doctrinis, debitisque vivendi formulis magis exprimitur.—Hic vero libellus quem tantopere in delicijs habere constituimus, nobiscum omnino vel hospitari vel cohabitare debet.

The first of these Paragraphs does, I think, sufficiently shew it to be ye King's, since these words fit no other person: the same, & the last shew his main Design in printing this Edition, tho' I wonder he should leave out *the* 20 *Son of Syrach* in this his first Tome. The second acquaints you with ye State of his Eyes about ye 26th year of his Reign, wch is not commonly taken notice of, & it likewise seems to infer that Spectacles were not then in England, since ye King must have his Bible printed with a gross Letter for his private use; as I suppose that ye Bibles, Missals, Breviaries, & other Religious Books, were written & printed at first in a large Hand, for ye use of old Priests & for other Antient people of ye Laity, who generally are ye most devout.

This Book has a large Index before it, & if it be valued according to it's Rarity, might bring me a very great Sum, but as 'tis mine, I will not sell it.

I hope Mr. Hearne will acquiesce in my Reasons for Ascribing the Bible to 30 King Hen. 8. I know not who it is that is writing the Antiquities of Middlesex, but rather hope for a good Performance of that Task, since few undertake such sort of works, but those who are able to give tolerable satisfaction to ye Publick. His Desires of a collection of all English Epitaphs, &c. (material ones) I believe will be fullfilled, for there have been as I have heard proposals of this kind published, & the work is said to be in good forwardness.

[Notes on Livy from Merula.]

Aug. 5 (Sun.). Anno 1674 was published in 4to. a Book *De nummis* under M^r. Selden's name by *Moses Pit*. 'Tis exactly ye same 40 wth that wch goes under ye Name of *Alexander Sardus*, first published in 1579, and afterwards at *Franckfurt* in 12°. in 1609, and again in *Grævius's Thesaurus*. We have y^e *Franckfurt* Edition in M^r. *Selden's* Library. So that it must be attributed to ye knavery of ye Bookseller, who has taken care to make no Alterations unless it be in ye Dedication for *Alexander Sardus Augustino Musto Patricio Ferrariensi* he puts *Joannes Seldenus Sim. Dewes Equiti Aurato*. And at ye end of it for *Moguntiaci Calend. Maij* 1579 he puts *ex Med. Templ. Calend. Maij*, 1642. — On Friday last (*Aug.* 3.) was publish'd, *The History of Holland*, with a particular Description of all it's Provinces, &c. in 2 vols. 8°.

Aug. 5. H. to Dr. T. Smith.—Glad the new ed. of Gruter is in so great forwardness. Sends MS. inscription on spare leaf at beginning of R. Soc. copy of Tarvisine Livy, containing a relation of the Actions for which Pompey had so glorious a triumph A. U. C. 692.—Joyner his informant about a Life of R. Bacon by Selden. Seller's will: his MS. bequeathed to Bodley.

Price 12^s. — M^{rs}. *Ann Cherry*, wife of *Wm. Cherry* Esqr, died in ye year 1702, in the 83^d year of her Age.

Aug. 6 (Mon.). On Thursday ye 2^d Instant the Dutchess of *Marlborough* presented ye Queen wth a fine Standard in commemoration of the Battle of *Hockstett* wch is to be continued yearly according to Act of Parliament.

[News from the Scottish Parliament, dated Edinburgh, July 28.]

Baron *Spaar* has pass'd the Canal between *Ghent* & *Bruges*, forced ye Enemie's Lines, & is got into ye Country of *Waes*. —

Out of ye Observations upon the essay towards a Proposal for 10 Catholick Communion, Chap. xi. p. 135. . . .

[Notes on Livy from Sebastianus Maccius Durantinus *de Historia*, Car. Sigonius and Balthasar Bonifacius *de Historicis*, Pamelij *Exercitatt.*]

The Author of y^e *Observations upon The Essay*[1] *for Catholick Communion* is M^r. *Edward Stephens*, as appears from the Book wch he quotes for *Prayers for ye Dead*, written by himself. D^r. *Hudson* also told me he was Author. This Person formerly writ one discourse at least in behalf of the *Quakers*, after wch He declar'd himself in several Respects to be a Roman Catholick. He was once very violent against y^e *Jacobites*, but at length, much about ye time that King William died, He 20 declar'd Himself for them, & wrote several Papers shewing himself to be of opinion that the *Prince of Wales* is legitimate. He is (tho' mutable yet) a very conscientious man, & has been a great sufferer upon y^t Account. He leads a most strict & severe life; but is a great *opiniator*. — D^r. *Wynne* (Hugh) tells me he has writ *An Historical Account, proving that it has been ye Opinion of the chief of our* English *writers since the Reformation, that the Lawfull civil Magistrate may, for Political Crimes, deprive a Bishop:* wherein he has discover'd some Errors of M^r. *Dodwell*, & shew'd y^t he has in some places contradicted himself. 'Tis not printed. — 30

[Notes on Livy from T. Fabri Epistolae, Pars II, various works of Lipsius, P. Benij Eugubini de Historia libri IV, &c.]

D^r. Crosthwait says that the Author of y^e *Essay for Catholick Communion* is one that is a *Welch*-man or at least lives in *Wales*. There is just now come out a Book containing some Papers about *Transubstantia[tio]n* wch pass'd between M^r. *H. Newcom* a minister in *Lancashire* & *T. B.* a *Romish* Priest. *Quære* whether this *T. B.* be the Author of *the Essay*. — From some words, wch pass'd between M^r. *Grabe* and another Gentleman in ye University, I gather that he saw M^r. *Stephens's Observations* upon the said Essay before they went to 40 the Press. Mr. *Stephens* quotes B^p. *Andrews's Prayers* to vindicate His Assertion for *Praying for the Dead*. I believe M^r. *Grabe* is of this opinion. I am sure He makes use of B^p. *Andrews's Prayers*, as an Extraordinary Book. M^r. *Stephens* amongst other things in these observations is for *Consubstan[tia]tion*, & that's the Reason M^r. *Grabe* receives the sacrament at his Hands, it being well known y^t he is a *Lutheran*, & that he never communicates with the church of *England*; wch I ye more wonder at, because He receiv'd orders from D^r. *Lloyd*, now B^p. of

[1] See above, pag. 33.

Worcester, & when he first came to *Oxford* propos'd to write a Book to shew that the *Church of England* excells all other churches. —

[Notes on Livy from notes to Hyginus and Polybius *de Castris* (ed. Amst., 1660).]

I am told by M[r]. *Grabe* that *The Essay for Catholick Communion* was written by M[r]. *Basset*, formerly a Church of *England* Man, and afterwards a Papist; upon w[ch] Account he was made by King *James* Head of Sidney College in *Cambridge*, tho' soon ejected thence. He is now living in *London*. It appears from some Passages in M[r]. *Stephens's*
10 *Observations* that *Bonaventure Gifford*, a *Roman* Priest, Doctor of the *Sorbon* & Bishop Elect of *Madaura*, (*in partibus infidelium*) did in some measure assist in this Essay. — . . Yesterday (being *Monday*) a fire hapen'd in S[t]. *Clement's* Lane in *London* in a Calender's House in w[ch] an Ancient Gentleman was burn'd to death, & a *Barbadoes'* merchant w[ch] lodg'd there had all his Books of Accounts burn'd tho' he offer'd 10000 lib[s] to save them. — According to y[e] *Paris* Gazet, the Duke of *Marlborough*, tho' he pass'd y[e] *Dyle*, yet being forc'd to retire back, came off with great loss, the *French* firing their Canon upon him for above an hour together. He lost at least 800 men, besides divers kill'd
20 in two or three other less Actions. — D[r]. *Hudson* tells me that M[r]. *Badger* has an old Edition of *Justin* w[ch] I have not yet seen. Remember to ask M[r]. *Badger* about it. — Ex 1[mo]. Vol. Scriptorum Historiae Augustae, per Sylburg. p. 485. in praefatione nimirum Andr. Schotti demonstranti Aurelium Victorem auctorem esse Libelli *de viris illustribus*. . . . — At y[e] End of *Diarium Italicum* publish'd by Mons[r]. *Monfoucat* are very considerable Emendations of the *Prologues to Trogus Pompejus* from MSS[ts] at *Rome* and other Places, w[ch] I did not know of, when I was about *Justin*. D[r]. *Hudson* talks of Printing them in a sheet in 8[o], so that it may be bound wth such copies as are not
30 disperst. However they must be remembred at least when another Edition of *Justin* comes out. . . .

[Notes on book-titles from Vaillant's *Numismata Aerea*.]

A Gentleman this afternoon told me that lately in Ireland in a Bog was found the Body of [a] man w[ch] seem'd very firm; but being open'd the Bones appear'd quite wasted being turn'd into Moss. —

Out of a Letter from D[r]. Mich. Geddes to Dr. Hudson dated Jul. 19. 1704.
I have in print promised two Books to your Library, the one is, *The Archbishop of Goa's Visitation of the Council of Diamper*, in Portuguese. The other is, *the Dominicans Romantick History of the Church of Ethiopia*, in Spanish. If
40 you Have them not already I will take care to send them to you by the first opportunity that shall offer. I find you have a great many MSS. Calendars, you would oblige me much, if you would let me know, whether you have, A *Large Heathen Roman Calendar* which mentions the *Festivitys of* old Rome, & if you have such a Book, & will be so kind as to let me have *a Copy* of it, I

Aug. 8. Jam. Ashenhurst to H. Enquires on behalf of a friend the number of vacant places & candidates at All Souls'. **T. Cherry to H.** Sorry the Lexicon cannot be found. Dodwell & Cherry cannot answer his queries. 'My Cozen has gotten the *Memorial of y[e] C. of E.*, but he feares the D[r]. would never make a Jubilee for it.' Thanks for the Mercury. News about the Duke of Marlborough. Dodwell has almost finish'd his work on Immortality of the Soul.

will to the full satisfy any person you shall be pleased to employ to transcribe it for me. I have a short one published by *Aldus Minutius* in the year 1591, &c.

Aug. 9 (Th.). [News from the Scottish Parliament, dated Edinburgh, August 1.]

On yᵉ 29th of July last Dʳ. Tennison Bᴾ. of Meath in Ireland departed this Life. . . .

[Notes on Livy from Boxhornius' *Quaest. Romanae*, Ryckius *de Capitolio*, Is. Vossius ad Scylacem, &c.]

Dʳ. *Hudson* tells me there is a Letter of Mʳ. *Dodwell's* printed in one of Mʳ. *Hen. Layton's* Pieces, concerning *yᵉ Immortality of yᵉ Soul*, & yᵗ his Name is to it. I have look'd them over, but do not find it, unless it be yᵗ Letter in p. 35. of his Pamphlet intituled *Arguments & Replies in a Dispute concerning the Nature of the Humane Soul. Lond.* 1703, wᶜʰ however has no Name added. I received a Letter from Mʳ. Tho. Cherry, from Shottesbrook, (where Mʳ. Dodwell lives) dated Sept. 2. 1705, satisfying me that this is Mʳ. Dodwell's Letter. — Dʳ. *Sloane* is very busy in writing *The Natural History of Jamaica*; which is yᵉ reason I hear, yᵗ he committed the care of *the Philosophical Transactions* to Mʳ. *Thorpe*.

[Notes on Livy from G. J. Vossius *de Arte Grammatica, de Origine ac Progressu Idololatriae, Commentarii rhetorici*; book-titles, &c.]

In *Drusius's Epistles*, printed *an.* 1595. 8ᵒ. . . are 4 to Sʳ. *Thomas Bodley*, whence it appears yᵗ the learned men of yᵗ time had a very great Esteem of his Learning, especially in the *Oriental* Tongues. See after the Answers of Sir *Thomas*.

VOL. III.

Aug. 10 (Fri.). Yesterday was admitted into the Publick Library, *Henningius Friman Danus.* —

[Notes from Cluverij Italia Antiqua.]

To day was publish'd Mr. *Tilly's* (*Will.*) Assize Sermon upon Prov. 24. 10, 11, 12. Bishop *Sanderson* has two excellᵗ Assize Sermons upon yᵉ same Text. — Dʳ. *Mill* told me to day yᵗ Dʳ. Alix has not yᵉ copy of the *Councils* ready for the Press, & that yᵗ is yᵉ reason we hear nothing now of it. — From some discourse tonight wᵗʰ Mʳ. *Grabe* I gather'd yᵗ he is inclin'd something to yᵉ church of *Rome*, and spoke but indifferently of yᵉ *English* Clergy, greatly blameing the Majority of them as being very negligent in visiting the sick *&c.* — . . Mʳ. Spinks[1] a nonjuror writ to Mʳ. *Thwaits* about a Passage concerning the Pope's Supremacy mention'd in yᵉ late *Essay for Catholick communion*. This made me think He was writing an Answer to this Book. But Mʳ. Thwaits assur'd me of the contrary, & yᵗ he was not able to do such a thing, tho' he be otherwise a cunning plodding man. Upon wᶜʰ I find he makes collections for another *non-juror* who is upon such a Design. — Mʳ. *Hoffman* seems to agree with Mʳ. *Grabe*, in Points of *Religion*. — There is a new Book lately come out call'd *the Principles of Laws*

---

[1] Mr. Thwaites mistaken. Mr. Spinkes came out with a Learned and Judicious Answer.

in General, in 8º, translated out of *French* by Dʳ. *Wood* of *New-Coll.* being design'd as an *Introduction* to his *New Institute of the Imperial or Civil Law*, publish'd last year in 8º.

Aug. 11 (Sat.). [News from the Scottish Parliament, dated Edinburgh, August 2.]

Several Persons of yᵉ Whigg Party were indicted & tryed this Assizes at Coventry for a Riot, by them committed at the Elections of Members of Parliament, some of wᶜʰ were found guilty & fined. — Norton Pawlet Esqr. a Member of Parliament for Petersfield is dead.
10 — Coningsburgh Aug. 2. An Express arriv'd here of an entire defeat of 8000 Swedes under comand of General Lewenhoft by 3000 Muscovites, most of wᶜʰ were slain. 30000 Muscovites have invested Riga. The *Czar* is marching wᵗʰ 50000 directly for Warswa. — On Tuesday morning Sʳ. Edw. Nevil one of yᵉ Judges of yᵉ *common Pleas* departed this life. — At Salisbury Assizes at a tryal about yᵉ Toll and Stallage of Swyndon Market, one Mʳ. Will. Wild was produced as witness, who was an hundred & fifteen years of Age. He well remembred Queen Elizabeth, & rode to Wilton to seek James 1ˢᵗ when he was at yᵉ Earl of Pembrooks. He was born at Friborne where he has lived all his time,
20 his Eyesight and Hearing are very good. His cheeks not sunk, & walked upright. His Grand-Daughter was in court, and was 60 years of Age.

[Extract from Petri Fabri *in Libros Academicos Ciceronis Commentarius*, p. 26.]

Quære whether a Pamphlet printed in the year 1650. 4ᵗᵒ, & intitled, *A Brief Resolution of that Grand Case of Conscience (necessary for these Times) concerning the Allegiance due to a Prince Ejected by Force out of his Kingdome, & how far yᵉ Subjects may comply wᵗʰ a present usurped Power*, was not written by Dʳ. *Hammond*? — In yᵉ year 1689. came out in 4ᵗᵒ *A Letter to Bishop* [sic] *concerning the Present Settlement & the New Oathes*. *Quære* who was the Author? As also who writ the
30 the New Oathes. *Quære* who was the Author? As also who writ the Answer to it, part of wᶜʰ was printed in 1690, tho not all, because 'twas seiz'd? Some say Captain *Hatton* writ the latter.

[Extracts from Cluverij *Italia Antiqua*.]

Falmouth 6th. Great shooting has been heard off of yᵉ Lizzard wᶜʰ makes us believe yᵗ Admiral Bing's Squadron has fallen in wᵗʰ the Brest Squadron.

Aug. 13 (Mon.). The great Shooting heard off of the Lizzard was occasion'd by two French Men of war wᶜʰ were engag'd & taken by the Worcester and Chatham Men of war. — Mʳ. Baron Price who sate
40 on the crown side at yᵉ Assizes at Winchester gave an Extraordinary fine charge to yᵉ Grand Jury in wᶜʰ amongst other things he took notice of yᵉ Slanders and Aspersions wᶜʰ yᵉ Fanatick Party in yᵉ Libells &c. cast on yᵉ Church of England, & reminded them yᵗ yᵉ present Liberty wᶜʰ they enjoyed was purely yᵉ effect of yᵉ Bounty of yᵉ Church of England &c. This is yᵉ Brave Britaine yᵗ so strenuously opposed in yᵉ Late Reign yᵉ Grant of yᵉ Principality of Wales to a Dutch Man. —

[Extracts from Frontinus, cum notis Rob. Keuchenij ; Cluverij *Italia Antiqua* ; J. C. Bulengerus *de Theatro* ; book-titles, &c.]

Aug. 14 (Tu.). I hear ye Queen has lately urg'd D^r. Mill (sending an order for that End) to hasten wth his Testament.

[Extracts from Q. Curtius, cum Com. Sam. Pitisci; Cluverij *Italia Antiqua*, &c.]

Aug. 15 (Wed.). D^r. *Charlett* lately told me y^t the reason why D^r. *Bathurst* did not give to the Publick Library such of his Books as were wanting there, was because D^r. *Hudson* told him y^t we wanted but very few of them: wch made him think y^t 'twas not worth while to put a clause in his will upon so small an Account. But I believe this to be a story, having been inform'd that the chief reason was because D^r. 10 Charlett desired D^r. Bathurst to let us take an Account before his Death of w^t Books we wanted. W^ch he seem'd a little to resent, as if he were not to be relyed on, & would dispose of the best of his Books to other uses. However he lent his Catalogue, which I carefully compar'd with the Library Catalogues, putting down all such Books as we wanted, wch was a considerable Number, & most of them valuable Books. So that I cannot for this reason think D^r. Hudson would say any such matter to D^r. *Bathurst.* — M^r. *Hoffman* is in quest after the Sermons or Homilies of *Jacobus Nisibenus.* He is looking over also the Homilies of *Ephræm Syrus* in the Publick Library. He has some 20 design of making them publick both in *Syriack* and *Greek,* if he could meet with suitable Encouragement to carry on the Impression.

Aug. 16 (Th.). M^r. *Milles* (Tho.) writ formerly a Letter to M^r. *Grabe* concerning his Dissent from him (M^r. *Grabe*) about relying upon the Judgment of the Father's insisted upon by him in his Preface to the 1st vol. of *Spicilegium Patrum.* 'Twas in *Latin,* & was design'd I believe to be printed, but I cannot tell what hinder'd it. — D^r. *Mill* gives but a very indifferent Character (wch I much wonder at) of D^r. *Beveridge,* now B^p. of St. *David's,* particularly upon Account of his not taking sufficient care of things belonging to his Prebend of Canterbury 30 wherein D^r. *Mill* succeeded him. — D^r. *Mill* tells me he has been at 400 lib^s charge at least upon S^t. *Edm.* Hall, and that amongst other things he finish'd mostly with his own money the Library wch was only began when he came to the Hall. But I do not believe this. — Amongst D^r. *Pocock's* MSS^ts *in Bib. Bodl.* is one of *Syriack* containing Homilies of *Mar* or *Dominus Jacobus,* & *Ephræm Syrus.* 'Tis probable this *Mar Jacobus* is the same w^th *Jacobus Nisibenus*; because, as M^r. *Hoffman* tells me, in the title Page, he is also call'd *Sanctus,* wch was a proper Title for

---

Aug. 16. Dr. T. Smith to H. Remarks on the inscription of Pompey. Still has doubts about Selden and Dee; thinks Joyner's memory has played him false—is he the translator of the Life of Pole, &c.? Thinks Bp. Godwin's *Nuncius inanimatus* was 'merely in the way of wit.' Expects Fabricius' *Bibl. Graeca* at once; glad he designs to publish Eunapius. Pritius seems merely a laborious collector and transcriber. Will ask Lister for a copy of his *Apicius.* Wonders at Seller's vanity in wishing for a Greek inscription, considering the 'horrible blunders in his *Antiquities of Palmyra.*' 'The *Chronicon Lichfeldense* is a curious & usefull MS. It formerly belonged to Capt. Spragge, sometime Fellow of Trin. Coll. Camb., whom I knew full well, who pawned it with some other MSS. to Mr. Pate, a woollen draper: from whom Mr. Seller obtained [it] in the way of barter and exchange for printed books.'

Jacobus Nisibenus, he being a very holy devout Man, & very much cele-brated in the East upon that Account. — Letters from Salisbury say that Dr. *Young* Deane of yt cathedral departed this Life last Thursday (Aug. 11). — Mr. *Tyrrell* tells me he cannot tell who 'twas yt translated Monsr. *Le Clerck's* Life and Character of Mr. *Lock* but that he will make Inquiry. — I am told that Mr. *Rymer*, who has Published two Volumes of *Records* from the Tower, is a very good sort of Man, & that he designs to carry on the work, being now upon a IIId volume. Dr. *Hudson* has lent him for a month the MSt of Instruments &c. concerning
10 the Reigns of *Edw*. III. & Hen. V. which he received from Sir *John Osborne*.

August 17 (Fr.). Dr. *Wynne* tells me that Mr. *Spinkes* is a very prudent Man, & that he thinks him qualifyed to answer Mr. *Basset's Essay for Catholick communion*, notwithstanding I was told by another he was not. He has it seems writ one book already about *Patience*, wch I have not seen. He with Mr. *Wagstaffe* is imploy'd to distribute such moneys as are given by the chief Jacobites for charitable uses. Dr. *Hickes* has given this Mr. *Spinkes* a very worthy character in his General Preface to his *Thesaurus Linguarum veterum Septentrionalium*. — Mr. *Cherry (Francis)* has drawn
20 up a Chronology to *Herodotus*, wch Mr. *Dodwell* tells me is done very well. I suppose he had once a design to publish anew this Excellent Author ; but I believe, upon the Death of his Father, he has laid aside all thoughts of this kind. I have seen in his Study, in an *octavo* Book, a great many particulars relating to Mr. *Dodwell's* Life, wch I suppose he will take care to publish if he survives him. He has been at the charge of an Exact Picture of Mr. *Dodwell*, painted in his studying gown, writing, & with Books about him. This he designs to bequeath to the University, to be hung amongst other Learned Men in the Publick Gallery belonging to the *Bodlejan* Library.

30   **August 18 (Sat.).** [News from the Scottish Parliament, dated Edinburgh, Aug. 9.]

Plymouth 12th. Yesterday morning about 1 aclock was a terrible storm, in wch divers merchant ships were lost homeward bound from Lisbon, Leghorn, Barbadoes &c. The Men of War indeed are all safe, but upon a true compu-tation from the Accounts hence, & other places particularly Portsmouth where of 150 outward Bound Merchant Men above half are missing the Merchants have suffer'd more in their shipping than they did last great storme.

A Proclamation come out for further Proroguing the Parliament to the 23d of October next, when they are to meet & do Business. — They
40 write from Andover in Hampshire that ye storme blew down intirely the Steeple there, reckon'd the biggest in yt Country; but that no other damage was done by the fall than breaking down part of a House. — Yesterday one *Sanford* came to the Publick Library, with *Cole* the Ingraver, on purpose to look over our Coyns, & to take the Impressions of some of them. *Cole* says he has got a good Collection of his own, &

Aug. 18. Charlett to H. 25 copies of amended advertisement of Theatre books to be sent to him at Windsor Castle. Is to ride over to Maidenhead to meet Dodwell and Cherry over a 'Dish of Coffe,' and will do justice to H. as sub-librarian. Mr. Ceely to send the two 8vo. Common Prayer Books bound.

that he is acquainted wth the chief *Virtuosos* in London, who have any Coyns. *Quære* whether this be true?

[Extract from M^r. Selden's Notes to his Verses upon M^r. *Hopton,* praefixed to his *Concordance of Years,* pr. *An.* 1615. 8°.]

B^p. *Godwin's Nuntius inanimatus* was translated into English by D^r. *Tho. Smith* (as he tells me in a Letter) and published in 1657. Desire him to send us one to the Library (if he has duplicates) we having there neither the *Latin* nor ye Translation. — Mr. *Priaulx* is said to be Author of those two ingenious Poems, call'd *Faction display'd,* and *Moderation display'd,* whereof there is lately come out in 8° (price 2*s.*) a new Edition printed from a correct copy, with Improvements.

[Inscription on a coin of Gordian.]

Aug. 19 (Sun.). On *Friday* last D^r. *Lloyd,* B^p. of Worcester, return'd from the Country to *Oxford,* where he designs to stay 'till the Sitting of the Parliament, with intent to prosecute his *Exposition upon Daniel,* whereof there are already about 13 sheets printed, the whole being to be 30. He says that he must finish this work before he can proceed with his *chronology,* whereof 30 sheets were printed several years since. So that no one expects to see this Work from his Hands, and he is now become sensible that he cannot finish, & therefore intends to leave it to his son, whom he thinks able to carry it on, having already settled matters so as 'twill be no difficulty for any one a little skill'd in chronology to put the remainder in good order. The last time he was in Town he shew'd me a *Summary* of his whole *Exposition upon Daniel,* which seem'd to be extraordinary well done, and adapted to the meanest Reader.

Aug. 20 (Mon.). [News from the Scottish Parliament, dated Edinburgh, August 11.]

We hear ye Queens design'd Procession to St. Paul's on the 23^d Instant is put off tho' things were prepared for solemnizing ye day by Te Deum & a sermon. 'Twas thought w^n ye Proclamation was issued for a thanksgiving it was expected y^t some thing more signal would have followed upon forcing the Enemy's Lines to have made ye victory compleat & signal but unforseen Difficulties hapned & ye Elector of Bavaria in an Intercepted Letter of his to the French King assures his Majesty y^t he'l observe his orders in not fighting & will defye the Duke of Marlborough to force him to it. So y^t upon the whole most are of opinion that there ought rather to have been a publick Fast Day than one for a Thanksgiving, especially since 3 Holland Mails just arriv'd assure us that the Duke of Marlborough having attempted a Battle was obstructed by the Dutch who are unwilling to hazard one, upon wch he complains in a Letter to the States of the small Authority he has in the Army by indirect Practises of those who do not seem to favour the good of ye common cause. And the Prince Lewis has joyn'd his Army, yet Marshal Villars, the French General declines to fight. Nor do Letters from Lisbon give any better Accounts, a Great Plot in favour of Charles III^d having been discover'd and several of the Principal concern'd in it executed.

[Note on Livy from Gruteri Fax Artium, p. 324.]

Aug. 21 (Tu.). In the 9th Vol. of D^r. Langbain's Collections, given to the Publick Library by M^r. *Ant. à Wood,* are divers Matters, by way of

Objection and Answer relating to *Purgatory* and *Prædestination*, put down by him I suppose upon Account of some Publick Dispute in Divinity. Of Free Will in pag. 43. ibid. p. 69. An Ecclesia errare vel deficere possit? — I am told by one of the Fellows of *Merton-College* that M^r. *Ant. à Wood* formerly us'd to frequent their Common Room; but that a Quarrel arising one night between some of the Fellows, one of them, who thought himself very much abus'd, put some of the rest into the Court; but when the Day for deciding the matter came, there wanted sufficient Evidence. At last M^r. *Wood*, having been in company all the time the Quarrel lasted 10 and put down the whole in Writing, gave a full Relation, wch appear'd so clear for the Plaintiff, that immediate Satisfaction was commanded to be given. This was so much resented, that M^r. *Wood* was afterwards expell'd the common Room, & his company avoyded as an observing Person, & not fit to be present where matters of moment were discuss'd.

[Extract from Ant. Mureti Var. Lectt., lib. 16, c. 8.]

Yesterday D^r. *Mill* sent to me a *Testimonium* to be sign'd for Cyprian & Paul Appia, Vaudois, that they may be admitted into H. Orders. But whereas they never lodg'd, nor convers'd with any, in Edm. Hall (at least not to my knowledge) I return'd it again wthout giving my Hand. 20 The B^p. of Worcester has maintain'd them for sometime. & now designs to put them into Orders, being mov'd to it by D^r. *Mill*, who does not consider that 'tis not canonical, they having not been ever of any University before they came hither; & tho' they did sometimes receive a Lecture from one in *Edm*. Hall, yet they were never either of y^t House or any other in this university as Members, and therefore ought not to claim the Privilege of university men. Besides 'tis not 3 years since they had first a Lecture from the said Person, being admitted into the Publick Library Apr. 11. 1704, a little before wch they agreed about a Lecture.

Aug. 22 (Wed.). The true Title of the MS^t wch M^r. *Hoffman* thought 30 contain'd some *Homilies* of *Jacobus Nisibenus* is, as he has found out since, *Codex Sermonum, in dies Festos, Dominicos, aliorumque generum Domini Doctoris Jacobi, Episcopi Bathanæi in Syria, cum paucis quibusdam S. Ephræmi.* — M^r. Swift Author of *The Tale of a Tub.* —

In Bibliotheca Bodlejana inter MSS. codices super D. Art. num. 86. est liber bene magnus rythmis Anglicanis tractans de Oratione Dominica, ejus septem petitionibus, septem donis Spiritus Sancti, septem peccatis mortalibus, septem virtutibus, septem beatitudinibus, & septem *aureolis* seu praemijs; cujus principium est,

> Almiȝty God in trinité,
> In Iwome ar persones þré.

40

Aug. 21. Hudson to H. To ask Mr. Thwaits whether he has anything to say to Hudson (who is at Northampton). H. to watch the coin-monger, and to report anything worth communicating. Directions how to address him. He returns in less than a fortnight.

Aug. 22. Charlett to H. Commissions. 'Mr. Tillys Sermon pleases very much some considerable Persons at Court.' Defeat of the French in Italy by Prince Eugene. Messages to Sherwin, Thwaites, Smith, and Prichet (has received the Key and Spatter Dashes).

Præmittitur toti libro minio perscripta hæc notatio.

Anno Domini 1384 compilatio ista hoc modo Cantabrigiæ erat examinata unde à quodam sacerdote ad ligandum ibid. fuit posita, à quibusdam scolaribus diligenter erat intuita atque perlecta. Et Cancellario Universitatis ejusque Concilio præsentata, propter defectus & hæreses examinanda, ne minus literati populum per eum negligenter fallant, & in varios errores fallaciter inducant. Tunc jussu Cancellarij coram eo ac toto Concilio universitatis per 4 dies cum omni studio ac diligentia fuit examinata, atque in omni Collegio undique comprobata. Die quinto omnibus Doctoribus utriusque juris & magistris Theologiæ cum Cancellario dicentibus & affirmantibus eam de sacris legibus ac 10 libris divinis bene ac subtiliter tractatam, et ex auctoritate omnium doctorum sacræ paginæ sapienter allegatam, id est affirmatam, necnon & fundatam. Ideo quicunque fueris, ô lector, hanc noli contemnere quia sine dubio si aliqui defectus in ea inventi fuissent, coram Universitate Cantabrigiæ combusta fuisset. ▬

Yesterday M^r. *Gilby*, Bach. of Law, Fellow of All-Souls Coll. & one of the Proctors in the vice-chancellor's court died of a consumption, wch he said a little before he died he thought verily to have proceeded from a piece of cherry stone which some time since went down his [1] wind-Pipe & caused a corruption in his Lungs. Which tho' it might be one cause, 20 yet 'tis said the chief was hard Drinking. He is reported to have been a person of parts, and some Learning. ▬ D^r. William *Healey*, Dean of *Chichester*. His Brother, Bach. of Arts, lately of *All-Souls* Col. is Præbendary of the same Place, & I am told is reckon'd a celebrated Preacher in *London*. . . .

Aug. 23 (Th.). By a Letter from Prince Eugene to ye Duke of Marlb. we understand y^t on ye 16 in ye Morning he Attackt ye Army under ye Duke of Vendosme near Calvensano y^t ye fight (wch was betwixt ye Infantry) continued obstinate till past 3 when the Enemy quitted ye Field of Battle & he gained an entire victory, but having himself rec^d a slight 30 wound would not pursue the Enemy & referrs ye Particulars to his next, for wch victory the Gunns at Whitehall & ye Tower have been fired, & tho' the Paris Letters of the 24th make ye victory on their side yet in conclusion they say ye Battle was like y^t of Luzanna, where neither side had reason to boast of ye victory. ▬ By the Letters wch came last Night we hear that ye Queen will certainly go in Procession to S^t. Paul's this day, notw^thstanding she had declar'd once her Resolution to ye contrary. ▬ D^r. Younger is made Dean of Sarum.

[Extract from Pauli Leopardi *Emendationes*.]

To-day, being the Thanksgiving for the Duke of Marlborough's forcing 40 the French Lines, M^r. Evans of S^t. John's preach'd at S^t. Mary's upon *Judges* viii. 34, 35. . . I believe he pleas'd the Whiggish party very well, in extolling so much the Bravery & courage of K. William & the Duke of Marlborough, but chiefly by recommending union and Moderation, & not suffering our Zeal to carry us so far as to bespatter our Governours in libellous Pamphletts, such as he insinuated had lately appear'd, meaning w^thout doubt y^t usefull one *The Memorial of ye Church of England*. Tho' it must be acknowledg'd that in the general 'twas a good sermon & sufficiently laid open the Sin of Ingratitude, & the Mischiefs that will infallibly

---

[1] I have been since inform'd that his throate was cut by some Atheistical People of the College.

ensue if due return of thanks be not given to God for his Deliverance of us from the Publick Enemy, & a just respect not shewn to those whom he makes his Instruments.

Aug. 24 (Fri.).   M[r]. *Wharton* writ a Pamphlett in English, intit. *The Enthusiasm of the Church of Rome,* &c. 4°. Printed at *Lond.* — D[r]. Hudson writ the Inscription upon the Monument of D[r]. *Plot,* which M[r]. *Llhuyd* has added to the Account he drew up of his Life, printed in the Supplement to M[r]. *Collier's Dictionary,* and at the Beginning of D[r]. *Plot's History of Oxfordshire,* Edit. 2[d]. — *The Superintendency of*
10 *Divine Providence over Humane Affairs,* in a Sermon preach'd at St. Paul's London before the L[d] Mayor *&c.* on the 29th of May 1705, by *Francis Fox,* A.M. & chaplain to his Lordship. *Lond.* 1705, 4°.   The said *Francis Fox,* having served above 6 Years as an Apprentice to a Mercer[1] in *London* left off his Trade & came to *Oxford,* & entred himself Commoner of *Edmund*-Hall as a Member of which he took his Master of Arts Degree in the year 1704, & soon after going to London, became Chaplain to Sir *Owen Buckingham,* Mayor of that city for the year 1705.   So that whereas he once scrupled the Oath of Abjuration, yet upon reading the Preface to Vol. I. of my Lord *Clarendon's* History
20 he immediately took y[t] Oath, without having any other Argument to offer for it, as he not long after told M[r]. *Dodwell* in my hearing, which so astonished that Pious & learned Person that he told him he thought him a Man of no conscience nor consideration; since granting there had been any Argument in that Preface 'twould have been so far from justifying w[t] he did that 'twould be directly ag[t] him being not writ by the Author himself but the Editors all of which except one had taken the Oath.   But indeed there is no Argument or any thing like an Argument to defend the taking of this Oath in that place, as M[r]. *Dodwell* plainly shew'd him.   And yet he was so far from hearkening
30 to the pious Discourse of this Excellent Man, that he went away smiling, & with so little concern that he affirm'd to me that he could take the Oath if it had been ten times worse, & yet could give no manner of reason for it.   He is got in with the Whigs, & tho' he was once ag[t] the Occasional Conformissts he is now very warm for them. When he was in Oxford he went every Sunday to Christ-Church Prayers in the Morning, to receive the Sacrament; which gain'd him the character of a Sanctify'd Person.   But after he had taken the Degree of Bachelor of Arts, he left off that Custom quite, to the Amazement of his Acquaintance.   In short he is a Man of great Boldness and As-
40 surance, but has neither parts nor Learning; and the Sermon above mention'd is an injudicious rhapsodical discourse of Providence in General collected from several Authors with little in particular relating to the day. — 'Tis observable that last Night were no Illuminations in Oxford on Account of the Thanksgiving but in D[r]. Mill's Lodgings.

Aug. 25 (Sat.).   In the Publick Library is a MS[t] *Ægidius Romanus de Regimine principum,* with this Distich at ye End,

Quod pica, quod bubo, quod graculus est vel hyrundo,
Hoc liber est iste, simulator namque sophistæ.

---

[1] or a Glover, Quære.

Here is also added a Copy of the lasst Will of *Will. Kyghton* of *Brigeford* (ut videtur in Comit. *Nott.*) aº. 1528, wherein is nothing Material, save yᵗ he makes his Father & his wife his Executors, wᵗʰ this Provision, yᵗ if his Sonne *Lawrence* happen to live after his Father yᵗ he shal succeed in yᵉ Roome of his Father as Executor. — Dʳ. *Langbain* gives a particular Account of all the Tracts in the MS. U. 3. 7. Jur. (according to the old placing) of the Publick Library. There is a Catalogue of the Consuls & other Historical Pieces wᶜʰ may be of use in Livy. See Langb. coll. ex dono Ant. à Wood, num. 7. — Mʳ. *Gilby* of *All-Souls* coll. was buryed last night. His Body was opened, & a large impostume was found in his Lungs. . . .

In the Beginning of the Edition of *Livy* (at *Rome* 1472) in *Corpus Christi Coll.* Library is this *Memorandum* :

> *Orate pro anima Reverendi in Christo Patris ac Domini Ricardi Fox olim Wintoñ Episcopi Collegij corporis christi Fundatoris. qui hunc librum dedit eidem.* At the end: *liber Jo. Shirwod Se. Apᶜᵃ Protonotarij Archidiaconique Richmondiæ emptus Romæ in fine Januarij anno Domini 1475.*

Edinb. 17. This day the Parliament met, & went upon Limitation of a Protestant Successor. At last they pass'd a Bill that for the future the Lords of the Privy-Council, Treasury & Exchequer, as also the Lords of the Session and Justitiary shall be solely nominated and appointed by the Parliament. So yᵗ yᵉ next King of *Scotland* is like to be King of Clouts. — Dʳ. *Ellis* is made Bᴾ. of *Kildare* in Ireland, the Bᴾ. of *Kildare* being removed to the Diocess of *Meath.* — We hear at last that the *Muscovites* did not vanquish the *Swedes,* as was at first reported; but that the *Muscovites* were defeated with the loss of 7000 Men. — 'Tis generally concluded that Prince *Eugene* had not a compleat victory over the *French* in *Italy,* but that both sides after great loss parted, tho' the better was on the part of Pr. *Eugene.* — On *Friday* the Paper call'd *the Review of the Rehearsal* writt by Tutchin did not come out as usual. Upon wᶜʰ 'tis thought a stop has been put to it by order of Court; it being a most scandalous, nonsensical thing, and such as gives offence to both sides.

Aug. 26 (Sun.). The Pamphlett call'd *A Cat may look on a Queen, or A Satyr on her present Majesty,* seems to have been written[1] by J. *Tutchin* or some such pitiful Fellow, being a very silly thing, & stuff'd with Raillery upon the Fathers & other Friends of the Church. — Dʳ. *Hudson* was chosen Keeper of the Publick Library in *Oxon April* 11. 1701. — Mʳ. *Rogers* (afterwards Dʳ. of Divinity) was chosen President of *Magdalen*-Coll. *Oxon. Apr.* 12. 1701. — The IIᵈ Edition of *Livy* at *Rome* was printed from the first by *Joannes Antonius Campanus Episcopus Interamniensis,* & is exactly the same only 'tis somewhat more correct, whereof the chief things of note are observed by *Gronovius* & other Editors of *Livy.* At the End are these Verses :

> Aspicis illustris lector quicunque libellos,
> Si cupis artificum nomina nosse: lege.
> Aspera ridebis cognomina Teutona : forsan
> Mitiget ars musis inscia verba virum.

---

[1] Others say J. Dunton, the broken Bookseller, was Authour, wᶜʰ is not unlikely.

Conradus Suuenheym : Arnoldus Pannartzque magistri
Romæ impresserunt talia multa simul.

In domo Petri de Maximis M.CCCC.LXXII, die XVI. Julij,

M^r. Lesly, in his *Discourse ag^t Marriages with those of different communions*, pag. 50. attributes the mischiefes wch befell King *Charles* I. in a great measure to his marrying a Popish Lady. This Tract of M^r. Lesly's seems from several passages in it about the B^{ps}. depriv'd by King W^m, & one concerning Sir *Hen. Spelman's History of Sacrilege* to have been written for the Jacobites, notwithstanding he says the
10 Substance of it was preach'd at Chester before the *Revolution*. From pag. 59 he seems to insinuate that when all the present dissenting B^{ps}. are dead those who are against such as have been substituted in their Places will not submit, but will joyn to forreign B^{ps}. who are against the Depriving of B^{ps}. by the Civil Magistrate. In pag. 59 he clears the objections offer'd about our English Reformation, because of the Lay-Power employ'd in it, from the Pope's unjustly pretending to a universal & Unlimited Supremacy, & his imposing upon us things Sinfull & Heretical, which make a Seperation justifyable.

[Note on Livy from Gruteri *Fax Artium*.]

20 D^r. *Mill* tells me B^p. *Walton* did not write the *Prolegomena* to the *Polyglott* Bible all himself, but that 'twas done by several Hands.

Aug. 28 (Tu.). Yesterday came to the Publick Library the Countess of *Bridgwater*, being one of the Youngest of the Duke of Marlborough's Daughters, together with her Mother-in-Law the old Countess. — D^r. *Langbain* in the year 1641 sent a Transcript from the *Bodlejan* Library, (*MS. Digb.* num. 218.) of *Aldredus Rieval. de vinculo Perfectionis*, & another Tract. of his *de Vita inclusarum* (in ye same MS.) to *Jacobus Merlon Horstius* a Divine of *Cologne*, with a design to have it printed in the Edition of S^t. *Bernard*'s Works, then fitting for ye Press
30 by ye said *Merlon Horst.* See D^r. *Langbain*'s Collect. Vol. 4. p. 410. b. in Bib. *Bod.*

In dicto MS. *Digby* num. 218. pag. 106. habetur pars libri sexti Polychronici *Ranulfi Cestrensis*, ubi de *Aluredo* Rege et Scolis publicis variarum Artium apud *Oxonias* per ipsum institutas ad consilium *Neoti* Abbatis. Ex Willelmo de Regibus. lib. 2°. Ubi in margine habetur annotatio quae sic incipit,

Atulphe Rex, dilecte Dei, quid moraris. mitte filium primogenitum ad Romanum pontificem, ut ab ipso inungatur in Regem Anglorum. Et sic ab ipso procedat unctio regalis ad caeteros Reges ipsius Regni in perpetuum duratura &c.
40 Haec in vita S. Alfredi scripsit S. Neothus. Similiter alia nota (e regione loci ubi Ranulphus Cestrensis meminit Grimbaldi). Iste Grimbaldus, ut primo Cancellarius & Doctor ordinarius praesente Rege victoriosissimo Alfredo, caeterisque regni magnatibus, in Universitate Oxon. legit primo lectorem Scholasticam ; qui paulo ante fuit Parisiensis Cancellarius. Haec in vita Alfredi Regis.
MS. Digb. 205, 224 [titles only].

The Countess Dowager of Bridgwater talk'd very much of Coyns, when at the Library, which she seem'd to understand well, & declar'd a great Affection for Learning.

[Notes on Livy from Yvonis Villiomari in Locos Controversos Roberti Titij
50 Animadversorum liber, Lipsius, &c.]

Aug. 29 (Wed.).   Just publish'd M^r. Spinks's *Answer to* M^r. Bassett's Essay for Catholick Communion. 8°. — Ex cod. Langbain in Bib. Bodl. num. 5 . . . Epistolae Gilleberti quondam Abbatis Hoylandiae. (Codicem hunc descriptum ad Jacobum Merlonem Horstium Coloniensem una cum Bernardi Epistolis aliquot alijsque jam tum ineditis, cum Bernardo cujus editionem adornabat, una edendum transmisi. Quod ab eo praestitum est.) — . . . *Scheffer* in the Catalogue of his Works, printed in the said *Lcctt. Acad.* makes mention of a Justin with Notes prepared for ye Press by him. *Quære* whether ever printed?—*Quære* also whether his *Liber adversariorum, in quo Notæ ad Scriptores plurimos, veteres & recentes,* was ever printed? — . . . ¹ 'Tis said that M^r. *Holland* (*John*) of *Merton College,* went to M^r. *Sam. Parker,* the Non-Juror, soon after he had married M^r. Clements (the Bookseller's) Daughter, on purpose to dispute with him against his drawing his wife over to the Communion held up by the greatest part of Non-Jurors in behalf of the deprived Bishops; but that M^r. *Parker* was too hard for him, & thereupon his wife communicated with the Non-jurors, & so continues to do. . . .

In MS. NE. A. 3. 6. M^{ri} Thomae Gascoigne sacrae theologiae Doctoris Oxoñ, Relatio de decollatione Ricardi Scroop Archiepiscopi Ebor, facta 8° Junij 1405 jussu Henrici 4^{ti}, judice Willelmo Fulthorp, ubi inter alia sic scribit—

Et in quinta percussione collum Archipraesulis super terram cecidit, & corpus super dexterum latus ad terram cecidit in tertia sullione, quinque enim erant sulliones seminatae cum ordeo, & in terra ubi Archipraesul decollatus erat fuit ordeum seminatum quod pridie in calamis ad modum fusi apparuit, & pedibus conculcantium in die decollationis ejus penitus distractum erat, & eo non obstante in eadem aestate, absque novo semine, & absque opere humano deus tale incrementum dedit supra communem usum naturae, quod aliquis calamus quinque, aliquis calamus quatuor spicas ordei produxit. Et qui pauciores produxit non minus quam duos calamos protulit.

Immediate post hanc narrationem Langbain (in coll. vol. 5. p. 56) aliam, quae sequitur adjecit, viz.

Huic affine admodum est quod aliquando a testibus fide dignis accepi de agro quodam in Cornubia ubi praelium commissum est inter partes Regias sub Radulpho Hopton milite & Parliamentarias sub Domino Stamford a° Domini 1643, viz. triticum an hordeum eo in agro seminatum pedibus equorum hominumque penitus conculcatum; autumno sequente singulos fere calamos tres aut quatuor; alios sex, septem, octo, novem immo & decem spicas produxisse.

[Extracts from Malala, pp. 225, 233, 276.]

The Appendix to ye Life of ye R^t. Rev. Father in God Seth L^d. B^p. of Sarum, written by D^r. Walter Pope, in a Letter to the Author, Lond. 1697. 8°. was written by D^r. Tho. Wood of New college, notwithstanding he does not own it. He also was Author of, *The vindication of the Historiographer of ye University of Oxford & his Works, &c. Lond.* 1693. 4°. — . .
I am inform'd M^r. Will. Smith Fellow of University College finds great Fault with M^r. Wood's *Antiquities of Oxoñ,* as being taken in a great measure from M^r. Twyne's Papers in the Schoole Tower, & containing

---

¹ This is certainly true. But M^{rs}. Parker now communicates, as M^r. Dodwell & several other Non-Jurors do. They began upon the Death of D^r. Lloyd B^p. of Norwich. Tho. H. Jan. 20. 1710-11 Saturd.

a great many errors. He has himself labour'd several years upon the same Subject; but being known to be a man of but little Judgment, there is no great heed given to him. For 'tis well known Mr. Wood took a vast deal of pains in that work, & that tho' he might have some Notices from Mr. Twyne, yet he examin'd all the Records & Register Books himself, wᶜʰ occasion'd Dʳ. Lloyd in his *Geogr. Dict.* to give an ample Testimony of the Book. — ... Mr. *Wagstaffe*, who formerly writ in vindication of King *Ch. I.* Εἰκὼν Βασιλικὴ, & was once a member of *New-Inn-Hall*, where he took his Master of Arts Degree, practises
10 Physick now in *London*, with great Success. He is a Man of very good Parts, & considerable Learning. — Mr. *Collier's Geographical & Historical Dictionary* gave but very little satisfaction to the subscribers, upon Account of it's being several Sheets less than was promised; besides the unaccurateness of divers particulars. Upon wᶜʰ he publish'd a Supplement with a design to correct the Faults, & satisfy for the Defects and omissions thereof. But this being done in hast, there are still abundance of faults, & more omissions. So that 'tis far from being a perfect work, it being requisite that a thing of this Nature should be undertaken by a set of men of great Industry & knowledge,
20 to procure Materials not only from Authors but from such Places where 'tis to be supposed are preserved any Evidences wᶜʰ may give light into the Life of any great Man. — Praefatio in tertiam Decadem Livij ex Editione Fr. Asulani (*Ven.* 1519. 8º.) ...

Aug. 31 (Fri.). Ad calcem cod. NE. A. 3. 7. est nota Historica quod capella B. Mariæ Radingiæ cœpit ædificari per Nicolaum Abbatem 13. Kal. Maij. 1314. — ... Mrs. Hesther English, a French woman, writ the Proverbs in French, very neatly, in variety of Hands, wᶜʰ is now in the Publick Library. She was nurse to Prince Henry, & married Bartholomew Kello, a Scotchman. Their Grandson is now Sword-Bearer
30 of Norwich. . . ,

Sept. 1 (Sat.). [News from the Scottish Parliament, dated Edinburgh, August 23.]

We hear from Launceston in Cornwall yᵗ one John Davis, having caused a Person to be press'd, with whom his Daughter was engag'd, she, out of Revenge, one night set the House on Fire, whereby her Father, Mother & her self were burnt. — From Hampshire that in the late Storm about 20 Acres of wheat were burnt, occasion'd by a Tobaco-

---

Aug. 30. H. to Smith. Is inclined to think Joyner's story of a Life of R. Bacon by Selden a mistake. Extract conc. Dr. Dee from Hopton's *Concordance of Years.* Did not know before that Smith was translator of the *Nuncius Inanimatus.* Pritius has left: Fabricius' characterisation of him in letter to Hudson. Halley will reprint in *Phil. Trans.* the inscription relating to Theophrastus incorrectly given by Prideaux. Mr. Simon Priest, Vicar of Bisley, Glo., proposes to translate Graevius on the Roman Denarius and on Egyptian Pyramids. Asks for Smith's opinion thereon.

Aug. 31. Hudson (Theddlethorp) to H. Has some gold and silver coins for Bodley. Has catalogued the curiosities of the Earl of Exeter's library; it contains *Icones Livianae.* The Earl has a noble collection of coins, esp. gold, all in cases in due order, wrapt up in papers with their descriptions upon them.

pipe being blow'd out. — .. To-day I saw at the Public Library D^r. *Stearn* Dean of S^t. *Patrick* in Ireland. He is son to *John Stearn,* D^r. of Physick, & Professor thereof in Dublin, who was Tutor to the Learned M^r. Hen. Dodwell. This D^r. Stearne, the Dean, has published a Discourse in Latin *de infirmorum visitatione,* & a Sermon. But he has printed nothing else yet, as himself·was pleas'd to tell me. — Wanting in ye Publick Library D^r. John Stearne's Examen Herebordi de Concursu, (2) Dissertatio de Electione & Reprobatione. He also writ a Preface to Roger Boyle's *Inquisitio in fidem hujus sæculi.* But this does not goe along with the Copies, & so is not to be met with : there being 10 some reason why 'twas not publish'd with the Book itself, viz. either a difference between D^r. Stearn's widow & the Bookseller, who would not allow a sufficient gratuity for ye copy, or else something æquivalent.

Sept. 2 (Sun.). D^r. Lloyd, B^p. of Worcester, was so well pleas'd with M^r. Evans's Thanksgiving Sermon before the University, that he said soon after *that he was very glad there was one even* in Oxford *that would speak for King* William. It seems too he sent for him to his Lodgings & told him he would get him good preferment for it. The Sermon is reported to have been made by D^r. Tadlo, this Evans, and some others at a Merry-Meeting. As for Evans, there are very few in Oxford bear 20 so bad a character, being noted for &c. — I have been told y^t the B^p. of Worcester is now in the ¹88th year of his Age. — M^r. Hoffman a Lutheran. Being to day at dinner with the B^p. of Worcester, M^r. Lloyd, his Son, (who was lately made Chancellor of Worcester by his L^dship) happening to mention Coyns, seem'd to shew some Resentment towards D^r. Hudson, to whom he says he formerly offer'd his service for putting the coyns in order in the publick Library given by Consul Ray, & that he seem'd shy in ye Matter. When Dinner was ended M^r. Lloyd shew'd his collection of Coyns, wch indeed is a good one, they being for the most part very fair. He has not many Consular ones, but those of the 30 Emperors are many, & valuable, for the most part. He has also a good number of Gemms, stones &c. He spoke several times ag^t the High-Church-men at dinner, wch his Lordship did not seem to like very well. — D^r. Stearne, (who dined at ye B^{ps}. too, and preach'd this Morning at Magd. Church, upon his Lordship's Request, who received ye Sacrament there) says that he lately amongst MSS^{ts} he purchas'd had 2000 Evidences thrown into his Bargain, which he has communicated to D^r. Kennett. Amongst the MSS. were some Irish, wch he has communicated to M^r. Llhuyd of ye Musæum. — The two Sheriffs have been with D^r. Willis, Dean of Lincoln, with the Thanks of the Ld Mayer & court of 40 Aldermen, for the Sermon preach'd by him last Thanksgiving day (for forcing the French Lines) at S^t. Paul's. This Sermon, wch is just publish'd is variously talk'd off, & cannot, as is thought, escape wthout an

---

Sept. 2. T. Cherry to H. It was a mistake that Layton was to publish Dodwell's Arguments and replies. *Various messages from Dodwell.* He very often receives letters from Perizonius and Le Clerc about his schism. *Useless for Mr. M. Gibson to think of being Minister of Maidenhead. Local news and sundry commissions.*

---

¹ A Mistake.

Answer, there being several Reflections in it upon some of the Principal Men of the Church of England. — The Grand Juries for London & Middlesex, the last Sessions, presented *the Memorial of the Ch. of England* (whereof there is a Vindication come out) as a dangerous Pamphlett. But this is not at all to be wonder'd at, if we consider of w^t Persons the juries consist, & who are the Presenters. — 'Tis now agreed upon for certain that the Ld Pembroke (President of the Council) is speedily to go over to Holland, to expostulate with ye States for their obstructing the Duke of Marlborough in his design'd Engagement wth ye French. —
10 'Tis said (M^r. Lesley) the Writer of *ye Rehearsal* is taken up for being Author of *The Memorial*, & that he has given 1000 lib^s bayle. — M^r. Dodwell has just finished a Discourse concerning *the Immortality of ye Soul*, & is going to put it to the Press. — M^r. Grabe, as 'tis said, & he seem'd to insinuate as much to me, will print only the Alexandrian Copy of the *Septuagint*, w^thout Notes, only Parallel Places of Scripture. But if he lives & has his Health he will add a Volume of Annotations afterwards. This I believe he will do provided he does not meet wth better Encouragem^t for carrying on the Expenses. But if there be suitable Encouragem^t he will print Notes at ye Bottom, wch will be very large,
20 & will require a great deal of time. — M^r. Lloyd tells me he knows Sanford, who came to see our Coyns, & that he is one who makes it his business to pick up such curiosities, & to sell them afterwards, being a Person of no skill in History or any other Parts of Learning, as having not been bred up to it.

Sept. 3 (Mon.). Cod. MS. in Bib. Bodl. NE. C. 4. 3. Compendium Historiarum ab orbe condito usque passionem Apostolorum Petri & Pauli. — The B^p. of Worcester told me that formerly he look^t over all the Coyns in the Pub. Library Gallery, wch was before the considerable Additions made by Nourse, Consul Ray &c. . . .

30 **Sept. 4 (Tu.).** M^r. W^m. Cherry[1] died (some time since) in ye 73^d year of his Age. — It seems M^r. Lesley was taken up for being Author of *the Memorial* upon an Insinuation in one of the Observators written by *Tutchin* who was lately in Devonshire, & other western Parts, on purpose to rake up all the Scandal he could against the stan[c]h members of the Church of England. W^ch being hinted to the Judges in one place (as they were on their Circuit) he was forced to fly immediately. — Sometime since I compar'd the Oxford Edition of S^t. Cyprian (as reprinted in Holland) with a MS^t in Lincoln College, & the Life of S^t. Cyprian with a MS^t in S^t. John's college, & put down the Variations
40 (wch are many & considerable) in a Copy of D^r. Mill's. — The Edition of Tatian, wch came out at Oxford, in 1705, tho' it bears M^r. Worth's name, yet most of the notes, wth the Dedication, & Prefaces were written by D^r. Mill. So that M^r. Worth did but very little to it. I was with him at Eaton, whither I went on purpose from Shottesbrook to compare a MS^t for this Edition. —

Sacrilege Arraigned and condemned; by D^r. Basire. *Lond.* 1668. 8°. At the Beginning is written by D^r. Barlow,

D^s. D^r. Isaac Basire Natione Gallus, Religione Reformatus, Professione

---

[1] I have a Letter about it written by Mr. Holden.

Theologus, Dignitate Northumbriæ Archi-Diaconus, Dunelmensis Ecclesiæ
Canonicus & Sacræ Majestati Regiæ à Sacris; Tyrannide à Cromwello occu-
pata annos 15 (ὡς ἔγγιστα) Exsul, post Gallias, Italiam, Græciam, Thraciam,
Asiam, Palæstinam & Ægyptum lustratas, Albæ Juliæ Professor Theologiæ
primarius à Transylvaniæ Principe renunciatus, Anno 1660, redijt in Bri-
tanniam. . .

Burnett's History of Reform. pag. 144. Part II.

Another difference between the Ordination Book set out at that (viz. An.
1550) time, and that we now use, was, that the Bishop was to lay his one Hand
on yᵉ Priest's Head, and with his other to give him a Bible, with a Chalice 10
and Bread in it, saying the words now said at the Delivery of yᵉ Bible. In the
Consecration of a Bishop there was nothing more than what is yet in use, save
that a Staff was put into his Hand, with this Blessing, *Be to yᵉ Flock of Xt. a
Shepherd.*

This is a great Error, there being no such Difference either in the
ordaining of a Priest or Bᵖ, as appears from the *Forms* printed in 1549, &
1552, both wᶜʰ I have look'd into. —

Reasons that Catholicks ought in anywise to abstaine from Heretical Conventicles. 8⁰. . . The Running title over every Leafe is *a Treatise of Schisme.*
Quære who the Author. At the Beginning is this memorandum in MSᵗ, 20

Mʳ. Carter hath confessed he hath printed of these Bookes 1250. *This was
found at* Wm. Carter's *in his House at the Tower Hill wⁱʰ the Original Copy sent
from* Rhemes *allowed under Doctor* Allein's *owne Hand & name subscribed thus :*
Hic tractatus est plane Catholicus, & nostris imprimis hominibus, hoc schis-
matis tempore, pernecessarius.
Ita testor GULLIELMUS ALLANUS Sacræ Theologiæ Doctor & Professor.

Mʳ. Wood, Athen. Oxon. Vol. I. col. 306, insinuates that 'tis Robert
Parsones the Jesuite, who certainly writ *Nine Reasons why Catholicks
should abstain from Heretical Conventicles,* if we may credit Ant. Possevin
in Apparat. Sac. Tom. II. in Rob. Persons, which seems to be no other 30
than this in Bodley's Library, the Title-Page whereof is torn out, otherwise we could give a more full Account of it. — . . . The Book call'd the
Memorial was burnt last Satʳday at yᵉ Sessions House by yᵉ Hands of yᵉ
common Hang-Man & this week the same will be done at yᵉ Royal Exchange & Palace yard Westminster. — Yesterday night late came two
Holl. Mailes, viz. from Millan yᵗ the D. of Vendosme lyes near Rivalto &
Pr. Eugene att Grivelgo, the former flying before him leaving all yᵉ Inns
full of his Sick & wounded. The French lost in the battle wᵗʰ Pr. Eugene
3500 Men, among them 400 Officers. The D. of Marlborough took Fort
Sᵗ. Lewis after 2 days Siege, making the Garrison Prisoners of War. — 40
Mʳ. Clements, the Bookseller, tells me that *the Antiquities of Middlesex*
will not be continued, meeting with but a very indifferent Reception. —
One Mʳ. Hunt of Baliol College has just put into the Theatre Press
Theodosius's Sphærica, to be printed in Latin only, at the charges of Mʳ.
Clements. — Mʳ. Grabe shew'd me to day a Specimen of his design'd
Edition of *the Septuagint,* wᶜʰ has the Text according to the Alexandrian
Copy, & where that is defective, from other MSS, without any Annota-
tions, only Parallel Places of Scripture ; which method, it seems, he has
been advis'd to take, &, if he lives, to publish yᵉ Annotations in a seperate
Volume. — 'Tis said the Archbᵖ of Canterbury will suspend the Pro- 50
locutor &c. the next Convocation if they continue as obstinate as they did

the last. — M^r. Grabe had lately sent him by Zacagnius, Keeper of the Vatican Library, a specimen, (taken very exactly) in a new manner, the impression being made upon the skin of an Oxe's Gut, of the MS^t from whence the Roman Edition of the Septuagint was printed. He has given part of it to D^r. Hudson to be put in the Bodlejan Library. I have not yet seen it. — D^r. Mill has put M^r. Hoffman upon perusing all the Coptick Pieces of the Bible in the Bodl. Library, & promises him Encouragement to have 'em printed. — Just publish'd a 2^d Edition, with great Additions of M^r. Keil's (John) Lectures, read when Deputy Pro-
10 fessor to D^r. Millington, in the Natural Philosophy Schoole at Oxford. — M^r. Grabe tells me that before he came into England he was Professor of Humanity for about 12 Years, & that he drew up a great many things in order to an *Ecclesiastical History,* wch he proposed to methodise and put into order when he came to Oxford, as he declar'd to D^r. Mill in a Letter, whereof I have a Copy. He had also thoughts of printing Ephræm Syrus in Greek, from MSS. in the Oxoñ Libraries ; but being diverted, D^r. Mill I believe designs it, having already procur'd a Transcript of most in the Bodl. Library.

Sept. 5 (Wed.). M^r. Evans, of S^t. John's Coll., talks mightily of Print-
20 ing his Thanksgiving Sermon. But here is none in Oxford will print a thing so scandalously partial against the Church of England. — Just publish'd *A List of the names of all those who were taken in the Poll for the County of* Middlesex *at* Brainford *last Election for Members of Parliament.* — 'Tis said B^p. Andrews writ an Exposition upon the *Book of Common-Prayer.* But I could never yet meet with it. . . .

Sept. 6 (Th.). Yesterday the Fellows of University had a meeting, and turn'd M^r. Smith (Senior Fellow) out of his Fellowship, on Account of a Parsonage he has. . . .

Sept. 7 (Fri.). Yesterday M^r. Smith of University College made his
30 Complainte to ye Vice-Chancellor for the Fellows turning him out. Upon wch Birkett, the Mancipal was sent for, who said that he never knew any Fellow turn'd out in the Heads Absence. — As they were digging the foundations for the Church of All Saints in Oxoñ, soon after the old church fell down, they found the Body of a Man firm & intire after it had been buried about 150 years. — . . . M^r. Hoffman is looking over the Coptick Translation of the Bible in ye Pub. Library. He has begun to translate ye New Testam^t, D^r. Mill promising to get incouragem^t y^t it may be printed. — D^r. Mill says my L^d. Pembroke is already gone into Holland to expostulate with ye States, & y^t Sir Andrew Fountaine is
40 gone along with him. . . .

Sept. 8 (Sat.). The Grand Jury of London y^t presented the Memorial were 10 of y^m Dissenters & only 2 of ye Pannel Ch. Men who refused to sign ye said presentment. — The L^d. Pembroke designes to set out for Holland this day being Satturday. — S^r. Ch. Shuckborough one of the Members of Parl. for ye county of Warwick & Master of ye Buck Hounds to the Queen died Suddenly on Sunday last at Winchester. — 'Tis whispered there has been a 2^d Battle in Italy to ye Advantage of Pr. Eugene. — . . . The original Author of the *Private Devotions,* wch D^r. Hicks & M^r. Dorrington reform'd, was M^r. *Austin.* — M^r. Bonnell's Life was written by W^m. Harrington, who has publish'd a New Book of M^r. Bonnells containing *Devotions* &c. wch is recommended to the world by M^r. Jo. Strype, M^r. Sam. Palmer, &c. all Whiggs. M^r. Bonnell himself, who is so commended by these Pharisaical People, was of the Whiggish side. . . .

Sept. 9 (Sun.). M^r. Hoffman tells me that Mollerus is upon continuing *Morhoffius de re Literaria.* — Leipenius has written a Book *de Ophir*, wch I have not yet seen.

[News from the Scottish Parliament, September 1.]

At the Beginning of last week D^r. Berwick, a Physician, died, who 10 was very gracious with King Charles II. — Tho. Fagg, a Member of Parliam^t for Rye in Sussex, died lately of ye Small-Pox. — The Earl of Pembrook's Voyage to Holland is deferr'd for some time; but all things are getting ready for it. — 'Tis said if Lesley be prov'd the Author of *the Memorial* the Jacobites will be greater Sufferers than they have been as yet; wch makes several, who are well wishers to them, (believing that ye greatest part of cm[1] are men of conscience) wish that it may not be proved upon him, & y^t he would imploy his Pen upon other subjects. — M^r. Hoffman tells me he has been at Padua, where he saw the Monument of Livy; but that he believes all the Inscriptions 20 relating to him to be modern. — . . . M^r. Grabe tells me that D^r. Smith had a design to publish the Septuagint from the Alexandrian Copy in the time of K. Charles II. from whom he had hopes of encouragement. But his death prevented the undertaking. — M^r. Grabe says that D^r. Bull's Letter against the Papists printed in D^r. Hickes' Book against y^m is the best part in the whole Book, tho' D^r. Hickes's is very good, & ought to be publish'd seperate by it self, to be distributed as there is occasion. — I hear from M^r. Worth that the B^p. of Worcester is in the 78th year of his Age, and not in the 88th as I was lately told. M^r. Worth is his Chaplain. 30

Sept. 12 (Wed.). M^r. Moreton, a Clergyman, is writing the Antiquities of Northamptonshire. — The Antiquities of Stamford in Linc.shire are writing by a Gentleman of that towne. I have his Name, I think, in a Lett^r from M^r. Willis. He is a Clergyman, as D^r. Hudson, who is just come from those parts, informs me. . . .

[Notes on Livy from Lipsius *de Amphitheatro* and *Saturn. Serm.* Letter to Hudson from Ericus Benzelius filius, dated Upsala, July 15, 1705.]

D^r. Hudson shew'd me a Lett^r to day wch he rec^d from M^r. Wanley,

---

Sept. 11. Dodwell to H. Refers H. to his Dionysius for his views on Livian chronology. Was Dr. Mills concerned in the persecution of the Nonjurors?

Sept. 12. H. to Smith. Is sending Grabe's Ep. to Mill; G. is going abroad to consult MSS. for his LXX. Sends a transcript of Wanley's Memorandum in *Index Expurg.* (Madrid 1614). Sir James Astrey is engaged on new ed. of Spelman's Glossary; unless he consults Junius' MSS. 'twill be very superficially done.

---

[1] There is no reason to think them otherwise, notwithstanding what Dr. Charlett & some other Republicans are willing to suggest.

wherein he desires to borrow certain Books MSS. out of the Publick Library, offering security for them, being for his purpose towards an Edition of the Bible in Saxon which he is undertaking. But this cannot be done, & 'tis a matter of wonder he should desire such a thing. . . .

Sept. 13 (Th.). On Wednesday Morning died S^r. Sam. Dashwood K^t & Alderman of London. As also did the same Evening S^r. Robt Clayton, K^t & Alderman, the Father of y^t City. — This day looking into the Monthly Account of Books, call'd *The works of the Learned,* for August I found that there was ready for the Press at Oxoñ *Jo.* Leland *de Illustribus Scriptoribus majoris Britanniæ,* (with Notes and Improvements) from ye Original in ye Pub. Library, by M^r. Ant. Hall of Queen's College. — We hear 'tis now resolv'd in council y^t the Earl of Pembroke shall not go for Holland, Matters being agreed on y^t no Officer w^{t}soever shall be in council but ye D. of Malborough, Monsr. Overkirk & ye 2 States Deputies & y^t his Grace shall have a double vote.

Sept. 14 (Fri.). M^r. Thwaits says M^r. Hall of Queen's college does not design to publish *Leland de scriptoribus*; & that 'twas put into the *works of the Learn'd* without his knowlege. — M^r. Milles of X^{t}church tells me he has some design of Travelling into Forreign Countries. — From Edinb. the 6th we hear that that day a Proposal was made in Parl. for arming & training an Army of 72000 Foot & 8000 Horse, & looks great, being design'd to frighten the Parliam^t of England, who have touch'd 'em in ye sensible p^t by prohibiting their cattle, & making Scotch men Aliens. — There is an Elegy come out upon the late famous Atchievem^t of burning the Memorial.

Sept. 15 (Sat.). S^r. Rob. Clayton is not dead as was reported, but lyes dangerously ill. — Monsr. Montfaucon designs other Tomes of his Diarium Italicum. See his Preface, & remember to ask D^r. Smith conc. that Matter. — I was told last Night that in the great Fire at London was burnt a MS. Bible curiously illuminated like the Historical P^t of the Bible in Bodley's Archives, & that 'twas valued at 1500 lib^s.

Sept. 16 (Sun.). In pag. 4 of Montfaucon is an Inscription taken by the Author at Arles relating to a Victory of Charles the Great, not mentioned in any Historian. — In pag. 5 is mention of D. Marcellus Tolosus's History of Arles. Quære whether yet published. In pag. 6. of Paulus Nemausensis' Antiquities of Nemausum 'twas preparing then for the Press. — It seems the Non-Jurors in Oxford receive the Sacram^t at M^r. Sheldon's chamber at X^t Church, who finds all the necessaries for it, this Sheldon is Nephew to Archb^p. Sheldon, & was some time since Steward of this Coll.

Blondi Flavij Forliviensis de Roma Triumphante libri III, &c., Bas. 1559. . . . In him there is something concerning the Bones of Livy at Padua, &c.

Sept. 13. Dr. T. Smith to H. Greatly regrets the loss of Dee's Apology for Roger Bacon; has lost Godwin's *Nuncius* and his own trans. The inscription in Prideaux (corrected by young Wren), and a more important one noticed by Halley. Earle's trans. of Hooker. Mr. Greaves' *Pyramidographia* and his *Roman Foot and Denarius* are put into Latin by Mr. Wotton, author of the *Reflexions upon Ancient and Modern Learning.*

Sept. 17 (Mon.).   D^r. Mill wishes *ye Memorial* had not been burnt; speaking, I suppose, the opinion of several other of the Whigges. — L^d. Rochester was in Town last week with ye Dean of X^t Church. — I believe *The Secret History of Queen* Zarah *and y^e* Zarascians lately publish'd, in 8°, is the same wch was said sometime since would come out as B^p. Burnett's *Secret History.* The Name of *Secret* might create the mistake. — Hartm. Schedelij Chronicon. . . . In his Acc^t of Livy, fol. 93, he says he wrote only 110 Books. But does not give his Authority.

[Note on Livy from Q. Aurelii Symmachi Epistolae.]

Two Warrants are out for seizing the Author and Publisher of the 10 Whipping-Post for Reflecting on D^r. Willis's Sermon preached before ye Queen. — M^r. Payne made to day Mayor of Oxon. — D^r. Sherlock, Dean of S^t. Paul's, dangerously ill. . . .

Tacitus, per Lipsium. *Antv.* 1589. Jam vero princeps Historicorum audit Livius, si magnitudinem operis, & varietatem rerum spectamus.

I saw M^r. Willis of X^t Church to day, who says M^r. Tanner will hardly ever publish Leland, & that M^r. Wanley's talk of the Edition of the Bible in Saxon will come to nothing.

[Note on Livy from Lud. Dorléans' Novae Cogitationes in libros Annalium Taciti.]   20

D^r. Aldrich, Dean of X^t Church, was Tutor to ye Present Duke of Ormond.

VOL. IV.

Sept. 18 (Tu.).   (Josephus κατὰ Πλάτωνος.) Ex Cod. Baroc. 26. [1–15.] — Eorum quae in praecedentibus aliquot paginis ad fidem MS. hiulca & corrupta habentur emendatio per cl. Langbain. (Vide ejus Coll. in Bibl. Bodl. Vol. II.) [16–21.] — Josephi, ex opere inscripto, contra Platonem, De causa Universi, de loco in quo justorum pariter & injustorum animae continentur: Interprete *Ger. Langbain.* [21–46.] — Yesterday was enter'd of our Hall M^r. Peirce of Lincoln College in order to succeed M^r. John Muston as Vice-Principal who has a Living of 150 lib^s per An. given 30 him.

[Notes on Livy from Lud. Dorléans in Cogitatt. Nov. ad. Tacit. p. 362. a; p. 487.]

Ferretij Musæ Lapidariæ Antiquorum. *Veronæ,* 1672. . . In pag. 321. there is mention of Livy's monument at Padua, with a Note y^t 'tis not of Livy the Historian. — . . . Arkheim a German has lately published a Book in ye German Language de Sacrificijs & cultu Cimbrorum Anti-

---

Sept. 17. Charlett to H.   Has not Mr. Hall of Queen's another name in Edmund Hall?

Sept. 18. Dr. T. Smith to H.   Only ignorance or impudence could deny the printing of the *Index Expurg.* at Madrid (reprinted at Geneva). Fears the designed new ed. of Spelman's Glossary will signify but little. Is disappointed as to the antiquity and importance of Halley's inscription; will H. transcribe it carefully from the original? Is greatly interested in Pompey's inscr., which is referred to by B. Marlianus in his *Urbis Romae Topographia* (1544).

quorum. — . . . Ger. Joannis Vossij Ars Historica. *Lugd. B.* 1623. Several things there relating to Livy's Writing, & the Number of Books wch his History comprehended. — . . . To day was at the Publick Library (where he designs to study a week or thereabouts) M^r. *Tho. Maddox,* who put out y^e *Formulare Anglicanum,* which is a very usefull Book for our English Antiquaries, particularly the Lawyers, being done wth much Judgment & Industry. He tells me that D^r. Johnson's designs of Publishing the Antiquities of Yorkshire will come to nothing, he having not skill to put his collections in order, & that M^r. Fortescue,
10 who had once some design of printing the unpublish'd pieces of S^r. John Fortescue, has alter'd his Mind. M^r. Maddox is ab^t another work, but w^t he has not yet told me. —

Epistola sive Praefatio Joannis Episc. Aleriensis ad editionem suam Livij Historiarum quae prodijt Romae, An. 1470, fol. [53–97.] . . . The Preface &c. to the 2^d Vol. of Aldus's Edition of Livy, *Ven.* 1518. 8°. [98–107.]

In pag. 55. l. 3. of Selden de Synedrijs vet. Hebr. is the Inscription on the Theophrastus taken from the Stone at White-Hall, wch M^r. Halley has lately taken anew. 'Tis also in P. Junius's Notes on Clement's Epist. Quære whether 'tis not more exact y^n 'tis publish'd in Marm.
20 Oxon. & whether it agrees with M^r. Halley's copy? — . . . M^r. Madox makes use of M^r. Dodsworth's Collections in ye Publick Library, to wch he has been recommended by ye B^p. of *Carlisle.* . . .

Sept. 20 (Th.). 'Tis reported that in a Meeting lately of some Great Persons, amongst whom the L^d. Rochester was one, a Discourse ariseing conc. Passive Obedience, a Question was propos'd who they thought of all the Jacobites would suffer Death if a Persecution should arise? And 'twas agreed by the Majority that there were only two who would stand firm, wch are the Principal of the Party, tho' they hop'd well too of ye rest.

30 [Note on Marm. Oxon. num. CXXXII. pag. 270, and p. 39 of Mr. Selden's Edition.] . . .

Pliny in lib. VII. Hist. Nat. § 27. has the Inscription containing Pompey's Triumph, wch he took from the Temple of Minerva. But 'tis somew^t different from that wch I find copy'd from the Stone it self in The Tarvisian Edition of Livy, wch I have transcrib'd above in some of these Papers. 'Twill be worth publishing anew in an Edition of Livy, at wch time Harduin's Notes must be consulted upon it. — In p. 322 of Reinesius's Epistles are divers Emendations of Justin, wch I must consider if I live to put out another Edition. Look also in pag.
40 375. 410. 436. 478. 550. 566. — . . . Yesterday M^r. Madox was admitted into ye Pub. Library. — D^r. Wallis made several Emendations (wch are very good) to Festus Avienus's Descriptio Orbis Terrarum, at D^r. Hudson's Request, who is now going on wth the 3^d vol. of his Geographers. This was the last Work D^r. Wallis did. — In pag. 269. of Reinesius's Inscr. is an Inscription taken from the Temple of S^t. Agatha at Rome the very words whereof occur in L. vii. c. 3. of Livy. Reinesius refers us to L. Faunus's II Book c. 4 de Antiquitatibus urbis Romæ, w^ch

---

Sept. 20. M. Gibson to H. (Farnham). Asks for lit. gossip.

Book is not in yᵉ Publick Library. Reinesius in pag. 457. ibid. has two Inscription[s], with a comment, wᶜʰ Luc. Langermannus the Lawyer transcrib'd from Cyriacus Anconitanus's Scholia in Greek (MSᵗ) upon Strabo. Quære wᵗ Scholia these are. Langermannus I suppose was never printed.

Sept. 21 (Fri.). To day Mʳ. Thwaits told me that he really believes Mʳ. Hall designs to prosecute Leland, & to publish it unless Mʳ. Tanner does it very quickly. Wᶜʰ I the rather believe because I have heard Mʳ. Hall say he had some such Intention.

[Plates containing ' The Inscription on a Stone found lately at Rewly, and 10 since put into the Anatomy Schools,' and ' An Inscription on one of yᵉ Stones in yᵉ Theatre Yard,' in Marm. Oxon. p. 270.]

The first Inscription above mention'd I found on a Stone dug up at Rewly in the Ground, where the Chappel of the Abbey formerly was. This Stone I purchas'd of Mʳ. Cox who lives now in the House wᶜʰ is pᵗ of the Abbey, and I have since put it into the Anatomy Schoole Adjoyning to the Publick Library. 'Tis the more valuable, because it discovers Ela Countess of Warwick to have Founded the Chapell ; wᶜʰ is not mention'd by any Author that I know of, tho' Her other Works of Charity at Oxoñ and else-where are reckon'd up by Sir Wᵐ Dugdale, in his Antiquities of Warwick- 20 shire & the History of the Baronage. She died in the year 1300, & so I suppose founded the chapell much about the time that the Abbey was built by Edm. Earl of Cornwall, wᶜʰ was An. D. 1281. temp. Ed. I. The Greek Inscription is that wᶜʰ I have mention'd above as being in the 270ᵗʰ pag. of Marm. Oxon. But 'tis here inserted exactly as I took it from the Stone in the Theatre Yard.

Sept. 22 (Sat.). Last Night I was with Mʳ. Wotton (who writ the *Essay on Ancient & Modern Learning*) at the Tavern, together with Mʳ. Thwaites & Mʳ. Willis. Mʳ. Wotton is a Person of general Learning, a great Talker & Braggadocio, but of little Judgment in any one par- 30 ticular science. He told me he had begun some time since to translate Greaves's Rom. Denarius, but had not finish'd & could not tell whether he should ever perfect it.

[Extract from Joseph. *Antiq.* l. 14. c. 8.]

Steph. de Urbibus (in voce Σάμος) tells us that the Gentile Name of Σάμος, is Σαμαῖος, &c. Upon wᶜʰ Account perhaps the Inscription above in the Theatre Yard should be supply'd in yᵉ first line Σαμαίων ; tho' Berkelius observes that Σαμαῖος comes rather from Σάμη, & that Σάμιος is the Gentile of Σάμος. But 'tis probable Stephens had observ'd Σαμαίων in some Inscriptions, & so he affirm'd Σαμαῖος to be yᵉ Gentile name. — 40 Mʳ. Wotton told me Mʳ. Baker of Sᵗ. John's col. Cambridge had writ the History & Antiquities of that Col. & that he is every ways qualified (being a very industrious & judicious Man) to write the Hist. & Antiq. of that University. He told me also yᵗ he really believ'd Cambridge to be much later yⁿ Oxoñ.

Sept. 23 (Sun.). Dʳ. Mill was installed Prebend of Canterbury Aug. 14. 1704. His is the 4ᵗʰ Stall. — To day in yᵉ Morning Mʳ. Penton of New Col. preach'd at Sᵗ. Maries, on *Prov.* 16. 32. *And he that ruleth his Spirit, than he that taketh a City*, where speaking of moderation, he took occasion to give a very great Encomium of the Duke of Marlborough & to insinuate yᵗ the Generality of the university did not pay him that Respect & Gratitude they ought. In his Application he shew'd himself a Whigg & a Countenancer of Fanaticks, and yet could not but blame such as comply'd for Interest, wᶜʰ however is certainly the case of the Whiggish Party, being generally biass'd by selfish Principles. So yᵗ he might have spar'd his words, being against his own Principles. ━

There was taken lately upon London Bridge, wᶜʰ has been attested before a Publick Notary, a Paper containing the following words, viz.

10 This is to certifie all whom it may concern that the Bp. of Sarum has recᵈ 5000 libˢ for voting for Occasional Conformity, & that he is to receive 30000 libˢ more, & the Revenue of his Bᵖᵖrick during Life whenever Presbytery shall be Establish'd in England, which he endeavours to have effected, & 'tis fear'd that he will succeed in the undertaking. ━

Mʳ. Evans's Sermon is said to be printing.

Sept. 24 (Mon.). There is a report yᵗ my Lᵈ. Shrewsbury is married to an Italian Lady in Italy where he now is. By wᶜʰ it seems yᵗ he is turn'd Roman Catholick, he being before engag'd to an English Lady, between whom & him the writings were drawn up.

20 **Sept. 25 (Tu.).** Dʳ. Tho. Wood of New-Col. married lately to Mʳˢ. Baker. ━ ... Famianus Nardinus in his Roma vetus c. 1. hath a Testimony conc. Livy.—In lib. 5. c. 3. of Marlianus's Topographia Urbis Romæ is mention made of Pompey the Great's triumph and of the Monument in Memory of it in the Temple of Minerva, but the Inscription is neither added by Marlianus Ursinus who writ notes upon him.— Nardinus in Roma vetus l. vi. c. 9. mentions Minerva's Temple too & gives part of the Inscription from Marlianus, who had it from Pliny, & not from the stone it self as Nardinus insinuates. ━ Cenotaphia Pisana per H. Noris. *Ven.* 1681... In diss. 4. c. 1. there is an account of *Livy's* 30 *Patavinity*.

Sept. 26 (Wed.). Mʳ. Madox says *The First Pᵗ of the Antiquities of Middlesex*, lately publish'd, meets but wᵗʰ an indifferent reception at London, & yᵗ he does not believe 'twill be carried on; but he does not tell me who is thought to be yᵉ Author. ━ .. Thesaurus Graecae Antiquitatis cura Jac. Gronovij. In vol. 3ᵈ of yᵉ Thes. is Livy's Effigies, with an account of him. ━ Mʳ. Berger tells me Bernardus Scardeonius has writ de Patavinitate Livij, wᶜʰ I have not yet seen. I believe 'tis in his Antiquitates Patavij. .. He likewise tells that Carola Patina an Italian Lady design'd to publish Livy with notes. Faccius has writ Politica 40 Liviana. ━ P. Lambecij Com. de Biblioth. Caes. l. ii. c. 7. p. 522. ... In pag. 943, &c. is a large and exact Account of [a] MSᵗ wᶜʰ must be

---

Sept. 23. H. to Dr. T. Smith. *Re Index Expurgatorius* and Astrey. Sends accurate copy of the inscription Halley is engaged on; with remarks and conjectures. Also, copy of the inscription discovered at Rewley on Thursday last [Ela, &c.], which he has purchased and placed in the Anatomy School. This benefaction of Ela is not mentioned in Dugdale. Hudson has returned from Lincolnshire and sends query concerning the Scholia upon Strabo attributed by Reinesius to Cyriacus Anconitanus.

considered when an Account is given of the MSS. & Editions of Livy.

Sept. 27 (Th.).   In pag. 997 is a short Dissertation *De Carnunto,* but he promises a larger ; wch was never publishe[d], as M^r. Berger tells me, who thinks 'tis amongst Lambecius's other Papers at Vienna. — . . . I am told by M^r. Hoffman y^t one Arkeim has writ in the German Language a Book *de Sacrificijs & Cultu Cimbricorum.* — We have an Account from ye North y^t vast Numbers of Scotch Cattle will come into this Kingdom before ye Act takes place, by wch they are prohibited, and y^t they are sold at very small Rates scarce yeilding 20^s. a Head. No English horses 10 are permitted to be carried into Scotland, not so much as for ye Coach. — Sept. 25th last were admitted into ye Publick Library these two Gentlemen, Henr. Joach. *Browne* Hannoveranus.   (2) George *Seidel* Lesna Polanus. — . . . To day M^r. Hoffman went to London, with 3 or 4 Germans, where he will stay about a Month. — The above mentioned M^r. Browne reported that he was to be made Chaplain to the Prince of Denmark ; but M^r. Hoffman has assured me he is not, M^r. Crucius a German Divine, & of some Learning, being to have that Place.

Sept. 28 (Fri.).   M^r. Wesley's Letter.

On my printing a Poem, on ye Battle of Blenheim, I was sent for to London 20 by a Person of Quality in Jan. last, the Duke of Marlb. having promis'd me a Chaplain's place in one of ye New Regiments and another Honb^le Person greater Favours.

I had writt two Books against ye Dissenters at which they were very angry. The Person who sent for me up told me I must drop that Controversy, & at last that I must publickly and in Print Recant or palliate what I had writ against the Dissenters. He added that those People expected so many Friends in the next House of Commons more than they had in ye last, that when they came to sit, they had resolv'd to call those to Account who had affronted them. This had a contrary Effect to what was expected. I left my Fortunes 30 in Gods Hands and resolv'd to Act according to my conscience, & as soon as I came into the country to use w^t little Interest I had in our Election to serve those who were not likely to be partial to the Dissenters. But before I would Act I was so nice as to write to Coll. Whichcott, because there had been some Intimacy betwixt us, giving him the Reasons why I thought myself oblig'd to vote against Him. This Letter he expos'd, and his Friends reported there was Treason in it, after wch I gave copies of it. They likewise threaten'd to write up against me, & throw me out of my Chaplain's place, which the Duke had given me, & throw me into Goal, all which (I thank 'em) they have fully effected. I wrote to London to know why I was turn'd out, without knowing 40 my Accusation. My Coll. Lepell answer'd, that a Person of the First Quality told Him 'twas for something I had published wch was not approved of at Court, & for having concern'd myself too much in some other Matters. The first must be my Books against the Dissenters ; the Latter my Acting in the Election for my own County, which I thought I had as much Right to do as any Freeholder ; God be prais'd these Crimes were link'd together. After this the Friends of the new Candidates the Dissenters and their Adherents charg'd me with Preaching Treason, and reported I was distracted (where then was their Mercy ?) but at last were content to throw me into Prison according to their Promise for no great debt to a Relation, & Zealous Friend 50 of one of the New Members. They knew 'twas sufficient to do my Business, I having been thrown behind by a series of Misfortunes. My Parsonage Barn was blown down 'ere I had recovered the Takeing my Living : My House great part of it burnt down about 2 years since. My Flax, great part of my

Income now in my own Hands, I doubt willfully fir'd & burnt in ye Night, whilst I was last in London. My Income sunk about one half by the low price of Grain, & my Credit lost by the taking away my Regiment. I was brought to Lincoln Castle June the 23^d last past. About 3 weeks since my very unkind People thinking they had not yet done enough, have in ye Night stabb'd my 3 Cows wch were a great part of my poor Numerous Family's Subsistence. For wch God forgive them.

                                                                    WESLY.

— Georg. Pritius has writ a silly Poem in Latin in Praise of the Queen, & the D. of Marlborough. — Upon the Knighting of Dr. Hann's & the Quack D^r. Wm Read.... — There is a Gathering making in ye University for Relief of M^r. Wesly, to the great mortification of ye Fanaticks. — M^r. Grabe went to day to London, with a Design to go thence into Germany, & so into Prussia, his Native Country, where he says he will not tarry long. One chief end of his going out of England, is to consult MSS. for his intended Edition of the Septuagint. — M^r. Cole, the Engraver, tells me he has hopes of procuring very shortly a very old Inscription ; but he will not tell where 'tis. I believe however there cannot be much in it, by reason he says there is but a letter or two visible in it. — *Quære* of M^r. Dodwell whether he writ a [1]Book ag^t Hobbs's *Leviathan*, proving it to be Heretical? . . And if he did, to give one (if he has Duplicates) to ye Publick Library.

Sept. 29 (Sat.). The Duke of Shrewsbury has written a Letter to ye B^p. of Oxford (his Couzin) that he has married an Italian Lady of Excellent Accomplishments, that she is turn'd from the Church of Rome, that he is coming with her into England, & desires his Lordship that when she is here, he would be pleas'd to give such Arguments to her as may settle and fix her in the Protestant Religion. — On the 19th came by a Flying Post a Pacquet from Court to Edinborough with orders to ye Commissioner not to give ye Royal Assent to the Act for Limitation, y^t for Triennial Parliam^{ts}, & y^t for sending Plenipotentiaries to Forreign Treaties. After wch several other Acts being confirm'd by the Commissioners giving ye Royal Assent, the Session was ended. — On the 30th of Jan. last M^r. Potter preach'd at Cairfax in Oxford. His Sermon was afterwards much censur'd as containing nothing relating to the Day, W^{ch} D^r. Mill coming to hear of he ask'd him about it. To wch he reply'd that 'twas so far from that, that the greatest part of it was wholly upon ye occasion. Some time after this, D^r. Mill happening to speak again of ye Sermon, on purpose to shew w^t groundless Censures were cast on the Whiggish Party, M^r. Pearse then present, a great Friend of M^r. Potters, having been one of his Pupils, & whiggishly inclin'd too (as some say) answer'd that he was then an Auditor w^n the Sermon was preach'd, & y^t there was too much ground for ye Report ; the Sermon being the very same wch M^r. Potter preach'd the year before at S^t. Peter's in ye East before the University one of the Lent Sundays, the whole Drift of wch was Church unity ; only wth an Additional Sentence at ye last, telling the Auditors that 'twas the Martyrdom of King Charles Ist & they might make ye Application themselves. 'Tis thought some of the Sneaking Fanatical Moderators put him on this, well knowing that to vindicate y^t

---

[1] He did not.

Pious King would be against their own Principles, wch are destructive to Monarchy & quite contrary to ye signal Actions of y^t Prince in defending ye R^ts of ye Church.

Oct. 1 (Mon.). Sir Thomas Rawlinson is chosen L^d. Mayor of London for ye year ensueing, notw^thstanding the Great opposition of ye Whigg Party. — Sir Stephen Fox's Lady is brought to bed of a Boy and a Girl, wch is ye more extraordinary because S^r. Steph. is almost 8o years of age tho' his Lady is but young. He has had a son before by her, who is living.

Oct. 2 (Tu.). M^r. Wesly's Letter has procur'd very considerable Benefactions not only in Oxford (where Magd. College has given him 10 30 lib^s., Jesus 16, & most of the rest proportionably) but at London & in divers other places, particularly my L^d. Nottingham (who is reckon'd none of ye most generous) has sent him 30 lib^s. — M^r. Bagford has made proposals for printing his Collections concerning the Original & Progress of Printing. — I hear Dr. Royse, Provost of Oriel-College, is going to print his last Sermon preach'd before the Queen.

Oct. 3 (Wed.). The Descriptions of some Brass Coyns a Gentleman of X^t Church shew'd me ... With 4 or 5 others very much defaced, wch seem to be Constantius's, Tetricus's & Claudius Gothicus's. But 'tis not easily guess'd whose. — Being to day at M^r. Abel's Chamber of Merton 20 College he was pleas'd amongst several other curious Books in his study to shew me one wch he bought out of D^r. Lydal's study late Warden of that college being in MS^t containing all the Fees of the Beadles, Registers &c. of Oxford as they were settled by D^r. Rives, Vicechancellor of Oxford, in ye time of Q. Eliz. & the Heads of Houses in ye University. He has Gryphius's Edition of Quintilian, Lugd. 1544. but I think there is not much in it. — I was told to day of a Brass Plate dug up at Godstow wth a very old Inscription on it. . . .

Oct. 4 (Th.). Last night M^r. Abel told me he had taken most of the Inscriptions in Merton Chapell, wch will be of use when another Edition 30 of Hist. & Antiq. Oxon. comes out. — . . . Jac. Perizonij prima & secunda ad nuperam Notitiam de Varij Aeliani, aliorumque locorum locis. *Lugd. Bat.* 1703. . . . In pag. 12 is An Account of Perizonius's Assistance to Gronovius in ye Edition of Livy, & of his suppressing the greatest part of the Observations, wch Perizonius could not recover again.

From S^r. John Walters to the Sollic[i]tor General (S^r. Simon Harcourt). In Imitation of Martial Epigr. Book II. Epig. 32.

We own your skill, S^r. Pleadwell, in the Laws,
Your Art to manage & defend a Cause:
But wth your wit & Eloquence we find
A Servile Temper & an abject mind.

Against Cadoggan I've commenc'd a Suit,
Now like a Friend, engage in ye Dispute:
Offend Caddoggan! No S^r. not a Word!
A Rising Man ye Darling of his Lord.

Well! against S^t. John's I've an Action got,
How mute again? refuse! & pray why not?
Plead against S^t. John's! no, excuse me there, 40
He's great at Court, & has Her Grace's Ear.

Harley invades my Right w^thout Pretence,
Now Justice calls to speak in my Defence:
Have Patience, you Reply! with Temper wait!
You'll not disgust a minister of State.

Oct. 2. F. Fox to H. Is Wall's *Infant Baptism* in Bodley?

My Servants the Great Dutchess keeps by
   Force,
Gives me Affronts, then bids me take my
   Course:
She's Rich, she's old you say, w^{th}out a son ;
Put up th'Affront there's nothing to be done,
No ! for the World you'l not provoke her
   Grace
Nor loose your expectations of a Place.

Is this the Boasted Service of your Tongue ?
Only for Fortunes Favourites well hung :

His Honest, Generous Temper I commend,
Who dares the Justice of a Cause de-
   fend :
But hate the Wretch whose Mercenary
   Fear
Makes him ye Slave of Courts, the Great
   ones Worshipper.

10   The Justices, this Sessions at Oxford, have given near 20 lib^s. to M^r. Wesley in consideration of his great Distress.

Oct. 5 (Fri.). M^r. Dalton, one of ye Junior Fellows of All Souls College, going out two or three days since to divert himself by shooting, met with some High-Constable, who not giving way, there was some Justleing ; but at last Dalton being forc'd to break way, he was so concern'd that he turn'd back presently, & shot the Constable, who being a lusty stout Man made up to him (notw^{th}standing his wound) & took his Gun from him, w^{th}out any other Damage, leaving the Issue of it to a Tryal, being resolv'd to prosecute him. This Dalton is a proud empty
20 person, & was put into the College by the Archb^p. of Canterbury, soon after the late Warden (D^r. Finch) died, & I believe may be of ye Whiggish Party. — Jac. Perizonij Oratio de Fide Historiarum contra Pyrrhonismum Historicum. *Lugd. B.* 1702. In this Oration are several Particulars concerning the Fidelity of Livy, wch must be consulted when I write an Account of him. . . .

Oct. 6 (Sat.). Last night died M^r. Martin, Vice-Principal of Hart-Hall, of the colick. — M^r. Wanley writ the Preface to the Catalogue of Septentrional MSS. in English, wch was afterwards translated into Latin by M^r. Thwaites, or else his Pupils, who supervis'd and corrected the
30 whole Catalogue, & order'd it as he pleas'd.

[Notes on Livy from Phil. Parei *Lexicon Criticum* (and also at pp. 164, 166–168).]

Macarij Ægyptij Opuscula nonnulla Græc. Lat. per Jo. Georg. Pritium. *Lips.* 1690. He is in quest after other Pieces wth a design to publish y^m. — One M^r. Ellison stands Candidate for Fellow of University Col. in room of M^r. Smith, whose Place is declar'd void upon his late Promotion to a Living. — An Examination of D^r. Willis's Sermon on the late Thanksgiving before the Queen is just come out. — M^r. Martin was first of Trinity coll. where he was servitor to Dr. Whitby, thence he
40 remov'd to Corpus Christi Col. where he took his M. of Arts Deg. 1683 & was Chaplain. Afterwards he was Vice-Principal of S^t. Mary Hall, & at length, upon some difference when M^r. Wyat became Principal (as

Oct. 6. Dr. T. Smith to H. Remarks on the Greek inscription; wishes for a new ed. of the inscriptions, 'without that bulk of riff raff notes, with wch both Mr. Selden and Prideaux have stuffed their bookes.' Congratulations on the Rewley inscription ; suggests slight amendments in H.'s reading of it. Almeloveen's ed. of Strabo to be finished by next Midsummer. Asks for information concerning Carthaginian, Mauritanian, Sicilian, or old Spanish coins stampt with Punic characters, and of books relating thereto.

is said) he remov'd to Hart-Hall, where he became Vice-Principal, & by his Industry & care made it flourish equally to any House in Oxford. . . .

Oct. 7 (Sun.). On Friday last (Oct. 5) about 9 in the morning Secretary Hedges came to the L^d. Keeper Wright, demanding of him the Great Seal, wch being deliver'd was immediately carried to the Queen at Windsor, & 'tis thought that in the council this day M^r. Cooper was made L^d. Keeper, to the Great Resentment of all the Honest Party. — M^r. Martin was buried this Evening, ab^t 6 of ye clock in S^t. Peter's Church in the East, in a very solemn Manner, there being a great Concourse of ye most considerable Scholars at his Funeral. He died worth 10 1500 lib^s. at least.

Oct. 8 (Mon.). M^r. Laughton (John) Keeper of ye Publick Library in Cambridge I am inform'd is a rank Whig, a great Talker, & very violent in his Aspersions of the true Ch. of England Men. —

In Aurel. Cassiodori Consules Cuspiniani Commentarius. *Franc.* 1601. pag. 193. . . .

This day came a Letter from the Court at Windsor to my L^d. Abbingdon, putting him out of all his Places, to the great Astonishment of all. — Some have reported that an Answer was written by M^r. Grascombe to the Essay for Catholick Communion & to have been 20 printed by M^r. Lichfield of Oxford. But Lichfield has shewn this to be a meere story.

Oct. 9 (Tu.). Out of D^r. Langbaine's Coll. Vol. 8. p. 88.

Jan. 23, 1617. John Shurle had a Patent from Arthur Lake, Bp. of Bath and Wells and Vice-Chanc. of Oxoñ. for the Office of Aletasting & the Making and Assiseing of Bottles of Hey, in wch Place were formerly Ed. Prickett. Before him Will. Indifferent. Before him Will. Ellis.

The Office of Aletasting requires, that he goe to every Ale brewer that Day they brew, according to their Courses & tast their Ale: for wch his Ancient Fee is one Gallon of Strong Ale & two Gallons of small wort worth a 30 penny.

The Hay Bottles are to be made according to the Price of Hay; & the Weight allowed by the wet, which at this time 1640 is thus: good Hay being 20^s. a load, the Penny Bottle ought to wey 3½.

Ibid. pag. 123.

DEO O. M. | ET | MEMORIAE SACRVM | OPTIMAE SPEI ADOLESCENTIS | HENRICI SMITH, | FILII ROGERI SMITH DE EDMVND THORP | IN COMITATV LEICESTRIAE | ARMIGERI, | COLLEGII REGINAE COMMENSALIS. | QVI, DVM AESTIVIS HORIS ANIMI | OBLECTANDI, SALVTIS FIRMANDAE | ERGO, CHERWELLI FLVENTIS FIDEN | TIVS QVAM PRVDENTIVS SE COM | MITTERET, NEC NATANDI 40 PRORSVS | RVDIS NEC SATIS PERITVS, | RAPIDI ADVERSI FLVMINIS VORTICE, | PROH DOLOR ! ABSORPTVS, INGENS | SVI DESIDERIVM MOESTIS | PARENTIBVS RELIQVIT | A.D. XII. KALEND. IVN. | ANN. DOM. CIƆ DCXL.

This Inscription D^r. Langbaine made and caused to be set up upon his Monum^t in Marble on the North Wall of S^t. Peter's church in ye East in Oxford. — Gaddius de Scriptoribus . . . There is an encomium of Livy. . . . — This day was read in Convocation the Chancellor's Letter nominating D^r. De Laune vice-Chancellor for the year Ensueing (wch is his 4th year) & 'twas approv'd by the convocation. — D^r. Hudson shew'd me to-day the Catalogue of M^r. Seller's Books, wch was 50

sent him by M^r. Prowse. 'Tis a very valuable Collection, & there are
a vast number. M^r. Prowse in his Letter says that a Gentleman offer'd
to give 150 Guineas at least for the MS^t M^r. Seller bequeath'd to y^e
Publick Library if it might be dispos'd of. I cannot tell why he should
offer so much the chief thing in it being The *Chronicon Lichfeldense.* —
M^r. Prowse also sent to D^r. Hudson, a Catalogue of M^r. Seller's Coyns,
wch are almost 200, But we cannot make an Estimate of the value, he
having not describ'd 'em. — The speech wch M^r. vice-chancellor made
to day upon his being re-elected was chiefly upon My L^d. Clarendon's
10 History, whence he took occasion to speak against the Fanaticks & the
Whiggs, & to commend the Zeal of ye university against 'em, concluding
wth a Request that they would proceed in the same care for the Church
&c. — . . . Gesneri Bibliotheca. See w^t he has s^d there of Livy. . . .

Oct. 10 (Wed.). 'Tis said by some Persons y^t B^p. Burnett gave M^r.
Wesly ab^t a year since 25 or 26 lib^s, on purpose as is thought y^t he
would not speak anything either in print or otherwise ag^t ye Presbyterians & the rest of ye Whiggs. But he was resolv'd to act like a conscientious Man, thinking himself for this charity the more oblig'd to
write in Behalf of ye Church of England.

20   A correct Copy of the verses on Dr. Hanns and Reade the Mounte-
banck, being Knighted together.

The Queen like Heaven shines equally on
    all
Her favours now wthout Distinction fall.
Great Reade and slender Hanns both
    knighted show
That none their Honours shall to Merit owe.
That Popish Doctrine is exploded quite,
30   Or Ralph had bin no Duke, & Read no
    Knight.
That none may Virtue or their Learning
    plead

The first wants Grace ye last can hardly
    read.
Such moderation now at court is seen,
That nothing Excellent can pleas ye Queen.
O Hanns ! the Royal memory restore,
This will advance thy character much more
Than Empty Titles fools & knaves adore.
And thou, o Read ! the Royal Eyeballs
    couch,
And then the Queen will see as well as
    touch.

ON THE TACK.

The Globe of th' Earth on which we dwell
    Is tackt unto the Poles :
The Little Worlds our Carcasses
    Are tackt unto our Souls :
The Parsons chiefest Business is
    To tack the Soul to Heaven :
40 The Doctor's is to keep the Tack
    'Tween Soul and Body even.
The Priest besides by Office tacks,
    The Husband to ye Wife ;
And that's a Tack (God help them both)
    That always holds for Life.
The Lawyer studys how to tack
    His client to ye Laws :

Th' Attorney tacks whole Quires & Reams
    To lengthen out y^n Cause.
The Commons, Lords & English Crown
    Are all three tack'd together,
And if they 'ere chance to untack
    No good can come to either.
The Crown is tack't unto ye Church,
    The Church unto ye Crown,
The Whiggs are slightly tack't to both,
    And so may soon come down.
Since all the World's a general Tack
    Of one thing to another,
Why then about one Honest Tack
    Do Fools make such a Pother !

Oct. 11 (Th.). M^r. Berger tells me y^t the Edition of Strabo wch is
doing in Holland will be very inconsiderable, Almeloveen the Under-
50 taker adding nothing new, from MSS. or other Authorities of y^t kind, but
printing Casaubon's Notes at large. — 'Tis reported the Great Seal will
be managed by 3 Commissioners ; whereof Secretary Harley is to be

one, but y^t is not believed. — D^r. Smith in a Letter I rec^d from him last Night desired me to intreat M^r. Tyrrel to bring wth him the next time he goes to London the Papers he formerly lent ye Doctor relating to ye Statutes of Trinity College in Dublin. I mention'd it to M^r. Tyrrel but it being a considerable time since he lent them ye D^r. he cannot now call to mind w^t they are, & therefore desires the D^r. would specify 'em & w^t volume they are in. — In Jac. Salomonius's *Inscriptiones Agri Patavini* are some things relating to *Livy.* . . . — Going down last Night to M^r. Nichols's, a Quaker's in Oxford, he shew'd me a thick folio Book containing the Lives of ye Saints. 'Tis a Popish Book in old English, 10 but being w^thout beginning or Ending I cannot tell when or where 'twas printed, nor who was the Author. I do not remember I ever saw one of them before.

Out of Mr. Lock's Will. [Bequests to the Bodleian Library]. ¹Printed. See Lock's Works, Ed. 1714, Epistle to the Reader.

Oct. 13 (Sat.). I saw last Night a Letter in Latin from M^r. John Friend, the Physician, to Mr Keil of X^t Church giving an Account of the Feaver raging in that ²place, with ye methods he us'd for Remedy. Amongst ye best Preservatives he mentions Malt & Oat Beer. — On Tuesday last my L^d. Mayor call'd a Court of Lieutenancy to Elect a 20 Colonel of ye yellow Regm^t of Train'd Bands of London in Room of S^r. Sam. Dashwood deceas'd & ye choice fell on S^r. W^m. Withers, K^t. and Alderman, a very loyal & honest Gentleman, tho' 'tis said one of another stamp was aim'd at. — On Wednesday Night the Queen & Prince wth their whole court return'd from Windsor to Kensington & a General Council was summon'd to meet them in ye Afternoon when 'twas said for certain that W^m. Cowper Esqr. was to be declar'd L^d. Keeper & have the Great Seal deliver'd him for wch High Dignity he has already got his Equipage ready. 'Twas expected also y^t my L^d. Wharton would be declar'd constable of ye Tower in Room of ye Earl of Abing- 30 don. 'Tis reported S^r. Nathan Wright when he deliver'd the same seal said he resign'd that office wth more content y^n he rec^d it, or words to y^t purpose. He injoy'd it 5 years & 5 months, & 'tis hop'd is no looser by it, he will for the future give up all Practise of ye Law, & live privately, having acquir'd an honest good Name. — M^r. Llh[u]yd, Keeper of the Ashmolean Museum, spent a Fortnight or three Weeks to compare some of D^r. Hicks's things in this Thesaurus with the British Language; but (for w^t reason I know not) there is no mention at all of him in the Work; wch should have been done by all means, especially since he has made such honourable Mention of several who are known 40 to be but mean worthless Persons in comparison of M^r. Llhuyd.

Oct. 14 (Sun.). M^r. Cowper was made L^d. Keeper on Thursday last.

Oct. 12. T. Watson (Beconsfeild) to H. Dunning H. for £3 in 3 weeks if he does not wish his father thrown into ' Windsor prisson.'

Oct. 14. H. to F. Cherry. Will be glad of any suggestions for Livy. The Tarvisine and Rewley inscriptions. The subscription for Mr. Wesley.

---

¹ [Printed . . . Reader. These words are written (? by Hearne) in pencil.]
² Portugal.

[Plate containing ' An Inscription wch I found in MS^t in a spare Leafe at the Beginning of the *Tarvisine* Edition of Livy, wch I had of the Royal Society.']

I just now saw ye Oxford Almanack for ye year ensuing, wherein is represented the L^d. Treasurer (Godolphin) playing at dice, & the Queen in a very disconsolate condition &c. if we may believe those who are suppos'd to understand ye Meaning. 'Tis s^d my L^d. Kingston will be made L^d. Chamberlain in room of ye Earl of Kent, my L^d. Sunderland Secretary of State, in room of S^r. Charles Hedges. 'Tis s^d now my L^d.

10 Wharton is to [be] made L^d. Lieutenant of Oxfordshire & the Earl of Essex Constable of ye Tower, both in Room of the Earl of Abbingdon. — The M^r. Cowper, who is made L^d. Keeper, is but 41 years of Age, being ye youngest L^d. Keeper ever known; but he is a man of P^ts & Learning tho' of very bad Principles & Morals, being well known to have had two Wives at a time, a Man of no Religion, &c. Some report that M^r. Harris, formerly of S^t. Gregorie's has a Grant to be his Chaplain. — The L^d. Gore, Chancellor of the Dutchy of Lancaster exspects next to be turn'd out; and then 'tis hop'd the Whiggs or Presbyterians will be contented, having got all into their Hands, except 4 or 5 L^d. Lieutenancies.

20 **Oct. 15 (Mon.).** In ye Publick Library amongst Archb^p Laud's Coyns are two silver ones, of ye 2^d Magnitude, of King Juba, the Description whereof is this : REX IUBA. Ejus cap. ℞. Templum octo Columnarum, cum aliquot literis Punicis, . . . — Some think, the Monthly Mercury is writ by the Author of ye Post-Man. — M^r. Tyrrell has promised to give to ye Publick Library several MSS. written by his Grandfather (by ye Mother's side) Arch-B^p. Usher, two or three whereof are in D^r. Mill's Hands, one of wch ye D^r. shew'd me containing theological Matters, & another he told me he had relating to some obscure Passages in the New Testament. — In D^r. Charlett's study is Ant. à Wood's Head taken in

30 Plaister de Paris, wch shews him to have been a melancholly thoughtfull Man.

Oct. 16 (Tu.). [Sketch of coin of Juba, with note, ' Duos hujus Regis nummos habemus in Archivis Bodlejanis.'—Ant. Augustinus in Dial. VI. de Nummis, p. 80. Ed. *Antv.* 1617. . . .]

To day was admitted into ye Publick Library, Ricardus Lovett Londinensis. — 'Tis s^d the Earl of Kent L^d. Chamberlayn of ye Houshold has laid down & will be succeeded by the L^d. Kingston. — 'Tis s^d the New L^d. Keeper will be made a Baron of this Kingdom. — A Ship come into Sheelds gives a dismall Account of ye Jamaica Fleet as if

40 most of 'em are lost. — 'Tis discours'd amongst some y^t the Duke of Ormond will be turn'd out of Ireland, & y^t ye L^d. Summers will be put in his Place. W^ch is ye more to be rely'd on, because 'tis certain (from w^t has been already acted) that there will be a total Removal of all Honest Men, & y^t ye Favourers of ye Faction will [be] put in their Room.

Death of Mr. Martin, V. P. of Hart Hall (5th inst.). Horse-race in Port-Mead in opposition to that at Woodstock. ' The Oxford Almanack for ye ensueing year is finish'd. My L^d. Treasurer is represented throwing dice, the Queen in a disconsolate condition &c. wch I do not question but will exasperate ye Whiggs.' Messages, &c.

Oct. 17 (Wed.). Being last Night with D^r. Mill, M^r. Pearce, who was then wth him too, was pleas'd to run down M^r. Alsop of X^t Churche's Sermon, preach'd upon these words: *And now that he descended w' is but that he also ascended,* &c. affirming that there was neither Style, sense or judgm^t shewn in it. D^r. Mill concurr'd with him, & from thence proceeded to call him the greatest Blockhead y^t ever liv'd. Upon wch knowing M^r. Alsop had the universal Character of being a man of singular modesty, wit, & good Learning, I spoke up for him, & told them that the Sermon bore an extraordinary character in the university, & y^t divers of the best judges concluded it to be a neat polite well-penn'd Discourse, & y^t he shew'd him- 10 self a Person of a very clear head in delivering ye several opinions ab^t Hades, & afterwards pitching upon w^t he thought the best, wch D^r. Mill so much resented (as if I detracted from his own Character beli[e]ving himself to be a better Judge yⁿ ye whole university besides) that he abus'd me very much, & afterwards being not contented wth this He and M^r. Pearce went on to the rest of ye Members of X^t Church, not sparing ye Dean himself, giving them no better Quarter than they had done M^r. Alsop: not to mention some other Colleges wch they fell foul upon also. All wch suits well with ye Character I rec^d concerning M^r. Pearce, just as he came to our Hall, that he was one of the most ill natur'd Men in 20 Oxford. — [1]D^r. King Archb^p of Dublin 'tis said will be suddenly in Oxon. He was Pupil to M^r. Dodwell. — .. Taylor a servitor of X^t Church lately stole 120 Guineas from a Gentleman Commoner, wch he ingenuously confess'd. He also stole several Books out of that College Library, cutting the Covers off and leaving them standing. This was discover'd by the Binder. He is since gone off, the college being not willing to expose him for his Father's sake who is a Clergy Man. — M^r. Lloy'd Son of ye B^p. of Worcester disputed yesterday & to day in the Divinity schoole for his B. of Divinity's Degree. . . .

Oct. 18 (Th.). I saw this Morning M^r. Smith of University College's 30 Case, wch I had not time to hurrye through, but by w^t I read it seems to be all Juggle. I saw also another Trifling Paper of his. — The Master of university college shew'd me a Copy of verses sent him by an unknown Hand from London last Night, wherein the New L^d. Keeper is reflected on especially for his Mistress Cullen. — My Lord Marlborough 'tis now s^d will be L^d. Lieut. of Oxfordshire, the Earl of Bridgwater L^d. Chamberlain, the Marquis of Monthermer Master of the Horse to Prince George in the L^d. Bridgwater's Room, & my L^d. Stamford Chancellor of ye Exchequer. — M^r. Lesley was in the Publick Library this Afternoon, with some Irish Ladies. He goes under ye Name of *Smith.* — The Allyance 40 Pacquett Boat has brought advice that Badajox is certainly surrender'd.

Oct. 19 (Fri.). This day was a meeting in the Pub. Library of the Curators, to examin ye Accounts of the Library, & there was 30 lib^s. put into ye Chest of S^r. Tho. Bodley.

Oct. 20 (Sat.). S^r. W^m. Pittett is in Custody for Writing ye Pamphlett call'd *The Bonefire,* wch reflects on ye Burning of *The Memorial.* — Selecta Numismata antiqua ex Musæo Jacobi de Wilde. *Amst.* 1692. . . There are there 4 Coyns of Amyntas (all Brass), the Father of Philip, Grand-

---

[1] He did not come.

father of Alexander yᵉ Great, & 4ᵗʰ of the Macedonian Kings. They have all on the Front Amyntas's Head cover'd with a Lyon's Skin (according to yᵉ Custom of the Ancient Heroes) & on the Reverse an Eagle treading on a Serpent & pulling it in pieces, denoting perhaps the Conquest of Thessaly by Amyntas, in wᶜʰ as Solinus has observ'd, there is a great number of Serpents; unless it belongs rather to some prodigy wᶜʰ happen'd to the King. But I like the former conjecture best. The first of these Çoyns has on yᵉ Reverse AMYNTA., the second ΠΥΔΝΑΙΩΝ, the 3ᵈ ΠΥΔΝΑΙΟΝ, & yᵉ 4ᵗʰ ΠΥΝΔΝΑΙΩΝ, By wᶜʰ it appears yᵗ yᵉ 3 last were
10 struck at Pydna a City of Macedonia, & upon that Account they are great Rarities, it having been observ'd that yᵉ Antiquaries had observ'd no Coyns struck at this City before these were found, wᶜʰ was in the year 1685, by Theodorus Van Haghe, who took yᵐ all four (and so 'tis likely the 1ˢᵗ was struck at Pydna also) in an Earthern urn about Thessalonica . . .

Oct. 21 (Sun.). The Master of University coll. told me to day that Mʳ. Hall of Queen's acquainted him in yᵉ Morning that he had given off his design of Publishing Leland de *Script. Brit.* upon Assurance yᵗ Mʳ. Tanner prosecutes it.

Oct. 22 (Mon.). Mʳ. Elston Member of Parliamᵗ for Chichester is
20 dead, by wᶜʰ Mʳ. Bromley has lost a vote for Speaker to yᵉ H. of Commons, as likewise have yᵉ Whiggs by the Death of Col. Dore. — . . . On yᵉ 16ᵗʰ Instant was admitted into the Publick Library Georg. Homerus Smyrnæus. — . . . In the 1ˢᵗ Book of Pliny's Nat. Hist. ad lib. 6. amongst the Author[s] *Livius filius* is reckon'd. See in the Index there giving an Accᵗ of the Authors quoted by Pliny, præfix'd by Harduin. There is a Testimony of Livy. — Dʳ. Mill is said to have but a very indifferent Character at Canterbury, where he is Prebend. . . .

Oct. 23 (Tu.). Mʳ. Bouche has in French a Learned Treatise abᵗ Annibal's Passing yᵉ Alps. See Harduin ad Plin. l. 3. p. 371. I never
30 yet saw it.

Oct. 24 (Wed.). Yesterday was admitted into yᵉ Publick Library Joannes Perry Comitat' Leicestr. . . .

Oct. 25 (Th.). Mʳ. Vatchell one of yᵉ Burgesses for Reading in Berks is dead. Interest is making by Sʳ. Owen Buckingham, yᵉ other Burgess, for his son to succeed. — On Monday was a meeting of a great number of Loyal Church Parliamᵗ men at yᵉ Fountain Tavern in the Strand to consider of yᵉⁱʳ strength for yᵉ choice of Mʳ. Bromley to be Speaker. The Whiggs laugh'd at it, & have laid two to one that they shall carry it for Mʳ. Smith. — The Guns have been fired at yᵉ Tower
40 for the taking of Barcelona, & all other Demonstrations of Joy as Bonfires,

---

Oct. 21. Hearne to Dr. T. Smith. Notes on the Tarvisine, Halley, and Rewley inscriptions. Has been to Godstow in search of a brass plate lately dug up. Hudson still on Strabo: H. would prefer Josephus. Only one Punic coin in Bodley; described in Augustinus, *VI. Dial. de Nummis* (Antw. 1617), p. 80. Dr. De Laune's speech on being appointed V. C. for another year. Mr. Seller's books and MSS. Death of Mr. Martin. Jo. Mollerus Flensburgensis is writing *Historia Cimbrica* in 3 vols. fol. Query about ed. of the Bible attributed to Henry VIII. Mr. Bassett reported author of *Essay for Catholic Communion.* Pritius has published pieces of Macarius.

Illuminations, &c. were made at London for this News. — On Sunday last Dʳ. Wake was consecrated Bᵖ. of Lincoln in Lambeth Chapell. Dʳ. Kennett preached & his Sermon is order'd to be printed. — Tuesday being yᵉ first day of yᵉ Term the new Lᵈ. Keeper made yᵉ most noble Cavalcade from the Middle Temple Hall to Westminster yᵗ ever was known, most of yᵉ Ministers of State attending his Lᵈship. His train consisted of about 60 Coaches. His Lᵖᵖ at his Entrance into Westminster Hall was ushered up to the High Court of Chancery by my Lᵈ. T[r]easurer walking on his Left Hand followed by yᵉ Dˢ. of Newcastle & Somersett, yᵉ Earls of Kent, Rivers, Samford Orford & Essex, the Lᵈˢ. Somers Colepepper & others. They sat some time wᵗʰ my Lᵈ. Keeper & then withdrew. His Gr. yᵉ Archbᵖ of Canterbury complemented my Lᵈ. Keeper in the Temple Hall, & in the Qu. Bench divers persons most Pamphleteers appeared upon their Recognizances. — . . . The Columna Rostrata (wᶜʰ should be printed in Livy) illustrated by Petr. Servius miscell. p. 25. . .

Oct. 26 (Fri.). Just publish'd, *Some Secret Memoirs of Robt. Dudley, Earl of Leicester*, From an old MSᵗ, with a Preface by Dʳ. *Drake*. 8°. Pr. 3ˢ. 6ᵈ.

Oct. 27 (Sat.). On Thursday (25ᵗʰ Instant) the Parliamᵗ met. Candidates for Speaker to yᵉ House of Commons were Mʳ. Bromley & Mʳ Smith. The former had 205 Votes, the latter 248. Divers speeches were made on both sides, & tho' several very good objections were made agᵗ Smith, as his voting for a standing Army, &c. yet yᵉ whiggs took no notice of them, but carried it against Mʳ. Bromley against whom they could object nothing but yᵗ he was a Tacker, & a true Friend of yᵉ Church. Mʳ. Tilly's Sermon was reflected on by their speechers & a great many bitter words dropt agᵗ the Universitys, especially Oxford. All good men now fear yᵗ 248 will prove 48. — The same day the Convocation met. Dʳ. Stanhope preach'd a Latin Sermon. After wᶜʰ they proceeded to the choice of a Prolocutor. Dʳ. Binkes Dean of Lichfield had 25 Votes, & Dʳ. Stanhope 37. — This day in the Afternoon died Mʳ. Wᵐ. Randal, Master of Arts, of Magd. Hall. He was a man of tolerable Parts, & a good Philosopher, & one yᵗ lov'd his pipe & pot. — The Master of the Mitre Tavern in Fleet-Street has a very large Table making, wherein are to be inserted, in large Golden Capital Letters, the Names of all those Worthy Patriots who were for passing yᵉ Bill agᵗ Occasional Conformity.

Oct. 28 (Sun.). There is a memorandum in yᵉ Courant that *Dudley's memoirs* is yᵉ same Book wᵗʰ *Leycesters common-wealth* (wᶜʰ has been printed several Times) and yᵗ yᵉ Author was Robᵗ Parsons the Jesuite. — Three of Terence's comedies, & near 3000 select verses out of Ovid's Metamorphoses, with English notes, likewise some Excerpta out of Castellio's Latin Testamᵗ by the *Author*[1] of the Peculiar use & Signification of several words in yᵉ Latin tongue. 8°. —

The Heads of her Majesty's Speech to the Parliamᵗ, viz.

That she was well pleas'd to observe so many at yᵉ opening of the Session wᶜʰ gave her great hopes of prosecuting the war wᶜʰ was of yᵉ greatest Importance to us to be timely in our Preparations. Nothing is more Evident than

[1] Willymot.

if y^t ye French King continues Master of the Spanish monarchy the Ballance of the Powers in Europe will be utterly destroyed & he will be able in a short time to engross ye trade & wealth of the world. No good Englishman would at any time sitt content an[d] still in such a Prospectt, and all the time we have good grounds to hope that by ye Blessing of God on our Armes wth our Allies we may Act offensively the next campaigne & restore the House of Austria to the Spanish Monarchy. Recomends to y^m ye union wth Scotland, but more especially amongst y^{m}selves & for Regulating of the Press.

10 There was a great contest on Thursday & a great many warm Speeches in ye H. of Comons before ye choice of a Speaker was made, each side endeavouring to Lessen the Ability of ye contrary Candidate. Ag^t the Honble Gent. y^t fills the chair they objected a Speech he made in ye House in ye Late Reign for keeping on foot a consid^{ble} body of Regular Troops as necessary in y^t conjuncture of being at a late meeting in wch a Peer was prest about agreeing upon a person to be Speaker &c. all wch was easily answered. Ag^t ye other they printed his Juvenal Travels wth a ridiculous Index made to the Book argued from Tilly's Sermon the want of Judgm^t that Body might have w^n such Principles were taught in the choice of their Members but this is not very material. 'Tis certain num-
20 bers carried the Election. Of those y^t voted for M^r. Bromley is G. Clarke for wch he is turn'd out of his Places. And this is w^t all must expect y^t vote honestly & conscientiously. — M^r. Wullaston made Purse-Bearer to the present L^d. Keeper because he is a good Dear-Stealer.

Oct. 30 (Tu.). I am told D^r. Leigh who writ y^e *Nat. History of Lancashire* has divers things fit for ye Press, but y^t he will not let y^m see ye Light because his History has not taken well.

Verses on ye New Promotions.   Sent to ye Queen.

O *Anna*! thy new Friends & Prick-eard Court
30 Cannot thy Dignity & Crown support.
The Awkward Loyalty of Whigs is known
To ruine Princes whom they make their own.
Like Mastives, feed & strike 'em, they will faun ;
But growl & seize you, when your hands withdrawn
Thou art like one that has a Wolf by th' Ears ;
Unsafe to hold, & if let goe he tears.

40 One *Cooper* to your Uncle was untrue.
Another, *Anna*, may be so to you :
Can *He thy* Honour & thy Conscience keep
Unspotted, when *his own* is fast asleep ?
Let *Cullen* witness this, whose wretched Ghost
Proclaims this--*She who trusts to him is lost.*

Think of thy *Martyr'd Grandfather*, & shun
That race by which *thy Father* was undone.
Th' Hereditary Hatred of that Crew
Persues the *Stewarts*, & descends to *you.*
Oh ! doe not in those fatal steps proceed,
Least thy *White Neck* at last be made to bleed.

No Wanton Muse does dictate this in spite ;
As Vile *De Foe* & *Touchin* weekly write.
Love to my *Church* and *Monarchy* & *You*
Has arm'd my Pen with *Truth* and Courage too.
By Zeal by Loyalty & Duty led
My Ears I hazard to secure *thy Head.*

Solus scripsi.

Oct. 30. Dr. T. Smith to H. Sorry that Bodley has but *one* coin stampt with Punic characters. Will discourse with Mr. Tyrrell when he comes to town about his grandfather the Primate. Laments Mr. Martin's death. Seller's books and MSS. Knows Mollerus' *Bibliotheca Septentrionis Eruditi.* Has not seen the *Sacrae Bibliae Tomus primus.* Dearth of libraries in London. Mr. Basset, of Cambridge, reputed author of the *Essay toward a Proposal for Catholic*

'Tis said by some that there is to be a Royal Visitation of yᵉ University of Oxoñ. — George Clarke, Esqʳ, who is dismiss'd, was Secretary to the Prince, and one of yᵉ Secretaries to yᵉ Admiralty. — 'Tis reported yᵗ the Queen, wⁿ she spoke her speech, trembled so much yᵗ she was hardly able to go through wᵗʰ it, as being sensible yᵗ wᵗ she said was derogatory to yᵉ Church of England, Securing the Toleration (as she declar'd she would inviolably) being look'd upon as too great a Favour given to the Fanaticks, & others of yᵉ Dissenters, & tending to the Destruction of the church of England. 'Tis given out yᵗ she is kept in ignorance & yᵗ only those Pamphletts wᶜʰ are writ in behalf of yᵉ church (some of wᶜʰ are very 10 luk warm) are represented to her, & yᵗ the scandalous infamous Pamphletts written by yᵉ Presbyterians are kept from her or at least represented fairly. — I am told yᵗ yᵉ Earl of Abbingdon gave yᵉ Gentleman a Purse of Gold who brought yᵉ news of his being turn'd out, & desir'd him to give his Duty to her Majesty & tell her yᵗ he would for yᵉ future live privately....

Oct. 31 (Wed.). The Queen has presented yᵉ New Speaker with a Purse of a 1000 Guineas as a token of her Satisfaction of his choice. — She is sᵈ also to have given her Uncle yᵉ Earl of Rochester an Estate near Cornbury, tho' the Dutchess of Marlborough did endeavour to obstruct it. And she certainly had effected it, had not yᵉ Queen sign'd 20 yᵉ Writings immediately, the Earl bringing 'em wᵗʰ him when he sollicited her Majesty for yᵉ Estate, well knowing the Dutchess would hinder it. The Dutchess would have had her Majesty revok'd the Grant (saying yᵗ the Estate lay very convenient for the Duke her Husband, & yᵗ he could not go on wᵗʰ his Building at Woodstock wᵗʰ out it) but the Queen reply'd she could not do it. — I saw this Morning in the Master of University's Study the Qᵗᵒ Edition of Florentius Wigorniensis, collated with a MSᵗ in the Publick Library at Oxford by Dʳ. Langbain (whose Book it once was) to wᶜʰ he has added several other notes, wᶜʰ will be of great use when that Author shall be 30 printed again. — The Master told me that Dʳ. Goodal has a mind to translate two Epistles Dedicatory prefix'd to the new Edition of Forbes's Works, as also pᵗ of his Life, all written by Dr. Garden the Publisher. I suppose it may be to be printed in his designed Accᵗ of the Church of England Sufferers in the late Rebellion. — Out of Dʳ. Hudson's Papers for Books to be consulted in the Publick Library for correcting & illustrating Authors. [Includes De Livij Statua pag. 30. I forget wᵗ Book yᵗ is in. 'Tis in French I remember....] — This day at nine of yᵉ Clock was a Convocation, abᵗ a Letter from yᵉ Chancellor to the University in behalf of Mʳ. Lloyd, son to yᵉ Bᵖ. of Worcester, desiring 40 they would let him accumulate the Degrees of Bach. & Doctor of Divinity. There was a full House; but yᵉ Letter being read, Mʳ. Waldow, of All Souls' Col. one of yᵉ Pro-Proctors read the vote of Parliamᵗ agᵗ his Father & him abᵗ Sir John Packington: upon wᶜʰ Dʳ. Woodrof made a speech, calling Waldow titubans Magister : wᶜʰ word so exasperated a great many of the Masters that they would not let him

---

Communion, fairly, honestly, and learnedly answered by Mr. Spinkes. Has, with Bp. Pearson, a low opinion of the Homilies of Macarius, Nilus, &c. Asks for a transcript of Dee's petition to K. James, dated June 5, 1604.

go on. So the Proctors went to a Scrutiny, wch being ended it appear'd that there were 46 more ag^t ye Passing the Letter than were for it. — Wⁿ a new Impression of Eutropius is made I must remember to add a note at pag. 45 signifying y^t it should be read M^o (or Manio) *Acilio Glabrione,* as 'tis read ad init. lib. 36. Livij, & in ye Epitome there, tho' the Metaphrast has Μάρκος. See Delrius's notes upon Florus's Epit. of Livy. — 'Tis s^d my Ld Seymour presently after M^r. Smith was pronounc'd Speaker, rose up, and told them, *Gentlemen ; you have got a Low Church man ; but pray remember that* 100 *Voluntiers are better than* 200 *press'd men.*

VOL. V.

Nov. 1 (Th.). On Monday the L^{ds} order'd an Address of thanks to her Majesty for her most Gracious speech. — S^r. James Mountague is made one of the Queen's Councell. — The Commons did nothing on Monday but take the oath of Abjuration, and they went as far as the Letter S.

To M^r. Bromley.

Had Parts and merit gained ye Chair	Be Sarah's Pimp, Go——ns Tool
Then Br——ly we had seen thee there	A Tricking Knave, an easy Fool
But for the future take this Lesson,	The Church & Honesty disown
This downright dealing's out of fashion	Do this & then the Chair's thy own.

This day M^r. Smith sign'd a Resignation of all Right to his Fellowship of University-College, tho' 'twas wth abundance of unwillingness, and he would have kept it if he could have found any shift. But ye Fellows would give him no other favour, than the sum of 10 lib^s. above his due : being not willing the matter should come to a visitation. — 'Tis said that the stones with wch they build the Duke of Marlborough's House at Woodstock are extreme bad, & y^t they crack by the Frost : so y^t in all probability they must begin ye Foundation again ; 'tis look'd upon as a bad omen.

Nov. 2 (Fri.). D^r. Wake B^p. of Lincoln is order'd to preach before the L^{ds} on the 5th of Nov., and D^r. Willis before the House of Commons. — M^r. Urry of Christ Church is desir'd to get transcrib'd for a Lady, Fisher B^p. of Rochester's sermon at ye Funeral of King Henry VIIth preach'd May 10th 1409. (2) A Mornyng Remembraunce had at the moneth mynde of ye noble Prynces Margarete Countesse of Richemonde and Darbye, Moder unto Kynge Henry the VII. & Grandame to oure Soverayne Lorde y^t nowe is, uppon whose soull Almyghty God have mercy. Both in 4°. in the Bodleyan Library. (3) The Mirrour of Golde to ye sinfull soule out of Latin into English by the said Countess. Also in ye Public Library. — Narcissus Marsh Archb^p. of Armagh gave 2500 lib^s. for B^p. Stillingfleet's Library, w^{ch}, like y^t of D^r. Isaac Vossius's, was sufferd to go out of ye Nation to the eternal scandal & Reproach of it. The said Archb^p. has built a Noble Repository for them. — The Library of Trinity College in Dublin, where the noble studoy of B^p. Usher was placed, is quite neglected & in no Order, so y^t 'tis perfectly useless, the Provost & fellows of y^t College having no regard for Books or Learning. — M^r. (Jos.) Barnes in a

Letter to D^r. Hudson mentions a Book wch he has seen call'd D. *Caroli Josephi Imbonati Mediolanensis Bibliotheca Latinorum Hebraica*, Rom. 1694. where in fol. 423. § 7246. is mention of M^r. Barnes's Hesther, with the whole Title Page. — J. Gadderar (a Scotch man) was the Author of the English translation of Craigg's Book against Parsons the Jesuite. Fabrettus's II^d Piece against Grunnovius (as he [calls him]) is in my L^d. Sunderland's study. This Book to be consulted in a new Edition of Livy. — Corpus Geographorum veterum edidit Petrus Bertius. Quere whether this be in ye Public Library? 'twas printed at Basil. — Dorrington has a Collection of Coyns, as D^r. Hudson informs me. But he cannot tell who this man is, there being no other mention of him in his Notes. — On the 30th of Oct. last D^r. John Arbuthnott was sworn her Majesty's Physitian Extraordinary, by her Majesty's special command, in consideration of his good & successfull services perform'd as Physitian to his Royal Highnesse.

Nov. 3 (Sat.). William Ashurst Esqr. Town Clerck of London is dead at ye Bath, for whose place it being worth 1500*l*. per. annum great Interest is making to ye Common Council in whose disposal it is. — On ye 1st Instant ye Lords attended the Queen wth ye Address at S^t. James's & afterwards adjourned to Monday. The Commons took into consideracion the Queen's Speech & appointed a Committee to draw up an Humble Address for ye same, ye substance of wch is to congratulate her Majesty for ye success of her Arms. That theyl effectually support her to carry on the war stand by her in suppressing ye Enemies of ye Government. That theyl keep a good Harmony amongst themselves. Thank her for her Assurance of her care of ye Church of England & for maintaining ye Toleration. —

The true Copy of *M^r. John Dee* his Petition to ye King's most Excellent Majestie exhibited: Anno 1604. Junij 5. at Greenwich. (transcrib'd from the Printed Copy in the Bodlejan Library, 4°. S. *Jur.*)

To the King's most excellent Majestie.

In most humble and lamentable manner beseecheth your Royall Majestie, your Highnesse most distressed Servant, *John Dee*: That, as, by the grace and providence of the Almightie, you are our King, our earthly Supreme Head, and Judge: So it may please your Sacred Majestie, eyther in your owne royall presence and hearing; Or, of the Lordes of your Majesties most honorable privie Counsell: Or, of the present assembled Parliament States, to cause your Highnesse sayd Servant, to be tryed and cleared of that horrible and damnable, & to him, most grievous and dammageable Sclaunder: generally, and for these many yeeres last past, in this Kingdom raysed, and continued, by re- port, and Print, against him. Namely, That he is, or hath bin a *Conjurer*, or *Caller*, or *Invocator* of Divels: Upon which most ungodly, and false report, so boldly, constantly, and impudently avouched: yea, and uncontrolled, and hitherto unp[un]ished, for so many yeeres, continuing: (Altho, your Majesties said Suppliant, hath published in print, divers his earnest Apologies, against it) yet some impudent and malicious forraine Enemie, or English traytor to the florishing State and Honor of this Kingdome, hath in Print (Anno 1592. 7. *Januarij*) affirmed your Majestie's said Suppliant, to be the *Conjurer* belonging to the most Honorable Privy Counsell, of your Majestie's most famous last Predecessor, (Queen Elizabeth) so that, seeing the said most abhominable Sclaunder, is become so highly haynous, and disgracefull, that it pretendeth

great discredit, and disliking to be had, also, of the said most Honorable Lordes, of your Majestie's Privie Counsell (as to use any *Conjurer's* advise: and your said suppliant to be the man.) It therefore seemeth, (upon divers respects,) to be very needfull, due and speedy order, to be taken herein; by your Majestie's wisedom, and supreme Authoritie: (by one, of the three foresaid meanes, or any other), to have your Highnesse said Suppliant, to be tryed, in the premisses: Who offereth himselfe willingly, to the punishment of Death: (yea, eyther to be stoned to death or to be buried quicke: or to be burned unmercifully) If by any due, true, and just meanes, the said name of *Con-*
10 *jurer*, or *Caller*, or *Invocator* of Divells, or damned Spirites, can be proved, to have beene, or to be, duely or justly reported of him or attributed unto him: Yea (good and gratious King) If any one, of all the great number of the very strange and frivolous fables, or histories reported and told of him (as to have been of his doing) were True: as they have been told, or reasonably caused any wondring among, or to, the many headed Multitude, or to any other whosoever cls. And, then, your Highnesse said Suppliant, (upon his said Justification, and Clearing, made herein,) will conceyve great and undoubted hope, that your Majestie will, soone after, more willingly, have Princely regard of redressing, of your Highnesse said Suppliant his farder griefes and hinderances;
20 no longer, of him, possibly to be endured: So long, hath his utter undoing, by little and little, beene most unjustly, compassed. The Almightie and most mercifull God, alwayes direct, your Majestie's royall heart, in his wayes of Justice & Mercy, as is to him, most acceptable: and make your Majestie to be the most blessed and triumphant Monarch, that ever this *Britysh* Empire enjoyed. *Amen. . . . —*

Dr. Hudson shew'd me a Letter to-day wch he recd from the Bp. of Norwich in Answer to one sent lately to him, complaining of his Ldship's Backwardness in Lending certain Books, (to ye great detriment of the Publick): His Ldship declar'd himself sorry yt the Dr. should
30 take it amiss, & promis'd to lend him for ye future any Book he should have occasion for out of his study. He also told him he would lend me any Livy I should want in ye design'd Edition of yt Author. — This Evening came the Lds Address to Town, wherein they thank her Majesty for her most Gracious Speech, declare that they will stand by her in her designs agt the King of France, & of Establishing a Union wth Scotland but especially among our selves, & for yt end advise her to prosecute the Incendiaries of the Nation (meaning the Church Party) with ye utmost Rigour & Severity. So yt poor Oxford (who stood so firmly to her Martyr'd Grandfather) must expect hard measure for their
40 Zeal agt ye Schismaticks. — Dr. Royses's last sermon before the Queen, (wch is newly published) is a well penn'd discourse, & pleases the Whiggs well. — I saw a Letter to-day to Dr. Hudson from Dr. Drake dated from Hampton Court the 9th of October last, in answer to one of ye Dr's desiring him to send his Books. He modestly excuses himself, thinking yt nothing he has hitherto done worthy so noble a Place; but however since some are pleas'd to entertain so favorable an opinion of him he promises to send wt he has written to be placed as Dr. Hudson shall think fit. —

Dr. Hudson also shew'd me a Letter from Laurentius Alexander
50 Zacagnius Keeper of the Vatican Library written to him (dated Feb. 11 Nov. Styl. 1703) giving an Account of wt he had done for him relating to his Noble Edition of Dionysius Hal. At ye End whereof he gives a short Relation of ye terrible Earthquake wch began when he was writing

ye said Letter; wch was so violent that he was hardly able to go on, as appears from several distorted Letters. The whole Passage here follows, viz.

Videas nunc, Vir Clarissime, an alia ulla in re opera, aut favore meo opus habeas, lubens enim curabo, ut mandata tua, qua par est diligentia exsequantur. Cum hæc postrema verba paulo ante meridiem scribo, validus terræmotus totam urbem de novo horrendum in modum concussit, cujus indicio sunt distortæ non nullæ eorundem verborum literæ. Placeat Deo Optimo Maximo peccatorum nostrorum Beatissimæ Virginis Mariæ, cujus Purificationis Festum agimus, intercessione misereri.   10

The Title of John Dee's Almanack for the year 1591.

A triple Almanack for the Yeere of our Lorde God 1591, being the thirde from the Leape Yeere. Wherein is conteyned, not onely the common accompt, which in this our Realme is used, with the Romane Kalender according to the late correction of *Gregorie:* but also, the true computation and reduction of the Monethes to their first and auncient seates, Christmass day being at the Sunnes entrance into *Capricorne,* or shortest day : whereby may easely be perceyved the great difference which hath happened for want of due observation of the Courses of Sunne and Moone Referred principally to the Meridian of London and for most respectes will serve for all Englande, and many other Countries 20 also. By J. D.

At the End is another Treatise relating to the said Almanack, & thus Entit.

A Prognostication for the same Yeere M.D.XCI. Conteyning a short discourse of the Eclipse of the Moone, and of the Quarters of the Yeere, with other necessarie Rules, for the better understanding of the Almanack going before : wherein are Rules for the finding the Planetarie Hower very easely and pleasantly, as also the rising and setting of the Sunne any day throughout the yeere, referred with the other, to the same Meridian. By J. D.

The Commons have agreed to An Address to her Maje[s]ty. There 30 was one observable Passage in it, viz. That they think ye Church is in no Danger; wch surprises several in Oxford, who were inform'd that they had voted 'twas in Danger, as it certainly is, when so many sects are countenanc'd & the true Church men scouted and declar'd dangerous Enemies. S^r. Wm. Blackett, S^r. Robert Clayton & S^r. Wm. Ashurst are dangerously ill. — D^r. Cliton one of the College of Physitians is sent over to the King of Portugal to assist him in his sickness wch is very dangerous.

Nov. 5 (Mon.). To-day M^r. Crosse of New College preach'd before the University at S^t. Marie's upon these words : *I will build my Church* 40 *upon this Rock, & the Gates of Hell shall not prevail ag^t it.* He shew'd first y^t the Establish'd Church of this Nation is founded upon the Rock mention'd in the Church. II^dly That the Methods carryed on by the Jesuits & other Emissaries of the Church of Rome for destroying of it are diabolical, & fitly answer the Expression of *the Gates of Hell.* III^dly that we ought to give Hearty Thanks to God for defeating all their wicked Designs, particularly that Grand one wch was to be effected as

---

Nov. 5. H. to Dr. T. Smith. Will ask Llwyd for inscriptions. Reasons for attributing the Bible before mentioned to Henry VIII. Transcribes John Dee's petition to James I (1604) from one of Burton's books. Convocation

upon this day. He spoke handsomly, & very little or nothing in behalf of the Whiggs, as was expected, he being known to be of y^t Party by his Stickling so much for D^r. Trimnel's coming in Warden of New-Col. — I have not yet compar'd the Book call'd *Dudley's Memoirs* with *Leyscester's Commonwealth*; but D^r. Charlett tells me that 'tis exactly the same with y^t Book, being printed *verbatim*: wch I the more wonder at, because that is a common Book, & 'twas almost impossible for Dr Drake to be ignorant y^t there was such a Book publish'd. The D^r. has wrot a Preface to it, wch has somew^t remarkable in it. *Leycester's Com-* 10 *monwealth* goes under the Name of *Father Parsons*; but *M^r. Ant. à Wood* insinuates that he was not the Author. — M^r. Ayliffe a Civilian of New College having taken Andr. Alciati Juris utriusque praxis out of the Publick Library (not at all regarding his oath & the force of the Statute) return'd it again to-day, it being down upon his name, & I suppose being first of all inform'd y^t 'twas missing.

Nov. 6 (Tu.). M^r. Bobart, the Botanist was greatly assisted in the II^d vol. of ye Oxford History of Plants, by M^r. Dale of Queen's College, who revis'd the whole & put it into proper Latin for him. Presently after the Death of the s^d M^r. [1] Dale, I had a sight of a Folio Book in MS^t drawn 20 up by himself, being Tables & Explications on Aristotle's Rhetorick. The whole seem'd to be done wth great Judgment, & was so much valu'd y^t several Gentlemen of the Middle Temple got Copies of it, for their use in ye study of ye Law. — M^r. Waller on the Earl of Berkley's Meditations, (Printed *Lond.* 1680. 8. to w^{ch} 'tis praefix'd) not publish'd I believe in the Collection of his Poems [2]. — There is just publish'd Three Years Travells over Land to China, &c. by E. Ysbrantes Ides, translated out of Dutch. — In the Bodlejan Library is an Acc^t of Rich. James (the Antiquarie's) Travells into Russia written wth his own Hand. There are some good Things not observ'd by others & may be worth 30 printing in a Collection. — Entred Commoner to-day of our Hall Tho. Sherley of New-Bury. — Some Advices say my L^d. Gallaway is dead of his Wounds. There will be suddenly several Promotions made at Court. — Yesterday being Gunpowder treason 'twas observ'd more than it us'd to be at Lond. — Our Parliament are so unanimous that 'tis thought they will settle the supply before Xtmass. — I was told to-day by a Merchant y^t he saw in *Portugal* a curious Piece of Writing, wch he thought exceeded that in our Publick Library written by M^{rs}. *Hesther English* a French Lady. — M^r. *Pullen* of *Magd.* Hall, last night told me that a certain Gentleman formerly bequeath'd a curious Manuscript *Virgil*, 40 in vellam, to their Library, wch coming into some Gentleman's Hands of *X^{t}Church* (but whose he cannot tell) they never could procure it. He likewise told me y^t there was once a very remarkable stone, wch was

---

negatived accumulation of B.D. and D.D. by Mr. Lloyd. In the debate Dr. Woodruff called Mr. Waldow *titubans magister.* Dr. Marsh has bought Stillingfleet's Library for £2500.

---

[1] This Dale was no great Scholar notwithstanding what follows. He corrected Dr. Smith's catalogue of Cotton's Library, but very ignorantly, & left out divers things.

[2] [Printed in the Edit. 1711.—Dr. Bliss.]

afterw^ds lent to D^r. *Plot,* who never return'd it, replying, when he was ask'd for it, y^t *'twas a Rule amongst Antiquaries to receive, and never restore.*

Nov. 7 (Wed.). Just publish'd *A Review of the Danger of ye Church of England,* wch is (as I am told) a very scandalous Pamphlet, & is reported by some to have been written by Dr Kennett. — D^r. Freind has seen at Lisbon two Libraries to be sold, each consisting of a thousand folios, & he suppos'd that two Hundred lib^s. would purchase 'em both. — M^r. Charles Bernard (Chief Physitian to her present Majesty) has given to the Publick Library a very fair MS^t containing the 5 last Books of Tacitus' Annals, & the 5 Books of his History, & at ye end are some 10 Epistles of Julius Cæsar & the Epistle of Pilate to Tiberius. D^r. Hudson has sent the Collations of Cæsar's Epistles to one M^r. Davies of King's College who is putting out a new Edition of Cæsar's Commentaries in 4to

Nov. 8 (Th.). By the Removal of Geo. Clarke Esqr. M^r. S^t. John is made Secretary of war for the Marine Forces as well as Land wch he enjoyed before. — On the 5th the B^p. of Lincoln preacht before ye House of L^ds in Westminster Abbey taking his Text ye 7th Matthew & the 15th verse. Beware of false Prophets wch come to you in sheep's cloath &c., from wch according to ye occasion of ye day being the Anniversary of the 20 Gunpowder treason he layd open the Principles and Practises of the Church of Rome. For wch Sermon the House of Lords the next day orderd his Lordship their thanks. At ye same time D^r. Willis Dean of Lincoln preacht before ye House of Commons in S^t. Margarets Church from the words in the 49th Chapter of Genesis & the 7th verse, Cursed be yeir Anger for it was fierce & their wrath for it was cruel, in wch he gave An Acc^t of the Powder Plot as also of the Assassination Plot ag^t King William. For wch the House of Commons the day after also orderd the Dean y^r Thanks wth a desire y^t ye same may be printed. D^r. Smalridge preacht before the Queen at ye Chapel Royal at S^t. James' upon the 16th 30 verse of the 10th Ch. of S^t. Mat. and the day was observd wth ye usual decency & ye night concluded wth ringing of Bells, Bonfires & Illuminations. — Last night M^r. Nevil of University-College told me that tho' D^r. Sloane had almost finish'd his Natural History of Jamaica, yet he would never print it, because he was well assur'd there were 2 or 3 ill natur'd men who would write ag^t it, & endeavour to expose it. W^ch tho' amongst men of Sense 'twould be no disgrace, yet he is too modest to publish w^t he finds must undergoe ye Publick Censure of ill natur'd men. — He also told me y^t an Extraordinary Acc^t of ye Alps (wth a great number of curious cutts) was committed to M^r. Thorp to be publish'd. W^ch he intends to 40 do with an Addition of some other excellent Observations of ye same kind. — To day between 8 and 9 of the Clock began the Visitation of the Bodlejan Library, & was ended before 11. But tho' there appear'd to be Wanting one P^t of the *Morning Exercise,* amongst the Folio Divinity Books, & *Ferdinandi's Quadragesimal Sermons,* amongst the Divinity Books in Quarto, yet ye Curators (for w^t reason I cannot tell) gave no

Nov. 7. Abr. Kent (Rickmansworth) to H. Wants a *testimonium* from the Principal and Dr. Garrett. A lady here has a large collection of coins; can't induce her to give them to Bodley.

order for finding of them out; nor did they sit to consult upon any other
matter after they had look'd over the Books alotted them : wch always
us'd to be, & the Result of their Consultations put down in a Book for y^t
purpose. 'Twas expected by some observing persons that they should
amongst other things have agreed upon Visiting D^r. Barlow's, D^r. Marshall's, & the other Books on the South and North p^{ts} of ye Library in the
middle Range wth those in Arch. C. &c. (they having not been yet
visited); because upon a private Examination of them there appear to be
wanting this year the following MS^t Books (all of w^{ch}, unless those w^{ch}
10 were never sent, M^r. Crabb can give no Acc^t of) besides some printed ones,
viz. (1) inter MSS. Hatton num. 12. I. Antonij Vita, Syriace. (2) Inter
MSS. Thurstoni num. 23. Institutiones puerorum Turcico-Persice. num.
24. Grammatica Arabica. Num. 53. Scheda continens superstitiosas for-
mulas & figuras. (3) Inter MSS. in Muséo, num. 131. Literæ impera-
toris Turcici patentes &c. num 227. Spelman of Testaments & Wills.
(4) Inter MSS. Gravij, num. 1. Historia Josephi, Persice (liber elegan-
tissime compactus). num. 19. Biblia Hebr. never sent. Num. 42. Catalogus plurimarum vocum Saxonicarum, cum Interpretatione Lat. 8°.
Num. 45. Ali Proverbia, &c. not sent. num. 47. Colloquium inter
20 Ahmed & Sinan, not sent. num. 48. Decem priores Psalmi &c. not sent.
50. Quæstiones inter Abdallah &c. not sent. Besides these things w^{ch}
should have been consider'd of are the new writing over the Curating
Books, the Account of the Duplicates, the Entring the Benefactors Names
&c. After the Examination of the Books, & a slight view of the Leads,
they went to M^r. Vice-Chancellor's where was Collation, & from thence
they went to the Natural Philosophy-Schoole, where M^r. Fouks of X^t
Church ye Junior Proctor made a very handsome Speech to ye Honor of
S^r. Tho. Bodley &c. In wch besides the usual things insisted on in those
Speeches, he touch'd upon the Danger of the Church & Learning at
30 this time, & concluded wth an Exhortation to ye Auditors to pursue the
Interest of both, w^n they had such Extraordinary Accomodations provided by their Benefactors, particularly S^r. Tho. Bodley. There was one
great omission however observable that he did not mention Archb^p. Laud,
who was so considerable a Benefactor, not only in giving a large Collection of Books, but also in contributing so bountifully tow^{ds} the building
of the spacious Room where M^r. Selden's Books are reposited. — On
Tuesday M^r. Quoiles the Watch-makers Son was married to a Quakers
Daughter Heiress of 30000 lib^s. Fortune. S^r. W^m. Penn performed the
Ceremony. There were present 3 Dukes, among y^m the D. of Ormond,
40 8 L^{ds}, 7 Forreign Envoyes & abundance of other Gentry.

Nov. 9 (Fri.). D^r. Hudson was told by a Person of unquestionable
Integrity[1], That K. William gave a 1000 lib^s. to those two infamous Villains
Blackett & Fuller that were embark'd in a Design to take away the Lives
of D^r. Sancroft, Archb^p. of Cant., & D^r. Spratt, B^p. of Rochester. Admiral Churchill told M^r. Charles Bernard, & another Person (whose Name
ye D^r. has forgot) that My Ld Romney assur'd him y^t he paid the 1000
lib^s. by King W^m's order to those two Villains.

[Alleged physical defects of William III.]

[1] M^r. Edm. Halley ye Ingenious Professor of Geometry at Oxon.

The *Columna Rostrata* is represented in *Lucius Florus* of Grævius's edition, & will be of use in an Edition of *Livy.* See there in pag. 50. — See also there in pag. 116. for a Coyn illustrating the Triumph of *Pompey ye Great.* — The Travells, call'd the Grand *Toure of France and Italy,* lately printed, and father'd upon M^r. *Bromley,* by the Whiggs, is a most ridiculous scandalous Book, being publish'd on purpose to lessen ye Character of that Worthy Gentleman. But they are so far from obtaining their End, that none or very few read the Book, & men begin (even some of ye Whiggs themselves) to have a better Opinion of him than they had before, believing he must be very free from Faults, and a real Honest 10 man, against whom they can bring nothing, but childish Stories invented by themselves. — M^r. Spencer Compton is Elected Chairman for ye Committee of Elections of ye House of Commons. — M^r. Shute, who writ *The Rights of the Protestant Dissenters,* is like to come in Town Clerk of the City of London. — I am told M^r. Tyrrell will go no farther with his *General History of England,* wch I can hardly believe, since 'tis certain he prosecutes his Studies y^t way, and is continually writing down w^t he finds observable in order to a Continuation. M^r. Eachard indeed is upon the History of England, but w^t he will do must needs be trite if we may judge from his other Performances wch are fit only for novices, 20 having nothing in them of Learning, or anything else but w^t is taken from common Printed Books. — M^r. Dodwell's new Book call'd *A Case in view consider'd ; in a Discourse, proving that (in case our present* invalidly *deprived* Fathers shall *leave all their sees* vacant, *either by* Death or Resignation) *we shall not* then *be* obliged *to* keep *up our* Separation *from* those Bishops, *who are as yet involved in the* Guilt *of the present Unhappy* Schism, is variously talkt of, some thinking 'twill do a great deal of good, & others (amongst whom are some of ye Jacobites themselves) y^t 'twill do mischief ; because most people thought M^1. *Dodwell* would never come in 'till such time as the present Compliers of ye Church of England should 30 declare their being ag^t ye Civil Magistrate's Power of Depriving Bps. Amongst these 'tis probable will be M^r. *Lesly,* if we may judge from his Discourse ab^t marriges in Different communions.

Nov. 10 (Sat.). Out of ye Benefactors Book of the Publick Library, pag. 68. vol. II.

Maria Newcomen Viri Humanissimi Nicolai Newcomen, de Theddlethorpe in Agro Lincolniensi, Conjux ; Fœmina animi nobilitate pariter ac formæ dignitate præcellens, pro singulari suo in Bibliothecam Bodlejanam affectu ex Cimelijs suis ad rem nostram nummariam augendam donavit quatuor Numismata aurea & tria argentea eximiæ raritatis & magni pretij : atque insuper ex 40 Muséo filij sui Nicolai Newcomen (Juvenis Ornatissimi morte immatura præ-repti) ad supellectilem hanc Librariam locupletandam dono dedit ista quæ sequuntur volumina, viz.— —

Whereas the House of Commons made an Order in one of ye Sessions of ye last Parliament y^t no one should preach before y^m unless he had taken the Degree of D^r. of Divinity either in Oxoñ or Cambridge, they, having not the fear of God before their Eyes, nor any Regard to their own Honor & Reputation, the first Sessions this present Parliament orderd one M^r. Willis, a Lambeth Doctor, (who has crept into ye Deanery of Lincoln) to preach before y^m on the 5th of Nov. last, & order'd his Sermon 50 to be printed because it is in favour of ye Whiggs. — On Wednesday

last was a great Competition between the Hon^{l.le} Spencer Compton,
Esqr, and S^r. Gilbert Dolben, to be Chairman for the Committee of
Elections in the House of Commons, ye first who was of Trinity College
in Oxford, being one of Toland's Disciples, carried it against ye latter
who is well known to be a man of singular probity & of an unblemish'd
Character in all Respects, and of rare Abilities for that Place. — To-day
was enter'd Commoner of our Hall *Will. Somervile.* He came from
Lincoln College.

Nov. 11 (Sun.). M^r. Garrett tells me y^t M^r. Hull an illiterate Fellow,
and singing Man of Salisbury, who was ordain'd by B^p. Burnett, came
lately to ye said B^p. and ask'd him when his L^dship would ordaine, saying That his Wife had a mind to be Ordain'd. The Bp. thinking he was
mistaken Said, *You mean when do I Confirm? Right,* says Hull, *for my
Wife wants to be Confirm'd, being a very flippant Dame.* And yet for all
this fellow was so shamefully ignorant, ye B^r. gave out when he ordain'd
him y^t he was an excellent Scholar & well vers'd in the Scriptures, tho'
'twas well known he could hardly read them in English.

Nov. 12 (Mon.). Above a Week since was a terrible Scuffle at X^t
Hospital of wch S^r. Francis Child is President between the Governors
about ye Choice of a Hall Keeper for Blackwell Hall. The Candidates
were M^r. Leak formerly a Goldsmith and one Stackhouse. The Churchmen
appeard for ye first & ye Dissenters wth their Friends for ye Latter, but y^e
first carried it upon the Poll by 5 or 6 voices. However the Latter would
have wrangled 'em out of it alledging that they had not told fair & de-
manded a new Election with hard words but the same was not granted.
But on the 9th Instant in another Court called by the President the election
was confirm'd. — Some few days since a Letter was distributed at y^e
House of Commons Door advising the Taking off ye Test Act. By wch we
see how modest ye Party are. The same contains Argum^ts against an
Occasional Bill. — Some say That the Whigg Members of Parliament
[are] much displeas'd at M^r. Tilly's Assize Sermon, and That they will
order it to be burnt: upon wch M^r. Tilly is printing another Sermon
preach'd at Cairfax in Oxon on the 5th Instant, wherein will be a Preface
vindicating himself from the many false Aspersions cast upon him. —
To-day M^r. Halley coming to ye Library, D^r. Hudson shew'd him M^r.
Selden's large MS^t Map of China (whereof there is a Copy amongst D^r.
Bernard's MSS. that is to be put into the Anatomy Schoole) to wch D^r.
Hyde added some Explicatory Notes. M^r. Hally having taken a view of
it, concluded it to be full of faults, from some wch he knew to b[e] so from
his own observations.

Nov. 13 (Tu.). Velseri Op: in Rer. Aug. Vind. lib. II. p. 199.... —
M^r. Stephens of All-Souls College tells me he has rec^d a Letter from his
Brother signifying That tho' the Whiggs carried it for a Speaker to y^e
House of Commons by a Majority of 43, yet they had only 16 more
than ye Church Party in the Election of a Chairman to the Committe of
Elections. So that, in all probability, the Whiggs will find it a very difficult
matter to carry things to their mind, especially if the Church Party keep
together in the House, as at present they seem resolv'd to do. — Tho'
there is nothing in print ab^t Ela Long-Espee, Countess of Warwick's

being a Benefactor to the Abbey of Rewley, yet M^r. Leland in his Itinerary has mention'd her giving several Lands to it ; but he does not say any thing of her founding a Chapel there. — M^r. Wotton is made Prebendary of Sarum, he being, it seems, a Whigg, or any thing else, as he finds 'twill be for his Interest. W^n he was in Oxford last I drank the Takkers Health with him wch he was not against; nor did he refuse to drink ye Health of the Author of *the Memorial of the Church of England.* — There are wanting in ye Public Library several of the Books of Coyns mention'd in Labbe's *Bibliotheca Nummaria.* — When S^r. Andrew Fountaine was last in Oxon̄ he was asking me whether we had in the Publick Library 10 any ms^t Books of Coyns? Remember to tell him that there are several things pertaining to ye English Coyns amongst M^r. Rich. James's Collections. — Patinus in his Introduction to the History of Coyns insinuates That Goltzius was no Scholar, and did not understand Latin. And yet he has written very learnedly upon the *Fasti Consulares,* &c. and seems to have accurately consider'd w^t Sigonius, Onuphrius, Pighius, &c. had written before him. — M^r. Dodwell acquaints me that at ye Beginning of ye Revolution D^r. Kennett, then Vice-Principal of Edmund-Hall, lent him a Book of his Writing in MS^t (wch was never printed) offering Arguments for taking the Oaths of Allegiance & Supremacy to King William & Queen 20 Mary, with a Design to Draw M^r. Dodwell to take them. But he was so far from being brought to y^e D$^{r's}$ Opinion that he has several times told me that he was rather confirm'd in his former Sentiments, & that upon mentioning this Book sometimes since to y^e Doctor, he blush'd at it, and seem'd to be asham'd of what he had written. This Book must not be forgot to be inserted amongst the Doctor's other Pieces by him y^t shall continue *Athenæ Oxonienses.* His translation of Pliny's Panegyrick also & the Preface must be there discours'd off at large, with a particular Account of his Contradictions. — D^r. Hutten has about 40 Volumes of MS^t Collections. They are all in 8vo, & he designs (as I am inform'd by M^r. Madox) 30 to leave them to some publick Place. They are agreed upon by all Hands to be very valuable; and 'twere to be wished some Application were made to him to leave them to the Publick Library in Oxon̄. — M^r. Willis of X^t Church has made some Collections relating to Cardinal Wolsey, wch he has committed to ye Dean of X^t church's Hands, with a desire that he would imploy somebody in Writing the Life of y^t Great Cardinal. But the Collections are not near enough, & I am told M^r. Willis has given over prosecuting the Matter any farther. — D^r. Smith told me the last time he was in Oxford that Dr. Bernard writ a large learned Preface to the Catalogue of MSS^{ts} wch he had seen after his Death in the Publick 40 Library; but upon Enquiry then for it, I could not find it, nor have I been able to meet with it since, notwithstanding I have carefully look'd all over his Papers.

Nov. 14 (Wed.). The Art of Longevity, or, A Diæterical Institution, by Edm. Gayton. *Lond.* 1659. 4°. This is omitted by M^r. *Ant. a Wood* in his Catalogue of that vain, trifling, Author's Writings. — The Book call'd *Leycester's Commonwealth* (reprinted lately under ye Title of *Dudley's Memoirs*) was written by Father Parsons the Jesuite, and at first was call'd *Greencoat* alias *Leycester's Commonwealth.* Vide D^r. James his Life of Father Parsons, p. 59. — The Book call'd *Jerusalem and Babel, or the* 50

Image of both Churches, dedicated to *Charles* the 1st, then Prince of *Wales,*
and printed at *Tornay,* 1623, then at *London* Anno 1633, (where this is
added to ye former Title, *being a Treatise Historically discussing,* Whether
Catholicks or Protestants be better Subjects?) was writ by one Mr. *Pattison*
a Lay Papist, & out of yt Popish-lying Book was another call'd *Philanax
Anglicus* almost *verbatim* taken. — *The Apology for the Ancient Right
and Power of ye Bps to sit and Vote in Parliaments.* Pr. at *Lond.* 1660.
4º. was writt by *Jeremy Stephens* formerly of All Soul's Coll. *Oxon.* &
beneficed in Northampton-Shire in 1661. — *John Sudbury* preached a
10 Consecration Sermon Oct. 28. 1660 (printed ye same year) on 1 *Tim.* 3. 1,
wch is ye same text Dr. Kennett preach'd his Consecration Sermon upon
(just printed) & may be trac'd in some things to have made use of him,
& another very Learned Sermon preached at a Consecration by Dr. Sancroft An. 1660. — In the Publick Library amongst Bp. Barlow's Books
is *Euripides's Hecuba* in Greek printed at *Lovain* 1520. 4º. with large
MSt Notes, neatly written, the Author whereof I cannot tell. Mr. Barnes
should be acquainted of them, tho' there seems to be little in them to
his purpose. — *The Defence of Priestes Marriages* 4º. *Lond.* was writt
by *Matt. Parker,* Archbp. of Cant. See Dr. *Jo. Cosins's* Book intit.
20 *Apologie for sundry Proceedings by Jurisdiction Ecclesiastical,* &c. Part. 2. ch.
12. p. 109. — *Smectymnus* is a feign'd Name, made up of the first Letters
of these 5 Divines (the Authors of it), Viz. (1) *Stephen Marshall.* (2)
Edmund Calamy. (3) *Thomas Younge.* (4) *Matthew Newcomen.* (5) *William
Spurstow.* Vide *John Saltmarsh* his Book, call'd *Groans for Liberty.* 1646.
p. 1. — Amongst other Books given by Dr. Hudson to the Publick
Library is one *concerning Images and Idolatry,* wch was never published,
but printed by Mr. *Obadiah Walker* (who was ye Author or at least his
Tutor *Abr. Woodhead*) in the Stables belonging to *University Col. An.*
1689. 4to. where ye greatest Part of the Edition was seised. But Mr.
30 Walker himself gave it (wth other Books of yt kind) to Dr. *Hudson.* —
The Answer to a late Pamphlet, intituled, The Judgment and Doctrine of
the Clergy of the Church of England conc. one Special Branch of the
King's Prerogative, viz. in *Dispensing with the Penal Laws,* is writ by way
of Letter to a Friend, & printed at *Lond.* 1687. 4to. *Quære* who ye Author?
The Author of *The Judgment &c.* was then suppos'd to be Dr. *Sherlock.* —
The Weekly Pacquet of Advice from Rome was writt by *Hen. Care,* & not
G. Care, as Dr. *Barlow* has asserted in one place. — Χειροθεσία τοῦ Πρεσ-
βυτέρου or a Letter to a Friend tending to prove, (1) *that Valid Ordination
ought not to be repeated.* (2) *That Ordination by Presbyters is Valid,* by
40 *R. A. Lond.* 1661. 4º. The said *R. A.* suppos'd to be *Hen. Hickman*
of *Magd. Col.* — *Church-Government* Pt. v. *Oxon.* 1687. Dr. *Barlow*
at the Beginning of a Copy of it in the Publick Library has noted that he
was told by a Person of Honour (who well knew) that the Author of this
Book was one *Perkins,* who was Author of *the Guide to Controversies,* and
of a Book call'd *Considerations of the Council of Trent* &c. 1671. 4º. But
Mr. *Wood* has given another Account, being wthout doubt better inform'd.
— There is just come out a New Book in 4to, about Embalming, written
by *Tho: Greenwood,* Surgeon. It seems to [1] be well done, & to contain several matters relating to Antiquity. 'Tis 10 shillings Price, &

---

[1] I have since look'd into it, & 'tis done very meanly & pitifully.

has a great Number of Cutts. — De Visibili Romanarchia contra Nich. Sanderi Monarchiam Προλεγομένων libri duo. *Lond.* 1573. 4°. The Author — *Ackworth.* — Dʳ. *Barlow* at the Beginning of *Geoffry of Monmouth* (amongst his Books in *Bib. Bod.*) has noted divers things wᶜʰ will be of use to one that shall put out a New Edition of that Author. — Amongst Dʳ. *Barlow's* Books is *Expositio S. Jeronimi* (or rather *Ruffini*) *in Symbolum Apostolorum* printed at *Oxon.* in 1468, 3 years after Printing began at *Mentz.* Dʳ. *Barlow* has Several Observations there about Printing, with References to some old Books. Mʳ. *Bagford* should carefully look them over. — The Author of the *Brief Examination of the Present* Roman 10 *Catholick Faith contained in Pope* Pius *his Creed* &c. (*Lond.* 1689. 4ᵗᵒ) was Dʳ. *Gardiner,* as his Son *Samuel Gardiner,* Rector of *Eckington,* near *Chesterfeild* in the County of *Darby* (who gave him a Copy) assur'd Dʳ. *Barlow.* — In the year 1668 came out at *Lond.* a Book call'd *Papa Ultrajectinus* &c. Auctore *Ludiomæo Colvino.* That is anagrammatiκῶς *Ludovico Molinæo,* (the Son,) who also writ *Jugulum Causa,* &c. *Lond.* 1671. — ... *Marci Meibomij* De Fabrica Triremium liber. *Amst.* 1671. .. This Book ought to be consulted well by Mʳ. *Grabe* in order to his Edition of the LXX. — A Discourse of the Religion of England &c. *Lond.* 1667. 4ᵗᵒ. The Author was Mʳ. *John Corbett,* a Non-Conformist Hamp- 20 shire Minister. — In the Month of *Nov.* 1666, was printed and published at *London,* a Pamphlett call'd, *The English-Papists Apologie.* The Author whereof was inquired diligently after by the House of Commons, but could not be found. The Printer fled, but his Presses being found, were broken by Command of yᵉ sᵈ House. Some time after Bʳ. Barlow was inform'd that the Author was one *Pugh* a Papist and a Physitian, and (as one of his Countrymen told him) a Welshman. 'Twas Answer'd by Dʳ. *Lloyd* now Bᵖ. of Worcester the yʳ after. — Amongst Bᵖ. *Barlow's* Books is a Copy of the *xxxix Articles* printed at *Lond.* 1633 .. with large MSᵗ Notes relating to them made by yᵉ Bᵖ. and will be of great use to one that gives 30 an History or Exposition of them. Wᵗʰ them are also Bound the Canons wᶜʰ have likewise large MSᵗ Notes added to them. — In the Year 1668 was printed at *Antwerp* a large insignificant, impertinent Book (in 4ᵗᵒ) call'd *Protestancy wᵗʰout Principles.* The Author *E. W.* i. e. Father *Edw. Worsley* or *Worresley* an Englishman. — Dʳ. *Francis Carswell,* Vicar of Bray, in Berks, and Author of two Sermons wᶜʰ contradict one another (being, it seems, resolv'd to keep up the old Proverb wᶜʰ had it's original from one of his Predecessors, *The Vicar of Bray will be Vicar of Bray still*) has a very curious study of Books, as I am inform'd by one of *Exeter* Col. a native of yᵉ Place, who lately perus'd them and drew up a 40 Catalogue for yᵉ Doctor. He is a very rich Man, and minds nothing but Pelf, as his Neighbours say. — Mʳ. [1]Kannell (Joseph) of Lincoln Col. writ a short Discourse against *Self-Murther* in opposition to Dʳ. *Donne.* He made some Application a little while since to get it printed, but could not prevail with any one to undertake it, being a Book for wᶜʰ there is no manner of occasion. I am inform'd he is now quite off publishing it, being laugh'd at by some in the College, who entitle the *Book, Dʳ. Donne undone.* — [2]Mʳ. *Creech* of *All Souls Col.* a few years before his Death

---

[1] This Mʳ. Kannell died in 1710.
[2] I am inform'd Mʳ. *Creech* help'd Mʳ. *Adams* to Most of his Arguments in his

propos'd to put out a new Edition of all *Justin Martyr's* Works, & had, for that end, drawn up a great many Sheets of Notes, as M^r. *Grabe* has inform'd me, who had the perusal of 'em. He says they were very well done, only that there were some things in them very singular, and would be accounted amongst men of Skill *Heterodox.* — He that shall undertake a 3^d Volume of the *Monasticon Anglicanum* must remember to give an Account of the Foundation &c. of *Shottesbrooke* Coll. in *Berks.* All the Chartularies of wch are now in the Hands of M^r. *Francis Cherry* L^d of the Mannor of *Shottesbrooke*, who procur'd a great many of them

10 lately of M^r. *Stephen Edwards* of *White-Waltham* an adjoyning Parish, who had them of M^r. *Charles Weldon*, to whom they properly belong'd, being left them by his Father, who was owner of ye Lands belonging to ye said College, wch were afterwards purchas'd of him by S^r. *Hen. Powel*, and so they came to the Cherry's. I have a Transcript of most of the Papers wch M^r. *Edwards* had, & upon Intimation of this to M^r. *Cherry*, he got M^r. *Edwards* to deliver all the papers of that nature in his Custody to him. — Within the Parish of *White-Waltham*, is a mannor call'd *Feens*, near to the mannor House where was once a Chapell of Ease. This Mannor lately belong'd to *John Finch*, Esqr, who dying without Heir Male

20 it came to 5 Daughters, one of wch is married to ye said M^r. *Francis Cherry*. The Chapell was at length turn'd into a Stable; but whether this was done by M^r. *Finch* or some of his Predecessors I cannot yet certainly tell. This however I am credibly inform'd of, that M^r. *Finch* observing his Affairs not to prosper very well, advis'd with M^r. *Rich. Cleer* then Rector of *Shottesbrook*, and Vicar of *White-Waltham*, who directed him to imploy the money, wch was wont to be given to the Minister for reading Prayers (20 *lib^r. per Ann.* I think) in charitable uses, wch accordingly he did, & I have reason to think that M^r. *Cherry* does ye same to this day. The undertaker of this Volume also must take a view of the

30 *Sepulchral* Inscriptions in the said Church of *Shottesbrooke*, where the Wardens of the College lie buried, the last whereof was [1] *Throgmorton* as appears from his Tomb in the Chancell of that Church. — *White-Waltham*, otherwise call'd *Abbot's-Waltham*, did belong, as I am told, to [2] *Waltham Abbey* in *Essex*, and it seems the Writings relating to it are lodg'd at *Winchester*. About the Bounds of this *Parish* and *Bray* is an old Record Printed by M^r. *Prynne* in one of the Volumes of his Work about the Incroachments of the Pope. — In the Windows of the Parish Church of *Warfeild*, within 3 miles of Windsor, is a great deal of Painted Glass, wch will afford much assistance to him that shall give an account of that

40 Church.

Nov. 15 (Th.). I was told this Morning by D^r. *Charlett* That M^r. *Ayliffe* of *New-College* vindicates himself upon taking the Book out of

---

Nov. 15. Dr. T. Smith to H. Agrees with H. as to the authorship of the *Bibliæ Sacræ tomus primus* (condemns Strype by the way); on the subject

---

Book against *Self-Murther*: wch must be sure to be remembered by ye Continuer of *Athen. Oxon.*

[1] I have since found y^t he was not the last. See at ye End of the 5th Vol. of Leland's Itin.

[2] False. It belong'd to Chertsey Abbey in Surrey.

the Publick Library, saying that he will not scruple to do the same again: and yet he has no other Argument, than *usu id exigente* in §. 8. of the Statutes, wch is express ag^t him, that Exception being added upon Account of Books to be sold, exchang'd or Bound, and relates only to the Library-Keeper, who cannot, w^thout guilt of perjury, carry any Book out upon any other Account. So that (if M^r. *Ayliff* were rigorously, and according to ye express words of the Statute, proceeded against besides his being guilty of perjury,) he ought to pay double the value of the Book & be perpetually expell'd out of the Library for not restoring it before he went out of the Library the same day he 10 had it. — Memorandum (1) That Father Parsons writt a Book intit. *The Judgment of a Catholick Englishman*, &c. against the Oath of Allegiance. (2) D^r. *William Barlow* (Bishop of *Lincoln*) writ an Apology for ye Oath of Allegiance, wth this Title—*Triplici nodo, triplex cuncus, or an Apology for the Oath of Allegiance* &c. printed *Lond.* 1609. (3) *An.* 1612. Father *Parsons* publish'd a Book call'd *A Discussion of the Answer of M^r. Will. Barlow* &c. wch is a Defence of the first & an Answer to ye second Book above mentioned. —

M^r. *John Goodwin* in his Book call'd Ἀπολύτρωσις Ἀπολυτρώσεως, *or Redemption Redeem'd*, brings (and brags of) this Argument for the 20 universal Redemption of all mankinde (*nemine excepto*) as *unanswerable, and clear, as the Sun at Noonday* (those are his Words), thus—

That which everyone in the World is bound to believe, that is true ;
But every one in the World is bound to believe that X^t dyed for him,
Ergo, 'tis true that he dy'd for every man in the World.

This Argument was by one (who never saw *John Goodwin*) believed to be evidently inconsistent, and the *Minor* manifestly false, and accordingly it was in a Letter signify'd to him, (subscrib'd T. S. for T. B.) upon these Grounds, (to set down the sum of that Letter).

1. The Law wch binds us to believe X^t dyed for us, is a *Divine, positive* 30 Law: because, 1. no Humane Law can, 2. the Natural Law doth not bind any to believe in X^t : for no man ever had any such Authority to oblige all Mankind ; and Natural Reason could not possibly discover that there was, or ever would be, a Mediator, or X^t a Saviour. 2. No positive Law of God or Man, can bind any to obedience without sufficient Promulgation, cum certissime constet, quod Promulgatio *sit ad obligationem legis necessaria.* 3. But the Law of the Gospel, which commands Belief in X^t, neither was, nor could be sufficiently promulgated, either 1. to *Infants*, 2. or to *natural fools*, and *madmen*, 3. nor to men *born blinde, deaf* and *dumbe :* all these having a natural Impossibility and Incapacity to hear or understand that Evangelical Command. 40 4. nor was it ever promulged (much less sufficiently) to any of those Pagans (before or after X^t) to whom the Gospel was never preached ; for w^t 'out a Preacher they could not hear, (*Rom.* 10, 14, 15.) much less believe or be bound to it: And therefore St. *Augustine* said well (speaking of the Gentiles, who

---

of spectacles refers H. to a dissertation of Francisco Redi, physician of Florence, printed in Spon's *Recherches curieuses d'Antiquité*, p. 213. The Archbishop of Armagh and his intention to found a Library at Dublin ; he writes that Dr. Stillingfleet's library is safely arrived there, and he is very well pleased with the purchase. Fears that H.'s account of the state of Trinity College Library is too true. Mr. Lloyd to be made a Lambeth Doctor ; it would be satisfactory to have this prerogative of the Archbishop cleared. Mill admits that he made too much haste with the Greek text of the New Testament.

never heard the Gospel) *Veniam habebunt propter infidelitatem, damnabuntur propter peccata contra naturam.* Upon Receipt of this Letter (of wch this is the sum as put down by Bp. *Barlow*) M^r. *Goodwin* in ye year 1681 published a Book call'd *the Pagans Debt and Dowry*, &c., but wisely conceales the s^d Letter, & prints it not all, (that men might see the Argument he endeavours to answer) nor the Reason or words of any part of it; onely he saith something (though most irrationally) as to Pagans, y^t all they heard the Gospel sufficiently to bring an Obligation upon them to believe in X^t. upon wch says ye Bp, *Legat cui vacat, & (per me licet) judicet.*

10   Upon Reading this Sum of the above mention'd Letter (wch I found inserted by D^r. *Barlow* in the Beginning of *The Pagan's Debt* &c. in the Publick Library,) I immediately consulted Bp. *Barlow's Remains*, & there find the Letter to have been written by the D^r. Himself, it being there printed at large wth another Extract of ye same Nature. — D^r. *Bull's Harmonia Apostolica, seu binæ Dissertationes* &c. has a great number of MSS^t notes by B^p. Barlow whose Copy is in ye Publick Library. M^r. *Grabe* should have consulted these, some of them seeming to be very material & fit to be taken notice of. — In relation to this Book of D^r. *Bull's* must be seen a Book in 8°. wth this Title—*An*
20 *Endeavour to rectify some prevailing Opinions, contrary to the Church of England* &c. *Lond.* printed by T. M. for Rob. Clavell in the Crosse-Keyes-Court in Little-Britaine 1671. wch Anonymous Author (pag. 2,) 1. *approves* & commends the first of the D^r's Dissertations, & the first 5 Chapters of the 2^d. 2. But he finds fault w^th & censures ye 2^d part from 6th Chapter (*inclusive*) & endeavours to disprove several of D^r. *Bull's* Positions. D^r. *Barlow's* Copy must be consulted by him y^t shall continue *Athen. Oxon.* — . . .

Anno 1662 was printed at *Lond.* in 4to a Pamphlet call'd *A Vindication of my L^d. B^p. of* Worcester's *Letter touching* M^r. Baxter *from the Animadversions of*
30 D. E. the Author whereof was then constantly reported to be S^r. Hen. *Yelverton.*—*Anno* 1689 came out a Book in 4to intit. *A Treatise of Monarchy in two Parts: 1. Conc.* Monarchy *in* General. 2. *Conc.* this Particular Monarchy:— The Author *Philip Hunt.*—*Anno* 1687. came out a Book (pr. at *Lond.*) call'd *An Answer of a Minister of the Church of* England *to this Question, w^t Respect ought the true Sons of ye Ch. of* England, *in point of Conscience & X^tian Prudence, to bear to ye Religion of y^t Church, whereof ye King is a Member?* The Author was then suppos'd to be, *Cartwright* B^p. of *Chester;* tho' he deny'd it.—The *Free-Holders Grand Inquest touching our Sovereign* L^d *the King & his Parliam^t*—pr. an. 1647. The Author S^r. *Rob. Holburne.*—D^r. *Heylin's* Book call'd
40 *Respondet Petrus*, &c. was (by order of State) call'd in, and commanded to be burn'd, about ye last of *June* 1658. —

Amongst D^r. *Barlow's* Books (B. 14. 15. *Linc.*) is a Volume with several Tracts conc. *Toleration*, with MS^t observations by the D^r. And amongst ye rest at ye Beginning is a Draught for a General *Comprehension*, wch was said and generally believ'd to be contriv'd and formed by *Matth. Hale* Chief Baron of the Exchequer. —

The Inconveniences of Toleration; or An Answer to a late Book, intit. A Proposition made to the King and Parl^t. &c. *Lond.* 1667. 4to. The Author M^r. *Tomkins.* The *Proposition* (to wch this Book is an Answer) came out about y^e
50 Beginning of *August* 1667, & in the same year, *Oct.* 25, he reprinted it again wth a short Reply to M^r. *Tomkins.*—*A Peace Offering* &c. in 4to. It came out *Nov.* 14. 1667. the Parliam^t then sitting, & the Author was *John Owen.*—A Discourse of Toleration: in Answer to a late Book, intit. *A Discourse of the*

Religion of England. Lond. 1668. 4to. But 'tis postdated, for it came out in *Mich.* Terme, 1667. The Author D^r. *Perencheife*, Prebendary of *Westminster* & Subalmoner to the King. The Author of the Book, to w^{ch} 'tis An Answer', was M^r. *Corbett*, a Non-Conformist.—Indulgence not Justified &c. *Lond.* 1668. 4°. D^r. *Perinchief* s^d also to be Author of this.—*Anno* 1661, in *Octob.*, came out *a Petition for Peace*, the Author said to be M^r. *Baxter*. It came out clandestinely, & the Printer was imprison'd for his Paines.—Amongst the B^p. of *Lincoln's* Books . . is a Copy of M^r. *Valentine Greatrate's* Letter to the B^p. of *Chester* (D^r. *Hall*) touching his Cures by Stroaking. In MS^t. . . .

The Tombes, Monuments, & Sepulchral Inscriptions lately visible in 10 S^t. Paul's Cathedral &c. written by *Pain Fisher* is a silly Book (abating only the Inscriptions,) there being nothing of Learning or Diligence shew'd in it, much after the same manner as the *Antiquities of Middlesex*, the first p^t whereof was lately publish'd, but no more. The said *Pain Fisher* in p. 32. of y^t Book (writt meerly to flatter some men (such was the vanity of the man) makes mention of a *great History of the Tombs & Monuments of London*, which he had written or at least design'd to write. *Quære* whether any such Book was ever publish'd? — I am told by one of S^t. *Peter's* Parish that when the Church-Wardens went to D^r. *Halton*, Provost of *Queen's*-Coll., asking his 20 Benevolence for Building ye Gallery in S^t. *Peter's* Church (wch would be for ye use of ye University as well as ye Parish) he put his finger out of ye Window pointing to ye Library, then building there, & desir'd them to see w^t he was doing another way: so would give nothing. After wch they went to D^r. *Mill*, who would give nothing because the Provost did not, tho' had he had as good reason as he he might have come off creditably. — To Night meeting with M^r. *Urry* of *Christ-Church* (who seems to be a Pious, conscientious, man, and a thorough-pac'd Scholar, wch is ye Character also he bears amongst the true Sons of the Church of *England*) he was pleas'd to tell me that he wish'd M^r. 30 *Dodwell* had not publish'd his two late Books about Schism, & much more wishes he will not publish a new Book he has ready for the Press about ye Natural Mortality of the Soul; particularly for this reason, because the World is too wicked already to have a notion, wch may do mischief, improv'd by the Writings of a good Man. He likewise told me that the three Pieces, in old English, the Lady would have tran-scrib'd out of *Bodley* are not very valuable upon account of any thing extraordinary in them, but she was willing to have them because one of them was done by a Lady of Extraordinary Worth (to whom also the other two belong) & she had a great veneration (not only for Antiquity) 40 but for all Pieces written by ye Female Sex.

Nov. 16 (Fri.). The Petition of M^r. *Hopkins* &c. complaining of an undue Election for *Coventry* is rejected[1], so y^t the two chosen members (who are Tackers) will continue in spight of all the Contrivances for ejecting them carried on chiefly by that malicious man. —

The Rational Account of ye Doctrine of Roman Catholicks conc. ye Ecclesiastical Guide in Controversies &c., pr. in 1673. 4to. was said to be written

---

[1] A mistake, it being refus'd to be heard at ye Bar of ye House, and referr'd to ye Committee of Elections. Their Refusing to have it heard there is a notable Instance of ye Impudence of ye Party, who had a few days before refus'd to have a Petition of Sr Roger Mostyns heard at ye Bar upon the same Acc^t.

by *R. Holden*, a *Sorbon* Doctor.—The Lawfullness of obeying yᵉ Present Government—1649. 4ᵗᵒ—The Author *Fr. Rouse*, Provost (*sed contra jus, fasque*) of *Eaton* Coll. Who was Author likewise of *The Bounds and Bonds of Publick Obedience.* Lond. 1649. 4ᵗᵒ.— *The Sea-man's Grammar and Dictionary* &c., *Lond.* 1692. 4ᵗᵒ. said in yᵉ Title Page to have been written by Captain *John Smith*, was really writ by Sʳ. *John Smith*, the Captain's Works being of another Nature. ◾

Mʳ. *Needham* (Peter) of *Cambridge* who lately publish'd yᵉ *Geoponicks* had divers considerable things from MSSᵗˢ in the Publick Library of
10 Oxoñ & from some printed Books wᶜʰ had MSᵗ notes in the margin. But he is so far from acknowledging this that he takes no notice of it, & tho' Mʳ. *Crabb* drug'd some time in transcribing an Index from a Book there of the *Geoponicks* (wᶜʰ he has publish'd as his own) yet (with shame be it spoken) he has not sent Mʳ. *Crabb* so much as a Copy, nor taken care to gratify him any other way. And wᶜʰ is as bad he has not sent a Copy neither to yᵉ Library, such is the Ingratitude of ' the man, yᵗ one would really think he had nothing but yᵉ Spirit of a Whigg in him, & yᵗ he was possess'd wᵗʰ the Soul of yᵉ Scandalous *March. Needham nimis notus omnibus.* ◾ . . . Parliamᵗˢ Power, in Lawes
20 for Religion. *Oxon.* 1645. 4ᵗᵒ. The Author Dʳ. *Heylin.* N.B. See a MS. Tract in English, by Sʳ. *Edward Cooke*, concerning the Power of the Church to make Canons, by the Act of 25 *Hen.* 8. cap. 19. His opinion is (and that most false, and contradictory to yᵉ knowne Laws of England,) that the Clergy in Convocation, call'd by yᵉ King's Writt, though the King give his Royal Assent, can make no Canons obligatory. ◾ Concordia Scientiæ cum fide è difficillimis Philosophiæ & Theologiæ Scholasticæ quæstionibus concinnata. Auctore *Thoma Bonarte Nordiano*, Anglo. *Col. Agrip.* 1659. 4ᵗᵒ. By a Letter from Mʳ. *C. Willughby*, dated *London May* 30. 1664. who (in his Travells abroad) was familiarly
30 known to this Author, Dʳ. *Barlow* was inform'd, that this Name *Thoma Bonarte Nordiano* is not his true, but a Counterfeit Name ; That beyond Sea, he assumed the Name of *Barton*; that his true Sirname is *Anderton* (and *Nordiano*, is an Anagram of *Andertono*) that he lived 18. or 19. Years at Sᵗ. *Omar's*, afterwards in *Portugal* and *Flanders*, and was in yᵉ Court of K. *Charles* 2. the 4 last years of his Exile. 'Tis prohibited in the *Index librorum prohibitorum Alex.* 7. *Pont. Max.* Rom. 1664. p. 388. ◾ A Discourse conc. Liturgies & yᵉ Imposition. *Lond.* 1662. 4ᵗᵒ. 'Twas then suppos'd to be writt by Dʳ. *Owen.* See in *Ant. Wood.* ◾ A Treatise of Taxes and Contributions. *Lond.* 1667. 4ᵗᵒ. 'Twas writt
40 by Sʳ. *Will. Petty*, who in the beginning of our Civil War, 1640, (being very poor) came to *Oxon*, studied Physick, cut up doggs and taught Anatomy in the War (after *Oxon* was taken) was made Fellow of *Brasennose*, the Visitors putting Loyal Persons out, to put him and such others in : afterwards he went into *Ireland*, was imployed to survey that *Kingdom*, then conquered by *Cromwell*, got a vast Estate there, (about 5000 *libˢ. per Annum*) & at the King's Returne (having got Money of the Rebells, &, 'tis fear'd, for Rebellion, for they did not so well reward Loyalty) he got Honor of the King, and was made a Knight. ◾

A Discourse of the Necessity of Church-Guides, &c.—1675. 4ᵗᵒ. By R. H.
50 i.e. *Abr. Woodhead.*—Reason and Religion, or The certain Rule of Faith, by E. W. (i.e. *Edw. Worseley*). *Antw.* 1672. 4ᵗᵒ.—The Christian moderator, &c.

—1651. 4ᵗᵒ.—Writt by Mʳ. *Austen,* a Catholick Gentleman & a Traveller, but not in Orders.—A Light shining out of Darkness. *Lond.* 1659. 4°. (By Hen. Stubbe.) ...

Enquire of Mʳ. *Dodwell,* or some body else, whether the MSᵗ. mention'd to be at *Paris* (probably in the King's Library) *concerning the famous Schism wᶜʰ was rais'd upon the Account of Josephus the Presbyter* (quoted by *Cotelerius* in his Notes upon the IIIᵈ Volume of *Monumenta Ecclesiæ Græcæ.* (& by Dʳ. *Hody* pag. 15 of his *Letter concerning a Collection of Canons* &c.) be the same with the *Baroccian* MSᵗ published by Dʳ. *Hody* & whether the Canons immediately follow it in the same 10 manner as in the *Bar. MS.* — In the Year 1648. was put out a most base and trayterous Pamphlett intit. *Several Speeches delivered at a Conference conc. the Power of Parl. to proceed against their King for Misgovernment,* (in 9. Speeches). 'Twas taken *verbatim* out of the first Part of *Dolman* (or *Parsons's*) Book touching Succession to yᵉ Crown, these 9 Speeches (as they are here call'd) being the 9 chapters in *Dolman.* 'Twas printed at yᵉ Charge of the Parl. 30 libˢ. being paid by them to the Printer, *in perpetuam eorum infamiam.* See the Collection of his Majestie's Gracious Messages for Peace, p. 125. 126. Wᶜʰ Messages were collected, and printed with Observations upon them by 20 Mʳ *Simons.* The said *Speeches* were put out by *Walker* an Iron-Monger; from that he came to be a Cow-herd; when the King came into *London* about the 5 members he threw into his Coach a Traiterous Pamphlett, call'd *To thy Tents oh Israel.* He afterwards writ The perfect Occurrences & in 1649 was made Minister by yᵉ Presbyterians. Mʳ. *Darby, Yorkshire,* and Parlᵗ Man bought *Doleman* of *Cornelius Bee,* at yᵉ King's Arms in *Little-Britaine,* who gave it to *Walker.* In the year 1655. was pr. and published at *Lond.* another treatise on the same subject, intit. *A Treatise conc. yᵉ Broken Succession of the Crown of England.* 4ᵗᵒ. wᶜʰ is the same with the former a little alter'd. So willing 30 they were (even those pretended Saints) to make use of the basest Artes, and Jesuitical Armes against the Established Government of their own Country: and having murder'd their King, by these & such other trayterous Arts, they endeavour'd to keep his Son from the Succession.

Nov. 17 (Sat.). Mʳ. *Dodwell's* new Book for Healing yᵉ Schism pleases extremely much yᵉ Generality of Readers, and even most of yᵉ Persons in Power cannot but commend it, and think yᵗ he acts like an Honest, Conscientious Man, and a true Son of yᵉ Ch. of England. But some Expressions in it give distast. — Mʳ. *Sherlock* has a Grant from the Queen to be Master of the *Temple* (worth two hundred libˢ. *per* 40 *An.*) after the Death of his *Father.* — Marginales linguarum collationes in Armenico Dictionario Rivolæ, per *Tho. Hyde.* These are added in a Copy of that Dictionary in the Publick Library, wᶜʰ in the year 1676 was order'd to be sold among other Duplicates by yᵉ Curators; but yᵉ Doctor sav'd it, & restor'd it again. At the beginning he has himself given an Account of yᵉ Notes. — ... Observations upon the Ordinance of the Lords and Commons at Westminster. *Oxon.* 1645. 4ᵗᵒ. 'Twas

---

Nov. 17. T. Cherry to H. Message from Dodwell about Livian chronology. Has given Dr. Kennett a copy of the inscriptions in Shottesbrooke Church.

writt by one *Bowen*, who flying from the Rebells *An.* 1643. had writt
a larger Volume of the Bishops w^ch (D^r. *Jer. Taylor's* Book of the same
Subject preventing him) he printed not.   This Treatise is an Extract
of that Greater Worke, or at least those Parts of it wch concern'd this
subject. — The *Observations upon some of his Majestie's* (K. Chr. I.) *late
Answers and Expresses* were written by *Hen. Parker.* — The Essay upon
Poetry, printed at *Lond.* 1682. 4to. was written by ye Earle of Mulgrave,
who was the same year turn'd out of ye Bedchamber to the King, &
Offices worth at least 4000 *lib^s. per Annum.* — The Reply to the
10 Pamphlet call'd *the Mischief of Impositions,* (the Author whereof was
Mr. *Alsop*) was written by M^r. *Clegate* Minister of *Graye's Inn.* Printed
Lond. 1681. 4to. — A Prefatory Discourse to a late Pamphlett, entit.
A Memento for English Protestants &c. *Lond.* 1681. 4to.   The Author
M^r. E. *Amy,* a Lay Gent. — In *Spon's Recherches Curieuses d'Antiquité,*
p. 235. Ξήνων, is writt thus—ΝΙΚΩΝ ΤΗΝΩΝΟΣ ΧΡΗΣΤΕ ΧΑΙΡΕ. In the
same Book p. 310. is an Emendation of Justin in the word *Pylæmenis.*
— Talking with M^r. *Joyner* (the *Roman*-Catholick) concerning my L^d.
Clarendon's History of the Rebellion, (wch D^r. *Hudson* advis'd him to
read,) he seem'd to have but a very indifferent opinion of it, not believing
20 it to be writ either in a good style, or wth y^t impartiality as 'tis said
to be; tho' he appear'd to be something prejudic'd upon Account of
y^t Great Man's being educated at *Magd.* Hall, the chief Members of
wch he said were always rigid *Puritans,* for whom he could not have
a very fair Opinion, upon account of their unmercifull Usage of Archb^p.
Laud, whose Head they cutt off, notwithstanding the great favours they
had rec^d from King *James* 1st, who made D^r. Geo. *Abbot* Archb^p. of
Canterbury, meerly to oblige (to use *Joyner's* Expression) some of the
Puritans, who thought the King was not favourable enough to y^m; w^ch
Preferment w^n *Abbot* had got, he rais'd a fund for maintaining the
30 *Puritans,* some of whom (namely the *Fanaticks*) cut off *Laud's* Head,
who was a man of such admirable Judgment & Learning y^t he knew
w^t Danger the Nation was in & whence it proceeded & did declare y^t
if they wou'd take his Advise he could heal all Breaches; wth the
Fanaticks (or *Puritans* as *Joyner* calls them) well perceiving they dispatch'd him as soon as possible, wch when they had done, they us'd
these words,

> All praise & Glory to the Lord,
> & *Laud* unto ye Devil.

When *Laud* was thus taken off they thought they had done most of
40 their Work, King *Charles* the 1st having no body now to stand his
Friend so much as *Laud,* that King being of so easy a Temper y^t by

---

His Sermon at consecration of Dr. Wake.   Mr. D. has another girl: still out
with Mill.   Burnet has been preaching against Occasional Conformity.   The
Dean of Christ Church and his 'inclinations for trimming.'   Money matters.
Has ordered his sister to send H. a barrel of the best oysters.   My Cozen
very much occupied.   Various messages.   Mr. Holden has left, thinking he
had not encouragement enough to stay.   **Dodwell to H.**   Asks for fresh
transcript of passage of Vettius Valens concerning the place of separate souls.
Has sent a copy of *The Case in View* for Bodley, and has one for H.

his Granting the Fanaticks so much he lost his Head at last as his Good
Friend *Laud* did.

As *Laud* was stiff ag^t the *Fanaticks*, so was likewise the Duke of *Buckingham* ; & therefore M^r. *Joyner* believes y^t had both these men liv'd the King's
head [had] not been cut off.   But besides other misfortunes wch befell the
Duke & made him Dislik'd was his Journey into Spain wth this King then
Prince, in order to consummate his marriage wth the *Infanta* ; wch coming to
no happy Conclusion, the King himself was somew^t displeas'd, & y^t too for this
(as well as other reasons usually offer'd) namely that the Duke (whose extraordinary Parts, besides the comeliness of his Person, made the King very   10
much delight in him) whilst he was there happen'd to receive a ——, by lying
wth a Spanish Beauty whom he much admir'd, & wch prov'd so violent, y^t he
could not rid himself off it before he was oblig'd to return into England wth y^e
Prince, where 'twas soon divulg'd, & I am told, by a Person who well knows,
y^t there is a Letter relating to this whole Business in some private Hands in
Oxford. This Juvenile Adventure did the Church men (to whom ye Duke was
a great Friend) also much Prejudice, & after the Duke was unfortunately
murder'd, & the Fanaticks saw they should gain ye Day, they made this
Rime,—

> If *Grex* & *Rex* had had their will,
> Then *Bucks* & *Ducks* had had their fill.   20

— Amongst other Discourse also wth M^r. *Joyner* He told me y^t when
some of ye Fanatick Puritans complain'd to S^r. *Hen. Savile* of their want
of Preferment, he advis'd them to go to hungry Courtiers ; wch advise
they made so good use of, that soon after *Abbot* was made a B^p., afterwards Archb^p., & some of ye Rest were prefer'd too, to ye no small
profit of ye Fanaticks. —

A Brief and Impartial Account of the Nature of ye Protestant Religion &c.,
Lond. 1682. 4to. The Author was D^r. Owen.—M^r. *Emmerton's* Marriage with
M^rs. *Bridget Hyde* consider'd. *Lond.* 1682. 4to. The Author said to be M^r. 30
Hunt ye Lawyer.—An exposition of ye Doctrine of ye Catholick Church in
Matters of Controversie, By *James Benigne Bossuet. Lond.* 1685. Translated
into *English* by M^r. *Dryden*, then only a Poët, afterwards a Papist, & may be
so before, tho' not known.—The Pamphlett call'd *A Vindication of the Obser-
vator* &c., printed *Lond.* 1685, was writ by the Author of ye Observator himself, S^r. *Rog. L'Estrange.*—The *Answer to the B^p. of Condom afterwards of
Meaux's Exposition of the Catholick Faith*, *Lond.* 1686, was written by M^r. *John
Gilbert*, M^r of Arts of *Hart-Hall* in *Oxon*, & afterwards Curat of *Ashwell in*
the County of Hertford. —

M^r. Professor *Halley* tells me he has 6 or 7 Copies of ye Inscription 40
in the Theatre yard relating to Zeno the Archon printed at ye Theatre,
only as a Specimen, to see how people like it ; being minded to print
it more accurately in the Transactions. — M^r. *Joyner* says that, M^r.
Hobbs us'd to say that M^r. *Selden* understood nothing of Mathematicks,
wch M^r. *Selden* being inform'd off, he reply'd that if M^r. Hobbs understood no more mathematicks than he did Law, he understood nothing
at all of them.   And indeed M^r. *Selden* had such a Mean opinion of
that *Malmsbury* Philosopher, that he us'd to say, *All comers were welcome
to his Table, but* Tho. Hobbes & *one* Rossingham. — On ye 14th Instant
in ye Evening came on the Hearing of ye Election of S^t. Albans & ye 50
Committee sate 'till 3 in ye Morning & adj^d the farther hearing till
Friday Evening ; but carryed the main Question ag^t Honorary Freemen
having Right to vote by a Majority of above 40 voices so y^t twas

guess'd the same would go for Adm. *Killigrew* the Pet. against M^r. *Gape*
the sitting member. — The Lords on Thursday in a full House went
upon the Consideration of the State of the Nation, ye Q. & Prince present
at ye Debate, & amongst other Matteres the L^d. H——m proposed y^e
calling over ye P^ss. Sophia in wch he was seconded by the E. of A——y,
but this was overbore so y^t it came not to ye Question, but 'twas like to
end in further consideration how to strengthen the succession of y^e
House of Hanover. — On ye 2^d Instant, (being *All-Souls* Day) was
made Fellow of *All-Souls* College (there being but one Vacancy) *Bar-*
10 *zillai Jones*, A. B. of *Jesus College.*   He had great Interest, amongst the
rest the Duke of *Ormond* & the Duke of *Beaufort*, the latter of w^ch (as
I have been inform'd) came hither on purpose to make Friends in y^e
College for him.   He had so good Friends, it seems, upon Account of
his Father, nam'd also *Barzillai Jones*, who was formerly of *Jesus Coll.*
(where he took ye Degree of Master of Arts in ye year 1674) and afterwards was made a Dean in *Ireland*; whose Father being an Anabaptist
hinder'd this Jones his son from being baptis'd whilst young, insomuch
y^t 'twas not perform'd 'till he came to *Jesus Col.*, where S^r. *L. Jenkins*
(then Principal) got it done.   I am told y^t he became great wth ye Duke
20 of *Beaufort* upon Account of a Wife he married who was (tho' far off)
related to that Family : wch also made him great wth the Duke of
Ormond (who is related to ye Duke of *Beaufort*) & so he was preferr'd
to a Deanery; but whether he really deserved it I cannot tell.   This
however is certain that (notw^thstanding his being at present a Non-
Juror) he is a proud, haughty Man, as one of his own Country-men has
told me. — We hear from *Berwick* that several Gentlemen have been
taken up there, and put into the Town-Goal, there being divers Letters
of ill Consequence found about them, and some 100^s. of Arms taken in
ye House where they were seis'd. — M^r. *Joyner* thinks that *Davila's*
30 History of *France* is preferable to *Thuanus's* & y^t the latter's is more
esteem'd amongst the Protestants because he generally gives them very
great Characters. — One *Goddard* is made Chaplain to ye House of
Commons, who when he was of *Magd.* Col. in *Oxoñ* was commonly
call'd *Honest Tom Goddard*, because of his being a true Friend to the
Pot & Pipe, & was a good natur'd Rake : wch Character suits very
well with him still, it being observ'd that the very first time he read
Prayers after his being made Chaplain he read the Evening for the
morning Service, having drunk to y^t Excess the night before that his
head was giddy when he should perform his Duty ye day after.   Upon
40 wch there goes about a witty Copie of verses in Latin. — The Chief
Monument in ye Church of *Merston*, near *Oxon*, is y^t of S^r. *Rich. Croke*,
(Son of *Unton Croke*,) where he is characteris'd as being a Man of Great
Virtues, & belov'd by King *Charles* I & II, & by all good Men, & was
universally lamented at his Death.   W^ch is so false, that 'tis well known
that for his Breach of ye Articles made to *Penrudduck*, after he had
surrender'd himself up to him, upon the Defeat of his Enterprise in
behalf of the King (then in Exile) at *Salisbury*, as that he should have
his Life &c., he, the said *Croke*, was made a Serjeant by *Oliver*, and
became so universally hated, for y^t treacherous Action, & several other
50 most notorious Instances of Knavery, that no one could give him, or

his Son *Unton Croke*, who was as bad, a good Worde; tho' 'tis acknowledg'd y^t he was a very fair spoken Man, & by his insinuating way of Behaviour got a large Estate, wch however never prosper'd — ... D^r. *Beau*, the present B^p. of *Landaff* is 88 years of Age, & his Brother (a plain, Honest, true-principled man living at *Merston*) 75. H[is] Father and Grandfather, wth some others of ye Family, [lived] to be extraordinary old too, & it might have been taken notice of in ye new Edition of D^r. *Plot's N. H.* of *Oxon-sh.* — D^r. *Charlett* tells me that he does not think Father *Parsons* was the Author of *Leycester's Commonwealth*, and that this is the Opinion of divers others besides; but I 10 cannot hear any good reason offer'd for this Opinion: all they say, it seems, is, y^t the Author personates a Protestant, & y^t there is little or nothing of Popery in it, wch is no Argument y^t it should not be writ by a Jesuit, it being sufficiently known that *Parsons* was a Cunning, subtile Man, of a clear Head, great Learning, & very well vers'd in our *English* Constitution: & such a man was ye Author of this Book. — When Sir *Godfrey Kneller* (as D^r. *Hudson* informs me) came to *Oxon.* by Mr. *Pepys*'s order, to draw D^r. *Wallis*'s Picture, he, at dinner wth D^r. *Wallis*, was pleas'd to say, upon the D^rs. Questioning the Legitimacy of ye Prince of *Wales* that he did not in ye least doubt but he was the son 20 of K. *James* and Q. *Mary*: and to evince this, he added, That upon the sight of ye Picture of ye Prince of Wales sent from Paris into England, he was fully satisfy'd of w^t others seem'd to doubt so much of: For, as he farther said, he had manifest Lines and Features of both their Faces; wch he knew very well, having drawn them both several times. When this was said, were present at Dinner with D^r. *Wallis* the following Persons, D^r. *Aldrich* Dean of X^t Church, D^r. Charlett Master of University Coll., D^r. Hudson Head Library Keeper, & D^r. Gregory (the Scotch Man) one of the Savilian Professors. — *Ant. à Wood*, as D^r. *Hudson* told me, consulted with him (knowing y^t he had great Corre- 30 spondence wth ye chief Men in Holland) how to get his third vol. of *Athenæ Ox:* printed there. When he was ask'd the reason why he would not have it printed in England, he answer'd That his other Books had suffer'd so much, by the Liberty that some men took of expunging w^t they pleas'd that he would never suffer any Book of his to be committed to an English Press again. He moreover added (to use his own words) *when this Volume comes out* I'll *make you laugh again.* — D^r. *Charlett*, Master of University College was brought into y^t Place by the Interest of the Worthy Dr. Hudson, who might have had it, before M^r. Bennett, when D^r. Charlett succeeded. — Upon a Competition between D^r. 40 *Oldish* of New-Coll. & M^r. *Clarke* of *All-Souls* for being Burgesses for the University of *Oxon.* Dr. *Hudson*, who was then Master of Arts of *Queen's* Coll. was by the Interest & malice of D^r. Halton (Provost of that Col.) hinder'd of a Fellowship, for voting conscientiously for D^r. *Oldish*, & not for *Clarke* who was then a young Pert Master of Arts, & not comparable to the other for Abilities. About two months before this, the said M^r. *Hudson* had a Testimonium from D^r. *Halton* & all the Fellows, he then intending to go into Holy Orders, wch he not using at y^t time luckily kept by him, & did him afterwards (as it were Providentially) most signal Service. For when he miss'd of a Fellow- 50

ship at yᵗ College, he, intending to take Holy Orders, ask'd a Testimonium from the sᵈ Provost & Fellows, wᶜʰ he then, forgetting what he had done before, obstinately deny'd him.   Upon this he, taking his Testimonium dated a little time before, went to *Farnham*, & was ordain'd Deacon by Bᵖ. *Mew* ; with whom he left the said Testimonium. When he happen'd to stand for a Fellowship of University Coll. he petition'd the said Provost for a Testimonium, as is usual; but he deny'd it him.   Dʳ. *Crosthwait* Mʳ. *Hudson's* Friend ask'd the Provost whether he had been guilty of any Misdemeanour since such a time,
10 meaning the time when this Testimonium was dated?   The Provost answer'd, no.   Then replies Dʳ. *Crosthwait*, the Testimonium that you gave him a few months since is good.   Upon this Mʳ. *Hudson* was advis'd by the said Dʳ. Crosthwait to send to the Bᵖ. of Winchester for the Testimonium, wᶜʰ the Bᵖ. readily transmitted to him, and was accepted of by the Master & Fellows of University Coll. who thereupon elected him Fellow.   But it is to be observ'd that when Mʳ. *Hudson* stood Candidate for that Fellowship, Mʳ. *Obadiah Walker* the Master, seeming to have a kindness for him (well knowing him to be an ingenious Young Man, and a very good Scholar) without his Privity
20 procur'd a Mandate from King *James* ; wᶜʰ Mandate, when Mʳ. Hudson was acquainted with it by Mʳ. *Walker*, absolutely refus'd, saying, He had rather live by his Wits than come into a College without the Consent of the Fellows : wᶜʰ being known to the Fellows, those who were most for another Person came all over to his Interest ; so that he was unanimously Elected Fellow.   The Reason of Mʳ. Walker's getting yᵉ Mandate was, that he thought Mʳ. Hudson was not of a right County as the Statute requires : but upon Examination it appear'd that he was in yᵗ respect statutably qualified.   This mandate is an Instance of yᵗ Kings Assuming a Power of dispencing with Statutes of Colleges.   The
30 Copy of the Mandate is as follows,

To our Trusty and Well-beloved the Master and Fellows of University College in our University of Oxoñ.

JAMES R.

Trusty and well-beloved We greet you well.   Having receiv'd a good Character of John Hudson, Master of Arts of Queen's College, in that our University, and being inform'd that he is well-qualified by his Learning and Good Manners, to be chosen Fellow of your College, We have thought fit hereby, in a particular manner, to recommend him yᵉ said *J. H.* to you to be chosen accordingly a Fellow of your College, in the Place now vacant, notwithstand-
40 ing his not being of the County required by the Statute, or any other Disability, with all which we are pleas'd and do hereby dispense in his Behalf : And so, not doubting of your ready Complyance herein, We bid you farewell. Given at our Court at Whitehall the 21st Day of March 168⅚, in the second year of our Reign.   By his Majesty's command,

SUNDERLAND P.

The said Mʳ. *Hudson* having a Right to some money, due to him as Master upon the Foundation of Queen's College, when he was Fellow of University College requested the same of yᵉ Provost, and Burser of Queen's.   One Morning at a Meeting of yᵉ Provost and Fellows, it
50 was put to yᵉ vote, and by the Interest of the Provost and his Party

carry'd against him: wᶜʰ being told the said Mʳ. *Hudson* at the Coffee
House by his singular good Friend Mʳ. Joseph Fisher, a solid Divine,
and well skill'd in Orientals, he said in jest that he would Appeal to yᵉ
Ecclesiastical Commissioners.   This being overheard was carry'd to yᵉ
Provost, who (to shew he was a man of no great Courage) call'd
another Meeting of yᵉ Fellows, and procur'd a Vote to pass for his
having the Money.   The said Mʳ. *Hudson*, tho' he was so much in-
jur'd, still retain'd a mighty Affection for his Country College, and has
been often heard to say, That he could forgive the Provost a thousand
Injuries for his great Care and Generosity in Building and Furnishing 10
that noble Library: And has often since gratefully acknowledg'd his
Kindness for prevailing with some of the Fellows (who had been lead
aside by the cunning Dealing of Magd. Coll. men) to espouse his
Interest heartily when he stood to be Library Keeper to the university
of Oxford.   When Dʳ. *Hudson* stood to be Library-Keeper, Dʳ. Aldrich,
the Worthy Dean of Xᵗ Church, was his particular Friend, and did not
only engage his whole House to be for him; but came purposely
down from London himself, with several other Persons whose charges
he most generously bore.   The said Dʳ. Aldrich, as Dʳ. Hudson told
me, who had it from his own mouth, writ the Dedications to the Queen 20
prefix'd to the IIᵈ & IIIᵈ Volumes, and the Prefaces to the first, of my
Lᵈ. *Clarendon's* History. — To shew the Archbᵖ. of Canterbury's (*Tennison*) small Concern for the university of *Oxon*, when the Warden-ships
of All-Souls & Merton Coll. were to be fill'd by his Nomination, he
chose the Persons yᵗ were least deserving, Dʳ. *Martin* for *Merton*, who
was not comparable to Dʳ *Bateman* (a Man of great Integrity, Excellᵗ
Learning, & other noble Accomplishments), & Dʳ. *Gardiner* for All-
Souls, far inferior to Mʳ. *Waldron*, who was one of yᵉ Greatest Wits of
yᵉ Age, and justly esteem'd a second *Hudibrass*; whereas the other was
violently suspected to be an Egregious ————, & known to be a 30
Person of very little Learning & less Honesty, standing for all Places yᵗ
He can make any Interest to procure, as to be Custos Archivorum,
wᶜʰ Office he neither is nor ever will be qualified for.   Besides this,
he has done great Prejudice to yᵉ University by being a main Instru-
ment to bring in Dʳ. *Farrar* of *Magd.* Coll. (a Fellow all Gutts without
Brains) to be Natural Philosophy Professor, & Mʳ. Wallis of yᵉ said
College to be Arabick Reader, who hardly knows the Alphabet. —
When Birmingham School was void (by the Factious Town's men
turning out yᵉ Worthy Dʳ. John Hickes, Fellow of Magd. Coll.) the
Towns-men, thinking themselves not proper Judges of yᵉ Qualifica- 40
tions of a Schoolmaster, refer'd the choice of one to Dʳ. *Tillotson*
Archbᵖ. of Canterbury.   This Fanatical Prelate, having Liberty to chose
out of the two Universitys & all the world besides, could not think of
any Person to prefer to this Place, but one Perkinson, who was
Expell'd yᵉ University of Oxford for Fanatical Anti-monarchichal Principles. — Dʳ. Radcliff's Character of Mʳ. John Naylor Fellow of University (a Huge great lubberly Fellow) was, that he was only fit for
cleaving Wood. — After Mʳ. Walker was turn'd out of University
Coll. for being a Papist, he liv'd obscurely in London, his chief Maintenance being from the Contributions of some of his old Friends and 50

Acquaintance; amongst whom was D^r. *Radcliff,* who, (out of a gratefull Remembrance of Favours rec^d from him in the college) sent him once a Year a new Suit of Cloaths, with ten Broad-Pieces, and a dozen Bottles of the Richest Canary to support his Drooping Spirits. This D^r. Hudson (from whom I rec^d this story) was inform'd by D^r. *Radcliff* himself.

Nov. 19 (Mon.). In the Letters wch came last night 'tis said that the Upper House of Convocation, having drawn up an Address to Her Majesty for her late Gracious Speech, sent it down to ye Lower House for their Concurrence; but when they had read it, (whether it was because of their agreeing y^t ye Church was in no Danger, or w^t else I cannot as yet tell) they return'd it, and are resolv'd to draw up, and present Her Majesty, a Loyal one of their own. — *Kusterus,* in his Notes upon *Suidas,* in voc. "Ἀπρος p. 339. makes mention of D^r. *John Cowell's* (Head of *Bennett* Coll. Camb.) Itinerary thro' *Greece,* containing several curious matters relating to ye Language, Antiquities, Rites & Religion of that Country, wch he says would be of great Advantage to ye Republick of Letters to have publish'd. Ask D^r. *Smith's* Opinion of them, if he has seen them. —

A Letter to a Lady furnishing her wth Scripture Testimonies ag^t ye Principal Points and Doctrines of Popery. *Lond.* 1688. 4to. 'Twas written by *Charles Barecroft,* of Lin[c]olnshire.—Protestant Certainty, &c. *Lond.* 1689. 4°. Written by *Guil. Dillingham.*—The History of Passive Obedience since the Reformation. *Amst.* 1689. I am inform'd that ye Author was *Abednego Seller.* —A Defence of the Profession wth D^r. *Lake* B^p. of Chichester made upon his Death-Bed conc. Passive Obedience & the New Oaths, &c. *Lond.* 1690. The Author was *Rob. Jenkin,* chaplain to his L^dship. —

There is in y^e *Bodlejan* Library an unpublish'd Greek Scholiast upon *Aristophanes's Lysistratus;* some things whereof are printed in the Notes of *Kustar* to *Suidas.* — Some seasonable & Serious Queries upon ye Late Act against Conventicles. 1670. 4to. B^p. *Barlow* was told (by one who should know) that M^r. *Lockier,* a Non-Conformist-Minister was Author of this Seditious Pamphlett. after wch he fled beyond Sea. — A Commentary upon the Present Condition of the Kingdom, and it's melioration. 1677. Pen, then an Anabaptist, now a Quaker, was suppos'd to be ye Author. — A short Answer to several Questions proposed to a Gentleman of Quality &c. shewing the Author's Judgment conc. ye Publick Exercise of several Religions &c. *Lond.* 1678. 4to. B^p. *Barlow* was inform'd that ye Author was S^r. *John Monson* of *Lincoln-shire.* — Tragi-Comœdia Oxoniensis—4to. The Author M^r. *John Carricke* of X^t Church. — On Friday Morning (being the 16th) died the Dutchess of *Norfolk.* — M^r. *Gibson,* one of the Attorney's in the L^d. Mayor's Court is made Town-Clerk of ye City of London. There was neither Whigg nor Tory appear'd in ye Election, & my L^d. Mayor (to his immortal Hon^r) manag'd all things wth great Impartiality, notw^th-standing his son's being one of the Candidates. — Aristotelis & Platonis Græcorum Interpretum typis hactenus editorum brevis conspectus, per P. Labbæum. *Par.* 4to. 'twill be of admirable use either in cataloguing of the Translators of these two Authors, or giving a Relation of their Works.

The Rebells Plea—1660. By M^r. *Tomkins.* — A needfull Corrective or Ballance in Popular Government—4to. 'twas writ by Sr *Hen. Vane,* at least by his Advise and Approbation. — De Monarchia Absoluta Dissertatio Politica. *Oxon.* 1659. The Author was *Ed. Bagshaw* Stud. of *X^t. Ch.* — D^r. *Homack* was Author of ye Pamphlett call'd—*Aronbimnucha, or, Antidote to cure the Calamities of their trembling for Fear of the Arke. Lond.* 1663. 4to. — Oxonium Poema. *Oxon,* 1667, per *F. V.* i.e. *F. Vernon* (of Ch: Ch:) 4to. — The Conflagration of London Poetically delineated. *Lond.* 1667. The Author D^r. *Sim Ford,* who also writ *London's Remains* in *Latin & English.* He was Minister at *Northampton,* and once of the Presbyterian interest in the Rebellion, but he turn'd afterwards. In the year 1668 He publish'd Londini Renascentis Imago Poetica. — The Elegy on the Death of M^r. James Bristow, Fellow of All Souls, *Oxon.* 1667. 4to, was written by *Ed. Palmer,* commoner of Queen's Col. & Son of S^r *Ed. Palmer.*—Irenæi Philadelphi Epistola, ad Renatum Veridæum, in qua aperitur mysterium iniquitatis novissime in Anglia redivivum, & excutitur liber Josephi Halli, quo asseritur Episcopatum esse Juris Divini. *Eleutheropoli,* 1641. 4°. Auctor hujus libri, seu potius libelli famosi fuit P. *Molinæi* filius medicus Lond. qui à Patre venerando penitus rejectus huc se, & vitia simul transtulit. — Episcopacy, not abjured in his Majestie's Realme of Scotland. 1641. 4to. 'Twas written by . . . . . . *Maxwell* Bp. of *Killaly* in *Ireland,* and before Bp. of *Rosse.* — A Discoverie concerning Puritans—1641. The Author *John Ley,* Pastor of *Budworth* in *Cheshire;* who also writ, *The Defensive Doubts against the Oath in the New Canons.* — The *Key to y° King's Cabinet, Oxon.* 1645. 4to was writ by D^r. *Tho. Browne,* sometimes Student of *X^t Ch.* — The Unlawfullness of Subjects taking up Armes against their Soveraigne, in what case soever—1643. The Author *Dudley Diggs,* Fellow of *All-Souls, Oxon.* — The Relation of the Battle at Newbury Sept. 20. 1643. was writ by the L^d. *George Digby.* — In the Story of Thebes compiled by *John Lidgate,* pag. 374. at ye End of Chaucer's Works, is a Testimony of *Martianus* Capella; wch ye Gentleman of *Cambridge* (of *Queen's* Col. viz. M^r. *Wasse*) who is publishing *Capella* anew should remember to put down among y^e *Testimonia.* — The Character of a London Diurnal—1644. 4to, was writ by *Jo: Cleveland Cant.* — Parliam^ts Power in Lawes for Religion—Author D^r. Heylin. *Oxon.* 1645. 4to. — The Life of S^r. *Hen. Gage. Oxon.* 1645. The Author *Ed. Walsingham* a Papist, and under-Secretary to ye L^d. *George Digby,* principal Secretary of State. — The Great Assizes holden in *Parnassus,* by *Apollo* and his Assessors. *Lond.* 1645. 4to. The Author *George Wither.* — A Petition to his Majesty of ye Three Revolting Counties in ye West, *Wilts, Somerset,* and *Devon &c. Lond.* 1645. 4to. 'Tis a spurious Bratt, bred and borne at *London,* as appears clearly by that Rebellious Language it speaks; wch was not ye Language of *Devon,* or *Wilts,* but of *Westminster.* — A Brief Relation of ye Present Troubles in *England,* translated out of *French. Oxon.* 1645. The Translator *Tho. Tully.* — A Corrector of ye Answer to the Speech out of Doors, &c. *Edinb.* 1646. 4to. The Author supposed to be *Hen. Martin.* — An unhappy Game at *Scotch and English,* &c. *Edinb.* 1646. 4to. Supposed to be writ by Lieut.-Col. *John Lilburne.* 'Twas burn'd at *Lond.* in *Nov.* 1646. — *Absalon* & *Achitophel* in Latin. The Author D^r. *Atterbury.* — A Discourse conc. Prayer *Extempore*—1646. D^r. *Jer. Taylor* Author. The *Short Censure of ye Book of* W. P. *entit.* The University of *Oxford's* Plea,—1648. 4to, was writ either by D^r. *Allestrey* or *Rob. Waring. Quære? —* . . .A Word to *Will.* *Prynne* Esqr. &c. *Lond.* 1649. The Author *Hen. Martin.* — . . .

Nov. 20 (Tu.). On *Friday* last in the Evening the Committe of Elections went again on that of S^t. *Albans,* & finish'd in favour of S^r. *Hen. Killigrew* against — *Gape,* Esqr. the sitting Member. The Managem^t of the Election caus'd a great many warm speeches, especially on acc^t of the Dutchess of *Marlborough's* Intermeddling. — In pag. 372 of

Phil. à Turre's Monumenta Veteris Antij are several things concerning *Pliny the Younger's* Epistles, wch must be made use of in a new Edition of y^t Author. — I have been told, by one that knows, that M^r. *Wilkinson* Minister of *Lawrence Waltham* in *Berks* being a Person inclin'd to ye Study of *English Antiquities*, had collected a great many things of y^t nature, wch would be of use in a new Edition of *Camden*; but he cannot tell to whom they came after his death, or where they now are[1]. — In pag. 7 of ye said *Monumenta Vet. Antij* is a Note conc. *Valerius Antias*, the Antient *Roman* Historian, (so often quoted, & sometimes condemned, 10 by *Livy*) his going to *Rome*. In pag. 15. He quotes a MS^t Dissertation of *Hieronymus Aleander Junior*, wherein he show'd in opposition to *Lipsius* that *extenuatas* and *attenuatas* in *Livy* is not to be chang'd into *extacniatas*. He promises there to give a more full relation of this Diss. & ye other MSS. of *Aleander* in another *Place*. *Quaere* whether he ever perform'd his promise, & whether ye Diss. was ever yet printed? The said *Aleander* also made an Addition to Sirmondus's Comment upon ye Inscription of *Scipio Barbatus*. See there pag. 27. Quaere whether this was ever printed? In p. 66 he tells us that Fabrettus died the 7th of y^e *Ides* of *Febr. An.* 1700. in ye 80th year of his Age, leaving an excell^t 20 Work, wch he had began, unfinish'd, viz. *Descriptio Agri Romani antiqui*, for compiling of wch he had collected a vast treasure of Materials, & prepar'd a most accurate Map, & several excell^t Tables besides. There was nothing of it digested. Quaere where his *Adversaria* are reposited? —

Today being at M^r. *Abell's* Chamber of *Merton*-Col. he was pleas'd to shew me the following *Roman* Coyns, viz. . . .

[Here follow the descriptions of eight coins; at pp. 175-6 of five other coins, and at p. 177 of two more.]

Nov. 21 (Wed.). I am told by a Person, who well knows, having rec^d it from his own Mouth, that D^r. *Kennett* designs to give at large, in a 30 Work he is now consulting, all the material Inscriptions in any Church wch belong'd to some Religious House in *England*. —

The Inscription on ye monum^t of M^r. *Rich. Walker*, buried in S^t. Michael's Church in Oxon:

> Hic | Juxta Parentis sui Exuvias | situs est | Ricardus Walker hujusce urbis oenopola | notissimus | et ob | singularem erga Hospites Humanitatem | Liberam erga pauperes Munificentiam, | Eximiam erga amicos Benevolentiam, | Summam erga Cognatos Pietatem, | Debitam & Academiae, & Ecclesiae Reverentiam, Desideratissimus. | De omnibus, quibus innotuit | Bene meritus est; Prae omnibus, de Johanne Freeman | e sororum una nepote; | Quem, 40 liberorum expers utut bis maritus, | Filij loco vivens habuit, | Haeredem moriens reliquit. | Haeres ille | Accepti beneficij memor | monumentum hoc poni curavit. | Obijt decimo die Nov. 1704. aet. suae 52.

This Inscription was made by the Ingenious M^r. *Alsop* of *X^t Church*, & was communicated to me by my singular Good Friend D^r. *Hudson*. — The New Edition of *Euclid's* Works wch came out at the Theatre in fol. in D^r. *Gregory's* name, was chiefly owing to the Care of the Learned D^r. *Hudson*, who at ye Request of D^r. *Aldridge*, Dean of X^t Church, submitted to be a joynt Editor of that Book, it being agreed upon at ye Dean's, That D^r. *Gregory* should see y^t ye mathematical things were

---

[1] (N.B. Peter Le Neve Esq. had many of them. Tho. Hearne June 4. 1732.)

Right, & D^r. *Hudson* should take care of the *Greek* and *Lat.* Text in all other regards, wch he effectually perform'd, first by settling the *Greek* Text, wch he corrected and supply'd in many Places, by the Assistance of MSS. and printed Copies in ye Publick Library, and first of all with abundance of Pains transcrib'd the *Phænomena* out of an old MS^t, and accurately prepar'd it for the Press, having been never publish'd before. 2. As to the *Latin* Version, it cost him a great deal of time in ye Books following the first 6 (wch were published by S^r. *Hen. Savile* and judg'd to need no Emendations, wch the D^r, (relying too much upon D^r. *Gregory,)* found he was mistaken in; for in ye Publick Library the Version of those Books are all along mended by D^r. *Bernard* with great Skill and Judgm^t) in making use of D^r. *Bernard's* Emendations of ye version in most of ye Book, especially in y^e *Data*; and afterwards adjusting the Version of those Parts wch D^r. *Bernard* had not touch't to the Original Text.   (3) The chief Part of correcting the whole in *Greek* (wch D^r. *Gregory* knew nothing of) lay upon him, as also the *Latin* in a great measure.   (4) D^r. *Hudson,* supposing y^t he should be joyn'd wth ye D^r. in the Dedication (wch Dedication D^r. *H.* by himself made an offer of to ye Dean of X^t *Church,* not doubting of D^r. *Gregory's* Concurrence wth him) when that was to be drawn up, he mentioning something about it to D^r. *Gregory,* the s^d D^r. told him, y^t he had nothing to do wth that, and moreover added to w^t purpose should he have his Name to a Book of Mathematicks wch he did not pretend to: to wch D^r. *H.* replyed, He had as good reason to have his Name to a Book as Mathematical, as D^r. *Gregory* had to a Book *quatenus Greek.*   Upon this, D^r. *H.* at ye Request of D^r. *Wallis* and D^r. *Mill* was content to let him have the sole Honour of it, upon these two considerations, first y^t D^r. *Gregory* having Children might have all the Dean's Gratuity for ye Dedication, wch prov'd to be twenty Guineas to ye D^{r's} son.   Secondly that he might do S^r. *Hen. Savile's* Professor ye utmost Honour, tho' he was sensible D^r. *Gregory* deserv'd none.   The Dedication of this Book was writ by one of ye Students of *Christ Church.* The Preface wch is most of it but indifferent Stuff was first drawn up by D^r. *Gregory* himself, and afterwards mended (as to the gross faults of it) by some other Hand. W^t is said of D^r. *Hudson* was penn'd by D^r. *Mill,* who promis'd to do it when he prevail'd with D^r. *H.* to yield to D^r. *Gregory.* W^t relates to *Euclid's Musica* was drawn up by D^r. *Wallis,* and printed *verbatim* as ye s^d D^r. Wallis had done it. 'Tis true D^r. *Gregory* has mention'd the Assistance of D^r. *Wallis,* but in the same place has not been so ingenuous (resolving to act y^e *Scotch* Man all along) as to acquaint his Reader y^t w^t follow'd was D^r. *Wallis*'s own words, wch indeed should have been distinguish'd by commas (as ye Printers call y^m) at the side, as was but highly reasonable, seeing D^r. *Wallis* had ye chief care of it, D^r. *Gregory* beeing at *London* wⁿ 'twas printed. *Memorandum* that when D^r. *H.* was so kind as to yield the whole Honour of ye Dedication & consequently of ye Edition to him, he told D^r. *G.* that he hop'd his contending for y^t point & carrying of it, would not be made use of as an Argument why D^r. *H.* should not have an equal share with him ye s^d D^r. *G.* in w^t ye Curators of the Press should allow for ye Pains taken in the Edition of this work. D^r. *G.* then protested to D^r. *H.* y^t he never design'd any thing else but that they should be equal sharers.   Yet after this (to shew yet

more fully how perfect a *Scotch* man he was) he made Interest to several
of yᵉ Curators to have a great many more Copies allow'd him than Dʳ. *H.*
wᶜʰ by the under-hand dealing of Dʳ. *Charlett* (the known Patron of the
Scotch Men) he at last effected, Dʳ. *H.* never troubling himself to
represent wᵗ he had done to yᵉ Curators. This is every tittle true, & may
be rely'd upon, it coming from Dʳ. *H.* himself. Here also it must be
remembred that Dʳ. *Hudson* first put Mʳ. *Milles* upon Sᵗ. *Cyrill* (whereof
I have given an Accᵗ in one of these Vols. already) procuring him Books
collated wᵗʰ MSS. from the Bᵖ. of *Norwich,* &c. — I was told by Dʳ.
10 *Hudson,* who had it from Mʳ. *Halley,* that Sʳ. Isaac *Newton's* Lectures,
wᶜʰ he read when Mathematick Professor at *Cambridge,* are kept in
Trinity Coll. Library in *Cambridge,* and yᵗ some Scotch men, (who
would make a great Figure in Mathematical Learning) got access to
them, & transcrib'd abundance of things out of them, wᶜʰ afterwards
they publish'd as their own Inventions, getting Credit and Reputation in
yᵉ World by stealing another man's Works, wᵗʰout any manner of
Acknowledgmᵗ. — In yᵉ first Edition of Mʳ. *John Keil's* Lectures, there
were abundance of Faults as to yᵉ Mathematicks, wᶜʰ the sᵈ *John* was
friendly told of by Mʳ. *Halley* and others, wᶜʰ he has since corrected in
20 the 2ᵈ Edition. It may here likewise be observ'd that Men well skill'd in
Mathematicks scruple not to say that Dʳ. *Gregory* has stole most of his
Astronomy from *Isaac Newton,* whom he has mention'd wᵗʰ some little
acknowledgmᵗ but not so often as he should have done : wᶜʰ as 'tis said
has put Sʳ. *Isaac* on a new Edition of his *Principia &c.* —

I was told that my Lᵈ *Haversham* made yᵉ first Speech in yᵉ H. of Lᵈˢ for
Bringing over yᵉ Princess *Sophia* & the Young Prince of *Hanover,* & yᵗ he was
seconded by the Earl of *Anglesey,* to whom reply'd the Lᵈᵉ *Somers* & *Hallifax,*
who were answer'd by the Earls of *Nottingham* & *Rochester.* One of these
Noble Lords said in his Speech that he had observ'd from our *English* His-
30 torians that when ever yᵉ next successor happen'd to be out of yᵉ Kingdom, at
yᵉ Death of any King or Queen, they never came to yᵉ Crowne, and that in
the time of either *Rich.* or *Edw.* II. a Famous Bp. of *Sarum* (wᶜʰ was mention'd purposely to glance upon yᵉ present Bp. of *Sarum*) was us'd to maintain
that unvoluntary oaths did not oblige, wᶜʰ (sayd that noble Lᵈ) is a Doctrine
he had heard preach'd wᵗʰin those Walls. Next yᵉ Earl of *Devon* made a
speech shewing the Great Charges it put yᵉ Kingdom to in maintaining the
Port & Grandeur of yᵉ sᵈ Princess : To wᶜʰ a certain Lᵈ reply'd, That tho' a
Young Woman was very Expensive to keep (as yᵉ Earl of *Devon* has found
by Experience) yet a little matter would serve to keep an old one. —

40 In *P. à Turre's Mon. Vet. Antij* are divers things conc. *Josephus,* wᶜʰ
will be of use to him yᵗ shall put out a new Edition of that Author. This
Author in pag. 134. of his *Mon.* has a laudable Character of *Montfaucon*
and *Mabillon* ; especially for their Travells in order to consult *Greek*
MSS. &c. In pag. 136. He has an Excellᵗ Emendation of *Eutropius* ;
the want of wᶜʰ made *Lazius* committ a great Blunder in *lib.* 5. *de Rep.
Rom.* as is there discours'd of at large. — *Commodianus* the Poët, who
flourished in the time of *Constantine the Gr.* was first publish'd by *Rigaltius,* an. 1650. See there pag. 162. In pag. 163. He tells us that
Hieronymus Alcander's Philological Dissertations are *in Bibliotheca Bar-*
50 *berina.* He has there publish'd some things from them concerning
Mithra. In pag. 168. is a laudable Account of Dʳ. *Hyde's Historia*

Religionis veterum Persarum &c. In pag. 222. He tells us that *Hiero-nymus Aleander*, the Younger, writ a short Dissertation upon the VIIIth of the *Kalends of Jan.* of the old Kalendar (or the 25th of *December* as we reckon) w[ch] is now extant, amongst his *Adversaria* in Cardinal *Bar-berine's* Library, & publish'd by *Turre* in this Work pag. 223. but, he farther adds, that his intire Comment upon the old Kalendar is quite lost, & y[t] to prevent the like Fate to his other Writings *Justus Fontaninus* design'd to publish them in his *Scriptores Forojulienses*. In pag. 243. is an Observation upon *Dionys. Halicarnass.* — *Joan. Antonius Astorius* writ an Elegant Dissertation upon y[e] Image of *Bronto*, w[ch] he afterwards 10 publish'd. That Image, with other *Aquileian* Monuments, is now pre-serv'd at *Venice*. See there pag. 291. In pag. 296. he cites a Collection of Inscriptions made by *Capodaleus*. W[t] are they, and who was this *Capodaleus?* In pag. 290. It seems this *Capodaleus*'s Xtian Name was *Joseph*, and that he writ a Book in *Italian* call'd *Udine Illustrata*, wch is publish'd. Besides wch he likewise compos'd the s[d] *Collection of Inscrip-tions*, which *P. à Turre* has acknowledg'd to have made use of, the original Copy sent him as he was writing these *Monumenta*. These In-scriptions relate to *Aguileja*. In pag. 331. He relates y[t] y[e] first who collected Inscriptions was *Joannes Marcanova*, wch was *an.* 1465. He 20 there quotes a Passage out of the Original at *Venice*. . . .

Nov. 22 (Th.). The Upper House of Convocation having sent down their Address (w[ch] they design'd to present Her Majesty for Her Speech) to have their Concurrence, D[r]. *Freeman* was so much taken with it, that he stood up and made a Speech, desiring that they would Address the Upper House for it, and he was seconded by D[r]. *Kennett*; upon w[ch] one of y[e] others desired that D[r]. *Freeman* and D[r]. *Kennett* might be Address'd also for this their Hearty Zeal against y[e] Church, w[ch] they thought in no Danger, notw[th]standing the Extraordinary Favours shew'd to all manner of Dissenters, & the great Dis-couragement of all Worthy Men who were real Friends of y[e] Church, &c. — 30

D[r]. *Gardiner*, Warden of *All-Souls*, being, it seems, the only Person of the Doctors, who voted in *Oxon* lately against M[r]. *Lloyd's* Accumu-lating the Degrees of Bach. and D[r]. of Divinity, D[r]. *Kennett* sent him a Letter, expostulating the matter with him, and desiring his Reasons, being, as he said, continually ask'd about it, by Persons who were amaz'd at it, thinking a Doctor should have more sense and Discretion than a Young Master of Arts, especially too one y[t] was *Custos Archi-vorum* & should understand the Customs & Privileges of the University better than others, & conseq[tly] presently see y[t] the Reason alledg'd relating to y[e] Parliam[t] did not concern the University. D[r]. *Gardiner* 40 soon after writ an Answer, giving his Reasons at full, and granting him Liberty to print y[e] Letter, if he thought it might prevent any farther Inquiry. — In the *Ashmolean Museum* is a Collection of Epitaphs in the County of *Berks*, made by M[r]. *Ashmole* in the year 1666, & written in 3 fol. Volumes. Number'd in y[e] Cat. 7057. w[ch] is 850, &c. as they stand in the *Mus.* Look into these Volumes for y[e] Inscriptions in the Church of *Shottesbrooke*. — The Design of Christianity &c. By *Edw. Fowler*, Minister of God's Word at *Northil* in *Bedfordshire. Lond.* 1671. 8[o]. B[p]. *Barlow* was told by one, who seem'd to know it, that *Fowler* was not the Author, but one *Godman* of *Hatfeild* in *Essex*. — Sure- 50 Footing in Christianity Examin'd, by *G. H.* i. e. *Huish* sometime of

Pembrooke-Col. in *Oxon.* (*Lond.* 1668. 8º.) — The Principles and Practices of certain Moderate Divines of the Church of *England* (greatly misunderstood) truly Represented and Defended. *Lond.* 1670. 8º. This Discourse is a Justification of a *Latitudinarian* (the word was first hatch'd at *Cambridge*) against yᵉ Zealous Nonconformists, and it looks so like some Discourses of Dʳ. *Hen. Moore* of that University, that Bᵖ. *Barlow* thought at first he might be Author of it ; but he was afterward inform'd from *Cambridge* (by those who should know) that one Mʳ. *Fowler* (the same yᵗ is mention'd above) an *Oxford* man, was Author
10 of this Discourse. — Quakerism is Paganism, &c. By *W. R.* (i.e. *Russell*) *Lond.* 1674. 8º. — Inscriptions¹ in the Church of Shottesbrooke in the County of Berks. [202-210.]... — In one of Mʳ. Ashmole's MSS. conc. Berks I found a Letter from Mʳ. *Tho. Wilkinson*, Minister of *Laurence-Waltham*, to Mʳ. Ashmole giving an Account of a Plate dug up in the Church of *Laurence Waltham*, whereon were Armes, wᶜʰ are Blazon'd by Mʳ. *Wilkinson.* — The Dutchess of *Norfolk* left all yᵉ Estate wᶜʰ belong'd to yᵉ *Peterburgh* Family to her Husband Sʳ. *John Germaine*; but her Joynture, wᶜʰ was 2000 *libʳ. per an.* returns to yᵉ *Norfolk* Family. — The Duke of *Argyle* is to be created a Peer of this
20 Realme & to have the Title of Baron or Earl of *Bristol*; tho' 'tis said the Lᵈ. *Digby's* Family claime the same, & that his Gr. will have some other Title. —

On yᵉ 19ᵗʰ & 20ᵗʰ the Lᵈˢ were upon the State of the Nation (the Q. present at all yᵉ Debates) & a Bill is ordered to be brought in for the more effectual securing the Succession of the Crowne in the House of *Hanover* by appointing the ensueing great Ministers & Officers of the Crown to administer the Government as Lᵈˢ Justices in case of the Q'ˢ Demise till the next successor arrives in the Kingdom, viz. the Archbᵖ. of *Cant.* in time being the Lᵈ High Admiral the Lᵈ Chancellor or Keeper of the Great Seal Lord Treasurer
30 & Lᵈ Presidᵗ of the Council Lᵈ Steward of Her Majᵗⁱᵉˢ Household & yᵉ Lᵈ Ch. Justice of *England.*

The Address of the Upper House of Convocation to her Majesty. [213-220.]

Mʳ. *Tilly's* Sermon, preach'd at *Cairfax* 5ᵗʰ *Nov.* last, is newly publish'd, & there is prefix'd a Preface vindicating himself upon Account of the Aspersions cast on him, & defying all they can do to him, & submitting his former Discourse to their Wills, being resolv'd to stand firm to his Principles wᶜʰ he thinks so usefull to yᵉ Church of *England.* — The Buckler of State & Justice—*Lond.* 1673. 8º. The Author of this Ingenious & Judicious Tract was the Baron of *Isola.* — The
40 History & Fate of Sacrilege, by Sʳ. *Hen. Spelman. Lond.* 1698. 'tis an imperfect Work, being never finish'd by the Excellent Author. Dʳ. *Gibson* publish'd his Posthumous Pieces, but this was left out, upon Account that some Gentlemen might be disgusted at some Relations in it. — When I went over to *Shottesbrooke* from *Oxford* in the year 1698, I lodg'd at Mʳ. *Cherry's*, where I met with Dʳ. *Gibson's* Transcript, wᶜʰ he had made from the *Bodlejan* Library (where 'tis amongst Bᵖ. *Barlow's* MSS.) & I fairly transcrib'd it from that for Mʳ. *Cherry*, who a little while after either writ a Preface himself, or else got some Body else (I believe Dʳ. *Kennett*) to do it, and so sent it to yᵉ Press, & 'twas printed
50 from my Copy. — Pauli Colomesij Opuscula. *Par.* 1668. 8º. . . There

¹ See also in Ashmole's Inscriptions of Berks Vol. 1. p. 289.

is an intire Chapter about *Livy*, the Title whereof is (Ch. xvii.) *An Titi Livij Imagines Patavinæ digitum ori appressum habeant?* — A Serious and Compassionate Enquiry into the Causes of the present Neglect and Contempt of yᵉ Protestant Religion and Church of *England, Lond.* 1674. 8º. Dʳ. *Goodman* (formerly of *Cambridge*, then a Country Minister) was Author of this Inquiry. But whoever was the Author, he was a feirce Remonstrant, highly confident (ne quid pejus dicatur) & sufficiently Ignorant. — In Dʳ. *Hudson's* Copy of *Tanaquil Faber's* Edition of *Anacreon* at yᵉ End he has added these References—vid. *Canteri* Novas Lectiones l. v. c. 7. & l. 2. c. 13. Vid. Fabri notas ad Longinum. vid. 10 Fabri Epist. p. 292.

[Notes on Livy from *Tho. Bartholini* de Armillis vet. (*Amst.* 1676) and Stephens' Schediasmata.]

I must read over *Giffanius's* Index to *Lucretius* to see whether there be any Emendations of *Livy* there or Illustrations. Dʳ. *Hudson* has it from whom I have borrow'd it. — A Letter to a Deist. *Lond.* 1677. 8º. The Author Bᵖ. *Stillingfleet.* — The Triumphs of *Rome* over despised Protestancy. *Lond.* 1667. 8º. The Author Dʳ. *Geo. Hall* Bᵖ. of *Chester.* — ... Whereas 'tis sᵈ above by Mʳ. *Ashmole* in yᵉ Epitaphs of *Shottes-brooke* that Sʳ. *John Trussel* & Maud his wife founded the Church of 20 *Shottesbrook,* I cannot tell wᵗ Authority he had for it. I find indeed that Sʳ. *Wᵐ. Trussel* founded the college of Shottesbrooke & a Chantry here, but there was wᵗʰout doubt a Parish Church before. — *Sallust* corrected in *Giffanius's* Index to *Lucretius*—voc. *anquirere. Catullus* in voc. *antistare. Q. Curtius* also in yᵉ same word. *Virgil & Bede* in voc. *aqua.*

Nov. 23 (Fri.). Faith vindicated from Possibility of Falshood. *Lovain,* 1667. 8º. The Author of this Apocryphal Pamphlett (wᶜʰ is an impertinent Piece of Error & Metaphysical Nonsense) was Mʳ. Will. *Serjeant* (the same who writ *Sure-Footing*) who was first (really or in 30 shew) a Protestant, & Secretary to Dʳ. *Morton* Bᵖ. of *Durham,* & then turn'd Papist. — Discursus Divinissimus de Polygamia, Auctore *Joanne Lysero. Friburgi,* 1676. 8º. In relation to wᶜʰ it must be observ'd, 1. That *Bernardinus Ochinus* (an *Italian,* borne at *Siena* in *Tuscany,* first a Friar, then turn'd Protestant, then an Apostate &c.) writt two Dialogues, for Polygamy in *Italian,* wᶜʰ were translated into *Latin* by *Sebast. Castalio,* then into *English,* and printed London 1657. 2. *Beza* answered *Ochinus's* Dialogues *Tractat. de Polygamia* &c. *Genev.* 1587. 8º. 3. A Booke was printed in 1674, wᵗʰ this Title: *Discursus Politicus de Polygamia,* per *Theophilum Alethæum* &c. & much of it out of *Ochinus.* 40 4. Now this *Discursus Divinissimus* (above mention'd) is onely the said *Discursus Politicus,* &c. wᵗʰ Additions &c. 5. *Lyserus* came, & B[r]ought his Books to *London* wᶜʰ (in *Febr.* 1675) were seis'd on by the Right Revᵈ *Hen. Compton* Lᵈ. Bᵖ. of *London,* & at his Intreaty the King banish'd *Lyserus.* ...

Bonasus Vapulans, &c. *Lond.* 1672. 8º. The Author *Hen. Hickman* of *Magd. Coll.*—A Letter from a Protestant Gentleman to a Lady revolted to

---

Nov. 23. Kent to H. Can't get the coins. What writers on Mystical Divinity? Does the non-compliance of the invalidly deprived Fathers make

yᵉ Church of *Rome. Lond.* 1678.   The Author Dʳ. *Arth. Horneck.*—A Reply to yᵉ Answer of the Catholique Apology. 1668.   The Author *Pugh* a *Welchman.*—Discourse conc. yᵉ Spirituality and Simplicity of New-Testamᵗ Worship. *Lond.* 1667. 8⁰.   The Author Mʳ. *Wilson* a Non-Conformist.   He liv'd abᵗ *Chester.*   He was also Author of *Nehushtana, or A sober and* Peaceable Discourse conc. yᵉ Abolishing of Things abused to Superstition and Idolatry. *Lond.* 1668. 8⁰.—Vindicatio Generalis & Specialis Librorum Apocryphorum & Veteris & Novi Testamenti. *Lubecæ* 1638.   Auctore *Hen. Lemmichio.*   Most or all of it is taken out of the Learned *John Reynolds's* Book *de libris Apocryphis,*
10 wᵗʰout any Acknowledgmᵗ.— Sacrilegious Desertion of the Holy Minstery Rebuk'd, &c. 1672. 8⁰.   The Author Mʳ. *Baxter.*—A Prospect of the State of Ireland from yᵉ year of yᵉ World 1756 to the year of Xᵗ 1652. *Lond.* 1682. 8⁰.   The Author *P. W.* i.e. *Walsh.*—A Defence of Humane Learning in the Ministry.   By *H. Th.* (i.e. *Thurman*) St. of *Ch. Ch. Oxon.* 1660. 8⁰.—*Prodromus,* or the Character of Mʳ. *Sherlock's* Book called, *A Discourse of the Knowledg of Jesus Xᵗ. Lond.* 1674. 8⁰.   The Author *S. R.* i.e. *Samuel Rowles,* a Non-Conformist.—Acta Sanctorum Apostolorum [ad] literam explicata, per *Carolum Mariam Du Veil. Lond.* 1684.   Auctor iste fuit primo gente & religione *Judæus,* dein Papista, postea (Roma relicta) reformatus, & tandem Ana-
20 baptista Hæreticus.—Prologus de Coma.   The Author was *Salmasius.* N.B. *Joan. Rossus Warwicensis* in Historia sua MS. in *Will. Rufo,* queritur de Seculi sui (vixit sub *Ed.* 4. *Angliæ,* & sub initio *Hen.* 7. fatis cessit) viris, quod comam nimirum alebant—*Nonne etiam adinventiones hominum malum aliquod futurum minantur ; longitudine crinium faciem in Baptismo Sanctæ Crucis signo signatam abscondunt, pudenda palam faciunt, & de vitijs non pudent,* &c.—*Tho. Godden* was Author of *the Just Discharge to Dʳ.* Stillingfleet's *unjust Charge of Idolatry against yᵉ Ch. of* Rome. *Par.* 1677. 8⁰.   As also of *Catholicks no Idolaters.*— The Life of Bᵖ. *Bedell* was writt by Dʳ. *Burnett* the *Scotch* Bᵖ. of *Sarum.*— *Velitationes* Polemicæ : or, Polemical short Discussions of certain particular &
30 select Questions. By *J. D.* i.e. *John Doughty,*formerly of *Merton* Col. *Oxon.*— ... A Manual of Controversies. By *H. T.* (i.e. *Hen. Turbervill,* Priest.) *Doway,* 1654. 8⁰.—Observations, Censures, &c. on the 12, 13, & 14 Chapters of *Hobbs's Leviathan. Lond.* 1657. 8⁰.   The Author *W. Lucy* Bp. of Sᵗ. *David's.* —*Judicium Discretionis,* or A just and necessary Apology for The People's Judgment of Private Discretion &c. *Lond.* 1667. 8⁰.   By Mʳ. *Wilson,* the Non-Conformist.—The Presbyterians unmask'd. *Lond.* 1676. 8⁰.   The Author *Sam. Thomas.*

A Private Letter of Satisfaction to a Friend conc. (1) The Sleep of the Soul.   (2) The State of the Soul after Death, 'till the Resurrection.   (3)
40 The Reason of the Seldom appearing of Separate Spirits.   (4) Prayer for departed Souls whether Lawfull or no. 1667. 8⁰.   Conc. wᶜʰ in the Beginning of yᵉ Copy in yᵉ *Bodl.* Library, Bᵖ. Barlow has made this Remark :

---

us all guilty of Schism?   **H. to Dr. T. Smith.**   Wanted, a more accurate History of Hen. VIII's reign than that of Strype or Burnet.   Points out an alleged error of the latter *re* the Ordination Book of 1550.   Is pleased with Redi's Dissertation on Spectacles ; is now of opinion that it can't be inferred from the Preface to the Bible that spectacles were not in use in England before.   Looks forward to the publication of Smith's Life of Dee.   Kennett is making a collection of epitaphs in all such churches in England as belonged to religious houses, and has taken those of Shottesbrooke.   H. has transcribed the copy in Ashmole's Epitaphs in Berks, and will compare them with the originals : he has copies of the Cartularies concerning the foundation of the College by Sir W. Trussell, formerly in the hands of Mr. Stephen Edwards, but now of Mr. Cherry.   A mistake in Ashmole pointed out.

Literis hisce privatis (jam juris publici factis) Author (quisquis demum fuerit) effuso verborum non bene cohærentium flumine, Rhetorem agit potius quam Theologum, aut subacti judicij Philosophum. Confidentia in asserendo satis valida utitur, consequentijs in probando non item; adeo ut rudi popello aut Philosophorum plebi nonnihil forte suadere potest; sed doctis, qui non ex affectu sed judicio, non ex verborum turba fastuve, sed ex præmissis de conclusione judicant, satisfacere non potest. Qui serio leget (ni meus me fallit animus) juxta mecum sentiet.

It must be here noted that M[r]. *Milles* (the same I mean that has his Name to S[t]. *Cyrill*) soon after the last Act that was celebrated in *Oxon* in 1703 writt a Letter to M[rs]. *Brace-Girdle* (one of the Actresses) giving her great Encomiums (as having himself been often to see Plays Acted whilst they continued here) upon Account of her Excell[t] Qualifications, & persuading her to give over this loose way of Living and betake her self to such a Kind of Life as was more innocent and would gain her more Credit. W[t] Effects this Letter had I cannot tell; tho' I believe it did not answer his Design, it being certain she continu'd the same Course of Life afterwards.

Nov. 24 (Sat.). The D. of *Argyle's* Titles are settled, and he is to be Baron of *Chatham* and Earle of *Greenwich.* — M[r]. *Addison* has just publish'd *Travells through some Parts of* Italy in 1701, 1702, 1703. — In the 16 of E. 3. S[r]. John *Trussell*[1] wrote himself of *Acton* & his Brother *Will.* of *Cublesdon*; & bore for his Armes *Or frettè gules, with a Besant on each joynt of ye Frettè,* & for his *Crest an Asses Head couped, issuing out of a Coronet.*

Epitaphs in Whitewaltham Church, in *Berks,* as M[r]. *Ashmole* took y[m] ab[t] ye year 1660. [242–246.] . . .

Errour non-plust, or D[r]. *Stillingfleet* shown to be ye Man of no Principles. 1673. The Author M[r]. *Serjeant.* — Patronus Bonæ Fidei, in causa Puritanorum, contra Hereticos Anglos. 1672. 8⁰. The Author *Lewis du Moulin,* the Physitian, who was imprison'd for publishing this Book, but set at Liberty a few days after. — . . . Observations upon a Treatise entituled *Of Humane Reason. Lond.* 1675. 12⁰. The Author was M[r]. *Edw. Stephens* of *Glocestershire,* who has writ a great many other small Pieces, several of w[ch] are in y[e] *Bodlejan* Library. They are most very hard to be got, he printing them at his own Charge, & so having but a very few (sometimes not above 30 or 40) Copies. — An Account of D[r]. *Still.'s* late Book against the Church of Rome, &c. 1672. 8⁰. The Author was one Father *Canes* an *English* Man, and a *Franciscan* Frier, and was afterwards reprinted by him in a Pamphlett by him publish'd, with this Title : Τῷ Καθολικῷ Stillingfleeton, *or An Account given to a Catholick Friend,* &c. *Bruges* 1672, who also writ *Fiat lux.* This *Account* is the first p[t] of that Book, call'd Τῷ Καθ. &c. —

The Ancient Rites, and Monuments of the Monastical & cathedral Church of *Durham,* publish'd by *John Davies of Kidwelly. Lond.* 1672. 8⁰. Before the Copy in ye Publick Library B[p]. *Barlow* has put this Remark,

Liber hic omnino apocryphus, μυσαρᾶς &° legendæ putidæ plurimum, veræ Historiæ (praxi &° cultu monachorum superstitioso exceptis) parum habet; adeo ut

[1] *Dugd. H. of Warw-sh.* p. 538.

mirari subit inscitiam ejus qui condidit, imprudentiam ejus qui edidit, & ὰβλεψίαν & negligentiam (veritati & Ecclesiæ Anglicanæ damnosam) ejus qui prælo permisit.

— A Letter from M^r. *Ralph Thoresby* to M^r. *Llhuwyd* of the *Musæum.*

[1]Reverend Sir,

    I have not had the Satisfaction of a line from you of a long time, nor has anything occurr'd here worthy your notice, except you will please so to account of a late discovery of some *Roman* Coyns found at *Clifton* near *Edlington* 3 miles from *Doncaster*, the *Roman Danum*, where the *Præfectus Equitum* 10 *Crispinianorum* resided. They were found by some Labourers so near the High-way that the Cart-Tracks had almost bared the Top of the urn. Upon further search they found another *Theca Nummaria* both full of the *Roman* Copper Coyns, which were mostly of *Gallienus, Victorinus,* & of *Tetricus* & his Son, tho' there were some few also of *Salonina, Posthumus* & *Cuintilius*. Some of them appear very fair now y^t they are cleansed from the Rust contracted by lying so many Ages in the Earth. These tho' they have not added one Emperor, yet have made considerable Addition to ye Variety of Reverses in my Collection. So that I have now above 30 of *Gallienus* all different, one of his w^th *LIBERO Patri CONS.* AVG. & *Posthumus*'s COS. V. (wch my Edition 20 of *Occo* has not) are the most remarkable of any that have come to ye sight of

                        S^r, Your most humble Servt,

                                RALPH THORESBY.

Leedes, 19th *Nov^r.* 1705.

I have inclos'd one of them wch I beg your Acceptance of.

    At the same time he writ a Letter to M^r. *Cavendish Nevil* A.M. & Fellow of University Coll. wth two more of these Coyns; the first is of *Victorinus* wch has on the Reverse *VIRTVS AVG.* The other *Tetricus Cæs.* wch has on the Reverse *SPES AVG.* We have three of *Victorinus* the very same wth this M^r. *Thoresby* has sent, wch are thus 30 describ'd IMP. C. VICTORINVS P. F. AVG. Caput Radiatum. R. VIRTVS AVG. Statua Militaris stans, dextra Hastam, sinistra Clypeum. The *Tetricus* is *Tetricus Junior.* We have in the Pub. Library Eleven wch are the very same wth y^t of M^r. *Thoresby*'s wch he has sent to M^r. *Nevil.* The Description of wch follows, C. PIVESV. TETRICVS CAES. Caput radiatum. Reverse SPES AVGG. Dea spes. We have four in the Publick Library, wth LIBERO P. CONS. AVG. & the Best Edition of *Occo* has [*sic*] of them. We have likewise one of *Posthumus*, with cos. v. The Best Edition of *Occo* has y^t too. So y^t I do not look upon M^r. *Thoresby's* Collection relating to the Thirty Tyrants of any Extraordinary value. — *Antiquitas Theo-* 40 *logica & Gentilis.* Or, Two Discourses, the first, conc. ye Original of Churches, & their Direct or Collateral Endowments. The second, Touching the Religion of the Gentiles, their Temples, Priests, &c. *Lond.* 1670. 8°. The B^p. of *Lincoln* (D^r. *Barlow*) in the Copy in the Publick Library has made this note:

Est hic Codex, (si vel molem vel virtutem spectes) vere libellulus: in quo nec perorat probe Auctor, nec disputat. Antiquitatem crepat, sed ignorat. Omnia hic, si rationem spectes, invalida, confusa si methodum παροράματα (ex incuria aut inscitia) multa occurrunt. Adeo ut emendo pecuniam, legendo operam perdidi. Hæc volebam (Lector) nescius ne esses; indicavi scopulum, ut tibi caveas & naufragium 50 *fugias; ut infortunio meo doctus, sine pecuniæ & operæ dispendio sapias. Vale.* —

    Catholicks no Idolaters. 1672. 8°. The Author was *T. Godwin* (or *Godden,* 'tis an assumed Name) an *English* and *Cambridge Man*; Confessor

         [1] He is not in orders.

or (at least) Preist or Chaplaine to Queen *Catharine.* D^r. *Barlow* was told his Name was *Tilden.* M^r. *Thorndike* (who is cited in the Title Page) left this for his Epitaph. *Hic jacet Corpus Herberti Thornedike Prebendarij hujus Ecclesiæ, qui vivus veram Reformatæ Ecclesiæ rationem & modum precibus studijsque prosequebatur. Tu Lector requiem ei & beatam in Christo resurrectionem precare.* — Flavij Josephi de Jesu Dom. Testimonium suppositum esse Tanaquilli Fabri Diatriba. 1654. 8º. Tis judiciously & learnedly Answered by *Hen. Valesius* in his notes to *Eusebius's* Hist. lib. i. cap. ii. p. 20. Col. 1. c. 2. A. — M^r. *Thoresby* is now Writing *The Antiquities of Leeds.* 10

[Notes on Livy from Voss. Observatt. ad P. Melam, lib. III. c. 1, and Tennulij Not. in Jamblichum, p. 157.]

In ye Press now at *Camb.* M^r. *Whiston's Essay or an Exposition of ye Revelations. The B^p. of Worcester is an Assistant.* S^r. Isaac Newton's Algebra, D^r. Bentley's Horace not to be finish'd till X^tmass come twelvemonth. — *Fontana* has writ a Treatise on *Vespasian's* Amphitheatre, who is now esteem'd one of ye Best of y^e *Roman* Architects. This Piece wⁿ M^r. *Addison* was at *Rome* was unpublish'd : but I cannot tell whether it be come out since. — M^r. *Oddy* of *Cambridge* is upon *Dion Cassius*, & 20 designs to come to *Oxon* next Summer, wth an Intent, I suppose, to look after materials. Tho' I believe his Design to publish this Author will come to nothing, his character being not extraordinary for publishing Authors that I hear of.

Nov. 25 (Sun.). In the Reign of King *James*, D^r. *Plot* upon ye Decease of D^r. *James* Warden of *All-Souls* Col. made Application to the Earl of *Peterborough* & S^r. *Edw. Hales*, (who had then a great Influence upon ye King) to be Warden of ye said College ; but M^r. *Leopold* (*William*) (afterw^{ds} D^r.) *Finch* got ye start of him, & had ye Place conferr'd upon him before D^r. *Plot's* Friends knew of his Intention to move for y^t Place. 30 This said *Finch* who had so great obligations to King *James* was one of those Heads of Colleges in *Oxon* who sign'd an Association to stand by the Prince of *Orange;* & 'tis moreover credibly reported that he was one of ye three or 4 Heads who intended if they could have prevail'd wth Colleges to deliver up all the College Plate to ye said Prince, in order to be imploy'd against their undoubted L^d. and Soveraign King *James*, who had not at y^t time left *England.* D^r. *Ironside* happen'd then to be Vice-Chancellor of *Oxford*, who was a great stickler for this Prince purposely as 'twas generally believ'd that he might get a Wife & a B^{pp}rick, wch he did not long after. This said D^r. before ever King *William* had any pre- 40 tended Right to ye Crowne from ye Convention administred ye Oath of Allegiance to King *William* in the Congre[g]ation House at *Oxford*: which particular I had from a worthy Person, who had it from the Mouth of M^r. *Bingham* of University, who was at y^t very time admitted to a Degree. The foresaid Warden stood in Competition wth ye Learned M^r. *Dodwell* to be *Cambden's* Reader of History, & upon his Disappointment was so inrag'd that he turn'd *Jonas* Proast (a Worthy Learned Conscientious man) out from being Chaplain of *All-Souls* because he honestly voted for M^r. *Dodwell.* Upon wch M^r. *Proast* appeal'd to D^r. *Tillotson*, Archb^p. of *Canterbury*, & visitor of this Coll., who was very dilatory in doing him 50

Justice. When D^r. *Levins* President of S^t. *John's* & *Greek* Professor in this university died, D^r. *Hudson* had certainly succeeded him in ye s^d Professorship if ye B^p. of *Sarum*, D^r. *Burnett*, had not us'd this Argument for D^r. *Humph. Hody* to King *William*; That he had writt for ye Government, & y^t ye other Person (D^r. *Hudson*) was rather suspected to be no Friend to it. — In King *William's* time when ye Disposal of Ecclesiastical Power was in ye Hands of Commissioners, these said Commissioners were so far from Gratifying any but y^{e}ir own Creatures, & Army Chaplains, & Persons related to Officers in the Army, y^t 'twas next to an impossibility for any
10 man of worth to get any Thing. An Instance of this is the above mention'd D^r. *Hudson* who having many Promises from most of the Bishops in Commission was yet shamefully postpon'd by them: For when the Parsonage of *Green-Norton*, in *Northamptonshire* became void, the D^r. having very timely notice from a Friend of his in y^t Neighbourhood, went to *London* wth great Expedition and made his Application to ye B^{ps}, several Days, before one Collonel *Woods* heard of it, who prevail'd with ye Commissioners to confer it (to their Eternal Dishonour) upon a Brother of his, an ignorant, illiterate Fellow, who (as 'tis s^d) was a Broken Shopkeeper, & never saw an University. — M^r. *Harrington* of X^t Church (a
20 Barrister of Law) writ the second Preface (the first being done by the Author himself) to the first Volume of *Athenæ Oxon.* He also writ the Preface to the II^d Volume. — By ye Death of ye said *Harrington* Christ Church lost a 1000 lib^s. that he was intrusted to Receive from the Executors of D^r. *Wood*, B^p. of *Lichfield*, who left 2000 lib^s. to the Senior Students Table, and 2000 lib^s. to the Juniors. The Seniors got theirs & laid it out in Land, & now enjoy the Benefit of it. The Juniors intirely lost theirs, the Executors refusing to pay the last 1000 lib^s. unless they would make good that wch was lost by M^r. *Harrington*. — In ye latter End of B^p. *Fell's* time there was of *X^t Church* one M^r. *Bennett* (Bro. to the Bookseller)
30 who apply'd himself to the Study of Physick, & 'tis suppos'd he would have been a Man very Eminent in y^t Faculty, if he had enjoy'd a longer Life. This Person examin'd by D^r. *Hudson* for his Master of Arts Degree. — W^{ch} D^r. *H.* when he was Master of Arts was Prior-Opponent in ye Divinity Schoole, M^r. *Entwistle* of Brasennose College being respondent. The Question was, *An Christus satisfecerit pro Peccatis mundi?* M^r. *H.* after an Elegant opposition Speech oppos'd with so much Clearness & Subtility y^t he rais'd ye Admiration of ye Professor & the Auditors. — M^r. *Beurdsall* of *Brassennose* College a little before he died was married to one M^{rs}. *Middleton*; but never bedded her, as she
40 and her mother declar'd, he upon his Death own'd his marriage & left her w^t he had, wch was about ye value of 2 or 300 *lib^s*. — When the Lower House of Convocation were order'd by the B^{ps} to assent to the Address to her Majesty of their drawing up, or else give Reasons why they dissented from it. The Lower House instead of giving Reasons for their Dissent drew up Reasons why they should give none. — D^r. *Wills* of Trinity Coll. publish'd an Assize Sermon. He was look'd upon as one of ye best Preachers in the University of his time. He married a Daughter of S^r. *Will. Walker's*, who being Mayor of *Oxford* was Knighted by King *James* at his first Accession to ye Crown as is usual for the Mayors of
50 *Oxon* to be. He left behind him several Sermons in MS^t & divers other

Treatises, wch are now in the Hands of his Son now of *Trinity* Col. aforesaid.

Nov. 26 (Mon.). On Friday the Report being made to ye H. of Commons from ye Committee conc. the *S^t. Albans* Election, it was carried ag^t *Gape* in favour of S^r. *Hen. Killigrew* by a great Majority. — The House of L^ds have agreed to Thank her Majesty for her Care of a Union w^th *Scotland*, & confirming the Succession of the House of *Hannover*. They have order'd a Bill to be drawn up for Repealing all the Clauses pass'd the last Sessions relating to *Scotland*, except that for a Union. —   10

A Discourse of ye Nature, Offices & Measures of Friendship &c. *Lond.* 1657. 12°. The Author B^p. (*Jer.*) *Taylor.*—The Modern Pleas for Comprehension, Toleration, &c. *Lond.* 1675. 8°. Written by D^r. *Tomkins*, Domestick Chaplain to the Archb^p. of *Cant.*— . . . D^r. Stillingfleet still ag^t D^r. Stillingfleet. 1675. 8°. The Author *J. Wolsey.*—The Prerogative of Humane Nature. By *G. H.* Gent. *Lond.* 1653. 8°. By *H.* must be understood one M^r. *Holland*, a *Cambridge* Man, & afterwards a *Romish* Priest. He is the same Person y^t answer'd my L^d. Vicount *Faulkland's* Treatise *de Infallibilitate*, wch was Reply'd to in a most Excell^t Learned Postumous Piece by that noble L^d. —Schism Disarm'd, By *S. W.* (it should be *W. S.*, i.e. *William Serjeant*). 20 *Paris* 1655. 8°.—A short Discourse of ye Truth & Reasonableness of the Religion delivered by *Jesus X^t. Lond.* 1662. 8°. The Author said to be S^r. *Hen. Yelverton.*—An Endeavour to Rectify some Prevailing Opinions contrary to ye Doctrine of ye Ch. of England. By ye Author of *A Discourse of Natural & Moral Impotency.* He was M^r. *Trueman* a Minister and a Non-Conformist. The Book was pr. at *Lond.* 1671. 8°.—The Nature, Power, Deceit, & Prevalency of the Remainders of Indwelling-Sin in Believers. *Lond.* 1668. 8°. The Author D^r. *Owen.*

The Conforming Non-Conformist & the Non-Conforming Conformist pleading the Cause of either side against violent opposers &c. *Lond.* 1680. By *J. C.* He was a minister in *Lancashire* at *Warrington*, which 30 he left by reason of some Dissatisfaction wth the Termes of Conformity, & our New Liturgy. Having left his living, he sett himself seriously to study the point, & to examin all the Reasons he could get *pro* or *con* both for and against Conformity : and at last, was satisfy'd (and that after long study) that he might conform, *salva conscientia*; & then he writ this Book to justify himself, & give ye Reasons of his Conforming, &c. — When D^r. *Hall* Master of *Pembrook* Col. & *Margaret* Professor of Divinity was made B^p. of *Bristol*, D^r. *Maurice*, a Man of Excell^t Learning was chosen to succeed him ; he enjoying this Place but a little time, by Reason of his Death, D^r. *Sikes* of *Trinity* Col. by 40 a Corrupt Intere[s]t amongst ye Electors got ye Place from the famous D^r. *Bull* (now B^p. of S^t. *Davids*). This D^r. *Sikes* is so dull[1] a Reader,

---

Nov. 26. H. to F. Cherry. Thanks for draught of coin of Amyntas. Sends remarks and queries on Inscriptions in Prideaux *Marm. Oxon.*, p. 270. Sends a copy of the epitaphs, &c. in Shottesbrooke Church, as transcribed by Ashmole, with notes and queries. Note on a letter from Mr. T. Wilkinson, Minister of Lawrence Waltham, to Ashmole, on a brass discovered in that church.

---

[1] This Dullness was only in his old Age not when he was a young Man. See the following Volume.

stuffing his Lectures wth nothing but long Quotations out of *Fathers*, that after a few Lectures he could get no Hearers, & so makes ye Place in a manner a *sine-cure*, as most other Publick Readers do, by reason of *De-Laune* who is now in the fourth year of his Vice-Chancellorship, & has hardly been once at any Publick Exercise except ye Bodlejan Speech, wch he could not avoid being present at. This same *De Laune* was made President of S^t. *John*'s Col. after the Death of D^r. *Will. Levins*, upon ye Account of his supposed Riches, some Relation of his having left him a vast sum of Money, which as 'tis reported he squander'd
10 away in shaking his Elbow; whence a certain *terræ Filius* in the Publick Act in 1703 beginning wth some Hesitation to speak something of ye Vice-Chancellor broke out with a Resolution to do it wth these words, *jacta est alea.* — M^r. *Milles* of *X^t Church* ab^t a year ago talk'd of Publishing *Synesius*, & began to collate some MSS^ts for that Design; but he presently after laid it aside, by reason the worm (wth wch he is possessed) mov'd in his head another way, or else because the Book-sellers were unwilling to have any thing more to do wth him. — In ye Edition of *Edm. Spenser*'s Works at *Lond.* in 1679. fol. there is a short Acc^t of his Life. —

20 The Countermine: or a Short but true Discovery of the dangerous Prin-ciples, & secret Practises of ye Dissenting Party &c. *Lond.* 1677. 8°. The Author *John Nalson.*—A Letter of a Gentleman to his Friend, shewing y^t ye B^ps are not to be Judges in Parliam^t in Cases Capital. 1679. The L^d. *Hollis* Author.—Divine Dialogues, in two Volumes. *Lond.* 1668. 8°. The Author D^r. *Hen. More.*—Contemplations Moral and Divine. *Lond.* 1675. 8°. The Author was Judge *Hale*, & they were published by his Intimate Friend M^r. *Edw. Stephens*, a Lawyer (and now a Divine) who likewise writ ye Preface to them.—A Discourse conc. Evangelical Love &c. *Lond.* 1672. 8°. The Author D^r. *Owen.*—Artis Logicæ Compendium. *Oxon.* 1696. It has been
30 reprinted. The Author was D^r. *Aldrich* Dean of *X^t Church. Oxon.*— . . . . *Ecclesiastica Methermeneutica*, or Church-Cases cleared. *Lond.* 1652. The Author D. N. *Homes.*—A Brief History of ye Unitarians, called Socinians. 1687. 8°. Neither ye Author nor printers Names are to it; because the Author was a *Socinian.* D^r. *Barlow* was assured y^t they were written by one M^r. *Firmyn*, a Lay-Man, and a *London* Merchant, at least that he own'd them. —Elenchus Motuum &c. was written by D^r. *Bates*, first of *Queen's* Col. *Oxon.* afterwards of *Edm. Hall* and at length of ye College of Physitians at *London.* —The state of *France* as it stood in ye IXth Year of this present Monarch *Lewis* XIIII. *Lond.* 1652. 8°. The Author M^r. *John Evelyn.*—The Funeral
40 of the Mass, &c. *Lond.* 1673. The Author was *David Derodon* (who also writt Logick, Phys. & Metaphys.) & 'twas translated out of *French.* An Answer to it came out at *London* 1675, with this Title, *Missa Triumphans, wherein all the Sophistical Arguments of M^r. Derodon in his Funeral of ye Mass are fully answered by* F. P. M. O. P. Hib. 'Tis in 8°. But the Author subscribes his Epistles Dedicatory to the Queen, & Dutchess of *Yorke*, with these 2 Letters, C. W.—A Sober Enquiry into the Nature, Measure & Principle of Moral virtue, &c. by R. F. i.e. *Fergeson* a Scotch Man. *Lond.* 1673. 8°.—Several Conferences betw. a *Romish* Priest, a Fanatick Chaplain & a Divine &c. *Lond.* 1679. 8°. The Author D^r. Stillingfleet.

50 **Nov. 27 (Tu.).** A Private Conference between a Rich Alderman & a poor Country Vicar &c. *Lond.* 1670. 8°. D^r. *Barlow* was inform'd (by a Person of Quality who should know) that D^r. *Pittis* Minister of *Holy-Roodes* in *Southampton*, was ye Author of this Conference: who

having had some Contests with some of y⁰ Aldermen there, the Discourses between them and him, are here represented, little to their Advantage. So y⁺ D⁺. *Pittis* is y⁰ *Vicar,* & by the *rich Alderman,* one or more of y⁰ Aldermen of *Southampton* are meant. —

Truth and Innocence Vindicated &c. 1669. 8⁰.   The Author D⁺. *Owen.—* A Peaceable Resolution of Conscience touching our present Impositions. *Lond.* 1680. 8⁰.   The Author M⁺. *Humphrey,* a Non-Conformist Minister.— *Erastus Senior,* Scholastically Demonstrating, that (admitting their *Lambeth* Records for true) those call'd *Bishops* here in *England,* are no Bishops &c. 1662.   The Author *Joh. Lewgar.—*The Rule of Catholick Faith, translated 10 into *English* by *E. S.* (i.e. *Edw. Sheldon*) Esq.   *Paris,* 1660. 8⁰.—A General Draught & Prospect of Government in Europe, And Civil Policy. *Lond.* 1681. The Author M⁺. *Rimer* of *Gray's* Inn.—A Discourse concerning Supreme Power and Comon Right. *Lond.* 1680. 8⁰.   The Author S⁺. John *Monson* of *Lincolnshire.*— . . . The History of y⁰ *English* & *Scotch* Presbytery. 1659. 8⁰. Written, as D⁺. *Barlow* believ'd, by D⁺. *Isaac Basire.* —

Authors that have writ of *Mystical Divinity* :

And. de Azitores Theologia Symbolica S. Hieroglyphica pro totius SS. Comment. *Salm.* 4. 1597.   (2) *Vinc. Caraffæ* Thcol. Mystica. *Col.* 8⁰. 1660. (3) *Nic. Eschij* Exercitia Theologiæ Mysticæ. *Col.* 12. 1676.   (4) *Vict. Geleni* 20 Summa practica Theol. Mysticæ. *Col.* 4. 1646.   (5) *J. Jac. Grafti* Speculum Theol. Mysticæ. *Argent.* 8⁰. 1618.   (6) *Honr. Harphij (Herpij) Mechlin.* Lib. III. Theol. Mysticæ. *Paris.* 4⁰. 1580.   *Brixiæ* 1601.   *Colon.* 1612. 4. *Car. Harsentius* in *Dionys. Areopagitam* de Mystica Theologia.   *Par.* 8. 1626.   *Brixiæ,* 1601 & 1644.   (8) *Chr. Hoburgi* Theol. Mystica.   *Amst.* 8. 1656.   (9) *Hugonis de Palma* Theologia Mystica.   *Amst.* 12.   1649.   (10) *Maximil. Sandæi* Theologia Mystica cleric. *Colon.* 4⁰.   1623.   1640.   (11) *Aloysij Siderei* Theologia Mystica. *Col.* 8.   1660.   (12) *Joh. Theophili* Theol. Mystica. *Ludg.* 16.   1580.   *Phil. à SS. Trinitate* Theol. mystica. *Lugd. f.* —

Julian the Apostate : Being a short Account of his Life &c. *Lond.* 1682, &c. 30 The Author *Sam. Johnson,* who had a living in *Essex,* & from writing this Book wch has made a great Noise in y⁰ World, & has been excellently well answer'd by the most Learned D⁺. *George Hickes,* was, to his dying day, commonly called *Julian Johnson.—*A full and clear Answer to a Book written by *W^m. Petit* Esq⁺, pr. in y⁰ year 1680.   By wch it appears y⁺ he hath mistaken the Meaning of y⁰ Histories & Records he hath cited &c. *Lond.* 1681.   The Author D⁺. *Brady* of *Cambridge.—*The Prodigal Return'd home ; or the Motives of y⁰ Conversion to y⁰ Catholick Faith of *E. L.* Master of Arts in y⁰ University of *Cambridge.* 1684. 8⁰.   The Author of this Book was *E. Lydiott,* Fellow of King's Coll. in *Cambridge,* who travell'd wth y⁰ Earl of *Castlemaine,* was turn'd 40 out of his College, turn'd Papist, and (as B⁺. *Barlow* was inform'd) had a Pension allow'd him by the said Earle.— . . . Of Scandal &c. *Lond.* 1680. 8⁰.   M⁺. *Alsop,* a Non-Conformist Minister, y⁰ Author.—Apologia pro Ministris in Anglia (vulgò) Non-Conformistis. Eleutheropoli. 8⁰.   The Author *Hen. Hickman* of *Magd.* Coll.—*J. G.* (i.e. Jacobus *Greimesius* Montissosanus Marchio) De rebus Auspicijs Serenissimi & Potentissimi Caroli Magnæ Britanniæ Franciæ & Hib. Regis. 1647. 8⁰.   This was Extracted from the Marquiss of *Montross's* own Diary written by himself in *English* & translated into good *Latin* by *Geo. Wisehart,* whose name is not to it, onely these Letters *A. S.* nor is the Place where 'twas printed added ; but 'tis certain that was y⁰ *Hague.*—De Augustini 50 Doctrina, & Tridentina Synodo Dissertatio Posterior. *Par.* 1650. 8⁰.   The Author *Dionys. Petavius.—*Advice to a Son.   *Oxon.* 1656 &c.   The Author *Franc. Osborne* a Lay-Gentleman & an old Atheistical Courtier.   His Son was Fellow of *All-Souls* Coll. w^n this Book was writ.—Lactantius cum Notis var. *Lugd. Bat.* 1660. 8⁰. . .—An Essay in Morality. *Lond.* 1682. 12⁰.   This Book was convey'd & came to D⁺. *Barlow's* Hands by M⁺. *John Wright* (unknown to him) *Nov. 12. 1681*, who told him y^t D^r. *George Bright* (there being only G. B. express'd in the Title-Page) was ye Author of it, who going into *Holland* the Week before to wait on ye Princess of *Orange* by my L^d. of *London's* Order left this Book to be convey'd to him. . . —

Tho. Fermin above mention'd a ranck *Socinian* was a great Man wth D^r. *Tillotson* Archb^p. of *Cant.* & others of ye same Leaven promoted by K. *William* to some of the best Dignities & Preferm^{ts}. — *Rob. Ferguson* the *Scotchman* has been in all Plots from that of y^e *Rye-House* to this day; & 'tis suppos'd that he is a Jesuit in Disguise. — The Low^r H. of Convocation's Address to ye Queen. [303–307.] . . . D^r. Smalrige, M^r. Needham & M^r. Kimberley made Speeches in the Lower H. of Convocation of ab^t a Quarter of an Hour long each, shewing y^t ye Church was in Danger, wch forc'd those of ye contrary side to acknowledge it, & thereupon they declar'd that the B^{ps}. in their Address did not mean y^t the Ch. was in no Danger in general, but y^t 'twas not in danger from ye present Ministry, as a virulent Pamphlett (s^d D^r. Kennett) call'd ye Memorial & had insinuated, from wch Imputation he thought ye Clergy ought to free themselves by Detesting y^t Book, or to y^t Effect. — My L^d. Haversham has made another Speech, wherein amongst other things (the Q. & Dutchess of *Marlborough* being present) he told them that a certain L^d. told King *James* 1st that his Ear was besieg'd by the Duke of *Bucks*, And he thought he had as good reason to believe y^t the Queen's Ear was besieg'd : and he farther s^d he had ye Person (meaning ye Dutchess of *Marlborough*) in his Eye by whom ye Queen's Ear was besieg'd. — *The Display of Heraldry*, wch goes under ye Name of *John Guillim* (and whereof there have been very many Editions, wth Improvem^{ts} by other men, much to the Discredit of ye Book) was really written by *John Barcham*, of *Corpus X^{ti}* Coll. who gave it M^r. *Guillim*, by whom there were some inconsiderable Additions made.

Nov. 28 (Wed.). The Royal Charter granted unto Kings by God himself. *Lond.* 1649. The Author D^r. *Tho. Browne*, Prebend of *Windsor*, sometime Student of *X^t Church Oxon.* — *Memorandum* That there are a great many small Books in 8°. of 1^s. or something more price, said to be written by *Richard Burton* in y^e *Title Page, such as The Wars in England, Scotland, & Ireland; England's Rarities; Wonderfull Prodigies of Judgment & Mercy.* These Books bear a feign'd name, being really scribl'd by *Nath. Crouch* ye Printer, from *Wanley's* (Father to *Humphrey Wanley*) History of Man, *Beard's* Theatre &c. — . . .

A Short view of ye Life & Reign of K. *Charles* (ye 2^d Monarch of *Great Britain*) from his Birth to his Burial. *Lond.* 1658. 8°. The Author D^r. *Heylin.* —The Heart it's Right Sovereign. *Lond.* 1678. 8°. The Author *T. J.* i.e. *Tho. Jones* of *Oswestry* in ye County of Salop, sometime Domestick & Naval Chaplain to his Royal Highness ye D. of *Yorke.*—The Novelty of ye Modern *Romish* Religion. *Lond.* 1682. 8°. The Author *S. F.* i.e. *Sam. Felgate* M.A. & Vicar of *Milton* in *Craven.*—Schism unmaskt; or, a late Conference between M^r. *Peter Gunning* & M^r. *John Pierson* Ministers, on ye one part, & two Disputants of y^e *Roman* Profession on the other : wherein is defined both what Schism is, & to whom it belongs. *Par.* 1658. 8°. B^p. *Barlow* was told at

---

Nov. 28. Hoffman to H. Complimentary letter in Latin, introducing *Schmidius.*

first, that *Tho. White* (Author of *a Letter to a person of Honour in Vindication of Himself & His Doctrine*—1659. 8°) was he who did principally manage, & put out this Disputation.   But afterwards he was assured by D͏ʳ. *Breton* master of *Emanuel* Col. in *Cambridge* that his Name was *Spenser*, (who was the same yᵗ answered Archbᵖ. *Laud's* Book) & yᵗ Dʳ. *Lentall* was his Associate.   He was first of *Xᵗˢ* Coll. in *Cambridge*, then fellow of *Pembrooke*-Hall, a Preacher & in Orders ; then turn'd Papist, would have profess'd Civil Law, but his superiors made him professe Physick.—*Alphonsi de Vargas Toletani Relatio ad Reges & Principes Christianos, De Stratagematis & Sophismatis Politicis Societatis Jesu ad Monarchiam Orbis terrarum sibi conficiendam*. 1642. 12°.   There 10 were two Editions before this, viz. in 1636. & 1641.   *Hermannus Cingallus* (in tract. cui tit. *Scriptura S. Trinitatis Revelatrix*, Goudæ 1678. pag. 68. ex Sandio) thinks yᵗ *Casp. Scioppius* was Author of this Book.—*Iter Boreale* &c. *Lond.* 1660.   By a Rural Pen. i.e. M͏ʳ. *Wild* a Presbyterian then Rector of *Ayno* in yᵉ County of *Northampton*, the Place wᶜʰ Dʳ. *Hutten* the Antiquary now has.—.. *A Blow at Modern Sadducism in some Philosophical Considerations abᵗ Witchcraft* &c.   *Lond.* 1668. 8°.   The Author was *Jos. Glanvill*, who afterwards enlarged it very much.—*The Harmony of Natural & Positive Divine Laws. Lond.* 1682. 8°.   The Author *Walter Charleton.*—*Vade Mecum*, Or a Manual of Essays Moral, Theological. *Lond.* 1629. 12°.   The Author 20 *Daniel Tuuil* minister.—*Anti-Sozzo sive Sherlocismus Enervatus* &c.   *Lond.* 1675.   The Author M͏ʳ. *Alsop* a Nonconformist Minister in *Northampton-shire.* ▪

Flosculi Historici delibati nunc delibatiores redditi.   Sive Historia Universalis tam sacra quam prophana Rerum memorabilium, tam pace quam bello gestarum, usque ad Annum 1656. 8°. *Oxon.* 1663.   Editio quinta.   This Book compiled by *Joh. de Bussieres*, a Papist & a *French-man*, was brought to Dʳ. *Baylie* President of Sᵗ. *John's* and Vice-Chancellor of *Oxon. An.* 1663. by M͏ʳ. Will *Wyatt*, B.D. of yᵗ House ; who said he had read it, & assured the vice-chancellor, that it was innocent, 30 & had nothing prejudicial to yᵉ Church of *England*, (licet πᾶν τοὐναντίον), & yᵗ it was M͏ʳ. *Levins* of Sᵗ. *Johns* who made yᵉ *Appendicula*.   M͏ʳ. Vice-Chancellor read yᵉ *Appendicula*, and being inform'd by M͏ʳ. *Wyatt*, yᵗ yᵉ whole Booke (like yᵗ *Appendicula*) was innocent, he licenced it. ▪

The Great Propitiation or Xᵗˢ Satisfaction & Man's Justification by it, upon his Faith &c.   *Lond.* 1669. 8°.   The Author M͏ʳ. *Trueman* a Nonconformist Minister who dyed in 1671.—*The Authority of yᵉ Magistrate about Religion discussed* &c. by *J. H.* i.e. *John Humfreys* a Non-Conformist Minister. *Lond.* 1672. 8°.—*Vindiciarum Catholicorum Hiberniæ Authore Philopatro Irenæo ad Alitophilum libri duo. Par.* 1650. 8°.   The true Author's name was *Gallaghan*, 40 a *Sorbon* Doctor & Jansenist.   The 2ᵈ Part is written agᵗ a Book the author whereof was one *Kinge* a *Franciscan*.—*Questions propounded for Resolution of unlearned Protestants. Par.* 1652. 8°.   The Author was one *Spencer* a *Lincolnshire* Man & a *Jesuit*.—*Satyræ duæ Hercules tuam fidem sive Mun-sterus Hypobolimæus & Virgula divina. Lugd. Bat.* 1617.   The Author was *Jos. Scaliger.*—*Paraphrasis cum Annotatis ad Difficiliora loca Catechismi An-glicani.   In Lat. & English.* 1674. 8°.   The Author *Willᵐ. White.*

No sacrilege nor sinne to aliene or purchase yᵉ Lands of Bᵖˢ., or others whose Offices are abolished. *Lond.* 1659. 8°.   By *C. B.* i.e. 50 Cornelius Burges, D.D.   This *Cornelius Burges* was a fierce Presby-terian, a great Stickler for the Parliament against yᵉ King & Brˢ., *Anno* 1644.   Afterwards he bought good Store of Church Lands, especially Lands belonging to yᵉ Church of *Wells*; where he had, & built (or

rebuilt) the Dean of *Welles* his House, at yᵉ Expense of 1500 or 2000 lib.
He was bid for his Purchase, not long before yᵉ King's Returne (wᶜʰ
was Anno 1660) about 20000 *lib⁵.* but refused it; And yᵉ King un-
expectedly (to him) returning in yᵉ said year 1660. & Bishops & Deans
being restored, he lost all his purchased Church-Lands, & became so
poor (*ingens Justitiæ Divinæ documentum*) that he had not Bread to eat;
as appears by his own Letter to Sʳ. *Rich. Browne*, extant in Dʳ. *Isaac
Basire's* Book call'd *Sacrilcdge-arraign'd* &c. *Lond.* 1668. pag. 22. of
yᵉ Preface. — One Mʳ. Dale, belonging to yᵉ *Herald's* Office told Dr.
10 *Hudson* that the first Edition of *Guillim's Heraldry* is much yᵉ best, yᵉ
rest having been almost spoyl'd by ignorant Persons taking care of
it. — Dʳ. *South* told Dʳ. *Hudson* yᵗ he was resolv'd never to pocket
a Farthing of yᵉ Income of yᵉ Parsonage of Islip, & yᵗ he had already
new built & beautified yᵉ Chancel of yᵉ Church, built a noble Parsonage
House wᵗʰ out Houses & other Conveniences both for yᵉ Parson and yᵉ
Tennant; and yᵗ besides he had all along put several Boys to schole
& bound them out to Apprentiships, & has lately purchas'd some Land
to be settled upon yᵉ Parish for ever for these Uses. And yᵗ moreover
he intended to lay out wᵗ he had receiv'd from his Canonry of *Xᵗ Church*
20 upon small vicarages, & as Dʳ. *Hudson* infer'd from something in his
Discourse upon such Vicaridges as belong'd to *Xᵗ Church.* — When
K. *James's* Declaration was to be read in all Churches & Chapells Mʳ.
Ob. Walker order'd yᵉ Bible Clerck of University Col. to give it to yᵗ
Fellow of yᵉ College yᵗ should read Prayers that Morning. Upon this
the Bible-Clerck went to most of yᵉ Fellows then in Town to acquaint
them wᵗʰ this, but none of them but Mʳ. *Hudson* would read Prayers,
who ventur'd to read them wᵗʰout taking any Notice of yᵉ Declaration.
wᶜʰ Mʳ. *Walker* did not at all seem to resent, as People imagin'd yᵗ he
would do. — A little after Mʳ. *Hudson* was chosen Fellow of University
30 College, Mʳ. *Walker* contriv'd the matter so yᵗ he and one Mʳ. *Deane*
a *Popish* Fellow were to go to make an Election of a Scholar at *Maidstone.* In the Coach yᵗ carried yᵐ to London, it happened that all yᵉ
Company were Papists but Mʳ. *Hudson* and Mʳ. Alderman *Wright.* So
yᵗ Disputes arising Mʳ. *Hudson* was forc'd to maintain yᵉ Protestant
Cause against them all, the Alderman (though there were Disputations
all yᵉ way for two Dayes) saying not one word, but keeping silence as
he us'd to do in yᵉ House of Commons, yet afterwards frequently expressing his good Opinion of yᵉ sᵈ Mʳ. *Hudson* for his Noble Defence.
When they got to *London* Mʳ. *Hudson* was attack'd by one Mʳ. *Nicholson*
40 (formerly one of University Coll.) & reputed one of yᵉ Ablest Champions
for yᵉ *Roman* Catholick Cause. When his Arguments would not do,
the sᵈ Mʳ. *Nicholson* brought Mʳ. *Hudson* a Message the next day from
Sʳ. *Edw. Hales*, Lᵈ. Lieut. of yᵉ Tower that he was to dine wᵗʰ his
Lᵈship, and afterwards to be conducted to yᵉ King to Kiss his Hand,
wᵗʰ Assurance yᵗ yᵉ said Mʳ. *Hudson* should be preferr'd, if he would
not act (i. e. neither preach nor talk) anything against yᵉ King's Religion,
but be moderate as yᵉ Phrase was then. This Offer he refus'd, upon
several Accounts, and, as he told Mʳ. *Nicholson*, particularly to avoid
yᵉ Imputation of Popery yᵗ would be thrown upon him if it were observ'd
50 yᵗ he was introduc'd to yᵉ King. — 'Tis said that upon the Bᵖ. of

Worcester's waiting upon yᵉ Dutchess of *Marlborough*, at his coming to *London*, she was pleas'd to ask him abᵗ yᵉ news at *Oxford* & to declare her Resentment for the Members of yᵗ University's being so hot in relation to yᵉ present Administration of Affairs. The Bᵖ. acknowledg'd yᵗ generally they were very faulty, but yᵗ there were some still left in yᵗ place who were men of Prudence, & spoke well of King *William*'s Government, & instanc'd particularly in Mʳ. *Evans*'s Sermon, wᶜʰ he said was a very rational Discourse, & shew'd him to be a good principl'd man, & to have a great Esteem for his late Majesty, he speaking mightily in his Commendation, & magnifying the Exploits of yᵉ Duke of *Marl-* 10 *borough*. wᶜʰ so pleas'd her Grace, yᵗ she presently order'd a good Fat Doe to be sent to Mʳ. *Evans* wherewith he was to treat the Warden of *Wadham* Coll. & such other Persons as he should think fit yᵗ were of yᵉ same Kidney wᵗʰ himself. wᶜʰ 'tis reported he has done. — The Queen having recᵈ per Express certain Information of yᵉ Surrender of *Barcelona*, she has been pleas'd to communicate yᵉ same to both Houses of Parliamᵗ, & to make a Speech to them (wᶜʰ is in print) declaring yᵗ 'twill be expedient for prosecuting Affairs to yᵉ best Advantage to send speedily a supply to yᵉ Earl of *Peterborough*, & desiring yᵗ they would not fail in yᵗ point. For wᶜʰ they have resolv'd upon an Address 20 of thanks, certifying yᵗ they will Gratify her out of Hand. — Mʳ. *Addison*'s Travells is a Book very trite, being made up of nothing but scraps of verses & things wᶜʰ have been observ'd over & over, wᵗʰout any Additions of things not discover'd before; & even some of those wᶜʰ he has inserted, yᵗ have been already taken notice of are ridiculous; tho' it must be acknowledg'd that the Book is written in a clean stile, & for yᵗ reason will please Novices, & superficial Readers.

Nov. 29 (Th.). . . . . Pharamus sive Libido vindex, Hispanica tragœdia. *Lond.* 1650. 8⁰. The Author *Tho. Snellinge* of Sᵗ. *Joh. Coll.*— .. Animadversions written by the Right Reverend Father in God *John*, Lᵈ. Bp. of Sarum, upon a Trea- 30 tise, entitled *God's Love to Mankind. Cambr.* 1641. The Authors of this Tract call'd *God's Love* &c. (to wᶜʰ this Book of Dʳ. *Davenant* Bp. of *Sarum* is an Answer) were Mʳ. *Mason*, & Mʳ. *Hoord*. So *Hen. Hickman* in His *Historia quinque Articularis exarticulata* (printed 1673.) pag. 379.— . . . Julius Secundus Dialogus Anonymi cujusdam Auctoris &c. *Oxon.* 1680. 8⁰. The Publisher was Mʳ. *Tho. Gilbert* A.M. of *Edm.* Hall.— . . . The true Nature of a Gospel Church. The Author believ'd by Bᵖ. *Barlow* to be Mʳ. Elys of *Devonshire*. 'Twas an-swer'd by Dʳ. Owen. in a Little piece publish'd at *Lond.* 1690. 8⁰.—A Catechism being an Enlargemᵗ of yᵉ Church Catechism, The Method alter'd &c. *Lond.* 1677. By *N. M.* i.e. *Mathew.*—An Appendix to yᵉ late Antidote against 40 Idolatry. *Lond.* 1673. 8⁰. The Author Dʳ. *Hen. More* of *Camb.*—An Exposi-tion on yᵉ Chu. Catechism or yᵉ Practise of Divine Love. *Lond.* 1685. The Author Bp. *Ken.*—The Irregularitie of a Private Prayer in a Publick Congre-gation. 1674. 8⁰. The Author Dʳ. *Rob. Sharrock* (as Bp. Barlow was credibly inform'd.) printed by Mʳ. *Lichfield* in *Oxon*, & it came to him from the D. of C. —Elenchus Elenchi : sive Animadversiones in Georgij Batei Elenchum mo-tuum &c. Autore *R. P.* i.e. *Pugh. Par.* 1664. 8⁰.—The Church Catechism wᵗʰ a Brief & Easie Explanation thereof &c. By *T. C.* i.e. *Tho. Comber*, D.D. *Lond.* 1681. 8⁰.—'Εκλόγαι : or, Excerpts from yᵉ Ecclesiastical History &c. *Lond.* 1704. 4⁰. The Author *Simon Lowth*, who also writ, *Historical Collections* 50 concerning *Church Affairs. Lond.* 1696. —

De Epochis Syromacedonum per *Hen. Noris. Lips.* 1696. 4⁰. . . In pag. 241 is a laudable Accᵗ of yᵉ Bᵖ. of *Worcester's* (*Lloyd*) Chronology.

In pag. 476 the Text of *Josephus* is explain'd. In this Book are likewise divers other Places of *Josephus* illustrated. At the End of this Book are *Fasti Consulares Anonymi Auctoris* à clariss. Norrisio è codice MS^to Bibliothecæ Cæsareæ editi, cum dissertatione luculentissima. . . .

Out of Monday's *Gazette.* Nov. 26.

Henry Chivers, of *Quemerford* in ye County of *Wilts*, Esqr having very often & in divers places publickly reported things dishonourable of ye L^d. Bishop of *Salisbury*, his Lordship brought against him an Action of *Scandalum Magnatum*, wch was appointed to be tryed on ye 30th day of this Instant
10 *November*; but his L^dship hath forgiven the said M^r. *Chivers*, & discharged the said Action, on his giving a Bond to pay 50*l*. to ye use of the Poor, signing a Paper in ye words following :—

> *November* 11th. 1705.
>
> I *Henry Chivers* have reported on many occasions, & in many Companies, that I wth some others had seen the Bishop of *Salisbury* in an infamous Place, & in a scandalous Deportment: I do declare it was groundless & false; for wch I humbly beg God & his Lordships Pardon ; & do consent that this be printed & published in w^t manner ye said B^p. shall think fit.
>
> HEN. CHIVERS.

20   Signed by the above-named *Henry Chivers*, in ye presence of
MICHAEL GEDDES, HEN. BLAAKE, JOHN HASKINS.

See pag. 361. of this Vol.

Salust corrected in *Giffanius*'s Index to *Lucretius* voc. *Effetus.* ▬ Remember to consult *Ludolf*'s Historia Æthiopica. There are sometime Authors mended in him. ▬ Ambrosij Camaldulensis Hodaporicon. I never saw it yet. He translated something of *Chrysostome.* *Quære* whether in ye Publick Library? ▬ *Witsij* Exercitationes in Symbolum Apostolorum. Quære ab^t it ? ▬ Petri Petiti Observationes Miscellaneæ to be lookt into. ▬ . . . In the 2^d Vol. of the *Acta Lips.* is an Acc^t of the
30 *Dauphin* Ed. of *Livy.* ▬ . . . D^r. *South* has another Volume of Sermons ready for ye Press, wch he sufferd D^r. *Hudson* to peruse who judges them equal if not superior to those already publish'd. He does not design they should be printed till after his Death. There is a Preface to one of these Sermons that concludes with a very severe Reflection upon D^r. *Birch*, a Prebendary of *Westminster*, who, as D^r. South told D^r. *Hudson* had ye Impudence to preach one of his printed Sermons in ye Collegiate Church of *Westminster* when ye Author himself was present. ▬ D^r. *Talbot* B^p. of *Oxon* was a very great Rake all the Time he liv'd in ye University ; and afterwards when in orders was very much addicted to Gaming, being
40 observ'd by several *Oxford* Gentlemen at ye Wells at *Astrop*, & that he when Dean of *Worcester* plaid very much at ye Royal oke Lottery, to ye great Scandal of his Gown and Dignity. He with B^p. *Burnett*, B^p. *Fowler*, B^p. *Williams* (of *Chichester*) B^p. *More* (of *Norwich*) B^p. *Crew* of *Durham* &c. has been twice married, wch rarely or never us'd to be practis'd by the B^ps of ye Church of *England* or any other Church. The said B^p. of *Oxford* made a *Cambridge* Man Chancellor of the Diocess of *Oxon* to the great Grief of y^e *Oxford* Civilians. And he made a *Leyden* D^r. of Physick (one *Goodwin* an Hypocritical Puritanical Fellow) his Domestick Chaplain, wch was no less resented by the Oxford Divines.

Nov. 30 (Fri.). Verses on M^r. *Prickett* Buttler of University Coll. made by M^r. *Elstob*, A.M. & formerly Fellow of y^t Coll. now Rector of S^t. *Swithun*'s in London [1].

To The thrice Noble and Illustrious Pincerna, King of Pocillator's, Senior Proto-Butler, And Chief Minister of the Smallbeer, To The Senior College of ye most Antient University in Europe.

This following Poem, in memory of his transcendent worth, is humbly dedicated & presented,

By his most humble Admirer, & Observer, W. S.

THE DEDICATION.   10

Accept most noble Promo, don't refuse
This worthless Present of an Humble Muse,
Who suppliant waits on you, & from her Store
Gives you her hearty Choice, altho but poor.
The Poet's soil when wet with generous wine,
May yield rich Fruits & give you somew^t fine.
Where small Beer & it's Sister Water flow,
What wonder is't if weeds will only grow?
Poor as the soil and heartless as ye field,
Will be ye barren product it does yield.
But where the Sun does quick'ning warmth dispense,
And gives new Life & vigorous Influence:
Where fatning Streams impregnate as they run,
Help'd by y^o livening Virtue of y^o Sun;
A Plenteous Harvest there must doubtless bless
The Farmers labours with a full Increase.
Just so, did your bright Lamp supply the day
When absent in our Heaven & display
His glorious Light, did jolly Bacchus reign
And vital Spirit with our Water joyn.
A nobler soul would repossess y^o Age
And fill our Breasts with true poetick rage.
Now for excuse to these insipid Rhymes
Say 'ts not ye Poets fault, but ye dull times.
Help Cerevisia while I try to sing
The Subulonian Hero, wisest King
Of all those Antient Promo's of Renown,
That ever sway'd Oxonium's chearfull Town,
Ere since the Royal Alfred made the Place
Sacred to 'th Muses and to every Grace.

Whose aid combining loudly shall proclaim,
His matchless worth, & propagate his Fame.
In lofty numbers shall his deeds be told,
Bright as his Spirit, as his Courage bold
Worthy a Prince of the Tonsorian Race.
The best that er'e with steel mow'd human face,
From Fuzz and Bramble to the downy beard   20
He whisk'd them off, all quickly disappear'd ;
O'er all as nimbly glanc'd the shining blade,
As shadows on ye water's surface plaid :
To finish all he'd make his Fingers crack,
And grace ye matter with a double Smack.

Streight as an arrow was this proper wight,
His justaucorps brac't to his body tight.   30
His Shoulders square, then from his slender wast
The Skirts hung dangling as he walkt in hast.
Fix't on their Pedestals of polisht jet,
Two Taper Columns bore his body's weight.
His trowzes wch with loops emboss'd he tyes,
Make Capitals of ye Ionick size.   40
He spreads his Arms which with a seeming grace
Draw round, and wth his periods hold an equal pace.
But if o'er all a pendant Robe he wore,
It made another figure than before.
From his small neck ye wid'ning space encreast,
As by a sugar loaf is well express'd :   50
Or as you see some lofty Pyramid,
Grac't on it's Top with a Colossus Head ;

---

[1] These verses were made principally upon occasion of M^r. *Prickett*'s Journey wth D^r. *Hudson* & M^r. *Elstob* to *Cambridge*, where it seems they were very merry, & *Prickett* was so comical as to cut a poor fellow's tongue on purpose to make him sp[eak] French &c., wch caus'd abundance of Mirth.

Such was his Form, & from his Sparkling
   Eyes
Th' enlivning Beams like darted light-
   ning flyes.
The Radiant Glory of his Silver Hair
Rivals yᵉ Sun, & Phebe's not so fair
As awfull Promo seated on his Throne,
Arm'd with his Pen, & ready to put on.
When looking down he eyes yᵉ greasy
10   Rout,
Of gaping thrums, stand listning round
   about :
Fixt, as to chains, his powerfull Eloquence,
Holds them so fast, they dare not stir
   from thence.
Such plenteous Streams pour from his
   liquid voice,
He drowns the thirsty Cellar with the
   Noise.
20 Each empty Hogshead catches at yᵉ
   Sound,
And Thrumkins voider Noddle eccho's
   yᵉ Rebound.
   Should I his various Talents here re-
      hearse,
It were a Task too tedious for verse,
Yet that some nobler Instances be told,
A matter worthy of our Art we hold.
First hear him exercise that warlike Note,
30 When ratling Gutturals slake his Artfull
   throat,
Then as 'twere drumming with a slower
   Tone,
Each lowing Hogshead murmurs back a
   Groan.
But if more sprightly Accents urge to war,
Hark yᵉ shrill Trumpet clanging thro'
   yᵉ Air.
Mais ditez moi Monsieur, commong le
40   Noble Twang
Peut allumer la guerre, ou devant, ou
   dereire le Twang, noble Twang.
Such is yᵉ Language of yᵉ Gallick Court,
To wᵒʰ all Europe's Princes do resort,
Taught there to ring the modish clang of
   France,
Bridle their Tongues, & teach them how
   to prance.
Maugre chagrine, full stretcht wᵗʰ such
50   bizarre
The Palate struck, does thro' his Nos-
   trils jarr.
Here lay the Subulonians chiefest Art,
See him, admire him, & you have his
   Heart.
Then shall you hear how chuckling
   throats have squall'd,
With gripes & pinching rendred hoarse
   & gall'd,
60 Of noses red, & swell'd wᵗʰ hoisting round,
To give advantage to yᵉ Screaming sound.

But that for wᶜʰ he's most of all rever'd,
It's History is worthy to be heard.
   At that glad season when the joyfull
      year
In all it's gayest Beauty did appear,
When ev'ry object lookt benign & kind,
And banish't cares & sorrows from yᵉ
   mind ;
A time thus fit for Mirth, & made for
   joy,
Did Granta's Sons thus solemnly employ.
Proclaim'd a Feast, & summon'd from
   afar,
The Friends thought worthy in her joy
   to share.
To see the Triumphs of contending wit,
And raise th' Applauses of yᵒ clam'rous
   Pit.
Of all the pressing throng, to this delight
Oxonia justly first did claim her right.
Nor was there any of her sons whose
   Name,
Or voice could ever equal Promo's Fame.
Much less could Rival Granta shew a son,
Of Promo race, by him not far outdone.
They all surpriz'd & pleas'd, around him
   sate
And heard him story's of his skill repeat ;
How Throats well manag'd by his learned
   skill,
Untun'd & stubborn once, were brought
   to Trill.
And how some fetter'd Tongues that once
   were mute
By him set loose could nimbly dispute.
Pleas'd with his Art, at yᵉ Relation fir'd
To see some operation most desir'd.
And 'twas not hard this Favour to intreat
So truly generous was his Soul, & great.
Obliging was his Life, & to do good
He made his choice whatever Art with-
   stood.
Beside the Time & Place did both per-
   swade,
'Twas fit some choice Experiment were
   made.
Behind yᵉ numerous croud of Standers by,
One undiscern'd to most yᵉ company,
Who shoulder'd & wedg'd in on eveıy
   side,
And thro' a peep-Hole what had pass'd
   espy'd.
Rais'd by this talk did breaking thro'
   advance,
Imploring to be taught yᵉ Twang of
   France.
In suppliant posture & an earnest Tone,
Beg'd that on him this Practise might be
   shown.
Were he but taught, & his glew'd tongue
   set loose,
No pain in yᵉ Experiment he'd refuse.

Then Promo smil'd, & reaching him his
Hand,
Said, courage Friend I'll answer your de-
mand,
I'll make you Master of y° Gallick Twang,
Bizarre commang bizarre, bizarre com-
mang.

And strait, he fixt him in an elbow chair
Requiring help of all that round him were,
Some legs, some Arms, & some to hold
his Head
For fear of starting.   Then he flourished
By way of Prelude, in his hand did fly
The wavering Fillet of a purple dye.
To bind the Neck & fill the panting vein,
Till it the Struggling Bloud could scarce
contain.
But first he gagg'd him to y° fullest
stretch,
That he the patient's Tongue might better
reach.
Of clay bak't white, he made his Instru-
ment
In form of Cilinder for this Intent.
Some Stroppers call them, some the very
same,
Broken Tobacco-pipes, & by another
Name.
Things thus prepar'd, he took his Silver
Groat.
Thin as a wafer, or a thread-bare Coat.
Which fairly brandishing, in his Right
Hand,
(The other did the Patient's Tongue
command.)
He aim'd the edge aright, & at one push,
The striving goar, from out the wound
did gush.
Then he ungagg'd him, & fort[h]with
around
A Peel of Acclamations did resound.

The Groaning Patient's carry'd off y°
Stage
And Promo own'd the wonder of y° Age.
But let us once more see him on his
Throne,
Arm'd with his Pen, & ready to put on,
Sometimes he makes a whistling in y°
Air,
Like chirping Birds, but no Bird do's
appear.   10
The listning Thrumms look staring upon
high
And think y° voice they hear is in y° Sky.
Till sweep, his circumbendibus comes
round
And lays poor thrumkin sprawling on the
ground.
Stun'd and amaz'd the wondring rable
stand
And all their Passions work at his Com- 20
mand.
Joy, Hope, & Fear, are lodg'd in each
man's Face,
In different Postures with a strange
Grimace.
More various windings, nor more dif-
ferent ways,
The stragling water with his cost conveys
Thro' subterraneous Tracts, did never
know,   30
Than those by which he turns their Pas-
sions, now
Oh might I but, at his Lamps purer light,
Have catch't the flame, by which I this
indite.
What glittring lines had shone in ev'ry
page
To grace the subject, that do's them in-
gage.
But now great Promo, let our want of 40
skill
At least be pardon'd, for our better will.

FINIS.

Ex Epistola VII. Gudij ad Ma. Heinsium, pag. 9. writ from Florence. . . .

In pag. 51. In an Epistle of Grævius's to *Gudius* he makes mention of
Perizonius's having notes to *Valerius Maximus*, & a large work preparing
de Romanorum nominibus. — In a Letter to D^r. *Hudson* from D^r. *J.*
Woodward he tells him y^t he has read *Montfaucon's Diarium Italicum* &
Fabricius's Bibliotheca Græca wth abundance of Satisfaction, that my L^d.
Pembrooke has y^e *Columna Constantini*, wch he says is well graved, but ye 50
work of y^t Pillar falls vastly short of y^t on y^e *Columna Trajana*, & on y^t
of *Antoninus* at *Rome.* — They have lately translated & printed *M. Ides's*
Journal of his Journey from *Mosco* to *Perkin* in an Embassy from
ye Czar to ye King of *China.*   His Secretary M^r. *Brand* had formerly set
forth some Acc^t of it, wch also was printed here ; but y^t was much inferior
to this.   He says also, that he's just entering upon the Perusal of M^r.
Addison's Voyage of *Italy*, wch is at last publish'd. — Since the Dutch
have open'd a Trade wth France we have had 2 Vols. of ye Hist. de

l'Acad. des Sciences for yᵉ years 1701 & 1702, Mʳ. *Huet's* Antiquités de Caen 8º & M. Pezron's Antiq. de la Langue & de la Nation Celte 8º. The last of wᶜʰ Dʳ. *Woodward* says is but a very mean Performance. — Some men who pretend to know yᵉ whole mystery of *Chivers's* Recantation, in relation to Dʳ. Burnett Bᴾ. of *Sarum,* say that he did it for fear of a Pack Jury, wᶜʰ no honest man in this Age can be secure from : for 'tis very probable that yᵉ Bishop of *Sarum* in his younger years (the Fact mention'd by Chivers being done before he was Bᴾ.) being a brawny Lecherous *Scotchman,* might have occasion for such an infamous Place of
10 Pleasure : it being notorious that after threescore he married a barren widow, & impregnated her with two children at once.

These following Books to be got for the Publick Library. [pp. 362–379.] ...

VOL. VI.

Dec. 1 (Sat.). *Anton. à Wood* was prosecuted by the Earl of *Clarendon* in yᵉ Vice-Chancellor's court, for wᵗ he had said of *Edw. Hyde* Earl of *Clarendon* his Father in yᵉ *Athenæ Oxonienses* ; and when Sentence came to be pass'd his Book was order'd to be burnt & he himself to be fin'd 40 libˢ, wᶜʰ sum Poor *Anton.* was forc'd to pay to yᵉ Vice-Chancellor, who laid out yᵉ Money upon three Statues wᶜʰ are plac'd in the Nitches of yᵉ Gate of yᵉ Physick Garden. After this Mʳ. *Wood* told several
20 Persons particularly Dʳ. *Hudson* that if he had Liberty he could justify every particular yᵗ he had writ about yᵉ Earl of *Clarendon* from Authentick Papers, publish'd by Authority. — Dʳ. *Wallis* when he was fourscore years of Age or near it could, purely by yᵉ Help of his Memory, multiply 20 numbers by 20, & then extract yᵉ Cube Root ; wᶜʰ as well as his Art of Decyphering is an Instance of his Extraordinary Parts. — In the *Acta Lips.* for the Month of *July* 1696 is a large Account of some objections made by Mʳ. *Grabe* agᵗ yᵉ *Lutheran* Religion, & of an Answer made to yᵉ same by *Spener.* Mʳ. *Grabe* is represented there as being much inclin'd to Popery. In pag. 317 of the same Acts in *An. eod.* is
30 an Accᵗ of an Answer made to Mʳ. *Grabe's* Doubts by *Bernhard Von Sanden.* — Some of the Musical Authors, publish'd by *Meibomius,* were transcrib'd out of yᵉ publick Library at *Oxoñ,* & compar'd with other Copies by Dʳ. *Langbain* of Queen's College, for yᵉ use of *Meibomius,* who procur'd this of Mʳ. *Selden.* Vide *Gudij* Ep. p. 56. — Hen. *Oldenburg,* in an Epistle to *Georg. Morhofius* (vide Gud. Ep. p. 74.) told him that then, viz. 1673, they were preparing for yᵉ Press at *London Photius's* Lexicon & upon yᵗ Accᵗ he desired *Morhofius* to transmit to them (for wᶜʰ he would give security) a very fair Copy in the Hands of *Gudius.* *Gudius* writ learned notes upon the *Geoponicks. Quære* whether ever
40 printed ? — *Majoragius* writ Notes upon *Quintilian.* See ibid. p. 170. ...

Dec. 1. Dr. T. Smith to H. The Votive Shield of Scipio Africanus. Kennett and his design of publishing epitaphs. Sir W. Dugdale, before the Civil War, had carefully surveyed St. Paul's and other Churches : ' wᶜʰ worke of his he would mention to mee with great complaisance and joy, and blesse God for his conduct and providence in it.' There are abundant materials for several new volumes of the *Monasticon* ; see the writer's *Synoptical History of the*

— The House of L^{ds} have pass'd ye Bill relating to ye Repealing all the Clauses, but y^t conc. ye Union, pass'd ye last Sessions ab^t *Scotland.* They have gone thro' y^t for settling the Protestant Religion & the Succession. — *Pliny's* Ep. 8. l. iv. illustrated in *Falconerius's* Notes to the *Inscriptiones Athlet.* p. 36. . . . — M^r. *Smirke,* or the Divine in mode, being certain Annotations, upon ye Animadversions of y^e *Naked Truth.*. 1676. *E. Hickeringall* said to be ye Author. — *Sebastiani Faschij* de Nummo Pylæmenis Euergetæ Regis Paphlagoniæ Epistola. *Bas.* 1680. 4°. This will be of great use in another Edition of *Justin's* Epitome of *Trogus.* — Truth will out &c. by E. W. (i. e. *Edw. Worseley* yè Soc. Jesu.) 10 1665. 4°. — D^r. *Hudson* tells me y^t ye last time he saw M^r. *Ab. Seller,* wch was not long before his Death, and after, he (M^r. *Seller*) told him, that he had furnish'd D^r. *Cave* with Abundance of Materials for his *Hist. Literaria,* and complain'd y^t ye D^r. had rarely acknowledg'd what he receiv'd from him. — D^r. *Cave,* in ye Preface to his II^d vol. of *Hist. Literaria* gives a great Commendation of *Rich. Bury* B^p. of *Durham,* and then adds to this Effect, *utinam opulenta ista sedes semper haberet talem Episcopum* : wch no doubt is a just Reflection upon ye pres^t B^p. of *Durham*[1] to whom ye said D^r. *Cave* had Dedicated some of his Works, wch y^t B^p. had not acknowledg'd as he was oblig'd in Hon^r to have 20 done.

Books to be got into ye Pub. Library. [9–14; 15–18.] . . .

In *Lipsick* Acts for ye Year 1699, Mens. Mart. p. 114. in the Acc^t of the *Oxford* Edition of *Vellejus Paterculus* is a gross Blunder, D^r. *Charlett* being there made to be ye Editor of that Book (perhaps because himself, being very forward always to boast of more than is his due, had so reported to young *Menckenius* when he was here in *Oxford*) whereas 'tis well known y^t D^r. *Hudson* was the Publisher of it. . . .

Dec. 2 (Sun.). In y^e *Philosoph. Transactions,* num. 145. for ye Month of *March* 168⅔ is D^r. *Lister's* Relation of a *Roman* Monum^t found in 30 ye B^{p}prick of *Durham,* & of some *Roman* Antiquities at *York.* In the same *Transactions* for ye month of *Dec.* 1685, Numb. 178, D^r. *William Nicolson* (B^p. of *Carlisle*) hath two Letters conc. two *Runic Inscriptions* at *Beaucastle,* and *Bridekirk.* — *Ludolf* in his Comment. upon his Hist. of Æthiopia Pr. p. 39. has a Remark about *Livy,* whether it be now intire or no ? — In ye Master of University's Copy of *Flor. Wig.* is at ye Beginning a Reference to a Book in the Pub. Libr. containing the *Fasti Consulares.* It stood according to ye old Placing U. 3. 7. *Jur.* I believe 'tis *Marianus Scotus.* 'Tis intimated so also at ye Beginning of ye Book. D^r. *Langbain* compar'd all *Marianus Scotus* wth *Florence,* & concludes 40 y^t *Florence* has little of his own, transcribing all from *Marianus.* See

---

Cottonian Library, p. xxxviii. Mr. Ashmole a very exact and careful antiquary. Are there any familiar letters of Henry VIII and his son and daughters in Bodley? Asks for particulars of Ep. Ded. and Preface to Dee's *Propædeumata Aphorismatica.* **Dodwell to H.** Thanks for transcript of Vettius Valens. Must be wary in his title. Explains his views with regard to Lay Deprivation, communion with usurping Bishops, &c.

---

[1] D^r. Crew.

p. 393.   He has in some places compar'd *Florence* wth y^e *Saxon Chron.*
In p. 449 he seems to have look'd into Domesday Book from a Note
in *Marg.* He has compar'd a MS^t in Corpus X^{ti} Col. See pag. 492.
There is a Marginal Note from a MS^t y^t *Asser* translated *Boethius* &
not King Alfred, he doing it at ye Command of ye King. — The
Master has likewise a large folio Book in MS^t containing a great many
things relating to ye University of *Oxon* & some relating to Cambridge,
with other Things concerning some other Places, wch will be of good
use to one that gives an Acc^t of this university &c.

10   **Dec. 3 (Mon.).**   M^r. *Somervile* (Commoner of Edm. Hall) told me,
last night, that amongst ye Ruins of *Warwick*, caus'd by ye Fire, there
were lately found, two Roman Urns, full of Brass *Roman* Coyns, w^{ch}
are now in the Hands of M^r. *Smith* at or near *Warwick*, an Eminent
Antiquary as he said. One of these Coyns he said was of *Julius Cæsar.*
I ask't him w^t size it was, supposing that if it had been of ye lesser size
it might not be so antient. He reply'd ab^t as big as a Half-crown, & y^t
there were others of ye same Bigness. If they could be seen they might
probably give us some light in the Antiquities of *Warwick*, wch was
certainly a *Roman* Garrison. — This Gentleman likewise told me that
20 at *Warwick* amongst other Tombs was taken up one, wch being open'd
(some persons having a great desire it should upon account of it's
belonging to a considerable Noble man) there appear'd an Intire Man;
but when 'twas toucht it fell all in pieces but ye Skull. He died, as
was gather'd from ye Inscription, in ye Reign of Q. *Eliz.* —

Out of the Master[1] of University College's Copy of *Athen. Oxon.* in a
spare Leaf at ye End:
Memorandum that M^r. *Antony A Wood* told M^r. *Martin* several times before
his Sickness, that he intended to receive the Sacram^t at his Hands in the
Church of Witham the following Christmass.
30   That during his sickness he was almost constantly attended by M^r. Martin,
M^r. Biss &c., who can certifie y^t he always desired the Ch. of England Prayers,
which he had constantly read to him twice a day for ye last week of his sickness; that he desired the Sacrament to be given him by M^r. *Martin*; that He
himself particularly ordered that it should be inserted in his Will wch was
made 3 or 4 days before his Death; that he died in the Communion of y^e
Church of England as by Law Established: that there was no Papist or reputed Papist that visited him during his last Sickness.
This was transcrib'd at the Master's Desire from the original of M^r.
Tanner. —

40   A Noble L^d. (L^d. *Rochester*) moved on thursday last for ye Limiting the L^{ds}
Justices in ye Act of Succession from consenting to any Act in prejudice of y^t
of uniformity declaring y^t unless this was done tho he would not say ye Ch. of
England was in danger during her Majestie's Life, he could not help thinking
that it w^{ld} be so upon her demise. This was spoken wth such a peculiar Zeal
& Emphasis, y^t it had a notable Effect on ye House who presently ordered the
Judges to attend the next day wth y^{eir} Advice how to provide ag^t any Hazard
of this Kind. —

M^r. *Wesley* has printed a new Book intitled *The History of ye Old & New-
Testam^t* in verse, in 3 vols., dedicated to ye Queen. — The last day of y^e
50 Term a cloud of Informations was brought in by ye Attorney General

[1] D^r. Charlett.

against yᵉ Publick writers & Printers, & the oldest of the Tribe (Mʳ. *Dyer*) was fin'd by yᵉ Queen's Bench upon an obsolete Information of 6 years standing. — De Epist. 205 *Basilij* ad *Julianum* notae quaedam MSS. admodum Rev. *Tho. Barlow* Episc. *Lincoln.*, ut occurrunt ad Pag. 225. Exemplaris *Basilij* in Bibl. *Bod.* Edit. Par. 1638. [26–36.] ... — Happening to see Mʳ. Kent to Night, as he came thro' *Oxon.* in a journey to *Warwick*, he told me yᵗ the Lady *Franklin* to whom he is Chaplain has a Daughter who has a Noble Collection (abᵗ 300 in number) of *Roman* Coyns; [1] but yᵗ she dispos'd to give them to Trinity College in Cambridge, of wᶜʰ House she had some time since a Brother a member, & yᵗ she has no inclination at present, chiefly for yᵗ reason, to give them to our Publick Library: but nevethelesse hopes still to prevail wᵗʰ her, at least to give us such as we want, provided we will part wᵗʰ duplicates for yᵐ. He likewise told me yᵗ she has yᵉ whole 26ᵗʰ Chapter of *Matthew* cut in Greek Letters in paper by a curious Lady, very artificially, of wᶜʰ nature we have nothing in the Publick Library.

Dec. 4 (Tu.). Being at Dinner yesterday with Dʳ. Charlett, he was pleas'd to tell me yᵗ upon Mʳ. Ant. à Wood's falling ill, he went to him (having more interest wᵗʰ him yⁿ any other Person in *Oxon*) & told him yᵗ 'twas the Opinion of Physitians and others yᵗ his Disease (being a Stoppage of Urine) was very dangerous, & therefore desir'd him to prepare himself for Death by Prayers, and putting his Papers (of wᶜʰ he had a great number) into good order: This had so good Effect upon him, yᵗ he presently told the Doctor he would take his Advise, & desir'd him to let no other Person read Prayers or administer yᵉ Sacrament to him but Mʳ. Martin, who promis'd he would not. After this he ask'd the Doctor whom he thought the fittest person to leave certain Papers with, & to put the rest in order to be dispos'd of as he should give order. He told him Mʳ. Tanner. Accordingly Mʳ. Martin came constantly to Mʳ. Wood & read Prayers to him, & Mʳ. Tanner sorted all yᵉ Papers, some of wᶜʰ Mʳ. Wood laid by in order to be burnt when himself should give a sign to Mʳ. Tanner by stretching out his Hand. When he found himself ready to leave the world, he gave this sign, & Mʳ. Tanner burnt those Papers wᶜʰ were put by for yᵗ intent. The rest Mʳ. Wood left to yᵉ Ashmolean Museum & the Public Library, besides divers to Mʳ. Tanner, upon condition he would be honest, & take care (as indeed Mʳ. Tanner promis'd & so did Dʳ. Charlett too should be faithfully perform'd) to digest & make them publick. The Dʳ. farther told me yᵗ Mʳ. Wood died with a great deal of Patience & Submission, much like a Christian & Philosopher. — ... Goltzius had a Design of engraving all the Coyns of the Roman Emperors, as appears from his MSS. now in the King of *France*'s Library. See there pag. 3. — ... To day at 10 a Clock was a Convocation, and a Letter being read from yᵉ Chancellor on behalf of *Sam. Hill* Archdeacon of *Wells*, desiring yᵗ wheras he had taken his Bachelor of Arts Degree above 30 years since, & was sufficiently known

---

[1] These Coyns I have had since a view of, being put into my Hands by Mʳ. John Thompson, Fellow of Queen's Coll. who succeeded Mʳ. Kent as Chaplain to the Lady. He committed them to me on purpose that I might describe them; wᶜʰ accordingly I did. He promised to get me a gratuity from the Lady. But he never did it. The Coyns are of no great worth, being very much defaced.

for his Learning & Zeal to the church, he might be admitted to the Degree
of Master of Arts, w^{th}out performing any Exercise or keeping Terms,
paying only the usual Fees : wch was granted, nemine contradicente.
   [Note on Livy XXXVIII. *ad fin.*, from Aul. Gellius cum Notis var.]. . .
   On Sunday last about eleven Clock in ye Evening died *Sir William
Blackett* by whose death an Estate of ten thousand lib^s. per An. is
come to his Son, a Gentleman-Commoner of University College, whose
Tutor is M^r. Clavering, who lately publish'd a piece of Maimonides, he
being well skill'd in *Hebrew*, and had some considerable Hand too in
10 the New Hebrew Grammar publish'd by Rabbi Levi : but how it came to
pass that D^r. *Beverige* B^p. of S^t. *Asaph* would not accept of a Dedication
of Maimonides propos'd to him I cannot imagine unless it be because
M^r. Clavering is of the Trimming Principles, or because the thing was
offer'd him by D^r. Mill, whose Sincerity he had good reason to doubt
from his being ready to side with any party y^t he sees uppermost. M^r.
Blackett has a Subtutor namely M^r. *Burman* a Master of Arts of ye same
College, who set out ye late Edition of D^r. Plot, & who has ye Character
of an Honest Man. — . . . M^r. Elstob who has printed some Sermons,
& done some other little Jobs in Learning (vide D^r. Hicks Thesaur.
20 Ascham's Ep., S^r. John Cheek's Life by Strype in wch last he has made
a very scurvy and undeserv'd Reflection upon M^r. Obadiah Walker) when
he was of Queen's College appear'd a Candidate for a Fellowship of All
Souls passing for a South Country Man, but missing this became a
Northern man, & was upon that elected one of Skirlaw's Fellows of
University College. The same Trick was plaid by one D^r. Stapleton,
who had a Yorkshire Scholarship in University Col. & afterwards a Fellowship of All Souls as born in ye Province of Canterbury. Likewise one
M^r. Rob. Grey, first a Commoner of Queen's Col. and afterwards Fellow
of All Souls, his Parents and Friends living all in New-Castle upon Tine,
30 upon pretence y^t he was accidentally dropt in London, obtain'd a Place
in Chichley's Foundation. — M^r. Bingham of University Coll. reading
D^r. Sherlock's Books imbib'd his false Notions about ye Trinity, &
preach't some of y^m in a Sermon before the University at S^t. Peter's in
the East on S^t. Simon and Jude, in ye year 1695 ; upon wch M^r. Beauchamp of Trinity College, commonly call'd ye Heretick-Hunter, complain'd to ye Vice-Chancellor of them who call'd a Meeting of the Heads
of Houses &c. in wch Assembly M^r. Bingham's Sermon was censur'd.
After this it being fear'd y^t unless he publickly recanted his Doctrines he
should be expell'd, ye Master & Fellows of University College suffer'd
40 him to enjoy a Year of Grace (upon his Promotion at y^t time to a Living)
w^{th}out having a Name in the Buttery Book. The Master of University
College can tell more about this Gentleman. — On the 2^d Instant
S^r. Cloudsly Shovel had Audience of her Majesty & ye next day was in
ye House of Commons. The Discourse still continues y^t he will be made
a Peer of this Realm. — M^r. Jones who is lately come in Fellow of All
Souls had vast Interest, divers of the chief Nobility appearing in his
Behalf as ye Duke of Ormond, Earl of Rochester, L^d. Digby, Duke of
Beaufort, &c. besides all the Heads of Houses in Oxford, that are firm
to ye Church besides a vast Number of others. His Father has a good
50 Estate as I am inform'd, & is an ingenious & good Man, & not proud as

I was once told. — At the end of the first Edition of Livy at Rome in 1470 are these verses : Proderat haud multum . . . lectitet ipsa diu. [52-54.]

Dec. 5 (Wed.). . . . We hear to day y^t M^r. *Hen. Bird*, M.A. & fellow of *Queen's* Coll. is dead in ye North, whither he retir'd for his Health's sake, he being in a Deep Consumption wch he got (notw^thstanding his being of a strong body and hardly 30 Years of Age) by continual Bibbing. — . . . M^r. J. Wasse Fellow of Queen's Coll. in Cambridge I am told by one who corresponds with him has laid by (at least for ye Present) his design'd Ed. of Marianus Capella de Nuptiis Phil. because one in Holland is upon ye same work.   He drives at a great many things, & to day his Friend was in the Publick Library on purpose to consult a passage in the MS^t Copy of Servius's Com. on Virgil for his use; whence I suppose he may have some design of publishing anew this Author.

Dec. 6 (Th.).   Last thursday (Nov. 29) came on an Election of Fellows into Merton College.   There were seven elected y^t were members of the College, & one y^t was of Pembroke, whose Name is Wintley. They stile it ye Golden Election because they are all Excell^t Scholars, especially three or four of them are said to be as good as any in Oxford of their standing.—Wintley's Father died just before the Election, & within a day or two after he had news of his Mother's lying upon her Death-Bed.   One of the Candidates was M^r. Tanner a Bachelor of Arts of Queen's, Brother to M^r. Tho: Tanner, Chancellor of Norwich.   I am told he appear'd very well as to Scholarship, & y^t he took his being put by very chearfully, & paid his Respects afterwards to the Fellows, whereas ye rest, who mist coming in, sneak'd away & seemed to resent it. — Last Week D^r. Aglionby her Majesty's late Envoy to ye Protestant Cantons departed this Life. — . . . M^r. Browne Willis is elected Parliam^t Man for Buckingham. He is an Honest Gentleman, & is well known for his Diligent Search into our English Antiquities, in w^ch (having a very good Estate) he may do very considerable Matters, if he think fit to be generous. . . .

Out of ye Gazette for Monday.

Dec. 3.   Wheras I William Lenthall of Lincoln's Inn, Gen^t. have writ and published a Poem call'd, A Trip to Leverpool, where there are scandalous Reflections on M^r. Manley and M^r. Walker; I do hereby own them to be false and groundless, and humbly beg their Pardon; and do consent that this shall be published in what manner they shall think fit.   Witness my hand this 30th day of November, 1705.

WM. LENTHALL.   Witness, WM. THOMSON, THO. BARSHAM.

— In a Glass Window of the Chancell of the Church of Thame in Oxfordshire is this Coat-Armour, Argent, a Tiger Passant, Regardent, gazing in a Mirrour or Looking-Glass, all proper, impaled on the sinister side with the Coat-Armour properly pertaining to the Family of de Bardis.   Neer to this Escocheon is placed this Inscription, Hadrianus de Badis Præbendarius istius Ecclesiæ.   See Guillim's Heraldry pag. 144. Ed. Lond. 1610. — In the Year 169⅘ came out a Treatise in 8°. intit. *Usury Explain'd; or Conscience quieted in the Case of putting out Money at Interest.*   By Philopenes, i. e. Jo. Dormer è Soc. Jes.   In the Copy of this Book in the Bodlejan Library, is a MS^t Letter added, written by the B^p. of Condom, in answer to the Author's Arguments, wch here follows.

In Castro Rᵒ. Upsaliarum die 26 Febr. an. 87.

Ad casum quem proponit V. Clarissimus, facilis & plana responsio est, hac scilicet fixa Regula : lucrum ex mutuo, quod est lucrum ex usura per sese est iniquum, & obligat ad restitutionem neque ea obligatio tolli potest per eas rationes quas affert V. C. 1ᵃ. quod fœnus exercuit cum fœneribus : sed nulla est hæc ratio, cum nec liceat inique agere cum iniquis. nec juvat quæ 2ᵃ. ratio est; quod hi quibus suam pecuniam mutuatus est ea locupletati sunt : sive enim illa divitiarum accessio æqua sive iniqua fuerit, non potuit is qui pecuniam mutuo dedit in hujus lucri partem venire, nisi ex contractu legitimæ
10 societatis, quæ hic locum non habuit. 3ᵃ. ratio, metus infamiæ, sed 1ᵐ. res potest agi clanculum, tum vero si publice agatur, honoris magis erit quam dedecoris.

Quod autem vir Clariss. existimat, posse vel tolli vel minui restituendi fœnoris necessitatem propter gravia mala damnaque, quæ causa religionis pertulit, nulla est hæc ratio : cum suæ patientiæ mercedes expectare debeat non ab hominibus per usuram & lucrum injustum sed à Dei misericordia cumulatissime remuncrante fidem ejus atque pietatem.

Quod V. C. pauperibus quasi aliud agens restitutionem fecit, optimum & ad minuendam restitutionem imputandum adversus eos quidem quibus satisfecit :
20 sed alijs quoque licet ditioribus satisfacere oportet.

Neque juvat quod V. C. eo animo fuerit, ut pecuniam quidem acciperet sponte oblatam, lege autem agere nollet. Neque enim refert quo ipse animo fuerit, cum ita videatur egisse cum cæteris, ut ipsi existimarent se ad præstandam usuram ex pacto teneri. Quod V. C. ait licuisse illi sortem capitalem aliter expendendo ad suum emolumentum legitime convertere : nihil est, nisi forte eo loco res fuerint ut emolumentum illud verum reale & præsens fuerit : tunc enim locus datur remunerando lucro cessanti, ut ajunt; sed spes lucri inanes ac vagas, non licet certa ac presente pecunia repensare.

Hæc sunt V. C. quæ pridem respondere debuissem ad doctissimam tuam
30 consultationem nisi me aliæ curæ prohibuissent. more posco veniam tibique V. relᵐᵉ in Xᵒ sum addictiss.

J. BENIGNUS EPISC. MALDENSIS.

A Sober Answer to yᵉ Friendly Debate betw. a Conformist & a Nonconformist : By Philagathus (i. e. Dʳ. Roll) Lond. 1669. 8ᵒ. — . . .
The English Translation of Herodian, Printed at London, 1698, 8ᵒ., & sᵈ in the Title page to have been done by a Gentleman of Oxford, I am inform'd was made by Mʳ. ¹*Dennison*, M.A. & Fellow of University Coll. & one of yᵉ Pro-Proctors for this year; the same Dennison I mean who thro' the means of Hum. Wanley & yᵉ indirect, malicious, & foul Prac-
40 tises of some other Informers, (amongst whom was John Prickett the Butler) came in to the room of Mʳ. Usher, who had been duly Elected Fellow of yᵉ College; but the Master not having any kindness for him (notwᵗʰstanding his being a very Excellent Scholar & a man of Parts) by the help of the foresaid Sycophants got him expell'd the University, upon an old Story of above two years standing, to yᵉ Great amazement of all truely Honest Men in the University & the no small Disgrace of yᵉ Master himself. But yᵉ Case being in print by Mʳ. Usher, it must be consulted. — The Old Religion demonstrated in its Principles &c. *Lond.* 1684. 8ᵒ. The Author Dr. Goodman. — . . . Remember to
50 inquire of Mʳ. Professor Halley how the Kit Cat Club came to have it's

---

¹ 'Twas not done by Mʳ. Dennison but by one Mʳ. John Thornhill of University Col. now a Barrister of Law.

Name from one Christopher Catling[1]. — Quære whether any Acc[t] was
sent to Harduin when he publish'd Pliny of the Notes written by John
Claymond upon y[t] Author, & whether they are now in Corpus X[ti] Coll.
Library? Quære also whether his Notes upon Aulus Gellius, Com. in
Plautum, & Epistolæ ad Grynæum be there also? & whether any of them
printed? — Memorandum that whereas Ant. à Wood says (Ath. Oxon.
Vol. 1. p. 35.) that John More Son of Sir Tho. More was little better
y[n] an Ideot, the contrary to this may be evinc'd from Grynæus's Dedications præfix'd to his Editions of Plato & Proclus's comments upon Plato,
printed at Basil in the year 1534. — D[r]. Wells has just put into the 10
Press at Oxford a Letter to a Dissenting Parishioner, wch is to be in
3 Sheets in 8o. — M[r]. Sherlock Son to D[r]. Sherlock is enter'd upon the
Mastership of the Temple, he having (as I have hinted before) rec[d] a
Grant of it from the Queen. — D[r]. Baily President of Magd. Col. was
one of y[e] King's Chaplains at y[e] Revolution, & supply'd his turn and
preach'd before King William once: but not caring to take y[e] Oaths he
never appear'd at Court any more. — When the Election for a Member
to serve for the Corporation of Buckingham came on, my L[d]. Wharton
& several others of his Gang appear'd there, & made Interest for one
Captain Tyrrell (Son to James Tyrrell Esq[r].) who was prevail'd with to 20
leave his Regiment in Flanders & come over to stand for this Place. He
y[e] said Capt. Tyrrell (when they came to Poll) had six votes & M[r].
Willis six; upon w[ch] the Mob who were concern'd to have a Representative for y[e] Town made diligent Enquiry after y[e] 13th Person, who
was missing, and at length found y[t] he was in Prison. After this he was
brought out, & conducted to y[e] Market Place where they took y[e] votes,
& being askt who he was for, resolutely declar'd he was for M[r]. Willis.
The said M[r]. Willis among other Good things is a man of Great
Zeal for y[e] Church w[ch] he has eminently shewn by laying out a considerable sum of Money in Beautifying and adorning the Church where he 30
lives. — This Afternoon I saw M[r]. Pawle, Fellow of Jesus Col. in Cambridge, at y[e] Publick Library, who told me y[t] D[r]. Bentley had suspended
the Publication of Horace, as I had also been inform'd before, & y[t] he
had most egregiously abus'd D[r]. Talbot y[e] former Editor, notw[th]standing
his being highly serviceable in some things to him relating particularly
to this work, w[ch] however D[r]. Bentley had not y[e] civility to acknowledge.
He also told me y[t] he had no acquaintance w[th] M[r]. Wasse but y[t] his
Character in Cambridge is that he is an ingenious Man; but I am afraid
his Parts are but rambling, since M[r]. Wasse as M[r]. Pawle told me among
other things had also some design ab[t] a Sallust some time since & had 40
done somew[t] towards it.

    Dec. 7 (Fri.). M[r]. Abell (Joseph) of Merton Coll. who took his
Master of Arts Degree *June* 18. 1702. was originally of S[t]. Edm. Hall;
but when D[r]. (then M[r].) Kennett left y[t] Hall, whereof he was Vice-
Principal, in 1695, M[r]. Abell, as several besides did, went to Lincoln
College; from whence, when Bach. of Arts, he was Elected Fellow of
Merton Col. He has several Translations of Verses &c. into English in
M[r]. Potter's Greek Antiquities, and has made a Collection of most of the

---

[1] It came to be call'd so from him (a Pudding Pye man) wth whose Puddings &
Conversation the first Founders of the Society were extremely well pleas'd.

Editions of Aristotle's Ethicks ad Nicomachum wth an Intent (if good Fellowship does not hinder) to put out a more accurate & compleat Edition of this work yⁿ is hitherto extant, with Notes. See more of him in some of the foregoing Volumes. — . . . The Scotch are so well pleased wth her Majestie's Governm^t y^t they will raise 10000 men to prosecute the War in Catalonia. — M^r. Neocorus has stole Alemannus's Correction of Suidas wthout acknowledgment. See Alem. notes upon Procopius's Hist. Arcana p. 22. — Just publish'd The Memoirs of y^t Great Minister of State Cardinal Wolsey, giving an Acc^t of his Rise &
10 Fall &c. Publish'd on purpose to prevent the Queen's being ingross'd by any particular Favourite. . . .

    Sir Edw. Acton Bar. of Queen's Coll. was created M.A. of the University of Oxon. in the Year 1667, Apr. 23. There was one Edw. Acton of Hart-Hall, who went out A.M. May 9. 1674. There have been other Actons of this University, as Francis Acton of Braz-nose Coll. who went out A.M. Jul. 4. 1681. John Acton of Hart-Hall, who took the Deg. of Bach. of Civil Law March 2. 1684. Paul Acton of New-Coll. who took his A.M. Deg. June 3. the same year. Tho. Acton of X^t Church, who took his A.M. Deg. June 28. 1665. and that of Bach. of Div. July 14. 1683. Mich. Acton of New
20 Coll. who took his A.M.'s Deg. Janu. 14. 1689. One M^r. Acton was 4 or 5 years since a Gentleman Commoner of S^t. Edm. Hall. His Tutor was M^r. Tho. Mills, between whom there was a great Intimacy, & Milles expected some preferment from him. He has now a Brother Commoner of Baliol College, where he was enter'd last Summer, being design'd for Edm. Hall, but Milles perswaded him (contrary to his Brother's Intention) to go to Baliol. —

    Rich. Adams of Braz. Nose Coll. who took his A.M.'s Deg. May 29. 1651, and has publish'd divers Sermons, as may be seen in Ant. a Wood's Athen. Oxon. & the Appendix to ye Bodlejan Catalogue, is not to be taken to be ye same with Rich. Adams of All-Souls Coll. who went
30 out A.M. Oct. 16. 1675. B. M. Dec. 11. 1679. and Doct. of Phys. Jul. 9. 1684. the former being a Non-Conformist Preacher and ye latter Principal of Magd. Hall, whither he never comes but once or twice a Year to receive his Cash. Besides these two there have been of this university Charles Adams of Braz. nose Col. who took his A.M.'s Deg. Jul. 9. 1663. Fitzherbert Adams of Lincoln Coll. who took his A.M.'s Deg. Jun. 4. 1675. his Bach. of Divinity's Jan. 23. 1682. & was upon the Death of D^r. Tho. Marshall made Rector of his college May 2. in 1685. in opposition to his most Learn'd & Conscientious Tutor D^r. George Hickes, who was put by chiefly for this reason, because he was like to prove
40 a good Disciplinarian. However it must be acknowledg'd that tho' M^r. Adams (who took his Doctor of Divinity's Deg. Jul. 3 the same year he came in Rector & was at length made Prebendary of Durham) be not a Scholar, yet he has been a considerable Benefactor to ye College. He was Vice-Chancellor in the years 1695 & 1696. and is now living. —

    Other Men of the name of Adams of this university are Rich. Adams of Magd. Col. who went out A.M. June 27. 1684. and B.D. Feb. 4. 1695. He is Brother to the Rector of Lincoln. Sam. Adams of Linc. Coll. (who was
50 originally of Cambridge) & took his A.M.'s Deg. as a member of this Coll. Apr. 16. 1670. & y^t of Bach. of Div. Nov. 20. 1677. Sam. Adams of Exet. Col. who went out A.M. June 23. 1679. & Bach. Div. Aug. 6. 1690. Sylv. Adams of Alb. Hall who went out A.M. Jan. 19. 1663. Will. Adams of

Linc. Coll. who went out A.M. March 16. 1663.   Will. Adams of Bal. Coll.
who went out A.M. Apr. 22. 1670.   Another Will. Adams of Linc. Coll. who
went out A.M. Jun. 8. 1683.   Sam. Adams of Magd. Col. who went out A.M.
1693. & has been since one of the Head Proctors.   He is now fellow of y^t
House, Moral Philosophy Reader (tho' he does not understand one word of
Aristotle) & an Affected, proud Person.   Simon Adams of Univ. Col. who
went out A.M. Jun. 25. 1694.   Will. Adams of X^t Ch. who went out A.M.
May 19. 1698.   And another of y^t name who went out ye year after March
20. one of wch has publish'd Cornelius Nepos a pretty Edition, is a quaint
Preacher & has ready for ye Press Horace with Notes, which perhaps may 10
come out when D^r. Bentley shall be pleas'd to publish his Edition & Another
of y^t Name too who went out A.M. of this House Jul. 4. 1704.   Knightley
Adams of Linc. Coll. who took his A.M.'s Deg. Jun. 18. 1702.   He is related
to ye Rector but being a good companion, when he stood for orders was turn'd
by for Deficiency, tho' he has got them since.   Sam. Adams of New Col. who
went out A.M. Nov. 19. 1702.   John Adams who publish'd an Essay conc.
Self-Murther, Lond. 1700. 8°. is a Cambridge Man.   He has Sermons in Print.
—One J. Adams has printed in a thin folio, Lond. 1680. Index Villare, or an
Alphabetical Table of all ye Cities, Market Towns, &c. in England & Wales;
wch is a Book of good use.   See more of him at ye Beginning of y^t Work. . . 20

Rights of ye Kingdom: or, Customs of our Ancestors, touching y^e
Duty, Power, Election, or Succession of our Kings and Parliam^ts, &c.
Lond. 1682. 4°.   This Book (which is exceedingly erroneous and sedi-
tious, decrying Monarchy and magnifying the Extravagant Power of
Parliam^ts) was printed in Oliver Cromwell's time under ye Name of
M^r. Bacon of Grayes Inn, but now it came out without ye Author's
Name. . .

Dec. 8 (Sat.)   Lancelot Addison of Queen's coll. took his Bach. of
Arts Deg. Jan. 25. 1654. that of Master Jul. 4. 1657, and July 6. 1675.
accumulated ye Degrees of Bach. & Doct. of Divinity.   He died a year 30
or two since being then Dean of Lichfield.   Amongst other things he
hath written, The present State of the Jews. Lond. 1676. 8°.   The
present State of Mahumedism. Lond. 1679. 8°.   Seasonable Discourse
about Catechism. Lond. 1674. 8°.   His Son Joseph Addison, who took
his A.M.'s Deg. Feb. 14. 1693. being then of Magd. Coll. is an ingenious
Man, & besides the Travells lately publish'd & other things has verses
in the Musæ Anglicanæ, to wch he præfix'd a Preface.   D^r. Addison has
another Son of Magd. Coll. who went out A.M. Feb. 3. 1702.   He was
originally of Queen's, whence he was elected Demy into Magd. Coll.
but I think he has writ nothing yet, tho' as to parts qualify'd for it. — 40
Anthony Addison of Queen's col. took his A.M. Deg. Jun. 14. 1681. &
y^t of Bach. of Div. Jul. 10. 1691. being then Fellow of the College.   He
was afterwards made vicar of S^t. Helen's in Abington & Chaplain to his
Grace the Duke of Marlborough.   He has printed, A Sermon preach'd
at S^t. Helen's in Abington on the Day of Thanksgiving to Almighty
God, Sept. 7th. 1704. for the late Glorious Victory obtained over y^e
French & Bavarians at Bleinheim &c. on Psal. 68. 28. Oxon. 1704. 4°.
Dedicated to ye D. of Marlborough. —

Propaedeumata Aphoristica Joannis Dee, Londinensis, de praestantior-
ibus quibusdam naturae virtutibus. London 1568. 4°.   50

['Typographus Lectori.' Abstract of the Dedication to Mercator, with
extract. Preface. (94–103).]

D^r. Hyde has interpreted in Latin some of the Chinese words in Confucius's works. See Arch. Bod. A. num. 1. &c. & so also of some other Chinese Books in y^t Place. — In Bodley's Archives A. 73. are M^r. Rich. Greenham's works Printed at Lond. 1605. covered wth velvet & boss'd with Silver, given by M^{rs}. Priscilla Pownoll of Bristol, whose Arms are there drawn, viz. . . Sable, A Cross argent, charg'd wth another of the first, between four Escallop Shells, of the 2^d. There is one M^r. Edward Pownoll of the same Family living now in the Parish of Shottesbrook in Berks, who was formerly Register of Bristol, & had a good Estate besides part of wch lay in the Parish of White-Waltham in ye said County of Berks; but he at last lost his Register's Place, because he did not look after it himself, but imploy'd a Deputy: upon wch entring into a tedious suit of Law he was forc'd to sell all his Estate to defray the charges being overthrown. He is a non-juror, & speaks with a great deal of Indignation ag^t K. William &c. — The L^{ds} on Friday Resolved that the Church of England redeem'd by K. W^m. is in a safe & flourishing Condition under her Majesty's Government & y^t whoever goes about to suggest y^t the Church is in danger is an Enemy to the Queen, ye Church & ye Kingdom. — Moderation in fashion, or an Answer to a Treatise, written by Francis Tallents, Entit. A short History of Schism &c. wherein his scandalous Abuse of the Primitive Fathers &c. is plainly detected & Refuted, by S. G. (suppos'd to be Sam [1] Grascomb) a Presbyter of ye Church of England.

Dec. 9 (Sun.). D^r. Smaldrich having some Acquaintance wth B^p. Burnett went to present him wth his Sermon preach'd before ye Queen last 5th of November. He was presently admitted to ye B^p., but was receiv'd and dismiss'd by him wthout one single word from ye B^p. The reason whereof is suppos'd to be the D^{rs}. Speech in Convocation to prove ye Church was in danger. — M^r. Wotton is made Prebendary of Sarum in Room of M^r. Scarborough deceas'd. — M^r. Ant. Addison a little after he got a Fellowship of Queen's College was made Chaplain to D^r. Gulston B^p. of Bristol, with whom he liv'd till the B^p.'s Death, & preach'd his Funeral Sermon upon these Words of Scripture, A man of understanding is of an Excellent Spirit. This same Sermon, mutatis mutandis, he preach'd on a Sunday Morning at St. Maries when ye Judges happen'd to be at Church, & one Robin Parsons, (formerly of University College, now Archdeacon of Glocester, who preach'd mad L^d. Rochester's Funeral Sermon) hearing M^r. Addison, when he came out of the Church said, He was an impudent Fellow for stealing before the Judges. For, says he, this Sermon was my Friend M^r. Pindar's of University College: wch was certainly true, several Persons comparing M^r. Pindar's printed Sermon with w^t they could remember of M^r. Addison's. — This same Addison who was one of those concern'd in turning by M^r. Hudson from a Fellowship in Queen's College, was a proud, Huffing, conceited Fellow, but abundantly mortify'd by the Discovery of this Sermon, & his marrying a nasty Cook's widow of neither Fortune, Beauty, nor Reputation. Upon wch he was contented to take a small Living from Queen's College call'd Hampton Powel near Oxford. —

---

[1] 'Tis he.

Dean Addison when he was a young man at Queen's had his Eye accidentally struck out by a small Bone flung at him in jest. He was Terræ Filius in yᵉ year 1657, & reflecting upon Dʳ. South in his Speech yᵉ Dʳ. stood up, & said ô monstrum horrendum, informe, ingens, cui lumen ademptum. Some time after wᶜʰ he was turn'd by a Fello[w]ship of Queen's, and after that he went along wᵗʰ Sʳ. Benjam. Bathurst into Spain who ever after had a kindness for him & help'd him to his Preferment. — Arch. A. Bod. 74. A Book of Prayers, curiously illuminated wᶜʰ belong'd (as is said) formerly to King Hen. VIII. About 400 years old. — Arch. A. Bod. 76. A Curious Book containing Pictures of all the Turkish Habits. — ib. 81. Basinij Parmensis Astronomicon Carmine Latino, cum Constellationum Figuris. 'Tis a 4ᵗᵒ. Book & yᵉ Constellations are curiously illuminated. Quære whether ever printed? — I find two or three things of his printed, but not this. At the Beginning is this Distich :

> Accipe & hæc manuum tibi quæ monumenta mearum
> Sint, precor & longum servi testentur amorem.
>   Ang.—Aquil.

Ib. 87. King James the first's Works in Latin, printed at Lond. 1619. fol. Bound in velvet. Given by the King Himself, whose Handwriting appears at yᵉ Beginning, viz. Jacobus Rex D.D. immediately under wᶜʰ is this written by another Hand viz.,

Jacobus D. G. Magnæ Britanniæ, Franciæ & Hiberniæ Rex, Fidei Defensor, qui majorum titulis literarum decus addidit, & musas pulla lugentes in veste solio imposuit purpuratas ; qui Catholicam fidem non ferro & igne (quod ijs relinquit qui nihil sibi reliquerunt in veritate præsidij) sed stilo & voce asseruit ; qui mitræ ambitione scriptis pessundata,[1] hoc regij otij negotium sibi ideo voluit superesse, ut posteris suis impensi temporis ratio constaret, exstaretque quod imitarentur, quodcunque res posceret, exemplum. Itaque suæ Oxoniensi Academiæ, sanctissimo Mnemosynes fano, fido Literariæ Reipublicæ tabulario, hoc depositum credidit, monumentum bonæ mentis, æternumque amoris sui pignus, quo sic literas prosequitur, ut inter earum cultores in Bibliotheca publica locum ambiat, qui quotus qualisque futurus sit, Almæ matris arbitrio permittit.

GEORGIUS CALVERT, Secretarius.

ib. num. 89. A Chronology from the Floud to our Saviour, folio. 'Twas formerly Mʳ. Tho. Underhill's A.M. who gave it here. It cost him, as appears at ye Beginning 3 libˢ. 6s. 8d. In the Register it is express'd that the Author was Hugh Broughton. Upon wᶜʰ having recourse to Mʳ. Broughton's Works, before wᶜʰ there is put a Preface giving some Account of his Life by Dʳ. Lightfoot, I find there yᵗ Dʳ. Lightfoot tells us that the first Book wᶜʰ made Mʳ. Broughton known to the World was his publishing his Book called A Concent of Scripture, which came out 1588. Mʳ. John Speed, a man well known, was Overseer of the Press for its Printing, a Taylor by Trade, but, by Acquaintance with Mʳ. Broughton, grown very studious in yᵉ Scriptures, & by His Directions grown very skillfull in them. While this was Printing, Mʳ. Speed, by Mʳ. Broughton's direction gathered all the Genealogies of the Bible into one view, & at last they were published under his Name, in the form we have them before our Bibles. But it

---

[1] [See original, an omission here.—Dʳ. Bliss].

was M^r. Broughton, that directed, & digested them, and there are yet fair Manuscripts of them to be shewed (amongst wch this in the Bodlejan Library I take to be one being a very fair Neat Book) some whereof have the Names in Hebrew, and Greek, and some in ye Latin Letter, & in some of them M^r. Broughton's own Hand. And one that attended him, Dorman, or Dalman, or of such a Name, had made such a Collection, by the Direction of his Master, before M^r. Speed had collected his *one view*. Yet notwthstanding this, when the Genealogie came to be published, because the B^{ps}. would not suffer M^r. Broughton's name
10 to be prefixed, M^r. Speed went away wth all the credit & profit; so y^t M^r. Speed would often confess y^t M^r. Broughton was a great Friend to him. & y^t he owed his Livelyhood in a manner to him: upon wch y^t Act of his is to be wonder'd at, which himself mention'd to some of M^r. Broughton's Friends, viz. That he had as many Manuscripts of M^r. Broughton's, as he could hold in his Arms, holding his Arms encompass'd: but, saith he, I have burnt them all; for w^t reason not known. Inquire farther about this, and remember y^t the Catalogue of MS^{ts} be alter'd in the Title of this Book. — Ibid. num. 90. Rob. Hare Collectio Privilegiorum & Libertatum universitatis Oxon. It com-
20 mences wth the time of Hen. 3^d & reaches as low as the 34th year of Q. Elizabeth. M^r. Hare made another such Collection for the use of Cambridge wch was done before this. It has a Preface, neatly & handsomly penn'd at the Beginning to the Chancellor &c. — Ibid. num. 91. Liber diversorum privilegiorum statutorum & rerum Memorabilium universitatis Oxon. fol.

Dec. 10 (Mon.). The Archb^p. of York, the B^{ps}. of London, Bath & Wells, and the B^p. of S^t. Asaph were the only spiritual L^{ds}. that spoke for ye Churches being in danger on Thursday last, particularly from the great number of Seminaries erected all over the Kingdom by the Dissenters
30 for instructing their children in different Principles. — ... Sixty of the L^{ds} voted ye Church not in Danger, 30 y^t 'tis. The same was consider'd of in ye House of Commons, on Saturday, & upon a Division 'twas carry'd that 'tis not in Danger, Noes 212 Yeas 161. — .. Arch. Bod. A. 136. The Crucifixion of our Saviour, wth Pictures colour'd of the S^{ts} & Inscriptions underneath in Greek. — In the same place num. 144. is a Book, containing a Collection of Indian Pictures most neatly done. — The Customers Replie &c. By Tho. Milles. *Lond.* 1604. Here are several MS^t Additions. It stands Arch. A. 145. — Ib. 153. Xenophontis Cyropædia Græce. Tis an old Copy fairly written, & should have been
40 compar'd by all means in the Oxford Edition by D^r. Wells. — Ib. 154. The History of the Bible from Genesis to Job most splendidly illuminated. Some have computed y^t it could not cost less yⁿ a thousand lib^s. to do it. — In a Book writ by D^r. Pitcarne a Scotch man, (who was for some time Professor of Physick at Leyden) intit. De inventoribus rerum, he has made D^r. Gregory, our Savilian Professor of Astronomy, the first Author of ye Quadratura curvarum linearum, upon wch several persons, taking Notice that this was sometime before treated of by S^r. Isaac Newton in his Lectures kept in Trinity College Library Camb. wch some Scotchmen got admittance to, (stealing several remarkable Things out of them)
50 D^r. Gregory & his Friends were so asham'd at this Discovery, that what

Pitcarne had said of D^r. Gregory was left out in ye 2^d Edition of it.   S^r. Isaac Newton has complain'd that D^r. Gregory, who borrow'd most of the best materials in his Book of Astronomy from Sir Isaac, has made little or no mention of him but just in his Preface : so y^t S^r. Isaac fearing least y^t in Process of time D^r. Gregory's Book might happen to be printed wthout this Preface, and consequently he be thought the Author of what S^r. Isaac himself had before him discovered, resolv'd to make another Edition of His Book call'd Principia Math. — To shew that the Dutchess of Marlborough (commonly call'd Queen Zarah,) has the Ascendant over the Queen I could not but remark these two Instances ; The first is, 10 That when the Queen had made a Grant to one M^r. Dobyns of a Living (wch Dobyns was a Master of University Coll. & Pupil to D^r. Hudson) the said Queen Zarah made the Queen recall the Grant before it pass'd the Seals, upon this suggestion of Zarah's, That His Father voted against Killigrew at S^t. Albans.   The second is this, That when Prince George (who is lookt upon as a man of little Spirit & understanding) sollicited the Queen his wife for a Place for some Friend of his, Zarah who happend to be by at that time, cry'd out, *X^t Madam I am promis'd it before.* — D^r. Tho. Guidott an ingenious (but vain, conceited, whimsical) Physitian at ye Bath, amongst other Books publish'd Theophilus de urinis out 20 of a MS^t in the Bodlejan Library, & never had ye Civility to send a Copy to ye Library, as he was oblig'd to do.

Dec. 11 (Tu.). . . Chronica Juridicialia or a General Calendar of the Years of our L^d. God &c. *Lond.* 1685. 8°.   The Author — Cook a Lawyer. — Rad. Fornerij Rerum Quotidianarum libri III. . . Pliny Jun. emended in. Fornerius. — Hen. Aldrich of X^t Church took ye Deg. of A.M. Apr. 3. 1669. & was made Canon of y^t House Feb. 15. 1681. in the Room of D^r. Sam. Speed. In wch year (Mar. 2) he accumulated the Degrees in Divinity, and on the 17 of June 1689 he was installed Dean of the same place, in room of M^r. Joh. Massey, who withdrew himself 30 from y^t office in ye latter End of Nov. going before.   This D^r. Aldrich, is a most ingenious, Learned man, &, wch is above all, a sincere Member of the church of England, as he has shew'd by divers of his late Proceedings, whilst Prolocutor to the Lower House of Convocation during the last Sessions.   He is likewise a most affable complaisant Gentleman & has nothing in him of Affectation.   Amongst other things he has written,

A Reply to two Discourses conc. the Adoration of our B. Saviour in ye Holy Eucharist. Oxon. 1687. 4°.   W^{ch} Discourses were written by M^r. Abr. Woodhead & publish'd by M^r. Obadiah Walker.—Artis logicæ Compendium. Oxon. 1696. 8°. for the use of the Honble M^r. Charles Boyle now Earl of 40 Orrery.   W^{ch} Book is scurrilously spoken of by D^r. Rich. Bently in his Answer to M^r. Boyle's ingenious Discourse ag^t D^r. Bentley's Dissertation upon Phalaris.

D^r. Aldrich has also critical notes in the Marmora Oxon. upon some obscure Places relating to musick not understood by the Publisher D^r. Prideaux.   He has also taken care to continue the new Years Gift since the Death of B^p. Fell, & there is one of his Relations (of the same name wth himself,) a Bach. of Arts of X^t. church (an ingenious young man especially in Poetry) who is now taking pains ab^t Homer's Odysses design'd for a new years Gift for the next Year.   50

Arch. Bod. A. num. 161. A folio Book containing the Statutes of the University & divers other things pertaining to it, collected by M^r. George Darrell Proctor of the University. An. 1604. — Ib. num. 166. Registrarium FF. sive Liber Epistolarum Universitatis Oxon. ab anno Domini 1508 usque ad an. 1597. In fol. 17. b. is the University's Letter to Cardinal Wolsey in 1514, 6 Kal. Jul. as also in fol. 18. b, fol. 19. b, fol. 21. b. &c. In this Book are a great many scribblings of William Smith A.M. of University Coll. most of them of very little or no moment, as most of his other things are w^{ch} (contrary to his oath) he has inserted in
10 several Books of the Library. There are some also of Ant. a Wood & Bryan Twyne. This Book of great use to him y^t shall write Cardinal Wolsey's Life. In fol. 54 b. is King Hen. VIIIth's Letter to the University desiring they would make M^r. Robt Porret under Beadle of Divinity that place being vacant dated at the Manor of Newehall 29 Sept. 1522. In fol. 58. a. is the same King's Letter (dated Nov. 25. an. 1522) to Tho. Shelton mayor of Oxoñ. commanding him to set at Liberty & restore to him his Goods Tho. Pantrey Squire Beadle of Arts in Oxon, whom he had seiz'd as being a Frenchman. The same King's Letter in fol. 64. a. to Walt. Gover and Rich. Wakelyn Bayliffs of the Town of Oxoñ com-
20 manding them to redress certain Abuses in Victuals sold & bought in y^e University, dated at Woodstock Oct. 18. 1523. Three Letters of the same King (in fol. 104. a. &c.) to the University relating to his Divorce, the first dated March 5. 15$\frac{29}{30}$, at Windsor—the 2^d at Windsor March 6th an. ejusd. The 3^d at Windsor March 27th. 1530. In fol. 105. a. is a Letter of the same King to the University about sundry matters to be declar'd to them by D^r. Bell one of his Counsell, dated March 6th at Windsor an. 15$\frac{29}{30}$. In fol. 106. b. is another of his to the University ab^t y^t Divorce dated at Windsor Apr. 13. 1530. In fol. 107. b. His Letter to the University for W^m. Standish A.M. & Fellow of Magd. Coll. to succeed Tho.
30 Key Registrarie of the University, wch Letter is wthout Date, but M^r. Wood in Ath. Oxon. Vol. I. p. 136 referrs it to ye year 1543. tho' here it comes under ye year 1541. Ibid. His Letter to ye University, dated at Greenwich Apr. 23. 1541. conc. the Electing of Proctors &c. Fol. 109. a. His Letter to ye University, desiring an Account of the Articles of Wickliff condemn'd by them, but also of the Confirmation thereupon of the counsel of Constance, dated Jul. the last, An. ejusd. In fol. 125. b. His Letter to ye University for Electing John Glyn Yeoman Bedle of Arts, dat. at Greenwich July 6th An. D. 1533. regn. 25th. — 'Tis reported for certain M^r. Jo. Addison is marry'd to the Countess-Dowager of Warwick. — M^r.
40 Bromley in the Close of his Speech (in the House of Commons) about ye Churche's being in danger gave this Instance of its being so, that the L^d. Godolphin was now the Prime Minister of State, who in King James's time was one of the Privy Councel for sending the B^{ps} to ye Tower. — M^r. Charles Boyle, now L^d. Orrery, is marry'd to the Lady Eliz. Cecil. — B^p. Patrick made a Speech in ye House of L^{ds} to have ye two Universities visited, especially (as he was pleas'd to say) that insolent University of Cambridge, wch put a slur upon a very Honble person (L^d. Godolphin's Son) who had the Royal Recommendation to be y^{eir} Representative. — I am told by D^r. Hudson that M^r. Thoresby of Yorkshire has a great
50 Collection of Original Letters of Persons famous for their Learning. He

has a good Collection of Coyns (as may appear by w^t I have said of him before) & other Curiosities.

Dec. 12 (Wed.).   A Letter from S^r. John Packington to D^r. Lloyd B^p. of Worcester communicated to me by D^r. Charlett.

Westwood, June y^o 6th, 1705.

My Lord,—The Esteem and Veneration I have always had for your order, & the Belief I have that some People, not only put you upon acting those things wch very much lessen your Character in the world, but also represent Matters by a false Light wch leads to Errour, together with a desire I have to free myself from any Imputation, is the occasion of your Lordships being 10 troubled with this.

Your Lordship has been extreamly misinform'd by those that have told you that I had any prejudice either to ye Bishops in general, or to your self in particular ; our Form of Church Government I believe to be the best in ye World, & consequently I respect ye Heads of it, neither should I have appear'd against your Person but in the necessary Vindication of my self and Friends.   I am not conscious of any Provocation I have given you, unless it's reckoned one to vote and Act in the House of Commons, according to the best of my Judgment for the Service of the Church and Nation ; when your Lordship first shew'd your Displeasure, and thought fit to asperse me in every 20 place, making me a Drunkard, Lewd and Guilty of all sort of Vice, & not content with this you rak't up the Ashes of the Dead, accusing my whole Ancestry with the same Faults, who are now uncapable of justifying themselves.

Your Lordship did not stop here but proceeded to treat with the utmost severity all my Friends y^t you had any Power or Influence over.   Some you turn'd out, others you threaten'd, & to all you appear'd very angry, for no other Reason than their Voting for me.   I think I may now say with Modesty That the Resentments you shew'd were very extraordinary for a Churchman, & that your Lordship did not do yourself much Honour by Acting after such 30 a Manner.   For admitt I was culpable as your Lordship represented me, you that are so good a Textuary cannot but be sensible I ought to be admonished first privately, & then in the presence of two or three Witnesses before being publickly expos'd ; & even Hereticks are not to be rejected, 'till after the first and second Admonition ; & if I was in an Errour as to Principles, your Lordship should have endeavour'd to convince me before you condemn me.   This I must confess is very strange to me that I should disoblige a Bishop of the Church of England, & that the Dissenters should be more in His Favour than a Member of it, or that it should be reckon'd Persecution of them to keep them out of y^t Power they have ever made ill use of, which so many Families 40 do yet feel & particularly my own.   My Lord I have represented things to you wth much Truth and Plainness, not to pursue Pique or Revenge.   And it will be your own Fault, if this appears upon the Stage again.   I have dayly brought to me greater Cause of Complaint than ever against your Lordship ; I have several Letters to produce on occasion & am urg'd by many of my Friends to right them as far as lyes in my Power.   There are some who are Sufferers upon my Account already, & others that are like to become so themselves and Families, & I find the Strictness of the Canon only made use of to the Disadvantage of my Friends.   I forbear to mention many vexatious and unneighbourly Proceedings against your own Tenants.   But your Lord- 50 ship must give me leave to tell you once more, that this way of Acting neither consists with Christian Charity in respect of yourself, nor with the Liberty of a Free Parliament in respect to ye Votes ; it being contrary to ye Constitution, that threats or any Compulsive Methods should be made use of to gain or hinder any Elector from voting for whom he pleases.   I have nothing more to add but to assure your L^{d}ship that it lyes wholly in your Power to put an End to these Disputes by ceasing to persecute my Friends; But if your Lordship does not I must with great Regret endeavour again to right myself & them. I am with all imaginable Duty (unless your Lordship give me cause to ye contrary) as you were pleased to conclude in one of your Letters,

Your Lordships most obedient

humble Servt

J. P.

There is an Index come out pointing to divers of the Ridiculous, childish observations made by M^r. Addison in his travells. In one sheet
10 in 8°. — The Arms of the University of Oxon are A field Jupiter, a Book Expansed in Fesse, Luna, garnished, having seven Labels with Seales, Sol, & this Inscription, Sapientia & Felicitate Saturne, between three Crowns of the Third. This Bearing appeareth to be very ancient, from y^t which is ingraven in the Top of S^t. Samson's Church at Grekelade, in ¹ Gloucestershire, wch is an Argument that this University (as is commonly held) was first planted there in the old Britains' time. The Book it self some have thought to signifie y^t Book mention'd in ye Revelations, having Seven Seals; but these here are taken rather to be the seven Liberal Sciences, & ye Crowns to be the Reward of Learning and
20 Wisdome; & the Triplicity of the Crownes are taken to represent the three Cardinal Professions or Faculties before Specified. The Inscription has varied according to variety of times; some having Sapientia & Felicitate; others (& that very Ancient) Deus illuminatio mea; others this; Veritas liberabit, Bonitas regnabit; & others thus; In principio &c.; In the Beginning was the word, & ye word was wth God. Vide Guillim's Heraldry. This must be consider'd of in my Notes to S^r. John Spelman's Life of King Alfred. — M^r. Tho. Wise, B.D. & Fellow of Exeter College, has just publish'd The Reason and Philosophy of Atheism confuted, being for ye most p^t either an Abridgment or Improvem^t of D^r. Cudworth's
30 Intellectual System. 4to. The Bulk of it deters most from either buying or reading it. — In the Register above mention'd FF. Arch. Bod. 166. in fol. 127. b. is K. H. 8th's Letter to the University for chosing the B^p. of Linc. (D^r. John Longland) chancellor of the University, & conc. a Question about the Power and Practise of the B^p. of Rome, dat. at Greenwich May 18. 1534.—In fol. 129. a. His Letter to them for chosing John Powlet M.A. Proctor in room of Dunstan Lacie deceased, dat. from the Manner of Langlay Sept. 13. a^o. 1534. the 25th (or rather 26th) Regni. — Arch. A. Bod. 168. Principal Passages of Affairs between ye two Kingdoms of England & France under ye Reigns of K. Edw. III. &
40 K. H. 5. of France, &c. dedicated to K. Charles the I. &c. Quære who the Author? He says in the Dedication that he translated it out of an old MS^t in Latin. He gives a great Commendation of Titus Livius who writ the Life of Hen. V^th. It may be worth printing in a Continuation of D^r. Gale's Collection. I suppose it may have been taken out of some such Book as S^r. John Osborne lent to D^r. Hudson. — In this Vol. also is S^r. Fra. Vere's Journey of Cales, His Island Jorney, & his Defeat at Turnhoult. — Ib. num. 169. Argumenta facta pro successione Regis Angliæ ad Regnum Franciæ, cum alijs id genus. — Ib. num. 170. A Dutifull

¹ Wiltshire.

Defence of the Lawfull Regiment of women by Hen. Howard (Son to Hen. Howard Earl of Surrey & afterwards) Earl of Northampton. in Fol. This Book wch is most learnedly written was never yet printed. This Earl of Northampton was reckon'd the most learned of the Nobility in England, & for y^t Reason had his Earldom conferr'd on him by K. James I^st. — Ib. num. 171. Catalogus Codic. MSS. in Bibliotheca Cæsarea Viennæ. — Ib. 172. Catalogus MSS. Bibliothecæ Vaticanæ. Done by Sam. Slade of Merton College, wch is not taken notice of by Ant. a Wood, who nevertheless in the Fasti mentions his Great Assistance to S^r. Hen. Savile in his Edition of Chrysostome.—In this vol. is also a 10 Catalogue of the MSS^ts given by Cardinal Bessarion to the Basilica of S^t. Mark at Venice, made by Bessarion himself whose Epistle is prefix'd to Xtophe Maure Doge of Venice, which will be of good use to him that shall give an Acc^t of ye MSS^ts here or of those sav'd since the taking of Constantinople &c.—In the same Vol. likewise is Catalogus Librorum MSS. Mediceæ Bibliothecæ Florent: And of the Elector Palatine's at Heidelberg. — Ib. 176. Arguments for ye succession of ye Kings of England to France. — Just printed at ye Theatre Josippon seu Josephi Ben-Gorionis Historiæ Judaicæ Libri sex integri hactenus inediti, nunc primum ex Hebræo in Latinum translati, & Notis illustrati opera & studio 20 Joannis Gagnier A.M. 4to. This Book is dedicated to the Archb^p. of Canterbury, and was printed at the charge of the B^p. of Worcester, with whom M^r. Gagnier lives, & receives from his L^dship great kindnesses, w^ch, together with those receiv'd from the Archb^p., have induc'd him to promise other things of this Nature provided this present work be well receiv'd. There is likewise finish'd at the Theatre, Sophoclis Ajax Flagellifer, & Electra Gr. Lat. cum Scholijs antiquis & Annott. per Tho. Johnson Etonensem. 8°. Which M^r. Johnson, is now one of the Ushers of Eton-Schoole, & so being not able to be in Town imploy'd M^r. Andrew Rinman, a Swede to transcribe the Scholia (such I mean that 30 were not publish'd before, wch are a considerable number) from MSS^ts in the Bodlejan Library, & to fit them to the old Edition, & one of Oriel col. to correct the sheets as they came from the Press. This M^r. Johnson has done some other small things for the use of Schools, with notes taken from the larger ones of others, w^thout adding anything from MSS^ts or other monuments of y^t nature, wch might make them acceptable to curious & learned Men. It were to be wish'd he would go on wth Sophocles in the same manner as this is printed. M^r. Aldrich's Edition of Homer's Odysses is also just finish'd.

Dec. 13 (Th.). Tullij opera per Jac. Gronovium. 8°. The Table of 40 the old Bachanalian Laws publish'd by ye Younger Gronovius in the first Vol. of his Edition of Tully. But he does not tell us where the Original is, & gives but a very brief Acc^t thereof. Quære of D^r. Smith whether he can inform any thing more conc. it? Desire D^r. Hudson also to ask, when he writes, his Friend Perizonius ab^t it. — The Case stated conc. the Judicature of ye House of Peers in the Point of Appeals. 1675. 8°. Ld Hollis then s^d to be Author, Who also was s^d to write the Book printed at Lond. the year after in 8°., call'd, The Case stated of the Jurisdiction of ye H. of L^ds in ye Point of Impositions. — The Authority of the Magistrate ab^t Religion discussed, in a Rebuke to ye Prefacer 50

(i. e. D^r. Parker) of a late Book of B^p. Bramhalls, by J. H. i.e. John Humfreys. Lond. 1672. 8º. who likewise was Author of The Obligation of Human Laws discussed, pr. at Lond. 8º. 1671. . . .

Amongst Arch. B^p. Laud's MSS. in Bib. Bodl. A. 29. is Lexicon Harmonicum, in quo ostenditur Harmonia Linguæ Græcæ, Latinæ, Anglicæ cum Hebræa. The Author was Will. Lamplugh A.M. & there said to be a very great Linguist. He died in the year 1636, leaving the work unfinished. M^r. Wood in his Athenæ has not mention'd him. — MS. Laud B. 65. Mexican Hieroglyphicks. — Ib. B. 155. Fragmenta quaed. 10 de rebus gestis Angl. & Francorum, Gallice ad. Picturis elegantissimis. Fol. — Ib. B. 167. A folio Book containing Draughts of a great Number of Arms. In fol. 5. b. are the Arms of Wm. Inglysh ; . . . in fol. 6. a. Those of Lyonell Fitz de Roy ; . . . in fol. 8. a. of Robert Luttrell ; . . . in f. 17. a. Monsor Willyam Paynell ; . . . Monsor Thomas Paynell. — When ye Question was Debated in the House of Lords about ye Churche's being in Danger, the Duke of Leeds made an Excell^t Speech, in wch there was this particular very remarkable : I am (saith he) too far advanced in years to be suspected of any Design of Ambition ; so y^t my words may be look'd upon as proceeding from the greatest Sincerity. 20 And here I confess 'tis my Persuasion y^t ye Church is in very great Danger, & for this Reason in particular, y^t I have heard the Queen herself say that she thought the Church could never be safe unless the Occasional Bill should pass.

Dec. 14 (Fri.). . . . This Morning about 7 of the Clock died of the Gout in the Stomach D^r. Tho. Sykes President of Trinity College & Margaret Professor of Divinity in this University, to wch last Place he was elected 6 Nov. 1691, on the sudden Death of D^r. Hen. Maurice of Jesus Coll. & to the former upon the Death of D^r. Ralph Bathurst in the year 1704. He took ye Degree of M.A. Febr. 12. 1666, that of B. of D. 30 Jul. 3. 1677, & y^t of D^r. May 12. 1692. When he was Fellow of the College he was a great Tutor, & in his younger Years accounted a man of Quick Apprehension ; but when Years grew upon him, he became infirm, & had not y^t ready utterance as might be expected from a Professor. However he has left behind him the Character of an Honest Man, & a learned Divine. After he became President he spent near 400 lib^s. in Repair of the President's Lodgings. He has printed a sermon, preach'd at ye consecration of the New Chapel of Trinity College. — In the Book of Heraldry above mention'd (vid. p. 155.) fol. 22. a. Monso^r. Willyam Heron ; . . . in fol. 23. b. Monsr. Thomas Trussel ; 40 . . . ib. fol. 37. a. John Paynell ; . . . ib. fol. 38. a. Monsr. William Trussel[1] ; . . . Ib. fol. 33. a. Monsr. Johan Paynell ; . . . Ib. fol. 39. b. Monsr. Thomas Paynell ; . . . Ib. fol. 45. a. Monsr. Odynell de Heron ; . . . Monsr. Roger Heron ; . . . Monsr. Jhon Heron ; . . . Ib. fol. 45. a. Mons. Symond Weltdene ; . . .

All the Armes in this Booke before mention'd, tho' not express'd whence taken, (to pag. 40) seem to have been drawn from some old Monuments. — John Trussel, sometimes a Winchester Scholar, after-

---

[1] Quære whether this W^m. Trussel be not S^r. William Trussel who founded the College of Shottesbrooke in Berks ?

wards a Trader and Alderman of that City, continued Daniel's History of Eng. He likewise continued a certain old MS. belonging to the Bᵖˢ of Winton, containing, as it were, an History of the Bᵖˢ and Bᵖrick, wᶜʰ continuation came down to Curles time. He also writ A Description of the City of Winchester, wᵗʰ an Historical Relation of divers memorable Occurrences touching the same, fol. Also a Preamble to yᵉ same of the Origen of Cities in General.—Quære whether this Trussel be any ways descended from the famous Trussels in Edw. 3ᵈˢ time & before? — In the Middle of the Book of Heraldry above mention'd, are Armes taken from a very antient Rolle of Parchment, so worne as scarcely to be discern'd, A.D. 1589. Amongst wᶜʰ those of Sʳ. Geff. Luttrell. . . Afterwards follow Lese sont Nosmes and les armes des Banaretes de Engleterr in le Temps le Roy Edward le prime a Conqueste, amongst wᶜʰ, Sʳ. John le Estrange . . . & Sʳ. Roger Le Estrange . . . Sʳ. Rychard Baskervylle . . . Sʳ. Jhon Paynell . . . Sʳ. Jhon de Heron . . . Sʳ. Jhon Paynell . . . Sʳ. Will. Paynell . . . Sʳ. Jeffrey Luttrell . . . Sʳ. Rafe Paynell . . . Sʳ. Hamond L'Estrange . . . Sʳ. John Le Strange . . . Sʳ. Jhon le Estrange . . . Sʳ. Odynell Heron . . . Sʳ. Roger Heron . . . ━ Then follow, Cy Comence les Nosmes and les Armes de Seigneuirs Noble Homes qui estoyent avecques le Roy Edwarde Prymer a la Seige de Karlaverocke in Escoteland 1300. Amongst whom Jhon le Strange . . . Jhon Paynell. . . . Next follow,—Memorandums in a peice of the old Role set in the old Booke. Amongst these Sʳ. Will. Paynell . . . Sʳ. Walter Baskervile . . . Sʳ. William Paynell . . . Sʳ. Foulke Strange . . . Sʳ. Jhon le Strange . . . Sʳ. Hamond Le Estrange. . . .

Dec. 15 (Sat.). . . . The Dissenting Lᵈˢ gave four Reasons for their Dissent: yᵗ yᵉ Church is in no Danger. There were only the Bɪˢ of London and Bath & Wells & 24 Temporal Lᵈˢ yᵗ sign'd it. — Sʳ. Robᵗ Miller of Chilchester is dead. — The Countess of Abingdon is removed from being one of yᵉ Ladies of yᵉ Bed-Chamber to yᵉ Queen & is succeeded by the Dutchess of Sᵗ. Albans. — Quære wᵗ Armes are now in the Church of Ewe-Elme in Oxfordshire. There are several of them in the last Editions of Sʳ. Jeoff. Chaucer's Works. His Arms were parted per Pale, Argent and Gules, a Bend Counter-changed. . . .

[Notes and Queries on Arms in the windows of Shottesbrook, White Waltham, and Lawrence Waltham churches. (170–176.)]

Dec. 15. H. to Dr. T. Smith. Will have the shield engraved for Livy. Dr. K. ought to travel up and down himself (like Mr. Weaver) for his work on epitaphs. Mr. Browne Willis (now M.P. for Buckingham) and his designs for a new volume of *Monast. Angl.*; Peckwater Quad.; Life of Wolsey, &c. Transcribes an account of the work from Dee's *Propaedeumata Aphoristica* (London, 1568, 4to, ed. 2). Discovery of Roman coins at Clifton, near Edlington, Doncaster (now in possession of Ralph Thoresby). ? Author of *Letter to a Bishop conc. the present Settlement and the New Oaths,* 1689; also of answer thereto (? Capt. Hatton). Tanner's account of Wood in his last sickness. 'Pray be pleas'd . . to let me know wᵗ Character Mr. Addison's travells bears at London. It seems to me to be very trite, and as such tis esteem'd by Scholars here.' Laud B. 167 contains the arms of T. and W. Trussel, Robt. and Geoff. Luttrell, and W. and T. Paynell. 'Yesterday morning, being Friday, abᵗ 7 of the Clock, died of the Gout in yᵉ Stomach

Dec. 16 (Sun.). D^r. Sikes made a Will ab^t 4 years before his Death, whereby he left 300 lib^s. to ye College. The Executors in Trust are M^r. Allemont Senior Fellow of Trinity, M^r. Hinton Chaplain of Corpus X^ti, & Heywood Junior the Atturney. — This day in the Morning preach'd at S^t. Mary's D^r. Baron, master of Baliol College, upon Rom. 16. 17. . . . The main drift of his Discourse was about Occasional Conformity, shewing how dangerous it was to the establish'd Church of England, & w^t little reason there was to trust the Presbyterians, & other Schismaticks, who had already once ruin'd the Church & Government. He likewise at large
10 shew'd w^t little reason the Presbyterians & other Sectaries had for Dissenting from us, both from the nature of our Church Governm^t & from Testimonies drawn from the chief of our moderate Divines, & from the best Writers of the Protestant Churches beyond Sea. This he did, wth good Judgment, in relation to Episcopacy, our Liturgy & Ceremonies ; & concluded the whole wth a pertinent Application, warning all the Auditors to take care to follow the Injunction of the Text, & avoid those y^t cause Divisions, namely the Presbyterians &c. ; who are certainly guilty of the many schisms wch now unhappily disturb ye Church. — Tho' M^r. John Chamberlayn has in ye Preface to his Father's Present State of Eng. in
20 the Edition of 1704, represented to the World the Knavery of M^r. Guy Miege in his New State of Eng. who transcrib'd for the most part the present State, w^thout due Acknowledgment ; yet he has not at ye same time been pleas'd to mention the Assistance his Father receiv'd from M^r. Andrew Allam of Edm. Hall, who drew up several sheets & communicated them to his Father taking a journey on purpose to London for y^t End, where he got the small Pox, & dy'd of it ; but his journey was not satisfactory to him, he being deny'd the sight of D^r. Chamberlayn, whom he went in a great measure to see, & if his company had been vouchsaf'd he would have imparted to him several other useful matters wch would have
30 added much to the worth of the Book. But the D^r. was not only unkind to him in this, but likewise when a New Edition of the Book was set out, he would not declare who was his chief Friend in the Additions, & his Son has follow'd his Example. Memorandum that the Account of the Publick Library in Oxford in the said Edition of 1704 was written by M^r. Humf. Wanley.

Dec. 17 (Mon.). Those old, thick and strong Walls at ye West Gate of the Cathedral Church of Winchester the Remains of a College in the Time

---

Dr. Sikes President of Trinity Coll. and Margaret Profess^r. He died rich, & has left the Character of an Honest Man behind him. He spent near 400 lib^s. presently after he became president on the President's lodgings, wch makes well for his successor, who 'tis thought will be either Mr. Allemont or Mr. Barker. Candidates for Professor are Dr. Baron Master of Balliol and Mr. Wynne of Jesus College (the same that epitomiz'd Lock's Hum. understanding) ; but the X^t Church men, as 'tis said, have put a 3^d Person, viz. Mr. Grabe, to the great Resentment of some, who do not think it creditable for the University to chose a Foreigner, who never receiv'd the sacrament after ye Church of England way, into a Place for wch we have so many in England qualify'd beyond Mr. Grabe, whose skill does not lie in controversial Divinity.'

of the Romans, where Constans the Monk resided, whom his Father Constantine (when he put on the Purple in Opposition to Honorius the Emperor) made Cæsar and afterwards Augustus.   Quære more about this. See Camden's History of Hampshire, & his Introduction to ye Brit. in the Roman Affairs.—After the said College was ruin'd Kenewalch, King of ye West-Saxons, founded here, in it's room, a Cathedral Church and B^{pp}rick.   See Camden ibid.   In a new Impression of Ductor Historicus must be better consider'd w^t is there said concerning K. Lucius's founding a Monastery here. Perhaps y^t to be understood of the Monks here in the time of ye Romans before mention'd. If so M^r. Tanner's Notitia Monastica 10 to be corrected.—Consider also w^t M^r. Camden has there said about the New Minster's being founded by King Ælfred, & see whether 'twas not rather Founded by King Edward ye Elder according to the Will of his Father ye s^d K. Ælfred.   This must be specify'd in the Notes to ye Life of King Ælfred by S^r. John Spelman.   In the s^d Notes also, when an Account is given of Domesday Book must be mention'd the Cross of King Canute ye Dane wherein was describ'd the yearly Revenue of all England; wch Cross was reposited in the New Minster after it's being translated to Hide by King Hen. I. & was burnt in the fire wch happen'd there soon after ye Translation.   His Cross seems to be something like 20 Domesday Book. ▬ Ninnius tells us y^t Silchester in Hampshire was founded by Constantius Son of Constantine ye Great, & y^t he died here. This fabulous, it being certain y^t he died in Cilicia, & was buried at Constantinople.   However 'tis probable here was also an Honorary Monument Erected to him, it being certain y^t this was a flourishing & noted Town in those Times from the Coyns dug up here of Constantine Junior Brother to Constantius wch have on their Reverse PROVIDENTLÆ CÆSS.   There are still Remaining large and magnificent Reliques of ye Walls, two Miles in Cumpace and deserve an accurate view by such as study the Antiquities of this County. ▬ ... Petrus Cratepoleus in Catalogo Academiarum totius orbis 30 makes Cambridge to have been founded by Sigebert or rather by Cantaber, & restored by Sigebert. He speaks more honourably of it than of Oxford, whereof he makes K. Ælfred Founder. ▬ ... M^r. Will. Worth Fellow of All-Souls Coll. is made Archdeacon of Worcester, in Room of M^r. I. Fleetwood deceas'd.   This Person was of Queen's Coll., afterwards of Edm. Hall, and at length Chaplain to ye B^p. of Worcester, D^r. Lloyd, who by his Interest wth the present Archbishop of Canterbury got M^r. Worth in Fellow of All-Souls upon a Devolution of the Election of Fellows to ye said Arch Bishop by the Death of D^r. Leopold W^m. Finch.   This Person has publish'd Tatian, concerning which and how carried on, I have already 40 spoken enough in one of the preceding Volumes.   The valuation of this Archdeaconry, according to the Book of Taxations made in the Reign of Edw. I. a Copy whereof is in the Bodlejan Library, is in the Queen's Book, 30 marks per An. besides a Parsonage annext. ▬ [Arms at the Beginning of a MS^t Copy of Peter Comestor's History, C. 122. Laud.] .... ▬ Amongst the same Books C. 123. is Missale Fratrum Prædicatorum, wch tho' in the Catalogue put down as being a MS^t yet is a printed Book. 'Tis a very splendid Letter, & an antient Book, and a very great Rarity. ▬ D. 17. Laud. The Works of S^t. Columb in Irish verse. At ye Beginning of this MS^t is this written in a loose Paper.   50

Oxford the 9th of August 1673.

This Book is call'd the Works of St. Colum in Irish Verses, and the Reader may see many famous things in it, as well of his own Life, as also of Prophesies, from himself and other saints, many good Advertisements, for Kings, Princes & Ecclesiastical Persons, how to govern and regulate in the Commonwealth. I pray Reader make use of it, at ye Perswasions of S^r

Your Friend & Servt

TULLY CONRY.

— M^r. Bromley in a Letter last Night to ye Vice-Chancellor relates, That two Bishops intimated to a Member of the House of Commons, That if any person should chance to speak against ye Fanatick Seminaries, it would be proper to retort upon him Parker's Academy at Oxford, wch was done accordingly by a Member of ye House of Commons, who said he had his Information from two Bishops. Now the Business of Parker's Academy is only this, that he has a Son of Collonel Tufton's, who boards with him, & is suppos'd to be instructed by him. — The L^{ds} and Commons have agreed to Adress the Queen and Congratulate her upon their Resolution, That ye Church is in no Danger, whereas towards ye latter End of the last Sessions, the L^{ds} were for bringing in a Bill, to prevent ye Danger the Church was in from ye Growth of Popery.

Dec. 18 (Tu.). ... Amongst M^r. Selden's Books in the Pub. Libr. ... There is a Copy of the first Edition of ye 39 Articles, Lond. 1563, wth the Subscription of the lower House of the Convocation of Canterbury in MS^t, under the Subscribers own Hands.

VERSES UPON THE L^{ds} RESOLVE THAT Y^e CHURCH IS IN NO DANGER.

Good Hallifax & pious Wharton cry
The Church has Vapours, there's no
    Danger nigh.
those we love not, we no Danger
    see;
Were they all hang'd, where would the
    Danger be?

What e're you see there is no ground for
    fears,
You must not trust your senses but the
    Peers.
So the lewd Ravisher that's voyd of shame
First stops the Mouth, and then deflowres
    the Dame.

Archiv. Laud. D. 28. Guilelmi de Saona Rhetorica. 'Tis a printed Book, & at ye End is added,

compilatum autem fuit hoc opus in Alma universitate Cantabrigiæ, Anno Domini 1478, die 6 Julij. quo die festum Sanctæ Marthæ recolitur: Sub protectione Serenissimi Regis Anglorum Edvardi quarti. Impressum fuit hoc presens opus Rhetoricæ Facultatis apud Villam Sancti Albani, Anno Domini M^o.CCCC^o.LXXX°.

'Tis in 4to. — Arch. Laud. D. 135. A Large Vellam Missale in Folio. 'Tis a Printed Book at Herbipoli or Wirtzburg in the year 1481, in a large Splendid Letter; being printed by Jeorius Ryser at ye Command of Rudolph B^p. of Wirtzburg, & the Chapter there, as appears by their Preface dated the same Year, at ye End of wch are their Arms ingraven on Copper, wch is a very considerable Curiosity, being in all probability one of ye first Specimens of Ingraving in Copper. — Arch. Laud. D. 138. Officia Divina ad usum Ecclesiæ Herbipolensis. A large folio. This was also printed at Herbipoli, but in w^t year appears not, two or three Leaves at the beginning and Ending being wanting. However 'tis not of the same year wth ye former, the Letter being considerably lesse.

Dec. 19 (Wed.). I am told by one who understands English Books well that besides D^r. Thomas James, D^r. Watson also (a Romish Priest) has made Father Parsons Author of Leycester's Commonwealth; but he could not then tell me in w^t piece this was to be found, nor have I yet made any search. — . . . To day D^r. Hudson shew'd me the following Coyns [six in number], wch he rec^d to be explain'd from M^r. Wase (Son to the ingenious Xtopher Wase late Beadle of Law in this university). . . . The said Coyns are all Brass of the 3^d magnitude. M^r. Wase (who is 10 a man of Parts & some Curiosity) has other Coyns in his Custody, wch he designs to leave to the College, where there is already a Collection, as I am inform'd by one who knows. — Rich. White, commonly call'd Basingstoke, amongst other things that he writ (where of there is only his History of England in ye Publick Library) is Ælia Lælia Crispis. Epitaphium antiquum in agro Bononiensi adhuc videtur; a diversis hactenus interpretatum varie : novissime autem à Ric. Vito Basingstochio, amicorum precibus explicatum. Patav. 1568, in 6 sh. and a half in 4to. This I must see. — Arch. Laud. E. 18. Petri Cameliani liber carminum in Beatæ Katerinæ Ægyptiæ X^ti sponsæ vitam. The Dedication to 20 Robt. Bracunbure Keeper of the Tower of London, & in it is a fulsom commendation of King Rich. III. — MS. Laud. E. 31. In this Book are verses taken from the Windows of the Church of St. Alban's before the Dissolution of Monasteries, & the Destruction of painted Glass by the Fanaticks, as likewise verses in the Windows of ye Library of S^t. Albans transcrib'd at y^t time; by these last it appears w^t Books were then in that Library, the Authors being mention'd wch were there, but amongst them there is no Livy, so y^t it seems y^t Author was not then in ye Library. These ver[:]es are all printed in ye Monasticon Anglicanum, being taken from this MS^t as appears in the Margin.   30

Dec. 20 (Th.). Last Night was buryed D^r. Sykes in Trinity col. Chapell. There was a Speech made on him by Tho. Hasker *A. M.* of y^t Coll. B.D. . .

Out of a Letter I saw to day.

I forgot in my former to tell you that M^r. Nash Rector of Binfield is lately dead and has left a good place for some one or other that can get it. They say M^r. Frinsham of Wargrove has made Intercession to M^r. Nevil to be his Friend to ye New Lord Keeper whose gift they say it is. But 'tis thought that the Dutchess of Marlborough being the Queen's chief Favourite will interceed for some of her Friends & if she does no question but they will carry 40 it. 'Tis a considerable Place and deserves a good laborious Preacher, being worth 9 score or 200^li per annum : but all good places have not good Preachers nor deserving Men good Preferments.

The said M^r. Nash (Salomon) was of Pembrook Coll. in Oxon, & took his A.M^s. Degree May 31. 1662. He has nothing in print y^t I know of only some stupid verses before M^r. John Brandon's Book (who was of Trinity Coll.) call'd Everlasting Fire no Fancy. I have been inform'd that M^r. Winder (Tho.) of Trinity College (whose Father, a rich man, lately died at his House call'd Bullock's Hatch near Windsor) makes great Interest for Binfield. — MS. Laud. E. 33. M^r. W. Lisles Saxon 50

English Remains. This Book of great use to such as begin to Learn the Saxon Tongue, because the Saxon is English'd in an opposite page. — ... [MS. Laud.] E. 65. The History of the Revelations of S[t.] John in Latin, wth figures, & a Comment in the German Language. The Comment is written, but the rest printed on one side only, & is one of those Books w[ch] were printed at Harlem w[n] this Art was first invented. 'Twas done in wooden Cuts & is a great Curiosity. I shew'd it M[r.] Bagford when he was in Oxford. Hence 'tis plain that y[e] true way of printing began first at Mentz, & not at Harlem as some would
10 make believe. — Ib. E. 72. Terentij Comoediae—At the Beginning— Terentius genere exstitit Afer civis cartaginensis. ... This may be inserted in Livy, perhaps. — ... This Day at two of y[e] Clock began the Election of a Margaret Professor of Divinity in room of D[r.] Sykes deceas'd. Candidates were D[r.] Baron, Master of Baliol-Coll. and M[r.] John Wynne Bach. of Divinity of Jesus Col. the same y[t] Epitomiz'd M[r.] Lock's Essay. The former had 27, the latter 35 votes. They are both Worthy Men, and of good Affection to the Church of England; but there is this Difference, that whereas D[r.] Baron has something of Pride and Haughtiness in him, M[r.] Wynne is a man of singular [1] modesty
20 & Humility, great Prudence, and in point of Learning superior to the D[r.], who however is a thorough pac'd Divine, and qualify'd for the Place. No sooner was the Breath out of D[r.] Sykes's Body, but an offer was immediately made by some of X[t] Church to the Pious and Learned M[r.] Grabe, then in London; but he being a Prussian by Birth, and having other reasons besides ag[t] his Accepting it, modestly declin'd it. The like did also D[r.] Hudson who was desir'd by divers to put up; & I am perswaded that if he had done it ([2]his Excellent learning, sound Judgment, great Affection to the Church of England joyn'd with an Affable Temper,) would have carry'd [3]it in opposition to any one else
30 that should appear. After these two Worthy Divines had declin'd it, M[r.] Tho. Smith (B.D.) of Brazen Nose Coll. put up; but finding that he had not Interest enough to carry it, before the Election he desisted, and most if not all his Party went over to M[r.] Wynne, who had otherwise infallibly lost it.

(N.B. The said M[r], now D[r.] Wynne, is a great Lockist, and his Lectures do not answer the Expectation conceiv'd of him. However he is an ingenious Man and a good Scholar, but better skill'd in Natural Philosophy than in Divinity. He is withall a man of Republican Principles, & a great Defender of them in the Coffee-House.—May 11th. 1710.)

40   D[r.] Baron hath prov'd a poor snivelling Fellow, & to be in many respects a Knave. Feb. 10. 17$\frac{8}{19}$.

Dec. 21 (Fri.). Upon carrying of y[e] self-Denying Bill by the Tories, there were divers Speeches made on both sides, and some of the Whiggs saying 'twas ill Nature to suppose they were ill Men because they did not vote so and so, S[r.] Tho. Hanmer replied That he was not y[e] worst

---

[1] Not so. He is rather a Man of Pride, and of no great Judgment, nor Prudence, as I find by those that know him intimately. Sept. 14. 1712.
[2] All this may be left out. May 7. 1711.
[3] So I thought then; but I have great reason to think since that he would have certainly lost it.

Natur'd Man in yᵉ World, & he hop'd he had no more ill Nature than wᵗ was necessary for self-Preservation, but yet when he saw some Men turn'd out of their Places for not voting as they were bid, he could not help thinking yᵗ others were kept in because they had voted as they were bid. — The Lᵈˢ who enter'd their Protestation agᵗ the Resolution That yᵉ Church was not in danger, enter'd also these Reasons for their Dissent [209–213]. . . .

Out of Mʳ. Bromley's Letter to Dʳ. Charlett Master of University Col. Dated Dec. 18. 1705—

—Indeed one Gentleman blamed you for not Burning the Memorial by yᵉ 10 Hands of yᵉ Common Hangman, but was very well told, you had no university Hangman.

— I am told by one yᵗ should know yᵗ Mʳ. Milles of Xᵗ Church gave his vote, in yᵉ Election of a Margaret Professor, neither way. A day or two before yᵉ Election he told one yᵗ he wish'd Dʳ. Mill would stand, & yᵗ he would give his vote for him before any one else in Oxford, tho' 'tis well known yᵗ he us'd always to speak agᵗ the Dʳ. & hop'd to live to see Edm. Hall have no one left in it, he being not able (as he said) to wish the Hall might flourish as long as Dʳ. Mill liv'd; tho' otherwise he had a Kindness for it.   20

Epitaphs in Sᵗ. Peter's Church in yᵉ East, Oxford.

In the Chancel is no Epitaph, nor any Stone Monumᵗ.

SOUTH ALLEY.

A Grave Stone, the Plates on wᶜʰ the Name of the Person interr'd torn off ; but on two other Plates, one of wᶜʰ somewᵗ broken, are these Verses in-grav'd.

> Terram terra tegat, demon peccata resumat,
> Mundus res habeat, spiritus alta petat.

As you be so was . . . . | As I am so shall you . . . | . . . ray you for mee for | . . . requirith charyte.   30

On the Right Hand of wᶜʰ another Grave Stone, on two Brass Plates whereof is a Man and Woman, with Hands elevated on their Breasts, in a praying posture, & underneath on a Plate, this Inscription.

Hic loci jacet Wiᵗmus Robinson quondam pincerna Collegij Reginæ. | Oxon & Johanna uxor ejus qui obijt xxº. die Mensis Junij anno Domini millesimo cccclxxviij cujus animæ propicietur Deus. Amen.

On the Rᵗ Hand of these two on a grave stone.

Hic sita est Maria uxor Edwardi | Potter Septem liberis juxta | jacentibus stipata obijt 10º | Julij Anno Domini 1676 Ætatis suæ 32.

In the wall just by the Minister's Pulpit, a curious Stone Monumᵗ and 40 thereon,

P.M. | Edvardi Potter | nuper hujus Parochiæ generosi, | Reverendi admodum viri | Christopheri Potter S.T.P. | olim Collegij Reginensis Præpositi | necnon Ecclesiæ cathedralis apud Vigorniam Decani, | filij : | qui ex hac vita discessit | Feb. 8º. Anno Dom. 1701. Ætat. 61. | Mem. etiam sacrum | Sampsonis Potter A.M. | haud ita pridem Collegij BaliolensisSocij | Edvardi Potter Filij natu-maximi | qui obijt Jan. 26. Anno Dom. 1699. Ætat. 35. | Christopherus Potter | Eorundem Filius & frater unice superstes | Pietatis & gratitudinis ergo | Monumentum hoc | P. | [The Arms follow.]

Opposite to this on the South Wall another curious Stone Monumᵗ wᵗʰ this 50 Inscription.

To the pious Memory of the most Religious | Gentlewoman Elizabeth Langbaine late of this | Parish Daughter of Charles Sonnibanck D.D. and | Cannon of Windsor. She was first wife of Christopher | Potter D.D. Dean of Worcester and Provost of | Queens Coll. afterwards married to Gerard | Langbaine D.D. & Provost of the same Coll. | who deceased the 3ᵈ day of December 1692 | in the 79ᵗʰ year of her Age. | As also in Memory of Mary Potter | Daughter of Sir Sampson White of this City | & late the virtuous and loving wife of Edward | Potter of this Parish Gent. She departed this Life | the tenth day of July 1676 | in the 32ᵗʰ Year of her Age.

Just below Mary Potter a Grave Stone, with yᵉ following Inscription:

Mortalitatis Exuvias heic deposuit | D. Christophorus Potter | D. Christoph. Potter
10 S.T.D. Coll. Reg. Præp. | filius naturæ secundus | conjugio nexus conjugi semper charus | vita integer | moribus comis | Pietate insignis | qui hanc vitam meliore | commutavit anno ætatis suæ | XLIII Aprilis XXVI. A.D. 1678.

Near to this on wᶜʰ are the Arms of yᵉ Potters upon the Ground, are these following, viz.

Thomas Killigrew, Son to Thomas | Killigrew, Esqr. one of his Majesties | Groomes of the Bed-Chamber was | borne in Mastricht the 19 of February in the Yeare 1657 | Dyed the 3 of June 1674.

Theron his Arms.
One omitted being not legible for the dust wᶜʰ has fill'd up the Letters, and
20 some are broke off.

Here lieth yᵉ body of Margret Daughter of Henry & Elizabeth Clements who died May the 6ᵗʰ 1703. aged 10 years.
Walter | Gnatus Wᵐⁱ Dunch militis quarto genit. | in Academia Oxoniensi libere | Educat. Juris (illius quæ Anglos æquat exteris) apud Glocestrenses | digne Bacchalaureus. Vixit dum vixit | fidus charus comis amicis suis | omnibus dedit se vivens Deo sua | moriens propinquis undecimo | Januarij 1648. Hic Waltere tui quod erat mortale relicto | Lætus es in Christo jam sine fine tuo.

On a Stone Monumᵗ on the South Wall.

Hic jacet | (nisi quod ejus supra est) | Gulielmus Day | Richardi Day | de Abbots-
30 Langley in comit. | Hartford Generosi filius, vir, bacchante | populo. sobriæ pietatis, grassante perfidia, | subditus fidelis, antiquorum morum cultor | severus, in facultate Chirurgica, quam apud | Exteros adornaverat, Arte, cura, & summa | in pauperes humanitate plurimos annos | Oxonij celeberrimus: qui hydrope extinctus diem | clausit Septembris XXIX. salutem expectans sibi | partam abinde annis MDCLXV. ann. Ætatis suæ LXI. | Tantum ut scires, Lector, Nicolaus Stratford S.T.D. | Consanguineus & ex asse hæres | mœrens & memor | P.

On a Stone raised pretty high from the Ground in a Chapell on the North side of the Chancell:

Here lyeth the bodie of Richard Atkinson late Alderman of Oxoñ wᶜʰ hath borne
40 the | Office of the Mayoralty fyve tymes, and was both Justice of the Peace and Quorum and so departed | out of this transitory Lyfe in the Faith of Christ the last of May in the Yere of our Lorde | God mccccclxxiiij. Together with his late wife Annes Atkinson. | (Above this Inscription An Alderman in his Robes & on each side two Women, & underneath eleven children, 5 Boys & 6 Girls.)

On the walls of the sᵈ Chapell:

M. S. | Joshua Crosse L.L.D. | Generosa stirpe agro Lincoln. | ortus, fortunæ non parcæ nec ipse | parcus. Vir acri ingenio, judicio solido, | memoria tenacissima, varia & expedita le | ctione, prudentia in rebus gerendis parum vul- | gari, vita integerrima, injuriam pati quam | facere paratior, beneficium conferre, quam | accipere propensior
50 moribus gratis & sincera fide spectabilis Amicus, fidissimus | Conjux & amantissimus, Parens providus | Aulæ magdalen. primo Alumnus, | Col. Linc. post Socius, & Acad. Procurat. | Socius demum Col. Magdalen. & | Phil. Nat. Professor Sedleianus | Obijt Pleuriticus IX Maij, | Anno Domini MDCLXXVI. | Ætat. LXII.

Thereon his Arms, quarte[r]ly parted per Cross, Gules & Or. in the first Quarter a Cross of the 2ᵈ.

Anna Oldisworth uxor Jacobi Oldisworth Rectoris de Kencot in Diœc. hac Oxon.

Filia & Hæres Guil. Mountesteven de Cote in Diœc. Glouc. Cleric.   Prudentia Oeconomica, fide, charitate, Sanctimonia, & alijs, quæ mulierem vere Christianam decent virtutibus exornata Obijt 19 Die Octob. Anno 1700, Ætat. suæ 51°.

In a Brass Plate, a Doctor of Physick & his wife kneeling at Prayers, & thereunder,

Richardus Ratcliff in Medicina Doctor | Obijt Januarij 18. 1599. Sepultus | Est Jan. 21.   Ætatis suæ 54 | Quem probitas, virtus, pietas doctrina tueri | Non poterant vivum, vel prohibere mori, | Conjunx chara viro Monumentum triste superstes | Defuncto statuit, constituitque sibi.

The next to this almost worn out, & so I could not read it when I view'd 10 it, it being towards Evening, & so must be inserted at another time.

All those before in the East wall of the Chapell.   In the South wall thereof,

M. S.

Helenæ Low filiæ Johannis Low Equitis Aurati | in agro Dorcestrensi | Benignæ, comis, & generosæ Virginis ; | urbanitate morum, perinde ac vitæ sanctimonia celebris, | quarum utramque adeo pulchre, adeoque ingenue commiscuit, | ut, quemadmodum pietas ipsi, enituerit ita & ipsa ornamento pietati, | Virginis. infirmiori sola valetudine infelicis ; quæ fuit tamen mentis, isti infelicitati paris ; | Quæ secreta liberalitate tot egenos aluit, miserisque ita gestijt opitulari | ut, dum alienos sublevavit, suos. quadam quasi sympathia delenitos | Vix omnino visa sit dolores persensisse ; Ægrota, sed 20 placida semper, & vultu pariter, & animo sereno, | Quem & in ipso mortis articulo, cupida & secura cœli, exhibuit | Oct. 28. An°. Dom. 1683. Ætatis suæ 26. | Hoc monumentum Ed. Low & Rob. Hyde, Executores | Mœsti posuere in memoriam munificæ Testatricis. |

West Wall of yᵉ Chapell.

Memoriæ | Maximæ spei, omnibusque virtu | tibus cumulatissimi Juvenis | Godescalci ab Alefeld no | bilis Holsati, quem Ethic- | es, Politices, Historiarum & | Jurisprudentiæ, Latinæ ex- | terarumque aliquot lingua- | rum feliciter jactis funda- | mentis in ipsissimo ætatis | flore, ac medio studiorum ! & peregrinationis cursu | præmatura proh dolor mo | rs A.D. 7. Augusti anno | 1635 summo bono- | rum omnium cum luctu 30 in- | tercepit, cineres Angliæ | reliquit, animam vero | beatissimæ angelo- | rum patriæ transcripsit | Positum.

In a Brass Plate (as was yᵉ former) In obitum Abaelis Wilcox Magistri in artibus | ex Aula divi Edmundi nuper studiosi. |

Epitaphium | Cui multas artes Pallas Phœbusque dedere | Arte tamen nulla vincere fata valet ! | Sed precor in tuta requiescat molliter urna | Wilcoxus, levior cippus & ossa premat. | Obijt 28 die Martij: Anno 1613.

South Wall.

To the Memory of that venerable & most Religious Matron Mʳˢ. Ursula Sandys the Relict of Emanuel Sandys of South Petherton in the County of Sommerset Esqʳ. who 40 died the 7ᵗʰ of July 1671 aged 69 and lies here interred in her second Son Mʳ. Saɱ Sandys his Grave.

The Arms on the Monumᵗ are, parted per Pale or and argent, In the first, A Fesse indented between three Crosses fitched Gules : In the second, two Chevronelles betw. 3 Martletts sable.

See in the following Vol.

VOL. VII.

Dec. 21 (Fri.).   Epitaphs on the Wall of the North Isle of Sᵗ. Peter's Church in the East Oxon.

M. S. | Viri Eruditi, benefici | pij, bonis omnibus, & Deo chari | Petri Eliot M.D. qui | Equestri Eliotorum Surriens. | Familia oriundus, Tavistokiæ Devon. natus 50 Oxoniæ enutritus est; C.C.C. & totius Acad. | decus: sæviente bello civili, armis emicuit, in exercitu Reg. Car. I. præfectus, & resumpta demum toga, pacis artibus patriæ saluti usque consulebat : Donec | morti quam sæpius alij protelaverat, | placide cesserit ipse, decedentium | stator, ad cœlestem vitam evocatus, | 5º die Mart. anº. Æt. suæ LXIII. | salutis humanæ 1681. | Vidua mœrens | P.

In a Brass Plate.

Here resteth the Bodies of Simon Parret, Gentleman, Master of Arte, late Fellowe | of Magdalen Colledge, and twise Procter of the Universitie of Oxford, and Eliza | beth his Wife, Daughter of Edward Love of Aenohe in the County of North | ampton Esquier: Which Simon departed this worlde the 24 day of September in the yeare of our Lorde God MCCCCC 84, and in the Yere of his Age 71 : | and Elizabeth de-
10 parted in child bed the 24 day of December in the yere of | oure Lorde God mcccclxxij, and in the Yeere of her Age xlij. |

Above them Ten Men & Eleven Women kneeling, with their Hands lifted up to Heaven in a praying posture. Above them these Arms viz. (1) Parted per Fesse, in the first a demy Lyon rampant, in the Second 3 Paires & a Mullet. (2) A Field of three Coats, the first with a Demy Lyon rampant, the second 3 Pairs & a Mullet, the 3d a Lyon Rampant. (3) A Lyon Rampant.

In Memory of the most pious and vertuous Gentlewoman Elizabeth the wife of Ed-mund Dickinson Dr in Physick who died in child-bed on the 12th day of August in the Yeare of our Lord 1670. in the 21th Year of her Age. |
20   Deo Opt. Max. | Et | Memoriæ sacrum | Henrici Smith | Optimæ spei adolescentis, filij | Rogeri Smith de Edmund Thorp | in Comitatu Leicestriæ | Armigeri | Collegij Reginæ commensalis | qui dum Æstivis Horis (animi oblec | tandi salutis firmandæ ergo) Cher | welli fluentis fidentius quam | prudentius se committeret, nec na | tandi prorsus rudis, nec satis peritus | rapido adversi fluminis vortice | (proh dolor) absorptus | ingenti sui desiderio moestis parentibus tantum relicto | Ex hujusce tempestæ vitæ | fluctibus in æternitatis | portum enatavit | A.d. XII Kalend. Iun. | Ann. Dom. | 1640. |

In a Monumt of White Marble on the Wall just by the Font.

Near this place lyeth the Body of Daniel Fogg Gent. who departed this Life May yº 15th 1702. aged 85 years. As also several of his children, Daniel & William who
30 dyed Infants, John aged abt 30, Mary abt 20, & Thomas M.A. abt 35.

Charles Cæsar Esqr., one of the Burgesses for Hertford, happening to speak some Words on Wednesday last in the Debate of the H. of Commons wch arose upon Acct of the Bill for the better security of her Majesty's Person and Government, wch were judg'd reflecting on her Majesty, he was presently committed Prisoner to the Tower. . . .

Dec. 22 (Sat.). . . . In Arch. Laud. E. 81. B. Brunonis Comment. in Psalterium, in Cantica Bibliorum : in Te Deum, Symbolum fidei &c. 'Tis an old printed Book at Herbipoli for the use of the Bp. and Chapter there. — Laud. F. 41. Annales Hiberniæ ab Anno Xti 1162 usque ad
40 annum 1370. At the Beginning is this Memorandum.

The Author of this Book is unknowne. It was brought (as supposed) out of Ireland, by yº Lord Thomas Howarde Duke of Norfolke, Ld. Treasurer, and Earl Marshall of England, when he was Earle of Surrey, and Lorde Lieutenant of yt Realme in anno 11 Regni Henrici octavi, and of late Yeares given by yᴶ Ld. Wm. Howarde, Youngest Son to Thomas late Duke of Norfolke, unto the Learned and Judicious Antiquarye Mr. Wm. Camden, who put the same in print, inserting it into his Britannia, and by him given to George Lord Carew in anno 1619.

Dec. 23 (Sun.). The Words for wch Mr. Cæsar was committed to
50 the Tower, are, There is a noble Lord wthout whom the Queen does nothing, who was known all last Reign to keep a constant Correspond-ence with the Court of St. Germains. — This Morning preach'd at St. Marie's Mr. Sacheverell of Magd. Coll. upon, in Perills amongst false

Brethren, in the Prosecution of wch words he did with a great Deal of Courage and Boldness, shew the great Danger the Church is in at present (notw^thstanding the Parliam^t has voted it to be in none) from the Fanaticks & other False Brethren, whom he set forth in their proper Colours[1]. — Being to day with S^r. Andrew Fountaine, he told me that he has been lately in Holland, where he has purchas'd a great Number of Curious Books and Coyns, some for himself but most for my Lord Pembrooke. He likewise told me that he design'd to write a Dissertation in Latin upon Carausius and Allectus, and to explain all their Coyns wch he could procure, wch will be of great use to all curious Persons, this part of the Roman History having not yet been sufficiently written of, for want of such undertakers as are skill'd in Coyns. D^r. Sikes besides a very good Collection of Books had likewise a good Number of Coyns, wch however he did not leave to any publick Place, but they are come into ye Hands of his Relations. He once said he would give some to ye Publick Library, & his Executors, particularly M^r. Hinton, say they will take care to procure y^m for y^t place if they can. Sir Andrew Fountaine formerly saw them, & he assures me y^t one of Carausius's amongst y^m is very valuable, there being on the Reverse VICTORIA CEA, the like whereof he never saw before in his life. — I saw to day at D^r. Charlett's the Lower House of Convocation's Reasons for not assenting to ye Lords Address, penn'd with much modesty, & Affection for ye Church. — I saw also M^r. Westley's Letter to the Master dated from Linc. Castle Jul. 31. 1705. wherein is the sum of all his Debts, viz. 357^l. 16^s. 10^d, wch he says he did not contract thro' Extravagance, it being impossible to be free from them when he has such a Family and has had so many Crosses. He acknowledges wth a great sense of Gratitude the Master's Kindness to him, & declares he has rec^d divers unexpected Kindnesses from others wch he hopes he shall always have sense to mention wth the greatest Deference and Humility. — Petri Victorij Observatt. in Columellam, Catonem & Varronem. Lugd. ap. Gryphium 1542. 8°. not in ye Publick Library I think. I saw it at ye Mast^r of University's Lodging. There goes wth them Georgius Alexandrinus in libb. de re Rustica. P. Beroaldus in Columellam. Aldus de Dierum generibus.—Ciceronis Epistolae per Manutium. Antv. Plantin. 1567. 12°. Quære wheth^r in ye P. Library. — Quære ab^t the Motto of the Arms of the East Indian Company. I am told by M^r. Thwaites that 'tis INDVS VTERO SERVIET VNI, wch he very ingeniously conjectures to be VTERQ. wch w^thout doubt is right, being in Imitation of Hor. Et uterque Pœnus serviet uni. — Memorand. to consult the new Author of Embalming, who speaking de lucernis sepulch. takes notice of an Author who asserts y^t a Lamp was found Burning at ye opening of a Vault; but says he such a one does not believe it, nor such a one, but Judæus Apella does believe it, wch Error arose from credat Judæus Apella.

Dec. 24 (Mon.). M^r. Greaves in his Description of ye Roman Denarius mentions an Attick Drachme of his, found in the Black Sea, wth this Inscription, ΑΘΕΤΙΝΑΡΝΙΚΑ ΑΡΧΕ, wch shews that in Livy l. 37. c.—

---

[1] This is the very Sermon that he preach'd afterwards in Lond. Nov. 5. 1709. before the L^d. Mayor, for wch he was impeach'd & punished. See in that Year—May 12th. 1710.

where the Description of the Naval Triumph of L. Æmilius is given Tinarnica is to be read & not tetradrachma as is conjectur'd by Budæus & Rhodiginus; wch is also confirm'd by the first Edition of Livy, wch has Tetracina, wch is an errour that came wthout doubt from the carelessness of ye Scribe. Ask S^r. Andrew Fountaine ab^t this.—I shew'd him this Particular, & he immediately thought it should be rather ΑΘΕΝΑΙΩΝ ΤΙΝΑΡΝΙΚΟΣ . ΑΡΧΙΕΡΕVΣ. But suspended [his] positive Judgm^t. — There is in the Taberders' Library at Queen's Coll. a Livy in Folio, with Wooden Cutts, printed at *Franc. ad Moen.* 1578.

10   **Dec. 25 (Tu.).**   In a Letter I saw to day at ye Master of University's conc. M^r. Bromley's Father, 'tis there said y^t he was a Gentleman Commoner of Hart-Hall, matriculated in Apr. 1636. He afterwards travell'd, & upon his Return Home, took w^t proved the wrong side. He was in Arms, & rid in ye Troop of L^{ds} & Gentlemen y^t was called ye K's Troop, commanded at Edge-Hill Feight, & (as the Author of this Letter thinks) was in other Battles. He was taken Prisoner in ye War, & lay 15 Mo. in Prison, & afterwards upon His Releasm^t gave 10,000 L. Bond not to stir above 2 Miles from home, under wch Confinem^t he continued till ye Restauration: And then all ye Recompence he had for his Sufferings was
20   ye Honour to be created a K^t of ye Bath at ye Coronation.—The main Drift of this Letter is to vindicate him from the Aspersions cast on him as being a Presbyterian & I know not w^t; wch if true S^r. W^m. Dugdale would not have given him so good a Character in his Antiq. of Warw. Sh.—He was (continues ye Letter) eminently in those Interests both of Ch. & State, & his Son has follow'd his Steps, 'tho' to his Loss. The Author of ye said Letter M^r. Bromley his Son.

UPON Y^e D. OF SHREWSBURY.

O yes! from henceforth sit omnibus notum
30 That a great Duke of England, and Statesman of Gotham,
Hath robbed y^o Publick by stealing a Woman
And pounding in Wedlock a beast of ye Common.
So Dotage concludes ye great Feats of his Life,
And Brachiano's cheap Mistresse proves Talbot's dear Wife.

— In a Letter from M^r. Nelson to D^r. Charlett he is pleas'd to speak very favourably & wth abundance of Concern for ye D^{r's} Interest, & for M^r. Westley, & desires to know, w^t character M^r. Dodwell's new Book bears in ye university, being of opinion y^t neither side can like it well (wch however is far otherwise) & wishes his Book ab^t ye Soul were not in ye Press, being too sensible y^t such a Book coming from so great a
40 Man will do much Mischief, & be entertain'd wth a great deal of Pleasure by ye Scepticks of ye Age. — Memorand. y^t M^r. Edm. Chishull has writ a Letter to D^r. Hicks, p^t of wch is printed in the D^{r's} Book ag^t ye Papists. The same M^r. Chishull has ready for ye Press a Book of Inscriptions collected in his Travells, wch were never published by any Collector. — The Master of University shew'd me a Ballad printed in the Year 1648, & now reprinted call'd, Rustica Academiæ Oxoniensis nuper Reformatæ Descriptio, in Visitatione Fanatica Octobris 6to, &c. An. D. 1648. cum Comitijs ibid. Anno sequente: Et alijs notatu non indignis. Doctore Alibone nuper Lincolniæ (false, he was of Magd.)
50 Oxon. Auctore. — Edward Son of King Alfred (as Marianus relates)

rebuilt Maldun in Essex, after it had been destroy'd in yᵉ Danish Wars, & fortify'd it with a Castle. See Camden in Com. Essex. He also built a Castle at Colchester. See ibid. — Mʳ. Camden notes yᵗ Colchester was call'd by yᵉ Britains Caer Colin, & yᵗ he saw a great number of Roman Coyns dug up here, amongst wᶜʰ some of Carausius. Quære whether the *Victoria Cea* upon Dʳ. Sikes's Coyn does not belong to this place, & whether it should not be *Victoria Caer*—? — In Cumberland Mʳ. Camden mentions an Inscription to a certain God, thus—DEO CEAIIO AVR II RTI &c. Quære whether this Coyn may not relate to him? In Cheshire he tells us yᵗ the Cangi or Ceangi were a British People, which he places in yᵗ County, conquer'd in the time of Domitian.

Dec. 26 (Wed.). Sir Andrew Fountaine among other Curious Books shew'd me Yllustrium Ymagines, Lugd. 1514. 8º. wᶜʰ is the first Book of Medals ever printed.—A folio Book in MSᵗ containing divers Pleas of yᵉ Crowne.—Traicte des cinque Ordres d'Architecture, dont se sont servy les Anciens, traduit du Palladio, augmenté de novelles inventions pour l'Art de bien bastir, Par le Sʳ. le Muet. Par. 1645. 4º. All done in Copper. Sʳ. Andrew tells me there were not above 20 printed, being design'd for yᵉ use of yᵉ Dauphine.—Constitutiones Provinciales in Concilio Oxon. editæ per Stephanum Cant. Archiepiscopum Anno 1222 Regis Hen. filij Johannis 8º. MS. fol. in Vellam.—A large Folio Book in MSᵗ containing Original Letters, &c. The first is a Letter from yᵉ University of Cambridge dated nonis Jul. 1628. to the Duke of Buckingham wᵗʰ the Duke's Answer, Dat. at Chelsey Jul. 30. 1628.—Paul. Manutius & Sigonius from a Place in the 5ᵗʰ Book of Livy cap. 7. equis se suis stipendia facturos promittunt, gather yᵗ there were two sorts of Kᵗˢ at Rome who serv'd in the Wars, one sort wᵗʰ a Publick Horse at yᵉ Charge of the State, & another wᵗʰ a private Horse, at their own Expense; but from these words the most Learned and judicious Grævius in his Præface to yᵉ 1ˢᵗ Vol. of his Thes. Antiq. Rom. has prov'd the direct contrary.

Dec. 27 (Th.). On the 24ᵗʰ Instant Mʳ. Dobson & Mʳ. Allemont were elected at Trinity & sent up to the Bᵖ. of Winchester for him to make choice of one of them to be President. — On the 25th Mʳ. Rob. Pearce A.M. was made Vice-Principal of Edm. Hall in room of Mʳ. Musson. Here it must be observ'd that tho' Dʳ. Mill seldom or never speaks well of other Houses as being (in his Language) wᵗʰout Discipline, yet he has taken successively 3 Vice-Principals from other Places, viz. Mʳ. Milles in room of Dʳ. Kennett, when there were several of the Hall who would have accepted of it, particularly Mʳ. Grandorge, a worthy ingenious Man, now Fellow of Magd. &c. (2) Mʳ. Musson of Linc. when there were, Mʳ. Walker, & two or three more who would have had it. (3) Mʳ. Pearce of Linc. when at the same time that Mʳ. Musson talk'd of leaving the House Mʳ. Kent said he would readily accept it, if yᵉ Principal should think fit. But he does not care it seems for his own Men; wᶜʰ however has almost ruin'd his House, wᶜʰ if he had made a choice of Mʳ. Kent, would have recover'd he being a Man of Parts, Learning, Address & Aquaintance. But he is now better preferr'd, having got a good Living.

[Note on the spelling of Carseoli, from Grævius, Pref. to Vol. I. of Thes. Antiq.]

Dec. 28 (Fri.). D^r. Aldrich Dean of X^t Church told D^r. Hudson y^t the Pope inquir'd very much how he ye said D^r. Hudson did. — At the Church of Pauler's-Pury near Towcester in Northamptonshire there are several Monuments of the Family of ye Throgmortons, who were Lords of Pury, wch Lordship was sold to S^r. Edw. Hales governor of ye Tower in King James II^{d's} time which he sold again to S^r. Benjamin Bathurst who made it his Lady's Joynture, and will descend to his Eldest Son M^r. — Bathurst after her Death. In this Parish of Pauler's Pury was the famous D^r. Edw. Bernard born, his Father being only Curate to the Rector of y^t
10 Place. — At Easton near Towcester lives ye Lord Leominster, who has ye best Collection of Ancient Marble Statues, bigger than ye Life that perhaps are any where in being. They were the famous Lord Arundell's who collected the Marbles in ye Theatre Yard at Oxoñ. This said L^d. Leominster has been twice married, his second wife (now living) is Daughter to ye Duke of Leeds. He pretends a mighty Affection to ye Church, but like most others of the Lay Pretenders has no real Kindness for it, as may be gather'd from this, That he disposes of his Livings always with a Bond of Resignation, and is at this time sueing an Honest Gentleman one M^r. King who was unawares drawn in to give him a Bond, & intends to do
20 so wth another Gentleman who lives in ye Neighbourhood. — Laurentij Pignorij Mensa Isiaca. Accedit Tomasini Manus ænea. *Amst.* 1669. 4to. This Book to be got into ye Publick Library. I saw it at S^r. Andrew Fountaine's. I should look it over for Livy . . . Harduin de Nummo Pantheo. Wanting in ye Publ. Library. . . . Horae B. Mariae. 12°. MS. I saw this in S^r. Andr. Fountaines chamb^r. — When they were Repairing the Church of Rochester they took down a Beam on wch was written *1004*. — Sir Andrew Fountaine has a printed Book call'd Kalendarium Benedictinorum in 4 Vol^s. A most Curious, rare Book, & to be got into ye Library. — Laurence Nowel a very learned Man & ye first who
30 reviv'd the Saxon Language. Camd. in Cornwal. — In the same County M^r. Camden has [an] Inscription . . . which he reads thus, Doniert rogavit pro anima, or if it be thought the 3 Pricks are the remains of an E Doniert erogavit pro anima. Dug up near S^t. Neots. Quære ab^t this Stone, & w^t Doniert this should be. There was one Dungerth a petty King of Cornwall who according to the Annals was drown'd An. 872. — Arundell the Family, call'd in Latin by some *de Arundine*, not improperly, Arondell signifying swallow in French, & their Arms are Sable, six swallows argent.—Whence a Dragon in the Banners of our English Kings, see Camden in the same place. Where may be consider'd the Roman
40 Eagle & ye Danes Reafan. Quaere whether Livy may be in any thing hence illustrated?

[Cicero and many other Latin Authors corrected in Graevius' Thesaurus (and throughout this volume passim).]

Dec. 29 (Sat.). . . . MS. Laud. F. 82. The Acts of the Apostles in Greek with a Latin Translation ad verbum in an opposite Column. A very old MS. in Capital Letters. At the End in a more modern Hand, but in Capitals also, is the Apostles Creed. From a Note there it appears to have formerly belong'd to the Dukes or Governors of Sardinia. . . . — When a new Edition of Herodian is undertaken Bockler's Edition at

Argent. 1662. must be consulted.   At yᵉ End of his Notes he Defends the Version of Politian against yᵉ Corrections of Hen. Stephens, wᶜʰ Corrections some say the Oxford Editor has recᵈ into yᵉ Latin Text. — ¹ Ptolemie's φάσεις ἀπλανῶν ἀστέρων, καὶ συναγωγὴ ἐπισημασίων, a Book never yet printed, but fraught with divers pieces of yᵉ Parapegmata both of Meton & Eudoxus ; and wholly another thing from that wᶜʰ goes under a like Name for Ptolemies, published at yᵉ End of some Editions of Ovid's Fasti.   See Mʳ. Selden's Discourse conc. yᵉ Birthday of our Saviour p. 16.   The said MS. wᶜʰ was communicated by Sʳ. Hen. Savile to Mʳ. Selden is now in the Savilian Study at Oxford. — Abraham de Balmis 10 translated a Book intitled Isagogicon Astrologiæ Ptolomæi, wᶜʰ appears to be yᵉ same wᵗʰ Geminus's Phænomena.   See Mʳ. Selden ibid, who has some observations abᵗ it.

_____

An Exact Catalogue of all the Pieces in the MSᵗ Collection wᶜʰ Sʳ. John Osborne lent Dʳ. Hudson.

1. Epistola Domini Benedicti ˙XII. Edwardo Regi Angliæ tertio directa, dehortatoria ne utatur nomine & Armis Regis Franciæ.   Pr. Benedictus Episcopus servus servorum Dei carissimo in Christo.

2. Procuratorium pro Domino Rege, or K. Edward 3ᵈˢ Letter of Procura- 20 tion for several Persons therein named to appear for him and make his Appeal from the Parliamᵗ of Paris.   Pr. Quorundam insinuatione nuper audivimus.

3. Procuratorium pro Domino Rege concernens statum suum & Regna, or another Letter of Procuration from K. Edw. 3ᵈ. to several Persons to appear for him & justify his Proceedings before the Pope.   Pr. Pateat universis per præsentes quod nos Edwardus.

4. Provocatio pro Domino Edwardo Rege Angliæ & Franciæ ad audientiam Concilij Generalis ad judicem supremum in qua quidem provocatione fit mencio de Lodowico Imperatore.   Pr. In Dei nomine Amen.   Ego W. de S. Procurator.   30

5. Domino Papæ, Dominis Cardinalibus & alijs volentibus intelligere justitiam causæ suæ intimat Rex Angliæ Edwardus tertius jura sua in Regno Franciæ & injurias sibi factas per Regni Franciæ intrusorem cum excusatione eorum quæ facit pro sua defensione & sui juris prosecutione & cum Notificatione suæ intentionis devotionis & fidei.—Pr. Jus naturale primævum pariter animalia cuncta docens.

6. Argumenta è jure Civili et Canonico petita summoque Pontifici oblata per Domini Regis nuncios ostendentia Edwardum tertium jure Hæreditario Galliæ Regem esse.—Pr. Factum ex quo Dominus Edwardus Rex Angliæ jus habere se dicit.   40

7. Epistola 2ᵈᵃ. Regis Edwardi tertij missa Domino Papæ pro Jure suo ad regnum Franciæ.—Pr. Sanctissimo in Christo Patri Domino C. Divina providentia—Dated 1ˢᵗ June 19ᵗʰ of his Reign.

8. De jure & titulo Regis Angliæ ad coronam & Regnum Franciæ ac primo factum præsupponitur & sequuntur rationes & argumenta pro utraque parte— Pr. Philippus filius Sancti Lodowici Rex Francorum genuit.—In this Discourse the King of England's Title to the Kingdom of France is more largely handled than it had been before.   Upon this occasion there is inserted at the End a Genealogical Table of the Kings of France & England from Sᵗ. Lewis to K. Henry VI.   50

9. Tractatus alter de eadem re, Gallice.

10. Excerpta quædam de eadem re è libro qui dicitur sompnium viridarij qui est Dialogus inter clericum & militem.

¹ Tis printed in Petavius's Uranologion.   But yᵉ MS. in Sʳ. H. Savile's study is much more correct.   There are two MSS. in Sʳ. H. Savile's Study.

11. Copia tractatus Magnæ Pacis in Latino inter Reges Angliæ & Franciæ factæ apud Bretigny juxta Carnotum Anno Domini 1360, & confirmata seu jurata eodem anno Calesiæ & Bolon.—Pr. Johannes Dei gratia Francorum Rex universis salutem.

12. Responsio Gallicorum in tractatu apud Loulyngham, Gallice.

13. Litera Renunciationis Joannis Regis Franciæ, cum clausula Cestassavoir, Gallice.—Pr. Johan par la Grace de dieu Roy de France.

14. Duodecima & ultima Egloga Francisci Petrarchæ Bucolicorum, continens bellum Edwardi Regis Anglorum & Joannis Regis Francorum.

15. Tractatus pacis finaliter conclusæ & in quibusdam articulis de novo apud Calesias correctæ inter Reges Angliæ & Franciæ predictos. Gallice.

16. De Allegamijs inter Reges & Regna. Gallice.

17. Litera super liberatione fortalitiorum in diversis partibus. Gallice.

18. Tractatus Calesiæ cum Articulis subtractis aliter subscriptis, or A full Account of the Treaty of Calice betw. K. Edward 3 and K. John of France: declaring what Lands and Territories each Prince shall hold &c. with all other Instruments belonging to y^t Treaty in French.

19. Requisitio facta per Henricum quintum Regem Angliæ & Franciæ adversario suo Franciæ de & super corona & Regno Franciæ ei pacifice dimittendis.—Pr. Mediator Dei & Hominum Christus Jesus à summis ad ima.

20. Articuli continentes modum & ordinem observatos ab Henrico quinto Dei Gratia Rege Franciæ & Angliæ in prosequendo jura sua Hæreditaria coronam videlicet & Regnum Franciæ injuriose ab Adversario suo detenta.—Pr. Inprimis licet eidem Regi competierit.

21. Forma Redemptionis sive Financiæ & Liberationis Arturi de Britannia Prisonarij Regis Angliæ Henrici 5^{ti} per Indenturam.

22. Forma Commissionis ad tractandum super Elargitione ejusdem Prisonarij scilicet Arturi de Britannia.

23. Forma elargiandi dictum Arturum Prisonarium.

24. Juramentum Arthuri de Britannia de observanda pace conclusa Trecis & de serviendo in Armis Henrico Regi Angliæ Hæredi & Regenti Franciæ.

25. Forma oblationis factæ pro Arthuro de Britanniæ Prisonario.

26. Commissio pro ligis faciendis cum Delphino.

27. Commissio pro treugis faciendis cum Delphino.

28. Treugæ generales factæ cum Duce Britanniæ cum Appunctuamentis diversis.

29. Confirmatio prorogationis Treugarum factarum per Comitem Armaniaci.

30. Commissio ad procedendum super attemptatis contra Treugas Britanniæ prædictas.

31. Appunctuata ante Redditionem Villæ Rotomagensis.

32. Oblationes factæ per Regem Henricum quintum parti Franciæ pro pace finali.

33. Petitiones eorum de Francia factæ Henrico quinto.

34. Commissio ad reformanda attemptata contra Treugas factas cum Adversario Franciæ.

35. Commissio ad tractandum cum Delphino de pace.

36. Oblatio facta per Ambassiatores Regis Franciæ Henrico 5to Regi Angliæ in Medunta, or the Offers made by ye Ambassadors ot the King of France to King Henry the 5th at Melun, with all ye Proceedings of y^t Treaty.

37. Articuli tractatus magnæ Pacis inter Henricum 5^{tum} Regem Angliæ &c. & Carolum Regem Franciæ apud Trecas conclusi, Anno Domini 1420, 21 die mensis Maij. There are two copies, one in Latin in ye Name of King Charles of France & ye other in English in ye Name of King Henry.

38. Another Copie of the said Articles in French in ye Name of King Charles.

39. Litteræ Testimoniales super Juramento de non veniendo contra dictam pacem facto per Capitulum Ecclesiæ Cathedralis Parisiensis, &c., or several

Letters & Certificates concerning the Oath y^t was taken by the Clergy & Noblemen of France to observe ye said Treaty, & also of ye Homage & Fealty they then made to K. Henry with other articles & Agreements with the Count of Troyes to serve King Charles & King Henry & to do him Homage. viz. (1) the said Litteræ Testimoniales de juramento &c. (2) Testimoniales super simili juramento præstito per studentes Universitatis Parisiensis. (3) Similes super juramento præstito per vicarium generalem & officialem Episcopi. (4) Similes super juramentum præstitum per Præsidentem & Officiarios Curiæ Parliamenti. (5) Alia forma pro Canonicis & Ministris Ecclesiæ Cathedralis. (6) Similes pro Juramento Domini Ducis Clarentiæ, & Dominorum Britanniæ. 10 (7) Modus faciendi Appunctuamenta per Commissarios, cum alijs multis id genus, inter quæ est, Propositio Abbatis de Bello-Becco Magistri sacræ Theologiæ facta coram Papa post conclusionem pacis factæ in Civitate Trecensi, uti etiam ejusdem Protestatio. Deinde sequuntur, Appunctuata & Concordata desuper terris & dominijs Ducatus Aquitaniæ; Articuli pro conservatione pacis firmandæ inter Reges & Regna &c. necnon super modificatione & limitatione superioritatis & restrictione resorti. Item Responsiones datæ in scriptis per Gallicos ad articulos super modificatione & limitatione ultimi resorti.

40. Extractum ab originali libri Antiqui Cronicorum Sancti Severini Burde- 20 galensis. Gallice.

41. Transcriptum de Registris Parliamenti Parisiensis de Alligantia olim facta & jurata inter Delphinum & ducem Burgundiæ qui occisus, with several other things, amongst wch one immediately precedes this Transcript, relating to ye said Treaty of Troyes.

See pag. 58.

Dec. 30 (Sun.). Annals of England by N. Trivet, wth ye Continuation of Adam Merimuth. Never printed. — Peter de Ickham's English Chronicle.—History of England by J. Ross.—The Chronicle of S^t. Swithun's Monastery.—Annals of England by Th. Otterburn.—Chron. 30 of England by Gualt. Gisburn.—Chron. of England by Jo. Merilynch.— Chron. of ye Monastery of S^t. Edmund.—Title of Edward the 3^d to ye Kingdom of France. None of the said Books yet printed, tho' in a Paper wch came out some years since at ye Theatre there was an offer made for it, & 'twas said y^t they were then actually ready for ye Press; but I suppose want of Encouragement hinder'd the Good Design, as it did of printing several other usefull Pieces of Antiquity not hitherto published. — Out of a Paper I saw at ye Mast^r of University's Lodging, containing the Reasons those offer'd who dissented to the Bill ab^t Security of the Protestant Succession, & the Names of those who dissented also to ye 3 40 Riders [50-57] ...

A Continuation of ye Catalogue of Pieces in S^r. John Osborne's MS^t.

42. Scriptum Magistri Johannis Rivell contra Ducem Burgundiæ & relaxationem Juramenti sui Regi Angliæ, & cætera. Gallice.

43. Acta & Processus in Conventione Attrabatensi, or The Acts & Proceedings at Arras between K. Hen. VI. & Charles of France with all ye Argum^{ts} urged on both sides.

44. Conventiones Pacis initæ inter Regem Karolum & Ducem Burgundiæ in dicta Conventione Attrabat.

45. Declarationes Ambassiatorum Concilij Basiliens. factæ in Attrabato. 46. 50 Acta & Gesta in Conventione pro Tractatu pacis habita in Marchijs Calesiæ Anno Domini 1439. &c. or The Acts & Proceedings at ye Convention or Treaty of Peace held in ye Marches of Calais An. Domini 1439 wth all ye Commissions from ye Kings of France & England, Instructions to ye English

Embassadors & yᵉ offers of Peace made by yᵉ Duke of Orleans & Dutchess of Burgundy in Behalf of yᵉ French & yᵉ Answers of yᵉ King of England there-unto wᵗʰ yᵉ last Results & Breaking off of yᵗ Treaty written in Manner of a Journal by Tho. Beckington Dʳ. of Laws & one of yᵉ Commissioners for yᵗ Treaty.

47. A short History of yᵉ chief Actions of K. Hen. V. in Hexameter & Pentameter verse. By yᵉ same Author.

— Dʳ. Hicks has put out a New Edition of his Private Devotions wᵗʰ some Additions, & in yᵉ Preface I am told has made an Answer to some
10 Objections made agᵗ some pᵗ of yᵉ Book. — I saw a Letter to day at yᵉ Master of University's Lodgings in MSᵗ from Beza to Archbᵖ. Whitgift dated Cal. Febr. 1593. Genevc. I suppose never yet printed. Quære. — Talking to-day wᵗʰ Mʳ. Smith of University College, he seem'd to be of opinion yᵗ the Passage in Camden's Edition of Asser Men. relating to the University of Oxoñ is forged, & affirm'd yᵗ tho' Mʳ. Camden had establish'd a good Character of being an Honest Man yet he did not act fairly in this particular; because he did not tell yᵗ this Passage was omitted in the Edition of Archbᵖ. Parker, & notify whether in the MSᵗ he made use of it was in the Text, or in yᵉ Margin : wᶜʰ is no Objection at
20 all, it being certain yᵗ Mʳ. Camden had no mind to engage in so useless a Controversy ; and his making no mention at all how it was written in the MSᵗ shews yᵗ twas in a continued Manner wᵗʰout breaking off or being added by a latter Hand. But he sufficiently vindicated himself afterwards to Mʳ. Twyne as I have insinuated in my Notes to Sʳ. John Spelman's Life of King Alfred. He also seem'd to disbelieve altogether yᵉ Story of Theodorus Archbᵖ. of Canterbury, wᶜʰ howevcr is not utterly to be rejected any more yⁿ several other stories wᶜʰ are not confirm'd by undoubted Authority ; especially since there are divers Proofs from other things of yᵉ Truth of this, particularly from the Arms of the University
30 of Oxoñ in the Church of Grekelade, (see Vol. immediate præcedens p. 142) a British Passage publish'd by Mʳ. Burman in the New Edition of Dʳ. Plot's Nat. History of Oxoñshire, & other Authorities, as I have shew'd in yᵉ foresaid Notes upon Sʳ. John Spelman.

A Catalogue of the MSᵗ of Letters &c. of Sʳ. Andrew Fountaine, men-tion'd in this Vol. p. 20.

1. A Letter from the University of Cambridge in Latin, dated the Nones of July 1627, to yᵉ Duke of Buckingham their Chancellor, giving his Grace Thanks for his Great Care of the University, especially in relation to printing, & desiring his Care for yᵉ Future.
40 2. His Grace's Answer in English, dated from Chelsey July 30ᵗʰ 1628, signifying yᵗ tho' he should be absent for some time yet he had taken effectual Means for preventing the ill Designs of the Enemies of yᵉ University &c.

3. An imperfect Index to some Common Law Book, either printed or written.

4. An Extract out of Antoninus History tit. 17. c. 9. § 28. aᵒ. 1196. & § 31. aᵒ. 1201. As also out of Genebrard's Chronicle aᵒ. 1198 & 1199, & Paulus Æmil. p. 302, concerning Philip the 1ˢᵗ King of France's marrying Vigeburg or Ingeberg, Daughter to Canute King of Denmark, his Divorce of her, & his being afterwards Excommunicated for it. pag. 1.
50 5. A Reconciliation made between the King (K. James I.) and his Subjects, touching the Demand of his Right in old Debts and Landes quietly enjoyed tyme out of mind &c. wherein yᵉ Root is discovered from whence both these

and other principal Grievances between yᵉ Said Prince and his People have been branched : the Error of such as fathered the said Grievances upon the Lawes and Privileges of yᵉ Crowne sufficiently made knowne, seeing the Thief wᶜʰ (all this while) robbed both King and Country is here openly detected, and a Remedy to prevent the like Mischiefs to yᵉ Crowne & every Man's Posterity safely propounded : written by Sʳ. Edw. Coke.—Pr. When I had well observed the Grievances. p. 4.

6. A Parliamᵗ Writ, directed to Marmaduke Bᵖ. of St. David's, dat. at Westm. 12 Oct. 26 Year of Q. Eliz. Reign. p. 13.

7. A Letter from Anthony Bory to yᵉ Lord Cromwell against yᵉ Pope's 10 Lawes for denying Prohibitions &c. contrary to yᵉ Lawes. p. 15.—Pr. After my Bounden Dutye unto your good Mastershipp for your most lovyng Letters.

8. Concerning the Act of Appeals. H. 8. pag. 17.

9. Notes & Copies out of the Tower Records, conc. Tolle Office, Custom Office, Impositions, Subsidies granted upon Condition the Grant made to yᵉ King in Parliamᵗ, 6. H. 4., the Subsidie to be delivered to Will. de Walleworth & John Phillpot, of 15ᵗʰˢ, two Tenths &c. in yᵉ 2ᵈ Year of Rich. 2ᵈ, Tax upon Wool in Ireland, & lastly conc. the Tax upon Wine in yᵉ time of Rich. 2ᵈ. pag. 19.

10. Petitiones Parliamenti 8 E. 2. p. 23.   20

11. Ethelbald King of Mercia's Charter for founding the Abbey of Crowland, dated an. 716. p. 29.

12. K. Hen. 4ᵗʰ'ˢ Patent, an. Regni 7ᵐᵒ, for Naturalizing Albertus de Andernaco Goldsmith. p. 31.

13. K. Wᵐ. Rufus's Charter to yᵉ Monastery of Evesham, Anno 1100. p. 32.

14. Extracta de Moneta & Cambio Domini Regis scilicet quis fecit Monetam seu Cambium sine Domino Rege, &c.

15. Other things about yᵉ Corps of this Kingdom, particularly abᵗ Transporting of Gold &c. as also abᵗ yᵉ Exchange : with John Fordes Case conc. 30 his Vending Wool to Forreigners, 17. H. 6. See page 72.

Mʳ. Thwaits assures me that Dʳ. Barrow's Euclid in 8ᵒ. is taken from Herigonus, as also are most of his Scholia and Corollaria & Monita. He likewise tells me yᵗ yᵉ *figures* & very Letters thereof are exactly the same. — The Archbᵖ. in his Quarto Edition of yᵉ Bible has so mangled the first Prophecy in Genesis concerning our Saviour yᵗ nothing can be made of it. Quære? — Mʳ. Thwaits has in his Study Hierom de Bara's Blazon of Armes in French, pr. at Lyons 1581. folio. Quære whether in yᵉ P. Library? — John Dee's Preface to Euclid was prefix'd by Capt. Tho. Rudd to his Euclid's Elemᵗˢ of Geometry yᵉ first 6 Books in a com- 40 pendious form contracted & demonstrated, Lond. 1651. 4ᵒ.

Dec. 31 (Mon.). . . . Livy in yᵉ 4ᵗʰ Book ch. 16. tells us yᵗ L. Minucius had a golden Statue given him in shape of an ox wᵗʰout yᵉ Porta Trigemina ; wᶜʰ shews yᵗ Golden statues were in use before yᵉ time of Acilius Glabrio, contrary to wᵗ is asserted by Valerius Maximus. But Lipsius assents to Valerius, & reads in Livy *Bove & agro* for *Bove aurato* : wᶜʰ is probably the true Reading, it being certain yᵗ statues of Gold were

---

Dec. 31. Dr. T. Smith to H. Remarks on Browne Willis and materials for Life of Wolsey ; condemns Dr. Burnet as a historian. Thoresby, his writings and autographs. The author of the Letter to a Bishop (1689) was Dr. Comber, who received the rich Deanery of Durham as a reward of his unrighteousness. Is wholly ignorant of the author of the designed Answer, of which only about seven sheets were printed. Advises H. to give the bulk of

not known so early.   See Rupertus upon Val. Max. p. 150. — . . . Consider a Coyn amongst those given by M^r. Ray, in wch is ΣΙΠΥΛΗΝΗ.   In one of the Oxoñ Marbles there is διὰ τὴν Μητέρα τὴν Σιπυλήνην, by whom they us'd to swear.   Vide Græv. Thes. Vol. 5. p. 661. — Consider also a Coyn there of Philetærus.

A Continuation of ye Heads of S^r. Andrew Fountaine's MS^t.   See pag. 68.

16. A Memorandum relating to one John Campoh Merchant's giving English Money in Exchange to Forreigners, an. 3° Hen. 8. p. 66.

10   17. Breve Regis Edwardi 1^{mi} & Inquisitio inde contra falsam & corruptam monetam & pollardos per quosdam Mercatores importat'. anno 29 & 31° Regni dicti Regis.

18. p. 68. Carta Regis Eadwini filij Regis Eadmundi & fratris Regis Eadgari de terris in Jeakelea, an. 956. p. 73.—Pr. Regnante ac gubernante Domino nostro Ihesu Christo, memoria quia hominum.

19. Extract out of ye Statutes relating to Armor. p. 77.

20. Extract out of ye Statutes relating to Archerye. p. 77.

21. Extract out of ye Statutes relating to Gunns & Crosse-Bows. p. 77.

22. Extracts out of ye Statutes relating to Merchants, Merchants of y^e
20 Staple, Victualers, Hostlers, Weights & Measures, Draperye, Money, Corne, Crowes and Rookes, Husbandry, Wyne, Yarne, Golde & Silver, Hatts & Capps, Tynne, Wax, Pynns, Rogues & Vagabonds, Relief of ye Poor, Chaplains, Highways, Passage, Ale Houses, & Sewers. p. 78. &c.

23. Another Copy of all ye said Extracts. p. 90.   All these Statutes whence these Extracts made obsolete.

24. Some observations of S^r. Edw. Coke conc. the Seal of ye Court of Common Pleas. fol. 99.

25. Carta Regis Johannis pro Electione Episcoporum, cum Annotatiuncula quadam Domini Edv. Coke ad eandem spectante. fol. 101.

30   26. Extracts out of the Records conc. Escheats in ye County of Chester. f. 103.

27. Cardinal Woolsey's Inditement, in French, with a Collection of several Reports. f. 111.

28. Ex Placitis coram Dom. Rege Ed. 4to. Rot. 143. Termino Mich. 5to anno Regni. f. 131. b.

29. Ex placitis coram Domino Rege apud Westm. de Termino Sancti Hillar. Anno Regni Regis Edwardi 3^{tij} post Conquestum tricesimo 8vo. Rot. 14. f. 133.

30. Presidents out of ye Treasurie relating to Prohibitions. f. 136.

40   31. Notes conc. Resumptions & Disabilities to take. f. 139.

32. Form of Premunire. f. 140.

33. Another forme of the same. f. 142.

34. Note conc. the Clerk of Chancery. fol. 145. b.

35. Out of a Parliam^t Roll of 11th of H. 4. concerning the Recovery of certain Castles, Honours, &c. to ye Crowne. fol. 146.

36. An Order resolv'd on by ye Judges & Barons of ye Exchequer concerning

his time to nobler and more useful studies than English Antiquities.   Believes that Grabe received the Sacrament at his ordination.   ' I often, several yeares since, urged Mr. Antony à Wood, who then seriously protested to mee, that hee was no Papist, for the worlds better satisfaction to receive the H. Sacrament in Merton-College-Chappell, or in our College-Chappell with mee; but this hee utterly refused.   But soon after, upon a Solemne Festivall, hee went over to Ifly, and communicated there: of which he brought a certificate, . . . & which hee shewed mee.'

ye dealing wth and disposing of Woods, Trees, and Coppices wthin Parkes, Forrests, & Chases. f. 148.

37. Revocatio Litterarum Patentium de Officio Assaiæ Uluagij de Woosteedes in Civitate Norff. An. quinto Edw. 3^{tij}. f. 150.

38. Out of ye Records of King's Bench, containing divers Inditements for Treason, &c. f. 152.

39. A Catalogue of Inditem^{ts} for Treason temp. Eliz. Reginæ. f. 164.

40. A Collection of some other Inditem^{ts} for Treason in the time of K. Edw. 4. & Q. Eliz. with some things conc. Inditem^{ts} for ye same Crime in ye time of K. Hen. 7. & 8. f. 166.   10

41. Case of ye Murder of John Imperial Embassador of ye state of Venice, in the 3^d Year of ye Reign of Rich. 2^d. f. 179.

42. A Note conc. King John's offering to make his Kingdom tributary to ye Great Emperor of Turkey, & (upon his Refusal) to ye Pope. f. 192. b.

43. The Disannulling of the said Offer to ye Pope by K. Edw. 1. & Edw. 3. f. 193.

44. A True Copy of ye Articles Exhibited against Cardinal Woolsey. f. 195.

45. Concerning Ecclesiastical Jurisdictions as well out of ye Lawes and Ordinances of Spaine, as of ye Story both for ye Point of Prohibition and of Supremacy. By S^r. Edw. Coke.—Pr. The Clergie of Spaine besides their rich 20 Indowments. f. 209.

46. S^r. Edw. Coke's long Epistle to ye Princes & States of Germany, warning them of ye Dangers impending from the House of Burgundy & the Spanish Monarchy.—Pr. When I call to remembrance most gracious Lordes. f. 223.

47. De Superioritate Maris Angliæ & jure Officij Admiralitatis in eodem. f. 244.

48. King James ye first's Proclamation touching Fishing. f. 246.

49. Other Things concerning the Sea & Fishing. f. 248.

50. Reasons to maintaine ye Navigation of ye English Merchants into ye East & West Indies. By S^r. Robt. Cotton. f. 253.—Pr. I doubt not my Honble 30 Lord, but in this Accompt.

51. Typus totius Orbis terrarum in quo & Christiani Militis certamen super terram (in pietatis studiosi gratiam) graphice designatur à Jud. Hondio.

52. Carta Brithrici Regis, ex libro vocato Abendone Landbooke Ca. 19. f. 9.—Pr. In nomine Omnipotentis pijssimi genitoris, qui cunctorum bonorum. f. 261.

53. Carta Etheldredi Regis, ex eodem libro. f. 96.—Pr. Ego Ethelredus totius Albionis Dei providentia imperator.

54. Alia Carta ejusdem Ethelredi Regis de donatione 25 mansorum sive Hidarum Terræ in Ichington facta ad Clofiam.—Pr. In nomine excelsi tonan- 40 tis, cujus nutu & miseratione à pio Patre præditus. f. 263.

55. Ex Eodem libro excerptum cap. 38. de Donatione Cufwlfi Monasterio Abendon. f. 264.

56. Aliud Excerptum ex eodem libro c. 38 de Donatione Ethelswith Reginæ dicto Cufwlfo, ministro suo, in usum dicti Monasterij de Abendon. f. 264.— This Donation of Æthelswith dated A.D. 868. The Charter wch is here added beginns thus, Ego Æthelswith Regina Deo largiente Merciorum, cum consensu meorum seniorum, concedens donabo &c.

57. A Note about the Antiquity of Davies alias Tavies Inne.

58. Some very good Notes about our Ancient English Coyn, beginning wth 50 y^t of the Britains, by S^r. Edw. Coke. f. 265.

59. A Patent of K. Edw. I (An. Regni 20°) to Osbert de Spaldington and John de Suthewell constituting them Justices for ye Isle of Man. f. 267.

60. Out of ye Pleas of the Crown of the 21st Year of the Reign of Edw. I. relating to Master Gwynand de Briland's Poysoning of Salomon de Roffe. f. 269.

60. Some short Notes conc. Coyns, Woole &c. f. 240. b.

61. A Computation of ye Value of all Merchandizes exported & imported

out & into yᵉ Realm of England shewing yᵉ Difference betwixt yᵉ Value of yᵉ Exportation & Importation for 2 years successively, viz. the years 1612, 1613.

62. A Brief Computation of yᵉ Value of all Goods imported & exported into & out of yᵉ Port of London by Merchant Strangers according to yᵉ Printed Booke of Rates excepting the Wines inwardes & Clothe outwardes. Both of yᵐ rated by a Medium being not valued in yᵉ said Book of Rates viz. for one whole year begun from yᵉ Feast of yᵉ Birth of our Lord God 1610 & ended at yᵉ same Feast 1611 being by yᵉ Space of one whole year.

63. Sʳ. Lionell Cranfeild's Ballance of Trade.

10   64. Some Notes of Sʳ. Edw. Coke conc. yᵉ English Coyn. f. 271.

65. Testamentum Henrici Secundi Regis Angliæ. Dated anno 1182.

66. Pope Alexander's Letter to King Henry 2ᵈ for yᵉ Government of Ireland.—Pr. Alexander Episcopus servus servorum Dei, Christianissimo in Christo filio Henrico Illustri Anglorum Regi.

67. His Letter to yᵉ Barons & Nobles of Ireland relating to yᵉ same Matter. —Pr. Alexander Episcopus servus servorum Dei, Dilectis filijs, nobilibus Viris.

68. A Brief Collection of yᵉ Alterations wᶜʰ have been made in yᵉ Monies of this Realme since the time of Edward yᵉ first. f. 273.—Pr. In the 28ᵗʰ year 20 of Kinge Edwarde yᵉ first there were Workemen sent for.

69. A Brief Note of all yᵉ Monies of Gold and Silver Coynes in yᵉ Time of Queen Elizabeth with yᵉ true value thereof in Monie. f. 290.—Pr. Coyned in Sterlinge Monies in the Myntes in yᵉ Tower of London.

70. The like Note for the 1ˢᵗ 15 Years of King James the first's Reign. f. 292.

71. An Estimate by Reasonable Conjecture of yᵉ present State of England in Currant Standard Monies. f. 296.—Pr. There hath beene coyned since yᵉ first Year.

72. Some short Notes conc. the Baillive of Sandwich, Fees &c. f. 299.

30   73. The Manner of making the Monies and the Forme of yᵉ Remedies from the Standard as well for Weight as Finenesse. f. 300.

74. Notes out of Sundrie Indentures whereby the Mint-Master is to have Allowance if his Monies fall out better than Standard. f. 301.

75. A Memorial of such Resolutions as were taken by his Majᵗʸ K. James the 1ˢᵗ abᵗ certain Grievances presented to Him by the Parliamᵗ. f. 303.

76. De Terris in partibus transmarinis, Constitutio facta 17, & 42 E. 3. f. 308.

77. King Henry the 4ᵗʰ'ˢ Letters Patents about certain Privileges of yᵉ Monastery of Evesham, an. Regni 7ᵐᵒ. f. 310.

40   78. A Form for Raising a Loan.

79. King James yᵉ first's Letter to Sʳ. Edw. Coke about Raising a Loan, dated yᵉ last day of Oct. the 9ᵗʰ year of his Reign, wᵗʰ yᵉ King's own Hand at yᵉ Beginning. p. 314.

80. A Privy Seal from King Richard the 3ᵈ to William Swan Gentleman Enabling him to leavy Armes, wᵗʰ the King's own Hand at yᵉ Beginning. f. 315.

81. A Letter of Dʳ. Geo. Abbot Archbᵖ. of Cant. to Sʳ. Edw. Coke conc. some Injury done to his Lᵈship's Courts & Ecclesiastical Jurisdiction, by such Prohibitions as flowed by Sʳ. Edw.'s Means from the Court of Common Pleas. 50 dat. Jan. 11. 1611. f. 317.—f. My very good Lord. Since yᵉ time that his Majesty out of his gracious favour.

82. A Discourse conc. the said Prohibitions. f. 317.—Pr. To omit the larger Discourse of Prohibitions.

83. A Letter of Tho. Lake conc. the same, dat. March 5, 1610.

84. The Petition of the Judges in yᵉ Ecclesiastical Courts to yᵉ King abᵗ the same. f. 320.

85. A Schedule of certain Speeches delivered by Sʳ. Edw. Coke in Vindication of those unjust Prohibitions. f. 320.

119. Le Case de Office de Supersedeas, Termino Paschæ Aᵒ 29. Eliz. Reginæ. f. 410.

120. The Certificate of yᵉ Judges of yᵉ Court of Common Pleas to yᵉ Lo. Chancellor delivered to Mʳ. Attorney General Term. Paschæ 8 Regis Jacobi. f. 412. b.

121. Another Copy of yᵉ same. f. 413.

122. Epistola Cardinalis Bellarmini ad D. Georgium Blacwellum Archipresbyterum Anglorum, dat. Rom. Sept. 28. 1607. f. 415.—Pr. Venerabilis in Xᵗᵒ Domine frater. Anni sunt fere quadraginta.

123. Hales's Project for Reforming Abuses in yᵉ Commonwealth. f. 419.— Pr. It is a lamentable thyng to here howe every Man complaineth.

124. Certain Notes out of Mʳ. Foxe's Acts and Monumᵗˢ. f. 430.

125. Ex Rotulo Patentium de Anno Nono Regni Regis Henrici 3ᵗⁱʲ de Admiralitate. f. 431.

126. Certain Notes about yᵉ Admirality. f. 433.

127. A Letter of John Doddridge conc. a Book of old Talbot conc. Admirals. f. 434.

128. Whether yᵉ Master of yᵉ Rolles being a sworne Privy Counsellor 7 yeares before yᵉ Chancellor of yᵉ Excheqʳ be to give him place at yᵉ Council Table or elsewhere being his Puisne Councellor by 7 years and more. f. 435.

129. A Record relating to yᵉ Fishery. f. 437. There are two more Copies in fol. 442. 443.

130. Revenue rising from yᵉ Ports. f. 438.

131. Extracts out of the Pipe Roll abᵗ yᵉ Fishery. f. 440.

132. The Reasons of yᵉ poor Fishermen & others of yᵉ Counties of Devon & Cornwall against yᵉ Patent of yᵉ fifth of August in yᵉ 7ᵗʰ year of his Majesties (K. James I.) Reign, granted to Henry Heron. f. 444.

133. A Collection of Notes from Records in yᵉ Tower conc. yᵉ King's Prerogative. f. 447.

134. The Declaration made by John Fortescue Knight upon certen Wrytynges sent owt of Scottland ayenst the Kynges Tytle to hys Realme off Englond. f. 497.—Pr. A Lernyd Man in the Law off thys Lond. f. 449. See pag. 103.

135. King Henry yᵉ 8ᵗʰ'ˢ Pardon of Cardinal Woolsey. f. 462. Dated. 12 Febr. an. Regni 21ᵒ.

136. King Rich. 2ᵈˢ Pardon of Willᵐ of Wickham Bᵖ. of Winchester. f. 469.

137. K. James yᵉ 1ˢᵗ'ˢ Warrant to yᵉ Lᵈ. Keeper for Pardons to Popish Recusants. f. 474. Dated 9 Sept. 1623.

138. K. Ed. 4ᵗʰˢ Letters of Exemplification relating to Jaquett Dutchess of Bedford. f. 475.

139. Robert Fitz-Harding's Grant of yᵉ Church of Berkley, Wotton, &c. to his Priory of Black Canons of yᵉ Order of Sᵗ. Augustine at Bristol. f. 481.

140. Henrici Regis Concessio 3ᵗⁱʲ Denarij de Placitis Comitatus de Oxon ad Comitem Albericum. f. 482.

141. Shippes and Mariners imployd by King Ed. 3 in the Expedition made by him into France in yᵉ 20ᵗʰ year of his Reign. f. 493.

142. Copie of a Letter of Stephen Gardiner Bᵖ. of Winchester to ye Lᵈ. Protector. (See Acts & Monumᵗˢ pag. 470. of Mʳ. Foxes 1ˢᵗ Edition) conc. yᵉ Honour of yᵉ Lawes of yᵉ Realm in those Dayes. f. 496.

143. A Brief Note of Instructions & Orders made for staye of Executions &c. f. 498.

144. King James 1ˢᵗ Creation of his Eldest Son Henry Prince of Wales.

145. The true order & manner of yᵉ Execution of Mary Qu. of Scotts together wᵗʰ Relacions of all such Speeches & Actions spoken and done by her or any others and all other Circumstances & Proceedings conc. yᵉ same from & after her Delivery to Thomas Andrewes Esqʳ High Sheriff of Northampton

unto yᵉ End of yᵉ said Execution, written by R.W. to Lᵈ. Burleigh. f. 499.—
Pr. It maie please your good Lordship to be advertised that according as your
Honour gave me Commaunde. Dated 11ᵗʰ Febr. 1586. Here are several
very remarkable things in this Accᵗ & the whole very well worth Printing if
not done already.

146. A Copie of Mʳ. Anthony Babington's Letter to the Queen of Scottes.
—Pr. Most Mighty most Excellᵗ, my Dread Sovereign Ladie and Queene
unto whome onlie I owe all fidelitie & Obedience. It may please your
Gracious Majestie—

147. The Queen of Scotts Answer to yᵗ Letter.—Pr. Trustie & well-be- 10
loved. According to yᵉ Zeale & intire Affection.

148. Another Relation of yᵉ Execution of yᵉ Queen of Scottes. f. 508.—
Pr. Upon Wednesday the 12ᵗʰ of October 1586. The Lordes Commissioners
for yᵉ Hearing of the Scottish Queene.

149. Queen Elizabeth's Letters Patents directed for the Execution of yᵉ
said Queen of Scottes. ▬

There are several Copies of Sʳ. John Fortescue's Declaration in England. There is one in the Cottonian Library, another in the Bodlejan;
but the latter is imperfect. Mʳ. Dodwell has a Copy accurately taken
from that in Cotton's Library, and compar'd wᵗʰ that in Bodley; and 20
Mʳ. Cherry has a fair Transcript from Mʳ. Dodwell's. Mʳ. Fortescue
also I believe has another. . . .

Jan. 2, 1706 (Wed.). Dʳ. Adams Principal of Magd. Hall intends to build
six Rooms & come to live in Oxon, intending now to keep Residence, which
to His Eternal shame he has neglected ever since he was made Principal.
▬ Mʳ. Will. Dobson is made President by the Bᵖ. of Winchester of Trinity
Coll. in Roome of Dʳ. Sykes. This Mʳ. Dobson, who took his Master
of Arts Degree Nov. 4. 1672, & had his Grace for Bach. of Divinity's
Degree proposed & granted some years since (tho he is not yet presented
to it) is an Honest Man & a good Scholar, who by his Prudence 'tis 30
hop'd will raise the Drooping Credit of yᵗ Society, wᶜʰ formerly had men
of Note in it, but now has not one. When He left his Fellowship Mʳ.
Arthur Charlett succeeded him, of whom you may expect more anon. ▬
Series Chronologica Olympiadum, Pythiadum, Isthmiadum, Nemeadum,
Quibus veteres Græci tempora sua metiebantur. Per Guil. Lloyd, A.M.
Episcopi Wigorniensis filium. Oxon. e Th. 1700. fol. This Piece was
done for the better understanding of Pindar done by Mʳ. Rich. West &
Mʳ. Rob. Welsted of Magd. Coll. with wᶜʰ Edition 'tis commonly bound.
But 'tis to be noted yᵗ tho' the same bears the name of Mʳ. Lloyd (who
is lately made Dʳ. of Divinity by the Archbᵖ. of Canterbury's Diploma 40
upon his being denied by the University of Oxon as I have before related)
yet the Author was the Bᵖ. himself as I have been credibly inform'd. ▬
As for yᵉ said Edition of Pindar tho' 'tis printed in a Good Letter &
Paper, yet yᵉ Editors being careless & not much versed in old MSS. (a
fault common to most of the Fellows & even others in Oxon) & being
not withall diligent enough in collecting Materials & consulting Authors
there are a great many Blunders in it, besides divers material Omissions
to yᵉ no small Blemish of the undertaking. These Chronological Tables
are printed also wᵗʰ Pindar itself, wᶜʰ came out at the Theatre in 1697,
but being faultily printed there by the Negligence of the Compositor or 50
rather yᵉ Ignorance and carelessness of yᵉ Undertakers occasion'd this new
Edition in 1700, wᶜʰ is enlarg'd. ▬ . . . Mʳ. Allemont of Trinity Coll. who

has been twice return'd to the Visitor by the Fellows of Trinity Coll. for their President has for a great many years lived so obscure a Life in ye College (confining himself to ye College & never appearing at or doing any Exercise in the University) that 'tis a hard matter to know his just Character; yet this may be observ'd by the by, that when he was a Tutor he notoriously neglected his Duty as D^r. Wallis's son who was his Pupil has frequently told several Persons. D^r. Bathurst was so sensible of this, that to oblige him to leave off Pupils he made him his Curate at Garzington, wch Curacy he continu'd in'till D^r. Sykes was made President. (He died in 1710,
10 or else 1709. Quære?) — In the Theatre Yard is an Inscription to ye Memory of Laodice Daughter of Seleucus Philopator the Son of Antiochus ye Great & Wife of Perseus the last of ye Macedonian Kings whom P. Æmylius triumph'd over, as is related by Livy. This Laodice is mention'd only in this Stone, & for y^t reason 'tis very valuable, & must be reprinted in ye Notes to Livy. As printed in Marm. Oxon. 'tis thus : . . . Quaere whether it be taken right?

   Jan. 3 (Th.). . . . MS. F. 83. Laud. Opusculum de Natura legis Naturæ & de ejus censura in successione regnorum supremorum, per D. Joan. Fortescue. N.B. A year or two since I saw and talk'd wth M^r. John
20 Fortescue a Barrister of Law & descended from this most Learned & Judicious S^r. John Fortescue, who came on purpose from London to Oxford to look into certain MSS pieces of S^r. John, intending to Publish some if not all ye Pieces he could procure not hitherto published. About 4 or 5 Years since at ye Request of M^r. Alexander Denton, a Common-Lawyer, who was once Commoner of Edm. Hall, I transcrib'd out of S^r. Tho. Bodley's Library S^r. John's Piece in English De Dominio Politico & Regali, for ye use, it seems of this M^r. Fortescue, who was put upon ye Work by ye Learned & Conscientious D^r. George Hickes. But I am now inform'd (but whether truly or no I cannot tell) y^t he has laid aside this
30 Design [1]. — Sagittarius de Januis Veterum. 8°. The Scholiast of Aristophanes corrected there. pag. 105. — It must be noted that tho' Robortellus long since discovered Sigonius to be ye Author of that Piece wch goes under ye Name of Tully de Consolatione, & is now known to every one to be a spurious Piece, yet B^p. Burnett has asserted (being ignorant of the matter & having no Judgment, or but very little in Tully's Style) that 'tis the best Piece that was ever writ by Tully. Tho' Robortellus writ several Pieces in opposition to Sigonius, yet Sigonius (as Grævius has well observ'd) much the greater Man, being more ingenious & of more solid Judgment : however there was one great Infirmity in Sigonius that he
40 was not promptus linguæ, being not able to discourse in Latin with any-one, wch was also observ'd in Morhofius, who was otherwise an ingenious & learned Man. — . . . In pag. 588. in Donatus's Descriptio urbis Romæ is the Columna Rostrata engrav'd wth the Inscription printed at large. Consider of this w^n Livy is printing.

   Jan. 5 (Sat.). Stow in his Annals has printed Cavendish's Life of

---

Jan. 5. Dodwell to H. Notes on Hearne's coin of Carausius. Messages

---

[1] He hath since published from my Copy the Tract de Dominio &c. Tho. Hearne, June 17. 1732.

Cardinal Woolsey. Quære whether it be exactly ye same wth that newly printed by D^r. Drake? — S^r. Andrew Fountaine tells me y^t he found his Curious MS^t (the Heads whereof I have given above) in ye Cellar of his Father's Study in the Middle-Temple, where he found a great many others, most of wch he says are valuable Rarities, & some whereof are now in his Hands, but the rest were spoyl'd. — Sir Andrew also tells me that after he had drawn up his Excell^t Dissertation conc. the Saxon Coyns, pr. at ye End of D^r. Hickes's Thesaurus, he sent it up to the said D^r. Hickes that he might revise it; upon wch ye D^r. drew up a Diss. of his own & sent it to S^r. Andrew, who however did not think fit to publish it as the D^r. had done it, but printed it exactly as he had drawn it up himself, only wth this Alteration that whereas before he had said nothing of the Catalogue of MSS, he now added studio aut saltem auspicio viri istius Doctissimi, meaning D^r. Hickes, the said D^r. having put it in ye Diss. he sent him studio & cura, intimating y^t he had been at ye whole care and pains of doing this Catalogue, wch is pr. under Humph. Wanley's Name. — . . . Memorandum that M^r. Tanner has a MS^t of a Piece of Bale wch is for ye Publick Library. (He hath since [sent] it thither. I plac'd it myself.) — Imperatorum & Cæsarum vitæ, cum Imaginibus ad vivam effigiem expressis, per Huttichium, cum Elencho & Iconijs consulum. 1534. 4°. This piece at ye End is the first Collection of ye Consular Coyns y^t ever was publish'd. — Ludolphi Smids Romanorum Imperatorum Pinacotheca. *Amst.* 1699. 4°. Frid. Adolfi Lampe de Cymbalis veterum libri III. *Traj. ad Rhen.* 1703. 8°. Almeloveen Romanorum Consularium libri II. *Amst.* 1705. 8°. All these Books in this Page I saw at S^r. Andrew Fountaine's.

A Catalogue of some other MSS. besides y^t above mention'd wch I have seen in S^r. Andrew Fountaine's Hands.

1. Constitutiones Provinciales in Concilio Oxoñ celebrato editæ per Dominum Stephanum Cantuar. Archiepiscopum Anno Domini millesimo ccxxij^o, & anno Regni Regis Henrici filij Johannis octavo.—Pr. Ex auctoritate Dei patris omnipotentis, Beatæ Virginis, omnium sanctorum.

In the margin under this Head, De vita & Honestate clericorum & de prælatorum habitu & conversatione & ne clerici concubinis suis ad . . . . at these words addentes ne clerici maxime beneficiati vel in sacris ordinibus constituti in Hospitijs suis *vel alibi* tenere puplice *vel occulte* concubinas præsumant, nec alibi cum scandalo accessum puplicum vel occultum habeant ad easdem is the following Note added by Sir Edw. Coke, videlicet, in exemplari impresso anno 1504 arte Magistri Wulfangi Hopitij hæc verba maxime beneficiati, vel occulte omittuntur : et vel alibi & occultum omittitur. Sic in alijs exemplaribus impressis.

2. Constitutiones Domini Bonifacij Archiepiscopi Cantuariensis, in Concilio Westmon. anno 1261, anno 44 Henrici 3tij.—Pr. Universis Sanctæ Matris Ecclesiæ filijs per Cantuar. Provinciam constitutis.

to Sir A. Fountaine and 'my candid Adversary.' 'I do not know whether the scrap of my Letter be worth inserting in my copy of the Case in View. I was at Oxford when the Schism commenced. And all that were pleased to take any notice of my behaviour then may remember that I was at New Colledg Prayers at 4. of the Clock, that Whitsun Tuesday whereon the news came that evening to the Cophee house, that the Altars were erected against the old Altars on the Sunday before. So far I was from separating for any cause but that which I have here insisted on.'

3. Constitutiones de Redyng editæ ibidem per fratrem Johannem Peccham
Cantuar. Archiepiscopum 3^tio Kalendarum Augusti Anno Domini millesimo
cclxxix°. & Consecrationis anno iij°.—Pr. De Institutionibus & Destitutioni-
bus. Audistis fratres conscripti istius Constitutionis tenorem. (4) Constitutiones Provinciales Domini Roberti de Winchelsea aliter Domini Stephani de
Langton Cantuar. Archiepiscopi apud Merton editæ de Decimis & Nutrimentis
animalium Anno Domini millesimo ccclx°.—Pr. Quoniam propter diversas
consuetudines in petendo decimas. (5) Constitutiones de Lambethe per
Dominum Stephanum de Langton Cantuar. Archiepiscopum editæ, & in qui-
10 busdam libris istæ Constitutiones præcedunt Constitutiones de Merton.—Pr.
De Modo dandi Mortuarium. Statutum felicis Recordationis Reverendi præ-
decessoris nostri de Mortuarijs. At the End of these Constitutions of Stephen
Langton is this Note of Sir Edw. Coke: In libro vetere Manuscripto intit. ma-
tricula de Camera Abbatis Sancti Aug. Cant. fol. 168. sunt statuta quædam
Stephani Cant. Archiepiscopi in sinodo, De irregularitatibus quæ indigent
dispensatione &c. (6) Constitutiones fratris Johannis Peccham Cantuar.
Archiepiscopi apud Lambethe editæ anno Domini 1281.—Pr. Ab exordio
nascentis Ecclesiæ Christianæ orthodoxi. (7) Constitutiones venerabilis Patris
Domini Symonis Mepham Cantuar. Archiepiscopi totius Angliæ Primatis in
20 Concilio Provinciali apud Sanctum Paulum London. celebrato Mense Febr.
viz. die Veneris post Conversionem Sancti Pauli Anno Domini Millesimo
cccxxviii.—Pr. Zelari oportet Domino Deo suo ecclesiarum prælatos qui non
de sola. (8) Hæ Constitutiones sequentes secundum aliquos libros sunt
Constitutiones Provinciales Johannis Startforde Cantuar. Archiepiscopi editæ
London. in Consilio Provinciali x° die Mensis Octobris Anno Domini 1342.—
Pr. Ne in privatis Oratorijs Missarum sollempnia sine licentia Episcopi de
cætero celebrentur.—Quam sit inhonestum in reverentiæ Divinæ. (9) Con-
cilium celebratum Westmonasterii tempore Archiepiscopi Cantuar. anno
Domini 1065 de clericis habentibus Matrimonium.—Pr. Si quis sacerdos vel
30 Clericus in sacris ordinibus constitutus. In margine hæc habetur manu re-
centi Annotatiuncula, viz. *Richardi ut in Chronica Hovedeni anno* 1175. *& in
Gervasio* 1175. *est Rici ut in alijs libris antiquioribus.* Quære? (10) Constitutiones Provinciales Sancti Edmundi Cantuariensis Archiepiscopi.—Pr.
Qui sunt irreverentes & suspensi mero jure. Inprimis igitur in virtute spiritus
Sancti districte præcipimus. (11) Constitutiones Provinciales Domini Stephani
(in margine Symonis) Mepham Cantuar. Archiepiscopi editæ apud Lamhithe,
de ornamentis Altaris & Clericis circa illud ministrantibus.—Pr. Cui thora-
mina, corporalia, pallæ, tuellæ, manitergia. (12) Constitutio Dominorum
Roberti Winchelsey & Walteri Reynold & secundum quosdam Symonis Islep
40 Archiepiscoporum Cant. Quid Parochiani invenire debeant insuper etiam &
quid Rectores.—Pr. Ut Parochiani singulorum Archidiaconatuum Cantuar.
Provinciæ. (13) Constitutio Domini Symonis de Islep quondam Archiepiscopi Cantuariensis de Presbyteris annualia celebrantibus & alijs non curatis ut
curis deserviant desolatis ad serviendum curis hujus (f. huiusmodi) compellen-
dis.—Pr. Symon permissione divina Cantuar. Archiepiscopus totius. (13) De
Juramento Sacerdotis & obedientia Rectoribus & Vicarijs præstanda : & est
Constitutio Domini Roberti de Winchelsei Cantuar. Archiepiscopi facta in
Visitatione sua Anno Domini 1305.—Presbyteri necnon alij sacerdotes stipen-
diarij proprijs. (14) Casus in quibus Judex Ecclesiasticus potest cognos-
50 cere regia prohibitione non obstante concessi per Cartam Regiam.—Pr.
Edwardus Dei gratia Rex Angliæ & Scotiæ Dominus Hiberniæ. (15) Litera
Domini Regis (Edw. primi) directa Justiciarijs suis pro moderanda prohibitione
Regia.—Pr. Rex Justiciarijs suis salutem. Circumspecte agatis de negotio.
(16) Constitutio Domini J. Islep Cantuariensis Archiepiscopi de Festis per
annum observandis ; aliter, Incipit Constitutio Domini Symonis de Islep de
Festis Sanctorum observandis & de Parochianis ut intersint Horis Canonicis
per ordinarios debite exortandis.—Pr. Simon permissione Divina Cantuariensis
Archiepiscopus, totius Angliæ Primas. (17) Constitutiones Domini Joannis

de Stratford Cantuariensis Archiepiscopi editæ anno Domini 1342°, aliter 3°, die Mercurij proxime post festum Sancti Edwardi Regis & Martyris in Ecclesia Sancti Pauli London.—Pr. Sponsam Christi sacrosanctam Ecclesiam privilegio libertatis celitus decoratam. (18) Constitutio Domini Thomæ Arundell Archiepiscopi Cantuariensis edita in concilio provinciali celebrato Oxon. Anno Domini 1407. — Pr. Thomas permissione Divina Cantuariæ Archiepiscopus.

The said MS^t in a thin fol. in Vellam.

II. Preparatory Thoughts for Receiving ye Holy Sacrament, Dedicated to ye Lady Rich, & written by B^p. Gauden. 8°. 'Tis written in a very neat 10 Hand, S^r. Andrew Fountaine says by the B^p. himself.

The Beginning—Opportunity being offered me of coming to the Holy Sacrament of the Supper of our Lord.—Quære whether this be not ye very same Book with y^t wch goes under the Name of the B^p. call'd *The whole Duty of a Communicant* &c., whereof there are several Impressions, the first came out in 1681. 12°. Ask S^r. Andrew whether there be any other Pieces of B^p. Gauden (who was his Great Uncle by ye Mother's side, as I think he told me) in MS^t wch have not been printed? Ant. à Wood intimates there are, wch however he never saw.

III. Modus tenendi Parliamenti, in English. There are some things left 20 out, wch are in ye Latin Copies, whereof there are divers, as M^r. Selden notes in his Titles of Honour, but he does not think the Treatise Ancient. 'Tis certain from the use of the Words *Parliament, Baron* and *Justices of the Bench* &c. y^t it must have been writ after ye Reign of Hen. III^d. This English Copy (wch is in a Vellam 4to) appears to have been written in the Time of Hen. VIIIth whose Effigies in two or three places is illuminated, wch shews illuminations to have been frequently us'd at y^t time all the great Letters at ye Beginning of Chapters and Paragraphs in this Book being illuminated.

IV. A Book of Heraldry, in 8°. the Coats neatly drawn.

V. Extractus Inquisitionum & aliorum extra turrim London. Feodorum &c. 30 in Comitatu Norff. viz. (1) Escaetr. tempore Henrici Tertij de Comitatu Norff. (2) Ex Bundell. Escaetr. & Inquisitionum tempore Edwardi Primi, Com. Norff. pag. 14. (3) Cartæ tempore Edwardi primi. p. 42. (4) Escaetr. de tempore Edwardi 2^di. p. 62. (5) Inquisitiones ad quod dampnum Edwardi 2. p. 88. (6) Cartæ Edwardi 2. p. 108. (7) Patentes Edwardi 2. p. 114. (8) Escaetr. & Inquisitiones tempore Edwardi tertij. p. 122. (9) Cartæ Edw. 3. p. 180. (10) Patentes Edw. 3. p. 190. (11) Escaetr. & Inquisitiones tempore Regis Ricardi secundi. p. 204. (12) Patentes Ricardi 2^di. p. 239. (13) Henrici Quarti. p. 247. (14) Henrici 5. p. 257. (15) Inquisitiones ad quod dampnum Henrici 4^ti. p. 263. (16) Inquisitiones ad quod dampnum tempore Hen- 40 rici 5^ti. p. 268. (17) Patentes Henrici 4^ti. p. 271. (18) Patentes Henrici 5^ti. p. 272. (19) Escaetr. Henrici 6^ti. Norff. p. 280. (20) Cartæ Henrici 6^ti. p. 303. (21) Patentes Henrici 6^ti. p. 304. (22) Edwardi Quarti. Norff. p. 312. (23) Ricardi 3^tij. p. 329. (24) Edwardi Quarti Carta. p. 330. (25) Patentes Edwardi Quarti. p. 331.—This MS^t in a Thin folio, in Paper.

VI. Liber antiquus Feodorum Militum in Comitatu Norff. & Suff. in a thin paper folio.—fol. 8 b. in Hundredo de Hempstede : Petronilla de Narford tenet Manerium de Shotesham per Servicium xi & tres partes feodi Militis de Comite Marescallo & idem de domino Rege per I. feod.—fol. 14 b. in Hundredo de Weylounde : Petronilla de Narforde tenet in Asshele Saham & 50 Honton unum feodum Militis de Honore de Clar. & ille de Domino Rege in Capite.—fol. 16 a. in Hundredo de Southgreve Howe : Petronilla de Nerford tenet in Narbourgh medietatem unius feodi Militis de Roberto filio Rogeri & ille de Comite Richemond.—f. 17. in eodem Hundredo Thomas de Narforde tenet in Narforde dimidium feodi Militis de Comite Warenn. ut de Manerio de Lynge per servicium unius & idem Comes tenet ultimo de Comite Richemond, eidem de Rege.—f. 20 a. Willelmus de Kerdeston tenet Manerium suum in Sidestern per servicium unius feodi Militis de Hered. Willelmi de Nerford &

idem de Comite   & Comes de Rege.—f. 22. In Hundredo de Clakelose: Abbas de Dereham tenet in Dereham vi^tam partem unius feodi Militis in puram & perpetuam Elimosinam de Hered. Willelmi de Narfforde & idem Her. de Comite Gloucestriæ & ille de Rege.—Willelmus de Nerforde tenet in Crymplisham VIII. partem unius feodi Militis de Comite Gloucestr. & idem de Domino Rege.—Johannes de Stokes tenet in Wirham voc. Yronhall per servicium unius Quarterij feodi militis de Hered. Petri de Narforde eidem ser. de Comite Gloucestr. & idem de Rege per decimam partem unius feodi.

In Suffolk.

10   Fol. 28 b. Hund. de Bosemere: Johannes de Hudebomle & Johannes de Narforde tenent in Breset quarterium unius feodi Militis de Willelmo de Narfforde & idem de Comite Gloucestriæ & idem Comes de Rege.—f. 29 a. in eodem Hundredo Radulfus de Narfforde & Hugo de Rykynghale tenent tria quarteria unius feodi militis in Dominio & servicio in Crosfilde de prædicto Comite & Comes de Rege.

VII. An old Book of Pleas of ye Crown in the time of Ed. 2. & Ed. 3. A large folio, in vellum.

Vellejus Paterculus corrected by Rupertus in his Observatt. in Sallust. p. 152. ▬ Died out of the Parish of White-Waltham Berks since April 20 14. 1705 to Dec. 17. 1705 [here follow the names of 22, 19 grown persons and 3 children]. ▬ There is a Pamphlett come out of 6^d Price call'd A Letter to ye Author of ye Memorial, wch tho' it pretends to Wipe off the Slurs cast upon the Ministry of K. Wm. by ye Memorialists, yet it blackens ye Character of ye Duke of Marlborough, reflecting upon his Management in last Campaign & insinuates y^t his Journey to Vienna was onely to pick up Presents, not out of a Design to obtain any Accommodation wth the Hungarian Rebells, or making the Emperor act wth more vigour & Life than he did last year. It also Reflects upon M^r. Secretary Harley &c. But the Author discovering thro' the greatest p^t 30 of ye Letter y^t he is a Whig, he may Libell with Impunity. ▬ M^r. Dodwell in his VIIIth Prælect. § x. tells us y^t Paul Petavius had prepar'd for ye Press a Collection of Inscriptions, & y^t Is. Vossius transcrib'd thence the Fragments of the Libri Lintei whence Hadrian Beverland took a Copy, & communicated it to M^r. Dodwell, who has publish'd it wth Notes. Quære whether ye said Collection of Inscriptions is like to be publish'd, or where 'tis now? ▬ ... M^r. Boyle in his Preface to his Examination of D^r. Bentley's Diss. upon Phalaris acknowledges that in his Edition of Phalaris he was assisted often by M^r. Friend (now second School Master of Westminster) the Director of his Studies, it being 40 nothing but prudence for a Young Writer (or indeed any one else) to consult others who are suppos'd able to inform them when there is any Doubt. [1] This day viz. Jan. 7. D^r. Mill treated wth his Venison & a dish of Fowle at his Chamber. Persons invited were D^r. Dunster Warden of Wadham, D^r. Royse Provost of Oriel, D^r. Colnet & D^r. Irish of All-Souls, M^r. Vermin of Exon Col., & M^r. Caswell the Beadle, & M^r. Sloper of Pembroke. But there were present only D^r. Colnet, M^r. Vermin, M^r. Caswell & D^r. Irish. Of all these Persons M^r. Caswell is a Man of the best Character for Zeal Probity & Honesty. ▬ Rubenius's Book de Vita Mallij was communicated to D^r. Bentley by S^r. Edw. 50 Sherburn to be sent to M^r. Grævius to be publish'd, but wth this Con-

---

[1] This to be referr'd to pag. 142. under Jan. 7.

dition that S^r. Edw. should be mention'd as the Person who oblig'd the world wth it. W^{ch} D^r. Bentley neglected to inform Grævius of, & so it happen'd y^t Grævius knowing nothing of it's coming from S^r. Edw. dedicated it to D^r. Bentley, & attributed y^t Honour to him wch was due to S^r. Edw.

Jan. 6 (Sun.). We hear several of ye Persons, concern'd in Writing the Memorial, are discover'd and warrants out for seizing them. — D^r. Mill having by the Interest (as I suppose) of the B^p. of Worcester receiv'd a Present out of Woodstock Park of a Doe from the Dutchess of Marlborough, treated his Hall this day with a Haunch of it; but w^t is observ- 10 able (and wch is the reason I mention it) is that he did not give a glass of Wine or Ale to drink her Health, nor did he so much as mention her all the time he was at dinner. This same D^r. Mill when he was lately at Canterbury being at dinner wth a certain Gentleman, desir'd a Glass of Wine to be fill'd & drinking to y^e Gentleman said, *come S^r here is the Archb$^{t's}$ good Health.* To wch the Gentleman said, *Pray S^r w^t Archb^t do you mean?* W^{ch} being an unexpected Question, after a short pause the D^r. in a low sneaking voice (as his way is upon such occasions) reply'd *the Archb^t of Yorke,* thinking 'twould have look'd like ingratitude if he had said *Canterbury,* when the Archb^p. of York was his Great Friend 20 in getting his Prebend for him.

Jan. 7 (Mon.). See pag. 138. — There is a great Contest at New College ab^t ye Dysposal of a Sinecure, the Competitors being M^r. Loggans Chancellor of Sarum & M^r. Ford, M.A. & one of ye Senior Fellows in orders of y^t College. This last is reckoned a good ingenious Honest Man, but ye first a dully stupid Creature of ye B^p. of Sarum's, of whom there goes this Story, that speaking one day ab^t ye Different ways of spelling his Name, a certain Gentleman reply'd to him, that tho' ye Spellings might differ in ye End of ye Word, some making it Loggen, some Loggin & others Loggan, yet 'twas remarkable y^t they all agreed 30 in ye first syllable Log. — The Constitutions wch are attributed to the Archb^p. of Cant. in ye year 1065 in S^r. Andrew Fountain's Book of Provincial Councils, & there said to have been made at Westm. seem to belong to Richard Archb^p. of Cant. who was created An. 1175 as appears not only from Hoveden & Ge[r]vase, but also from Birchington's Catalogue of Archb^{ps} in the first Vol. of Anglia Sacra, unless they are rather of Richard Wethersted, Archb^p. of Cant. sernamed the Great, who was consecrated in ye Year 1229. — Josephus corrected by M^r. Dodwell, Praelect. p. 661. — . . .

Jan. 7. Thoresby to H. Account of a Roman monument lately discovered at Coning-Street, York. Inscriptions proving that the 9th as well as the 6th Legion was stationed at York, &c. Remarks on the reverse of the Carausius. Roman coin relating to Britain in his possession. Begs for autographs. **T. Cherry to H.** . . . ' Yesterday came Mr. Purcival of X^t Ch: (who has lately returned from Ireland). He informed us of more Particulars of Mr. Secheveral's Sermon out of a Letter he receiv'd from Dr. Charlott. Our neighbouring Clergy and all Honest Men do very much approve of his Courage and hope 'twill animate the well-affected in the Univ.' Mr. Fopps in difficulties in pleading before the House of Commons. Dodwell on the Soul almost finished. Don't send the *Mercury*; would like an Oxford Almanack.

Jan. 8 (Tu.). Remember to consult Donatus [in Grævius's III Vol. Thes.] p. 753. concerning yᵉ Temple of Minerva when Livy is printing, to wᶜʰ at yᵉ End must be added yᵉ Inscription conc. Pompey's Acts & Triumphs. — ... MS. Laud. F. 86. A large MSᵗ Treatise in English call'd Disce Mori wᶜʰ contains in a manner the whole Body of Practical Divinity. This was given to the Archbᵖ. by Mat Griffith as appears from his Letter at yᵉ Beginning to his Grace, wᶜʰ here follows:

To yᵉ Rᵗ Honᵇˡᵉ and Rᵗ Reverend Father in God, William Lord Archbᵖ. of Canterbury his Grace Primate and Metropolitan of all England, his much
10 Honoured Lord.

Your Graces many real Favours (so much transcending my desert and Expectation) have so wholly captivated me, that I can think of nothing but David's Quid retribuam? and yet having mustered up all my Forces to testifie my unfeigned thankfullness, I find my store to be but two poore Mites (my self, & this Manuscript) and these I willingly prostrate at your Grace's Feet, humbly craving your Gracious Acceptance of both. For howe're the one be in Sᵗ. Paul's Quorum ego minimus, & so not worthy your least Consideration, much less your Countenance: yet by the Phrase & Tenets of yᵉ other, your Grace's peircing Eye will soon discerne, that it merits to be receiv'd, & re-
20 verenc'd for Antiquitie; & being a None-such in yᵉ Kind, vouchsafe it, I beseech you, some corner in your Librarie: Soe shall you confirme me in your Grace's good Opinion; & oblige me dulie to pray that your Grace (than whom even Envie it self must ingenuously confesse that Christendome cannot shew in one person, either a Prelate more vigilant in the Church; or a Divine more powerfull in yᵉ Pulpit; or a Priest more Reverend at yᵉ Altar; or a Minister more faithfull to his King, and Country; or a more grave Counsellor of Estate; or a more just Magistrate on yᵉ Tribunal; or a more Resolute Defender of God's Cause; or a more Zealous promover of good Works; or a more Angelical Life, unspotted of yᵉ Worlde & the Flesh; and enamell'd with all
30 saving Gifts & Graces;) may long and long continue, & encrease in Health and Happiness, on Earth; and have your Mitre seconded with a Crown of Glory in yᵉ Heavens. And in this posture rests

The Humblest of your Grace's Servants

MATT. GRIFFITH.

Octob. 10ᵗʰ. 1638.
St. Maudlin Old fish Street London.

— Dʳ. Plot in his History of Oxonsh. notes yᵗ there is a MSᵗ in yᵉ Cottonian Library whence it appears yᵗ King Ælfred translated Boethius de Consolatione Philosophiæ at Woodstock, & thence inferrs yᵗ here was
40 a Royal Seat in yᵉ Saxon Times long before yᵉ Reign of Hen. I. — ... Yesterday they began to pull down the Building of Peckwater Quadrangle at Xᵗ Church in order to erect a New Fabrick. — ... Enquire abᵗ Astypalæa in Crete where Phalaris was borne. See Mʳ. Boyle's Examin. of Bentl. p. 36. See in the Coyns of Goltzius Sicil. & Magn. Gr. ex numism. p. 126. where tis call'd Astyphalis, & so also by Farellus Rer. Sic. Dec. 1. L. 6. c. 1.

Jan. 9 (Wed.). Mʳ. Wright Recorder of yᵉ City of Oxoñ is out of Favour with yᵉ Dutchess of Marlborough, the Lᵈ. Wharton & other Great Persons at Court, because he did not appear for Mʳ. Carter last Election
50 for Burgess of Parliamᵗ for this City. This is no small Grief to him, being a Man who has all along acted out of self Interest, & meerly to get Prefermᵗ; to accomplish wᶜʰ End he has stood firm to no side; but

now experiences that notw^{th}standing his Cunning (for he is a Man of Parts & Policy) he is like to get nothing more than w^t he has, the Whiggs themselves it seems hating men of shuffling, Latitudinarian Principles. — ..
Noris has illustrated a Coyn of Carausius, Diss. 1. fol. 22. Tristran Tom. 3. f. 379 mentions one of Carausius, on the Reverse whereof there is PAX AUG. c. Pax dextra Ramum, sinistra Hastam. — ... M^r. Jones of Sunning-well near Oxoñ (Brother in Law to ye B^p. of Worcester) has taken the Oaths, & qualified himself for ye said Rectory of Sunning-well, after he has stood out for several Years. But this will not be any great wonder to ye Conscientious-Non-Jurors, who know his Character well 1q enough, namely a shuffling—designing Man &c.

Jan. 10 (Th.). The H. of Commons have order'd D^r. Kennett to preach before them next 30th of Jan. — ... Bibliotheca Maxima to be got into ye Publick Library. . . .

Jan. 11 (Fri.). [Notes from Graevius's Thesaurus. (153–160.)]

Jan. 12 (Sat.). M^r. Thwaites tells me y^t M^r. Addison's Book of travells wch he has read all over is not so contemptible, as most would make it, being (as he says) writ not only in a very clean handsome style, but with good skill, & contains several Curiosities, wch are not so clearly told by other Authors. At ye same time he inform'd me y^t having lately 20 read over Vitruvius, he found nothing hardly done to y^t excellent Author, & y^t 'twould be an Excell^t work for some fit Persons (for one Man is hardly able, considering ye Variety of Learning in it) to undertake a New Edition. But alass! where are ye Patrons to Encourage it in England? — ... Sir Geo. Wheeler says (Pag. 23. Voyag.) y^t he went on purpose to Trau (a seaport Town belonging to ye Venetians, situated ab^t 18 or 20 miles west from Spalato) to see a MS^t wch hath made much Noise among ye Learned for it's Antiquity; viz. the Fragment of Petronius Arbiter wch was wanting in His works. This having not been seen for some Ages, was reckon'd a Spurious thing; & among others Monsr. 30 Valois esteem'd it fictitious: But Signior Lucia, & ye Abbot Gradi at Rome were of ye contrary opinion; the first of whom had undoubtedly seen ye MS^t, Trau being his Native Country. Sir George tells us y^t ye MS^t hath Tibullus Catullus & Propertius at ye Beginning & not Horace, as is affirm'd by the Preface of ye Paduan Edition. In Propertius is to be noted the *Cognomen Nautæ*, that Scaliger taketh Notice of in his Notes. After this followed Petronius Arbiter, just as printed, the title whereof written in red Letter is as followeth: Petronius Arbiter Petronij Arbitri Satyri fragmentum ex Libro Quinto Decimo & Sexto Decimo. In wch among others the Cœna Trimalcionis is very amply related as it is 40 printed at Padua, & in Holland. After wch in a more modern Hand is Claudian. The MS^t is eaten on ye Edges pretty much wth worms, & discovers in every respect y^t tis a very venerable Piece of Antiquity; & ye world need no longer doubt of ye Genuiness of ye Fragment. 'Twas then in ye Hands of D^r. Statelius (a man of Parts & Learning, but sickly, however not a Young Man as he was with some ill nature & pride styled by Monsr. Valois, being almost 3 score years of Age. — ... Out of a Pap^r D^r. Hudson lent me wch he rec^d from M^r. Ibbetson Fellow of Oriel

Col. containing Debates &c. in the House of Lords abᵗ yᵉ Churches being in Danger [Dec. 6, 1705; see Vol. VI. p. 209. (164–184.)]

Jan. 13 (Sun.). I saw today a Letter from Dʳ. Wake Bᵖ. of Lincoln to yᵉ Master of University-College concerning another Volume of the English Historians not yet published. He tells him of several Authors of Value still remaining in MSᵗ later than any yet published, particularly another Book of Hemingford, or at least wᶜʰ goes under his Name, wᶜʰ he thinks is in Magd. Coll. Library, of good Note and would deserve the Light. Walter Coventre wᶜʰ is in yᵉ Cotton Library might
10 be fit to begin such a Vol. but yᵗ he writes of the same times wᵗʰ Mat. Paris; yet for all yᵗ yᵉ Bᵖ. thinks good use might be made of him. For others he refers to Mʳ. Tanner. —

An Estimate of the yearly Income of one Prince (i. e. the Duke of Marlborough).

	Pounds per An.
Plenipotentiary to yᵉ States	7000
General for yᵉ English Forces on Mʳ. H——'s Establishmᵗ.	5000
General in Flanders on Mʳ. B——g's Establishmᵗ	5000
Master of yᵉ Ordinance	3000
Travelling charges as Master of yᵉ Ordinance	1825
Collonell of yᵉ Foot Guards, being 24 Companies	2000
Pension	5000
From yᵉ States, as General of their Forces	10000
From yᵉ Forreign Troops in English Pay, at 6ᵈ. per Pound, as per Warrant	15000
For Keeping a Table	1000
Keeper of yᵉ Great & Home Parks	1500
Mistress of yᵉ Robes	1500
Privy Purse	1500
Groom of yᵉ Stole	3000
	62325

The States General, on yᵉ Battle of Blenheim, presented a Blank Bill of 50000 libˢ. besides Presents from Germany and Flanders, from Officers and others for Employmᵗˢ, & yᵉ Profits on Exchange of Money, & by Safeguards, &c. The Estate of Woodstock is not reckon'd, because it cannot be yet known wᵗ it will cost to build & furnish a Palace there. The Emperor gave this year to yᵉ value of 50000 libˢ. besides wᵗ was presented by the King of Prussia, the Elector of Hannover, & other Courts. —
40 Mabillon in Iter Ital. Tom. 1... p. 188. tells us of some Excellᵗ Fragments of Livy preserv'd in yᵉ Library of yᵉ Cathedral Church of Sᵗ. Martin at Luca. Montfaucon does not mention them; but tells us of two MSS. at Naples wherein are preserv'd some of the Decads of Livy. But wᵗ he does not mention.

Jan. 14 (Mon.). The Romans us'd to swear by the Genius of the Emperors, & they were upbraided by some of yᵉ Fathers for observing

---

Jan. 14. H. to Dr. T. Smith. Willis's sources for Life of Wolsey; will try to get a copy of Storer's book. Original letters; Mr. Thoresby's

these Oaths more sacredly than those they made to Jupiter their chief God. — M[r]. Secretary Harley has bought the Library of S[r]. Simon Dewes, w[ch] is suppos'd to be very valuable: Humph. Wanley is now imploy'd by him to put it in order. — Nic. Bergierius in Lib. III. §. 6. de vijs Publ. & Mil. Imp. Rom. has a large Acc[t] of y[e] Author of the Itinerary, w[ch] goes under y[e] Name of Antoninus. As also in §. 7. ib. of y[e] Author of the Peutingerian Table, & of y[e] Reason of y[e] Name. — Augustus after an universal Peace was concluded, distributed the Legions into all parts of the Empire, to take care of y[e] Publick ways.

Jan. 15 (Tu.). XIV Caroli 2[di] was made an Act for Regulation of 10 the Press, wherein was a short Clause relating to the Libraries of the King, and of the two Universities to give a Copy of every printed Book. When this Act was renewed in the Beginning of the Reign of King James, our Oxford Burgesses did then forget to renew a Material Clause, which had been engrossed in the abovesaid Act, which Clause was added in XVII[o]. Caroli 2[di]. And therefore we do entreat, That with the said Act may be renewed the said Clause, together with the Amendments, Paragraph the 2[d] and 3[d] inserted in the Roman Character, and especially that instead of *Printers* may be every where read *Proprietors*, blotting out the word *Printer*, and inserting *Proprietor*, with what follows it. 20

XVII[o]. Caroli II. Cap. XV.

I. Be it enacted by the King's most Excellent Majesty, &c.

II. Be it further Enacted. That from and after such a day &c. every Proprietor of Books and Maps and Charts and Cutts and Pictures, and all Prints whatsoever within the City of London, or in any other Place, except the two Universities, shall reserve 3 Printed Copies of the best and largest Paper of every Book & Map and Chart, & Cutt and Picture and of all Prints whatsoever now printed or reprinted by him wth Additions or Alterations; and shall before any publick Vending of the said Books or Mapps or Charts, or Cutts, or Pictures, or other Prints, bring them to the Master of the Company of 30 Stationers, and deliver them to him; one Copy whereof shall by the said Master of the said Company of Stationers, within ten days after he hath receiv'd the same, be delivered to the Keeper of his Majesty's Library; and the other 2. within the said ten dayes be sent to the Vice-Chancellor of the 2 Universities respectively, for the use of the Publick-Libraries of the said Universities.

III. And it is farther Enacted, That the Proprietors of Books and Maps and Charts, and Cutts and Pictures, and all Prints whatsoever in the said Universities and every of them respectively, from and after such a day &c. shall deliver one printed Copy as aforesaid, of every Book, or Mapp, or Chart, or 40 Cut, or Picture, or of all Prints whatsoever so new Printed or Reprinted, in the said universities, or in either of them, to the Keeper of his Majesty's Library, as aforesaid; as also to the Vice-Chancellor of either of the said Universities for the time being, two such other Printed Copies for the use of the Public Libraries of the said Universities respectively. And if any Pro-

---

collection. Asks for opinion of Addison's Travels. Statement of Grabe's abstaining from the Sacrament founded on personal knowledge. Mr. Wynne made Margaret Professor, and Mr. Dobson President of Trinity. Dr. Sikes' Coins; including a Carausius, with VICTORIA CEA on the reverse; passes on Dodwell's conjecture. Thanks for information concerning the *Letter to a Bishop*, and Gronovius' Tables of the old Bacchanalian Laws. 'A certain curious gentleman talking with him about his Livy has informed him of the Coning-street, York, inscription.'

prietors aforesaid, or the Masters of the Company of Stationers shall not observe the Direction of this Act therein, That then he or they so making
Default in not delivering the said Printed Copies aforesaid, shall severally for-
feit besides the value of the said Printed Copies, the sum of 5^{li}. for every Copy
not so delivered; the same to be recovered by his Majesty, His Heirs and
Successors; and by the Chancellor, Masters, and Scholars of either of the said
universities respectively; by Action of Debt, Bill, Plaint, or Information, in
any of his Majestie's Courts of Record at Westminster, wherein no Essoyn,
Protection, or Wager of Law shall be allow'd.

10   **Jan. 16 (Wed.).**   The IXth Legion of the Romans is not mention'd
by Robortellus where resident.   See his Short Acc^t de Legionibus Rom.
— Out of Sertorius Ursatus de Notis Romanorum ...

Jan. 17 (Th.).   The Author of ye Letter in Answer to *The Memorial
of y^t State of Eng.* tho' he has been said to be a Jacobite or High-
Churchman (because of his abusing the Duke of Marlborough, M^r.
Secretary Harley, & others of the Fanatick Party in a most virulent
manner) yet is discover'd to be M^r. Stephens a Benefic'd Clergy Man
in Surrey, the same who sometime since preach'd a most notorious,
Republican Sermon on ye 30th of January, & is known to have asso-
20 ciated himself all along with the Whiggs and Presbyterians.   So that
now ye Duke of Marlborough, & his Gang, may see (if they think fit)
that the best way to live securely is to act fairly and Honestly, not to
make ye End thereof to get Wealth & Honour, when they are sure to
be tax'd for it openly & in print by Men of their own Kidney. — In
the 3^d vol. of Gronovius's Thes. Græc. the Votive Shield relating to
Scipio Africanus explain'd, & Livy may be illustrated therefrom.   See
there in Letter *n*.

Jan. 18 (Fri.).   There is a 2^d Part of the Antiquities of Middlesex
published. — Theod. Gronovius in Explicat. Marmoreae Basis Colossi
30 Tiberio Caesari erecti &c. c. 16 [on a Latin inscription in Appendix to
Marm. Oxon., p. 301].   Livy may be illustrated from this place.—This
Theodorus Gronovius Brother to Jac. Gronovius. — Nonnus who writ
the Commentary on Gregory's Invective, not the same wth Nonnus the
Poët, the Author of the Dionysiats, and the Paraphrase of S^t. John's
Gospel.   See D^r. Bentley ag^t Boyle p. 24. & remember to see that this
Distinction be made in the Catalogue of the Public Library. — The
Emperor is borrowing 200000^{li}. here wch is advancing by Subscription
& a great Duke (as a Leading Card) has subscrib'd 30000^l others
12000^l & some Citizens of London very largely so y^t ye Sum will soon
40 be compleat. — Letters from ye Hague of ye 22^d says that ye Provinces
of Guelderland Utrecht Frizeland Groningen & Overisle have approved
of ye Conduct of General Hangenburg last Campaign upon wch he has
resumed the Command as General of the Infantry under Monsr. de
Overquirke wch no doubt M^r. Stephens will look upon as a sort of a
Justification of his Pamphlett upon the Duke of Marlb. he laying a
great stress upon y^t General's Letter to ye States ab^t the Design of
Attacking the French Army at Over Isch by reason his Account is
something different from y^t sent to ye States by his Grace but this
won't save his Bacon if the Attorney General Attack him, for Scandal
50 is not to be justify'd (if it be so wch however is to be prov'd & 'twill be

expected he should have a neat Answer made to his Paper) upon his Examination he readily own'd himself to be Author of the Book he was charg'd with & said it contained nothing ag^t Law or good Manners.

Jan. 19 (Sat.). In some Editions of ye Genealogies set before ye Bibles, there are pictur'd two Owles, holding either of y^m a burning Torch, wch signifieth y^t M^r. Hugh Broughton was Author, at least had ye chief Hand and gave light to y^t Work. His Arms being a Chevron betw. three Owles. — B^p. Carleton in his Life of Bern. Gilpin (commonly call'd *the Apostle of the North*) says that this M^r. Broughton was bred up by the s^d Gilpin, & that he afterwards very ungratefully endeavour'd 10 to ruin him combining with some other of ye Clergy of the B^{pp}rick of Durham for y^t Intent, but y^t this was luckily prevented. However this seems a very unlikely Story, there being nothing of it in M^r. Broughton's Life. Besides Broughton's Parents were rich & did not want any one's Exhibition to breed their Children, as appear'd from their Breeding one of their Sons to the Law who became so eminent in it as to be made a Judge. — Cybele was the Local Goddess of the Smyrnæans & is represented wth a Tower'd Head on ye Coyns, on some of wch is at her feet a Lyon, & her left Hand upon a Cup, wch denotes Plenty of Wine in those Parts. Whence Pliny lib. xvi. § L. *M. Varro auctor est, vitem* 20 *fuisse Smyrnæ apud Matroum biferam.* Matroum is the temple (at Smyrna) of Cybele the Mother of the Gods. In the old Editions of Pliny 'tis *Smyrnæ apud mare*, wch Harduin from several good MSS^{ts} has corrected *apud Matroum*, & is confirm'd from Strabo lib. xiv. p. 646. where he tells us y^t Μητρῷον was a Temple at Smyrna dedicated to Cybele the Mother of ye Gods. — For ye same reason also upon some Coyns of ye Smyrnæans we have ϹΙΠΥΛΗΝΗ; not that this is a corrupt name of Cybele, but because she was styl'd so from Sipylus a Mountain of Lydia, as is plain from an Inscription in Spon. (Misc. Antiq. p. 350.) where are these words ΜΗΤΡΙ ΘΕΩΝ ΣΙΠΥΛΗΝΗ : which tho' some may 30 think to refer to Magnesia, wch from its being near Sipylus was called *Magnesia a Sipylo*, (to distinguish it from another Magnesia ad Meandrum, or upon the River Meander,) yet the Inscription's being found at Smyrna, & the other p^{ts} of it relating to y^t City will not admitt of it. Besides too ye Coyns wch have ϹΙΠΥΛΗΝΗ upon them have on the Front ϹΜΥΡΝΑΙΩΝ. And w^t makes more to this purpose, in the Covenant preserv'd on the Marble at Oxoñ as well the Smyrnæans as Magnesians swear per Μητέρα Σιπυλήνην, wch shews that she was call'd Sipylene in both places. — There is a Statue of the Queen going to be plac'd in a Nitch of the Tower where the Great Bell hangs at X^t 40 Church, being given by M^r. Secretary Harley. — A Gentleman today told me that at Silchester in Hampshire are frequently found great Numbers of Roman Coyns, as M^r. Camden also noted in his Time, observing that they were mostly Constantine Jun. The said Gentleman gave me one of the 2^d Magnitude in Brass, wch he says was found there. 'Tis of Nero, but the Letters on the Reverse are quite worn out, but there is a Military Figure with a Shield in the left Hand.

Jan. 20 (Sun.). There is Reprinting a Sermon of Bramhall's, and

---

Jan. 20. H. to Dr. T. Smith. Mr. Halley wishes for the address of Mr.

```
166      HEARNE'S COLLECTIONS.      [1706:
```

two of Archb͞p. Bancroft's. — M͞r. Tanner tell's the Master of University of a 2ᵈ Edition of Whitlock's Memoirs. Quære? — The Low-Church Men and Fanaticks designing in yᵉ Ward of Cripple-Gate, to put and keep out of any Place and Office all Persons well-affected to yᵉ Church, D͞r. Fowler B͞p. of Gloc. & Minister of Cripple-Gate hearing of this inveigh'd bitterly agᵗ them in a Sermon, telling them that under the Pretence of Moderation they only endeavour'd to strengthen a Party, & yᵗ he was resolv'd to do his utmost to oppose them. Upon this yᵉ next day one of yᵉ Leading Party came to him, and wonder'd yᵗ he should express himself after such a manner in his Sermon, telling him that yᵉ Archb͞p. of Cant. was of quite different Sentiments. To wᶜʰ he reply'd, That he depended upon none, & resolv'd yᵗ he would not be under any one's Girdle. — Memorandum to inquire of D͞r. Smith whether he knows how a Letter may be directed to M͞r. Baynard, a non-juror, who has a Greek MSᵗ of Pappus, wᶜʰ M͞r. Halley wants? Memorandum also to ask him whether he knows one M͞r. Jones a Non-Juror, who has (as S͞r. Andr. Fountaine informs me) a Collection of Coyns, from whom S͞r. Andr. purchas'd some. — M͞r. Sᵗ. John's sent M͞r. Barnes a Hogs-Head of Wine for his Dedication to him of Anacreon Christianus; but M͞r. Barnes's Wife dash'd it with Water & so made two HogsHeads of it. — D͞r. Hudson Elected Fellow of University Coll. March 29. 1686. See yᵉ Register of yᵗ Coll.

Jan. 21 (Mon.). M͞r. Secretary Harley having acquainted her Majesty of David Edward's the Printer of the Memorial of yᵉ Ch. of England's surrendring himself, & yᵗ in yᵉ Depositions taken several Members of the lower House of Parliamᵗ appear'd concern'd, She was pleas'd to answer yᵗ being tender of yᵉ Privileges of yᵗ House she would do nothing before she had made it known to them; upon wᶜʰ the House order'd an Address of thanks & desir'd she would give farther Orders in relation to this Matter.

[Descriptions of some (7) small Brass Coyns wᶜʰ D͞r. Hudson recᵈ of M͞r. Halley. (215–216.)] ...

Memorandum. M͞r. Halley has given the said Coyns to yᵉ Publick Library. — M͞r. Stevens has given a 1000 libˢ. Bayle. Notwᵗʰstanding the Scandal of his Pamphlett, yet yᵉ Grand Juries of London and Westm. did not present it last Sessions, tho' put in mind of it. 'Tis reprinted with an Answer Paragraph by Paragraph by De Foe, Author of the Memorial of yᵉ State of England. — ... Remember in yᵉ Notes upon Livy, ad Lib. 1. 18. to make some observations abᵗ yᵉ Age of Pythagoras, & refer to D͞r. Bentley's Answer to Boyle, p. 49. M͞r. Dodwell de ætate Phali & Pythag. & his Diss. de Cyclis.

Jan. 22 (Tu.). In the Year 1607. was printed at Naples *Speculum Concionatorum*, 8º. & said in yᵉ Title-Page to have been written by Gerardus Leodiensis, wᶜʰ is false it appearing from John Leland & yᵉ

Baynard, a non-juror. Does he know one Mr. Jones and his coins? Sends copies of the York inscriptions, showing that the 9th Legion was stationed there. Harley has bought Sir S. Dewes' Library, and employs Wanley to set it in order. Has received a coin of Nero found at Silchester.

MS^{ts} y^t Robert Grosthead, B^p. of Lincoln, was the true Author. — . . .
All Coyns wch have on ye Reverse ΣΜΥΡΝΑΙΩΝ wth a Lyon, & on the
Front A Woman's Head with a Tower'd Crown, do not relate to Cybele
the Local Goddess of Smyrna; for those wch have a Woman's Head,
with a tower'd Crown & an Ax r[e]late to Smyrna an Amazon who first
built this City & from whom twas denominated. See Seguin (*Numismata*) p. 25. — Quære whether ye B^p. of Norwich has ye first part of
ye 33^d Book of Livy found at Bamberg by Horrion & first published
at Venice 8°. 1616. by Franc. Bartholinus Urbinas with Quærengus's
Notes, & afterwards more correctly at Paderborne by Horrion himself, 10
an. 1617. 12°. — There is newly printed ye Characters of Robt. Earl
of Essex & George Duke of Buckingham, wth a Parallell betw. them,
s^d to be written by the Earle of Clarendon, wch is exactly the same wth
one of the Pieces of S^r. Hen. Wotton printed in his Remains p. 37. &
call'd the Difference & Disparity betw. ye Estates & Conditions of Geo.
D. of Buck. & Robt. E. of Essex. I have been told y^t notwthstanding
this, in the latter Editions of ye Remains 'tis really ascrib'd to ye Earl
of Clarendon & said to be written by him in his Younger Days. But
Quære? — . . . We hear from Lisbon y^t on ye 31st of Dec. last n. Style
Catherine Q. Dowager of England died. She was born Nov. 14. 1638. 20
& married to King Charles 2^d. in 1662. — Her Majesty's Answer to
ye lower H. of Commons in relacion to ye Memorial is that she is glad
to find y^t House express so much Resentm^t ag^t ye Libel mention'd
in her Message & takes very kindly the Confidence y^t House reposes
in Her, wch she will make ye best use of for ye Advantage of y^e
Publick. . . .

   Jan. 23 (Wed.). . . Julius Pollux is almost printed anew at Amsterdam.
'Twill be a very curious Edition, as M^r. Sentiman (who was of Linc.
Coll.) tells D^r. Hudson in a Letter. — To day D^r. Mill, D^r. Dunster,
D^r. Royse, D^r. Irish, D^r. Colenet & M^r. Worth went to Woodstock to 30
wait upon the Duke of Marlborough, who is there to visit his princely
Palace, & for whom it seems these Gentlemen have a very great Respect,
tho' some think that their Design in it is *in ordine ad &c.* — . . . John
Keile dropt at ye Dean of X^t Church's Table by chance, y^t my L^d
Pembroke was inform'd that M^r. Halley did not translate Apollonius
out of Arabick himself, but got one Jones to do it, wch M^r. Halley
cannot but resent as a great Indignity. — M^r. Halley has a Letter
printed in Hevelius's Annus Climactericus, & M^r. Hevelius in divers
places of y^t Work gives a great Character of him. — . . . In the Roman
Missal, pr. at *Antw.* 1619 fol. in the Publick Library A. 2. 12. *Th.* B^p. 40
Barlow has several very good Observations about the *Canon of ye Mass.*
— In the Letters wch came last night 'twas hinted that 'twas resolv'd
by the House of Commons that it shall be a Premunire for any one to
deny that ye Q. & Parliament has Power of altering & settling the
Succession as they please. But we shall know the truth of this when
the Succession Bill is past into an Act. — E Georgij Syncelli Chrono-
graphia p. 318. Edit. *Par.* 1615. sub An. Mundi 5513, X^{ti}. 13. . . . —
The Earl of Orkney has they say purchas'd ye late Duke of Buckingham's
House near Taplow in Buckinghamshire. — I am well inform'd y^t a
piece of Roman Copper Money, ab^t ye Bigness of Half a Crown, was 50

lately found in Waycock in yᵉ Parish of Lawrence Waltham in Berks. Try to get this. It may give some light into yᵉ Antiquities of the place. — Consider Mʳ. Dodwell's Account of *Clisthenes*, whom he compares to *Brutus*. See Dʳ. *Bentley's* Answer to Mʳ. *Boyle*, p. 88. — Quære whether Phintia & Hybla in Livy? Consider also abᵗ Phintias Tyrant of Agrigentum. See there p. 98.

Jan. 25 (Fri.). In the Publick Library among Mʳ. Selden's Books in B. 1. 5. Th. Seld. is an imperfect Copy of the first English Translation of the Bible, wᶜʰ is valuable not only for it's Antiquity but for divers Divine Notes in the Margin written by the most virtuous Xtian Lady Dame Ann Greie Wife to Sʳ. Hen. Grei Knt. & Grandmother to the Rᵗ. Honbˡᵉ. Henrie Earl of Kent, who caus'd the Book for yᵗ reason to be new Bound in Novemb. 1598. — Alegambe in his *Bibliotheca Scriptorum Societatis Jesu* does not mention *Leycester's Commonwealth* among Father *Parson's* Writings, wᶜʰ I see no reason he should not, if *Parsons* had really been yᵉ Author of it. — . . . 'Tis said some Great Men have given Bayle upon Mʳ. *Stevens* the Printer's appearing Evidence against them, in relation to the *Memorial of yᶜ C. of Eng.* — *Joan. Croij* Observatt. in Novum Test. . . See there abᵗ Livy's Patavinity in c. 34. — . . . In the Roman Edition of yᵉ Septuagint, among Mʳ. Selden's Books in Bib. Bodl., are several MSᵗ Notes, wᶜʰ will be of good use to Mʳ. Grabe or any one else who ingages in a new Ed. — . . . This ¹day (being Sᵗ. Paul's Convers.) the Ceremony of founding the new Building in Peckwater Quadrangle at Xᵗ Church was perform'd, when the Earl of Salisbury, & other Noble-men of Xᵗ Church were pleas'd each of them to lay a stone, on some of wᶜʰ were Inscriptions & particularly on that wᶜʰ was laid by my Lord Salisbury a Copy whereof follows.

Jacobus | Comes Sarisburiensis | hunc lapidem locavit | gratitudinis suæ & gaudij testem | quod ipse dum hæc surgerent mœnia | sub auspicijs decani | eorundem Architecti, | optime de se meriti, | feliciter adolesceret. | Præceptoribus usus Antonio Alsop & Johanne Savage A.MM. | Quorum dulcem memoriam tam conservari | voluit quam suam.

Jan. 24. Dr. T. Smith to H. Severe remarks on Grabe. 'I have read over Mr. Addisons travells and like them wel enough. The Criticks here have passed a very severe, and oftentimes too, a very unjust censure upon the impropriety of his style, and the meannes of his observations: wᶜʰ are agreeable to the poetical genius of the Author, who has blemished his booke by his large and numerous citations of the old Roman Poets, tho' the descriptions of the same places given by Livy and other Historians cited by him had been a more pertinent and advantageous fault. But this spoyles the series of his narrations, and notwithstanding the elegance of the language, wit, and phansy, with their equally elegant translation into English verse, instead of delighting, does nauseate and disgust the Reader.' Advises H. to find whence the Table of the Bacchanalian Laws was derived. Notes on Pappus; Books I and II, which are wanting in Greek, are extant somewhere in Arabic. Mr. Jones is utterly ignorant of medals; they are merely put in his hands to dispose of. Is there any mention in Gaddius *De Scriptoribus Florentinis* of Franciscus Puccius, admitted into Dee's diabolical society during his stay at Prague? if so, please send list of his books. Asks for a copy of Junius' eulogium on Usher in his edition of Cædmon's *Paraphrasis Poeticæ Geneseos* (Amsterdam, 1655).

---

¹ I am misinformed, yᵉ Ceremony being the day after.

And as this signal Act of Piety was done on this Festival, so (to shew the great Respect this Noble Society of X^t Church has to her Majesty,) the day before they fixed her Statue in a Nitch of the Great Tower where the large Bell Hangs, being done (as I have intimated above) at ye Cost & Charges of M^r. Harley.

Jan. 26 (Sat.).   *Labyrinthus Cantuariensis*, or Doctor *Lawd's* Labyrinth. By *T. C. Par.* 1658. B^p. *Barlow* was told his Name was *Spencer. Quære?* — S^r. *Jeff. Jeffreys*, being wth M^r. Secretary *Harley*, told him, that he thought he could tell from what corner the *Memorial* came. M^r. Secretary hearing this, desir'd he would inform him: to 10 whom he reply'd that he did not doubt but it came from ye Whiggish Party & Low Church Men, & was writ by them on purpose to throw the *odium* on ye Honest part of ye Nation. — ... The Terme beginning on Tuesday several Persons bound over for Writing & Printing appeared upon y^eir Recognizances and among^t ye rest M^r. Stephens ye Parson of Sutton for writing the Scandalous Lybell upon his Grace ye Duke of Marlborough & M^r. Secretary Harley. He appeared not in His Canonical Habit but in a grey Riding Coat wth a Whip in His Hand & look'd very bluff; but ye Attorney General has orders to prosecute him. One Straghan a Bookseller is taken into Custody of a Messenger upon the Information 20 of Edwards ye Printer not y^t he accused him of being concerned in ye Memorial of the Ch. of Engl. but y^t ab^t 3 years agoe he printed a Book for him intitled De Aris & Focis the Copy of wch was in ye same Hand as y^t of ye Mem. & therefore there is strong Presumption y^t he must know ye Author of it. but he's not so ingenuous as to confess. — ... D^r. *Mill* and ye other 5 who went with him to *Woodstock* to wait on ye Duke of *Marlborough* & his Dutchess (who it seems was there too) were so poorly rec^d y^t they had certainly din'd wth Duke *Humphrey* had not they put in at a House, where a dinner was provided at their own Expence. It seems the Dutchess expected the University should have complemented 30 the Duke, & therefore when these Gentlemen came to the House, the servant who was there to wait, ask'd whether they were sent by the University; & understanding they were not, the Reception was order'd accordingly. — ... Hospinian de Diebus Festis ... [p. 79 on *Mater Deum Cybele*].

VOL. VIII.

Jan. 27. 1706 (Sun.).   The Master of University Coll. communicated to me this Morning two other Inscriptions put upon two Stones laid yesterday at X^t Church, wch here follow :

Ad honorem Dei optimi Maximi | Quo nitidius & laxius habitarent Ædis 40 Christi Alumni. | Antonius Radcliffe S.T.P. | Istius Ecclesiæ Canonicus, | Hoc atrium Peckwatriense instaurari voluit | Et legato bis mille librarum | Benefactoribus cæteris præivit. | Ejus ex Testamento Hæredes | Henricus Aldrich S.T.P. | Istius Ecclesiæ Decanus. | Johannes Hammond S.T.P. | Ejusdem Ecclesiæ Canonicus | Imum hunc lapidem angularem | Locavere | Die 26° Januarij Anno Domini 170⅝ | Regnante Anna.

Cum hoc atrium Peckwatriense instaurarent | Henricus Aldrich istius Ecclesiæ Decanus S.T.P. | Johannes Hammond ejusdem Canonicus S.T.P. | Antonij Radcliffe Hæredes, conjunctissimos in | Capitulo fratres habuere |

Thom. Burton subdecanum | Rob. South, Ben. Woodroffe, Guil. Jane | Francisc. Gastrel, Rog. Altham Guil. Stradford | thesaurarium | Communi cum Hæredibus amore | Hanc ædem prosecutos. | Nec minore affectu | Perennem hisce mœnibus felicitatem auguratos.

— They cannot find out ye Author of ye Memorial. All y^t affects S^r. *Humph. Mackworth*, M^r. *Poley*, & M^r. *Ward* is y^t 150 of 'em as soon as printed off were sent to ye first as many to ye 2^d & 100 to ye last. —

Out of a Letter of M^r. *Rowney* to D^r. *Charlett.*

10 As to your Friend *Stephens* he stands to his Book & gives defiance and believes neither ye Duke of *Marlb.* or *Robin (Harley)* will prosecute him. He says the Secretarys are in the Dark ab^t the Author of the *Memorial of the Ch. of Engl.* & do not know who to fix it on. —

Out of a Letter from the Vice Chanc. to ye Master of Univ. Col.

The Queen is laid up wth ye Gout: she has order'd *Stephens* to be prosecuted, who had ye Impudence when he was taken to say, that he believ'd *Robin Harley* would not prosecute him; if he did, that he knew how to pull an old House upon his Head; & y^t he thought the Duke of *Marlborough* would not neither, but if he did, y^t he knew w^t to say to him too. —

20 D^r. *Mill*, who was one of those that went to wait upon ye Duke of *Marlborough* at *Woodstock* to complement him for a poor piece of Venison wch the Dutchess, without the Duke's Privity, sent to ye Whiggish Heads of Houses, slyly left his Company & went to his Parsonage at *Bletchingdon*, & the next Morning borrowing a Couple of Horses went early to attend his Grace's Levee, & let him know who he was (for it seems his Grace knew not one of those Persons who were the day before to wait upon him) viz. *a Tutor some years ago to his Youngest Brother, who was Commoner of Queen's Col.* & took ye Degrees of Bach. & Master of Arts & entred into H. Orders on purpose to have 30 some great Preferment wch was design'd for him; but he dy'd of a Consumption before it fell. It must be further noted y^t ye Duke, understanding that these Persons were not sent by the university (but came of their own Accord) receiv'd them after a slight manner, as is before noted, and styl'd them *a Body of Divinity*, & to inliven their stupid Whiggish Clay sent them half a Dozen Bottles of Wine to a Little Inne at *Woodstock*, where they were content to be slenderly accommodated: and to make amends for this poor Entertainment D^r. *Royse* (who was one of them) invited those that return'd wth him to refresh themselves at his Lodgings as soon as they got home. — I rec^d the 40 following Acc^t conc. M^r. *Grabe* from his Intimate Friend D^r. *Hudson*, viz. He was put into orders by the B^p. of *Worcester*, at his Palace (as D^r. *H.* believes) at *Worcester* or *Hartlebury*; but whether the B^p. gave him the Sacram^t at his Ordination or not he does not remember. But the D^r. one day asking him ye Reason why he did not receive the Sacram^t at X^t Church, he gave him these reasons. (1) He acknowledg'd that he did not think it unlawfull to receive the Sacrament as we do according to ye Form in y^e *English* Liturgy. (2) He always receiv'd the Sacrament from a *Scotch* Episcopal Nonjuring Minister, who administer'd it to him and some others in the Form of y^e *Scotch* Liturgy, 50 drawn up by Archb^p. *Laud*, thinking it much better upon this Acc^t,

that it was more agreeable to King *Edward* the VI^{th's} Liturgy, wch he judg'd was alter'd for ye worse in Q. *Elizabeth's* time, upon the Suggestion of some *Calvinistical* Forreign Divines. This Alteration made in ye Liturgy was the Taking away the Oblation or Sacrifice of Bread & Wine before Consecration, & turning it into a Sacrifice of Praise and Thanksgiving after Consecration. Which opinion of his he defends & justifys by the Authority and reasons of M^r. *Mead* in some places of his Works. The said D^r. likewise told me, that he fully believ'd he was intirely an Enemy to the Gross Errors of Popery, & believes him to be a man of that Honesty & Integrity that he did not scruple to lend him 10 a 100^l. upon his Bear note to support him under the Expenses he is in preparing the Septuagint for the Press. — He likewise told me that M^r. *Grabe* went 4 or 5 times a year to *London* purposely to receive ye Sacrament, wch he says he did, not because he thought our Liturgy unlawfull, but because he thought it better to receive according to ye Form of Archb^p. *Laud,* as long as he had an opportunity of it's being administer'd to him, in y^t Form. — It must be remembred that D^r. *Hudson* who (to his immortal Honour) had contributed both Money & Books to ye New Library at *Hart-Hall* did likewise, ab^t two Months before the Pulling down of *Peckwater* at *X^t Church*, voluntarily & ye 20 first Man of all, after D^r. *Radcliffe,* (who left by his last Will above 2000 lib^s. for the Rebuilding that Court,) subscribe 20 Guineas to carry on the Work when it should begin. He formerly gave 10 *lib^s*. to the finishing of the Chapell of University College, & 5 lib^s. to the New Wainscotting of ye Common Room, & (as I am very well inform'd) has 50 lib^s. ready to give to y^t College whereof he is Fellow in order to purchase a Living. — M^r. *Charles Harris* an Attorney has given 20 *lib^s*, & M^r. *Dingley* Fellow of *Corpus*, & M^r. *Thwaites* of *Queen's* have subscrib'd each of them 10 Guineas for ye abovesaid Design of Rebuilding *Peckwater*. — This morning D^r. *Aldrich* the most Worthy 30 Dean of X^t Church, & Noble Patron of Learning, preach'd in the Cathedral at X^t Church before the University, taking his Text from Matt. 3. vers. 2. *Repent &c.* From wch he explain'd very clearly the Nature of Repentance, in opposition to some Heretical Notions of the Novatians & others, particularly ab^t the Sin against the Holy Ghost, &c. — To be got into ye Publick Library, Hierome Vignier. La veritable origin[e] de la Maison d'Austriche, de Lorrain, de Bade, & de Quantité des Autres. à Paris. — D^r. Eaton writ a Discourse of ab^t a sheet on Peonick verse, wch was his first publish'd Work, tho' never printed. (forsan non meruit). He also gather'd various Lections to ye Cambridge 40 Horace put out by Talbot in 4°. His 2^d. Work. He likewise collated Catullus Tibullus & Propertius for ye use of the Cambridge Editor. Occidit pendente opere. — M^r. Thwaites (as himself tells me) has ye s^d Discourse of Peonick verse, & designs to publish it.

Jan. 28 (Mon.). To shew the Ignorance and Negligence of ye Corrector of ye Catalogue of MSS^{ts} there is a good Instance in the MSS^{ts} of Queen's College, where num. the 16. the Beginning of *Huguicio Pisanus's Dictionarium Etymologicum* is thus printed, *Augeo, ges, xi. clum, clu,* wch should be Augeo; ges, xi, ctum, ctu. — ... D^r. *Hudson* Being last night with ye Provost of *Oriel* Col. & talking by chance of ye 50

Illness of yᵉ Bᵖ. of *Gloucester*, the Provost told him yᵗ he fancied Dʳ. *Mill* was yᵉ likeliest of any *Oxford* Man to succeed him.   For wᶜʰ he gave this Reason, viz. that the Court having resolved to prefer no High-Church-Men, especially of this university, he could not think of any Man so likely to have it as Dʳ. *Mill*; for as to his Part he was resolv'd not to take it if offer'd him, and he thought the Warden of *Wadham* could not take it because he was a poor beggarly Fellow & not able to pay yᵉ First Fruits : so yᵗ there remain'd none but Dʳ. *Mill* who is known to be rich, and of thorough pac'd Moderate Principles. — The same Dʳ. *Hudson*
10 was told this Morning by Dʳ. *Edzard*, Minister of yᵉ *German Lutheran* Church in *London*, that yᵉ Prince of *Denmark* had turn'd off his Chaplain (Dʳ. M . . . . . .) the reason whereof was as followeth.   When yᵉ Prince of *Denm.* was made Lᵈ. High Admiral of *England* he was oblig'd to take yᵉ Sacrament after yᵉ Manner prescrib'd by yᵉ Ch. of *England*, after which he offer'd to communicate with yᵉ *Lutherans*, wᶜʰ his Chaplain honestly told him was an unjustifyable Practise, & that he was oblig'd to stick to yᵉ communion of yᵉ church of *England*, or yᵗ of the *Lutherans* ; and yᵗ 'till he renounc'd all Communion with the Church of *England* he could not administer the Sacrament to him in their Church ; for yᵗ he
20 look'd upon such occasional Conformity to be a matter of great scandal, & never heard of in any Christian Church till within these few Years here in England.

Jan. 29 (Tu.). . . . There is just publish'd *Athenagoras*'s two Discourses, viz. *Apologia pro Xtianis* & *de Resurrectione mortuorum*, Gr. Lat. printed at the Theatre, in 8º.   To wᶜʰ are added Notes & various Readings, by *Edm. Dechair* A.M. of *Linc.* Coll.   What disgusts most buyers is that the Editor has swell'd the Book with all the Notes yᵗ have been written professedly upon it, a thing wᶜʰ some judicious Men advis'd against when first propos'd to be printed.   But Dʳ. *Mill* being the chief Manager of yᵉ
30 Edition, he would have it done in the same manner as yᵉ Edition of *Tatian* ; tho' 'twould have been more acceptable & usefull if *Tatian*, *Athenagoras* and *Theophilus Antioch.* had been printed all together in 8º, wᶜʰ if well done would have made no bigger a Volume than one of these now make.   The Editor has spoken well of Mʳ. *Worth* in the Preface (as likewise of Dʳ. *Mill*) who communicated the Lections of the *Paris* & *Eton* MSᵗˢ to him.   These of the *Eton* MSᵗ are yᵉ very same Lections wᶜʰ were made abᵗ 6 years since, when I purposely went over to yᵗ Place to meet Mʳ. *Worth* to assist him in the Collating the MSᵗ.   How correct yᵉ Edition is I can say no more, than yᵗ the Editor took so little
40 care about it, that tho' the Notes of the Persons who had writ professedly upon *Athenagoras* were very faulty, & in divers places nonsense, particularly the Quotations made from Antient Authors, occasion'd by the Carelessness of yᵉ former Printers & the Absence of the Authors themselves, yet he transcrib'd them exactly as he found them, not taking pains to compare them with the Original Authors.   This I know, because divers sheets were brought to me in the Publick Library, where I look'd some places over, & corrected a great many considerable & material Faults & do veryly believe that there are some Thousands in yᵉ Book, & yᵗ 'tis the most faulty Edition yᵗ ever came yet from yᵉ Theatre Press.

As to the Notes that are new added, they are in a great Measure owing to M^r. *Potter*, Tutor to ye Editor; not but that M^r. *Dechair* is able to have put out a correct Edition, if he had taken Pains; but this he has not done, & by that means has impos'd upon the World. For I am sure y^t if he had consulted good Books he would have light upon considerable Observations, not taken notice of by any Profess'd Annotator as yet, wch would have adorn'd the Work, & have gain'd him Credit. — M^r. *Wase* began a Translation into *English* of *Vitruvius*'s Architecture, whereof there are two Sheets printed off as a Specimen containing ye Preface to *Augustus* & ye 1st Chapter of ye first Book, wth some small 10 marginal Notes. Folio.

Jan. 30 (Wed.).   The Great Health now is the Cube of three, wch is the number 27, i. e. the Number of the Protesting Lords. — This Day, being the Martyrdom of King *Charles* I^st, there preach'd at S^t. *Marie*'s before ye University M^r. *Wiles* of S^t. *John*'s College, taking his Text from *Revel.* II. 10. *Be thou faithfull unto Death, and I will give thee a Crown of Life.*

Which Words tho' directed particularly to ye Church of *Smyrna*, wch with the other *Asiatick* Churches was violently oppos'd by Avouch'd Enemies to Christianity, yet may be applied to all other Christian Churches, & contain in them an 20 Exhortation and a Motive. The exhortation is to stand firm to the Faith in opposition to all our Enemies, and constant Adhæsion to it even to Death, wch we of this Nation ought to do above all other People, ye Church of *England* being the best Church in ye World, whether consider'd in it's intrinsick worth, or in the Influence it has upon ye State, For as to ye former, 'tis certain y^t it's Liturgy & all the Doctrines injoyn'd by it are the nearest of any other to those of the Primitive Church, the Church of *Rome* transgressing in divers gross Ceremonies & Innovations, & the other Reformed Churches on the other Hand erring in throwing off such Ceremonies as are decent, & were in use in the most early times, & some of them in not admitting of Episcopacy, 30 wch yet is well known to be an Apostolical Establishment. And as it excells if consider'd in it's intrinsick Worth, so also does it upon account of ye Influence it has upon the State, nothing being more plain than y^t if the Church be destroy'd the State must sinck wth it, wch made King *James* I^st say, *no Episcopacy no King*; & for the same Reason the Presbyterians & the other Fanaticks cut off Archb^p. *Laud*'s Head before they could have their Power over the Good King who suffer'd upon this Day, well knowing that so long as he liv'd, who was such a support to and Defence of the Church, they could not Effect their Designs upon that Good Prince, & y^t ye surest way of Destroying the State was first to ruine the Church. M^r. Wiles having ingeniously & judi- 40 ciously made out ye Intire Dependence of ye State upon ye Church, & how both are inseperably united together, address'd himself particularly to ye Members of it, exhorting them to be constant & resolute in defending it, & even suffering for it, imitating their Martyr'd Sovereign, who did not only stand up for it by Pen & Sword, but even when thro' the obstinacy of his Enthusiastical Enemies he was not able to conquer them, patiently submitted to the Block. for wch there is no doubt he is rewarded with a Crown of Life, that being the Motive for all such to act as he did, & wch M^r. *Wiles* insisted on in ye next place, wch he shew'd they could not expect who were Friends to ye Church no longer than they saw suited with their present Interest, & would 50 for Preferment desert it, & close with them who were it's profess'd Enemies, a thing too notorious at this time.

M^r. *Thwaits* tells me ye Dean of X^t Church formerly drew up an Epitome of Heraldry for ye use of some Young Gentlemen under his

Care, but y^t he has no Copy now, all of them being got from him, & he does not know where to have one.   He says 'twas done very well, & ye best in its nature ever made. — *Justin* illustrated in *Gevartius's* notes upon *Statius* pag. 48.   D^r. Hudson has ye Book.   *Pliny's* Paneg. explicat. ib. p. 206 . . . Look over *Rupertus* upon *Florus* in ye P. Library, & *Kuhnius* upon *Aelian.* . . . Quaere about Tauromenium?   See D^r. *Bentley* ag^t *Boyle* p. 181.

Jan. 31 (Th.).   Out of ye Letters dat. Jan. 29 wch came last Night I hear S^r. Geo. Rook is lately married to a Daughter of S^r. Tho. Knatc[h]-
10 bull of Kent. — Last week S^r. Francis Russel of Strensham in Worcestershire departed y^s Life in this City & this Morning was carried into ye Country to be interr'd as was M^r. Hill one of ye Commissioners of the Navy who dyed some days past.   On Thursday last ye E. of Dorset & Middlesex dyed at ye Bath.   'Tis s^d he has left 1500^li per An. to his Lady besides his personal Estate.   On ye other Hand several great Marriages will be in a few days consummated as y^t of his Grace ye D. of Beaufort wth Madam Noell, ye L^d. Bruce wth Madam Sevill & ye L^d. Scudamore wth Mad^m Digby all Ladys of Great Fortunes. — This day one Sheers Servt of S^r. H. Mackworth taken into Custody of a
20 Messenger ab^t ye Affair of ye Memorial bro^t his Habeas Corpus & was admitted to Bail.   M^r. Straughan taken into Custody upon the same Acc^t has bro^t also his Habeas Corpus. — Just now meeting with an Honest ingenious Country Gentleman at ye Coffee-House, (with two others in Company,) he told me y^t he was well acquainted with M^r. Sheers, above mention'd, and assur'd me y^t the whole design of taking him & ye rest into Custody was only to pump and Fish some things out of them, with a design, if possible to fix the Memorial on S^r. *Humph.* & some other Honest Gentlemen. — Consider w^t D^r. *Bentley* says ab^t *Susarion* from the *Chronicon Marmoreum,* p. 205. of his Answer to
30 *Boyle.* & compare the passage wth the Marble itself.   He quotes D^r. *Mill* ab^t reading ye Marble, & says that he assur'd him, 'twas exactly as he conjectur'd it should be.   But D^r. *Bentley* should first have rec^d the Drs Reading from ye Stone before he had offer'd his conjecture.   But if he had not, there is enough to object ag^t D^r. *Mill's* reading of Marbles, for a Correction of his in one of these Volumes. — Consider also another part of y^t Marble insisted on by D^r. *Bentley ibid.* p. 231. ab^t *Thespis's* being the first Tragœdian.

Feb. 1 (Fri.).   *Quære* in y^e *Museum Ashm.* for *Noctua Athenis ; sive Ingressûs Comitis Pembrochiensis in Oxoniam xi Apr.* 1648. *vera nar-*
40 *ratio.* in one Sheet 4to.   Beginning: *Cavete vos Togati ; periistis, ilicet, Venit Pembrochiensis Comes, scilicet.* as also for *Tragicomœdia Oxoniensis.* Beginning, *Devictas aquilas, geminamque in clade ruinam, Subversamque Aciem, querulæ suspiria Musæ,* Writ by *Adam Littleton* of Christ Church. One sheet 4°. — A Passage relating to Comedy out of *Marm. Oxon.* as published by M^r. *Selden.* pag. 3. . . . — Passage out of ye same Marble ab^t Tragedy. as publish'd by Selden pag. 4. [31-33.] . . . — I saw to day

---

Feb. 1.   Hudson to H.   Have we *Col. Trajana* ; if so, has it any explication of the figures?   Have we a folio in Old English writ by John Bochas or Boccace?

at Christ-Church Library a most curious Book in 8º. written by Mʳˢ. *Hesther English*, & containing the *Psalms of David*. Before wᶜʰ is her Picture. There are exactly the same Hands in it with that of the Proverbs *of Solomon*, written by the same Lady, wᶜʰ is in the Publick Library, wᶜʰ has also her Picture before it. But wᵗ is further remarkable in this at Xᵗ Church is that 'twas Queen *Elizabeth*'s own Book (presented to her perhaps by the Ingenious Lady her self) who from a note (wᶜʰ for wᵗ reason I know not is scratch'd out) at yᵉ Beginning seems to have given the Book to the Library herself. Wᶜʰ is not at all improbable, being it may be mov'd to it upon Accᵗ of her Father who finish'd the Foundation here begun by Cardinal *Wolsey*. At the same time I saw a thin Folio MSᵗ Book, wᶜʰ was cardinal *Wolsey*'s & is most curiously illuminated. But time being short I could not have yᵉ Perusal of it. Likewise were shew'd to me some other Curiosities, as divers Coyns *Greek*, *Roman* and *English*, & amongst Natural Rarities a strange stone taken from a Man by Dʳ. *Willis*. — Dʳ. *Charlett* has a Cabinett (wᶜʰ stands in a Room on the East side of his Study, & upon it the Head of the famous *Ant. à Wood* in Plaister *de Paris*) wherein is a Collection of Antient *Roman* Coyns, put in order (as the Dʳ. says) by Mʳ. *Elstob* and Mʳ. *Wanley*. But the Dʳ. (who is otherwise forward enough to shew things) being not willing to give any one a sight of them (tho' he has often been desir'd by some curious Gentlemen, particularly by the Excellᵗ Sʳ. *Andrew Fountaine*) it makes some Persons suspect that *Wanley* (when he belong'd to it) stole them from the Collection in the Publick Library, where he did wᵗ he pleas'd, Dʳ. *Hyde* being infirm and not able to look after yᵗ place so well as he should. — Dʳ. *Kennett*'s Sermon before yᵉ House of Commons (as 'tis said) was suitable to yᵉ Occasion on yᵉ 30ᵗʰ of Jan. & was much different from wᵗ he preach'd formerly upon yᵉ same Occasion. — Dʳ. *Atterbury* preach'd before yᵉ Lᵈ. Mayor &c. a High-Church Sermon wᶜʰ was much commended.

Feb. 2 (Sat.). This day being the Purification preach'd before yᵉ University at Sᵗ. *Marie*'s Mʳ. *Woodford* of *New-College*, upon Mat. v. 5. . . .

Having stated the Nature of Meekness in opposition to Anger, he proceeded to shew that the Meek man possesses all temporal Advantages: as 1. He is well belov'd. 2. He will take advice, finds Friends to give it him, & has a quick Apprehension to know when good Advice is given him. 3. He is steddy and fix'd in all his Actions, and 4ᵗʰˡʸ. is never troubled with Anger & those other Passions wᶜʰ are the Effects of it. After he had made out each of these, he answer'd an Objection taken from Experience, namely that yᵉ Meek man oftentimes does not inherit the good things of this Life. As first the Text is not to be taken in so large a sense as to extend to every particular Man. 'Tis sufficient if Meek men generally enjoy these Blessings. 2. The meek man is rich if he be contented with wᵗ he has. 3. Some men appear to be meek who really are not so. 4. Perhaps a man may be meek and yet want some other necessary Qualifications wᶜʰ should entail yᵉ Blessings on him. Wᶜʰ done he concluded wᵗʰ a motive to yᵉ Duty.

— On the East End of the Library at Xᵗ Church is the Picture of King *Henry* VIIIᵗʰ. It seems the Library being decay'd & come to ruine was restor'd by Otho Nicholson Esqʳ., to whose memory on the South side of it near to yᵉ sᵈ Effigies of King *Henry* VIIIᵗʰ is an Honorary Monumᵗ with the following Inscription :

Hospes quisquis es, | circumfer oculos : | Perantiqui & prænobilis hujus Domicilij | Corpus intermortuum, foris | intus refinxit, | Unis impensis suis, & nova donavit anima | Totius, quam vides, exquisitæ pulchritudinis, Otho Nicholsonus, Armiger, Armarijque | Istius Literarij Memorabilis Instaurator. | ᴀᴅᴇo ʟɪʙʀᴏʀᴠᴍ ᴏᴘᴠʟᴇɴᴛɪᴀ.

Above wᶜʰ are His Arms.

Mʳ. *Woodford*'s (above mention'd) Eldest Brother has a Translation of
10 the *Psalms* in MSᵗ by that celebrated Poet Sʳ. *John Denham,* wᵗʰ Excellᵗ Remarks upon them by yᵉ same Hand.

Feb. 3 (Sun.). The Non-Conformists took up yᵉ word *Hold-Forth,* in yᵉ year 1642, wᶜʰ was never known before. See Dʳ. *Wallis's Xtian Sabbath,* Part II. p. 27.

Verses made by Dʳ. *Garth* when the K. of *Spain Charles* IIIᵈ was wᵗʰ the Queen at *Windsor.*

Pallas destructive to the Trojan Line,   Preserved a Hero & restor'd yᵉ Race.
Raced their Proud Walls tho' built by   So the Famed Empire where yᵒ Ebre
      Hands divine.   flows
20 But Love's Bright Goddess with pro-   Fell by Eliza & by Anna rose.
      pitious Grace,

Puffendorf in Hist. of the Affairs of Brandenburg lib. 15. § 32.

Erat iste (meaning Sʳ. *Joseph Williamson*) Williamsonus malitiosi ingenij vir, valde insuper dissolutus & negligens ; vespertinum tempus inter lætos sodales consumere, & mane in horam nonam stertere solitus, qui mores ipsius cum munere minime quadrabant.

Upon yᵉ D. of *Marlborough.*

When a Church on a Hill to yᵉ Danube   And 5 on all 4 run to Paris again.
      advances,   The wife of St. Albans a Princess shall
30 Then near to his Fall the Great Cock of   be,
      France is.   By right of her Spouse from yᵉ Father
Then 3 shall beat 5, be inaugur'd in Spain,   of 3.

Anno 1704. The sᵈ Prophecy was found long since under Ground by one yᵗ was lately in Packington's Pound. — When Mʳ. Thwaits was at yᵉ Bath he brought away the following Inscriptions. In horto prope Port. Occid. 2 Inscriptiones 2. urnae erutae prope Walcot ... — Dʳ. Venner a Bath Physitian died in 1660. He wrote a Book intit. Via recta ad vitam longam in wᶜʰ is this Memorable Observacoñ. That a Gamon of Bacon is of yᵉ same Nature with yᵉ rest of yᵉ Hog.—These
40 things I transcrib'd from Mʳ. *Thwaits*'s Notes. —

One Mʳ. *Brown* is committed to *Newgate* for Handing to yᵉ Press Half a Sheet on one side call'd *The Country Parson's Advice to yᵗ Lᵃ. Keeper,* which severely reflects (but Ironically) on divers Great Men, as Lᵈ. *Somers,* Lᵈ. *Halifax,* Lᵈ. *Orford,* Bᵖ. of *Sarum,* Secretary *Harley,* & others.

Feb. 4 (Mon.). In the School Tower is Sᵗ. *Jerom*'s (or rather *Ruffinus's*) *Expositio in Symbolum Apostolorum* (whereof there is a Copy also in the Publick Library) printed at *Oxon.* 1468. At the End of wᶜʰ are these Notes by Dʳ. *Wallis :*

Liber Universitatis Oxoniensis inter Archiva reponendus; ex dono Mosis Pitt, Bibliopolæ .Londinensis, 31 Januarij 16⅞⁹₀. Primus omnium liber qui vulgo perhibetur fuisse impressus, est, Ciceronis Officia; Moguntiæ, Anno Domini 1465. Hic autem, qui dicitur Hieronymi in Symbolum Apostolorum, (sed est Ruffini potius) impressus & finitus Oxoniæ Anno 1468. 17 Decembris, (non nisi triennio postquam ille primus;) Baker, in Historia sua perhibet Artem Typographicam, Londinum advectam esse anno 1471, & in Abbatia Westmonasteriensi, primo exercitam fuisse, a Caxtono quodam, (eodem cujus opera Oxoniam pridem advecta fuerat, ut qui Curcelleum quendam typographum ab Harlemo huc invitaverat.) Nescio tamen an ullus extet antiquior 10 Codex Londini impressus quam est Caxtoni Chronicon Anno 1480.

Jo. WALLIS. Cust. Archiv. Universitatis Oxon.

This Book, (the outer Margin being cut away more at yᵉ side than at the Top and Bottom; & because it hath 8 Leaves in one Signature, or Letter, as A, B, C, &c.;) appears like a large octavo: But is indeed a small Quarto, with two Sheets in one Signature, and one Sewing: As appears, both by the Rules in the Paper, which do not ly from Top to Bottom (as in Folio's and Octavo's) but cross the Page, from side to side, (as in Octavo's and Decimo-Sexto's:) And by the Mark of yᵉ Paper; which is to be seen, (near to the Sewing,) not at yᵉ Top of yᵉ 20 Page (as in Octavo's) but near the Middle of it, as in Quarto's. As for instance, in the leaves signed, a i. a iij. b, i. b, iiii. c, ii. c. iii. c iiii. d. ii. and (those wᶜʰ answer to them) a 8. a 6. b 8. b 5. c 7. c 6. c 5. d 7. (whence also it appears to be printed by Half-Sheets: for c hath the Mark oftener, and d seldomer, than for two Sheets: that having three Half-Sheets marked, & but one unmarked; this one marked, and three unmarked. The Signature e hath five Half Sheets (or 2½ Sheets;) of which e iiij, e v, (and those answering to them e 6, e 7,) are marked; the other three half Sheets, being unmarked. The Custome being then, (as now it is) to set the Mark of the Paper in each Sheet, in the Middle of one 30 of the Half-Sheets, & not of the other. — In Brazen-nose College Library there is a Parchment Book in folio, printed at Oxford A.D. 1481. viz. Alexandri (Aphrodisiensis) Expositio super tres libros de anima. At the End of it are these words printed: Impressum per me Theodoricum Wod de Colonia in Alma universitate Oxoñ Anno Incarnationis Dominicæ M.CCCC.LXXXI. XI die mensis Octobris. Another copy of this same Edition is in Oriel College Library. — Inter MSS. Laud. F. 92. is John Dade's Treatise of Heraldry curiously illuminated, and at yᵉ End is Caxton's Chronicle, with Illuminations too. — Coyns of Pergamus wᵗʰ Æsculapius's Head consider. — The Abbat of Oseney held yᵉ 40 Mannors of Weston and Water-Eton by Service of two Knᵗˢ Fees. See Mʳ. Dodsworth's Collections Vol. 6. f. 188. b.

Feb. 5 (Tu.). I am told by a very good Hand yᵗ yᵉ Oxford Almanack is now in Consideration before yᵉ H. of Lords & yᵗ Bennett yᵉ Bookseller has sent to Mʳ. Hall to send up to London wᵗʰout fail an hundred of them. — The Master of University College shew'd me a Petition of yᵉ Clergy to yᵉ Queen (Q. Eliz.) desiring yᵗ she would be pleas'd, in her princely Wisdom, to take Care yᵗ all Impropriations be restor'd to yᵉ Church, wᶜʰ they do not question she will do since she has promis'd to be so great a Friend to it, particularly when she came first to yᵉ Crown, 50 & at yᵉ same time the Bᵖˢ offer towards her Necessity certain Sums, provided they may be restor'd to them again, when the Crown shall happen to be inrich'd, viz.

Canterbury	.	.	.	.	200 libs.
Ely	.	.	.	.	200 libs.
London	.	.	.	.	100 libs.
Hereford	.	.	.	.	100 marks.
Cicester	.	.	.	.	100 marks.

In the same Paper were added Considerations why Bishops Temporalities should not be taken away. — There is come out a Half Sheet Printed on one side *The Oxford Almanack Explain'd, with the Reverse of y͞e same.* I saw at yᵉ same time a Letter from Dʳ. Edwards to yᵉ Master giving him an Account of an Answer, some pᵗ of the Lower House of Convocation had made to a Protestation of the other part, with a Declaration wherein they insist upon their Rights in Opposition to yᵗ Party, & the upper House, wᶜʰ he says are very well penn'd, tho' being long he could not send a Copy. Dated Feb. 1ˢᵗ. — A Letter likewise from Dʳ. Smalridge dat. Feb. 2. abᵗ yᵉ same Matter, and particularly that Dʳ. Cawley said not one word in opposition to the Answer or Declaration, tho' he be known to be a Low-Church-Man, & 'tis thought he was sent as a spy at this time. — The Almanack he says explain'd in a Jacobite sense. — A Letter also from Mʳ. Percival upon yᵉ same Accᵗ, wherein he farther says that Dʳ. Cawley was the more taken notice of upon Accᵗ of his Being one of the Protestors. That no Body knows what will be yᵉ Fate of yᵉ Regency Bill for yᵗ yᵉ Lords have so amended yᵉ Amendmᵗ of yᵉ Commons yᵗ by wᵗ he understands by yᵉ Conversation he has it wont go down. &c. Dat. also Feb. 2. — In the 3ᵈ Vol. of Dʳ. South's Sermons pag. 423. is a remarkable Passage relating to Dʳ. *Pocock*'s opinion abᵗ Grotius's Exposition of Is. 53. &c.

The Country Parson's Honest Advice to that Judicious Lawyer & worthy Minister of State my Lᵈ. Keeper. (By Dʳ. Brown.)

Be wise as Somerset, as Somers' Brave,
As Pembroke Airy, & as Richmond Grave;
Humble as Orford be ; & Wharton's Zeal,
For Church & Loyalty, wou'd fit thee well ;
Like Sarum, I wou'd have thee love yᵉ Church,
He scorns to leave his Mother in the lurch.
For the well governing your Family,
Let pious Haversham thy Pattern be :
And if it be thy Fate again to marry,

And S—y—r's Daughter will thy year out tarry,
May'st thou use her as Mohun his tender wife,
And may she lead his virtuous Lady's Life.
To sum up all ; Devonshire's Chastity,
Bolton's Merit, Godolphin's Probity,
Halifax his modesty, Essex's sense,
Mountague's Management, Culpepper's Pence,
Tenison's Learning, & Southampton's wit,
Will make thee for an able Statesman fit.

The Romans believ'd their Emperors to be Gods more firmly than any others said to be so because they were visible whereas yᵉ rest never appear'd. Vide Val. Max. Pref. ad Tiberium.

Feb. 6 (Wed.). I am told That in the first Edition of one of Erasmus's Pieces, the title *de viduitate* or *castitate conservanda*, or something like it, there is a most scandalous fault, much to the Disgrace of Erasmus, tho' not to be laid upon him. It seems yᵉ Correcter of yᵉ Press, being not very well pleas'd with his pay, or else expecting some extraordinary Pay to drink with, wch Erasmus was not willing to give, he was resolv'd to be reveng'd, & accordingly in the Dedication, wch was to some great Lady, before y^t Sheet wherein 'twas wrought off instead of *menti tuae castissimae* he most maliciously put *mentulae castissimae*. Quaere?

Feb. 7 (Th.). I heard D^r. Miles Stapylton (who was formerly Fellow of All-Souls Coll., Tutor to ye Duke of Grafton, Chaplain to ye L^d. Jersey when Embassador in France, & Minister of * * * *, near Henly, & Author of the English Translation of the Life of Caius Marius, printed in ye 3^d Vol. of Plutarch's Lives,) say yesterday that when he 10 was at Paris, he made a visit to Father Simon (lately deceas'd) whom he found in a small Hut surrounded with Books, without any Fire, tho' a very cold day, being us'd to fortifie himself against weather by several Caps upon his Head, a thick Robe, and a large leathern Girdle. After some usual Complements, they enter'd into Discourse about Learning & Learned Men, & happening to talk of D^r. Mill the Father told him he did not think y^t his Greek Testament, so much talk'd of, would ever be printed. But being assur'd by D^r. Stapylton that 'twas all printed off but ye Prolegomena, he presently pull'd down 6 large Folios relating to the New Testament, being Collections of Lections, criticisms, &c. telling him y^t there were at least 100 Good MSS. he had made use of, 20 wch D^r. Mill never either saw or had any Account of; & y^t if he presum'd to publish his Book, he should rue the Day that ever he undertook it, being resolv'd if he liv'd to be upon his Bones when that should happen. — He likewise made a visit to Harduin, particularly to desire leave to consult a MS^t of Justin Martyr under his Custody for ye use of M^r. Creech then ingag'd in putting out a new Edition of y^t Author. But tho' 'twas well known that there was such a MS^t under his Care, yet the Jesuit protested with several oaths y^t he knew of no such thing, & was sure there never was any in the Library, telling him moreover that he wonder'd any man should be so sollicitous ab^t MSS^ts of an 30 Author that was spurious, all the Fathers, he saying, being Forgery and a Cento made up by some Cunning Fellows on purpose to deceive the World. W^ch made the D^r. smile, expecting this Talk from one who notwithstanding his Great Learning was of opinion (at least people believe so) that all the Classicks (Pliny's Nat. History publish'd by himself excepted) were spurious &c. When the D^r. had taken leave of him, he mention'd the Discourse to some of ye Sorbonists (who are Enemies to ye Jesuits) & was certified by them that there was such a MS^t in ye Library, & y^t the Denyal of it with an Oath was a Jesuitical Trick on purpose by the help of it to spoyle the English Edition, when it should 40 come out. Which is a method also us'd by the Hollanders. — M^r. Wase the Beadle translated all Vitruvius into English, & ye Copy, a Sheet or two only wanting, is now in ye Hands of His Son, Fellow of Corpus Christi College, as I am inform'd by D^r. Hudson. This M^r. Wase the Son has certain Roman Coyns, (about 50 or 60), found at Cirencester in Glocester-shire: but they are very much defac'd. All unless one or two of the Lesser Sort. — ... The D. of Beaufort married to ye Lady Rachel Noel on the 4th. She is Daughter and Coheiress of ye late Earl of Gainsborough. — One Ward is taken into Custody for publishing a Burlesque Poem call'd Hudibras Redivivus in 50

wᶜʰ he lays open some sort of People in a little too lively Colours. ▬
We hear from Exeter that on the 30ᵗʰ of Jan. a merchant of yᵗ City
(whose Father was deeply concern'd in yᵉ Murther of K. Ch. 1.) had yᵉ
Impudence in ridicule of yᵉ Day to send his Servants thro' the City,
with a Calf's Head hanging on a String where his own had deserved
better to have been. ▬ Dʳ. Mill tells me he formerly saw in a Book of
Bᵖ. Barlow's divers Ancient Inscriptions in loose Leaves, wᶜʰ he is
afraid may be convey'd away, & not plac'd in yᵉ Publick Library amongst
the Bᵖ'ˢ Books, being a Rarity, as not printed in Gruter. Above a
10 Week since I saw lying upon Dʳ. Charlett's Table in his Study certain
old Inscriptions in eleven Sheets, wᶜʰ appearing to be curious, Dʳ.
Hudson (who was then present) desir'd the said Dʳ. C. to permitt me
to take them to yᵉ Publick Library, & compare them with Books of
Inscriptions whether they were wanting there or not. Wᶜʰ at last he
granted. I found them at yᵉ End of a Copy of Augustinus de Legibus
in Mʳ. Selden's Study, but of a different Edition : & I really believe
Mʳ. Wanley stole them from Bᵖ. Barlow's Books, and gave them to Dʳ.
Charlett, as without doubt he did other Things. ▬

Writers to be consulted de Nummis—F. Ursinus, Augustinus, Vicus, Erizzo,
20 Sambucus, Occo, Strada, Goltzius, Sᵗ. Amant, Hemmelarius, Angeloni, Seguinus, Patin, Spanheim, Vaillant, Oyselius. De Epigrammatibus—Lipsius, Boissardus, Panvinius, Selden, Lucius, Capacius, Paradinus, Gualterus, Reinesius,
Guichenon, Chorerius, Ursatus, Marullus Spalatensis (Spon had it in MSᵗ.)
Peireskius (unpublish'd), Gruter. De Ædificijs—Serlio, Marlianus, Palladius,
Bosius, Poldo, Bellorius, Bergerius, Perrot. De Statuis—Mich. Angelus, Ursinus, &c. De Gemmis—Ursinus, Gallæus, Le Pois, Pierius Valerianus, Gor-
læus, Chiffletius, Kirkerus, Augustinus, Caninius, Bagarrius, Reicheltius.
Toreumata—Bellorius, S. Bartoli, Suaresius, Bosius, Aringhi, Boissardus, &c.
Angeiographia—Bayfius, Ferrarius, Rubenius, Scheffer, Smetius &c.

30   **Feb. 8 (Fri.).** The Columna Rostrata, for illustrating Livy, is printed
p. 59. of Gualtherus's Tabb. Siciliæ. ▬ Mʳ. Powell, an Honest Non-
Juring Gentleman, who had been formerly Secretary to two or three
true Church of England Bᵖˢ, and had liv'd some time in Oxoñ upon yᵉ
Charity of Dʳ. Bayly President of Magdalen College, was summon'd to
attend the Council at White-Hall abᵗ Sʳ. Humph. Mackworth, (whom
the spight and Malice of wicked Designing Courtiers would gladly make
yᵉ Author of yᵉ Memorial) & being then under some Indisposition of
Body, and oblig'd to wait from 5 to 12 Clock at Night in a cold
damp Room, increas'd his Distemper to yᵗ Degree yᵗ he paid his last
40 Debt to Nature with in a day or two after, & may be justly reckon'd to
die a Martyr for yᵉ Memorial. This Dʳ. Hudson had from the President
of Magdalen who had a large Account of yᵉ Matter from Mʳ. Gandy a
Friend of Mʳ. Powell's, who is a Person of unquestionable Integrity, &
had formerly been Fellow of Oriel College & one of the Proctors of
this University. ▬ A Place of Julius Obsequens illustrated in Paschalius
de Corona, pag. 529.

Feb. 9 (Sat.). Dʳ. Nicholson, Bᵖ. of Carlisle, writ a Letter lately to
a certain Gentleman, wherein he most severely and scandalously reflects

---

Feb. 9. Kent to H. Asks for account of the modern Mystic Divines.
Though he is in Low Church company, he shall never be brought to think

upon yᵉ most Learned and Pious Mʳ. Dodwell. A Copy of it has been communicated to Mʳ. Dodwell, who is far from being concern'd or troubled at such Aspersions. He has shew'd it to several Persons, who very much blame the Bᵖ. for it, thinking he had had more sense and Discretion than to abuse one, who has establish'd the universal Character of a Great Man. — Last Week four Letters for Degrees from the Chancellor (amongst wᶜʰ was one for the Degree of Dʳ. of Divinity for Mʳ. Potter, lately of Lincoln College, and now Chaplain to yᵉ Archbᵖ. of Canterbury) being read in Convocation, they were all hinder'd from passing by the Proctors. The Reason, because they were not acquainted 10 with yᵉ Contents of the Letters before they came to Convocation. This was never customary, but Mʳ. Bickley the Senior Proctor will have it done, and has perswaded his Brother Proctor to be of the same mind, intending to send Copies of all Letters the day before the Convocation to every particular College and Hall, that the Members of Convocation may be able to examin into the Characters of yᵉ Persons on whose behalf the Letters are sent. Which is a laudable Design, & will hinder it may be some People's having Degrees conferr'd on them, who are not statutably qualified. I am told also Mʳ. Bickley moves that the names of all Persons in the University may be publish'd in every College 20 & Hall the Day before their Graces are propos'd in Congregation, wᶜʰ is also a most reasonable Desire, & may do good Service, especially in relation to Scandalous Fanaticks and Presbyterians, it being well known that some of these Men send their Children to the University where they let them continue only in Term time & afterwards take them home & hinder them from going to Church, but take them to Meetings, & so make them guilty of the Abominable Crime of Occasional Communion, notwithstanding their having subscrib'd to yᵉ Articles of the Church of England. This Mʳ. Bickley who is Fellow of New-College, & Great Grand-son (I think) to the Learned & worthy Dʳ. Tho. Bickley, (who 30 was made Bᵖ. of Chichester in the time of Q. Eliz.) is a Person of great Integrity & Resolution, & has withall good Sense, & if he does but meet with others to joyn with him will do the University much Service, being punctual in executing the Statute, & exact in seeing yᵗ nothing be done to yᵉ Disgrace of yᵉ University. He is likewise a true Son of yᵉ Church of England, & an Enemy to all Fanaticism, Enthusiasm, &c. — MS. Laud. E. 58. . . The said Book written in a Modern Hand, & is hardly 200 Years old. . . No mention in Gaddius de scriptoribus of Franc. Puccius a Florentine. . . Out of Junius's Preface to *Paraphrasis Poëtica Geneseos* of Cædmon. . . . — Rupertus's Observat. in 40 Synopsin Besoldi minorem to be read over when another edition of Justin comes out. Dʳ. Hudson also to consult him upon Paterculus. To be consulted also for Eutropius. — A letter from Zacagnius to Dr. Hudson [dated Romae die pᵃ Dec. MDCCV.; (75-84)]. . . . At the same time came a Letter to Dʳ. H. from Passioneus, a Copy whereof follows [dated Romae ex mea Bibliotheca V. Idus Januarias MDCCVI. (84-91).] . . . — Remember to ask Dʳ. Smith whether he ever saw Schelstrate's Edition of Antoninus's Itinerary, mention'd in a Letter to Dʳ.

Hudson by Passionæus from Rome, who desires to have all the pieces Dr. Smith has publish'd in Latin. Ask him whether he can accommodate Dr. Hudson with all ye sd Pieces but yt of ye 7 Churches of Asia, or tell how he may get them?

Feb. 10 (Sun.). This Morning preach'd at St. Marie's before ye University Mr. Husbands one of ye Chaplains of New-College upon Job xxvii. 8. . . . 'Twas an Honest Sermon, shewing (1) the Nature of Hypocrisy. (2) The Sinfullness of it, both with respect to God and Man. (3) The Punishments of it, (4) Some Methods for avoiding it. — In 10 the Afternoon preach'd before ye University at St. Peter's in ye East (this being ye first Sunday in Lent) Mr. De-Langley of Xt Church on Luke xvi. 30, 31. . . .

He first consider'd the Charity of the rich Man in Hell towards his Brethren. (2) The Probability of the Argument us'd by him. (3) Abraham's Answer, in considering wch he shew'd that the Revelation in ye New Testament exceeds all other Proofs & Demonstrations for attaining future Happiness, & affords the most cogent Argumts for exciting to Repentance for past sins and intire Obedience afterwds. Concluded with a Motive to Repentance.

Feb. 11 (Mon.). Rob. Dormer Esq. one of ye Kts of ye Shire in 20 Parl. for Bucks made a Sergeant at Law, by the Interest of ye Duke of New-Castle & the Ld. Wharton & afterwards one of ye Judges. — The Title of the Basil Edition of Livy, Froben. an. 1531. . . . Then follows Erasmus's Epistle giving an Acct of this Edition, wch is amongst his other Epistles. — Title-Page of ye Dauphin Edition of Livy. . . .

Feb. 12 (Tu.). In the Folio MSS. of De Wits Catalogue (num. 42.) are said to be *Notæ quædam in Tit. Livium, manu J. Lipsij scriptæ.* Also among the Quartos, (num. 25.) Jan. Gruteri Emendationes & Schediasmata in Senecæ libros de Beneficijs & Tit. Livium. Item Collationes eorundem Auctorum cum varijs MSS. Omnia ipsa doctiss. 30 Gruteri manu descripta. — Paul Merula, as he testifyes in Cosmogr. P. II. L. IV. c. xiii. collected & writ a Discourse about ye Ancient Tongues of Italy, wch he sd he would leave to his children. Quære whether printed in his Posthumous Pieces? This would be of good use to Mr. Llhuyd. He has in ye same place printed Columna Rostrata. See pag. 780. compare it with other Editions when Livy is printing. — A Petition being offer'd against James Winstanley Esqr. by Laurence Carter both which were return'd Members of Parl. for ye Borough of Leycester, it was referr'd to ye Committee who resolv'd yt Winstanley (who is a very honest Gentleman) was not duly Elected, 40 for wch their was a Thanksgiving in all the Conventicles in and abt Leycester; but it being afterwards propos'd to ye whole House, the majority dissented from the said Resolution of ye Committee, & declar'd Mr. Winstanley duly Elected, to ye great Mortification of the Presby-

---

Feb. 11. H. to Dr. T. Smith. Account of Grabe's practice concerning the Sacrament. Laying the foundation stones of Peckwater Quad.; inscriptions on those laid by the Dean and Canons and the Earl of Salisbury. Did he ever see Schelstrate's edition of Antoninus' *Itinerary*? Dr. Hudson wishes a copy of Smith's Latin pieces for presentation to a correspondent at Rome. Extracts from Junius' Preface to *Paraphr. Poëtica Geneseos* by Cædmon.

terians & yᵉ Friends of yᵗ Knavish and Rebellious Crew. — Ex Doujatij
Praefatione ad editionem suam Livij in usum Delphini. [97-126.] ...
Adjumenta Doujatij ex codicibus MSS. .... — Mʳ. James Sᵗ. Amand
Junʳ. (not long since a Gentleman Commoner of Hart-Hall, and afterwards of Linc. Coll.) tells Dʳ. Hudson, in a Letter, sent to him from
Leyden that he has seen Almelovanus's Strabo, wᶜʰ will be in two Vols.
& be publish'd in June next, at wᶜʰ time will also be publish'd Julius
Pollux. That Gronovius has been about Josephus 14 Years, but 'tis
not known yet whether he will really publish it. Gronovius's Brother
went purposely to Vienna to consult the MSSᵗˢ there. Besides wᶜʰ he 10
has recᵈ a great many Assistances, particularly from an Edition, in wᶜʰ
the famous Cocceius had written several various Readings, as also
Conjectures and Notes of his own. Mʳ. Vander Aa, the Bookseller
who had first undertaken to print Gronovius's design'd Edition of
Josephus, but has now resign'd his Interest to another, told Mʳ. Sᵗ.
Amand, That Heinsius, to whom we are oblig'd for the late Edition of
Juvenal and Persius, had undertaken to make a Collection of all those
Authors who had written of Pyramids, and that he designed to have
translated Greaves's Treatise on yᵗ Subject, & put it among the rest.
He had made a considerable Progress in this Work before his untimely 20
Death, upon wᶜʰ all his Papers came to his Widow, to whom Mʳ. Vander
Aa has writ to know if she will part with the Papers that relate to this
undertaking; because he proposes that yᵉ Gentleman who would translate the said Book of Greaves would also revise those Papers and publish
as much of them as he shall judge fit. Mʳ. Vervey has got a Noble
Edition of Hesychius ready for yᵉ Press, but nobody will print it because
of yᵉ War. Mʳ. Le Clerc is putting out a new Anthologia, & he invites
all people to send him any unpublish'd Epigramms with promise of
a gratefull mentioning the Persons he is oblig'd to in yᵉ Book.

Upon yᵉ Debates concerning yᵉ Churche's being in Danger.   30

1.

Sore sick a Lady late did lye,
Whose Name I will not mention;
And six and twenty Doctors by,
Maintain'd by her in Pension.

2.

Her Children round about her stood,
Some weeping & some grinning:
Those wish'd her Life, yᵉ others hop'd
To see her wrapp'd in Linnen.

3.

Cry'd one of these Legitimate,
With great Concern & Pother,
After this grand Inquest of fate,
Pray how do you like my Mother?

4.

O Sir, said they, she's very well,
And therefore pray be still ô,
And tho' you see pray do not tell,
We'll pull away the Pillow.

5.

What tho' her Eyes are dry & sunk,
Her nose & Cheeks so thin â,
Her Spirits fail thro'out yᵉ Trunk,
You see she cocks her chin â.

6.

Her pulse indeed vermiculates,
Her Breath is short & little,
Yet sighs & Hiccops indicates,
She's healthy too a Tittle.   40

7.

O Sir crys one my mind suggests,
These Sighs are wondrous bad,
Peace fool, cry'd they, she's very well,
And thou art surely mad.

8.

Thus they upon Debate opin'd,
Her Health in good Condition,
And voted all her Children blind,
That call'd for a Physitian.   50

The Bᵖ. of Norwich (Dʳ. Moore) sent me the first Book of Livy revis'd by Lipsius (who design'd to have done ye whole) & printed by Plantin at Antw. 1579. 8°. The Title & Preface follow: [134–136; 137–144 blank.]

Feb. 13 (Wed.). On Sunday Morning last about 9 Clock just against the Master of University's Lodgings a Quaker being mov'd by ye Spirit held forth in the open Street. A great Number of people immediately got about him. But D^r. Charlett and ye Proctors coming home from S^t. Maries, where they had been to receive the Pence p^d yearly by ye townsmen, it being S^t. Scholastica's Day, they took him up and sent him to ye Castle. He was let out yesterday, but was no sooner dismiss'd than he began his former Rhapsodical Discourse exactly in ye same place where he did before. He was not taken up again. I am told by M^r. Bacche a Norwegian (who is a Student in ye Publick Library) & is acquainted with him y^t his Name is Meydel, y^t he is a Dane by Birth, & that he was Preacher to ye Danish Church at London, wch was worth to him at least 200 lib^s. per An. He said he turn'd Quaker since he came into England, & upon y^t left his place. He says withall y^t he is a Scholar, & was before this Accounted a Rational man, & had acquir'd a good Reputation.

Feb. 14 (Th.). M^r. Meydel being examin'd by D^r. Charlett said y^t he was born in Schene in ye Kingdom of Norway, that he is aged ab^t 45 years, & bred up there to y^t idle trade of preaching for hire, &c. — Tuesday being the last of ye Terme divers persons appeared upon their Recognizances in ye Court of Queen's Bench, & amongst ye rest M^r. Stephens ye parson of Sutton & was charged by M^r. Attorney General, with a long Information for Lybelling his Grace the D. of Marlborough & M^r. Secretary Harley. Also D^r. Brown was charged with an Information for Handing to ye Press a Lybell upon my L^d. Keeper & several Ministers of State. M^r. Straghan a Bookseller was also charged with one for publishing the Memorial of ye Ch. of Engl. — M^r. Emmason formerly of Edm. Hall now Chaplain to ye English Merchants at Hamburg.

Feb. 15 (Fri.). Yesterday I had shew'd me by a Gentleman of Christ-Church five pieces of Money, dug up at Rewley in ye West-Suburb of Oxon. All of Brass. Two of them had on them *Ave Maria. Gracia Ihesu.* The other three were Dutch pieces. One of the first had a Crosse on the other side. The Crosse was commonly put on ye Reverse of ye Coyns of those times. But it might be put on this piece upon Account of Richard Duke of Cornwall (who was the first Founder of the Abbey here) his Journey into ye Holy-Land, at wch time he made a vow if he return'd in safety he would found some Religious House, wch he did both in this place & at Hales near Winchcombe in Glocester-shire. Tho' 'tis most likely that these Pieces might be buried here after this first Foundation, they being found just where the Stone was dug up, formerly mention'd, & therefore in all probability some of those wch were scatter'd at ye Ceremony of ye Foundation of ye Chapell by Ela Longespee Countess of Warwick. The Abbey was dedicated to ye Virgin Mary. The German or Dutch pieces might be laid here in commemoration of Earl Richard's being made King of ye Romans.

— Ab^t a year since the B^p. of Oxon suspended ab Officio & Beneficio M^r. Fell minister of Astoll near Witney, for marrying M^r. Johnson an Apothecary in Witney to a Young Gentlewoman, who was both under Age, & had not her Parents consent. This is a great Blot on the B^p., M^r. Fell having a Licence for doing it, & consequently the B^p. could not in Justice have meddled with him: wch he knew well enough, & therefore, being resolv'd to punish the poor Honest Man, he found a Word or two added by M^r. Fell to ye Licence, wch tho' not material, being only the filling up the Blank wch was left for the name of ye Parish, yet he proceeded upon y^t, & accordingly depriv'd him for three 10 years. And it may be he was the more against him because M^r. Fell's Uncle (Daniel Hechstetter,) (being a Schoolmaster under whom the Learned D^r. Hudson was educated 'till he came to ye University) was a very honest Man, & a Cavalier.

Feb. 16 (Sat.). Talking last Night with M^r. Smith of University College, he was pleas'd to say that he did not believe M^r. Bryan Twyne was Author of the Book wch goes under his Name, call'd *Antiquitatis Academiæ Oxoniensis Apologia*, but thought M^r. Tho. Allen of Gloucester Hall writ it in English, and that M^r. Twyne only put it into Latin, it being hardly possible, as he thought, that a man so young as Twine 20 was when that Book was ready for ye Press, (being then scarce 28 years of Age) should have read over and perused such a vast Number of Muniments &c. as were requisite for Compiling it. There is no doubt M^r. Twyne rec^d great Assistance from M^r. Allen, as also from M^r. Miles Windsore, but I really believe the whole Composuere is owing to himself, & that (being a Man of indefatigable Industry) he made most of ye Collections himself. Nor is it likely M^r. Allen should write such a Book in English, & afterwards get another to translate it, since 'tis well known he was a profound Scholar & a polite Man, & very well vers'd in Greek and Latin. M^r. Smith has had for some 30 time the Privilege of looking over ye University Charters, Records, &c. lodg'd in the School-Tower, of wch M^r. Twyne was first Keeper, & made a great many Additions for the use of the university, wch were of so great use to M^r. Ant. Wood, y^t he oftentimes took w^t Twyne had done ready to his Hand, but without Acknowledgment. This M^r. Smith told me, who has compar'd M^r. Wood's Book with Twyne's Papers. Particularly he says the Discourse about Printing is wholly Twyne's abating some few things wch have happen'd since his Death. I remember once I went into the Roome where the said Charters &c. are kept, & looking over a Volume of M^r. Twyne's Hand Writing found 40 several particulars wch M^r. Wood has in his Antiquities, & believe upon y^t Acc^t w^t M^r. Smith said to be in great measure true. — D^r. Kennett borrow'd a certain Paper from among the Records of University College of the Master and M^r. Smith, with Condition either to return it or send a Copy of it, but he has done neither as yet, tho' 9 years or more since 'twas lent. — In Ch. Ch. Library is a large Genealogical Table, in MS^t, of all the Count Palatines of the Rhine &c. done by Adolphus Joannes Comes Palatinus Rheni, who styles it Tabulam Genealogicam Majorum suorum. Done by his own Hand, & given by him to B^p. Fell. — On Tuesday last ye Quakers deliver'd out a Pamphlett in ye Lobby of ye 50

House of Commons giving an Account of their Sufferings in ye Court
of Exchequer complaining of the Priests and Tyth Farmers in proceeding against y^m for y^er due. But this is nothing but w^t was expected:
for in ye Circular Letter y^t was sent by ye Heads of y^m in London last
Spring to y^er Friends in ye Country, directing them how to vote in y^e
late Elections for Members of Parliam^t they told them they should have
occasion to apply themselves to ye House for 2 things the one was to
exempt them from paying Tythes, the other to make y^eir Marriages
valid in Law. — On ye 14th Inst. in ye Morning came on ye Tryall
10 of D^r. Drake at Guild Hall Lond. before ye L^d. Chief Justice Holt upon
an Information brought by the Attorney General for a Pamphlett written
by him called Mercurius Politicus, bearing date the 18 of 7^ber last.
After a long Tryal the Jury found ye D^r. guilty of writing the said
Pamphlett but ye word (*Nor*) was laid in ye Information instead of
(*Not*) as is in ye said Pamphlet, so that ye Verdict is special & to be
consider'd by the Judges. — Letters from Virginia say that ye College
at Williamsbury, a most Stately Fabrick, & one of the best in all
America, & to wch the late King W^m. had been a Benefactor, was on
the 29th of October last, utterly consum'd by fire wch by an unknown
20 Accident broke out in the very dead of the Night, together with the
Library, to wch divers persons bearing any Love to Learning had been
Contributors, & in all probability would in some time have grown very
famous.

Feb. 17 (Sun.). This Morning preach'd at S^t. Marie's M^r. Carter of
Oriel Col. upon Phil. iii. 19. *Whose Glory is in their Shame.* Having
preach'd once before on ye same Words he now gave some Methods
for avoiding this Sin of glorying in our Vices, taken (1) from the
Hainousness of the Sin. (2) The ill Effects it has upon Men. (3) The
Mischiefs and Inconveniences it brings upon our selves. —

30 E Registro Caroli Boothe penes Johannem Episcopum Norwicensem.
Hic textus insculpitur in prima petra jacti fundamenti Collegij Cardinalis
Oxon.—
Reverendissimus in Christo Pater ac Dominus, Dominus Thomas Wulcy,
miseratione Divina, Titulo sanctæ Cæciliæ Sacrosanctæ Romanæ Ecclesiæ
Presbyter, Cardinalis, Eboracensis Archiepiscopus, Angliæ Primas, & Apo-
stolicæ Sedis Legatus, Episcopus Dunelmensis, exemptique Monasterij Sancti
Albani perpetuus Commendatorius, Cancellarius Angliæ, & dictæ sedis Apo-
stolicæ ad vitam suam etiam de latere Legatus, hanc petram posuit in Honorem
Sanctæ & Individuæ Trinitatis gloriosissimæque Virginis Mariæ, Sanctæ Frides-
40 wydæ, & omnium Sanctorum vicesimo die Martij anno Domini millessimo
quingentesimo vicesimo quinto. —

M^r. Daniel Hetchstetter above mention'd (see pag. 151.) was born in
Cumberland, and descended from ye Family of ye Hechstetters in Germany, who came over into England in Queen Elizabeth's time to order
the Brass Mines, wch were found near Keswick in y^t County. He was
from School sent to Queen's Coll. in this University, where he became
Poor-Child, then Taberder: but when he was a Foundation Master (as
they call them) the Civil Wars then running high, he left the College
and serv'd the King in his Army. Afterwards when ye Royal Cause
50 could not be supported, he return'd into his Native Country where he
taught several Young Gentlemen privately 'till the Restauration. After

this he was made Rector of Bolton in the Diocess of Carlisle, (viz. in Cumberland) & likewise continu'd to teach half a dozen Scholars till the time of his Death. He us'd a Grammar drawn up by himself, wch he printed & gave to his Scholars. — Oliver Cromwell had amongst his Remarkable Vices some little Sparks of Virtue ; as being Chancellor of ye University of Oxoñ he gave several valuable MSS^ts to ye Publick Library there, and such a Respect for ye Learned B^p. Usher that he was at ye Expence of his Funeral wch amounted to 2 or 300 lib^s., and made his Souldiers then in Ireland be content to have so much deducted out of their Pay as raised so considerable a sum as purchas'd his Library, 10 for the use of Trinity College in Dublin where it now remains. Quære whether this be in his Life written by D^r. Par ? — That *Swinging Orthodox* (as ye Women style him) G. Burnett B^p. of Sarum, publish'd an Account of the Life and Death of the Mad & Witty Earl of Rochester, wherein he gives a large Account of his being often with him during his Sickness, yet several Persons of good Credit have averr'd that he never was admitted to visit him at y^t time, as he pretends in ye said Book. — M^r. Basil Kennett of Corpus X^ti tells me that D^r. Kennett his Brother has several Papers of M^r. Andrew Allam (who was Tutor to him ye s^d D^r. K.) from whence I believe the D^r. has taken 20 divers notices in his publish'd Books, & y^t he will make great use of them in a Work ab^t Cathedral Churches &c. he is now upon. — Tho. Lindsey now B^p. of Killaloe in Ireland was Fellow of Wadham Col. a Man of good Parts but little or no Learning, spending his Time in ye University in Tippling, & (as some say) wenching too. So also D^r. Nicholson B^p. of Carlisle was Fellow of Queen's College, had good strong Parts, but had ye Reputation (and not undeservedly) of a drinking Fellow, & boon Companion. When Bach. of Arts he apply'd himself to ye Study of the Saxon Language, & was sent by S^r. Joseph Williamson into Germany to learn that Language. He did not stay 30 long in ye College after he was Fellow, being invited by Rainbow B^p. of Carlisle to be his Chaplain, wch B^p. made him Archdeacon of Carlisle, from wch Dignity he was advanc'd by the Interest of S^r. X^topher Musgrave to be B^p. of ye same Place. — D^r. Hough when Fellow of Magd. Coll. got to be Chaplain to ye Duke of Ormond. Upon the Revolution he was made President of the same College, & a little after B^p. of Oxoñ, & some time after that being found to be a Man of Revolution Principles advanc'd to ye see of Lichfield & Coventry. And here it may not be improper to observe that he heap'd a great many Preferm^ts upon one Goodwin his Chaplain, a Man of no great Worth 40 nor Merits, and (as one would think) of no very good Conscience, because he keeps all this Preferm^t with a Fellowship.

Feb. 18 (Mon.). The Bishop of Landaff (Beau) dyed Yesterday was 7 night. — A Book of ab^t 9 Sheets of Paper is come out call'd the History of the Revolutions. 'Tis Handed privately about. — We have an Acc^t from Bristol of a pretty odd pranke y^t was play'd there on the 30th of Jan. last in ridicule of y^t day. Some of the Fanatical Crew met together in a street call'd the old Markett in ye Parish of S^t. Stephen and drest up a Figure to represent ye Royal Martyr with a white Capp on his Head wch they sett on a Mastiff Dog & carryed it to the place 50 of the Mock Execution, when on a Block one of them chopt of his Head wth an Ax, wth loud Acclamations & Hussas & being askt what they meant by the Accoñ they reply'd 'twas the 30th of January & the Figure represented Charles 1st. W^{ch} is a piece of Impudence beyond y^t of ye Calves Head Clubb.

[Note on Plin. Ep. VI. 33.]

February 19. [Notes from Maussacus's Diss. Critica to Harpocration.] ...

When it was debated amongst ye Fellows of Magd. College, that ye Women Bed-Makers (who had been scandalously lewd and vitious) 10 should be discarded and for ever kept out of ye College, Doctor Fayrer (who to the great prejudise and Dishonour of ye University, by ye Interest of a few Corrupt Electors got to be Natural Philosophy Read^r) shew'd himself the great Patron of these loose Women, wch was severely reflected upon by some of ye Fellows, who knew he labour'd under a flagrant suspicion with regard to some of them. This came from one of the same Coll., a person of great Integrity and unquestionable veracity. The Persons concern'd in ye Election of this D^r. Fayrer were D^r. De Laune Vice-Canc. D^r. Bayly President of Magd. Coll. & D^r. Gardiner Warden of All-Souls, as ye Statute directs.

20 **Feb. 20.** One of the Terrae-Filius's Speech at ye Act in Oxon. in the year 1693.

Sed unde hic Poëticus furor ? Τίς ἐβάσκαινε, num ille grandiloquus Nugarum Proclamator Woodroffius? Qui Zenonem, Polemonem, Stratonem, Ciceronem, toties ebuccinat, quorum omnium intelligit neminem. Esto, si hoc sydere sim afflatus. Insanienti erit propitius. Nuper magnificentissimus ille furentium patronus apud nos hospitium mente captorum extruxit, Ipse Principalis. Ibi ego, sicut ille, parce victitans, alte dormiens, sine stragulis, non sine pediculis, multo squalore, nullo sole, cum Græculis esurire possum donec ad me redeam. O Domus antiqua! Quam non dispari dominare Domino. 30 Jure tuo harum laudum Laudum [*sic*] adsis particeps, [1]Etoni ; Tu ei hanc solitudinem tuendam, hanc famem fovendam, in manus tradidisti, splendidissimus harum ruinarum fundator : Te tamen, Woodroffi, innocue furentem dimitto : habeo alium è Coll. Exon. fratrem Polonum. Occurrit ille [2] Evangelij nudus, Collegij nudus, & ô quam vellet ancillam pariter nudam ! Hic iste est Pumi-

---

Feb. 19. Dr. T. Smith to H. Grabe and his position strongly condemned. ' Here is indeed now in towne Mr. Edward Stephens, .. who in his little congregation of daily Communicants, consisting of five or six women, makes use of the first Liturgy of King Edward VI, with some few additions and patches of his owne; and perchance hee is the man with whom Mr. Grabe communicates. However this may be, he is clearly still a Lutheran.' Cf. his grandfather Johannes Behm's *Problemata de coena Domini* (Königsberg, 1614). Has received a scheme or plan of Montfaucon's *Collectio nova Patrum et Scriptorum Graecorum.*

---

[1] Dr. Eaton was principal of Glocester Hall before Dr. Woodrof, but resign'd because his Lodgings were broke open one night, and robb'd by some who had been thought of the House.

[2] This Book call'd the Naked Gospel was burnt, & himself (Dr. Arthur Bury) turn'd out from being Rector of Exoñ College for opposing the Visitor, & other notori[o]us Crimes.

lio, hic, inquam, iste est curcutiunculus qui Terræ-filijs semper terrori esse voluit, & semper fuit ludibrio. Atque jam nunc istum ita contundam, ego istulum ita molam, ego istiunculum ita in nihil redigam, ut post hac despicatui futurus sit nunquam. Adesdum, Arthure, fas sit pro consueta tua modestia quantum possis caput abdere, modo pedem proro(porri)gas. Nondum nævum illum attigimus, quem nemo unquam vidit præter obstetricem, & Susannam à Secretis ministram. O inauditam protervitatem! Quisquamne illis faucibus, illo habitu; tam aridus, tam elumbis, vetus veternosus senex, amplecti, deosculari, amari sese, pedem titillari concupiverit? Bilem plus justo moves, non parcam diutius. Veni sub ungue pulex; crepuit, evanuit, nihil reliqui habet, 10 præter votivam pellem Knick-Knacatorio suspendendam. I would now talk of D^r. Halton: but my Brother has p—t in my Boots, as the Lady did in that D$^{r's}$ last Saturday. Turn over H, then comes I, here is Irish &c. let 'em goe. K. here is only Kennett. We have done with him already. L. then, ay marry L. Now perhaps you may expect Lawyers, but I have got five Physitians for ye, viz. Luff, Lydall, Lasher, Ludwell, & one they alway bring along with them D^r. Lethum [*sic*]. Two of 'em met in a place they fill'd, viz. S^t. Thomas's Church-yard, & talk'd this Dialogue. LUFF. What just come from a Patient Brother Physitian?—LUDW. Not I, all mine lye here. LUFF. I am come from one desperately ill, whom I have given over for the Tooth-Ach. 20 But I have forgot you have chang'd your Trade for a better, and are turn'd Mercer.—LUDW. I don't cast Water now, but Accounts, I write no Bills, but out of my Father's Shop-Book. LUFF. What then you have Books now.— LUDW. Yes, Instead of making Folks bespeak 'em, I there transcribe, Imprimis, Item. LUFF. I believe you seldom write Acquittances to C. C. C.— LUDW. That's no matter, why a Pox did not you buy your Daughter's Wedding Linnen of me?—LUFF. Good Alderman be not so sullen. My Patients take of all your Woollen. *Exeunt.*

Possum multa de tribus cæteris, sed volens nolens, nolens volens, ad Aulam S^{ti} Edmundi feror. Ubi sit Promus, ubi Coquus. Ubi, ubi Principalis. Re- 30 spondit ex adverso D^r. Crosthwaite, D^r. ille irrefragabilis. Hi omnes tanquam proprietates quarto modo unico conveniunt Principali, sed unicus Principalis nullo modo convenit sibi: Quodnam inquam huic pluralistæ nomen, ut Registro Nebulonum in Academia Sarisburiensi inseratur? Respondet honestus Rookius, memini tum cum albis pedibus i. e. nudis è Northumbria una ambularemus fuit Milvus; cum Togam & calceos Taberdarij sumeremus vocatus fuit Millus; cum sociorum privilegium jactaret, (quod mihi nondum Doctori Collegij statuta interdicunt) dici voluit suavissimus Millius, (as ye Learned D^r. Bentley has it) cum pendulus[1] hæsit de juramento fidelitatis, audijt Windamil-

---

[1] 'Tis well known that Dr. Mill has been all along of very wavering unsettled Principles. The university chose him once to be one of their Convocation men; at wch time he acted quite contrary to w^t they expected from him. When the Revolution happen'd & the Prince & Princess of Orange were declar'd K. & Queen he appear'd very zealous for King James, saying that he could not take an oath to them, King James being alive, to whom he ow'd Allegiance as his Soveraign Prince. He offer'd Arguments to several upon this occasion, and writ some Letters into ye North perswading some Clergy men there to stand firm, putting them in mind of ye Doctrines of Passive obedience & non Resistance, wch had such effect that two or three of them (as I have been told) refus'd to take the Oaths, & were depriv'd of their Places & are now living, at least were lately, in a poor condition. At the same time he offer'd Arguments to the Learned & Pious M^r. Dodwell, who lodg'd then in Edm. Hall (because he thought the D^r. had been an Honest Man) upon the same subject. W^{ch} however he needed not have done, M^r. Dodwell having already well consider'd the Matter, & being resolv'd to stand firm to his former Oaths. But notwithstanding all this, when D^r. Mill found he must either take the Oaths to K. W. & Q. M. or loose his Places, & y^t quickly too, he suddenly changes his tone, takes the Oaths, talks mightily against the Non-Jurors (as he does to this day, calling them Fools & I know not w^t) to the great Amazem^t of the university & others, so y^t he was ridicul'd & ye very children

lius, & cum variantes lectiones sui Testamenti ad Apocalypsin perduxerit, erit Millenarius. Sed nunc a Millo ad Hydum, i.e. a Græcia ad Nubiam, infelicem & desertam. He writ a Book in Hebrew of Chess while the Publick Library Books were in pawn for the Printing, tho' by the by he keeps something more publick than the Library, viz. his Wife. I wonder she has not been abroad this Act, but perhaps he has chain'd her up: for the Italian Padlock is wanting out of the Knick Knackatory. He says she sings well. Cætera desunt.

Part of yᵉ other Terræ Filius's Speech the same Act.

10   Causa hujus Convocationis est ut hæ literæ perlegantur, & cætera quæ ad Doctorum contumeliam spectant pro more peragantur. Amico suo ex Procuratori Magistro Kennett viro Insignissimo, Insignificantiss. Mrj White, Audivi nuper a nostro Luffio Professore Regio, non per literas, quas nescit scribere, sed per nuntium fore hoc anno, Dic Lat. an Act. Illius ego Physicam admiror, quantum ille meam Politicam, aut vicinus Dʳ. Eaton ejus Filiam. Si vacat ab impositionibus legendis, respondeas velim quinam sint hac vice Terræ-filij, quos ego, ut jocosus sum, appello Merry-Andrews: quod genus nebulonum nonagesimo nono Politicorum D[i]alogo, volente Coslæo, uberrime confutabo. Ego vehementer obstupesco, quod tu rebus ita turbulentis munere 20 Procuratorio sis amotus, cum magno dolore meo, certe Tuo. Fac si possis, ut nulli sint Terræ-filij, & filiarum mearum hostes nequissimi.

Dabam Shotoveriæ primo die Aprilis.   Tuus non suus.

¹J. T.

Placetne vobis ut hæ Litteræ rejiciantur ?   Placetne vobis Doctorum uxores ?
Ut sit hac vice Terrae-filius?   placeat an non placeat procedam.
Placetne vobis Doctores ?

Quæstio est. An omne magnum ingenium habeat mixturam dementiæ?
Dixit olim Horatius, aut insanit homo, aut versus facit, Præsto adest ille periculosus Juvenis, qui et insanit, & versus facit. En opera Politica Viri² in-
30 cipientis in Theologia quæ extant omnia.

Cantet Jo Pæan, modo tristis cantet Jerne,
Nam Lyra quæ cantet, gessit Hyberne, Leo.

I hope Gentlemen y'l thank me for making English of yᵐ. I am sure he'l thank any one that can make Latin or sense of them.

Let Ireland now no more cry Hitto,   The sense of wᶜʰ is very mystick.
Lyons do things would make an Harp-   Christ Church may prate, but sure no-
   string Jo.   body
This I have thrown you in a Distick   Could do the like but Humphrey Hody.

Now to shew you the Judgment of yᵉ World (for this being somewhat
40 shorter than his Baroccian Controversy is read) I'll give you some verses in Praise of yᵉ Author by his Chum Creech:

in yᵒ streets sung up and down to this purpose, *Wilt thou take the Oaths, little Johny Mill? No, no, that I won't, yes but I will.* To pass by other strange Inconsistencies, When the Occasional Bill was first propos'd. he seem'd mighty glad, & I heard him say that 'twas the best Bill had been brought into yᵉ House a great many years, & wonder'd it had not been done before, since 'twould tend (if it pass'd) so much to yᵒ security of Church & State. But when he found the majority of the Court &c. against it he chang'd his Note, & became a violent Enemy to such as were for yᵉ Passing of it, & he is now one of the Rankest Whiggs (nor can he deny it) in England.

¹ i.e. Jac. Tyrrell.
² Dʳ. Humph. Hody. These verses made by Dʳ. Hody & printed amongst those of the university upon the Death of Queen Mary.

Some think it odd that you a man so tall,
Should write a Work so wonderfully small.
But in my Judgm^t you've contriv'd ye song,
That tho' a Distick, yet 'tis very long:
Besides the Comment too is strangely good.

Because it makes ye sense less under-stood.
Since with two verses you've so well begun
Never, High S^r, neer' let your muse alone,
'Till you arrive at length at making one.

As to this Speech 'tis observable that D^r. Hanes, who was chiefly concern'd in making the Reflections upon D^r. Luff afterwards married his Daughter the Widow Bull, for ye filthy Lucre of her Money, he using her very barbarously as he did a former Wife whom 'tis said he kill'd with his unkindness. And 'tis to be fear'd that this will not hold out long with such usage as he gives her. — M^r. Urry of X^t Church shew'd me this Afternoon a Book containing several pieces, in folio ; wch he purchas'd at an Auction, amongst wch is Julius Firmicus, with some MSS^t Notes of Jos. Scaliger, & Manilius printed at Bas. 1531. by Hervagius, with MSS^t notes, from printed Books & MSS^{ts}. 'Twas M^r. Creeche's Book as appears by his Name at ye End, where he has given a memorandum y^t he transcrib'd ye said Notes himself from another Copy printed at Basil & now in the Publick Library, being one of those given there by S^r. Edw. Sherburne.

Feb. 21 (Th.). M^r. Sawbridge the Bookseller is found guilty of Reprinting the Memorial of ye Church of England with a pretended Answer, & M^r. Pittis is also found guilty of Writing ye said Answer. — The Queen's Birth-Day being the 6th Instant, wch was Ashwednesday, it was kept at Court ye Day before. But 'tis observable that D^r. Mill made Illuminations upon his Grand Fast Day, tho' he did not see or hear of anyone in Oxford that did it beside, all but he being very sensible that all Acts of Rejoycing ought to be laid aside at such a time, & to be observ'd either the day before or After, the Rubrick of our Liturgy so directing in these Cases. — 'Tis said that D^r. Hanns was ye Son of a Basket-Maker, and y^t when he had arriv'd to a little Eminency in his Profession, he would not own his Father, nor suffer him to come near him. — Casp. Barthius had a MS^t of Martial, wch tho' writ on very bad Paper, yet was very valuable, & would be of excell^t use in a new Ed. of y^t Author. See Barthius's Notes to Papin. Statius, Vol. 2. p. 368.

Feb. 22 (Fri.). There is a Paper I long to send you but I cannot yet get it. 'Tis Princess Sophia's Letter to ye AB^p., wch is short, & I have read it; & a letter under ye Name of S^r. Rowland Gwin to my L^d. Stamford, wch is very long, & therefore ye Company would not let it be read. It contains ye sense of ye Court of Hannover of our Whiggs opposing ye Princesses being sent for & 'tis said to be a very shrewd Paper. It seems to be printed in Germany, by the Letter, ye spelling & ye Paper ; & I believe there are none in England but w^t were sent over in Covers by ye Post, for I heard of but that one wch I saw. I suppose care will be taken to print them here.—This out of a Letter from D^r. de Laune to D^r. Charlett.

— As M^r. Barcham was the Original Author of the Heraldry wch goes under Guillim's name, & therefore the first Edition ought, as to ye greatest & best Part to be ascribed to him, so also the material Improvements in ye second Edition are mostly owing to S^r. Richard St.

John, Clarenceaux, as M^r. Guillim himself insinuates in one Part of it.
— In Mich. Pocciantius's Catalogue of Florentine Writers, pr. at
Florence 1589. 4°, pag. 65. is an Acc^t of Francis Puccius, but he tells
his Pieces wch he writ were not publish'd.   Multa ex proprio ingenio
elaboravit, & metro, & prosa & nonnulla è Græco turbine convertit quæ
cum ad libitum perpolire non valuisset in hominum manus pervenire non
permisit.   Tell D^r. Smith of this. — Memorandum that the Church of
Shottesbrooke in Berks is mention'd in ye old Valor Beneficiorum in y^e
Publick Library, made in ye Reign of Edw. 1st, wch shews that there
10 was a Church here before Edw. 3^ds time when the College was founded,
& that 'twas not built first by S^r. Will. Trussell as is insinuated by
M^r. Ashmole. — On the 29th of Jan. last was admitted a Student in
ye Publick Library John Disney of the City of Lincoln.   He brought
with him a Letter to D^r. Hudson from D^r. Inett, signifying that he is a
Man of a good Estate, studious, a lover of Books & of some Curiosity, &
came to Oxford on purpose to consult some Books in order to some
Publick Design.   He went out of Town again this Morning.   The
said Publick Design is a Genealogical Table of the Princes of Europe.
He seems to be a man of tolerable Parts & to have a genius to
20 Heraldry; but his Friends being Presbyterians, & himself educated in
that Perswasion, notwithstanding his being now, as appears by his
Discourse & frequenting the Church, of a contrary opinion, yet he still
retains many of their ill Qualities, as being pert, affected, proud &c.
Besides having not been bred up in any university, nor acquir'd much
Learning, he does not seem qualified for any Work proper for a Scholar.
I saw two or three of his Tables, neatly drawn by himself, wch however
I am afraid will not please men of Accuracy in these Studies, who are
very sensible that all things of this Nature should be thoroughly consider'd, confirm'd by undoubted Authority drawn from the most Au-
30 thentick Rolls, Registers &c. wch a private Man cannot command, nor
indeed any one else in a Work so extensive.   For wch Reason 'twere
far better he would imploy himself in illustrating the Antiquities of his
own Country, wch would be a Work of good use and deserve Encouragement but as I observ'd before he has not Learning enough for
such an undertaking.   He went yesterday to X^t Church to take a
Transcript of the Table of the Princes Palatine of the Rhine (wch I told
him of) but having not time, he took but part of it.

Feb. 23 (Sat.). [Notes from Morellus on Constantine Porphyrog. de The-
matibus, Heinsius and Gudius on Phaedrus.]
40   Burmannus's Edition of Phaedrus to be consulted for Justin's History.

D^r. Mayow of All Souls College was a very ingenious Man, & an
Excellent Scholar; but by resolving to marry a Wife of a Great Fortune
fatally miscarried to his unspeakable and insuperable Grief.   For when
he was one Year at ye Bath, and happening to lodge at ye same House
with an Irish Lady and her Daughter, as was pretended, who went for
vast Fortunes, when ye old Lady feigning an occasion went to London,
he courted the young one and quickly married her: but she proving
nothing like ye Fortune y^t he imagin'd he was so confounded with it
y^t he did not long enjoy his Life.   He had a Brother Student of X^t
50 Church who married a Daughter of M^r. Jackson's of the Vent near

Forrest-Hill ab^t four miles from Oxford. — D^r. Tyndall Fellow of All Soul's Coll. (Quære whether originally of Linc. Coll. & D^r. Hicks's Pupill as some have s^d?) tho' he was a Clergy Man's Son, & liv'd upon a Clergyman's Bread (viz. Archb^p. Chichley's) yet has always been observ'd to be very violent ag^t ye Church & Church men.   He has been a most notorious ill Liver (Register'd as 'tis said or deserving to be soe at All Soul's under ye Title of Egregious ——) & in King James's time turn'd Papist, purely in hopes to ingratiate himself wth ye Roman Catholicks & get Preferm^t.   Immediately upon ye Revolution he grew a mighty Williamite (renouncing his Religion, if he had any) & writ something ab^t Government &c.   And as an Instance that 'twas believ'd he had little or no Religion take this following Epitaph,

Here lies D^r. Tyndall whom Interest ut fertur
Not Zeal for Religion has made a Deserter.
*   *   *   *   *   *

But now y^t y^o Knave is as rotten as pelf
pray for his Soul who ner'e pray'd for't himself.

— Quære of M^r. Dodwell whether Heathens, (such as had no opportunity of coming to ye Knowledge of X^t,) are not lyable to Punishm^t after Death?   Because 'tis said, and he owns it in his new Book ab^t ye Soul, y^t ye condition of Tyre & Sidon, nay even of Sodom (People who never could be suppos'd to hear of Jesus X^t) will be more tolerable at ye Day of Judgm^t y^n that of Chorazin, Bethsaida & Capernaum, who heard ye Preaching of our Saviour.   From ye word tolerable it may be inferr'd they had some punishm^t alotted.   He has satisfied this Question in §. 36. of the Book.

[Notes on Livy from Ravennas Anonymus Geographus (Paris: ed. Porcheron) and Casaubon's notes on Polyaenus.] . . .

D^r. De Laune who has printed a 30th of January Sermon before ye House of Commons, was always observ'd to be a good Companion, & one who understood Eating and Drinking very nicely, & much better than any part of Learning belonging to his Profession.   But more of him hereafter. — M^r. Lowthe of S^t. John's College has written a Book ab^t ye Inspiration of the Holy Penmen in Answer to some Letters printed in Holland.   In wch Performance he has not answer'd the Expectation he had rais'd, being not near so well done as another Answer by a French-Man, y^t came out after his. — M^r. Leigh likewise of ye same College has printed a Book of Devotions in Latin in a small 8vo.   He was usually styl'd Rabbi Leigh, for some Knowledge that he had in ye oriental Tongues. — D^r. Thomas Wood of New Coll. first apply'd himself to ye Civil Law & ye Practise of it in ye Vice-Chancellors Court.   Afterw^{ds} he study'd ye common Law & was call'd to ye Bar.   But both these Imployments he did not think so advantageous to him as a good College Living, upon ye Prospect of wch he left these Professions & took Holy Orders, & afterwards was presented to a noble College Living in Bucks. & little afterwards to a Wife, one M^{rs}. Barker, a Founder's Kinswoman.

Feb. 24 (Sun.).   D^r. Mill told me last Night, that talking sometime since with the Bishop of Worcester, he was pleas'd to say that he thought M^r. Dodwells Arguments about the Spuriousness of Sanchoniathon's History, in his Discourse upon that Subject, were very weak, & yᵗ he had enough to say to prove it genuine. And he likewise declar'd that tho' Mʳ. Dodwell's Arguments were cogent, yet he thought it far better to hold it genuine; since 'twould do mischief to endeavour to overthrow an opinion wᶜʰ has been embrac'd for so many Years.

Feb. 25 (Mon.). Memorandum yᵗ Sʳ. Andrew Fountaine gave 4 Curious Prints to yᵉ Publick Library viz. (1) Parmigiano, a wooden print at Mantoua 1610. (2) Another Parmigiano, a wooden Print also. (3) Raphael, a Wooden Print. (4) Raphael by Marc. Antonio, Copper.
10 — See Joseph Scaliger's Notes upon Ausonius Lib. II. c. 27. where is a Distich of Verses of Pliny Junior's. — Memorandum That yᵉ first Sermon Mʳ. Tho. Milles of Xᵗ Church (then of Edm. Hall) preach'd at Sᵗ. Marie's in Oxoñ before the University was about 7 or 8 years ago on these Words, *He that cometh to God must believe that he is.* The Subject being Providence, he spoke very affectedly, & made a Discourse more fit for one yᵗ reads a Lecture for his Degrees in Physick than a Divine, the greatest part of it being about the animal Part of yᵉ Creation, particularly Man, in describing whom he touch'd upon every Part as far as he could in modesty in the same Manner as Dʳ. Gibson
20 has handled him in his Abridgment of Anatomy, wᶜʰ Mʳ. Milles had just read before. This made yᵉ Congregation smile, & he was ever after taken for a vain, affected Person. — Concerning Livy's Monument at Padua see Stephanus Zamosius's Analecta Lapidum vetustorum. *Patavij* 1593. 8⁰. p. 29.

Feb. 26 (Tu.). Mʳ. Dodwell has Dedicated his New Book about yᵉ Soul to The Honᵇˡᵉ Charles Hatton Esqʳ. commonly call'd Captain Hatton, a Man of good Parts, & no mean Learning. He is withall well acquainted with yᵉ World, of a pleasant Temper, & a tender Conscience, & is now a Sufferer for being a Non-Juror.

30 **Feb. 27 (Wed.).** Ask Mʳ. Dodwell whether those Heathens who had no opportunitys of Hearing yᵉ Gospel are not to be punished or rewarded after Death, according as they have neglected or kept the Law of Nature? — Laurence Pignorius in his XXVIII. Symbolic Epistle has a very good Observation upon Justin, wᶜʰ must be consider'd in a new Edit. of yᵗ Author. His XLIVᵗʰ Epistle is wholly in Defence of Livy against Benius. Wᶜʰ will be of use either in writing the Life of Livy, or in a Preface to a new Edition. — Livy in his XXXIV Book c. 17. does not distinguish yᵉ Turduli from yᵉ Turdetani (for wᶜʰ reason Sigonius reads Turdetani in both places, yet contradicted by Gronovius)
40 just as they are also confounded by Strabo. But they are made two different People by Polybius, quoted by Strabo, and Stephanus Byz. who, according to yᵉ Opinion of Artemidorus calls them Τούρτους, καὶ Τυρτάνους. Wᶜʰ Difference is also observed by Ptolemy. See Ludovicus

---

Feb. 26. E. Smith to H. Can't get a copy of 'that piece of Livy of Horrion's edition. You may believe it not to be found in Shops, when Bateman's and Brown's equivalent to all yᵉ rest in those scarce commodities afford it not.' Mr. de Seau is preparing an edition of Lucian, and Grabe printing a vindication of the passage in Josephus about our Saviour. Locke upon 2 Cor. and various posthumous pieces to be published by Churchill.

Nonius's Hispania, c. viii. p. 29. — Barthius in his Notes upon Statius, p. 1694, tells us, that he writ a Discourse about the Latin Poëts who had written upon Love: also that he made an Index to Appulejus, drew up Notes upon Tertullian, & other Authors, some of which were unfortunately burnt. Quære whether any printed?

Feb. 28 (Th.). This Morning preach'd before ye Judges at S^t. Marie's M^r. Crank of Trinity College, upon Psalm xxix. 2. *Give unto ye Lord the Glory due unto his Name.*

Having by Way of Preface explain'd the Words, & hinted what a Melancholy and lamentable Thing it is to have Religion ridicul'd, and it's Professors 10 laugh'd and scoff'd at, and oftentimes insulted, as Men of no Worth nor use, he proceeded to consider first the Duty & secondly the Motives to it. As to the former he shew'd that the Duty of Honouring God consists first in a Due Reverence of his Holy Name, & never to take it in our Mouths but with all Aw and Respect, contrary to ye Manner of those who think it a piece of good Breeding to swear and curse upon every Trifling Occasion, wch being freq^{tly} us'd makes Oaths y^t are lawfull disregarded, & not observ'd with that Religion & Caution as is requisite. (2) The Honouring God consists in a constant frequenting Religious Assemblies, & a carefull Observance of His Holy Sabbath, & other solemn times of Devotion. (3) A Due Esteem of his Ministers and Vice- 20 Gerents. This being dispatch'd he proceeded to ye motives to this Duty taken (1) from it's being the most proper way of Doing God Service. (2) 'Tis the best way we can take to shew our Gratitude. (3) The Rewards are inestimable. In speaking on wch last he pass'd a Complement on ye Queen, Duke of Marlborough &c. & observ'd that since her Majesty shew'd so much Zeal for and Care of ye Church, & was assisted by others with ye same Vigour and Resolution, & since his Grace & our other Generals had such unexpected Success in ye Field, the Mischiefs y^t come upon the Nation must proceed from our own Breasts, & be attributed to a loose & negligent Practise of Religious Duties, wch if persisted in in opposition to those Methods wch are provided 30 for putting a stop to it, we must expect, besides the Punishments of this Life, Everlasting Destruction in ye World to come. —

I am inform'd that M^r. Hugh Hutchin, who publish'd the 2^d Apology of Justin Martyr, and has some Translations of Verses in the English Edition of M^r. Potter's Antiquities of Greece, sometime since began an Edition of Polybius, being put upon it by his Great Friend, the most Worthy D^r. Aldrich Dean of X^t Church, of wch Place M^r. Hutchin is now one of ye Chaplains; but y^t he has laid aside this Noble Design, & is commonly call'd Pol Hutchin. He is for this Year one of ye Pro-Proctors of ye University. He was originally of Lincoln College, where, 40 when Bachelor of Arts, I suppose upon Advice of M^r. Potter, he began, with M^r. Dechair of the same House, a new Edition of Hermogenes; but not finding anyone that would undertake ye Impression, 'twas laid by, & the Collections have been since communicated by M^r. Hutchin (who is a good natur'd Man, of quick Parts, & proportionable Learning, and for that Reason made Master of ye Grammar Schoole at Christ Ch. upon the Removal of M^r. Rob. Cock) to D^r. Hudson, who if other more important Studies do not hinder, and he finds suitable Encouragement, will take care to oblige the World with a beautifull and correct Edition. — M^r. Sam. Philips lately of S^t. John's College has publish'd Miscel- 50 lanea Sacra, a Collection of Poems by several Hands, amongst wch some of his own. He has likewise done some other small trite Things, amongst wch is The Poetical Courant. He is a man of tolerable Parts, but laying them out upon Trifles, he is laugh'd at by his Acquaintance & gets no Reputation unless amongst frequenters of ye Play-House, and others of that Gang.

Mar. 1 (Fri.). M^r. Milles in his Dedication of S^t. Cyrill to the Earle of Pembrooke has committed a very gross Blunder making *infucata pietas* signifying sincere Piety, wch is always us'd in a contrary sense.

Mar. 2 (Sat.). The Privy Council met at Edinburgh the 21st of the last Month, but did no publick Business, only order'd that no Episcopal Clergy man, be he qualified or not, be allow'd to preach in any Parochial Church or Meeting House. Upon wch a great many Meeting Houses are shut up, and M^r. Mathers is discharg'd from preaching any more at S^t. Andrews, tho' he is legally qualified by having taken ye oaths, & was one of the first of Scotland y^t congratulated the Queen's Accession to ye Throne. From whence may be gather'd w^t a good natur'd thing Presbyterian Moderation is. — M^r. Dodwell makes the Air the Receptacle of all Souls good and bad, and that they are under the Power of the Devil, 'till the Day of Judgment, he being the Prince of the Air. Not that he can inflict any Pains upon the Souls of really good men, but only some Disquietudes & Molestations, wherein they may be relieved by ye Prayers of ye Living according to ye Opinion of Justin Martyr. And that's the reason, without doubt, of M^r. Thornedike's being for Prayers for ye Dead. See M^r. Dodwell pag. 258. He makes in p. 262 the lowest Region of Heaven, y^t is the space betw. Earth and the Clouds, the place of the less perfectly good Souls, where they are to remain till the Resurrection, and have some Punishments inflicted on them by ye Devils, to purge & qualify them for ye upper Region. — M^r. Wood in Athenæ Oxon. Vol. II. p. 878. having made M^r. Charles Allestree Vicar of Great Budworth in Cheshire, he afterwards talking with M^r. Collins, Master of Magd. Coll. Schoole, call'd M^r. Wood his Patron, because of his making him Vicar of a Place he was not Vicar of: wch M^r. Collins mentioning to M^r. Wood, he smil'd, & protested y^t he had put down nothing in that Book but w^t he had Authority for, and that if there were any Falsities in it his Informers ought to be blam'd. — [1] I am inform'd by a Person, who was formerly one of the Church Wardens of S^t. Peter's in ye East Oxoñ that in the Parish Chest in ye Church is the Transcript of a Book made in ye Year 1314, wherein 'tis recorded that ye said Church was repair'd at y^t time, & that fourscore Nobles were paid for the Repair, half of wch the Parish charg'd upon Wolvercot as being a Chapel of Ease to it. But ye Inhabitants of that place being displeas'd at it, the Matter was referr'd to ye Pope, who order'd it to be decided at Canterbury. The Result was that Wolvercot should not pay any of this Money, but for the future be a Parochial Church of itself, & pay to S^t. Peter's 10 Groats per Annum, wch it continues to do to this day.

[1] 1710. Oct. 15. I have since got a Transcript of this Book, & it appears to have been in the year 1416, & the sum for Repayr was not so much as here expressed, & Wolvercot was to pay the 3^d part, & as formerly were for the future always to pay the 3^d part on such occasions, however they came to composition afterwards when it became a parochial Church.

Mar. 3 (Sun.). Last Week M^r. Nicholson of University College was denied his Degree of Bachelor of Law, 3 times, notwithstanding his Letter from ye Chancellor pass'd in Convocation that ye Terms he had kept at Dublin might be equivalent to his having kept them here. The reason I hear deliver'd in to ye Vice-Chancellor was his not being matriculated ; but this I am inform'd since is false, & I believe there is something else, otherwise (there being no reason offer'd the next Congregation as ought to have been by statute) he would have been presented after this Denyal. He is Son to ye same Nicholson who has writ a Dialogue between ye Body and Soul, lately printed & recommended to 10 ye World by the Learned M^r. Dodwell, whose Estate in Ireland is look'd after by ye s^d Nicholson.

Mar. 4 (Mon.). On Friday last ye Convocation met, at wch time the Lower-House read a Letter to them from ye Queen willing and commanding them to be obedient to ye Archb^p. & his Suffragan B^ps. in relation to his Adjourning them from time to time. — The House of Commons having address'd her Majesty that she would prefer M^r. Goddard their Chaplain, she has answer'd y^m that she will do it, as soon as she shall see it proper. — M^r. Tho: Lydiatt of New-College was a Person of that singular Modesty, Humility & Learning, that by many 20 great Judges he was reckon'd to excell Joseph Scaliger, one of ye most Considerable Men these last Ages have produc'd. Yet for all this being ingag'd for ye Debts of a near Relation, and having but mean Preferment, he was reduc'd to y^t Extremity that he was forc'd to lye in Prison a great many years in Oxford and the King's Bench. All wch time he was observ'd to be chearfull, and to carry on his Studies wth the utmost diligence, being so intirely addicted to them that he laid out w^t Money he got upon Books, so that he was in a manner starv'd to death : wch made D^r. Potter, when he sent him a Benevolence of 5 lib^s., give him a strict charge to spend none of it in Books, but take care to get what 30 might recruit his macerated Body. M^r. Fuller also ye most eminent Critick had very little to support an ingenious Man. The like also is to be said of M^r. Hales of Eaton (whom all allow to have been in a manner starv'd) wch hath made divers Forreigners say that England is not worthy to have Learned Men ; tho' 'tis generally observ'd by them (particularly I have heard M^r. Grabe say it) that no Country brings forth so great a Number of Men of that quick Apprehension and solid Judgment as England doth, tho' not always attended with so much Diligence as in other Countries.

Mar. 5 (Tu.). Her Maj^s. Letter to ye Archb^p. of Cant. [on differences 40 in Convocation, dated Feb. 25, 1706]. . . . — Books to be consulted for Livy, (1) Robert Whitynton de veterum Romanorum Magistratibus, pr.

March 3. H. to Dr. T. Smith. Thanks for account of Scotch Liturgy, which proves that Grabe is highly to blame. Bryan Twyne and the charge of appropriating Allen's work. Various literary intelligence about Dutch Scholars. Has received Dodwell on the Soul ; it contains some notions which are singular and will do some mischief. Has printed the fragment from Vettius Valens. Hudson is recovering from fever. An account of Fr. Puccius in Mich. Pocciantius' Catal. of Florentine Writers (Florence, 1589, 4to.), p. 65.

at Lond. 1514. 4⁰. (2) Humph. Lhuyd de Armamentario Romano, pr. at yᵉ End of Sʳ. J. Prise's Historiæ Britannicæ Defensio. Lond. 1573. 4⁰. (3) Tillesley's Animad. on Selden's H. of Tyths. (4) Some of Sʳ. Hen. Savile's pieces. (5) Edmonds upon Cæsar's Comm. — Dʳ. Wallis was a Man of most admirable fine Parts, & great Industry, whereby in some years he became so noted for his profound Skill in Mathematicks, to wᶜʰ he was naturally inclin'd, that he was deservedly accounted the greatest Person in that Profession of any in his time. He was withall a good Divine, & no mean Critik in yᵉ Greek and Latin Tongues.
10 But notwithstanding his being so Excellent a Mathematician, he was but an indifferent Chronologer, as Mʳ. Dodwell has above once hinted, in relation to what he has done yᵗ way at yᵉ End of Bᴘ. Fell's Edition of Sᵗ. Cyprian. He was originally of Emanuel College in Cambridge & coming to Oxford was soon taken notice of as a Man of revolution Principles, wᶜʰ he sufficiently made appear by his decyphering the King's Cabinet, wᶜʰ Worthy Work is preserv'd in a quarto Book in the Bodlejan Library. Oliver had a great Respect for him, & by yᵗ means he got to be custos Archivorum in opposition to yᵗ Great Civilian Dʳ. Zouch. It must however be acknowledg'd that wᵗʰ his other Learning
20 he had good Skill also in the Civil Law, as appears from divers Specimens of it in the School Tower. And 'tis frequently said that he would plead as well as most Men; wᶜʰ can hardly be doubted if it be consider'd that he had an extraordinary knack of Sophistical Evasion, wᶜʰ made the Oxford Antiquary say he could make black white & white black when he pleas'd, a shrewd Instance of wᶜʰ he had experience of himself. His Works wᶜʰ are printed at yᵉ Theatre-Press alltogether in 3 Folios, are much made use of by men, who are Mathematically inclin'd, & I am told by one, who should know, yᵗ Mʳ. Keil's Lectures are in great measure extracted from them. (But Quære?) His Sight con-
30 tinu'd strong to yᵉ last (tho' 87 years old when he died) so that he could read yᵉ least Characters, printed or written, without yᵉ Help of Spectacles. Some time before his Death his Picture drawn to yᵉ Life was put in the School Gallery, adjoyning to yᵉ Publick Library, wᶜʰ the Dʳ. was so vain as to come on purpose to see, as he did his Books after they were put in yᵉ Library, & seem'd very well pleas'd with their Placing. — Justin corrected by Sʳ. John Prise in Hist. Brit. Defens. p. 98. — ... Mʳ. Joh. Pricket Butler of University Col.'s Grandfather Rich. Pricket, & Rich. Pricket his Eldest, & Hugh Pricket his second Son, liv'd so long that the full Sum of their Age made 312 Years, & 'tis
40 remarkable that they all enjoy'd, wᵗʰout Sickness, a continu'd course of Health. The said Mʳ. Pricket of University College, youngest Son to yᵉ sᵈ Rich. Pricket is now 3 score & six very vigorous, & is like to live as long if not longer yⁿ either of yᵐ.

[Note on Livy XXXVIII. 34 from Boecleri Notae ad Vell. p. 32.] ...

March 6 (Wed.). Mʳ. Timothy Nourse, formerly Fellow of University College, was a Gentleman of Excellent Parts as appears from the Books he has written. He was also a man of great Probity, & eminent Virtues, & for yᵗ reason continu'd Bourser of yᵉ College several years together, all wᶜʰ time he made it a considerable Part of his Business to rectify the Accounts & put a Stop to those Abuses w^(ch) had happen'd from ye scandalous Negligence of some of his Predecessors in y^t Office. W^(ch) he perform'd so effectually, y^t he is often mention'd w^(th) great Veneration among the Society to this day. He afterwards liv'd in Worcestershire, & to his other Accomplishments added this also of being a curious Collector of Antient Coyns & Medals, w^(ch) at his Death (w^(ch) was untimely to ye no small Reluctance of good Men) he bequeath'd to ye Publick Library at Oxford, where they now remain, & are some of the fairest and most valuable in the whole Collection. That part of his Will relating to this Donation I have given in one of the foregoing 10 volumes of these Memoires. — Ask D^r. Hudson whether he be any ways related to ye most Loyal D^r. Mich. Hudson who was barbarously murderd by the Hellish Rebells in 1648? He tells me he is of the same Family, as also was Hudson, from whence the name of Hudson's Bay. — Verses writ by way of Letter betw. D^r. Charlett & M^r. Percival Student of X^t Church. . . . These Verses have been since printed. — Books to be consulted for Livy. . . .

March 7 (Th.). A Bill to prevent ye farther Growth of Popery having been brought into ye House of Commons, (occasion'd by certain Complaints of ye B^p. of Chester, & some of ye Clergy of his Diocess, of ye 20 Insolencies of the Papists in Lancashire, in proselyteing several People, Erecting a Stately Edifice &c.) when it came to be read a 3^d time it was rejected by a Great majority, there being but 43 for it & 119 against it. 'Tis said the Chief Reason of it's being dropt is because of ye Queen's being in Allyance with Popish Princes. — M^r. Hoffman tells me that one Beneditti an Abbat in London, where he has liv'd about six Years, has the Impressions in Wax of all the Curious Medals, Coyns, Gemms, &c. in ye Cabbinett of the King of France, amongst w^(ch) he says are several w^(ch) would serve very much to illustrate and explain some Passages in Livy, particularly one about ye Bachanalian Rites. 30 The said Abbat was born at Lucca, and has a good Collection of these curiosities himself, w^(ch) he is willing to sell, but values them at 5 or 600 Guineas. Ask D^r. Smith whether he knows him, & what his Character is. Hoffman tells me he din'd with him every day almost all ye time he was in London (w^(ch) was about 5 months) that he is a good devout Man, but he will not discover where he lives. — Ask also D^r. Smith, or some body else who may be suppos'd to know, what Hoffman's Principles are? the rather, because tho' he lodges in our Hall, yet he does not come to Prayers, tho' when he first came thither about 6 or 7 months since he came to them 2 or three times. 40

An Account of ye intended Edition of Livy.

1. 'Tis design'd to be in a handsome 8°. (such as we commonly use) on good Paper and good Letter in 4 or 5 Volumes.
2. The Chronology will be plac'd at ye Top of every Page, and in other Parts of it as occasion will require.
3. At ye Bottom of the Page will be Readings of MSS. never before collated, Conjectures and Emendations of Learned Men (in a great Number) not yet taken Notice of in any Edition whatsoever, together with select Readings, Corrections and Illustrations that are in other Editions, but with ye greatest Brevity imaginable. 50
4. At ye End of every Volume (or in the last) will be such larger Annotations

& Explications as could not conveniently be put under yᵉ Text, & then will follow

5. Such Ancient Inscriptions & Coyns as may serve to illustrate several Places in yᵉ Author.

Lastly, There will be accurate Indexes; & perhaps two or three Maps.

The whole's intended to be with yᵉ utmost Exactness & Accuracy, as well as Beauty; in order to recommend it to yᵗ Youth of our Nation and others.

Mr. Wase of Q. Coll. in Cambridge (the same whom I have mention'd before) designs shortly to send Diodorus Siculus to yᵉ Press.
10 He has a Sallust in yᵉ Press wᶜʰ has stuck there these two years. He is also for printing a Catalogue of all printed Books in yᵉ Libraries at Cambridge. Wᶜʰ shows that he is a Man of no fixt Resolution, but is more for carrying on new Projects than finishing what he has in Hand. — Mr. Davies's Edition of Cæsar's Comm. in 112 Sheets just finish'd. — Sr. Isaac Newton's Body of Algebra to be finish'd in a fortnight's time. — Mr. Needham has prepar'd Hierocles for yᵉ Press. Mr. Piers of Eman. College (who publish'd two Tragedies of Euripides) is going to print Dion X'tome, a specimen of wᶜʰ will be done speedily. He has divers MSS. Readings & conjectures not printed from a Copy in Selden's
20 Library, communicated to him by Mr. Grabe. — Mr. Thomas Tanner, (to whom Mr. Ant. à Wood at yᵉ Repeated Importunity of Dr. Charlett left his Papers) getting Acquaintance with yᵉ Bᵖ of Norwich upon Account of his Library, was drawn in to marry a short fat, plump Daughter of yᵉ Bᵖ's., & had yᵉ Chancellor-ship of Norwich conferr'd upon him by yᵉ Bᵖ. a little before or a little after his Marriage. This Wife & Preferment together with his Intimacy wᵗʰ yᵉ low Church Party have put a stop (as 'tis believ'd) to the Publication of yᵉ 3ᵈ Volume of Mr. Wood's Athenæ, wᶜʰ Mr. Tanner has. He was originally a Clark of Queen's College, & apply'd himself to yᵉ study of Dugdale's Mo-
30 nasticon & other Books of English Antiquities, & when Bachellor of Arts publish'd Notitia Monastica 8º. for yᵉ Dedication of wᶜʰ to yᵉ Honᵇˡᵉ Leopold Wᵐ. Finch then Warden of All-Souls, he had by the Interest of yᵉ said Warden a Chaplain's Place conferr'd on him in All-Souls Colledge & afterwards was made Fellow of yᵉ same. The said Dr. Finch was a Younger Son to yᵉ Famous Earl of Winchelsea, who had been in King Charles the 2ᵈ's time Embassador to Constantinople, where or in Germany this Dr. Finch was born, & had for his Godfathers Leopold the Emperor & William Nassau Prince of Orange & at length (by the greatest Injustice in yᵉ World) King of
40 England. He was educated a noble-Man in Xᵗ Church, whence he was Elected Fellow of All-Souls. He was a Man of Excellᵗ Parts, as appear'd from his Conversation and all his Performances. When Bachelor of Arts he made a Handsome Dedication of Cornelius Nepos (translated into English by several Hands of this Univers.) to yᵉ Earl of Abbingdon. When Master of Arts & in orders he us'd to preach very neatly. He printed one Sermon preach'd before yᵉ Convocation, & made not long before he died when he labour'd under a great Indisposition of Body. He married a West-Country Gentlewoman of a good Fortune, but had no Issue by her. He was made Warden of
50 All-Souls by K. James, perhaps upon Consideration of his being Captain of a Company of young Scholars who were rais'd by yᵉ Uni-

versity in yᵉ Time of Monmouth's Rebellion. At that time there were 4 Companies of Scholars train'd & fitted for service by the Loyal University, in one of wᶜʰ, that was exercis'd & train'd at New-College, Dʳ. Hudson, then an Inceptor in Arts, bore a Musquet, to serve his King & country.

VOL. IX.

March 8. 1706 (Fri.). Yesterday came on yᵉ Election for a Fellow of University College, in room of Mʳ. Smith, who resign'd some time since as I have before hinted. Candidates were five, one of wᶜʰ, namely Mʳ. Ellison, was of Linc. College, & seem'd to have a plausible Pretence, 10 as being qualified as to the Place of his Nativity. But yᵉ Fellows having examin'd them, & sifted their Characters, they unanimously pitch'd upon Mʳ. Hodgson, Bach. of Arts, & of about 10 years standing, who for some time has been in Sir Wᵐ. Glynn's Family at Amersden, on purpose to instruct his Son, now a Gent. Commoner of All Souls Col., wᶜʰ he did with so much Satisfaction, that he has gain'd a good Reputation there, and Sʳ. Wᵐ. seem'd mightily concern'd for his Carrying this Place. He is a person well skill'd in Greek and Latin (as appear'd from his Performance when examin'd) and may be a Credit to the College, if he please, being of a Strong Body, and able to go thro' some 20 laudable Undertaking. Mʳ. Smith his Predecessor has been all along a severe Student, & is well skill'd in our English Antiquities, particularly those relating to Oxford; but his great unhappiness is that he cannot express himself well. However his Collections, wᶜʰ are judg'd to be large, will be of great use if they happen to come into skillfull Hands, & may be of yᵉ same Service Mʳ. Dodsworth's have been, who spent his whole Life time in Collecting; & it must be acknowledg'd that wᵗ he did that way is prodigious, his MSSᵗˢ wᶜʰ are in the Bodlejan Library being reckon'd an inestimable Treasure, & have set up several Persons for Antiquaries, especially Dʳ. Kennett, who look'd them all 30 over, & took from them most of the Materials in his printed Books. 'Twas from them also that yᵉ Monasticon Anglicanum was chiefly taken, & therefore the chief Honour of yᵗ Work ought to be given to him, Sʳ. Wᵐ. Dugdale being no farther concern'd than in digesting some of yᵉ Papers, and looking after yᵉ Press.

March 9 (Sat.). In the 9ᵗʰ Table of Saxon Coyns publish'd by Sʳ. Andrew Fountaine is one wᶜʰ has on one side *Plegmund. Archiep.* & on yᵉ other *Eicmund. Mo.* The same is publish'd by Mʳ. Selden in p. 217 of his Notes to Eadmer, more exactly as it seems than Sʳ. Andrew has done, who nevertheless does not seem to have seen yᵉ Coyn himself, 40 quoting Mʳ. Walker for it. For *Archiep.* Sʳ. Andrew has *Achiep.* — Mʳ. Camden tells us that the Royal Palace at Woodstock, commonly call'd The Mannor-House, was a most Magnificent Structure. wᶜʰ

March 8. E. Thwaites to H. Asks for a draught of the ancient figures of the Planets from Dufresne's Lexicon; 'a dispute about Semeiography causes you this trouble.' Messages to friends.

sufficiently appears from the stately Reliques now to be seen, wch shew
that 'twas much larger than the Palace now erecting for the Duke of
Marlborough. Twas first built by King Hen. I. who made ye Park,
and afterwards augmented by King Hen. II. with an Addition of a
strange Labyrinth wherein he kept his Concubine Rosamund Clifford,
as is related by Brompton in his Chronicle. There are no [1]Remains
of it now, but it seems to have been some where on the north side
of that Part of the Mannor now standing, perhaps just by the Spring
call'd Rosamund's Well, but as to the story of her being Poyson'd by
Eleanor, Wife to King Henry, who got to her by a Clue of Thread,
it seems to be a meer Fiction, & to have no Foundation, our Historians
being wholly silent about it. But tho' the old Palace might exceed y^e
New one, yet there were no such Gardens, as are now design'd to be,
wch from w^t is already done seem to be very extraordinary, & to exceed
any thing of y^t nature in England. The Walls round are already built,
but they must be pull'd down again, the stone being faulty & crumbling
to pieces. He that shall attempt the perfecting Sir Hen. Spelman's
History of Sacrilege must not forget this place, the Park whereof caus'd
the Destruction of several Churches, & the Palace with the Chapel
there was strangeley abus'd by the Rebells in the Civil Wars. Let him
observe also the Consequences if the Mannor House be wholly destroy'd,
as 'tis said it will: also w^t Success the Duke or His Heirs will have in
the Projects here. — D^r. Geo. Royse who has publish'd some Sermons,
was originally of Edm. Hall, where he was Servitor to D^r. Tho. Tully
then Principal. Afterwards he was elected Fellow of Oriel College, &
at length Provost of ye same, & afterwards made Dean of Bristol. He
is a man of good Parts, well read in Pamphletts, of great Cunning and
Design, and so forgetfull of Kindnesses, as not to mention the Hall
where he was Educated when he preaches at S^t. Marie's. Which however is more to be pardon'd then his neglect of his near Relations,
particularly his Nephew of Oriel College, for whom he promis'd some
time since to get a Parsonage, wch he could have easily done; but
when ye Vacancy happen'd he got it for another no ways related to
him, but perhaps may do him he thinks some Service in the way of
Prefermt wch is his greatest Aim at present. — An old Book of Vellam
written in Capital Roman Letters found at Ivy-Church, mention'd by
M^r. Camden in his Britannia, and M^r. Webb in his Vindication of Stone-
Heng restored, pag. 76. — M^r. Selden in his Notes upon Eutychius has
a Disquisition ab^t Camalodunum, & a Coyn to illustrate it. Therein
something of the VIth Legion at York. This may be of some use in
the Notes upon Livy, when the Inscription conc. the IXth Legion is
printed. — M^r. Burton Author of the Com. upon Antoninus writ a
Book call'd Britanniæ Romanorum. See there pag. 210.

Mar. 10 (Sun.). The Commons having taken into Consideration
the Princess Sophia's Letter to ye Archb^p. of Cant. & S^r. Rowland
Gwyn's Letter, after 5 Hours Debate the Question was put that 'twas
scandalous & highly Reflecting on the Queen, Princess Sophia & both
Houses of Parliam^t. Upon a Division 'twas carried in ye Affirmative

[1] There are Foundations of it to be seen by the Spring.

Yeas 141, Noes 71. Resolved y^t her Majesty be addressed to apprehend & prosecute the Author, Printer and Publisher, & y^t ye s^d Resolution be communicated to ye L^ds at a Conference. — The Register of Benefactors to University College Library An. 1674. . .

March 11 (Mon.). M^r. Wall having said some things in his History of Infant-Baptism in opposition to Archb^p. Tillotson (tho' respectfully) they are resented by ye present Archb^p. Tennison, & he will not give him any Preferment as he once said he would. M^r. Wall's Book bears a very good character, & he is desir'd to draw up the Arguments in short, & I am inform'd he is now actually doing it, & y^t 'twill be in about 3 Sheets. — Justin corrected in Gronovius's Notes upon Arrian, p. 31.

March 12 (Tu.). Upon ye Death of D^r. Wallis, no one appear'd Competitors to be Custos Archivorum but D^r. Gardiner, Warden of All-Souls & M^r. Perks, Fellow of Corpus X^ti. There was a great Opposition; but there being then an Election of Fellows of All-Souls, D^r. Gardiner got several votes more y^n otherwise he would have had, & so carried it by a small Majority, tho' not near so well qualified for ye Place as M^r. Perks, who is a sober Man & an Excell^t Scholar, & Author of a Book. wch commonly goes under ye Name of M^r. Sacheverel, as I have already hinted. 'Twas expected y^t M^r. Smith of University College should have appear'd for this Place, he being well known to have studied these things for several Years; & 'tis thought he would have done so, had he not been disswaded from it by D^r. Charlett, a great Friend to Gardiner: for wch Smith now seems to have but an indifferent opinion of him. — The 2^d Part of Æthicus's Cosmographia in Bib. Bodl. (at ye End of a MS^t Solinus) not publish'd. See Burton's Com. upon Antoninus p. 5. — About ye Word Gesum in Livy see Burton ib. p. 14. — Monsieur Menage in his Origines Linguæ Italicæ often referrs to his origines linguæ Græcæ. Quære whether ever publish'd. — Conc. Livy Scaliger upon Festus voc. favissa.

March 13 (Wed.). The Close of last Week departed [1]this Life M^r. Poley, Esqr., Member of Parliament for Ipswich. He was a Man of a very despicable Presence, being deform'd to ye Highest Degree. But w^t made amends for this was his Admirable Parts, being endu'd with a strong Memory & most solid Judgment, insomuch that he was accounted one of the best common Lawyers in England, & for y^t reason suspected to have had a Hand in Penning *The Memorial of ye Church of England.* He was likewise a Man of a very quick Apprehension, and extraordinary Elocution. — Pliny corrected in a Collection of Epistles. 8°. Jur. K. 9. — Lipsius stole a good number of his Notes upon Tacitus out of the MS^t Papers of Muretus & Chiffletius as Ob. Gifanius has

March 11. E. Thwaites to H. 'A good-natured man can never want employment, 'tis your case. Please to look into No. 31. Cod. Jun. and Laud. E. 65. The first as I remember has wooden cuts in it, very ancient. Bagford, who is upon the Art of Typography, would have one of the figures drawn out. Tell me who can doe it artfully; let me have an account of the other book, & what figures be in it.'

[1] I think this Account of his Death is wrong. Quære.

observ'd in an Epistle to Canterus. — Ab^t the Hamburg Edition of
Cicero see pag. 90th of the s^d Epistles. — Gifanius complains y^t Lambin
stole several things in his Notes upon Cornelius Nepos from him.   see
ib. 97. — Justin corrected ib. p. 150. by Jo. Is. Pontanus, who put out
a Justin, wch was printed at Amsterdam by Jansonius.   It should be
consulted. — Jo. Is. Pontanus writ Discussiones Historicæ against
M^r. Selden's Mare Clausum.   He put out a Salust, & a Suetonius &
Florus. — There is a good Valerius Maximus in MS^t at Cambridge.
— Something in Pontanus's Discourse ag^t Selden ab^t King Alfred. —
10 M^r. Brome, who drew up the Indexes to D^r. Hicks's Thesaurus has
a noble Collection of Coyns, Greek, Roman & Saxon, as M^r. Urry of
X^t Church informs me.

March 14 (Th.).   The L^d. Granville & other Proprietors of Carolina
having caused 2 Acts to pass in their Assembly there after ye Nature
of ye occasional Bill, the Matter having been brought before ye L^{ds},
they upon a Debate ab^t ye same, on Saturday last pass'd ye ensuing
Resolves, viz. That ye said Acts tend to promote Atheism & Irreligion,
was contrary to ye Original Charter, & tends to depopulate ye s^d Colony,
& order'd an address to her Majesty to prosecute ye Author. — M^r.
20 Grabe having resolv'd to print ye Septuagint according to ye Alexandrian
Copy wthout any notes, pitch'd once upon the same Letter wth D^r. Mills'
Testament, wch is a magnificent Letter & was pleasing to his best
Friends in this University.   But he has since alter'd his Intention, & is
resolv'd to print in a Less Letter & in columns, being perswaded to it
by D^r. Bentley (a known Enemy to the University of Oxford & no
Friend to M^r. Grabe in this undertaking) & some others amongst w^{ch}
perhaps D^r. Mill (I am sure I heard him speak ag^t the great Letter)
who are no considerable Encouragers of other mens undertakings.   The
first Volume is to be confin'd to ye Octateuch wch in this Letter will
30 not be above 70 Sheets, & M^r. Wanley (stil'd in ye Proposals the
Accurate M^r. Wanley) is to compare the whole with the MS^t tho' 'tis
sufficiently known he understands neither Greek nor Latin : & perhaps
that may be ye reason he is imploy'd, because one who understood the
Greek might be apt to pronounce as ye sense directed not as really
written. — Col. Finch a Non-Juror, & one of ye Younger Sons of Heneage
Earl of Winchelsey, has a very valuable Collection of Coyns, as I am told
by M^r. Urry, a great many of wch he rec^d from his Father, & he is continually improving them, being a Gentleman of Curiosity & Learning.

Mar. 15 (Fri.).   D^r. Mill having now finish'd his Prolegomena de-
40 signs to put it speedily to ye Press, & dispatch it.   I have seen y^e
Beginning & 'tis to contain 3 Parts, viz. (1) agit de libris singulis N.
Fœderis, & Canonis constitutione.   (2) Textûs ipsius S. Historiam qualem
qualem complectitur.   (3) hujus Editionis consilium & quid in ea præ-
stiterit fusius exponit. — Ab^t a Passage of Livy see Pet. de Marca de

---

March 14.   E. Smith to H.   Has been appointed to the Living of Castle-
Rising ; regrets to leave London.   Recommends the insertion in Livy of a
Map of the Roman Empire.   ? print Toland's letter in last volume by way of
Appendix.   Wants a cheap copy of Clarendon, ed. 2, 8vo.   Arrangements for
returning Begerus to Dr. Sloane.

Primatibus publish'd by Baluzius, p. 206. — *Cn. Flavius scriba* is call'd by Livy *Caius Fl.* & by Macrobius corruptly *M. Flavius.* The true Reading *Cn.* see Jac. Gronov. ad Macrob. p. 178. — The Queen has consented y^t the Author, Printer & Publisher of the Letter going under S^r. Rowland Gwin's Name shall be prosecuted, intending to give immediate orders for ye Same.   She has also promis'd to secure ye Rights of the People of Carolina (in the Fanaticks style) in opposition to ye two Acts pass'd by ye L^d. Granvil &c.

Mar. 17 (Sun.).   M^r. Smith of North-Nibley in Gloucestershire, formerly a Gentleman-Commoner of Edmund-Hall, hath made a Trans-   10 lation into English of Pliny's Panegyrick, wch he has dedicated in a long Epistle to ye Dutchess of Hannover.   He mentions a MS^t in the Preface, wch he never saw I believe.   He made this Translation immediately from the Italian Version, & not ye Original.   He has done some other small things, amongst wch is *The Vanity of Victory,* dedicated to ye Duke of Marlborough.

Clarissimo atque Eruditissimo Viro Johanni Hudsono S. P. D. Jac. Perizonius. [*Dated* Lugduni in Batavis a. d. xiii. Kal. Aprileis cɔɪɔccv. (23–26.)] . . .

Mar. 19 (Tu.).   A silly Explanation having been publish'd by some 20 foolish Fanatick upon ye Oxoñ Almanack for this year 1706, there is another written by way of banter upon ye Whiggs, (as 'tis said) by M^r. Hen. Hall of Hereford, call'd *A farther Explanation of the Oxford Almanack,* viz.

As Man in Westminster to each y^t comes
Expounds upon his constant Text y^e
  Tombs :
Cryes there a Duke & there a Lord was
  laid,
And tells a long, long story of ye Dead :
So I'le explain what all these figures mean,
As if Ide Burghers, or th' Inventer been.
Lo that's Britannia coming to assist us,
S^r. Cotterel'd in by Hermes Trismegistus,
See how he points as if these words he
  spoke,
Those Arms not always shall adorn ye Oke.
That other Tree our Oke does yet surmount
Is sauce for those that call y^o Cutt
  t'account.
The Scrowl that's near ye Fasces & ye Axes
The worst of all Memorialls is,— ye Taxes.
That Figure there between two Chaffin
  Dishes
Some say a Man, & others it a Fish is.
The Quæriest needs will have him Neptune
  meant
Quite chil'd with cold, & out of's Element ;

Kens to a hair, what Hieroglyphicks
  mean,
And intimately known was to Poussin.
That Head that looks in Hand so like S^t.
  Dennis
Some say seventeen, & some threescore 30
  & ten is :
Whilst Whiggs that would be witty in
  their Ale
Cry Zounds ! upon that Head there Hangs
  a Tale,
The Cock & Dog at play have lately bin,
Fifty to one y^o twirl'd tail'd Cur does
  win,
Who all this War but Hogan has thrown
  in?   40
I'm sure that Tarr Divine you all must
  love well,
That you maynt doubt S^r. Cloudsly see y^e
  Shovel.
But where to find ye Figure out I trow
That does ye Church in so much danger
  show
Their Lordships only, & ye Lord does
  know.

March 16. Dr. T. Smith to H.   Grabe's opinion of the Church of England a thousand times less valuable than that of Casaubon and Grotius. Twyne and Allen.   Regretted last election to the post of Custos Archivorum. Fears the consequences of Dodwell's book, which he has not read.   Remarks on Oxford affairs.

— M^r. Gagnier, besides ye Edition of Ben-Gorion, has writ and publish'd a Book call'd *L'Eglise Romaine convaincue de Dépravation, d'Idola-
trie, et d'Antichristianisme. A la Haye* 1706. 8°.   He is said formerly to
have been a Jesuit & to have been converted to the English Church by
ye B^p. of Worcester (Quære?) with whom he lives & from whom he
receives great Encouragement in his studies; & being a man of a steddy
Head & great Industry may do other things for the use of Learning.
He assures me the B^p. has not his Chronology in such order as to be
carried on by any one upon his Death. — M^r. Bache tells me y^t Will.
10 Wormes (Son of ye famous Olaus Wormes) has writ several Pieces in
Physick (wch was his Profession) & Phylology, whereof there are none in
ye Publick Library. X^{tian} Wormes is Son of the s^d W^m. Wormes, &
is now a famous Preacher in the City of Copenhagen.   He is a man of
excellent Parts, & whilst in Oxford he made use of ye Publick Library
purely for ye sake of improving himself in Divinity, & other Studies.
W^m. Wormes his Father was Justitiarius in ye High Court of Denmark,
& a man of great Note. — Torfœus a Learned Dane, and ye King's
Historian, has written three Historical Books in Latin, viz. (1) De Insulis
Orcadibus.   (2) Series Dinastarum vel Regum Danorum.   3. Descriptio
20 Grœnlandiæ.

Mar. 20 (Wed.).   M^r. John Caswell, formerly Vice-Principal of Hart-
Hall, & now superior (or Esquire) Beadle in Divinity of Oxford, besides
his Trigonometry, printed with D^r. Wallis's Works, has written several
other Pieces in Mathematicks, as I have been inform'd by one of his
Intimate Acquaintance; but his great Modesty will not let them come
abroad, tho' very deserving of it. — This day being appointed a
General Fast for Imploring God's Mercy for our Sins & Success on our
Arms there preach'd at S^t. Marie's M^r. Reynolds of Corpus X^{ti}, on . . .
Hos. 5. 15. . . .

30   After a short Paraphrase, he proceeded to prove (1) That 'tis in vain to expect for Blessings, whilst we ought rather to look for Judgm^{ts}, as long as we
continue in our Sins.   (2) That we forsake our sins we may expect Mercy.
The former he made out (1) from God's Hatred of sin.   (2) from the Nature
of his Judgments.   (3) From the Connexion between sin & Judgment.   The
latter from the force of Prayer, & the Nature of Repentance, joyn'd wth
Fasting.   There was nothing Extraordinary in ye Discourse, & it might have
serv'd for any other Day of Fasting as well as this, there being nothing particularly relating to ye present times, only in the Conclusion he just mention'd
the many Divisions, wch he exhorted to make up, y^t they might be no Hinder-
40 ance to our Success, nor prevent those Blessings we may otherwise hope for
from the Justness of the War, & the Victories we have already obtain'd.

Mar. 21 (Th.).   S^r. W^m. Glynn has such an Aversion to D^r. Kennett
for his late Shuffling Proceedings, particularly for his 30th of January
Sermon, that, as I am well assur'd by one of his Friends, he will not
endure him in his Sight, tho' before no man was so great wth him, S^r.
W^m. thinking he had been a man of Honesty and Probity.   And the

---

March 20. Jno. Williams to H.   Is Head Master of Ruthyn School
at £80 a year.   Asks for news of H. and other Oxford contemporaries.   A
friend, Mr. C. Williams, has lost his letters of Order; will H. help him to re-
place them?

more to shew how much he is displeas'd wth him he designs to give ye Parsonage of Haden in Chesshire 3 or 400 lib^s. per Annum, wch he once design'd for D^r. Kennett, to another Gentleman.   M^r. Cherry also of Shottesbrooke another Patron of the D^r's is much dissatisfi'd wth him upon Acc^t of these Matters, but being a Man who has a great Respect for ye Clergy, & being very cautious of disobliging any one of them (of whatsoever Perswasion) he always appears extraordinary kind to him, & tho' he hates his Principles, yet he takes care to reverence his Person[1]. — On Thursday last his Grace the Duke of Buckingham was married to ye Countess Dowager of Anglesee Daughter of ye Late King 10 James, a Lady of rare Quality, on whom 'tis said his Grace has not only settled her former Joynture, wch is 2000^li. per an. but a considerable Additional one. — 'Tis said her Majesty design'd to have made S^r. Rowland Gwynne her Resident at Hambourg (wch is a very good Post) before this disobliging Letter of his came out, wch hath given such high offence to both Houses of Parliam^t.

[Royal assent to various Bills, and Prorogation.] . . .

Mar. 22 (Fri.).   M^r. Thwaits tells me y^t he has rec^d a Letter from M^r. Hinton formerly Student of X^t Church, now at London wherein he tells him y^t an able Person is writing an Answer to M^r. Dodwell's 20 new Book, which he styles Dodwell's Visions, & that he will handle (as he believes) M^r. Dodwell very roughly. — When ye B^p. of Worcester was formerly in London where M^r. Dodwell liv'd with him he freq^tly was put to it for a Sermon, at the Week's End, having Studied very hard all ye other part of the Week, & therefore knowing M^r. Dodwell to be a quick Writer he would often ask him to draw up something upon certain Texts he gave him ; wch he accordingly did, & 'tis said by several y^t the B^p. has preach'd divers Sermons thus made by M^r. Dodwell.   But quære farther? — Memorandum y^t B^p. Sanderson made the Alterations in the English Liturgy as printed in 1641, wherein 30 Congregation is put for Church & some other innocent Alterations made of ye same sort.   See Athen. Oxon. Vol. 2. p. 213. — K. Charles ye first translated into English B^p. Sanderson's Admirable Book de Juramento.   See there pag. 213.   Quære where it is now, & whether ever printed ?   B^p. Sanderson began the Translation into English of King Charles' Εἰκὼν Βασιλικῆ.   Butt was prevented from proceeding by D^r. Earle. . . .

Mar. 23 (Sat.).   Charles Cæsar Esqr, one of the Burgesses for Hartford, was discharg'd from the Tower on Tuesday whither he was confin'd by the House of Commons before Christmass. — Great Search is 40 made after ye Author of the Rehearsal for Reflecting on the Kingdom of Scotland. . . .

Mar. 24 (Sun.).   In the Church of Pauler's-Pury near Toucester in Northamptonshire the following Epitaph.

Anno Unici Mediatoris 1626.

Spectator luge, boni defluunt.   Hic jacet Arthurus Magni Nicolai Throckmortonij F. & paternarum virtutum ingenuus hæres, Equestris census, politis

---

[1] The s^d Parsonage of Haden now possess'd by Mr Percival formerly of New College.

moribus, animi fortis, exculti ingenij, religiosæ mentis, œconomia splendida, candidissimo pectore. Juxta accumbit charissima ejus conjux, Anna Lucasiorum; quæ quum LX fere annos explevisset, per totam ætatem melior an formosior fuerat ambiguum reliquit. Attigit ipse annum LXXII. convixerunt annos XL dies XVII sine querela. quos tam unanimiter conjunctos Maria Baronissa Wottonia ex quatuor filiabus natu maxima, solaque parentibus superstite, in hoc fano condidit ubi & antea tres ex proprio partu suavissimae spei tenellos, Elizabetham, Carolum & Annam in gloriosum diem deposuerat.

The Estate of yᵉ Throcmortons at Pauler's-Pury afterwards came
10 into the Family of yᵉ Hales in Kent, supposed by Marriage. In King James yᵉ IIᵈˢ time 'twas sold by Sʳ. Edward Hales to Sʳ. Benjamin Bathurst, who lyes buried in a Vault of yᵗ Church wᵗʰout any Monument. — Mʳ. Stephens finding that his Project in his Pamphlett agᵗ the Duke of Marlborough & Mʳ. Secretary Harley will not take, has lately in an Advertisement inserted in yᵉ Flying Post made Acknowledgmᵗ that wᵗ he said of the Duke is false & begs his Pardon, but takes no Notice of his Reflections on yᵉ latter. — The Queen having order'd Good Friday to be kept strictly in London, 'twas accordingly observ'd in a most decent & Religious Manner by all Friends of the
20 Church, but very negligently & disrespectfully by the Presbyterians & the rest of yᵗ Brood. — Mʳ. Nevil Junior Parliamᵗ Man for Abbingdon being lately married, to entertain his Lady he had some Extraordinary Musick for about a Fortnight or three Weeks at his Father's House at Billingbear in Berks, for performing wᶜʰ were three Musicians, two of them Oxford men, one of whom told me that he had dancing & musick upon this Occasion one Sunday night for three or four Hours. Such is the Religion of these pretended Hypocritical Saints; who always have reviled King James.I. & K. Charles I. for allowing innocent Recreation in Publick on yᵉ Lord's Day, when they themselves give themselves up
30 to chambering & wantonness on the same day; but not wᵗʰ the like Innocence: it being farther observable that the said Person told me yᵗ all the time he was in yᵉ House he saw not the least shew or Appearance of Religion, nor indeed any thing becoming a Gentleman (wᶜʰ this Nevil so much pretends to, & for wᶜʰ he is cry'd up among the Rascality of Whiggs & Low-church men) they being forc'd to come wᵗʰ very little Satisfaction for their Pains. — The Prolocutor of yᵉ Lower House of Convocation & some Honest members of it had a great mind to have propos'd in yᵉ House yᵗ publick thanks should be return'd to Mʳ. Wall for his Excellᵗ History of Infant Baptism; but this
40 seeming a little unpresidented, 'twas wav'd & the two Members of yᵗ District to wᶜʰ he belong'd were desir'd to thank him in the Name of yᵉ Prolocutor & some other Persons.

Mar. 25 (Mon.). The Arms of Wᵐ. Cherry Esqʳ. of Shottesbrooke being put over the Hall door of the Mannor House, in memory of him (he Deceasing abᵗ a year since) viz. Arg. a Fesse ingrail'd Gules:

March 25. Thoresby to H. Remarks on coins with head of Cybele, etc. Wants *any* autographs; 'nothing can come amiss that is remarkable either for the person or the subject.' 'The Captⁿ. is now well recovered. I sate

charged with a Flour de Luce or betw. 3 Annuletts underneath there is this Escrolle, *Memoria pij æterna.* — Remember to enquire of some Body whether Horrion's Edition of the 33ᵈ Book of Livy be in Manchester Library, wᶜʰ I am inform'd is a very valuable one. Mʳ. Dodwell in his Copy of Philo has several MSSᵗ observations wᶜʰ will be of use to one that shall put out a new Edition of this Author. —

Mʳˢ. Anne Cherry's Epitaph in Shottesbrook church, in yᵉ N. Side of the chancel.

H. S. E.

Foemina dilecta suis & desiderata ANNA CHERRY | uxor Gulielmi Cherry de 10 Shottesbrooke Armigeri | Per XLVII ferme Annos. | Utrinque par foelicis Conjugij solatium & exemplar. | Deum infucata Pietate coluit. | Novit simul Maritum revereri | Amore & obsequio non simulatis. | Et Liberos una prosequi | Affectu plusquam Materno. | Amicos officijs indefessis. | Proximos suasu & auxilio | Egenos mercede & Donis | omnes denique consilio & Exemplo | sibi conciliavit. | Denuo dierum & operum plena | Piam absque suspirio efflavit animam | Anno Christi 1703, Ætatis suæ LXXXIII. Moestissimus conjunx | exiguum hoc amoris monumentum | poni curavit. —

A Scurrilous Letter of yᵉ Bᵖ. of Carlisle's, (viz. Wᵐ. Nicholson) wherein he shews himself to be a weak Man in speaking so slightly of 20 the Great Mʳ. Dodwell.

Rose, Sep. 16. 1703.

Sʳ,—I can easily guess at yᵉ contents of Mʳ. Dodwell's Book, but I shall not be satisfied with that. I hope Mʳ. Wyat will take care to send me 't. His private Discourses I know have run on that topick for these several years. But why he should venture to send his Notions to the Press, in this rather than in the last Reign, I cannot imagine. The poor Man could do well to let controversial Points alone. He has gotten the Reputation of being a profound Scholar ; & (for ought I know) deserves it. Perhaps his Arguments may have their Depths too ; for I could never see nor feel the Bottom of any of 'em. 30 If posterity understands either his Latin or English (which I much Question) he may possibly be as great a man in succeeding Ages as this : But 'tis an even Wager whether his Book proves himself or me a schismatick. I promise Repentance and Recantation if I am convinc't of any Error of that kind : for I heartily abhorr Schism. I have y᾽ confidence & charity to hope that nothing he has to say will prove that either the Jacobites or we (in our present unhappy Differences) are Schismaticks : And I dare say that some of his Judges to whom he directs his Appeal, will condemn us both.

I had the other Day an Account of some Roman Antiquities found (about a fortnight ago) att Cattericke in Yorkshire. Amongst the rest there were 40 several Urns : & on the Handle of one of these the following Inscription :

II AVRELIVS HERACE PAT ET FIL FBAR.

A Friend desires my thoughts of this ; as I do yours. Can we think that it can have any Relation to the Usurping Emperor (or Tyrant) M. Aurelius Maxim. Herculius ? He might perhaps be some time in this Island ; but we are pretty sure he left not his Ashes here. If you and your Friends can help me to explain it, you'l oblige   Sʳ

Your ever truely affectionate Servᵗ

W. CARLIOL.

with him yesterday at Church, wʳ was a vast appearance to see the Blue-Coat-Boys, who first appeared in their formalitys from the New Charity School, wʳ 40 of them are maintained.'

To be got into ye Publick Library D^r. Allix's Discourse of ye Judgment of the Ancient Jewish Church Ag^t ye Unitarians. —
In Shottesbrook Church the N. Side of ye Chancel.

H. S. E. | Virgo matura Cœlo | Sara Cherry | Filia natu secunda | Willielmi Cherry de Shottesbrooke | Armigeri & Annæ uxoris ejus | Quibus | triste sui desiderium reliquit. Febr. xxiv. mdcxci. | Cum vixerit Annos xxviii. Menses vii | & dies xx. | —

M^r. Dodwell Receiving a Letter from M^{rs}. Astell urging him wth the Consequences of his Case in view for present Communion wth the National Church, return'd her an Answer, wch will be of great use if publish'd to those that shall read ye Case in view. — When M^r. Dodwell was at Dublin a new Edition in English being made of Francis de Sales's Introduction to a devout Life, he was Desir'd to read it over & alter some of the English, wch he accordingly did & put a preface before it. —

Books written by M^r. Dodwell not printed.

A Discourse in Latin proving that ye Greek Translation call'd the LXX was not made in the time of ye II^d but ye IVth Ptolemy.—A Cautionary Discourse in English ag^t the Project of Comprehension during the time of ye Schism.— A Discourse Concerning the Chronology truly follow'd by Josephus : wch he was put upon by D^r. Bernard, when he was upon a new Edition of y^t Author, wch unfortunately miscarried.—A II^d Part (viz. the Historical Part) of his Separation of Churches. This done in Latin, but not perfected.—A Letter to M^r. Richard King of Exceter fixing the Age of Philopatris commonly ascrib'd to Lucian, to the Year X^{ti} 262.—Some considerable Notes adjusting the Chronology of Bede's History. He has begun a Discourse upon Philo & ye order of his Works.—A Discourse concerning Barnabas and a Paraphrase upon his Epistle ; design'd to go wth a New Edition of ye said Epistle, prepar'd for ye Press by D^r. Mill & D^r. Bernard.—A great Number of Letters (Copies of several of wch M^r. Cherry has caus'd to be taken fairly in a Book for y^t Purpose) relating to ye Schism & matters of Learning. Amongst wch a Letter to an unknown Gentleman ab^t his going over to some Forreign Church upon the Death or Resignation of the Abdicated B^p. of Norwich.—A Discourse by way of Letter in answer to some objections concerning the Satisfaction to be expected from the New B^{ps} in order to a Reunion & concerning the Unlawfullness of the Prayers.—A Discourse sent to Perizonius in a Letter de morte Judæ. His first Letter ab^t Susception of Holy Orders was writ to M^r. George Sing Nephew to D^r. Sing B^p. of Cork ; the Latter to M^r. John Lesley Elder Brother to M^r. Charles Lesley. M^r. Charles Lesley is the 7th Son.—Theses in Trinity College in Dublin (in all 10) from Oct. 22. 1663 (in wch year he took his A.M.'s Degree) to Nov. 17. 1673.—De Auctore Operis à Rigaltio editi ex Apographo Sirmondiano pro Baptismo Hæreticorum. —

In White Waltham Church in a Chapel on the South side of the Chancel, on t e Wall.

Gulielmus Neile, Pauli Neile Equitis Aurati natu max. Filius, Richardi Neile Archiepiscopi Ebor, Nepos, Academiæ Oxon. Alumnus, Societatis Philosophorum Regiæ socius, serenissimo Carolo II°. à Camera privata. Suavitate Morum & temperantia plusquam juvenili spectabilis, Geometriæ studijsque Philosophicis totus incubuit, & perspicacissimi ingenij varia dedit specimina, donec ingentibus coeptis amicisque lugentibus immatura morte valedixit, præreptus viii^o. Calend. Octob. A^o mdclxx. Pijssimo filio Pater moerens P.

Underneath on a Black Marble on the Floor :

Here lyeth interred the Body of W^m. Neile Esq., Eldest Sonne of S^r. Paule

Neile K^t. and Grandchild to Richard Neile Late L^d. Archb^p. of Yorke. He was borne at Bishop Thorpe in the County of Yorke ye 7th Day of December. 1637 & dyed in this Parish of White-Waltham ye 24th day of August 1670.

I am inform'd that this M^r. Neile did not dye by hard Study, but for Love (being greatly taken with one of K. Charles II^{ds} Ladys of Honour) wch brought him into a Consumption, & y^t he was in a manner craz'd sometime before his Death. — M^r. Dodwell of Opinion that Philostratus's Life of Apollonius Tyanæus is spurious; wch ought to be consider'd by a Gentleman now engag'd in a new Edition of him. — M^r. 10 Gilbert a non-Juror formerly of S^t. John's College in Oxford, afterwards minister of Medenham & upon his Resignation upon Acc^t of ye Oaths he liv'd at Great Marlow where he dy'd ab^t 6 Weeks since & is bury'd in Shottesbrook near his sister. He us'd to officiate at M^r. Cherry's to him & M^r. Dodwell's Family & others of y^t Party in the Duties of Religion. Upon his Decease one M^r. Brooksby does it, a Cambridge Gentleman, afterwards Minister in Yorkshire (where he had a Parsonage of 200 lib^s. per An.) & upon his leaving y^t place retired into Leycestershire. He is a pious & learned Man. — Presently after D^r. Kennett's last 30th of January Sermon before ye House of Commons came out, 20 his Preface to Pliny's Panegyrick reprinted by itself & cry'd ab^t London Streets for a penny & half penny a piece. — As soon as D^r. Hickes's Jovian came out, it pleas'd King James very well, & for it he conferr'd upon him y^e Deanery of Worcester. But soon after he shew'd some dissatisfaction upon Acc^t of y^e D$^{r's}$ having asserted in y^t Book y^t 'tis lawfull for the Subjects to say anything in opposition to an arbitrary prince &c. tho' not justifyable to take up Arms ag^t him.

Mar. 28 (Th.). The B^p. of Worcester says that M^r. Dodwell above 20 years agoe had y^e same Notions about y^e soul wch he has advanc'd in his New Book, & y^t he would have then divulg'd them only he 30 hinder'd him. — A day or two since I had a small Brass Coyn given me found at Weycock in ye Parish of Laurence Waltham in Berks, on one side of wch DIVO CLAVDIO. Caput radiat. Claudij Gothici. ℞ CONSECRATIO. Aquila. W^{ch} shews that in this Place was a Fortress before the Time of Constantius the Younger, who built Silchester in Hampshire, contrary to w^t I once thought. — The B^p. of Worcester says that it us'd to be said of Judge Hale y^t he had got an Estate honestly and that it would wear like Iron. — The B^p. of Worcester is of Opinion that M^r. Dodwell is in ye Right about ye small Number of Martyr's & y^t 'twould have been an easy thing for him to have answer'd 40 Ruinart : but D^r. Turner (President of Corpus Christi College, who is a close, reserv'd man) as I heard him say to day, being at dinner wth his Lordship, believes M^r. Dodwell to be in ye wrong, & y^t the same Arguments will bring all History into Question. W^{ch} however is certainly false, & may as well be said of other Forgeries of ye Romanists. — The B^p. of Opinion that Eusebius's Account of ye Cross appearing in ye Heavens to Constantine ye Great is a Forgery, as being contradicted by Lactantius. Quære? — The B^p. of Worcester when B^p. of Lichfield and Coventry going thro' Coventry (as I heard himself say) happen'd to be told of Humfrey Wanley, & to have a good Character 50

of him, as being an ingenious & diligent young man, & not to be very well pleas'd with the Trade to wch he was put (& for wch he had then serv'd almost 7 years): for wch reason calling at the House where he was, he desir'd to see him. Coming to him, he shew'd his L^dship three or four Manuscripts, & talk'd wth some confidence: upon wch his L^dship sent him to Oxford recommending him to D^r. Mill, who took care to enter him at Edm. Hall, where he staid a little while 'till D^r. Charlett got him to University College, where he staid for about 5 years, & assisted D^r. Hyde in the Publick Library (in wch place he did much Mischief) & was
10 commonly call'd the master's Pimp, as he is by some to this day. His being to collate ye Alexandrian MS^t was mention'd to day at ye B^p. of Worcester's, & three or four then present said He was one of the fittest in ye World for it, as being able to read it better than most beside, upon wch the President of Corpus said that it requir'd one y^t understood it, insinuating thereby that M^r. Wanley did not understand Greek: wch is true, & ye B^p. could not deny it, his aim in sending him to Oxford being not y^t he should be a scholar (thinking him not capable of it, as having not been bred to it at Schoole) but to be usefull in transcribing MSS^ts & writing for Scholars. — I heard ye B^p. of Worcester say that
20 Judge Hale was a man who courted Honour & that he sacrific'd Justice it self to Popularity.

Mar. 29 (Fri.). D^r. Charlett was sent for up to London lately to be catechis'd upon Account of some Scandalous Story about ye B^p. of Sarum's being to have a great Sum of Money when Presbytery is established &c. (W^ch has been inserted in one of these volumes) it being said y^t he was the divulger of it. — A Ballad being made upon D^r. Mill & the others mention'd before going to Woodstock the beginning was this : Great Sir Our Caravan huc ibat | Because we heard you would be private. — M^r. Francis Bugg (as he has told M^r. Thwaits in a Letter)
30 having presented the B^p. of Worcester with his 2^d Vol. ag^t Quakerism in folio, he refus'd to accept it, & shew'd very great Resentment ; the reason whereof may be because of S^r. W^m. Penn's being so great at Court, having perswaded them that there are 40000 Quaking Freeholders in England. — We have an Acc^t from Hertfordshire of the Extraordinary Reception Charles Cæsar Esqr. had on Wednesday upon his Return home after his long Imprisonment in ye Tower having been met at Wormly 5 miles from Hertford by the Mayor Aldermen and almost all the Voters of Hertford and at Hodsdon by several 100 of the Freeholders ab^t his Neighbourhood to ye Number of ab^t a 1000 who attended him thro' Hertford
40 where ye Streets were strew'd with Flowers & the Inhabitants in their best Cloaths lined ye same expressing all manner of Satisfaction upon his safe Return home. — M^r. Joseph Trapp M.A. & Fellow of Wadham College has just publish'd, *The Mischiefs of Changes in Government ; and the Influence of Religious Princes to prevent them.* In A Sermon preach'd before y^e Mayor & Corporation of Oxon on Friday March 8. 170$\frac{5}{8}$ being the Anniversary of Her Majesty's Inauguration. He is a Person of good Parts, and has got some Reputation among the Witts for Writing a Play call'd Abram mule. He has likewise some Verses in the Musæ Anglicanæ.

Mar. 31 (Sun.). This day being Low Sunday M^r. Dennison (Will.) Fellow of University College repeated the four Easter Sermons at S^t. Maries : wch he perform'd so readily & distinctly, that he came off wth Applause from the whole Auditory, & 'tis not remembred to have been done better since the year 1665 when M^r. Sam. Jemmat of the same College did it to ye Great Amazement of all present, w^thout ye least Hesitation or Stop. — In the Afternoon preach'd at S^t. Marie's M^r. Ridgway of Wadham, upon Prov. i. 10. . . . 'Twas an ingenious, well penn'd Discourse shewing the Ends and Designs of Bad men in alluring men to sin, & the usual methods made use of for it, & concluding with 10 some Directions for Resisting them.

Apr. 1 (Mon.). The Lady Eliz. Cecil only sister to ye Earl of Exeter married to the Earl of Orrery (M^r. Boyle). D^r. Hudson made Bursar of University College last Week, wch he rec^d wth some unwillingness, upon Acc^t of his being full of other Business.

[Justin, Herodotus, Lactantius, Eutropius, explain'd in D^r. Hyde's Historia Relig. Vet. Pers. . . .]

To be got into ye Pub. Library . . . Olaus Borichius de usu Plantarum indigenarum. 8°. An Excell^t Book in it's kind, & very scarce. He has writ another Book call'd Parnassus in nuce. 4°.—Sperlingius de Baptismo Ethnicorum. 20 8°.—Jonæ Rami Norvegia Antiqua. 4°. He has writt another Book called Outinus & Ulysses unus et idem. A curious Book. 8°.

Sperlingius is now Fellow of ye Royal Society in London, an ingenious Man, & Professor to ye Royal Academy in Copenhagen. Ramus is also a man of good Parts, minister in Norway, & well skill'd in Antiquities.

April 1. H. to Dr. T. Smith. A scurrilous answer to Dodwell in preparation. Remarks on Wood, ' whose industry I can never sufficiently admire,' and Mr. Smith. Halley preparing for observations on eclipse of May 1 ; to be assisted by Gregory and Caswell.

'Mr. Thwaits is in a very desperate condition. He is forc'd to go upon crutches, and has not been out of his Chamber this half year. The last time I was with him abroad was at ye Tavern with Mr. Wotton and Mr. Willis, where we had a great deal of Discourse, & he was (as always) very chearful, tho' often complain'd of a pain in his leg wch encreas'd to y^t degree that he has been given over by ye Chirurgeons, and is now under a Woman's Hands. His chief Distemper is ye Evil, wch he let alone too long, to ye great Reluctance of all y^t know his excellent Parts & Learning.' Letters for degrees (including D.D. for Potter) read in Convocation, but vetoed by the Proctors because they had not been previously acquainted with the contents. Has received a coin of Claudius, found at Laurence Waltham, Berks ; also copy of inscription from a Throgmorton's tomb at Pauler's-Pury near Towcester. ' Y^e L^d. Leominster who lives at Easton near Towcester has ye best Collection of Ancient Marble Statues, bigger than ye Life, that perhaps are anywhere in being, wch once belong'd to ye L^d. Arundel, who collected the Marbles in our Theatre Yard.' Particulars of Dr. Mill's Prolegomena. ' Most people here are angry with Mr. Grabe for pitching on so small a Letter in comparison to what he once resolv'd to have, & for putting the 1st volume (wch will be 70 sheets only) at so high a Price. I am told Dr. Bentley has advic'd him to this, and y^t the Booksellers are well pleas'd with it, designing to break ye form & to print it in octavo the same time 'tis printing off in Folio ; for wch reason they have contriv'd it in columns.'

Before the first Book of Wandalin de Jure Regio in Bibl. Bodl. B^p. Barlow has ye following memorandum, viz.

Hoc Joh. Wandalini Opus de Jure Regio, pro Amicitia & benevolentia sua singulari, (ea qua par est gratitudine æterno recolenda) Tho. Lincolniensi dono dedit (XII Cal. Decem. Anno CIↃDCLXXIX) Petrus nuper (quam nollem infaustum illud nuper) Griffenfeldiæ comes illustrissimus, magnusque & meritissimus Daniæ Cancellarius, et (æmulis fatoque nequicquam reluctantibus) Vir optimus & doctissimus, Daniæ suæ prius ornamentum, nunc triste deside-rium, [he was banish'd because of his aspiring to the Crown, as I am told] et
10 (quod nullus dubito) à posteritate sero venerandus.

April 2 (Tu.).   About King Alfred's Works of Learning see John Fox's Preface to ye four Saxon Gospels, inter Codd. MSS. Laud. G. 5. — Perhaps Weycock mention'd above p. 57. is no more than the Saxon word, Ƿic-ʄʈop, wch signifies, a Fort, Camp, or place of Ençamping. — D^r. Royse . . . was reckon'd a good florid Preacher, & it happening that ye Earl of Berkley being at Oxoñ when he preach'd one time at S^t. Maries took particular Notice of him, & (as I think) made him his Chaplain.   After wch living at London some time, he got to preach at Lincoln's In for D^r. Tillotson, by wch means he became acquainted with
20 him.   About wch time (viz. a little after ye Revolution) he by ye Recom-mendation either of ye Earl of Berkley or D^r. Tillotson was made Chap-lain to King W^m and went along with him in his Irish Expedition.   A little after this D^r. Sancroft with Others of his Brethren (who would not swear Allegiance to ye Prince of Orange as King of England) were depriv'd, & D^r. Tillotson succeeding Archb^p. Sancroft, D^r. Royse was made his Domestick Chaplain, from whom he rec^d the Rich Living of Newington in Oxoñshire wch had been possess'd by D^r. Maurice, (who was made Margaret Professor but died (to ye Regret of all good Men) before he had an opportunity of Reading) & a little after he got from that
30 Dutch pretended King the Deanery of Bristol, vacant by ye Death of ye Stout and Loyal M^r. Thompson.   Not long after this D^r. Say Provost of Oriel Dying, some of ye Fellows with whom Royse us'd to drink got a Majority together at Mother Shepherds at Heddington, where they agreed to choose D^r. Royse, & not M^r. Davenant, who was always
¹look'd upon by ye Men of Learning, and Integrity in ye University to be ye fittest for Provost.   When he was at London he was a Lecturer at S^t. Swithun's, by London Stone, w^{ch} (I believe) he held 'till he was Elected Provost.   He is a man of good Parts, ready Elocution, and some Learn-ing.   He was always fam'd for good Eating and Drinking, [&c.]. —
40 D^r. Charlett commonly called the Gazzeteer or Oxford Intelligencer & by some (I know not for what reason) *Troderam* was originally of Trinity College, where he became Scholar of the House, and after his taking the Degree of Bachelor of Arts was made one of ye Collectors.   As soon as Master of Arts he was noted for the variety of his Correspondents and Acquaintance, as well as magnificent way of Living.   He became Fellow of that College when D^r. Dobson the present President left it.   He was in some time after a Pro-Proctor and was very active in ye Discharge of

¹ In these times not now (1709) it being certain that he is a malicious. ill-natur'd Person, no Friend to the University, a mean Scholar & mortally hated in the College. (See hereafter in 1709. under Julij 19°.)

y^t Office. The next Year he was one of ye Head Proctors, & in ye Long-Vacation made an Excursion into Scotland, where he was kindly receiv'd & nobly Entertain'd by S^r. George Mackenzy & others of Note & Learning. Some years after the Mastership of University College being void (and those who were fittest for it in ye College declining the Trouble and Expense of it) he was at last thought upon, and by ye Interest of D^r. Hudson, & one or two more, was Elected Master. At his first coming to y^t College, he laid out two or three Hundred lib^s. upon ye Lodgings, & he kept up ye Discipline & Exercise of ye House very well, by wch means it flourish'd equally to any House in ye University; but afterwards it de- 10 clin'd very much partly by ye Remissness of ye Master, & partly by D^r. Hudson's quitting his Pupils when he was made the Bodlejan Library Keeper. He is a man of a strange Rambling Head, much addicted to maintain Correspondence, to hear and tell news in Company wch he is seldom free from. But of him perhaps more hereafter.

April 3 (Wed.). Remember to tell D^r. Hudson of an Error in his Notes upon Dionys. in the Life of Ancus Marcius, where he quotes Livy in this manner *Tellenis Fidenaque*, whereas it should be *Tellenis Ficanaque*, & so Sigonius has corrected Dionysius, but ye D^r. does not take notice of it. — On Monday last was a meeting of ye Heads of Houses in ye Apo- 20 dyterium of ye Convocation House about a Letter sent to our University from the University of Francfort upon the Oder inviting them to celebrate the secular day of the Foundation of their University, wch will happen in this month, it being now just two Hundred years since that University was Founded. The Result of this Meeting was y^t they should not send any Representatives as they had done at Cambridge, but that the day should be solemniz'd in our Theatre with Speeches verses & musick, & some of the Great Men of ye s^d University of Franckfoort should have eundem Gradum dignitatem & Honorem conferr'd upon them by Diploma in this our University. It was objected at ye Meeting y^t ye Form of ye 30 Diplomas was very mean & ordinary (as all confess'd it was) yet it was carried y^t ye usual Form should be retain'd upon Account of it's Antiquity. It was moreover agreed upon at ye Meeting that a Letter should be writ to his Excellency Ezechiel Spanheim to know the Names and Degrees of ye Chief Magistrates in y^t University, & D^r. Woodroff was pleas'd to offer his Service in y^t Matter, wch was accepted of. — D^r. Charlett has turn'd off his famous Boy (call'd Davus in the verses upon him & M^r. Percival wch I have inserted at ye End of the last vol.) for several Pranks wch he had plaid, & particularly for one that was put in the Review & Observator viz. his getting drunk one night at New-College, & lighting his Master 40 home with a Silver Tankard instead of a Dark Lantern. — This day at one a Clock was a Convocation for admitting new Proctors in room of those of the last year : when M^r. Bickley the former Senior Proctor made (as usual) a proper Speech ; but he being but an indifferent Orator (however otherwise a man of good sense) he came off somewhat to the Discredit of himself and University, there being a great number of Auditors, expecting to have had something extraordinary; whereas there was nothing remarkable in his Relation of the last years Transactions (but ye New Building of Christ Church upon occasion of wch he mention'd the Palace going forward at Woodstock, & thought y^t the Duke of Marlborough 50

might look with an invidious Eye upon this at Christ Church if finish'd as
successfully as began) : And whereas formerly there was always among
other things a short History at this time given of the State of Learning in
the University for yᵉ year past, & what Books of Note had been printed
or carrying on, he wholly omitted this particular, as he did divers others
wᶜʰ should have been hinted at. After he had finish'd the New Proctors,
viz. Mʳ. Carter of Oriel and Mʳ. Cranck of Trinity were admitted; but
whether they will stand up for yᵉ Privileges of yᵉ University as their Predecessors did, is much doubted, the latter being (as I have already for-
10 merly observ'd) a Man who is for siding with both Parties, I mean Whigg
and Tory, and not declaring directly for either. — Dʳ. Lancaster, Dʳ.
Waugh and Dʳ. Gibson were all poor Children, Taberders and afterwards
Fellows of Queen's College. The first of these viz. Lancaster, when
Bachelor of Arts, was sent by Sʳ. Joseph Williamson, then Secretary of
State, into France, where he accomplish'd himself, & upon his Return he
prosecuted his Studies in Queen's College. When he stood for his Master
of Arts Degree, one Mʳ. Clark of All-Souls (one of yᵉ Proctors & a pert,
ignorant Fellow,) denied his Grace. But when it came to be put to
vote in the Congregation, he carried it against yᵉ Proctors, there being
20 nothing but trifling Objections made against him. In the first year of his
Regency & two or three years afterwards, he had a mighty Reputation for
a Preacher, wᶜʰ Character he might have still maintain'd, if he had kept
less Company, and taken as much pains as he did formerly. When he
was a Junior Fellow he liv'd some time as Chaplain to yᵉ Earl of Denbigh;
but in a little time return'd to yᵉ College, & became Tutor to several young
Gentlemen, & particularly to a Younger Son of yᵗ Earl's. A little while
after this 'twas his good fortune to be remov'd from Oxford (where for yᵉ sake
of good Company he neglected most of his Business) to yᵉ Bᵖ. of London,
& became his Domestick Chaplaine. While he was with yᵉ Bishop, he
30 got yᵉ Rich Parsonage of Sᵗ. Martin's from his Lordship, & some years
afterwards was made Provost of Queen's, wᶜʰ Election was controverted,
as being directly against yᵉ Statutes of yᵉ College. A little after this he
was made (by yᵉ Bᵖ. of London) Archdeacon of Middlesex. He has
publish'd some Sermons &c. The second Dʳ. Waugh was a plain,
popular Preacher, & a great Tutor. He was Proctor of the University &
not long after fell in league with a Widow, the Relict of one Mʳ. Fiddes
(the Son of old Mʳ. Fiddes Minister of Brightwell) upon wᶜʰ being
necessitated to leave yᵉ College, he, by yᵉ Interest of some Friends
in London, got a Lectureship in Sᵗ. Bride's, & by yᵉ means of Dʳ. Lan-
40 caster supply'd one of yᵉ Chapells of Ease in Sᵗ. Martin's Parish. Now
it being known to yᵉ Archbᵖ. of Cant. & others that he had been all along
a Favourer of yᵉ Whiggs upon the Promotion of the most Worthy Dʳ.
Beveridge, that self-designing Party (who never regard any but those of
their own gang) procur'd for him of yᵉ Queen yᵉ Good Living of Sᵗ. Peter's,
Cornhill. He preach'd and printed Bᵖ. Bull's Consecration Sermon, &
'tis said that (to augment the Number of Low-Church men in yᵉ Convocation House) he has the promise of an Archdeaconry after yᵉ Death
of one Mʳ. Staino[1]. The third Dʳ. Gibson when he was under-

---

[1] Note that this Mʳ. Stainoe was Fellow of Trinity College, & a noted Preacher
whilst at Oxford. He married a jolly fat Daughter of one Haslewood an Apothecary

graduate or just Bachelor of Arts was by D[r]. Mill put upon publishing
the Chronicon Saxonicum, w[ch] tho' the first by the Revisal of y[e] said D[r].
was better y[u] any of his other Performances.   After this to gratify one
Cruttenden (a broken Printer and a great Acquaintance of D[r]. Charlett's)
he apply'd him self to y[e] Publication of Quintilian ; in w[ch] if he had submitted himself to y[e] Directions of D[r]. Mill he might have made a very
good Edition of y[t] Author ; but seeing this (being likely to take up a
great deal of time) did not suit with y[e] Interest of Cruttenden, he left
D[r]. Mill & quite broke with him upon y[t] occasion, & in a little time gave
us an Edition of Quintilian, w[ch] had no great matter done to it.   Some 10
time I think before this he publish'd a Catalogue of MSS[ts] w[ch] he
inscribed Bibliotheca Tennisoniana, & dedicated to D[r]. Tennison, whereas
these MSS[ts] were really the L[d]. Clarendon's, w[ch] he purchas'd in Ireland
when L[d]. Deputy there.   To w[ch] is added a Catalogue of Sir W[m]. Dugdale's MSS. in y[e] Ashmolean Museum.   Not long after this, when some
Roguish Booksellers had a Design to cheat y[e] World, with a new Edition
of Camden's Britannia in English (which they pretended should be all
translated anew with great Accuracy, & inlarg'd with considerable Additions & Curious Remarks) he was thought fit to be made the supervisor &
Corrector of that Work, & to this End he went purposely to London, & 20
had all y[e] Papers relating to it put into his Hands.   Of what value they
were 'tis not certain, but excepting what y[e] Learned M[r]. Llhuyd of y[e]
Ashmolean Museum did there is nothing of any great moment appearing
throughout the whole Book.   Before or a little after his being made
Fellow of Queen's College, upon y[e] score & merits of his flattering &
unjust Dedication of y[e] above s[d] Catalogue of MSS[ts] to D[r]. Tennison, he
was made Keeper of y[e] Library at Lambeth, & liv'd in D[r]. Tennison's
(then Arch[bp].) Family, & within a while after was made one of his
Domestick Chaplains, the Arch[bp] having two more at y[e] same time, viz.
D[r]. Hody and D[r]. Greene.   Sometime after his Coming to Lambeth he 30
kept a fair Correspondence with some considerable men in y[e] Church,
such as D[r]. Hooper Parson of Lambeth and afterwards B[p]. of Bath and
Wells.   But upon the unhappy Distinction of High and Low Church Men,
and y[e] Debates arising in y[e] lower House of Convocation, he struck in
with y[e] Low Church Party, as being most able to prefer him, and writ a
great many Pamphletts about y[e] said Controversy relating to y[e] Convocation : by w[ch] Party he was look'd upon to be so meritorious especially
in y[e] Eyes of the Archbishop (who commonly sees with other Peoples
Eyes) that he got to be precentor of Chichester (that being an Option of
y[e] Archbishop's) & afterwards by the Interest of a Parcel of Whiggs in 40
that Church was made Canon Residentiary, and about y[e] same time
obtain'd the Rich Living of Lambeth, and half a Lectureship at S[t].
Martin's in y[e] Fields.   Note y[t] y[e] abovesaid D[r]. Green was a little
spruce smugg'd fac'd & formal Court Chaplain to S[r]. Stephen Fox, & it
may be by him was recommended to the abovesaid Arch[bp]. to be his
Chaplain.   By his Sneaking and Cringing (for nobody knew of any other
Merits that he had) he insinuated himself mightily into y[e] favour of y[e]
ArchB[p], & was by him recommended to be Master of Bennett College in

in Oxford, & after y[t] got a Living in London.   He has printed some Sermons, & a
Book in 8[vo]. the title whereof is * * *

Cambridge of wch both himself and ye Arch^bp were. The Fellows of that College, as to ye Majority of them, being willing to gratify the great and heavy man at Lambeth made choice of him to be their Master, to ye Regret of all men of Learning and Probity in y^t University. Either before or a little after this he was made by ye Archbishop to be one of ye Prebendaries of Canterbury. & to strengthen his Interest among ye Whiggs married a sister of D^r. Trimnell's.

Apr. 4 (Th.).   Just publish'd A Letter to M^r. Dodwell, wherein all ye Arguments in his Epistolary Discourse ag^t ye Immortality of ye Soul
10 are particularly answered, & ye Judgm^t of ye Fathers concerning y^t Matter truly represented, by Sam. Clarke, M.A. Chaplain to ye B^r. of Norwich. 8°.   'Twas written in hast, & therefore divers things are omitted; but there are several good Observations in it, & if w^t he says be true M^r. Dodwell has all along misrepresented ye Fathers. — D^r. Haley was originally of All-Souls College, first a Querister then Clerk & then Fellow there : afterwards he went along wth S^r. William Trumball in ye Quality of his Chaplain, when he was made King Charles II^ds Envoy to Constantinople. He also accompanied him in Quality of Chaplain when he was Envoy to France.   Upon ye Revolution, he was
20 made Camp Chaplain in his Expedition into Flanders, and after y^t Rector of S^t. Giles's in the Fields (Lond.) and at length Dean of Chichester. He has publish'd some Sermons in English, and one in Latin wch was preach'd before ye Lower House of Convocation, by wch anyone may see that 'twas something else than Merits that advanc'd him.   I think 'twas this D^r. who call'd D^r. Willis from his Fellowship at All-Souls (who was originally of Wadham) to be imploy'd as a Preacher under him at London.   By the Interest of D^r. Haley and his Friends, this D^r. Willis was recommended to King William as well qualified to accompany him as Camp-Chaplain in one other, or more
30 expeditions, into Flanders. He was Sub-Tutor to the Duke of Glocester, B^p. Burnett being chief.   Now being improv'd in Impudence and all Arts of Insinuation, and being a Man of true Revolution Principles, to the Surprise of all good Men, he attain'd the Deanry of Lincoln, and a little while after got a great Living wch was either in ye Disposal of ye Dean or ye Dean and Chapter of y^t Church. He has likewise printed some Sermons and other Pamphletts in English, and one Sermon in Latin, preach'd before ye Lower House of Convocation.   By wch anyone may see that he is hardly fit to be a Country Curate or School-Master. — D^r. Trimnell was a Clergyman's Son, I think in
40 Huntingdonshire, & was bred at W^m. of Wickham's School at Winchester, where he had two Brothers also; & they all three became Fellows of New-College. He had another Brother at Eaton who was afterwards Fellow of King's College in Cambridge. When the s^d D^r. Trimnell was at New College he was look'd upon as a very sober studious and ingenious Man, & by some means was recommended to ye late Earl of Sunderland in King James's time to be a Tutor to his Son

---

April 4.   Kent to H.   Consults H. about a poor woman who has been excommunicated for above sixteen years, & whom he is trying to reduce to submission by stopping the contributions of the charitable. Messages to T. Cherry, &c.

the present Earl of Sunderland. The first Preferment he had was a Parsonage in Northamptonshire wch he resign'd to one M^r. Downes Fellow of New College (who has printed a Sermon preach'd before ye University of Oxoñ) upon ye score of marrying his Sister as 'twas generally believ'd. Afterwards ye Doctor got to be Prebendary of Norwich, & has an Archdeaconry, as I take it y^t of Norwich. He married a Daughter of D^r. Talbot B^p. of Oxoñ, wch if he had not done 'tis very probable he might have been Warden' of New College upon the Decease of D^r. Traffles. For upon ye Election he lost it but by one 10 Vote, and several who were against him declar'd they would have been for him if he had not been married. He has printed one if not more Sermons. He seems to be a fair condition'd Man, & one of the best of all ye Whiggish or Low-Church Party. — Being with D^r. Charlett this Afternoon he confess'd he was sent for up to London upon Account of a Paper he shew'd to M^r. Beauchamp . . . who reported that ye Master could prove ye particulars, whereas he only shew'd it as a piece of News not at all vouching for ye Truth thereof. But w^t the Issue of his Journey was I could not gather from him; only thus much I perceive that he is afraid of being prosecuted, & for y^t reason designs to wait upon the B^p. of Worcester who is great wth ye B^p. of Sarum, & 20 to tell him ye Truth of ye Matter.

Apr. 5 (Fri.). The Natural Immortality of ye soul asserted and proved from Scripture and Primitive Antiquity, in Answer to a Book written by M^r. Dodwell, Entit. The Distinction betw. Soul & Spirit. A sheet of this I saw to day composed, & 'tis printing at ye Theatre. M^r. Mills corrects it. Quære whether he be not Author? — Just publish'd D^r. Charlott's Letter to M^r. Percival, with M^r. Percival's Answer. price 2^d. 'Tis ye same thing inserted at ye End of ye preceding Vol. — To shew w^t a Disciplinarian D^r. Mill is (after all his talk) it may be observ'd that he advis'd M^r. Pearce his Vice-Principal 30 to go and sit as Member of the Convocation when the Proctors were admitted, tho' he has not been yet made Regent; wch accordingly he did, & ye D^r. commends him for it. — Some days since departed this Life S^r. Walter Clergis K^t Baron^t after a long Indisposition of ye Dropsy. — D^r. Mill when he went to Woodstock to wait upon the Duke of Marlborough (with ye rest of his Oxoñ Brethren) address'd himself in the following Manner to ye Duke, viz.

GREAT SIR we are hither come / Whom most Men Johny Mill do call,
For to behold Your Stately Dome, / And purposely to wait upon your Grace
And complement Your self & Dear, / Our Noble Patron, & Lord of this place, 40
For ye Venison we had last year : / Have left my Testament i' th' lurch,
I am ye Principal of Edmund Hall, / As some years since I did ye Church.

Apr. 6 (Sat.). Dionysius Hal. does not make ye two Persons who assassinated Tarquinius Priscus, to be Shepherds (as Livy does) but onely to have been pastoralibus indutos vectibus, & armatos falcibus lignatorijs. — A Certain Gentleman of Dublin (I think) discoursing

---

April 6. F. Bache to H. Letter of thanks to H. and the authorities of the University and Library ; presents a book.

wth M^r. Dodwell upon ye Case of Jaddus mention'd in Josephus, M^r. Dodwell communicated to him ye following note out of ye Samaritan Chronicle, amongst D^r. Huntingdon's MSS^ts. viz. M^r. Dodwell thinks it of Importance to render ye Story of Jaddus suspicious, because it appears from hence y^t the Samaritans apply'd ye Substance of ye same story to y^eir High Priest. This chronicle is writ in ye Samaritan Language, & D^r. Bernard having read it over and made some collections communicated them to M^r. Dodwell. — M^r. John Gardiner, Bachelor of Physick of University College, has writ a Book ab^t ye Circulation of
10 ye Bloud. — S^r. Edm. Warcupp was in ye year 1699 entred of University College, & for sometime kept a Name in ye Buttery Book; at wch time D^r. Charlett (one of his Admirers) was sponsor for Discharge of his Battles. — D^r. Crakanthorp writ a Book ag^t a Book of the Archb^p. of Spalato's, publish'd by way of Retractation after ye Archb^p. left England; but D^r. Couzin pag. 12. of his Book de Sacr. Symbolis & vera præsentia X^ti in Sacram. Euch. shews y^t ye said Archb^p. never retracted his former Opinions nor writ any such Book, but died in defence of ye Doctrines wch he had maintain'd in his other Writings.

Apr. 7 (Sun.). The good Living of Adderbury in Oxoñshire be-
20 coming vacant upon the Death of D^r. Beau, B^p. of Landaff, and it being to be dispos'd of by Vote by the Fellows of New-College (to wch it belongs) M^r. Loggans, Bachelor of ye Civil Law, Chancellor of Sarum and Fellow of y^t House was one of those who stood for it & carried it by one Vote, to ye great Amazement of the whole university & Resentment of all good Men, he not taking orders 'till this time when he was above 50 years of Age, & being so void of Parts and Learning, that as 'tis said by some sober, understanding Persons he is not able to read the Common-Prayer; wch he is so conscious of that he designs to do no dutys at ye Place himself, but to keep one there for y^t End: his
30 design in going into Orders being for nothing else but to inlarge his Purse, not to do God service. And tho' all this could not but be well known by B^p. Burnett, yet he ordain'd him w^thout any Scruple that I can hear of. To such a Height of Wickedness is the World grown! — This Morning preached at S^t. Marie's D^r. Hall B^p. of Bristol upon these words, *my yoke is easy and my Burden is light,* shewing from thence how easy a thing it is for any man to obey and follow all the Commands & Injunctions of X^t, if he do but apply himself chearfully and willingly, & wth y^t love he has for other things, to ye Performance of them. — D^r. Charlett tells me that he thinks M^r. Mills to be the Undertaker of
40 ye Book, a sheet whereof I saw at ye Theatre Press, ag^t M^r. Dodwell; because he talk'd to him that he would write such a thing. — M^r. Collins (with whom I was this afternoon) is of opinion that M^r. Dodwell is in the right about ye natural mortality of ye soul, & said he would be so 'till some better Answer come out y^n y^t written by M^r. Clark. He told me that M^r. Hen. Stubbs was mov'd chiefly to write against ye Royal Society, because he was not admitted Fellow of it; wch if he had been, he would have us'd his Pen in Defence. — S^r. Walter Clarges Son of S^r. Thomas Clarges, who was once an Apothecary in London, Burgess for ye university of *Oxon,* and was Brother in Law to General
50 Monke, who married his Sister.

Apr. 8 (Mon.). Mr. Bingham, lately Fellow of University College, has just publish'd a Book in 8º, call'd *The Apology of the French Church for yᵉ Church of England*; wᶜʰ he has dedicated to yᵉ Archbᵖ. of Canterbury, but does not in yᵉ least complement him; & I believe yᵗ yᵉ Archbᵖ. will grumble at his Writing agᵗ Dissenters, whom he (like a 2ᵈ Abbot) encourages & protects as much as possibly he can.

Apr. 9 (Tu.). Dr. Woodroff did not write yᵉ Letter sent to Baron Spanheim conc. the celebration of yᵉ Foundation of the university of Francfurt, but yᵉ Vice-Chancellor himself. 'Twas well recᵈ by his Excellency & he gave his Opinion that our University took the best way, 10 & yᵉ Duke of Ormond seem'd at last satisfied tho' at first he seem'd something concern'd that we should not do as Cambridge had done. Which as it would have cost the University 6 or 700 libˢ. and perhaps have created some Difference about Precedence, so would it not have been so great an Honour as wᵗ has been resolv'd upon. — Memorandum yᵗ when Tully's Epistles are reprinted a little Piece is to be taken out of Morhoffius's Book de conscribendis Epistolis, wᶜʰ has this Title, viz. pag. 284, Exempla Epistolarum secundum causarum genera è Cicerone collecta. — Dr. Barton, originally Scholar and Fellow of Corpus Xᵗⁱ Coll. when in Oxoñ was reckon'd a pretty good Scholar, but a man of 20 a morose severe Temper, & a little Puritannically inclin'd. He was made Chaplain to Mr. Foley when Speaker of the House of Commons, and upon yᵉ House's Petition, as is usual for yᵉ Chaplain, was made Prebendary of Westminster. He has also a Good Living in Southwark, wᶜʰ it may be he recᵈ from one of yᵉ Lᵈ. Keepers. He has publish'd some Sermons. Dr. Hallifax, originally Scholar & Fellow of Corpus Xᵗⁱ of the same Puritanical stamp with yᵉ former, was at Smyrna for some time, and copied yᵉ Inscriptions at Palmyra, wᶜʰ were publish'd in yᵉ Philosophical Transactions, wᵗʰ notes, wᶜʰ are full of Faults. He was likewise Chaplain to Foley when Speaker of yᵉ House of Com- 30 mons, & tho' the House petition'd for him, yet 'twas his Fortune to get nothing : whereas one Galloway, originally of Hart-Hall, who was a most notorious stupid Blockhead, without one Grain of Learning, for being Foley's Chaplain, when Speaker, got to be Prebendary of Worcester; wᶜʰ to yᵉ scandal of all Worthy men he still enjoys. He (Dr. Hallifax) translated De Chale's Euclid, whereof there are two or three Impressions.

[Notes on Livy XXVII. 24 and XXXVIII. 25. from Caesar de Bell. Civ. III. 98, and de Bell. Gall. I. 46, ed. Davies. (108–109.)] . . .

A Gentleman this Afternoon shew'd me a Coyn of M. Aurelius Vic- 40 torinus, of the lesser Brass viz. ɪᴍᴘ. ᴠɪᴄᴛᴏʀɪɴᴠs ᴘ. ꜰ. ᴀᴠɢ. Victorini Caput radiat. ℞ sᴀʟᴠs ᴀᴠɢ. Fig. stans, dex. serpentem, cui Pateram sinistra porrigit. — There is a Book going under yᵉ Name of Gorallus, wᶜʰ is a fictitious Name for *Joannes Clericus*. See Baile's Dictionary. — Remember to tell Dr. Hudson that he has made a Reference in pag. 233. Vol. 1. of Dionysius to the Notes at yᵉ End of the Work concerning *Vicus Orbius*, where however is nothing said abᵗ it. — Mr. Milles coming to see Dr. Hudson this Afternoon, the Dr. told him he heard he had a Book in yᵉ Press in Answer to Mr. Dodwell. When

Mr. Milles did not frankly own it, but seem'd to shuffle about it, the
Dr. told him that he had it from three several Persons of good credit,
& that moreover common fame made him ye Author of it.   To which
Milles reply'd that this was only their Conjectures, & that common
Fame was often a Lyar.   Then says the Doctor to him, if you do not
own the Book why do you not disown it, & free your self from ye
Reflections yt some Men make, yt it was not fair in you who are
honour'd with Mr. Dodwell's Friendship, not to propose your Objections agt his Book to him by way of letter, before you make them
10 Publick.   To this he answer'd that seeing Mr. Dodwell had made his
Book publick it was fitting the Answer should be as publick too; & yt
Mr. Dodwell could not well object against it, seeing he was treated by
the Author (whoever he was) with ye greatest Respect and candor
imaginable; & yt 'twas so far from being any prejudice to Mr. Dodwell, that it would be a means to keep off others from falling more
severely upon him.   After this the Dr. told him yt if he had taken his
advice, he should not have meddled with Mr. Dodwell: for he thought
it not only unfair to deal so with a Friend but likewise that it would not
turn to any Good Account to himself.   For he might be sure that ye
20 Christ Church Men & others, who are already incens'd against him,
would severely criticise upon his Performance, & expose it all that
possibly they could.   To wch Milles reply'd that the Author had communicated what he had writ to two or three Friends whose Judgmt he
could rely upon & yt everything was so nicely weigh'd & well consider'd, that he fear'd no Body's Censure, & would court no Man's
favour; & did not in ye least doubt but it would be unanswerable.
After this the Dr. told him that he had heard that Mr. Milles should
say that Mr. Dodwell had not quoted so much as one Father fairly; to
wch Milles did agree.   Upon wch the Dr. told him, yt he believ'd Mr.
30 Dodwell was a person of yt Honesty and Integrity that he would not
willingly so impose upon ye World, & yt he was moreover of such
Abilities, & so well vers'd in ye Fathers, that he could not imagine Mr.
Dodwell should be so much mistaken.   To this Milles reply'd That in
a little time men would be convinc'd of ye Truth of what he said.
The Dr. talk'd with him no more on that Topick, but then ask'd him
how big this Answer would be.   He said near upon as big as Mr.
Dodwell's Book: to wch the Dr. said no more, but only express'd his
Wonder that so great a Book should be writ in so short a time, & yt if
he (Milles) was the Author of it yt he should have so much leisure as
40 to make Visits.   To wch he said, that the Dr. did not well consider
how much time he had to himself yet.   From all this the Dr. cannot
bring himself to believe that Milles is the Author, but rather Humphrey
Hody, who was in Town just at ye time the Book was put to ye Press;
& yt Milles to court ye favour of ye People at Lambeth has offer'd his
service to ye Dr. to correct his Book.   (The Dr. is willing that this
should be communicated to Mr. Dodwell for his own private use.)

   Apr. 10 (Wed.).   I am inform'd that Mr. Oddy ye Gentleman who
designs to put out an Edition of Dion Cassius lives in London, was
never bred at any university (his Father being a Fanatick) that he is
50 about 33 or 34 years of Age, has been a very hard Student, has

Excellent natural Parts, is a great master of the Greek Tongue & very well skill'd in Sacred & Prophane History, & y^t he is of different Principles from his Father. But quære more? — Just publish'd, A Book call'd Justice done to Humane Souls in a short view of M^r. Dodwell's Book Entit. An Epistolary Discourse, proving the Soul to be a Principle Naturally mortal &c. In a Letter to a Friend by John Turner, D.D. Vicar of Greenwich.

[Query, whether four books named are in the Public Library?] . . .

Apr. 11 (Th.). The Proclamation for silencing ye Episcopal Clergy in Scotland is as rigorous against y^m as if they had been declar'd 10 Exiles. — M^r. Percival told me last night that there are 4 or 5 Persons engag'd in writing the Book printing in the Theatre against M^r. Dodwell. Quære whether White of Wadham be not one of them? I am sure he is consulting Books ab^t ye Soul. — Meeting accidentally this day with two Young Gentlemen, they told me they call'd a day or two since in their way to Oxoũ upon M^r. Dodwell, with whom talking upon the Subject of his New Book, he told them he had just then rec^d M^r. Clark's Letter to him, & was reading of it over, & wthall said that he (M^r. Clark) had dealt very disingenuously by him. — Just come out a Book call'd The Rights of the Christian Church asserted against the 20 Independent Power of the Romish and all other Priests : in wch Book are some things against M^r. Dodwell's Preface to his Defence of the Vindication of ye Depriv'd B^{ps}. shewing that he is in a great Error about the first B^{ps} of our English Reformation, & y^t his Notion ab^t the Civil Magistrate's having no Authority to deprive B^{ps} for Political Crimes cannot be reconcil'd with w^t was done at y^t time. — 'Tis only the first Part, & I am told by M^r. Clements that D^r. Tyndal of All-Souls is Author, whom he saw present one in London to a Friend of his of ye same Principles wth the Doctor.

April 12 (Fri.). As soon as D^r. Hudson was made Bursar of Uni- 30 versity College, he took care to regulate divers disorders relating to his Office, wch had crept in by ye Remissness (I suppose) of some of his Predecessors. But amongst these laudable Undertakings is chiefly to be mention'd the College Garden wch having been almost ruinated & quite out of Repair, he order'd to be cover'd with Green Turff, planted with Trees & flowers, & the Walks to be gravell'd, to the great Beauty of ye Place & Satisfaction of the rest of ye Fellows : & there was no one of ye College appear'd at present displeas'd wth it but ye Master ; wch perhaps being known to one Robinson (a Commoner of y^t House, & Nephew to M^r. Smith lately senior Fellow & now in London, who it seems was 40 always averse to this Reform) a day or two after it was finish'd with two or three more of ye College got into ye Garden in ye Night time, pull'd up some of ye Ews spoil'd others, & did other Mischief, to ye no small Grief of ye Doctor & ye rest of ye Fellows ; it being such a piece of Malice as one would think could not enter into the thoughts of any person of common Breeding, & indeed seldom or never heard of in the University, but in y^s College, where they have had some other Instances of ye same Nature, & have had some lads noted for this Diabolical Wickedness ; & wthout doubt 'twas from them M^r. Robinson was in-

structed, he being reckon'd at first a civil modest Youth, & to be very
good natur'd.   One reason wch instigated him I hear is because the D^r.
and the rest of ye Society had taken care y^t all the undergraduates &
Bachelors should dine and sup in the Hall, or to undergo a penalty for
it, wch it seems had been neglected before, to the disgrace somew^t of the
College, this being a proviso in all College and Hall Statutes, & if kept
up redounds much to ye Honour of ye University. — A Book in Arabick
written by Abdollatiphi, containing a compendious History of Egypt was
begun to be translated by D^r. Pocock and printed at ye Theatre in
10 B^p. Fell's time at ye Expense of D^r. Marshall Rector of Lincoln College,
& was a pretty way advanc'd; but on a sudden ye B^p. having an occasion
for ye Latin Letter the Book stop'd, wch so vex'd the good old Man D^r.
Pocock y^t he could never be prevail'd to go on any farther.   Neither
would D^r. Hyde, tho' often desir'd by D^r. Aldrich when Vice-Chancellor,
finish the same, unless somebody would give him a good Sum of Money
for it ; wch was highly resented by the said D^r. Aldrich, who still offers
to be at ye Expense of Finishing ye Book. — Remember to look upon
the MS^t of Pomponius Mela in New College Library, & see w^t Age it
is.   A gentleman of Exeter is preparing a new Edition of it, & I am told
20 has six maps already Engrav'd for it.   I am [1]told the Gentleman is M^r.
Reynolds who has a Brother Fellow of Corpus X^ti & another Fellow of
Baliol.   He is a Schoolmaster in ye Country.

April 13 (Sat.).   D^r. Hudson ad pag. 271. of Dionys. Hal. thinks y^t
the Vatican MS. reads Οὐϊνδίκιος rightly for Οὐϊνδίκης.   W^ch is wrong,
Plutarch having Οὐϊνδίκης also : and Sigonius and Vossius (in his Ety-
molog.) have remark'd that *Vindex* in Livy is to be read for *Vindicius*.
— In Arch. Bod. B. 2. Is the Apocalyps in French & English Illuminations,
wch are remarkable, but are but grossly done.

April 14 (Sun.).   D^r. William Lloyd the Depriv'd B^p. of Norwich had
30 a son died lately (named John Lloyd) of the small Pox, being about 30
years of Age.   He was a Gentleman of great Hopes, being a Barrister at
Law, in wch he had obtain'd great Skill.   His death happen'd about a
fortnight after he had married a Daughter of D^r. Humphreys B^p. of
Hereford.   His Father D^r. Lloyd, who was of S^t. John's in Camb. as
was also his Son, is a Person of Excellent Learning, Primitive Christianity
&c. as may be seen in the Preface to D^r. Hicks's Thesaur. Ling. Sept.
D^r. Humphreys was of Jesus College, is reckon'd a Man of Integrity, &
highly noted for his Skill in the British Antiquities, as partly appears
from the Tables Chronological drawn up by him in ye first Vol. of M^r.

April 13.   Dr. T. Smith to H.   Hopes Mr. Smith, of University, will
not quit his station there if he can well and fairly keep it.   Will send
H. a copy of his letter to Dr. Wallis (written Sept. 1690) concerning
Wood's blunders and injudicious collections out of the Archives, when he
can light upon it.   Remarks on Halley, Thwaites, Hudson, Roman antiquities.   Sir W^m. Farmor, now L^d. Leominster, bought the marbles at Easton
of the Dowager Duchess of Norfolk (Mrs. Bickerton) for a very inconsiderable sum.   See Smith's letter to M. Boier, since printed without leave.   Any
truth in the scandalous story concerning Dr. Charlett ?   Who is C. Veratius
Philellen ?   Is highly satisfied with Mill's *Prolegomena*.

---

[1] This is certain.

Tyrrell's General History of England. — This day in yᵉ Afternoon preach'd at Sᵗ. Marie's before yᵉ University Mʳ. Stevens, Fellow of Merton College (to wᶜʰ place he was chosen from Corpus Xᵗⁱ Coll.) upon Mat. 10. 28. . . .

The design of wᶜʰ Discourse was to prove the Natural Immortality of yᵉ soul, & was levell'd particularly against Mʳ. Dodwell, whose Hypothesis he said was dangerous and Irreligious. He prov'd his position from the Nature of the Soul, which he said is immaterial, it being in his Opinion impossible for mater to think. The Arguments for proof of this were no other than wᵗ have been before advanc'd by Sir Kenelm Digby, & therefore he need not have 10 insisted so much upon them; nor indeed were they much to the purpose in confuting Mʳ. Dodwell, since yᵗ learned Man is of opinion that yᵉ Soul is neither material nor immaterial but distinct from both & yet dependent upon mater. After he had done with this part of his Discourse, he proceeded to prove it's natural Immortality from Revelation; wᶜʰ however was but indifferently perform'd by him, not confuting one Explication of any one Text of Scripture given by Mʳ. Dodwell; but only saying in general that the Scriptures were express against him; as also he insinuated the Fathers were, tho' he did not shew it, but only referr'd to Mʳ. Clark's Answer, not doubting but all people would be satisfied from thence; whereas 'tis so far from being a satis- 20 factory Discourse, that most people are of opinion that Mʳ. Clark has dealt somewᵗ unfairly by Mʳ. Dodwell in yᵗ particular; and indeed Mʳ. Dodwell complains of him on yᵗ Account. Upon the whole he concluded the Soul to be a principle naturally immortal, & not immortaliz'd by yᵉ Divine Spirit in Baptism, & hinted how easy 'tis for Great and Learned Men to fall into Error, when they suffer themselves to be byass'd thro' partiality, or are stiff in maintaining opinions not thought off before.

April 15 (Mon.). Dʳ. Smith tells me of a Piece written handsomely & judiciously agᵗ Jac. Gronovius in the ixᵗʰ Tome of Le Clerck's Bibliotheque Choisie wᶜʰ he says is dated at Oxon last Jan. I cannot tell who 30 it should be. 'Tis not likely to have been done at Oxon. Perhaps Fabricius was Author who ows Gronovius a spight for publishing Manetho's Apotelesmata, wᶜʰ Fabricius had undertaken & promis'd before ever Gronovius thought of it. . . Mʳ. Owen Master of an Academy (I think in Staffordshire) who writ Moderation a vertue & some other things agᵗ Mʳ. Lesley died abᵗ 10 days agoe. — Mʳ. Jo. Cannel, whom I have before mention'd, of Lincoln College, took his A.M.'s Degree last Term, & is since made Chaplain to my Lord Haversham.

April 16 (Tu.). Dʳ. Lloyd late Bᵖ. of Norwich has an Elder Brother nam'd Ellis Lloyd, a Gentleman of abᵗ 900 libˢ. per Annum, 300 of wᶜʰ 40 he had settled upon Mʳ. Lloyd (John) mention'd above, just before he married. — Upon yᵉ Decease of Dʳ. Halton Provost of Queen's College, Archdeacon of Oxon & Brecknock, his Archdeaconry of Brecknock was given to Mʳ. Roger Griffyth, a Person who had been formerly a Presbyterian Teacher, & was then come over to yᵉ Church of England. He

----

April 17. T. Cherry to H. Wants 'old shews,' stockings, linen, &c. sent. Three more answers to Dodwell forthcoming; Dodwell is uneasy under Mr. Clark's observations, denying that his book can do harm to any. 'He bad me desire you would compare the edition of Rinesius's Variæ Lectiones by Camerarius . . yᵉ 14 chap. & 3ᵈ Book with the manuscript of Selden's relating to Vettius Valence in which book he is often mentioned.'

never was of any University, wch he thinking then something scandalous, there was some motion made for having his Degrees of Bach. & M. of Arts given him here; but finding y^t would not take he went to Cambridge, where he was made Bachelor of Divinity at y^t time ye Queen was there, & in some time will take that of D^r. especially if he be made B^p. of Landaff, a thing wch has been propos'd by the B^p. of Worcester tho' not likely to happen y^t I can learn as yet.

April 17 (Wed.). One of the Sceleton's in ye Anatomy Schoole was wired by one Wells a Smith in Cat-Street; by wch he became an
10 Eminent Bone-setter & a good Surgeon. — In ye year 1690 was published a Pamphlett (of very good Note) call'd the Judgm^t of ye Forreign Reformed Churches conc. ye Rites & Offices of ye church of England: shewing there is no need of Alterations. The Author N. S. Memorandum That D^r. John Baron (Master of Baliol Col.) made bold with this Pamphlet, in a Sermon at S^t. Marie's (An Acc^t whereof I gave at y^t Time) just when he was a Candidate for ye Margaret Professor's Place. Quære whether M^r. Bingham has not also been dabbling in it? — I am told M^r. Perks of Corpus Christi College is one of those ingag'd in writing an Answer to M^r. Dodwell. — Talking this Afternoon wth M^r.
20 Milles about ye said Answer, he denied y^t any had a hand in Writing of it but one Person, & said y^t there were but two who ever saw it, tho' he had before told D^r. Hudson that 3 or four had perus'd it. He also denied y^t M^r. Perks had look'd any of it over, but 3 or four pages. The Author he s^d was so familiarly acquainted wth M^r. Dodwell, & had so great a Respect for him, y^t he took all possible care to avoid abusive Language. When I ask'd him why being so much his Friend he did not first of all communicate w^t he had to say to M^r. Dodwell, who perhaps might retract some of his Errors in ye New Edition, he gave but a very shuffling Answer, & no more y^n what he had told D^r. Hudson before.
30 He would not acknowledge himself to be Author, tho' he confess'd himself to have look'd it over, & to have some Hand in it as it was at ye Press : upon wch I told him some people wonder'd he should meddle at all wth one who was so much his Friend, especially since he formerly vindicated M^r. Dodwell's Opinion ; & notw^thstanding this was a different Subject, yet some things are to be resolv'd into those principles handled in those other Books by M^r. Dodwell, & ye World would think hardly of him upon this Account. To wch he reply'd that he was still of opinion y^t ye Civil Magistrate has no Right of Depriving B^ps & would defend M^r. Dodwell on y^t score : wch is such a piece of Contradiction as can hardly
40 be parallell'd, himself sometime since telling me he was asham'd of w^t he had written formerly on y^t subject, & having all along communicated wth such B^ps as are Schismatical according to M^r. Dodwell's Opinion & w^t himself had laid Down in his Vindication of y^t Learned Man. Upon ye whole from w^t he said in relation to himself, & especially from his intimating y^t ye Author would not answer all (by wch it should seem he was almost weary, much like M^r. Milles's manner of proceeding in such Cases) as also from part of ye Copy wch I saw today being his hand, I conclude M^r. Milles to be Author, or at least to have a very great Share in it. Amongst other things upon this occasion he told me D^r. South
50 was writing an Answer too, wch would be by way of Appendix to a Book

he is writing against yᵉ Bᵖ. of Gloucester. — Just publish'd, Because Iniquity shall abound, yᵉ Love of many shall wax cold. A Sermon preached by Dʳ. Burnett Bᵖ. of Salisbury at Sᵗ. Sepulchres Church London on Easter Monday, 1706. — The Earl of Berkshire died last Friday & is succeeded by his Grandson Henry Howard of Elstor in Staffordsh., who is not 20 yʳˢ of Age. The Earl died in yᵉ 90ᵗʰ Year of his Age.

April 18 (Th.). This day was an Election of Fellows at Queen's College, when Mʳ. Hudson, Mʳ. Todhunter, & Mʳ. Hall were Elected, & Mʳ. Matt. Gibson (Brother to Mʳ. John Gibson, one of the present 10 Fellows) Mʳ. Charnley & Mʳ. Hodgson, were turn'd by, tho' Senior to Mʳ. Hall; wᶜʰ is an Irregularity, & wᵗ is resented by some, tho' perhaps yᵉ Reason might be because these three had been in yᵉ Country, almost ever since they were Taberders, coming only to Oxford to keep Terms, or sometimes for convenience : whereas Hall & Hudson were constantly resident, & so was Todhunter, only a year or two before the Election he had serv'd as Curate at Bath. — Mʳ. John Potter of Lincoln College was presented this morning to his Degree of Dʳ. of Divinity. He was originally Servitor of University College, where he was Pupil first to Mʳ. Bateman & upon his Death to Mʳ. Bingham, & recᵈ some In- 20 structions from Dʳ. Hudson. Afterwards being Bachelor of Arts he was Elected Fellow of Lincoln, & before he took the Degree of Master of Arts published a little piece of Plutarch in Greek & Latin (upon wᶜʰ he was put by Dʳ. Charlett) de Audiendis poëtis, & a piece of Sᵗ. Basil wᵗʰ it upon yᵉ same Subject. When Master of Arts he put out Lycophron, wᵗʰ various readings & Notes, whereof there are two Impressions (both at yᵉ Theatre) in folio, wᶜʰ got him some credit ; as likewise did his Greek Antiquities, in two volumes in 8°. written in English, & afterwᵈˢ published in Latin in folio, being the last volume of Gronovius's Greek Thesaurus. 'Twas translated by another Hand, but 30 revis'd by Mʳ. Potter himself before printed. At length being noted for a person of Whiggish principles, he was taken notice of by the Archᵇᵖ. of Canterbury, Tennison I mean, who has no regard for Learning or Learned Men, any farther than as they are of yᵉ same Principles wᵗʰ himself & knows hardly any thing of Greek, as appears particularly from wᵗ I heard Dʳ. John Mill one of his Great Admirers say of him, namely that when Mʳ. Grabe had published the first vol. of Spic. Patrum the Archᵇᵖ gave Mʳ. Grabe a Complemᵗ upon it saying that he was glad he had printed such a piece as old Thecla, of whom he had heard something, & suppos'd it might be of some use tho' he could not judge of it 40 (his studies lying another way) I say Mʳ. Potter being taken notice of by this Archᵇᵖ. he was made one of his Domestick Chaplains (upon Dr. Hody's leaving it when made Archdeacon of Oxon,) & a little after had a Parsonage given him by his Grace, purely to incourage him to go on in the Sneaking way, wᶜʰ accordingly Mʳ. Potter does, and may do yᵉ Archᵇᵖ. some service by it. — Dʳ. Will. Shippen, who has publish'd some sermons, was originally of University College, a Fellow there & Proctor of the University & a person of good Reputation for Learning, as appear'd by his Proctor's Speech, wᶜʰ was highly commended, and by some other Performances. — On Monday (Apr. 15) last Mʳ. Simon Ockley of 50

Queen's College in Cambridge was incorporated Master of Arts of this University. Of whom I shall say more hereafter. — D^r. Aldworth, Fellow of Magd. Coll. upon ye unjust Deprivation of M^r. Dodwell was made Camden's Professor of History. He has never yet shew'd himself in print, & whether he be well qualify'd for ye Place or no 'tis hard to judge from anything wch he does, seldom or never reading. — Charles Allestry M.A. of X^t Church has I think printed a Sermon. He is now Minister of Dentry. — Quære whether M^r. Nath. Alsop Fellow and Bach. of D. at Brasen Nose Coll. was not Father to M^r. Ant. Alsop Student of
10 X^t Church. — D^r. Roger Altham Senior Regis Professor of Hebrew in this University, had y^t place first of all conferr'd upon him by ye Interest y^t D^r. Radcliff ye Physitian had at y^t time with ye Earl of Portland; but ye said D^r. Altham either not taking some Oath, or not making some subscription in due time lost ye Place & was succeeded by D^r. Thomas Hyde the Library-Keeper. After ye Death of D^r. Hyde, as 'tis suppos'd by ye Interest of ye Arch^bp. of York & other Friends, he obtain'd ye Place a 2^d time. He is a good Scholar, & a most Excell^t Preacher, but as yet has done nothing remarkable in ye way of his Profession. He was Chaplain to Arch^bp. Dolben, had some Preferm^t from him in y^e
20 Church of York & somewhere in ye Country.

April 19 (Fri.). In pag. 358. of the III^d Vol. of Prynne's History of Popes Usurpations is a Memorable Inquisition retorned in the 13th Year of Edw. first, but not filed 'till ye Year after, not only concerning the Bounds, but Tithes and Oblations of ye Parish of Braye in Berks, part of wch Tithes the King had sequestred. This will be of great use to ye Parishioners of White-Waltham who have had for some years a Contest wth the Parishioners of Bray ab^t their Bounds, the former always encroaching upon ye latter. — Yesterday D^r. Wynne of Jesus College read his Inaugural Lecture as Margaret Professor wch was a
30 very good one, as I am told. — I am told there were yesterday six of ye Fellows against turning those 3 above mention'd off at Queens & 7 for it; & ye Matter was effected by ye Provost's agreeing wth ye latter. The reason alledg'd in relation to Gibson was his having a Brother upon ye Foundation already, wch might if he were elected prove of some prejudice to ye Society.

April 20 (Sat.). MS. Laud. B. 155. A thin Folio Book in Vellam, containing curious Pictures, with an Explication in French, relating to the Wars of Edw. 1st. The Pictures are done by a modern hand, as is the whole Book, & seems to have been copied by Arch^bp. Laud's order
40 from the Fragments of a larger work. — Arch. Bodl. B. 49. R. Mardochæi Nathanis Radicum sive Thematum Hebræorum Expositiones Latinè à Nicolao Fullero redditæ, ac multis in locis emendatæ Notisque

---

April 20. Dodwell to H. Criticisms on Clark; reflections on Mill and his pretence of friendship. Complains of the Bishop of Worcester's neglect. Recommends him to *print* his Livy at the Theatre, but to *publish* in London. **Fra. Brokesby to H.** 'My Kinsman the Library Keeper at Manchester tells me that he is sorry that their Library will not afford the Paderborn or Venice Edition of ye first part of the 33^d Book of Livy.' Sends a passage relating to it from Gronovius' Preface to Livy. Suggests that 'such as are gone

varijs locupletatæ & illustratæ. 'Tis in 4to & at ye Beginning is the Following Clause of M^r. Fuller's will, relating to ye Disposal of it:

I give & bequeath to Sir Thomas Bodley's Library in Oxford, my New Translation in Latin of ye Hebrew concordance, wth manifold Notes therein, though not thoroughly perused nor perfected by me; that if any good thing be found therein, it may be forth coming for the studious Reader.

— Anth. Wood to gratify ye Papists often speaks but indifferently of A.B^p. Laud. — Memorandum y^t John Piers (second Son, as M^r. Wood hints, of D^r. W^m. Piers B^p. of Bath & Wells) liv'd at Denton in the parish of Cudesden near Oxon. His Elder Brother was D^r. W^m. Piers; & 10 one of the said sons (I cannot say w^{ch}) left two sons John & W^m. Piers. John now lives at Denton in ye Parish of Cuddesden. W^m. was sent to Merchant Taylors' School & thence to Emanuel Coll. in Cambridge, of wch he became Fellow, & has put out two Tragedies of Euripides, in Greek and Latin with Notes & ye Greek Scholia; & being a man of Learning & Industry ye world may expect more from him. — The Low-church Men to obviate ye Reflections made upon them for preferring none but y^{eir} own Party, at length promoted D^r. Bull & Beveridge to 2 B^{pp}ricks; but they were Welch ones & such as their own Creatures would not accept of. — 'Tis to be wonderd that Arch^{bp}. Usher, in his 20 Antiquities of ye British Church should suspect ye veracity of M^r. Cam-den in his Edition of Asser Menevensis, upon Acc^t y^t ye Passage relating to Oxford University is not in Arch^{bp}. Parker's Edition of y^t Author; but perhaps ye Reason why Arch^{bp}. Usher favours Parker is that Trinity College in Dublin (of ye wch Usher was ye First Scholar) was as it were a Colony from Cambridge, & so might induce him to be partial in y^t respect. —

Ask D^r. Smith whether in pag. 52. of his Life of M^r. Camden by *nuperus scriptor* &c. he does not mean B^p. Burnett? Without doubt he does, for in a spare leaf at ye Beginning of a certain copy of Camden's 30 Epistles (to wch ye said Life is prefix'd) I find ye following observable passage relating to ye said words, to wch it is referr'd, viz.

Is est *Gilbertus Burnet*, fidei suspectæ in Historia Reformationis Anglicanæ scriptor; qui favore Gulielmi Principis Arausionensis (ad quem paulo ante Expeditionem istam Batavicam, genti Anglicanæ, Religioni, bonis literis infaus-tissimam, se contulerat) Episcopatu Sarisburiensi, nostratibus fere omnibus indignantibus, insignitus est. Plurima quidem idiomate Anglicano edidit, tam ad Religionem quam ad Historiam & Regimen civile nostrum spectantia, quæ à probis & eruditis parvi æstimantur. Ex eorum numero est qui Academias nostras summo odio prosequitur, & Fanaticorum partibus impense favet. 40

April 21 (Sun.). I am told of some Coyns & Medalls lately found in a Ground near S^t. Leonards Hill by Windsor. Quære w^t they are? —

---

from Cambridge to the Secular Solemnity at Frankfort on Oder' might make enquiry at Paderborn. **E. Smith to H.** M. de Seau has gone into York-shire; on his return will try to borrow the two books from the Sunderland Library; he has lost his notes on Livy. Sends two passages bearing on Livy from Dr. Lyster's *Journey to Paris*. Sir Philip Sydenham contemplates an *Athenae Cantab.*, and Dr. Coward an answer to Dodwell. 'I am told several Gent. in ye Counties has club^d y^r notions & contributed a part in Tindal's execrable Book ... I'll get Mr. Dyer to excuse me the other news.'

M^r. Wood in ye Character of D^r. Goodwin B^p. of Hereford has omitted
y^t he was one of M^r. Camden's peculiar Friends as is observ'd in ye Life
of M^r. Camden. — Quære whether M^r. Thomas Savile who has a Letter
in ye Collection of M^r. Camden's Epistles dated from Merton College
was an Author, & whether of that Coll.? — Upon ye Decease of M^r.
Tho.Baker, Rector of Haritsham in Kent, M^r. Thos. (Rich^d.) Coleir, Fellow
of All-Souls Coll. & originally of Brasen-nose, was preferr'd to y^t Place, just
after he had been Junior Proctor of ye University. After wch he marry'd
& is now Chaplain to a Ship, having run himself into Debt by Building.
10 He has printed a Sermon, preach'd at a Visitation, &c. — M^r. Thomas
Collins Master of Magd. School was originally of Trinity-College, &
afterwards of Baliol, then Vice-Principal of Glocester Hall, & at length
was made Master of the said Schoole, where he has been several years,
is a good Preacher, a good Scholar, & a most facetious Companion. —
D^r. Thomas Hoy of S^t. John's Coll. was first Fellow there, & afterwards
practis'd Physick in Warwicksh. a little after ye Revolution, by ye Interest
wch his Tutor D^r. Gibbons had wth ye L^d. Somers he got to succeed D^r.
Luff Regis Professor of Physick in this University ; wch place he has
miserably neglected ever since he had it. He has translated into English,
20 some pieces of Plutarch's Morals, & writ a Poëm call'd the Life of
Agathocles, & some other things I think. Quære? — To be added to
ye Acc^t M^r. Wood has given of M^r. now D^r. Edw. Wells of X^t Church.
He publish'd while in Oxoñ a Set of Mapps of ancient & Modern Geography, with a Discourse in 8°. shewing the use of them. (2) Xenophon's
Works in 5 Vols. 8°. Gr. & Lat. (3) Dionysius's Periegesis, wth the new
Geography inserted, in Greek Verse. After wch he left the university for
a small Living in Leycestershire, where he writ 3 Letters ag^t ye Nonconformists, wch are printed, &c. He is an ingenious Man, of great Sobriety
& Modesty, &c. — D^r. Roger Altham Junior Student of X^t Church, &
30 Proctor of ye University (as had been D^r. Altham senior above mention'd)
was a little after his Proctership preferr'd to be Chaplain to ye B^p. of
London, who first gave him the Church of S^t. Mary Ax, & then remov'd
him to a better. Quære w^t? He has publish'd some Sermons. — M^r.
James Badger, Fellow of New College, & Master of ye Schoole belonging
to y^t Place (wch by ye consent of ye college he remov'd to ye End of S^t.
Maries &) wch by his Industry he made flourish to a great Degree. He
has publish'd a Book for ye use of Schools call'd Synopsis locorum com-
munium. pr. at Oxon. 8°. — Harrington Bagshaw was Fellow of Magd.
Coll. wch he left upon Marriage, and took up wth the Mastership of y^e
40 Hospital at Bromley. He has printed one Sermon. — John Bernard of
Brasennose College in King James's Reign turn'd Papist, and got to be
Moral Philosophy Reader. After ye Revolution he chang'd his Religion
again, & has writ several things, amongst wch is his Translation into
English of ye Lives of the Roman Emperors, written by Vopiscus &c. in
two volumes 8°. — D^r. John Bateman of Merton College was always
reckon'd an Excell^t Scholar, & well vers'd in Physick (in wch he was D^r.).
After ye Taking of his Degree he practis'd in London for several Years,
& liv'd in very good Reputation. Upon ye Death of D^r. Lydal Warden
of Merton he was one of ye three chosen by ye Coll. & presented to y^e
50 Arch^bp. in order to succeed him. All honest Men thought him infinitely

preferrable to the other two (viz. Dr. Lane & Dr. Martin) yet for all yt ye Archbp, because Dr. Bateman was an Honest Church of England Man, and one who was likely to do good in yt College, wch extremely wanted such a one, made choice of Dr. Martin, who by a lazy, Epicurean Life & an utter Neglect of all Discipline, has very much prejudic'd that noble and ancient Seminary. He has translated one of Plutarch's Lives & may perhaps have done some other Things. He had a Brother Thomas Bateman Fellow of University College, a Person of good Learning and great Probity, whose unfortunate Death by a Fall off his Horse near Woodstock was very much lamented by ye College and the whole 10 University. — Dr. Ralph Bathurst, President of Trinity Coll. sometime before he died promis'd to give to ye Pub. Library all ye Books it wanted in his Study; but his Death being hastened by a sudden Fall, he might forget to add a Codicil to his Will as he once intended. However in his Will there were two Pictures, one of Dr. Allestry & ye other of Dr. South, & some Coyns left to ye Library. He was Dean of Wells, & might have been Bp. if he had affected that Height of Dignity. He was a Man of Polite Parts, and an Elegant Writer in Latin, whether Prose or Verse. He discharg'd the Office of Vice-Chancellor with great Applause, & made his College flourish while he was President. He was suspected of Hypo- 20 crisy & of mean Complyance. — Luke Beaulieu Bachelor of Divinity of Xt Church, was (if I am not mistaken) Chaplain to Chancellor Jefferies, & was by him preferr'd to a Prebend of Gloucester. He hath publish'd a Sermon or two. — Mr. Tho. Beckonsall Bach. of Div. & Fellow of Brasennose Coll. has publish'd a Discourse abt ye Law of Nature in opposition to Mr. Lock, & a Sermon upon ye Resurrection preach'd at St. Marie's, wch is also against Mr. Lock's Notions abt ye Identity of ye Rising Body. He is a strange Hypochondriacal Person; wch may be a reason why he was so great an Admirer of King William, & ye Ministers of Queen Anne. — Dr. Hen. Beeston Warden of New (who was just 30 such another smooth-booted Complyer as Dr. Ralph Bathurst) was suc- ceeded upon his Death by Dr. Rich. Traffles; & he not living long to enjoy it, was succeeded by Mr. Brathwayt Bach. of Civil Law, & after- wards Dr. in yt Faculty. — Dr. Bury who was expell'd Exeter College, where he was Rector, for his Socinian Principles, & other Notorious Crimes, has since publish'd some Books favouring ye said Principles one of wch is call'd Latitudinarius Orthodoxus. — Dr. Pet. Birch of Xt Church has publish'd several Sermons, & preach'd some yt are none of his own, particularly some of ye Bp. of Rochester's and one of Dr. South's whilst the Dr. was present at ye Hearing of it in ye Abbey church of West- 40 minster: wch occasion'd this Raillery of ye Poët:

Rochester in courtly Tone Said he had too much Honour to his Sermons done,	But rugged South made of a courser mould Said he was a Thief and scandalously bold.

He is a forward, illiterate Man, but has had good Luck by rich Wives. — Blackmore (Richard) of Edm. Hall, where he was Vice-Principal, leaving the Hall went a travelling, & in some University in his Travells commenc'd Dr. of Physick. and in a short time arriv'd to Eminence in ye Practise thereof at London, and has writ several large Books in folio, such as Prince Arthur, Eliza, a Translation of Job, &c. He married 50

a rich Conventicler & by that means got a mighty Interest among y^e
Whiggs, & was Knighted by King W^m. who always lov'd to conferr
his Marks of Honour upon Persons dissaffected to ye Church of England.
— M^r. Rob. Brograve of Magd. Hall has publish'd a Sermon or two.
One upon this Text, *Let your Light so shine before men* &c. — M^r.
Bromley of X^t Church fam'd for his great Abilities, Integrity and firm
Adherence to ye stanch Principles of ye Church of England, when he
declin'd to serve as Kn^t of ye Shire for his own County of Warwick,
was yet prevail'd upon by ye University of Oxoñ to be one of y^eir
10 Representatives; wch Office he discharg'd with the great Applause of
all good Men, & would once have been chosen Speaker of ye House
of Commons had it not been for ye Base Arts of ye Courtiers and
Whiggish Party : one of wch was to publish a Book of his Travells
written by him when very young, & wch they turn'd into Ridicule, as
any Book may be serv'd by a scurrilous Index. — Gevartius writ Notes
upon Manilius, in wch as Peireskius in a Letter to M^r. Camden (pag. 217.
Ep. Camdeni) informs us, he maintains y^t Manilius liv'd not in Augustus's
time as Scaliger would have it, but tow^ds the latter End of the western
Empire.   Quære whether they were ever printed? (Not printed ; but
20 ye Substance of w^t he says ab^t the Age of Manilius is in his Papinianæ
Lectiones.   He is however wrong in that point about Manilius's Age.)
— S^r. Hen. Savile in a Letter to M^r. Camden (ibid. pag. 224) corrects
an Error in Godwin de Præsulibus Anglic. — In Gevartius's own Letter
to Camden (ib. p. 266) he says he has invincibly prov'd that Manilius
liv'd in ye time of Theodosius & his sons Arcadius & Honorius, & that
he is ye same who is call'd by Claudian Manlius Theodorus, in y^t
Panegyrick wch he writ upon his Consulship : in wch he has made some
mention of his Astronomicks. — It is s^d in M^r. Camden's Epp. that
Lindenbrogius was ab^t publishing Geographica quædam. Quære whether
30 ever publish'd? — In the King's Library at S^t. James's when Patrick
Young was Keeper of it, there was a MS^t Theodoret upon the Psalms,
by wch Fr. Ducæus when he was ab^t the Edition of the Bible in Greek
promis'd himself to restore ye Text in a Great measure.   There is
likewise at Rome a Theodoret upon Isaiah from wch he expected great
Matters.

Apr. 22 (Mon.).   Dionysius Hal. mentions the siege of Bola, whereof
not a word in Livy : wch makes Glarean believe Dionysius's Copies
corrupted.   This not taken notice of by D^r. Hudson.   See Glarean
upon Livy Ed. Par. 1573. fol. p. 148.   There is a note I find of it since
40 in pag. 476. Dionys. Hal. — M^r. Wood in pag. 842. tells us that he
does not find whether or no Orlando Gibbons was admitted or licensed
to proceed in the Degrees of Musick; but it appears y^t he did from
a Letter of D^r. Will. Peirs Vice-Chancellor of Oxoñ dated May 18.
1622.   See in M^r. Camden's Epp. p. 329. —

A Catalogue of such Persons as have been of ye university & never
took any care to have w^t they have printed sent to the Publick Library.
   (1) D^r. Whitby.   (2) D^r. Kennett.   (3) D^r. Waple.   (4) D^r. Lancaster.   (5)
D^r. Smalrich.   (6) D^r. Gastrell.   (7) D^r. Atterbury.   (8) D^r. Hody.   (9) D^r.
Gibson.   (10) D^r. Wake^1.   (11) D^r. Nicholson, B^p. of Carlisle.   (12) D^r.

       ¹ He has since given them.

Hooper B^p. of Bath & Wells. (13) D^r. Fowler B^p. of Glocester. (14). D^r. Nicholls of Merton Coll. (15) D^r. Young Dean of Winchester & formerly Ypobibliothecarian. (16) Mr. Elstob, of University Coll. (17) M^r. Bingham of ye same Coll. (18) Dr. Waugh. (19) M^r. Stainoe. (20) Dr. Isham. (21) M^r. Kennett of Corpus. (22) M^r. Wagstaffe of New-Inn-Hall. (23) D^r. Trimnell. (24) D^r. Royse. [(25)] S^r. W^m. Dawes, Head of Clare-Hall Camb. & formerly Fellow of S^t. John's in this University. (26) M^r. Burscough Archdeacon of Totness in ye Diocess of Exoñ. (27) M^r. Smith of ye same Diocess, both of Queen's Col. (28) D^r. Hough B^p. of Lichf. & Cov. (29) D^r. Williams B^p. of Chichester. (30) Dr. Ellyson of Newcastle Archd. of Nottingham, formerly Fellow of Corpus X^{ti}. (31) M^r. West of Magd. Coll. Chaplain to the B^p. of Sarum. (32) M^r. Addison formerly of Magd. College, into wch he was Elected Demy (after wch he was Fellow) out of Queen's, now one of ye Under Secretaries of State. (33) M^r. Chiswell of Corpus. (34) Mr. White of Wadham, y^t notorious Low church Man or Whig (call him how you please) who is famous for Drinking of two Healths, one to the Princes of Hannover, wishing that her way to the Crown might be pav'd with ye skulls of High Church Men ; the other to ye Honest Church of England wthout Ceremonies : who has lately publish'd a sermon preach'd at y^d Assize at Aylesbury the last Circuit. (35) M^r. Hodges formerly of Wadham. (36) D^r. Hickman, an Irish B^p. formerly Student of X^t Ch. & Chaplain to ye Earl of Clarendon & Rochester who preferr'd him. (37) M^r. Estwick of X^t Church. (38) M^r. Sprat of ye same House. (39) D^r. Sprat B^p. of Rochester. (40) D^r. Barton of Corpus X^{ti}. (41) D^r. Woodward of Edm. Hall. (42) M^r. Hoyle formerly fellow of Exon. (43) M^r. Wise of Exoñ Coll. (44) D^r. Baron of Baliol. (45) D^r. John Wynne of Jesus who Epitomiz'd Lock. (46) M^r. Bagshaw of Magd. Col. (47) M^r. Norris of All-Souls. (48) D^r. Tyndall of ye same Col. (49). D^r. Finch late Warden there. (50) D^r. Haley. (51) D^r. Willis. (52) (53) D^r. Entwistle formerly of Brasen-Nose, afterwards Chaplain to Dr. Stratford Bp. of Chester. (54) D^r. Woodroffe. (55) M^r. Wake formerly Fellow of Trinity Coll. (56) M^r. Bragg formerly Fellow of Wadham. (57) M^r. Stubbs Fellow of ye same House. (58) Mr. Welchman first of Magd. Hall afterwards Fellow of Merton. (59) D^r. Rob. Wynne of Jesus College, nephew to D^r. Hugh Wynne ye Non-Juror, who was Chancellor of S^t. Asaph, & succeeded in it by his said Nephew. (60) Dr. Birch. (61) D^r. Altham Junior. (62) M^r. Badger.

Apr. 23 (Tu.). I heard M^r. Grabe say this day that Interest has been made these four months for D^r. Potter at Court to succeed D^r. Jane (if he should die) in the Regis Professorship of Divinity, & y^t Dr Mill is very hot upon it. — Arch. Bodl. B. 41. A thin Book in Folio writ by Queen Eliz. containing Greek Phrases out of Demosthenes &c. & Latin ones out of Tully made in ye 18th year of her Age. — M^r. John Bateman Fellow of University College tells me y^t a few years since as they were digging for ye Foundation of an House at Canterbury (near to wch he the said M^r. Bateman has a Cure) they light upon a great deal of Roman Brick, wch being taken up they found under them divers Coyns, some of wch had Romulus and Remus sucking the Wolf (wthout doubt of Constantine ye Great) Bosses of Bridles, Buttons, Urns &c. M^r. Battley who publish'd a new Edition of Somner's Antiquities of Canterbury (in wch nothing appears considerable, tho' answerable to his character of being no Proficient in these Studies) has some of them, but where the rest are he cannot at present tell but promises to make Inquiry. The said M^r. Bateman is a man much inclin'd to Botanny, & w^t spare time he has from his Divinity Studies he lays out y^t way, much to his Commendation and Credit.

Apr. 24 (Wed.). When I talk'd wth M^r. Milles ab^t M^r. Dodwell's
Book & ye Answer printing at ye Theatre, upon his Denyal y^t above
one writ ye said Answer I said y^t 'twould be a very difficult Task to
answer it fully; since I could not tell of any one person who had y^t
variety of Learning requisite for it, especially in ye Platonick Philosophy :
to wch he reply'd y^t ye Author when he first became acquainted with
M^r. Dodwell, upon his Advice studied y^t Philosophy throughly & is
a perfect Master of it. Upon wch I immediately concluded Milles to
be Author, because about 8 years since he read over (when he heard
10 M^r. Dodw. discourse of ye usefullness of y^t Philosophy) Alcinous's
Introduction to Plato to a pupil or two of his; but wth so little gust
that he did not seem to understand anything of it, & I believe (nay am
almost sure) y^t he has read over nothing else of y^t nature, unless it be
some of ye Octavo Book of Plato printed at Cambridge. He sayd also
y^t the Author was a universal Scholar, & was able to write ag^t M^r.
Dodwell upon any Subject. I saw this morning a sheet of w^t is
printing of the Answer, wch appear'd to be writt in an affected Style,
with very little of other Learning but w^t may be pick'd out of common
English Books, & (wch is worst of all) very disrespectfully of his Great
20 and Good Friend M^r. Dodwell. — In a Letter to D^r. Bernard sent in
the year 16⅞⁰ Feb. 23^d dated from London 'tis said the Learned
Arnoldus design'd to send a son of his into these Parts, to improve
himself, being a Young Man of great Hopes, as appear'd from a
specimen he gave in his Discourse De S. Petri Denarijs. He was
nam'd Andr. Arnoldus & was afterwards a Student in ye Publick
Library at Oxford, & from thence prepar'd for ye Press, wch he publish'd wth a Translation & Notes, Athanasius's Syntagma doctrinæ ad
Clericos & Laicos, &c.

Apr. 25 (Th.). Arch. Bodl. B. 37.
30   Instrumentum quo Rex Hispaniæ declarat Dominum Christophorum Polome-
que non esse plebeium sed Generosum, ideoque à tributis & taxationibus
publicis immunem. Ille autem degebat in villa quæ vocatur Burgo el Hondo,
ex ditione Urbis Abulensis. Veteri idiomate Hispanico jam antiquato exaratum
est, et in Curia Hidalgiæ seu generositatis quæ est in urbe Valladolid consigna-
tum, 12 novembris, anno 1577.

The first leaf is curiously illuminated, with a Man & woman in a
praying posture, & ye virgin Mary & her Son over them. — Upon the
Death of Hen. V^th Emperor of Germany Maud his Empress, Daughter
to Henry the I^st King of England return'd to her Father, & bringing
40 wth her ye Hand of S^t. James King Hen. built ye Abbey of Reading,
where ye said Hand was reposed. See Fox's Acts & Mon. p. 225.
Ed. ult. — M^r. Fox had divers very good MSS^ts of our English History
never printed, & 'tis uncertain where they are now. He freq^tly quotes
them in his Martyrology. Perhaps some in ye Cotton Library.

Apr. 26 (Fri.). M^r. Lesley in his Rehearsal has an Observation or
two shewing that ye Memorial of ye Church of England was written
by the Whiggish Party, & father'd upon the Honest men on purpose
to bring an odium upon them; just as M^r. Stevens (that Notorious
Whigg and Fanatick) his Letter, when it first appear'd, was layd upon

the High-Church Men, & believed to be writ by some one of y^t side, 'till he made Acknowledgment himself. From the Memorial it plainly appears to have been done by a Whigg, from ye odd Scheme of Government there laid down, wch savours of Hobbism or something worse. — Memorandum that tho' D^r. Hyde sold a great many of his Books de Religione Persarum in 4to. for 5 shil. a piece, yet they now go for 12 shill. a Book, and are mightily bought up in Holland & other parts of Germany, where they have a great opinion of D^r. Hyde's Learning, especially in Orientals (in wch there is no doubt he was the greatest master in Europe) tho' he was disrespected in Oxford by several men, 10 who now speak well of him. — M^r. Wood, when he was consulting materials for his Athenæ Oxon. would frequently go to Booksellers & generously give money to them purposely to obtain Titles of Books from them, & 'twas observ'd of him that he spar'd no Charges to make y^t Work as compleat & perfect as he could. — M^r. Milles's Pretended Answer to M^r. Dodwell is printed for M^r. Peisly, tho' his Bookseller be M^r. Clements. The reason whereof is, that M^r. Clements did but laugh at ye undertaking, & declar'd to some one y^t he would not print it, if he might have ye Copy for nothing. — Remember to tell D^r. Hudson of an omission in pag. 568. of Dionys. Hal. where one of the 20 Consuls for the year u.c. 280. is call'd Aulus Manlius. He should have given a note at ye Bottom y^t he is call'd by Livy C. Manlius. — This being the day agreed upon by the Heads of Houses for Commemorating the Foundation of ye University of Francfurt upon Oder by Joachim ye First, Marquess of Brandenburg, a Convocation was held in the Theatre beginning at two a Clock. The Vice-Chancellor having declar'd the Design and Intent of it, several of the s^d University had Diplomas granted them for ye same Degrees in this university as had been conferr'd upon them at Francfurt, and at ye same time divers of our Nobility, & others, particularly ye Duke of Beaufort, L^d. Craven &c. 30 had ye Degree of D^r. of Laws conferr'd on y^m by Creation, & likewise M^r. Grabe was created D^r. of Divinity, who being presented by D^r. Smalrich, a Noble Encomium was given of him by the said D^r. setting forth his great Piety, Learning & Industry; after wch D^r. Smalrich presented him with a Bible, & upon y^t occasion commended his Excellent Design of publishing the Septuagint from ye Alexandrian MS^t, exhorting him to go on as he had begun. He likewise mention'd his Zeal for ye Church of England, & ye Aversion he had to Popery and Calvinism. This done ye D^r. presented him wth a Cap, & after y^t with a Ring, signifying that ye University of Oxford & Francfurt were now 40 joyn'd together & become two Sisters, & y^t they might be ye more firmly united together as well in Learning as Religion, he kiss'd M^r. Grabe. As soon as this part of ye Solemnity was ended verses & Speeches were spoke by several Young Students, & Musick perform'd as usual upon such extraordinary occasions.

Apr. 27 (Sat.). On ye 25th Instant M^r. Pettis was order'd in the Court of Queen's Bench to stand in the Pillory three Times, and to

---

April 27. H. to Dr. T. Smith. ' I have divers Collections relating to Learning at Oxford, wch it may be may prove usefull hereafter to him y^t shall

pay 100 marks for Writing the Vindication of yᵉ Memorial of yᵉ Church of England. — At yᵉ same time Mʳ. Sawbridge yᵉ Bookseller was fin'd 200 Marks for printing the same, & order'd to be expos'd in Westm. Hall, with a Paper affix'd to his Hat signifying his Crime. — Dʳ. Smalridge of Xᵗ Church was born at Lichfield. His Father was a Dyer, & had more Children, & was but very poor as I am inform'd by one who liv'd in yᵉ Place 7 years. This Dʳ. Smalridge is a man of admirable strong Parts, great Elocution, & good Learning. — Tell Dʳ. Hudson that in pag. 570. of Dionys. Hal. Vol. 1. for Πόπλιος Βολέρων is to be
10 read Ποπλίλιος Βολέρων, as it is read in Livy, l. II. c. 55. See Sigonius's Note there. — To day Mʳ. Pridy of St. John's coll. (Bach. of Div. & Fellow there) shew'd me these 3 following Coyns, viz. 1. ANTONINVS AVG. PIVS. P. P. TR. P. P. TR. P. Caput Antonini Pij. ℞ BRITANNIA COS. IIII. S. C. Figura moerens insidens spolijs, dextram capiti admovens (of the 2ᵈ Brass). 2. IVLIA MAMMAEA AVG. Juliæ Mammææ uxoris Vari & Alexandri Severi matris, cap. ℞ FECVND. AVGVSTAE. Figura muliebris sedens, cum puerulo adstante, cui dextram porrigit. (of the 3ᵈ Silver). 3. IVLIA MAMMAEA AVG. Ejusd. Cap. ℞ VESTA. Figura stans, dextra Palladium, sin. Hastam puram. — I am told by one who has a great Respect for him, yᵗ Dʳ.
20 Hodges who was of Queen's College is a person of so little Literature yᵗ he does not pretend to any thing above yᵉ Greek Testament; & yet he has three places one whereof (namely the Chief Church in Warwick) was given him lately by the Queen, he being it seems a precious Brother, & having an extraordinary faculty in yᵉ Gift of Preaching in yᵉ Opinion of yᵉ Whiggs.

---

continue either the Antiquities or Athenae.' Mr. Thwaites has had his leg cut off. 'I never yet read yᵉ story in yᵉ Observator conc. Dr. Charlett; but remember it made a great Noise in Town. It seems he, with yᵉ President of Magdalen College and yᵉ Provost of Queens (and perhaps some others) were one Evening at yᵉ Warden's of New College; where they staid till 9 of yᵉ clock; but 'tis highly scandalous to say they drunk to excess; the Warden of New-College being not in a very good State of Health, & neither of yᵉ other noted for being hard Drinkers. However 'tis true that Dr. Charlett's boy (who is since turn'd off) instead of carrying the Lantern took away a Silver Tankard, wᶜʰ was not perceiv'd till they came home; because the President of Magd. & Provost of Queen's accompany'd him, & their men had Lanterns at yᵉ same time. The Boy has been guilty of some other such Crimes, & being given much to drink might be somewᵗ disorder'd before he came to yᵉ College. I am heartily sorry any one should hence take occasion to blacken yᵉ Dʳ'ˢ Character, who (notwithstanding some Failings, to wᶜʰ all are subject) is a man of several excellent Qualifications, & if he had Abilities would be one of yᵉ Greatest Encouragers of Learning yᵗ have appear'd of late.' Attributes C. Veratius Philellen to Fabricius, who was displeased with Gronovius for publishing Manetho's *Apotelesmata*. Mill's *Prolegomena* revised by the Bishop of Worcester. Account of the doings in Convocation in commemoration of the University of Frankfort. Mr. Oddy to publish Dion Cassius; some account of him. Dr. Pocock and his interrupted edition of Abdollatiphi's History of Egypt. Is *nuperus scriptor* at p. 52 of your Life of Camden Bishop Burnet? 'The Duke of Beaufort has purchas'd the statue of Flora, which stands in yᵉ South End of yᵉ Physick Garden (where 'twas plac'd on purpose by yᵉ Maker for somebody to buy it) & give[n] it to yᵉ University.'

Apr. 28 (Sun.). Mr. Tho. Yalding, Bach. of Div. & Fellow of Magd. College is made Chaplain to ye Duke of Beaufort. — The said Duke has purchas'd ye Statue of Flora, wch stands in ye farther side of ye Physick Garden (where 'twas plac'd on purpose by the Maker for some body to buy it) & given it to ye university. — Mr. Pittis who is prosecuted for writing in Vindication of ye Memorial was, I think Fellow of New-College, & has some Poëms in print. — This afternoon preach'd at St. Marie's Mr. Adams (Will.) Student of Xt Church upon Luke 7. 33, 34, 35. · · ·

'Twas a most Excellent, Rational and seasonable Discourse. For having 10 shewn ye occasion of the Words, & laid open ye obstinacy of ye Jews and Pharisees, who neglected the Doctrine of Our Saviour & St. John ye Baptist his Forerunner, tho' they led the most pure, sanctify'd lives that 'twas possible for men to lead: he thence gather'd these two propositions, viz. That tho' men live never so regularly & agreeably to ye most strict Rules of virtue, yet they will always find persons to traduce them. 2. That notwthstanding this, they ought to persevere & continue, with ye utmost Resolution & Courage in defending the doctrines of Christianity & Morality against all ye Affronts and Bad usage they should meet wth from such implacable Enemies. He discours'd upon ye first Proposition only at this time, shewing the Truth of it, & 20 afterwards giving the Reasons wch generally influence bad Men to traduce & blacken ye Characters of such as are Religious & act according to Rules of Conscience. The greatest part of the Discourse was adapted to ye present times, when we see far the greatest part of Men, under a pretence of Moderation & christian charity, stand up in Vindication of the most notorious Hypocrites, Schismaticks, Debauchees & I know not wt; whilst those who are innocent & maintain the doctrines of ye Establish'd Church and Government in opposition to Presbytery, Fanaticism & Anarchy are vilify'd, persecuted & spoke against as the greatest Enemies of ye Nation, men not fit to live in a Xtian Country, but ought to be banish'd & plac'd amongst Barbarians, & such 30 as have no spark of Humanity or Virtue: And even ye best Words they meet with are that they are imprudent & understand nothing of ye World, by wch Mr. Adams plainly told the Auditors must be meant & understood nothing else but yt they are not Knaves & self-Interested men, but are harmless, innocent, unspotted, & true Patriots of their Country, wthout any Disguise or Hypocrisy as becomes Xtians.

Apr. 29 (Mon.). Memorandum that Dr. Jane, ye Regius Professor of Divinity, who is now of a very niggardly mean Spirit, was once of a generous Temper, & yt this Sordidness is in great measure to be attributed to his long infirmity, chiefly occasion'd by intemperance, & 40 too free a way of living. — John Matthews formerly of Oriel College, now Minister of Tewkesbury in Gloucestershire, hath publish'd a Sermon upon *Luke* 23. 34. intit. *Forgiveness of Enemies, and their praying for their Forgiveness*, preach'd in the Church of Tewkesbury Febr. 17. 170⅚. *Oxon*. 1706. 4°.

Apr. 30 (Tu.). Memorandum that tho' Dr. Tyndal of All-Souls be a noted Debauchee & a man of very pernicious Principles, yet he is so sly and cunning, & has yt command over his Passions, yt he always appears calm & sedate in company, & is very abstemious in his Drink, by wch means he has no small advantage over those he discourses 50

April 28. John Williams to H. Presses for the letter of orders; thinks 20s. too much.

with, & is the more able to instill his ill Notions. — The Author of
the Memorial of y⁰ C. of Engl. is for y⁰ independent State of Nature,
& for all Government to have it's Original from y⁰ People, as Mʳ. Lesley
shews in his Rehearsal.   Which is an evident token yᵗ 'twas writ by
some Low-Church man or Whigg.   For besides Stevens's Letter the
Shortest Way, wᶜʰ was Father'd upon High-Church was written by De-
Foe, who was pillor'd for it, & glories in it to this day. — Abᵗ y⁰ year
1180, in y⁰ Reign of K. Hen. 2. Pisanus Burgundio, of good skill in
Greek and Latin, translated into Latin Xtom's Homilies upon y⁰ Gospel
10 of Sᵗ. John, as also a great part of his Exposition upon Genesis.   Quære
whether this translation be now Extant, & whether he might not have
a hand in y⁰ Comm. upon Mathew going under y⁰ Name of Xtom?   See
Fox Vol. I. p. 264.

May 1 (Wed.).   Last Night a certain Person, of y⁰ High-Church
Party, (as they are call'd) happening to be with Dʳ. Mill, and discoursing
particularly abᵗ some Affairs of y⁰ Hall, the Dʳ. fell into a great Passion,
& vented abundance of ill Language, as he is us'd to do upon such
occasions, saying, amongst other things, that no Master of Arts in the
Hall should for y⁰ future have any Privilege of sconsing or otherwise
20 punishing the Servants in the Hall when they are impudent or negligent
in their Duty to them, but should, when any such misdemeanour happen,
make complaint to him, & if he thought fit he would regulate it ; whereas
it has been always customary for the Masters to inflict such kind of
Punishments, & they have the same reason for it, as Fellows of Colleges,
who always use it ; & if they are hinder'd from it, it may turn in
time to so ill account that the Servants will trample them under feet,
& nothing will be done but at y⁰ Pleasure and will of y⁰ Principal ;
contrary to y⁰ Intent & Design of y⁰ Statutes, wᶜʰ Dʳ. Mill has broken
not only in this, but in some other particulars : whether designedly or
30 no I cannot tell, nor will pretend to judge : but this is certain that y⁰
Members of y⁰ Hall are kept in ignorance of them, whereas they ought
to be read 4 times, at least once a year ; wᶜʰ the Dʳ. is so far from doing,
or causing to be done, that for these 10 years (wᵗ was done before I
know not) he has not began to read them but once, wᶜʰ was abᵗ 7 years
since, when he went thro' a little part, & promis'd once a Quarter to
do y⁰ same, tho' he quickly forgot wᵗ he said.   This arbitrariness at
present was suppos'd by y⁰ said Person (from whom this Story comes)
to be purely design'd to gain whiggish Proselytes, he believing that y⁰
more he can have his will & pleasure over the Members of y⁰ Hall the
40 better he shall be able to instill Whiggish Principles, with wᶜʰ he is in
so much love at present.   But whether it be so or no matters not much.
This I am sure of, that his Vice-Principal Mʳ. Pearce has mov'd him to
it, as he has to some other things, much to y⁰ Dissatisfaction of several
in y⁰ Hall, wᶜʰ has caus'd some Disturbance, & may cause much greater ;
especially too if y⁰ Principal be guided (as some say he is, & they seem
to give good reasons for it) by y⁰ Directions & Instigation of a certain
Woman, who is a Bed-maker in the Hall. — Quære whether Antiquæ
Historiæ Synopsis pr. at Oxon. 1660. 8⁰. wᵗʰ the Initial & Final Letters
H. S. be not Hen. Stubbs? — The Books here accounted for I saw in
50 the Study of Mʳ. Joseph Abell, Fellow of Merton Coll. [203–206.

Some 'to be consulted for Livy.'] — Mr. Abell had once a Tully's Epistles in MS^t wch Mr. Wanley had of him. Mr. Abell design'd it for ye Publ. Library. Quære w^t Wanley has done wth it? He s^d he would put it there, but I believe never did[1]. — The Prymer of Salysburye use &c. prynted yn Paris within ye House of Thylman Kernet at ye Expenses of Johan Growte Bokeseller y^n London dwellyng wythyn ye Blak Freers next the church Doore 1533. 12º. — ... Owen's Epigramms *Lond.* 1612. 8º. I saw a Copy of this Edition in Mr. Abell's Study interleav'd, & partly translated by Josuah Sylvester, in MS^t wth his own Hand (as suppos'd) wch he intitles Epigrammes not new-cast, but new-cased, & some 10 of them new placed. Pr. These Lines are Mine, their Linings are well known | To be mine owen's; not to be mine owne &c. — ... Two Books in 8º. in ye Slavonick Language (wch I believe to be rarities) The one seems to be something for initiating Children in y^t Tongue, the other some Extracts out of ye New Testam^t. — Introductio ad Linguas Orientales, *Lond.* 1655. 8º. Ask Mr. Okeley ab^t it, & quære whether some of his things are not extracted out of it? ...

May 2 (Th.). Yesterday about 9 Clock was an Eclipse of ye Sun. 'Twas darkned 10 digits ½: The Sky was cloudy but Mr. Halley and Dr. Gregory, with others who were with them, made Observations upon 20 it, & w^t they wanted most they plainly perceiv'd the Ingress & Egress. — Mr. Wotton, who writ the Reflections upon Ancient & Modern Learning, has writ the Life of the famous Mr. Boyle; wch being offer'd to ye Royal Society, 'tis order'd to be printed by them.

May 3 (Fri.). Memorandum that White-Waltham in the Deanery of Reading in Berks is thus valu'd in ye old Book of Pope Nicholas made in 20 Ed. 1st Reign: viz. Ecclesia de Waltham Abbatis cum vicaria indecimabili xx marc. Pensio Abbatis de Certesey in eadem, *vs.* — Quære whether this place was not annex'd or appropriated to ye Abbey of Chersey in Surrey, & whether 'twas not call'd so from the s^d Abbey 30 to distinguish it from the other Waltham on the West-side of Shottesbrook call'd Laurence-Waltham? — Mr. W^m. Adams Student of X^t Church is son to Mr. Adams who writ y^o Index Villaris, & was of ye Middle Temple, & was also (as his son is) an ingenious Man, & had promis'd several other usefull Pieces to ye World; but not meeting (as I suppose) wth suitable Encouragement he ran in debt, & was cast into prison, & his designs were blasted. — Memorand. that Dr. Hudson abridg'd Dr. Beveridges Introduction to Chronology when Bach. of Arts wch afterwards he printed for ye use of his Pupils they making abundance of faults in transcribing it, of wch are two Impressions.—He printed 40 Erasmus's Dialogus Ciceronianus at Mr. Lichfeild's Press in Oxon, at his own charges. He printed also a Sallust in 12º. at ye Theatre wth various Lections. An Accurate Edition. It goes under ye Name of another. But ye Dr. did it. He put Mr. Ibbetson upon and assisted him in the Edition of Marcus Antoninus. The like he did in ye last Oxoñ Edition of Pliny's Epistles, as also in the Edition of Eutropius, & Justins History, the two last of wch he printed at his own charge,

---

[1] Dr Charlett has it. I have seen it there three or four years agoe. Oct. 4. 1709. N.B. I have got it since Dr. Charlett's Death, it being given me by James West, Esq.

& generously encourag'd the Editor (who has rec^d a great number of Extraordinary Kindnesses from him besides) in putting out those small Pieces. Besides the Works going under his Name, he has likewise assisted in most of the things wch have of late years come from the Theatre Press, in some of wch he is gratefully mention'd, in others not, & amongst ye rest must not be forgot the Speech of M^r. Wyatt ye University Orator at ye Ceremony in the Theatre for the Foundation of ye university of Francfurt, wch being pitifull stuff (occasion'd by the orator's being almost worn out) the D^r. made it anew & in a manner
10 ex tempore, doing it as fast as ye Compositor set it. — Enquire who is ye Author of *The Account of ye Growth of Deism in England* pr. at London for ye Author 1696. 4°. — M^r. Ayliffe of New College being one of ye Proctors in ye Vice-Chancellors Court, & having exacted over much for a Cause wch he manag'd for one Benj. Cole an Engraver, he was complain'd off by the s^d Cole for ye same to D^r. Wood Assessor or Judge of ye Court, who prosecuted him for y^t & other Crimes, & ye Matter having been examin'd divers times this day he was ejected ye Court; but being a Man of a resolute Temper he designs to make an appeal to ye Congregation, & upon failour there to ye Convocation;
20 & if he miscarry there too, thence to the Court of Chancery. This M^r. Ayliff is a great Crony of D^r. Tyndale's.

May 4 (Sat.). D^r. Brown has had his tryal & is found guilty of Writing *the Country Parsons Advice to ye Lord Keeper*. Warrants are out & great Search is made after ye Author of the Pamphlett called *The History of ye Revolution*, wch Reflects much upon King W^m. & his Government.

May 5 (Sun.). Some years since D^r. Pocock made or at least began a Translation of a Curious MS^t amongst his Collection of Arabick Proverbs ; but it being not ever publish'd, and nobody now knowing where
30 it is ; M^r. Marshal (Bachelor of Arts and Student of X^t Church) an [1]ingenious, modest Young Gentleman and of considerable Abilities in these Studies) about 2 or 3 years since had some design of doing it anew, and making it publick : it being a Book of admirable use in reading the Arabick Historians, and other Authors; but not finding, I presume, sufficient Encouragement, or at least not having any one (after D^r. Hyde's Death) to assist and direct him in some Difficulties (w^ch 'tis to be suppos'd a young Man could not well break thro') the Work was laid aside, & there is no probability at present of it's appearing abroad.

May 6 (Mon.). The D. of Queensbury made Commissioner by her
40 Majesty for the Approaching Session of Parliam^t in Scotland. — An Acc^t is taking in all ye Parishes of London of ye Number of Papists & orders are sent into ye Country to do ye like to lay the same before the Parl^t next Sessions. — Whereas M^r. Ant. à Wood in his Epistle to ye Reader before ye first vol. of Ath. Oxon. says that he never eat ye Bread of any Founder, D^r. Wynne, ye Non-juror, protests to me y^t he has often heard old M^r. Cooper, Register of the university, & formerly of Merton College, say that he M^r. Wood was Clerk there & y^t he had seen him often serve

---

[1] A mistake. He is neither ingenious, nor modest, nor judicious, nor of good Principles.

there. But quære further ab^t this? As also whether he often din'd with B^p. Fell and D^r. Edwards, as I am told he did?

May 7 (Tu.). I am told y^t M^r. Jonas Proast's Father was a German, & y^t he was one of ye Assembly of Divines. Quære? — Memorandum that tho' M^r. Dodwell's Dedication of his Annales Vellejani, Quintiliani &c. was printed yet 'twas not publish'd because the Vice-Chancellor put Cardinal Norris before B^p. Lloyd, contrary to w^t M^r. Dodwell had done in his Copy; wch so displeas'd M^r. Dodwell that he suppress'd it. This an Instance of his Zeal for ye Church of England in opposition to Popery. — In pag. 648. Vol. 1. Dionysij Hal. D^r. Hudson to give an 10 emendation of *T. Veturius*. It should be *Sp. Veturius*. See Pighius's Annals. — M^r. Du-Gain (an Irish Man I think or else a French man) having been in Oxoñ several years, where he taught the Arts of Fencing and Dancing (in wch he is a great Master) & sometimes the French Tongue to divers young Gentlemen, was on Saturday last taken up, for some words wch he spoke upon the Death of King W^m. wch were thought reflecting. They were spoke just ab^t ye time ye King died, & were taken notice of now purely out of Malice. He had several persons appear'd on his behalf, otherwise he had been sent into ye Army as a common souldier. He was always look'd upon as Jacobitely inclin'd, & some say 20 he is a loose debauch'd Man. but I believe y^t to be a scandalous Reflection. He is a Gentleman, & is much belov'd by ye Refin'd sort of Mankind.

May 8 (Wed.). Just publish'd No church Established, or ye schismatick unmask'd, in answer to D^r. Tyndal's Rights of ye X^{tian} Church. pr. 1s. — Talking with one this Afternoon who saw M^r. Dodwell very lately he told me y^t M^r. Dodwell thought M^r. Turner's Answer to his Book (abating the scurrilous Reflections) to be much better done than M^r. Clark's: but I am to doubt ye Truth of this, since I do not find y^t any one much admires it in Oxoñ, or thinks D^r. Turner to be a man 30 of any great capacity. — That part of the Abbey of Rewley now standing wch seems to have been part of ye Chapell to some did not at all belong to ye Chapell as appears from the whole Circumference of the Chapell lately discovered, when ye Foundation of the Walls were dug up. It was in the Garden on the East side as you enter into ye House, & did not come to ye said part now standing by a great many Yards. I cannot learn that any coffins or Bodys have been ever dug up; so y^t it should seem their burying place was at S^t. Thomas's Church, or else at Oseney, & perhaps this may be one reason why Ela Longespee (that built Rewley Chapell) was buried in the Chapell of Oseney, as appears from Evidences 40 cited by M^r. Leland. — George Keith hath just publish'd An Account of his Travells into ye Western Plantations. It makes a Book of 12^d. price in 4to. & is dedicated to ye Arch^{bp}. of Canterbury; but w^t Incouragement he is like to meet with for Writing against ye Quakers at this time of day may be easily guess'd from the Reception M^r. Francis Bugg met with from the B^p. of Worcester wch I have mention'd at ye Beginning of this Volume. — D^r. Mill lately talk'd very kindly to me of D^r. Bury some time since Rector of Exeter College, & seem'd to have a good Opinion of him, & said that he design'd to be a great Benefactor of the said

College. I was amaz'd to hear so good a Character of one who is so well known for being a person of most wicked Principles, & to have us'd such indirect & unjust methods in ye Case of M^r. Colmer, whom he endeavour'd to ruin, & had effectually done it, had not M^r. Colmer been sufficiently known for an innocent Person, & clearly made out all the Objections against him to be contriv'd & carry'd on by nothing else but the utmost Malice &c. Insomuch y^t at length it appear'd y^t D^r. Bury was guilty of Incontinence, & other Crimes, wch he would so unjustly have fasten'd upon M^r. Colmer. But perhaps he may be now a low
10 Church Man (for he is anything, unless Old Age has made him a penitent) or may talk for y^t party, & so gain their good word. — The Term ending on the 6th M^r. Stephens wth others appear'd on y^eir Recognizances, & M^r. Stevens was found guilty of being the Author of the Answer to ye Memorial of ye State of England, was fin'd 100 Marks & order'd to stand in ye Pillory twice.

May 9 (Th.). Quære whether there was not some Religious House, or some Hall just on the West side of the Tower in wch the great Bell at X^t Church hangs? There are some Ruines wch would make one think there was. 'Twas an Hospitall. — I rec^d to day a Brass Coyn
20 wch was dug up in Weycock, wch I have before mention'd. It is very much defac'd, but seems to be Plautilla ye Wife of Caracalla. — In the Inquisition above mention'd (in pag. 142.) ab^t ye Bounds of Bray, is nothing relating to ye Parish of White-Waltham but Fayrhok, Crukenfend and Wolveley. I am told ye first was an old Oak wch stood formerly at ye Lane End call'd Tutchin Lane next Bray-Wood side, & was a Bound-Oak. It has been down for about 50 years, & S^r. Edm. Sawyer of Heywood, planted an Elm-Tree in ye Place of it, wch is now the Boundarie to ye Parish of White Waltham & Bray; but the Parishioners of the Latter in their yearly Circuits goe much below it, & take in
30 almost all that wch belongs to ye Mannor of Heywood in ye Common. Cruckenfend seems to be the House where M^r. Henry now dwelleth at Hawthorne, & is now called Crutchfield House. Wolveley is w^t is now call'd Wooley. 'Tis a green, & without doubt was formerly overgrown with Wood; for in ye Appendix to the Best Edition of Matthew Paris put out by D^r. Watts, there is some Hint y^t whereas the Marle Country was overrun with Robbers, who took Refuge in ye Woods, orders were given that a great part of ye said Woods should be cut down; wch was

May 9. Dr. T. Smith to H. The late Theatrical solemnity in honour of the Lutheran University of Frankfort has been viewed with suspicion in London. Has learnt from Mr. Edw. Stephens that Grabe is a member of his congregation : see p. 9 of Stephens' General Preface to a Collection of his Tracts and Papers (1702). Is Grabe really in priest's orders? Mr. Stephens died about three weeks since, professing himself a member of the Greek Church; he received *confirmation* (? of priestly orders, or a superinduction of new ones) from the Archbishop of Philippopolis. He was buried at Enfield by the care of Dr. Udall, his son-in-law, a successful schoolmaster there. Remarks on Thwaites, Philellen, 'the adventure of the tankard;' Mill's dilatoriness; Abdollatiphi; Sydenham; Burnet (Dr. Charlett omitted some censures on him in Smith's *Synopsis of the Cottonian Library*). Asks for a transcript of two letters of Henry Briggs.

accordingly done. It seems here were Wolves once, & so it might have
ye Name: Wolveley being nothing but a place of Wolves. — Some
time since an old Brass Piece was found under one of the Buildings
belonging to Wadham College, on one side of wch 3 flower de luces &
Ave Maria Gracia Dei, on ye other a Cross Flore.

May 10 (Fri.). Amongst B^p. Barlow's Books in ye Publick Library
is an old printed Book, intit. Bartholomæi de Chaymis Interrogatorium.
It was printed at Mentz, in 1478, and at ye End are peter Scheffer's
Arms who printed it: to it are also added three or four Notes by B^p.
Barlow & another Hand ab^t printing. — Memorandum that M^r. Cun- 10
ningham a Scotch man, student in ye Publick Library, who has been
tutor to two or three Scotch Noblemen, yesterday told me y^t he knew
King W^m. order'd the Heinous Murther committed at Glencoe (wch is
a sufficient reason for any one to speak ag^t him had his Title been good,
wch it was not, he being no more than an Usurper, & having as bad
Vices almost if not quite as Oliver Cromwell) where of there is a printed
Relation call'd Gallienus Redivivus, wch was written (as I am well assur'd)
by M^r. Lesley.

May 11 (Sat.) There is lately dead at Vienna an Officer who was by
Nation a Scotch man & has left behind him to his Relations a Million 20
of Money, but ye Council of war has seized ye same to ye Emperors
use, alledging y^t no Man could acquire such an Estate in his Service
y^t had been honest in his Post. This is a Resumption w^thout a Parliam^t & a short way of doing a Nation justice.

May 12 (Sun.). At the Entrance into ye Chancel of Eynsham Church.
Here lyeth M^r. Wylliam Emott somtymes vicar of | Einsham wch died y^e
xvi day of February A^o. 1584.

Epitaphium ejusdem.

Hujus quem statuit custodem Christus ovilis | Divino baculo dilacerare lupos |
Surripuere gregi, proh! fata sinistra fideli | Saxa premunt corpus mens sedet 30
ante deum.

May 13 (Mon.). Out of Dyer's Letter.

'Twas expected y^t M^r. Stephens would have been set on ye Pillory on
Thursday & Friday last according to his Sentence; but I concluded as soon
as I saw his Recantation and heard y^t he made no Defence to ye Information
y^t ye way was paved to his Pardon and y^t he knew very well that his old
Friends ye Whiggs (whose Amanuensis he was) would not leave him in ye lurch,
if it was only for ye Merit of his 2 Excellent 30 of January Sermons. |
— M^r. Llhuyd, Keeper of ye Ashmolean Museum, tells me y^t there were
lately found near Witney a considerable Number of Coyns, all Roman, 40
(but of no value) except one of the Saxon, I forget w^t. He told me at
ye same time y^t among other Books he look'd upon when he was last
in Wales, was one wch he purchas'd, containing among other things
Divers discourses mostly by way of Letter written by Josephus Monachus
Eveshamensis, some of wch I think he told me were valuable, as being
full of Historical Matters. He cannot tell (nor do I as yet know) who

---

May 11. Hudson to H. Message about paper; has met with materials
for Livy: Bennet repents of his refusal. 'Nobody here but rank Whigs
believe ye news about Spain.'

this Joseph should be. Quære whether he was Monk of Evesham in Worcestershire or of Einsham in Oxfordshire, wch by some Inscriptions in ye Church (tho' of a modern Date) I find to be writ Evsham. I am told by some of ye seniors at Einsham y^t the Monastery there had 52 Fish-Ponds belonging to it, according to ye Number of Weeks in a year, which seems to be true from divers Holes near to ye Place where the Monastery stood, wch without doubt were once Fish Ponds. There is nothing now remaining of ye Abbey but an outer Gate on the West-Side; wch however in some measure shews it to have been a stately
10 Place, & ye Trees ab^t it also shew y^t 'twas very pleasant. Quære more ab^t it in the Book of Statutes belonging to it writ by Joan. de Wudetun in Bib. Bodl. MS. NE. F. 3. 7.

May 14 (Tu.). D^r. Kennett's Parochial Antiquities is done very injudiciously. He had put in all Papers he met w^th, some of wch are very badly transcrib'd. There is one particular instance of his Ignorance in Reading MSS^ts. namely w^t he has publish'd out of Pope Nicholas's Valor Beneficiorum in ye Publick Library, wch tho' almost as plain as print, yet he has blunder'd strangely, & made it Nonsense. — M^r. Edw.
Llhwyd being a person who was naturally addicted to ye Study of Plants,
20 Stones &c. as also Antiquities, he was made by D^r. Plot underkeeper of ye Ashmolean Museum, & upon his Death he became Head-Keeper: sometime after wch his Name became famous, particularly upon Publication of a small Book in 8°. ab^t Fossiles: wch is writ in Latin, & has (together with other Things in the Philosophical Transactions) given occasion to D^r. Sloan often to say that he thinks M^r. Llhwyd ye best Naturalist now in Europe. And as he has this character upon Account of his Searches into nature, so he deserves very well for his Study of Antiquity, as appears from the Additions he has made to M^r. Camden; but will appear more so, when his Great Work (ab^t wch he has been
30 ab^t 12 years already) relating to the Language & Antiquities of Cornwal, Wales &c. shall come forth, one Volume of wch is almost printed. D^r. Nicholson B^p. of Carlisle in his Historical Library has given him a very great Character, to wch you may be pleas'd to have recourse; whilst in ye mean time I tell you, y^t he is a person of singular Modesty, good Nature, & uncommon Industry. He lives a retir'd life, generally three or four miles from Oxford, is not at all ambitious of Preferment or Honour, & w^t he does is purely out of Love to ye Good of Learning & his Country; But notw^thstanding these Deserts he could never yet get anything, but to be Keeper of ye Museum, wch is but a mean Place
40 seeing there is no Salary, & his Business requires two or three under him. But tho' there be no Salary he is oblig'd once a year to pay 3 Guineas (half a Guinea a piece) to six visitors of ye Place, out of his Perquisites wch is hard, & w^t the Visitors ought to abate. But they are often men of no Affection to Learning, or Industry, minding nothing more than how to eat & drink well. — At Rewly, just as you enter into ye House now standing are ye Arms of ye Earls of Cornwall &c., and in a Closet on the south side are the Images in Glass of some of ye Apostles, as S^t. Andrew, S^t. Thomas &c. And as you go upstairs in the window are these Arms, viz. Azure a Bend Sinister argent, & parted per Pale
50 Azure & or.

May 15 (Wed.). Michaelis Lochmaier Parochiale Curatorum. 'Twas printed at Hagenow in ye year MCCCCXCVIII by John Gran, who is stiled there a diligent Printer; wch seems to intimate y^t he had printed other Books there before. I believe he was one of ye first Printers there; it may be he was ye first. 'Tis pr. in 4to. in a black Letter. — In ye year 1521 was printed in 4to. at Cambridge Balduin, Archb^p. of Cant., his Sermon de venerabili, ac divinissimo altaris sacramento. At ye beginning are these Arms Quarterly, 3 flowre de Luces, the 2^d three Lyons passant guardant, the 3^d as ye 1st, the 4th as ye 2^d. At the End it appears 'twas printed by John Siberch, whose mark is there added. . . . 10 This Book may be of use to him that shall write of the Antiquities of this University, or ye Original of Printing here. . . .

May 16 (Th.). We hear her Majesty has been pleas'd to declare ye Duke of Rutland L^d. Lieutent. of Leicestershire, in room of ye Earl of Denbigh ; Earl of Kingston Custos Rotulorum of Wilts in Room of the L^d. Viscount Weymouth, & L^d. Wharton L^d. Lieut^t. of Westmorl^d. in room of ye Earl of Thanet. She has also been pleas'd to appoint S^r. W^m. S^t. Quintin one of ye Commissioners of ye Revenue in Irel^d. in room of S^r. John Bland. — Siege of Barcellona rais'd, if we may believe some Letters. — News arriv'd at ye French Court y^t they have taken S^t. Xtophers & 20 6000 Negroes, wth a vast Booty. — Parl^t. of Scotland adj^d. to ye 20th of June next. — Saturday last Earl of Carrington Baron of Wooton in Warwicksh. & Visc^t. Barreford in Irel^d. departed this Life, & ye Title wth him Extinct. His Estate is descended to Lewis Smith Esqr. — Talking just now with M^r. Milles, I read to him y^t Passage in a Letter I rec^d from M^r. Dodwell wch relates to his new Undertaking of Writing ag^t M^r. Dodwell's Book wch put him somew^t to ye Blush, as being conscious he had not dealt like a Friend ; but yet he continu'd obstinate y^t M^r. Dodwell was all along mistaken, had misrepresented the Fathers in a strange manner, & y^t he could not do other wise than write publickly 30 ag^t him. W^ch is contrary to w^t all his Friends advis'd him, & in all likelyhood he will meet with few who will think well of him for it.

VOL. X.

May 18, 1706 (Sat.). On ye 8th of August in ye Year 1701 was admitted Student into ye Publick Library M^r. Simon Ockely, A.M. of Cambridge. He was of Queen's College in y^t university, & came hither on purpose to consult some Arabick MSS^ts. Being naturally inclin'd to ye Study of ye Oriental Tongues, he was, when ab^t 17 years of Age, made Hebrew Lecturer in ye said College, chiefly because he was poor & could hardly subsist. Sometime after he married (tho' but very young) 40 & got a small Place, where he now is, near Cambridge call'd Swavesey. But had it not been for a certain Accident, wch redounded much to his

---

May 17. T. Cherry to H. Dodwell concerned at South's becoming his enemy, on account of his violence ; surprised and pained at Mill's ingratitude, of whose learning and integrity Francis Cherry never had a high opinion. 'I hear by your Father (who gives his Love to you) that you design to goe into Warwickshire.'

Disgrace, he might have had a much better; the Fellows of his College having resolv'd to give him a Parsonage, wch became vacant some time agoe: but they chang'd their mind upon y^t Account, & have now but an indifferent Opinion of him.   He has several Children, & is yet hardly 30 years of Age.   He was admitted into Holy Orders (as I am inform'd) by the B^p. of Ely, D^r. Patrick, before he was 20.   W^ch B^p. pretends to be his Patron (tho' like some other Prelates) 'tis only Pretence, he having as yet given him nothing to support himself & Family; notw^thstanding M^r. Okeley's having dedicated to him a small
10 Book in 8°. lately publish'd by him, intitl'd, *Introductio ad Linguas Orientales.*   Of wch there were only 500 printed, & conseq^tly he ought to have rec^d a gratuity from some Generous Patron to satisfy him in y^t wch he could not expect from a Bookseller when ye Number was so small. About 2 Months since he made another Journey to Oxoñ, where he was Incorporated A.M. as I have told you before.   This Journey was also undertaken purely for ye sake of ye Publick Library, wch he constantly frequented till Yesterday when he went away.   He is upon other Publick Designs, & for y^t End consulted divers of our Arabick MSS^ts; in wch Language he is said by some Judges to be ye best skill'd of any Man in
20 England; wch he has in a great Measure made appear by his quick Turning into English about half of one of ye Said Arabick MS^ts in folio during his Stay with us, besides ye other Business upon his Hands.   He is a man of very great Industry, & ought to be incourag'd, wch I do not question but he will if he lives to see Learning once more incourag'd in England, wch at present is not. — M^r. Selden ye Son of a Fidler, as M^r. Cowley has told my Friend.   M^r. Selden I am told rec^d the Materials in a great Measure of his Book de Dijs Syris from M^r. Hen. Jacob.   M^r. Cowley was after his Death said by some to have died a Roman Catho-lick; but this was only a Malicious story: for M^r. Joyner who knew him
30 well, has told me that he could not be drawne into y^t Communion all the time he was in France, wch was ab^t 10 years; but y^t he continu'd firm to ye last.   He was not so much respected by the Cavaliers, as he ought to have been upon ye Restauration, wch much troubled him, & made him fly off something, as appears partly from the Preface to his Poems.   He was however a good natur'd man, of great Candor and Humanity, & no Party ever spoke ill against him upon that score. — I have heard it said by a Gentleman, who liv'd in those times that the Earl of Clarendon did take Bribes upon the Restauration, & y^t a great Number of Loyal Cavaliers suffer'd upon his Acc^t, & were not rewarded, because not able
40 to fee him: & y^t M^r. Wood was honest & just in y^t part of his History. This I took ye more Notice of; because he spoke with a great Deal of Vehemence & seem'd to be positive in ye Matter.

May 19 (Sun.).   A Specimen printed at Amsterdam of a new Antho-logia, by Le Clerck.   Quære whether this Work was ever propos'd to be printed at ye Theatre, as M^r. S^t. Aman tells D^r. Hudson in a Letter from Amsterdam it was. — M^r. Cunningham a Scotch Man ab^t a Corpus Juris Civilis.   He is now at Amsterdam. — Academiæ Oxoñ privilegia in unum corpus collecta per D^rem Zouch. fol.   'Tis in MS^t in D^r. Sloan's Study: who has also a MS^t Book written by M^r. Rich. Smith conc. ye Original
50 & Progress of Printing.

May 20 (Mon.).   Out of a Collection of Letters of M^r. Tho. Lydiatt, & other Learned Men to him, in Bib. Bodl. NE. 2. 8.

M^r. Brigges his Answer to M^r. Lydiatt, de Periodo sua annorum 592.

Periodus tua, Doctissime Lydiatt, annorum 592, mihi videtur solertissime excogitata, & omnium quas me vidisse memini commodissime restituere solem & lunam ad eundem situm et distantiam in fine periodi, quos in principio ejusdem obtinebant.   Et si annorum Sexcentorum spatio, quod tu rectissime admones, quinque Intercalationes omittantur, vix pluribus annorum millibus contingeret, ut solis introitus in signa cælestia in alios dies cujusque mensis inciderent, quam in eos quos initio periodi stabilitæ, tenuisse deprehensus fuerit. 10 Vel saltem si unius diei mutatio facta fuerit (quod vitari non potest) tamen ad initium proximæ periodi omnia in pristinam sedem proxime devenirent. Quod si ista periodus Julio Cæsari aut Sosigeni nota fuisset, cum annus vagus & inconstans erat necessario mutandus & stabiliendus, nullam existimo ab humano ingenio commodiorem rationem inveniri potuisse definiendi & formandi anni, ut ejus omnes tempestates in eosdem menses et dies perpetuis futuris temporibus inciderent.   Sed postquam mutatio à Cæsare facta, tot sæculorum usu confirmata fuit, ut vix 12 aut 13 dies mutatus sit anni status per spatium mille sexcentorum annorum; nulla satis probabilis mihi caussa occurrit, quæ Gregorium, ad illam, quam tanto conatu aggressus est, mutationem potuit 20 impellere.   Hanc itaque anni formam quam à majoribus accepimus semper retinendam suadeo. quam etiam Tycho Brahe ubique sequutus est.   Quod si mutatio sit necessario facienda, Gregorianam potius amplecti mallem, ut commercia per universum orbem à mercatoribus commodius exercerentur, quam novam aliquam mutationis inire rationem.   Non quod Gregorianam probem ; aut quod ejus auctoritati quicquam tribuam, aut quod non existimem tuam esse multo commodiorem, si rem ipsam spectemus : sed quod in hujusmodi negotijs, vel quod antiquum est obtinere, vel plurimorum consensui morem gerere commodissimum arbitrer.   Atque hæc pro hujus temporis angustijs in re magni momenti et immensi laboris in bonam partem accipias 30 quæso.   Vale.   Dat. Oxonij die Cal. Junij 1626.

Tui amantissimus

HENRICUS BRIGGIUS.

Another Letter of M^r. Briggs to M^r. Lydiatt [dated Merton Coll., July 11, 1623]. . . .

In l. xx. c. v. of Justin for Vergamum, as in the common Editions, is to be read Bergomum, as is observ'd by Grævius ; & is plain from an Inscription in Gruter, p. 392. CVRAT. REIP. BERGOM. & pag. 396. num. 8. BERGOMI PATRONO.   So also in ye Peutingerian Tables.   See Cellarius's Geogr. Antiq. p. 431. . .   40

May 21 (Tu.).   M^r. John Falconer the Gentleman who writt ye Letters to M^r. Dodwell wch occasion'd his Discourse upon ye Soul.   He is a Scotch Man & suppos'd to be a Divine. — M^r. Dodwell has writ a Discourse proving y^t ye Anonymous Tract ag^t Rebaptization put out by Rigaltius in his Edit. of S^t. Cyprian was writ by Pope Stephanus.   In Labbe's Edition of ye Councils Tom. 1. in the General Table of the particulars of the Tomes tis call'd (tho' wthout any Authority) Ursini monachi Afri. — M^r. Dodwell has prov'd y^t Semiramis that was five Generations before Nitocris according to Herodotus could not be ye Wife of any Assyrian King that reign'd at Ninive, & therefore not the wife of 50 Ninus.   This may be of use in a 2^d Edition of Justin.   This he has done in a Letter to Perizonius. — He also some time agoe writ a Discourse ab^t ye Sicyonian chronology : wch story he thinks to be Fabulous.   'Tis

writ in Latin. — Mʳ. Edw. Stevens born in yᵉ year 1633, as he told Mʳ. Dodwell in a Letter. — Mʳ. Grabe ordain'd at Worcester by Bᴾ. Lloyd on Sᵗ. John Baptist's Day, wᶜʰ he desir'd himself. Mʳ. Dodwell has a Letter from Mʳ. Grabe abᵗ it, & Mʳ. Dodwell thinks he was only ordain'd Deacon. — Mʳ. Dodwell tells me he was of the same Opinion about the Natural Mortality of yᵉ Soul before his Letters of Advice were publish'd, and yᵗ he has advanc'd something there about yᵉ same Opinion. So yᵗ Mʳ. Clark & others talk very inconsiderately in saying wᵗ he has deliver'd is crude & indigested : for Mʳ. Dodwell assures me he has not studied
10 anything with more Care. He tells me that Mʳ. Peter King, Author of yᵉ History of yᵉ Creed is in a great Measure of his Opinion, & yᵗ Dʳ. Sherlock has some things tending yᵉ same way. — Mʳ. Dodwell of Opinion yᵗ Geoffry of Monmouth's story of Britain is wholly to be rejected. — Dʳ. Coward nephew to Dʳ. Lamphire. Dʳ. Lamphire had the Pictures of all yᵉ Camdenian Professors of History. Quære where now ? Dʳ. Coward offer'd to sell them to Mʳ. Dodwell ; but he did not think fit to buy them. They should have been in the Library Gallery. — Mʳ. Dodwell tells me yᵗ he sent Mʳ. Stevens a Copy of his Discourse about yᵉ Soul, but recᵈ no Letter upon it, but only a paper wherein were wrapp'd two Discourses
20 writ by Mʳ. Stevens, one of wᶜʰ abᵗ the Convocation. He believes he was then ill of yᵉ Feaver (of wᶜʰ he died) & yᵗ this hinder'd his Writing. — Mʳ. Grabe did not tell Mʳ. Dodwell in his Letter upon his ordination yᵗ he recᵈ yᵉ Sacrament. Mʳ. Dodwell believes he did not, & excuses him for it, because he thinks yᵉ Bᴾ. might forget; especially if Sᵗ. John Baptist did not fall upon a Sunday. Quære whether it did or no ? The Reason why Mʳ. Grabe was ordain'd on such a day is because of his Xᵗⁱᵃⁿ Name John. — Mʳ. Whiston of Cambridge has lately printed a Book upon yᵉ Revelation of Sᵗ. John. I am told he is of Opinion there yᵗ yᵉ World will be at an End abᵗ nine years hence when there will be a
30 great Eclipse of the Sun. Quære? the Bᴾ. of Worcester of yᵉ same opinion. Before wᶜʰ time yᵉ Bᴾ. thinks Rome is to be burnt. Grounding his Opinion upon some places in yᵉ Rabbis. The Jews all of this Opinion as I hear. — The Saxon Dictionary printed at Oxoñ, wᶜʰ bears yᵉ Name of Mʳ. Thomas Benson then B. of Arts, afterwards Master in yᵗ Faculty, of Queen's College was done chiefly by Mʳ. Thwaites. Mʳ. Todhunter of yᵉ same College had some hand in it, as had also two or three more Young Gentlemen of yᵉ same College tho' not mention'd in yᵉ Preface wᶜʰ was writ by Mʳ. Thwaites, or rather Dʳ. Mill. 'Tis a Compendium of Mʳ. Somner. the Additions taken from Mʳ. Junius's Papers in the Bodlejan
40 Library. Mʳ. Benson now Chaplain to yᵉ Bᴾ. of Carlisle. Mʳ. Thwaites has a Brother, now Taberder of Queen's College, an ingenious man. He studys the Saxon Language, & receives an Annual Pension (as I heard Mʳ. Thwaites say) from the sᵈ Bᴾ. of Carlisle to incourage him in yᵉ said studies. — Ask Mʳ. Dodwell abᵗ yᵉ Libri Lintei, & desire of him in wᵗ place of Livy they may be printed ? also whether he has any thing more to be added to them ? — Desire of him also whether he has any more Inscriptions not publish'd wᶜʰ may be added by way of Appendix to Livy ? Likewise wᵗ Inscriptions he thinks proper to add out of Gruter, Reinesius, or any other Collector ? — He thinks yᵉ Table of yᵉ Bac-
50 chanalian Laws publish'd in yᵉ first vol. of Tully by Gronovius shᵈ be

printed in Livy. He cannot tell whence Gronovius had them. — Ethelfled, Daughter of King Ælfred, repair'd Warwick, after it had been destroy'd by yᵉ Danes. See Dugdale's Antiq. of Warwicksh. p. 298.

May 22 (Wed.). Desire Dʳ. Hudson to inquire whether the MSᵗ from wᶜʰ Sirmond transcrib'd the Anonymous Tract above mention'd abᵗ Rebaptization had any Author's Name, & how tis worded. Let him ask Zacagnius, the MSᵗ being in yᵉ Vatican.

MR. DODWELL TO MR. CLARKE.

Sʳ, I did not know yᵗ yᵉ Copy of your Book against me was a present from the Author till my Arrival at London. My Bookseller who sent it, sent no [10] Letter with it that might inform me that it was so. And I had no reason to expect that favour from a stranger so perfectly unknown to me. Yet, if I be not misinformed, I knew an unkle of your's in our Colledg in Dublin under Dʳ. Winter our then Provost, in the next Chamber to mine. He is, as I am told, dead many years since, & I am glad he has left behind him such an Honour to his Name as you are. I hereby return you my Thanks for your gift, which would have been more acceptable if it had been done with that justice to me that I hope to observe to you. I know no Atheist in England that can take Advantage from the Primitive Doctrine of Natural Mortality, if you had assured him that I allow none such the Benefit of Actual Mortality. [20] No not even in the Interval between his Death & Resurrection. Had you done so, you had not possess'd our pious Readers with those prejudicing passions which must first be removed before I can expect they can judg equally concerning the Merit of the Cause. But then you could not have insulted me with testimonyes of the same Fathers owning all the Heathens, to whom they wrote in order to yᵉ perswading them to receive the Christian Religion, to be intitled to Actual Immortality. As if I had ever doubted but that they held so. Your upbraiding me with Contradictions is only grounded on your Mistake that you did not know that my Premonition was written after my Book with a design of explaining & recanting some things in the Book it self. You who [30] invite me to such Contradictions, methinks, should not upbraid me with them. You might thereby have discerned how free I am from yᵉ Prejudices with which you charge me. As for yᵉ Crudeness of my thoughts, you cannot pretend to have bestowed more time on them than I have done. You may find them suggested in my 2ᵈ Letter of Advice for studyes to Mʳ. John Lesley Brother to Mʳ. Charles upon his leaving our Colledg. The first Edition of those Letters was perhaps before you were born. Yet the Letters themselves were written some while before.

What you pretend not to understand I am sure you cannot pretend to confute, yet the Instances you give of my Obscurity are not so convincing that [40] favourable application would not have made you master of my Meaning. And till you mark out yᵉ Difficulty you must excuse me if I be as unable to find it as you were to know my Design in it. What you charge me with as to my Integrity in my Quotations in that I am sure of yᵉ Advantage of you. You cannot pretend to know my own Thoughts better than I, though you may be more sagacious in finding out the sense of our Authors. Nor am I conscious of any ouvert Acts by which you or any other can judg of my fayling in that point of Integrity. As to my personal Disabilities as I am sensible that no Man ought, so I am conscious that none can have reason to think more meanly of them than myself. And, so far as they are not Sins nor Scandals, I am willing [50] to leave them to our Readers without troubling him with any Apology. Yet you have shewn a strange inequality in your Censures. What you have taken upon credit, in that you are Favourable far beyond my Merit. But you are most severe upon my Book where you had less reason to depend on any Man's judgment but your own. However I am sensible of your good Will in that

favour by how much I am the more conscious of not having deserved it. I
like withall your Zeal for Religion in an Age of so little Zeal, and should not
have been sorry for being the Object of it if I had deserved it. Nor shall I be
ashamed of contradicting myself again if you give me reason to do so, however
you are pleased to stigmatize Recantation by that unpleasing name. Perhaps
you also may see reason, not to imitate, but to rival, me in doing so. God
prosper your Studyes, & make them beneficial for his Church's Good. I am,
so far as you will be pleased to contribute thereto,

            Your most unfeigned and hearty well-wisher

10   HENRY DODWELL.
Oxford, May 22, 1706.

You may direct yours to me at Shottesbrook by the Maidenhead Post in
Berkshire.

Mʳˢ. ASTELL TO Mʳ. DODWELL.

Chelsea, Mar. 11ᵗʰ. 170⅝.

Sir,—That truly Christian Temper, as well as eminent Learning, yᵗ appears
in all your Writings; yᵗ great Charity & Love to Truth, which are when
united the Signature of a Real Xᵗⁱᵃⁿ, but wᶜʰ are of little Worth when sepe-
rated, makes me presume that you will pardon this Address, from one, who,
20 tho' a Stranger to your Person, sincerely Honours you for your Merit, &
faithfull Sufferings for yᵉ Testimony of your Conscience, & who makes it in
pursuance of your Pacific Design in your *Case in View*, by the Reading of
which I receiv'd much Pleasure and Information.

Let it then be humbly offer'd to your Consideration; Whether all the
Constant and Real Members of the Church of England, if they mean to approve themselves as such, are not oblig'd to *present* Communion with the
Actual Possessors of the English Sees, & yᵗ by yᵉ Principles of yᵉ *Cyprianic
Age*, & of the *Case in View*: Excepting only those who Reside in the Diocesse
of Norwich, whose Obedience is due to their Depriv'd Father 'till he discharge
30 them from it?

For since the Bᴘ. is the *Principle of Unity* to his own Particular Church, &
yᵉ Head of all Xᵗⁱᵃⁿˢ living within his District, so yᵗ they who are not with the
Bᴘ. are not in yᵉ Church, Disobedience to God's Bishops being yᵉ occasion of
Heresies & Schisms; since there can be but one Bᴘ. in a District, so yᵗ he who
*is alone in Possession is for this Reason presum'd to be design'd for this Office by
GOD himself;* (as is learnedly proved in yᵉ *Case in View*;) Since *Forreigners*
must not *intermeddle* in another Bᴘ'ˢ *Jurisdiction* wⁿ the Faith is not in danger,
(Ibid.) & *Forreigners* being oppos'd to *Incumbent*, (p. 46.) it seems to me yᵗ all
Bᴘˢ are Forreigners in another Bᴘ'ˢ District, unless the Metropolitan at most;
40 Since Subjects can't be discharg'd of yᵉ Duty owing to their Spiritual Father,
otherwise than by his Death, Cession, or Canonical Deprivation; And lastly,
Since it was yᵉ Practise of yᵉ Primitive Church & Cyprianic Age in Case of
Heresy or Schism, for yᵉ Metropolitan or Neighbouring Bᴘˢ to whom it be-
long'd to provide a Pastor for yᵗ Flock, to Excommunicate yᵉ Heretical or
Schismatical Bᴘ, & to chose another in his place, as appears by Sᵗ. Cyp.'s
Letter to P. Stephen concerning Marcian Bᴘ. of Arles: therefore, there being
now no Rival Bᴘ. but in yᵉ Diocese of Norwich, so yᵗ yᵉ present Possessors
are, & must be yᵉ only Rᵗfull Bᴘˢ, each in his Respective Diocess, & yᵉ *only
Principle of Unity*, no other Bᴘ. whosoever having any Rᵗ to meddle there, as
50 being but a Forreigner; & our late Excellent Metropolitan & his Depriv'd
Colleges, who were yᵉ only Persons who cou'd pretend to a Power of Discharging us from our Obedience to yᵉ *Actual Possessors*, & of substituting
others in their Districts (considering the Church as under Persecution, &
therefore to provide for it's own Subsistence wᵗʰout yᵉ Intervention of yᵉ

Magistrate) not having done it, whereby we may reasonably conclude y^t they did not think it necessary[1]; And further, *Schism from the Catholic Church being consequent to Schism from ye Local B^p. of ye Place, & fundamentally grounded on it*; it must needs follow, y^t unless ye People in ye several Districts (Norwich only excepted) be united to ye Present [2]*Actual Possessors* as their B^p. and Head, they can be united to none; & conseq^tly it [is] as necessary for y^m to live in Communion with him, as it is for them to be united to their true Pastor in order to Communion wth ye Catholick Church & wth X^t it's Head.

To this there is but one objection y^t I can find, & y^t is w^t some call y^e *Contagion*, or to use the words of y^e *Case in View*, p. 2. it is thought necessary to 'abstain from ye Communion not only of ye Rival B^ps themselves, who are ye principal Schismaticks, but of all others also who have made themselves *accessary* to ye Schism by any Sacred Communion with those Rivals.' To wch give me leave to answer, y^t this is already in part obviated: For

1st. We adhere to our present Diocesans for ye same Reason we adher'd to our Depriv'd Fathers in their Respective Districts, (viz.) because being once Lawfull B^ps they have not been Regularly and *Canonically* Depriv'd.

2dly. We have no other *Principle of Unity*: So y^t we must either be as Sheep w^thout a Pastor, wch were to unchurch us; or else we must be united to y^t one Depriv'd Father, who has not yet Renounc'd his Title; but this cannot be in Forreign Districts. For should he [3] *intermeddle in another occupied Jurisdiction agreeing wth him in ye same Faith*, he cou'd *not be excus'd from Schism by ye Catholick Principles of ye Cyprianick Age.*

3dly. Our present Metropolitans being R^tfully so, ye B^ps and Clergy in their Respective Provinces, are oblig'd by Oath to Canonical Obedience. W^ch Oath how far it may affect ye Depriv'd Clergy I shall not now inquire.

4^thly. If I rightly apprehend y^e *Case in View*, it [4]makes ye Danger & Guilt of Contagion to consist in being gain'd over to ye Opinions of ye Infected Party. Whence I gather, y^t possibly our present Diocesans may not approve a Rival B^p. tho' they do not reject him from their Communion: Or supposing y^t they don't disapprove y^t Schism, their Subjects may however live in union wth y^m without Contagion; for this y^e *Case in View* not only grants, but even proves with Respect to ye Doctrine of y^e *Independency of ye Church on State.* § 11th & 12th. Neither are their Subjects proper Judges of their Actions; for we may not *Judge GOD & X^t*, nor make our selves *B^ps of B^ps*; to y^eir own Master they stand or fall. For

5^thly. In my poor opinion, besides all the other ill Consequences of this Doctrine of Contagion, & ye Hazards and Endless scruples to wch it exposes ignorant & well-meaning Persons; it leaves ye People too great a Latitude, sets us up as Judges of our spiritual Fathers, giving us Liberty to withdraw our Obedience before they are Canonically Depriv'd, wch is the very thing that they who teach it mean to argue against.

Lastly, it seems to me y^t we have ye most unexceptionable Precedent of quiet Submission even to disputable Titles, without danger of being Infected with ye usurpers' Guilt, or Partaking in their Sins, & y^t is the Example of our most Holy L^d, who did not Refuse Communion wth ye Jewish Church, tho' the Succession of ye Priesthood (entail'd by GOD Himself) was shamefully broken.

These Hints, on wch I might easily have inlarg'd, & wch are but inartificially put together, I submit S^r to your candid Consideration, not doubting that a Person of your great Sagacity, & Blessed Peace-Making Temper will improve

---

[1] Case in View, p. 38.

[2] *Constantine* found the Ch. in possession of Dioceses, & all the *Xtians* of this time in *possession* of y^t *opinion*, y^t their Living in a *particular Diocess* made y^m obliged in *Conscience* to pay their *Duty* to y^t *particular* B^p. who had ye R^t to y^t Diocess. Ib. p. 68.

[3] Ib. p. 42.   [4] Ib. p. 51 & 57.

them all y^t may be in order to y^t happy Reunion of wch you appear so desirous, & wch is so heartily wish'd by all who pray for ye Peace of Jerusalem, & by none more than by her who is,

Sir,

Your faithfull Servant in all the Offices of X^{tian} Charity :

M. ASTELL.

If you think me worthy of an Answer, be pleas'd to direct to be left at M^r. Wilkins, at ye King's Head in S^t. Paul's Church-Yard.

^{1} M^r. Dodwell's Answer [dated Shottesbrooke, March 30, 1706 (85-110).] . . .

May 23 (Th.).   M^r. S^t. Amand tells D^r. Hudson y^t there are 2 Prodigious Libraries to be sold shortly by Auction, viz. Marquardus Guidius's at Hamburg and M^r. Bigott's at Paris.   Catalogues and Commissions are given and rec^d at M^r. De L'Orme Bookseller at Amsterdam.   M^r. Bigott's has 6000 folios & both of them a great many MSS^{ts} w^{ch} 'twould be highly proper to have bought into ye Bodlejan Library, if Money could be spar'd.   M^r. Dodwell tells me y^t in Gudius's is a MS^t of Photius's Lexicon, w^{ch} 'tis probable may supply the Defects of y^t in the Bodlejan Library.

May 24 (Fri.).   This Morning M^r. Dodwell going to make D^r. Mill a Visit, the D^r. gave a severe Censure (according to his usual Method) of M^r. Dodwell's new Book, tho' he has not read it as he confess'd, but only makes his Judgment from w^t People generally say, wch is unfair & not becoming a Scholar.   M^r. Dodwell hinted to him his Changeableness, particularly his Advising him to stand out ab^t the Oaths.   He likewise mention'd to him a Letter wch the D^r. advis'd M^r. Dodwell formerly to write to D^r. Kenn to stand out ab^t the said Oaths, & told him y^t if he had but that in view he would not act wth so much heat against the Non-Jurors.   Some other things also pass'd, wch occasion'd the D^r. to abuse M^r. Dodwell, who notwthstanding us'd him civilly and like a Scholar & a X^{tian}, & told him y^t 'twould be more suitable to his Function to act more steddily & consistently. — 'Tis s^d Gudius writ the Book de Scriptoribus Historiæ Philosophicæ wch goes under ye Name of Johnston.   Quære farther? — Eutropius lib. i. c. xvii. makes Veij to be 18 miles distant from Rome.   It ought to be corrected xii. being writt perhaps xiix.   For so is the Number in ye Peutingerian Tables, or else xii. & half agreeable to w^t Dionysius Hal. asserts l. II. p. 116.   See Cellarius's Geogr. Antiq. p. 462. . .

May 25 (Sat.).   Hadrian Beverland had so great Interest in Isaac Vossius y^t he prevail'd wth him to write Notes upon Catullus, wch were publish'd after his Death.   There are some obscene things in them, but are otherwise excellent, & answer the Character he bore in the world.

May 25. H. to Dr. T. Smith.   Agrees that the compliments to the University of Frankfurt and to Grabe were extravagant.   Doubts whether Grabe *has* taken priest's orders.   Death of Mr. Edw. Stephens (b. 1633).   Ockley has left Oxford : H. wishes Mr. Wallis would undertake Abdollatiphi.

---

^{1} (Pp. 55-84 missed.)

This Beverland had a very choice Study of Books wch were sold by him at a low price. He is now living, in a craz'd Condition at London. He was look'd upon always to be a man of quick Parts, wch he imploy'd on bad Subjects, viz. in writing obscene, prophane & other loose Books. He was once a Student in ye Bodlejan Library, & therefore something more than w^t M^r. Wood has done may be spoken of him by the Continuer of Athenæ Oxon. D^r. Hudson rec^d a Catalogue of His Writings from his own Hands, & may if he thinks fit oblige any person wth it. — Conc. ye Patavinity of Livy some Things in R. Titius's 3^d Lecture pag. 36... 10

May 26 (Sun.). M^r. Burton in his Notes upon Antoninus pag. 116. seems to be of opinion y^t the Book περὶ ποταμῶν, said to be writ by Plutarch is spurious. He quotes there the Passage ab^t Lugdunum's being so call'd from Λῦγος a Crow & Δοῦνος a Hill, in the old Gallick Language. — Quære who Re——s & Br——n are, quoted in D^r. Coward's new Book? They are two of M^r. Boyle's Lecturers, but who? Quære also to whom 'tis he writes his first Letter, which he has not signify'd at large but only by the Initial & Final Letters, W——m C——ck, D.D. & Rector of Sl——ge in Gl——shire. — Blondell writ something ag^t Baronius, which is not yet printed. Quære whether it be 20 at Amsterdam where M^r. Dodwell tells me ye B^p. of Worcester saw it?

May 27 (Mon.). M^r. Dodwell tells me y^t M^r. Wharton not only writ the latter part of D^r. Cave's Historia Literaria, but y^t he likewise was concern'd in ye whole Work, and for y^t reason expected to have been mention'd as a joynt Author. This M^r. Dodwell rec^d from one who knew M^r. Wharton. — Viro perquam Reverendo, Doctissimo ac longe Clarissimo, D. JOHANNI HUDSON, S.P.D. Gottfredus Christianus Goetzius. [dated Lipsiae d. 16. Februar. cıɔɔccvı (pp. 119–129.)] . . . The said Godofredus Xtianus Goetzius, who is a Brandenburger, was admitted into ye Publick Library at Oxon 16 Sept. 1697. — Gisbertus Cuperus 30 design'd to write a Comment upon ye Palmyrene Inscriptions as is intimated by Jac. Rhenferdius in his Letter to him prefix'd to his Literatura vet. Palmyrena.—Cuperus sent to ye said Rhenferdius accurate Copies of the said Inscriptions.

May 28 (Tu.). This day was a Convocation at 2 Clock about an Address to her Majesty upon Account of ye Success in Catalonia & the Spanish Netherlands.

May 29 (Wed.). This day being the Restauration of King Charles II preach'd at S^t. Marie's M^r. Monnox of Baliol College upon 2 Sam. xxii. 48, 49, 50. 40

Llhuyd mentions Roman coins found near Witney; has bought in Wales a MS. containing Discourses of Josephus Monachus Eveshamiensis. 'A scandalous Dutch story' that Le Clerck's new Anthologia was proposed to be printed at the Theatre. Asks for information regarding Sloane's MSS. of Zouch's *Academiae Oxon. Privilegia* and Rich. Smith on *Original and Progress of Printing.* Particulars of two approaching sales—those of Marquardus Gudius at Hamburg and M. Bigott at Paris. Sends copies of the two letters of Hen. Briggs.

Which being a Thanksgiving of David to God for ye many signal Deliverances & Blessings he had vouchsaf'd to bestow upon him, he hence took occasion to parallel the Sufferings of K. Charles I & II with those of David, & to point out the Authors of all the Calamities & miseries wch these Kingdoms for so many years lay under. Under this Head he took notice of the many pernicious Pamphlets & other Books at y^t time Publish'd, the Encouraging of wch he said was enough at any time to inflame a whole Country, & would again (if not timely put a stop to) ruin our Church & state, particularly such Books as y^t of D^r. Tyndal's conc. ye R^ts of ye Church, wch is stuff'd with ye most loose
10 Principles, & manag'd with ye utmost Rancour & Malice tho' there is but little shew of Reason appearing throughout ye whole.

May 30 (Th.). In Vettius Valens fol. 4. col. 1. is mention'd ἱππάρχειον περὶ ψήφου]. ἐν ποίῳ ζωδίῳ. Probably out of Hipparchus. — M^r. Dodwell has found other Notes ab^t ye Age of Vettius Valens, wch shew y^t he liv'd after ye time of Antoninus. Indictions mention'd in it. The use of Indictions not 'till ab^t ye time of Maxentius. — M^r. Dodwell has collated formerly Pomponius Mela with an old MS^t then in ye Hands of Sir James Ware, now in the Library of ye Earl of Clarendon. This will be of use to M^r. Reynolds, the Collations being good & in several Places
20 correct ye Text. — M^r. Cherry (as M^r. Dodwell informs me) has a Translation (into English out of French of a Discourse,) made by Queen Elizabeth, & written with her own hand when about eleven years of Age. — M^r. Dodwell was put upon his Considerations of present Concern by ye B^p. of Worcester D^r. *Lloyd*[1], who has a Discourse in 4to. to ye same purpose.

May 31 (Fri.). At ye End of K. James 1st's Works in Bodley's Archives is a Letter in MS^t of Queen Mary to Cardinal Pole wch here follows :

Superscrib'd Reverendissimo Domino Legato Compatri meo.
30 Digna Patre tanto salutatione præmissa, agnosco plurimum debere me Reverendissimæ sanctitati vestræ, cum jucundis de literis mihi à vobis ad Ampthille regiam traditis, tum (vel maxime) quod summo meo oblectamento, regis reginæque parentum (quorum utriusque salutem regum ille supremus quam diutissima felicitate dignetur) menstruo convictu vestro dudum beneficio mihi frui licuerit. Una vero me interim (alioqui felicissimam) torquebat visendæ sanctissimæ paternitatis vestræ negata occasio, quæ si votis respondisset meis cum sancta vestra benedictione humillime petita, merita in me vestra meosque frequentia (quibus licuisset) gratijs rependissem. Id quoniam mihi quantumvis desideranti coram assequi tum temporis non obtigit, quod mei jam
40 officij superest, vestram istam benedictionem nonnisi omni cum observantia mihi nominandam mitissima implorans, celsitudinem vestram majorem in modum obtestor, ut cœpto erga me animi candore perpetuo sit. Ita (quod multis alijs nominibus debeo) obnixius orandum erit, ut incolumitatem vestram

---

May 30. H. to F. Cherry. Dodwell has expostulated with Dr. Mill; ' I have experienc'd an extraordinary change in him of late, & am afraid, by some proceedings, he will turn his Hall into a Fanatick Seminary: for wch reason I am now ab^t leaving him, and retiring nearer ye Library, where my Business lies.' Yesterday Mr. Monnox, Balliol, preached on 2 Sam. xxii. 48, 49, 50, attacking Tindal. Notes from Llhuyd (*ut sup.*). His first volume of the British Language is almost finished.

---

[1] Query.

Britannæ rei publicæ nedum mihi Deus Optimus Maximus longissime pro-
trahat. Hertleburye.

Tua spiritualis filia
MARIA PRINCEPS.

'Tis yᵉ original, under her own Hand.
June 1 (Sat.). John Boyce Esqʳ is remov'd from being one of yᵉ
Commissioners of Excise, as is Rich. Bretton Esqʳ. one of yᵉ Commis-
sioners of yᵉ Custom House. — Mʳ. Ayliffe of New Coll. tells me the
present Warden of Winchester Dʳ. Nichols has made a Translation into
English of Xenophon's History.   10

A Letter from Ern. Martinus Plarren to Dʳ. Hudson.
Admodum Reverendo & Clarissimo Viro JOANNI HUDSONO. S.P.D.
Ernestus Martinus Plarren.

Insignis illa humanitas Tua, qua, ut extraneos omnes, ita me inprimis,
quum Oxoniæ essem, excipere dignatus es, tantopere me Tibi obstrinxit, ut
tunc mihi vel maxime satisfecisse credam, ubi eam qualitercunque prædicandi
occasio se mihi videtur offerre. Et hæc causa est, cur non sine magno dolore
meo Te insalutato ex Anglia discesserim; quum inopina optimi Parentis mors
iter meum supra modum præcipitaret; cui vero rursus alia intervenere, quæ
me in hunc usque diem inutiles in Belgio moras jusserunt, quas sine Cl. Peri- 20
zonij aliorumque doctorum amicitia tædiosissimas mihi futuras fuisse unusquis-
que haud difficulter crediderit. In amicorum, quorum modo memini, numero
fuit etiam Neufvillæus quidam, qui cum instructissima Bibliotheca non sper-
nendam possidet antiquariam supellectilem & in hac quidem statuam illam
cujus Tibi iconem transmitto. Super hac varios ille consuluit viros doctos,
atque non paucorum sententia ex conjecturis oppido probabilibus eo recidit,
statuam esse Hetruscam; litterarum in femore scriptarum, & nisi fallor ijs,
quæ in Operis Inscriptionum Gruteriani Eugubinis tabulis habentur, persimi-
lium expositionem frustra optavit à quoquam sibi dari. Ego ex Anglia redux
de viro quodam harum rerum gnaro ab eo interrogatus indicavi eidem Geor- 30
gium Hickes S.T.P. qui de varia lectione Inscriptionis, quæ in statua Tagis
exaratur per 4. Alphabeta Etrusca ad D. Hans Sloane scripsit Epistolam. Ille
Neufvillæus de hoc indicio sibi à me facto supra modum lætatus, voluit, ut quum
Hickesium solo mihi nomine notum dicerem, ad Te, Vir Clarissime; cujus
ego amicitia gloriabar, ea de re litteras darem; Teque & ejus & meo ipsomet
nomine obsecrarem, ut hanc imaginem ab Hickesio videri ejusque circa Inscriptionis lectionem sententiam à nobis resciri curares. Quod ubi nunc à Te
vehementer expeto, de danda audaciæ meæ venia omnino mihi rogandus esses,
nisi ingenua amico serviendi cupiditas, & Tua præsertim humanitas eam mihi
ultro pollicerentur. Age ergo, Vir Clarissime & hoc Tibi onus imponi patere 40
ab homine Tui studiosissimo, cui nihil adeo arduum aut difficile futurum est,
quod non tui amore ductus, quam lubentissime suscipiat. Ubi in patriam
fuero reversus, commoda occasione data, de litterarijs nostrorum locorum
novis, Tibi forsan non ingrata perscribam, ex animo interea vovens ut mea
opera meaque studia, quæ Tibi prorsus dicata volo, quodammodo utilia tibi
esse queant. Vale. Dab. Lugd. Batavorum prid. Kal. Junij CICDCCVI.
Responsorijs Tuis ita inscribas velim:

À Monsieur
Monsieur Robert de Neufville pour
Monsieur Plarren à Leyden.   50

The said Statue, by the Cut, resembles a very beautifull Person, &
being adorn'd with Laurell about yᵉ Head seems to be yᵉ Image of some
Poët or great General. 'Tis much like Virgil. The letters are upon the
left thigh . . . — Dʳ. Hudson recᵈ a Letter from Dʳ. Hickes Dated June

10. 1706. Wherein he tells him he does not know ye meaning of ye Inscription but referrs to ye Philosophical Transactions num. 302, where he has a Letter to D^r. Sloane concerning it, & gives ye Letters according to four Alphabets.

June 2 (Sun.). D^r. Browne is found guilty of Writing the Country Parson's Advice to ye L^d. Keeper, & for it is fined 40 marks, & to stand in ye Pillory once. — Quære ab^t ye Abbey of Culnham not far from Oxon, where the two Staffords took sanctuary in their Rebellion ag^t Hen. VII. See Martin's Chron. p. 259. — Quære ab^t Luffield in
10 Buckinghamshire? There was a Priory belonging to Westminster. — This morning preach'd at S^t. Marie's M^r. Strong of Baliol College, upon Hebr. 7. 7. And w^thout all contradiction ye less is blessed of ye better.

From wch words he prov'd wth abundance of Argument, great Judgment & proportionable Learning ye Dignity of ye Priesthood, from the Priests Sanctity, ye veneration paid them in all Ages, their Function & Office &c. After wch he answer'd some objections started of late ag^t it, particularly in D^r. Tyndal's notorious Book, & concluded with a suitable Application.

June 3 (Mon.). In ye Year 1526 was publish'd at Basil, typis Frob. Six Orations of Chrysostom de Fato & Providentia Dei in 8º. without a
20 Translation. The Editor Erasmus. He has Dedicated them to Doctor Claymond first President of Corpus X^ti Coll. in this university, whom he styles Collegij apum Præsidi. — Vaccary or Vacchary, Vaccharia alias Vacheria, a House or Place to keep Cows in. Fleta lib. 2. c. 41. sect. *item inquiratur* 12. Domus sive locus in quo vaccæ aluntur vel quo negotium quod ad eas pertinet, perficitur, saith Spelman. A Dairy House. W^thout Warrant no Subject may have a Vacary within ye Forest, Cromp. Jur. fol. 194. But in ye Stat. 37. H. 8. c. 16. Vacchary seems to be a special Name of a certain Compass of Ground w^thin ye Forest of Ashdown. — In the Bodlejan Library among the MSS. in Mus. num. 235.
30 are the Epistles of S^t. Paul, &c. printed in an old Black Letter in 12º, wch was Queen Elizabeth's own Book, & her Hand Writing appears at ye Beginning, viz.

August. I walke many times into the pleasant Fieldes of the Holy Scriptures, where I plucke up the goodliesome herbes of Sentences by pruning: eate them by reading: chawe them by musing: and laie them up at length in the hie seate of memorie by gathering them together: that so having tasted thy sweetenes I may the lesse perceave the Bitterness of this miserable Life.

The covering is done in needle-work by ye Queen (then Princess) her
40 self, & thereon are these sentences, viz. on one side, on the Borders: CELVM PATRIA . SCOPVS VITAE XPVS . CHRISTVS VIA . CHRISTO VIVE. In ye middle an Heart, & round ab^t it, ELEVA COR SVRSVM IBI VBI E. C. (i.e. *est Christus*), on the other side about ye Borders, BEATVS QVI DIVITIAS SCRIPTVRAE LEGENS VERBA VERTIT IN OPERA. In ye middle a Star & round it VICIT OMNIA

June 3. T. Cherry to H. Is coming to Oxford on the 15th inst. to take his degree. ' Pray tell Mrs. Wells to gett my Batchellors gown and Bands in order ag^st I come. As I don't question she & all Friends else will their Bills; but of this don't you put 'em in mind.' The Venetian Ambassador resents the Queen's prohibition of any of her subjects attending his Chapel.

E. ✱ C. PERTINAX VIRTVS. I think for *Elizabetha captiva* vel *Elizabethæ captivæ,* She being then, when she work'd this Covering a Prisoner, if I mistake not, at Woodstock.

June 4 (Tu.). In Bodley's Archives, B. 94 is a MS^t. Primer, curiously Illuminated, wch was formerly Queen Mary's, & afterwards Prince Henry's. 'Twas given by Rich. Connock Esqr, Auditor General, Sollicitor, and of his Highness Council of Revenue, Jul. 7°. Anno Regni Regis Jacobi 13. 1615. Just at ye Beginning of the Psalms, is the following Passage written by Q. Mary's own Hand, viz.

Geate you suche Ryches as when the Shype is broken may swyme away wythe the Master for dyverse chances take away the goods of fortune, but the goods of the Soule, whyche bee only the trewe goods nother fyer nor water can take away. Yf you take labour and payne to doo a vertuous thyng the labour goeth away and the vertue remaynethe. Yf thoroughe pleasure you do any vicious thyng the pleasure goeth away and the vice remaynethe. Good Madame for my sake remember thys.

Your lovyng Mystres
MARYE PRINCESSE.

June 5 (Wed.). M^r. Phil. Ayres (who liv'd in Spain several Years) tells M^r. Dodwell & my self y^t in ye Escurial is a considerable number of Greek MSS. among wch is Stephanus περὶ πόλεων. tis a thick folio & probably not epitomiz'd. — Remember to look over a Preface of Corderius to Cyril upon Jeremy in 8°. where he gives an Acc^t of a Journey he made into Spain to see ye Library in ye Escurial, & gives us a Catalogue at ye latter end of some of ye most remarkable Greek MSS^{ts}. — At the Beginning of Vettius Valens in Bib. Bod. Arch. B. Seld. 35. Longolius has added, Curavit hunc librum describendum Christophorus Longolius precio octingentorum sestertiorum nummum, hoc est vicenis aureis ducatis. De Longueil. Presently after wch by another hand is added an explication of ye several Notes in the Book. [158–161.] . . .

June 6 (Th.). M^r. Dodwell tells me he has found a Note in Vettius Valens, shewing the Author liv'd 40 years after ye 21st year of Antoninus Pius. For he mentions one who liv'd so long after y^t time. — Out of M^r. Dodsworth's coll. vol. 149. p. 9. [Inscriptions, &c.,] In Worsopp Church (in Nottinghamshire) sometyme part of ye Abbay, March 4. 1639. . . . In ye Church of Wodhill alias Wahull in Com̃. Bedford. 29 Feb. 1639. . . — The lowest Note M^r. Dodwell has met with in Vettius Valens shews him to have been in Severus's time, he mentioning a Death of a Person whose nativity he acc^{ts} for in the year 200 after X^t or thereab^{ts}.

June 7 (Fri.). Dodsworth's coll. vol. 149. f. 11. b. [Inscriptions, &c.,] In ye Church of Braybroke in Com̃. Northampton 2 March 1639. . . . — In ye Church of Luton in Com. Bedf. 27 Feb. 1639. . . . — In Bedford Church 27 Feb. 1639. . . . — In ye Middle Ile of ye East End of ye Quyre of Yorke Minster. . . . — M^r. Dodwell has found another considerable note in Vettius Valens (if the latter part be the same Valens, wch is to be doubted from the Title of one of the Books call'd βιβλίον δεύτερον

June 6. E. Smith to H. Hopes to send on loan shortly Fabrettus and Burton's *Britan. Romanorum.* Asks in return for a copy of Dodwell's letter about Lucian.

in fol. 181. b. whereas before the 6th and 7th if not more are mention'd, in their order) viz. Ὑπόδειγμα β Διοκλυτιανοῦ ἔτος ρμζ (or 147) Τυβὶ ιδ εἰς ιέ ὥρ. γ. (in fol. 177. b.) w[ch] brings him as low as an. X[ti] 431. There is another Note in fol. 178. a. w[ch] mentions the Death of Valentinian II[d]. in y[e] 36th year of his Age. And by y[t] He is brought down to ab[t] y[e] year 391. — I find by the Buttery Book for Edmund Hall w[ch] I have seen by chance (for 'tis not like other Places here to keep their Books in a certain place for y[t] purpose) y[t] in the year 1672, on the 13th of March, there were then at y[e] Hall who battled fourscore & eighteen, whereof 6 Masters
10 besides Principal and vice-Principal, 24 Bachelors, 66 Under-Graduates.

    June 8 (Sat.). Tis s[d] y[t] y[e] King of France us'd to lye wth y[e] Dauphin's wife, & for y[e] Expiation of so great a Sin the Pope by way of Penance injoyn'd him to extirpate y[e] Protestants in France, w[ch] is said to be the occasion of their Persecution. — On y[e] 5th one D[r]. West a Physitian was stab'd thro' the Body by M[r]. Lydell his Brother in Law who w[n] he was seiz'd and in custody of a Constable carrying before a Justice of Peace wth a Penknife w[ch] he drew out of his Pocket cut his own Throat but 'tis believ'd neither of y[e] wounds will prove mortal. —

    Yesterday D[r]. Hudson receiving certain Books from D[r]. Tyson for
20 y[e] use of y[e] Publick Library, he sent with it also y[e] following Letter.

London May 28, 1706.

    Hon[d]. S[r],—Having been so tedious in sending those Tracts of mine you desired for y[e] Publick Library; you may easily imagine I had not so good opinion of them as to think they deserved so honourable a place. However since you desired it, I have obeyed; and what are wanting are to be met with in y[e] Philosoph. Transact. But to make some amends for y[eir] Intrusion, there will accompany them a MS[t]. in velam of L. Apuleius de virtutibus Herbarum; & Sextus Placitus alias Platonicus de medicina de Animalibus &c. Between these two there is a small Tract de Medicina de Homine. Whether it be-
30 longs to either of them, I am uncertaine, since Gab. Humelbergius who hath given us an Edition of both these Authors with his notes at large upon them, takes no notice of it. Both, as you will find, are imperfect : & in many places uncorrect. But having the advantage of y[e] Figures of each Plant &c. tho' but rude it may give some light to y[e] knowledge of y[e] Plants themselves, and by

    June 8. Dr. T. Smith to H. Again urges H. to find out 'by a side-wind question' whether Grabe be in full orders. Will try to get a copy of Ockley's Introduction to his work on the Saracenical Chaliphs. Fears that Mr. Wallis' attendance on young Lord Wenman takes him off from the business of his profession; he has neglected two commissions of Smith's. Complains of Charlett and the Press corrector's dealing with him in the matter of the *Synopsis.* Remarks on Josephus Eveshamensis. 'Mr. Selden was beholden to that rambling Wit, Linguist, and Philosopher Henry Jacob, afterwards Fellow of Merton Coll., for several notices received from him, w[ch] he readily and gratefully acknowledges in his Prolegomena to his booke *De Dis Syris,* cap. 3 p. 46 of the Leyden edition, w[ch] is more to bee esteemed than all the late German editions, with their nauseous additions and illustrations.' The Bigot and Gudius Catalogues. Thanks for Brigges' letters. Dr. Bernard's papers were left to S., but he has not touched them for seven or eight years. Among them was a noble collection of letters from Bishop Pearson, Isaac Vossius, Huet, the two Spanheims, Ludolfus, Gronovius, Mabillon and 40 others, but very few of Bernard's in reply. Before applying to the addressees he will have those in his possession transcribed, but has lost his amanuensis. Can H. find him one? Intends to bequeath Bernard's papers to H. Sends copy of his letter to Dr. Wallis, dated Sept. 13, 1690.

comparing it wth ye Editions I have by me, I find several Places may be corrected, as in ye first Page of the MS^t. of Apulejus treating of ye Virtues of Centaurium maj: 'tis ad sugillationes & livores, in ye printed Editions ad sugillationes & dolores. I will not trouble you with more Instances. But if you think convenient to give it a place in ye Bodlejan Library, I shall take it as an Honour to add any thing to so noble a collection of Learning. I must intreat you likewise to accept a Copy of my Ourang Outang since you was pleased to cast a favourable Eye upon it. & if at your leisure you should favour me wth your Opinion of the Age of the MS. you will much oblige

Your most humble & obedient Servant   10
EDW^d TYSON.

Dodesworth's Col. Vol. 149. fol. 18, a. Manchester church in Com. Lanc. 12 March, 1639. [186–193.] . . .

June 9 (Sun.). This Morning preach'd at S^t. Marie's M^r. Smalbrooke Fellow of Magd. Col. upon John 5th 28, 29. . . .

The whole Discourse was levell'd ag^t ye pious and Learned M^r. Dodwell's Hypothesis ag^t ye universality of ye Resurrection & ye immortalizing of ye soul by Baptism, in wch he propos'd to prove 1st y^t the universality of ye Resurrection is constantly represented in ye New Testament. Here he examin'd the principal Texts of Scripture made use of by M^r. Dodwell, & concluded that 20 he had given false interpretations of them. The Fathers he did not meddle with but referr'd to a Book wch he said would shortly come forth (meaning I suppose y^t printing at ye Theatre) wherein he said all ye Passages from ye Fathers were accurately consider'd, & y^t the Learned Author (so he call'd the writer, by wch it should seem M^r. Mills is not ye Person principally concern'd) had set them all in a true light, & upon that asserted y^t M^r. Dodwell's Notion was uncatholick & y^t he had egregiously misrepresented ye Fathers. Thence he proceeded in ye 2^d place to shew y^t this Hypothesis was highly derogatory to ye Justice of God. And in ye 3^d place concluded y^t M^r. Dodwell's Arguments were erroneous & unconclusive. This done he clos'd all by declaring 30 to ye Auditory that he had not said any thing out of Design to insult so great a Man but in some measure to prevent ye Mischiefs wch may proceed from this Opinion wch was establish'd by so pious & Learned a person, who was to be pitied upon Account of this & some other dangerous Positions laid down by him, particularly relating to Schism, his Defence of ye small Number of Martyrs &c. So y^t if persons so eminent for Learning & piety & who have done so signal Service to ye church in other Respects as tis certain M^r. Dodw. has fall into great Mistakes & Errors he caution'd all to be watchfull & upon y^eir Guard & to take all due care not to imbibe new Principles ab^t Religion &c.

The character this Sermon now bears is y^t M^r. Smalbrook spoke too 40 confidently & that he did not do M^r. Dodwell Justice, especially ab^t ye Resurrection since he is not ag^t ye universality of y^t, but y^t all are not to be concern'd in everlasting Rewards & Punishments; & in short y^t tho' M^r. Dodwell has advanc'd some new notions (at least such as are not known now when generally people read but few old Authors) yet 'twould have been far better for him not to have discours'd of them in ye Pulpit; since y^t is the way to do farther mischief, & to make people have worse opinions than are to be found in M^r. Dodwell's Book it self. — In ye Afternoon preach'd M^r. Bingham (of whom I have said something before) formerly of University Coll. upon 1 Cor. 16. 13. . . . The Design 50

June 9. H. to F. Cherry. Sends specimen of Livy, with proposals. Mr. Smalbrooke, Magd., has attacked Mr. Dodwell—not quite fairly or successfully—at St. Mary's.

of the Discourse was to exhort to Constancy & perseverance in the Duties of Religion & to endeavour always to keep a good Conscience. — Dʳ. Tyndale of All Souls Coll. was originally of Linc. Coll. where he was Pupil to Dr. Hicks, wch Dʳ. Hicks has a Brother a Physitian, who was first a Presbyterian, & afterwards converted to ye Ch. of Engl by his Bro. & now practises Physick in London.

June 10 (Mon.). On Tuesday Morning last one J——F a Presbyterian Parson who was seized the night before by ye constable and his watch in Cheapside was brought before ye Court of Aldermen & ordered
10 to pay 5 sh. for being (as Sʳ. Owen Buckingham carried the matter in his favour) in drink & to beg a quakers Pardon who was ye Accuser for violently taking his wife by y^e —— as she was knocking at her own door for Entrance. The Quaker after he had read him a Jumper Lecture agᵗ Lewdness in a man of his Profession told him y^t he would pardon him upon condition y^t he found he could give him no farther legal trouble. These are ye pious cheats y^t cry up so much for Reformation of Manners. — Mʳ. Dodwell tells me he saw ye Book Mʳ. Llhuwyd mention'd to me written by Robertus Josephus Monachus Eveshamensis (as he thinks he is call'd in ye Book) & he says it contains very little History,
20 besides ye suppression of ye little Religious Houses by Cardinal Wolsey, & ye story of ye Person (Quære whom) who reflected in his Will & Testamᵗ upon ye use of superstitious Legacies & for y^t had his Body dug up & burnt by ye Sheriff. He was contemporary wth Erasmus, whom he mentions sometimes & ye Epistles are only for Exercise of Stile, & ye Latin is better y^n usual among ye Monks. Mʳ. Dodw. saw ye Book at Sᵗ. Asaph. . . .

June 11 (Tu.). Mʳ. Philip Ayres an antient Gentleman who lodges as Commoner in Sᵗ. John's College (on purpose to direct a Young Gentleman Commoner [1] there newly entred) having been a great Traveller has pickt up several Curiosities, as Books Coyns, &c. one of wch I saw last
30 night at ye Coffee-House viz. a Roll neatly written in Arabick wch seems to be ye Alcoran. He gives a very good Account of the Places where he has been especially as to ye state of Learning & is of a communicative Temper. — Dodsworth's coll. vol. 149. f. 22. a. On a stone in ye Church Yard of Halton juxta Lancaster. Robert Burton of Heighfeild lyes under this stone | Who lyv'd at Heighfeld one hundred yeares & one. . . — This day Mʳ. Wᵐ. Smith left University Coll. He burnt a great Number of Papers upon his Leaving ye College. — Mʳ. Wood in his Life of Sir Anthony Cope Vol. 1. Ath. Oxon. p. 65. mentions only one piece done by him, viz. his Meditations on ye Psalms, tho' he insinuates y^t he perform'd other Matters
40 of Learning, wch he never saw. I have by me The History of Annibal & Scipio, gathered & translated out of Livy & other Authors, & said to be done by Anthony Cope, Esqʳ. printed at *Lond.* 1590. 8°. I suppose 'twas done by ye said Sʳ. Anth. Cope, it being dedicated to K. Hen. 8th & he being only mention'd as Esqʳ I suppose 'twas collected before he was Kᵗed.

June 10. Dean Hickes to Dr. Hudson. Thanks for Abbot Passioneo's present. Returns Hudson's picture (for a Dutch book) with remarks. Thanks for transmitting ' the colleges noble present for my book.' Will do all he can for Livy.

---

[1] Mr. Drake.

June 12 (Wed.). Dodsworth vol. supradict. fol. 38. b. . . .
Dodsworth Coll. vol. 150. p. 107. a. [Inscriptions &c.,] In Gainsborough Church in Lincolne. . . .

June 13 (Th.). On Tuesday last M[r]. Dodwell had a conference wth M[r]. Smalbrook ab[t] his Sermon, preach'd at S[t]. Marie's, w[ch] M[r]. Smalbrook was so ingenuous as to read to M[r]. Dodwell, who was pleas'd very well with his civility, & thinks him a much fairer person than his old Friend Milles of X[t] church who would not vouchsafe either to talk wth M[r]. Dodwell upon this subject, or shew him anything y[t] was done relating to y[e] new Book printing at y[e] Theatre. M[r]. Dodwell desir'd Mr. Smalbrook 10 would print w[t] he had said by way of Appendix to y[e] said Book omitting all Encomiums, y[t] he might see the whole they could say together.

June 14 (Fri.). Dodsworth's coll. vol. 149. p. 107. b. [Inscriptions &c.,] In Mattersey Church in Nott. . . . — Epworth in y[e] Isle of Axholme was y[e] House of Lo. Mowbray neare unto w[ch] y[e] Duke of Mowbray of Norfolke was banished. He parted with his Dutchess not far from Epworth, in w[ch] place the Ewers sett up a Crosse for a Memorie w[ch] is called Parteney Crosse.

June 15 (Sat.). Ibid. f. 108. a. [Inscriptions &c.,] At Beltone in ye Iland of Axholme. . . . Noketon Churche 4 Sept. 1641. . . . — Memorandum 20 y[t] when M[r]. Dodwell was with M[r]. Smalbrook M[r]. Parker was then present, who says y[t] M[r]. Smalbrook was too hard for M[r]. Dodwell. but quære? for it seems to be only a story[1]. — M[r]. Halley says he can prove y[t] Vespasian reckon'd his Reign to begin at ye Death of * * * * because he reckons Vitellius to be no Emperor.

June 16 (Sun.). M[r]. Periam of X[t] Church preach'd this Morning at X[t] ch. before ye University upon 1 Tim. 5. 22. Neither be partaker of other Men's sins.

'Twas a neat Discourse, shewing how any one may be partaker in y[e] sins of another, & upon y[t] occasion he could not but take notice of y[e] Happiness of 30 those who had opportunities of being Educated in such Places as were always famous for their Loyalty, virtue, & good principles, & in how great Danger those are who thro' Flattery or Connivence do not rebuke Vice, but suffer those at least who are their superiors to go on in the most abominable & notorious Crimes without so much as daring to speak one word ag[t] them, or in the least declare the Mischiefs w[ch] are like to proceed from such wickedness. —

I am inform'd that M[r]. Smalbrooke is one of those ingag'd in writing y[e] Book printing at y[e] Theatre ag[t] M[r]. Dodwell, & y[t] he very freq[tly] visits Milles for this End. — Dodsworth vol. 149, f. 113. a. . . . — Wakefeld Quyer. . . — Doncaster Church North Quyer. . .   40

Xtopher Barker Printer to Queen Eliz. was borne in y[e] Vicaridge House in y[e] Towne of Marr in Com. Ebor. He did afterwards make y[e] Cawsey in ye same Towne to ye Charges of 7[li]. He likewise paved all y[e] Alleys in y[e] Church boarded & made all y[e] best Formes & Pulpit in y[e] Church. He likewise gave a great Bible well bound & bossed on wch there is a plate wth this Inscription. Ex dono Xtopheri Barkeri de London Armigeri & Regiæ Majestatis Typographi 1579.—Rob[t]. Barker son of y[e] s[d] Xtopher was afterwards Printer to y[e] Queene & to King James.

June 16. Thwaites to the same. Asks for a book from Rome. Message from Sergeant Bernard. Has been almost miraculously preserved.

---

[1] Mr. *Parker* continues to be of the same mind. *Nov.* 13, 1706.

June 17 (Mon.). On Thursday last M^r. Broughton Chaplain to his Grace ye Duke of Marlborough was chosen Lecturer of S^t. Andrews Holborne in roome of D^r. Humphreysville lately deceas'd. The L^d. Mordant is made a Brigadier General & is going to make his Campaigne in ye Netherlands. — Dodesworth Vol. 22. f. 14. b. E Registro Lufnam in Officio Registrarij Curiæ Prærog. London, fol. 14. b. . . .

June 18 (Tu.). Ib. f. 49. b. (E Registro Logge.)

15 Sept. 1486. I Richard Harecourt of Wigtham com. Berks knight bequeth my Body to be buryed in ye Church of our Lady in ye Abbay of Abing-
10 don. Item I bequeth to the Abbay of Abbendon all my Lands & tenements
in Tylgarsley & Fyrth to fynd a Preist to pray for ye Soule of Edyth my late
Wief, & Dame Kateryne my now wief. Item I bequeth to ye Reparation of
the Churche of Wyghtham xx^{lib}. William Harecourt the Testator's sonne.
The Testator bequeth[s] to Dame Kateryne his wief ye Wardship & Keeping
of ye Lord Say durying his Nonage. Item I give to Margarete Daughter of
Edward Harecourt c. Mark to her Marriage & to Symond Harcourt & Richard
Harcourt his Broder cccc. M. The Testator had ye Manors of Wight-
ham Sowtrewerth in Com. Berks, the Manors of Corffe Hubert & Corffe
Moleyns in Com. Dorsett & Landes & Manors in Godstone, Lagham &
20 Walkhamstede in Com. Surrey wch Dame Katerine his Wief hath for Lief.
remainder to W^m. Harecourt the Testator's son & Heŭ. &c. rem^r. to Richard
Son of Xtopher Harecourt &c. rem^r. to Symond Brother to ye s^d Richard.
Item I will y^t Myles Harecourt be in the Keeping of Richard Lewkenor Esqre.
& that the said Richard take ye Profitts of my Manor of Chalgrave, called
Senclers maner in ye County of Oxoñ & Lampham juxta Pemsey in Com.
Sussex for Exhibition of y^o s^d Myles durying his Noneage. rem^r. to ye Heyres
of Xtopher Harecourt. rem^r. to Willm Harecourt ye Testator's sonne. An
Estate to be made of Lands in Lye juxta Astall in com. Oxon. to Jane wief
of John Hodelston Esquyer sumtyme wief to Xtopher Harecourt for her
30 Lief, rem^r. to Richard son of ye said Jane, rem^r. to Symond Broder of ye s^d
Richard, rem^r. to my son William. Probatum 25 Octob. a^o. supradicto.

E Registro Mylles. Ib. f. 53. b. 7 Julij 1488.

I dame Harecourt widow late wief of Sir Richard Harecourt Knyght bequeth my Body to be buryed in ye Abbaye of Rewly in Oxford. Item I make
Thomas Croft Esqr. one of my Executors to dispose of my Goods for my
soule & of Syr Myles Stapylton my Husband & of our parents soules & D^r.
Fitzjames & Robard Restwold Esqr. Supervisors. Item in Codicillo the
Testator Names John Hudleston Esqr. & Jane his wief executors. probatum
23 Jan. 1488.

40   E Registro Vox. Ib. p. 61. b.   12 Martij.

1493. I Edward Mounteford Knyght bequeath my Body to be buryed in
our Lady Chappell in ye Church of Henley upon Thames in Com. Oxon & to
have a metely Tombe made there, wth this Inscription. Here lyeth Sir Edmund Mountford Knight sometymes Councellor & Kerver with ye most
Blessed Kyng Henry the sixt, and aftir Chamberlayn unto ye High & Mighty
Prince Jasper Duke of Bedford Brother to ye said Prince the said Kyng.
Item I will that my Maner of Rammyngham remayne unto John Preston &
his Heyres &c. rem^r. to Sir William Norreys & his Heyres. probatum 24 Maij
1494.

50   June 19 (Wed.). Ib. f. 63. b.—11 April 9 H. 7.

Ib. f. 73. b.—8 Jun. 1498.

I Dame Katerine Reed widow bequethe my Body to be buryed in the Holy
church. Item I give to the Church of Hampton Poyle in Com. Oxon vi^s.
viii^d. &c. probat. 18 Sept. 1498.

Ib. f. 74. a.—4 Octob. 1498.

I William Stavely Esquire bequeth my Body to be buryed in the Chancell of ye parish church of Burcester. Item I bequeth to ye Monastery of Burcester XXVI^s. VIII^d. Item I will y^t my Maner of Broghton in Com. Bucks wch I purchased of Geor. Tresham & my Maner of Briggenhall wch I purchased of John Stokys Esqr. in Com. Oxon remayne to Alice my Wief for her Lief, rem̃. to Georg Stavely my Son & his Heirs, rem^r. to ye University Colledg in Oxenford &c. William Stavely & Isabell Stavely the Testators. Da. probat. 1 No. 1498. —

Memorandum That about 3 years since at least D^r. Bentley borrow'd 10 a MS^t Horace of Queen's college in this University. D^r. Hudson procur'd it for him; & ye Society lent it, thinking that D^r. Bentley, who had us'd M^r. Boyle so scurvily about ye MS^t Phalaris, would not fail to return it in a short time: but he has not done it as yet; wch has occasion'd D^r. Hudson to mention it in a Letter to him, wherein he likewise reminds him of his Edition of y^t Author wch the world is in Expectation of, as they are also of his Brother Critick D^r. Mill's Testam^t. — Memorandum also y^t when M^r. Penton resign'd his Principality of Edm. Hall he bought twelve Knives and forks, the Handles silver, wch are now in the Principal's Lodgings with a silver [*sic*] and a Cover to it, all wch it seems he left for ye use of 20 ye Principals successively. — In ye Principal's Lodgings is also a large Plate given by D^r. Butler, D^r. Woodard & D^r. Kennett when they took the Degree of D^r. of Divinity. Also another neat Plate, of considerable Value given by M^r. John Bennett Gentleman Commoner of ye Hall when he left us. W^{ch} M^r. Bennett is now of ye Middle Temple, & is & was always noted for an ingenious, good Natur'd Gentleman; but if you ask D^r. Mill about him he will give you the Reverse of this character. —

Dodesworth vol. 22. (E Registro Blamyr.) Fol. 83. a.—21 Jul. 1500. 16 H. 7.

I Margret Twynyhoo of Redyng com. Berks wydow bequeth my body to 30 be buryed in ye Grey Fryers in Reding in the Chapell of St. Francis as nigh the Tombe I have made ore my Fader & Moder as may be. Item I give to ye church of More Kirchill wher my Husband Twynyhoo lyeth xiij^s iiij^d. Item to the Church of Bedyngton to pray for my Husband Carewe, Nicolas my son, & me xx^s. The Testator had a 3^d Husband called Carant. Item I do give to my son Carant my best Bordcloth marked with A. & C. Item to Anne Tropynell my Daughter my Coler of Gold &c. Item to my Sanche [*sic*] Ewerby my Daughter my best owche &c. Item to Elizabeth Twynyhoo my Daughter my Vurre of Gold, & after her Decesse to Margaret her Daughter. Item to my Suster Cowdrey my Hert of Gold & after her Decesse to my 40 Nece her Daughter. Item to my suster Newburghe my Blake beds of jett with gaidyes of Gold & after to my Nece Agnes her Daughter. Item to Edward Twynyhoo my chayne of Gold. Item to my suster Margaret my Coller of Gold sett wth stonyes & pearle. Item to Cecill somtyme wief of my son W^m. Twynyhoo a gret flat Bolle of Sylver wth a couer wch was her Faders for her Lief to remayne to the Daughter of William Adams late her Husband. Item to M^r. Wode chief Judge of ye Common Place my overseer my best standyng Cupp. probat. 4 Martij 1501.

June 20 (Th.). King of Prussia's Letter to ye Queen about ye University's Celebration of ye Secular of Francfurt. 50

Fridericus, Dei gratia Rex Borussorum &c. Serenissimæ ac Potentissimæ

June 20. E. Smith to H. 'I am told a 2^d part of Tindal's Book is coming out; if that cursed Argument is encourag'd some of ye Clergy may

Principi, Dominæ ANNÆ, Eadem gratiâ Magnæ Britanniæ, Franciæ & Hiberniæ
Reginæ Fidei Defensori &c. &c. &c. Sorori, Consanguineæ & Amicæ nostræ
Charissimæ salutem.
Serenissima ac Potentissima Princeps, Soror, Consanguinea & Amica Charissima.
Splendorem secularium Sacrorum, ab Academia nostra Francofurtensi
secunda vice haud ita pridem celebratorum, nihil magis illustrat, quàm illus-
trissimas atque celeberrimas Angliæ Academias, tanto terrarum intervallo
orbeque ipso divisas, ejus pietatis atque gaudij partem sibi vindicare voluisse.
10 Quarum quidem Cantabrigiensis cum Viros, Virtutibus eruditione atque omni
cultu ornatissimos, miserit votis suis instructos; altera vero Oxoniensis illius
Diei memoriam solenni celebratione atque pompa dignam judicaverit: deben-
tur utrique haud vulgares laudes atque gratiæ pro publica illa effusissimæ
voluntatis, studij & amicitiæ testificatione, proque felici illa animorum in
studiorum omnis generis incrementum ac in communia commoda conspiratione.
Agnoscit quoque Francofurtensis Academia grato animo beneficium & ornamentum in se collatum, neque eorum unquam obliviscetur, imprimis cum de
commodis atque splendore Academiarum Angliæ agetur. Nos verò quæ ab his
ad concelebrandum diei illius natalitij secularis memoriam facta atque gesta
20 sunt, honoresque Oxonij in nostros non præsentes solum, sed & absentes
insolito exemplo, summo tamen studio collatos, nobis esse omnia quam gratis-
sima, Majestati Vestræ persuasissimum esse cupimus. Cui imprimis gratias
maximas studiose agimus, quod pro suo erga literas favore, proque sua erga
nos amicitia & benevolentia benignè permiserit atque annuerit, ut hæc publica
mutuæ Academiarum conjunctionis ac amicitiæ monumenta ad Posteritatis
memoriam existerent. Deus O. M. celeberrimas Academias semper florentis-
simas esse velit, à quo Majestati Vestræ prospera quævis optamus, eandemque
de sincera nostra voluntate atque studio certissimam esse jubemus. Dabantur
in Arce nostra Charlottenburg die 31 Maij 1706.
30   Majestatis Vestræ Bonus Frater Consanguineus
                                             FRIDERICUS R.
Serenissimæ ac Potentissimæ Principi Dominæ ANNÆ, Dei gratia Magnæ
Britanniæ, Franciæ & Hiberniæ Reginæ, Fidei Defensori &c. &c. &c. Sorori,
Consanguineæ & Amicæ nostræ charissimæ.
Ad Reginam Angliæ.   COMES à WARTENBERG.

— The Lᵈ. Howard of Effingham is made one of yᵉ Gentlemen of yᵉ
Bedchamber to Prince George of Denmark in room of my Lᵈ. Stawell,
who is turn'd out, because he is an honest Gentleman. Mʳ. Bingham of
University College married to a Daughter of one Mʳ. Pocock[1] a School-
40 master. — Mʳ. Mews one of yᵉ Prebendaries of Winton is deceas'd & is
to be succeeded by one Woodard of Sᵗ. John's College. — Dʳ. Tho.
Brown formerly of Corpus Xᵗⁱ Coll. now of Bᵖˢ. Waltham is yᵉ most
scurvily us'd by his People yᵗ ever was heard of. They set up his Effigies
in Straw, wᵗʰ a Pot in one Hand & a glass in yᵉ other to ridicule him.
— Baluzius in pag. 621 of his Appendix to Regino de Disciplinis Eccl.

expect to be De Witted . . . Sir Phil. Sydenham is inform'd yᵗ yᵉ Goverment
has taken notice of yᵉ propos'd design for translating Mr. Bale's Critical
Dictionary, and will interdict its proceeding notwithstanding yᵉ Undertakers has
been as they say at above 1400ˡ cost already. You know I suppose its character for which it was damm'd in Fr. viz. that there is never a lascivious verse in
all yᵉ Poets nor never a sceptical Notion in yᵉ Fathers or Philosophers but he
has faithfully raked together.'

---

[1] Pocock above mention'd is somewᵗ related to my old Friend Milles of Xt. church.
Quære in wᵗ respect?

has published a prayer in Latin out of an old MS^t. Missal in the Colber-
tine Library wch is exactly the same wth that in our Common Prayer
Books at ye End of ye Litany, wch beginns *O God Mercifull Father
y^t despisest not ye sighing of a contrite heart* &c. — Amongst B^p. Barlow's
Books in Bibl. Bodl. is one (8°. C. 593) printed at *Lond.* 1574, containing
ye Liturgy of ye Ch. of Eng. in Latin, wch belong'd once to J. Johnson as
appears at ye Beginning who has added in ye Margin & elsewhere several
MS^t. Notes. — See whether D^r. Smith has taken notice of ye Testimony
of Camden by M^r. Johnston in ye Preface to his History of Scotland. —
In ye Publick Library at Basil are the Quatuor Evangelica Græce ab annis 10
circiter mille exarata. See pag. 15 of Analecta Tom. 4 by Mabillon. . . .

    June 21 (Fri.). Baron Spanheim's Letter to D^r. De Laune on Acc^t of
ye Performance in ye Theatre in Memory of ye Foundation of ye University of Francfurt upon Oder. [254-261.]

    June 22 (Sat.). Quaere where Obrechtus's Books are now ? He had
added on ye Margin of a great many of y^m Learned Observations. Vide
Mabillon's Iter Germanicum, Vol. 4, Analect. p. 89. — Dodesworth, Vol.
22. f. 88. a. (E Registro Blamyr). [261-265.] . . .

    June 23 (Sun.). M^r. Trapp of Wadham writt Ædes Badmintonianæ
. . 1701. — Also he writt A Prologue to ye University of Oxon. Spoke 20
by M^r. Betterton at ye Oxon Act in 1703. — M^r. Tho. Yalden of Magd.
writ among other things An Essay on ye Character of Sir Willoughby
Aston, late of Aston in Cheshire, a Poem. *London,* 1704. — M^r. Ro.
Whitehall Fellow of Merton, Author of Urania or a Description of the
Painting of ye Top of ye Theatre at Oxon. & A Poem. London, 1669,
fol. (2) The English Rechabite, or, a Defyance to Bacchus & all his
Works.—a Poem. Lond.—fol. — . . . M^r. Glanvill of Lincoln's Inn
formerly of Trinity Coll. where he took his A.M.'s Degree & from w^{ch}
he was expell'd is Author of A Poem dedicated to ye Memory & lament-
ing Death of her late Sacred Majesty of ye small Pox. *Lond.* 1695. fol. 30
(I have seen a Copy of this with MS^t. Notes in ye Margin by way of
Explication by ye Author himself.) Also he writ a Panegyrick to ye King
Willm 3^d—this also I have seen, with some short explanatory Notes in y^e
Margin MS^t. Twas pr. at Lond. in 1697. fol. — Articles conc. ye Sur-
render of Oxford 24 Jun. 1646. I have seen a Copy of this wch appears
to have belong'd to John Barker Cornet to ye Q^r Mr General Capt.
Clement Martyn in ye King's Horse Guard. — The Vice-Chancellor
(D^r. De Laune) has desir'd M^r. Trapp of Wadham-College & some other
Ingenious Gentlemen of this University to write Encomiastical Verses
upon the New Edition in folio of Baron Spanheim's Book de Nummis. 40
— Some Places belonging to University College . . . Donors of Scholarships to University Coll.

    June 22. H. to Dr. T. Smith. Grabe & his orders. Sorry that Wallis
did not give a satisfactory answer about the Cufic characters. Particulars from
Dodwell of the discourses by the Monk of Evesham. Accepts Selden *de Diis
Syris* (Leyden ed.). Will do his best as Smith's literary executor. Recommends
as transcriber *Williams,* translator of an Armoric Grammar, printed by Llhuyd,
assistant to Llhuyd (fee 12^d per sheet). Asks for particulars of the Abbey of
Culnham (Berks). Possesses the History of Annibal and Scipio, gathered &c.
by Anthony Cope (London, 1590, 8°) ; not in Wood.

June 24, 1706 (Mon.) Dr. Smalridge's Encomium upon Mr. Grabe, when he presented him to yᵉ Degree of Dr. of Divinity, Dr. Jane yᵉ Professor being then ill [1–12].[1] . . .

A Letter sent to Mr. Dodwell by Mr. Rich. Lloyd. The Author unknowne [12–26]. . . .

The above said Letter I took from a very bad and faulty copy. Remember to ask Mr. Dodwell for his.

June 25 (Tu.). Last night Mr. Edm. Perkes, A. M., & Fellow of Corpus Xti Coll. was taken at about 11 clock wᵗʰ a fit of an Apoplexy, of wᶜʰ he died at abᵗ 6 This Morning. This Gentleman, whom I have several times mention'd before, I am informed now at yᵉ Print-House had a very considerable Hand in yᵉ Book printing at yᵉ Theatre against Mr. Dodwell, and did design in a short time to have done another Book in abᵗ 25 sheets of Paper. But wᵗ I cannot yet tell. His untimely Death happen'd to yᵉ great Reluctance of all good and learned Men, he being a person noted in his College and the university for his Probity, Honesty, usefull Learning, and Willingness to assist and encourage all Bookish Men. . . .

June 26 (Wed.). On Thursday last Ralph Lᵈ Grey Baron of Warke died of an Apoplexy. 'Tis said he took something for yᵉ Gout wᶜʰ struck it into yᵉ Head and Stomack, wᶜʰ immediately caus'd his sudden end : whereby the Honour is Extinct. — Some years since Dr. Wood, then only Mr. Wood of New College, took a sly way of ruining the Reputation of Dr. Musgrave the Physitian, by writing Letters wᵗʰout any Name into yᵉ Country where yᵉ Doctor was; wᶜʰ being prov'd upon him, he had like to have been expell'd yᵉ College; but he being young, Dr. Beeston yᵉ Warden (whom he had also aspers'd) & yᵉ society was so favourable as to impose no other punishment yⁿ begging Pardon, wᶜʰ accordingly he did. This was not yᵉ only ill thing he did there, as some of yᵉ College have assur'd me. His refusing and neglecting to be resident at his Parsonage, tho' he solemnly promis'd it when 'twas given him, his aspersing yᵉ Clergy in a gross Manner before he had any thoughts of taking H. Orders, his malicious carrying on an Action against Mr. Ayliffe (chiefly because he would not appear for him when he stood for Warden upon yᵉ Death of Dr. Traffles) and yᵉ like are so notorious to yᵉ world, yᵗ they cannot be past over in silence. — The Continuer of Athenæ Oxoñ must not forget to inform his Curious Reader yᵗ Dr. Thomas Wood writt a Book call'd *Angliæ Notitia*, being an Epitome in Latin of Chamberlain's Present State of England; wᶜʰ said *Notitia* when in the Press at Lichfields, Dr. Wallis happen'd to see, and perusing some Passages in it, his Censure of it then was yᵗ there were so gross Anglicisms in it that the Author ought to be whipp'd severely for it. This book, however, being dedicated to Dr. Luffe and Dr. Bernard, 'tis remarkable yᵗ yᵉ latter receiv'd it upon his knees, being transported at yᵉ Honour done him.

---

[1] [Footnote on p. 2. Mr. Grabe is superstitious, & 'tis thought desir'd this day; it being certain yᵗ yᵉ university had pitch'd once upon another.]

Out of a Letter of one Mr. John Mould to D^r. Hudson, Dated 7th Sept. 1703.

Since I left Oxoñ I hapned into ye Conversation of one M^r. Holliday ye son of one Barten Holliday a person once famous in ye University of Oxon and elsewhere.   He was Chaplain to an English Ambassador in Spaine, & had been before acquainted wth Gondomor ye Spanish Ambassador, whom he found in Spaine under some Disgrace.   Gondomer had a mighty Kindness for him, & as a present gave him a Book, wherein ye whole Conspiracy of ye Powder Plot was set forth in Spanish, & before M^r. Barten Holliday left Spaine, ye Booke was suppressed, but M^r. Holliday brought his Book into 10 England, and kept it 'till ye Restauration of K. Ch. 2^d. and soone after died. One M^r. Dowey a Clergyman of Fordeane in Gloucestershire & had married M^r. Holliday's Daughter had his Library and about ye year 1661 or 1662 presented this Book to your Publick Library.   Now Sir if there be any such book in ye Library, I know some Gentlemen would be at ye Charge of Transcribing it & Translating of it into English.   If this Book be to be found, please to communicate your thoughts to me on this occasion &c.

June 27 (Th.).   The Letter of ye university of Francfurt upon Oder to ye University of Oxon inviting them to partake in celebrating their secular. [33-38.] . . .   20

June 29 (Sat.).   Out of Dodsworth, Vol. 22, f. 89. b. (Registrum Holgreve).

Ultimo Dec. 1503.—Ego Thomas Bothe give all my Lands in Fawle, Uffyngton, Kyngston, and Bagmor in ye County of Berks to Margery my wief for Lief, rem^r to Thomas Bothe my son & rem^r to John Bothe my son, &c. rem^r to John Bothe my Broder &c. rem^r to William Bothe my Broder &c. rem^r to Helen & Margaret my systers &c. probat. 18 Feb. anno supra dicto. — Ib. f. 90 a.—18 Apr. 1504.   Ego Willielmus Danvers miles unus Justiciariorum Regis de communi Banco lego corpus meum sepeliendum in Ecclesia parochiali de Thacham &c.   He was possess'd of Lands in ye said Parish 30 of Thacham in Com. Berks. — In fol. 91 b.   There is an extract out of a Will, 24 Feb. 19 H. 7. of John Blake Esquyer bequething his Body to be buryed in ye Ch. of Nether Wallop nighe the Sepulture of Margery his late wief.—Item y^t John Dantsey should have ye Moyety of all his Lands in ye Countyes of Southampton & Wyltes.   Except certayne Lands in Compton and Calne, for his Lief, rem^r to Richard Dawnstey sonne of ye said John & Alice late his wief and Daugh. to ye said John Blake & to Heires of Richards Body &c. rem^r to Jane Wrogtone Daugh. of ye said John Blake &c. remaynder to the right Heires of Robert Blake Brother to ye Testator &c. — Memorandum that in fol. 95 is mention of ye Priory of Borscough in ye County of Lancaster. — 40 Ib. f. 129.—23 Jan. 1512.   I Richard Harcourt dwelling at Abingdon bequeth my Body to be buryed in ye Abbey of Rewley &c. ━

H. Stephens in Epistola ad quosdam Amicos, p. 41 . . complaining of ye Hard Fortune ye Classicks (especially the chief) had suffer'd from ye conjectures of ignorant persons, says Livy had underwent ye same hard fate too some years before.—Ecce enim Titum Livium ante aliquot annos multa hujusmodi castigationum vulnera (proh facinus) passum. ━

June 30 (Sun.).   MR. WALDRON OF ALL SOULS COLL. TO DR. CROSTHWAIT OF QUEEN'S.

S^r,
Since at ye Tavern I can't meet ye
In Paper Embassie I greet ye,
T' advise you not to be so wary
Touching King Wm. & Queen Mary,

That Spight of Fellowship & Pupills   50
You'll weigh your Conscience out in
         scruples
For as Your Queen's Men must believe
Two Negs. make an Affirmative.

Why in yᵒ Name of yᵉ Predicaments
And all yᵉ Analytick Sense
Won't you allow poor Affirmations
In their turns too to make Negations.
This postulatum any Pate
Will grant that's not prejudicate.
Nay yᵉ Argument I assure yᵒ
Appears to some à fortiori.
Hoc dato & concesso thus I
10 In Baralypton blunderbush ye:
He yᵗ to two Kings takes an Oath
Is by yᵉ last absolv'd from both.
For each Oath being an Affirmation
Both, as it's own'd make a Negation.
Thus scientifically you see
The more ye're bound yᵒ more ye're free.
As Jugglers when they knit one more
Undoe yᵉ Knot they made before.

Tis strange your Smiglecian under-
Standing should make so great a Blunder,
As roundly to Affirm Subjection,
Wern't Cousin German to Protection.
Nay more they're Relatives unless I
Mistake Tom Hobbs secundum esse.
I've hopes tho' you have slyly taken
The Oaths elsewhere to save yʳ Bacon.
So spark, by Country . . half undone
Takes Coach & steals a Cure at London.

P.S.

Sending you this in Verse, no doubt
You'll think my Reason has yᵉ Gout.
For verse, as you will learn from hence
The feet Confinement is of sense.

July 1 (Mon.). This day was sent a Letter to yᵉ university of
20 Francfurt upon Oder in Answer to theirs to yᵉ University of Oxon.
Twas first drawn up by yᵉ Orator Mʳ. Wyat; but that being hardly
Latin, 'twas done anew by another Hand, & so sent. A Copy of the
Orator's may be seen in one of yᵉ Folio Volumes of my Collections.
Of the other I have no Copy.—Mʳ. Barnes of Cambridge not pleas'd
with Mʳ. Piers for putting out two of Euripides's Tragedies; because he
thinks he has not done him Justice.

July 2 (Tu.). Dodesworth, vol. 22, f. 176. a. [E Registro Bodfeld.]

I Thomas Fettyplace Knt. bequeth my Body to be buryed in yᵉ Abbaye
Church of Abbingdon if it fortune me to dye at Besylles Lygh. A Prest shall
30 sey Masse at Scala cœli at Oxford. Item I give to yᵉ Church of Lyttle Shif-
ford xlˢ. to be bestowed ther after yᵉ Discretion of My Nephew John Fettyplace the Elder, on yᵉ Mending of my Grand Mother's Tombe or otherwise.
Item I give to Elizabeth my wief all her Apparell & Jewells. Also to Katerin
my Da. my silver Basin with yᵉ Ewer &c. & 400 ˡⁱᵇ. Item I give to my
Nephew John Fettyplace th' Elder of Bessylsleigh my Gowne of Right Rus-
sett Velvet furred with Martyn &c. & 100 Marks to help to yᵉ Marriage of
his Daughters. Item to my Nephew James Yate xˡⁱᵇ. &c. Item I will yᵗ
Elizabeth my wief have yᵉ Manor of Shrevinham Lamcote Burton Ocolt &
Bray & yᵉ Manor of Stamford in yᵉ Vale of White-Horse in yᵉ County of
40 Berks &c. probat. 1ᵒ Martij 1524. — 16 f. 176 a.—2 Jun. 12 H. 8. I John
Heron Tresurer of yᵉ Chamber to H. 8 do bequeth my Body to be buryed
wher it shall please God. Item I will yᵗ my Lady Dynham be payd 300 Marks
for yᵉ Reversion of yᵉ Manor of Great Rycote & little Rycotte in Bucks &
Oxfordshires, wherof cxxˡⁱᵇ to be receyved of Sir Thomas Dynhams Lands in
Devon & Somersetshires. Margaret yᵉ test. wief, Ursula Margaret yᵉ Test.
Da. Gyles Heron yᵉ test. son Edmond Xpofer, Henry & John Heron the test.
sons. probat. 9 May 1525.

Dʳ. Mill tells me yᵗ yᵉ Duke of Lauderdale was in his younger Days
one of the best Scholars of any Gentlemen in these Parts, & yᵗ Dʳ.
50 Hicks learn'd Hebrew just before he went to be his Chaplain on purpose
yᵗ he might be able to discourse with his Lᵈship in Rabbinical Learning.
That he was a Curious Collector of Books, and when in London would
very often go to yᵉ Booksellers shops and pick up wᵗ curious Books he
could meet with; but yᵗ in his Elder years he lost most of his Learning
purely by minding too much Politicks.

July 3 (Wed.). Dodesw. vol. 22. f. 231. b. E Registro Dyngley.—

4 Dec. 1535.—27 H. 8. I Fraunces Harecourte Esqr. of Whitham in com. Berks give my body to be buryed in ye Chauncell of ye Parish Church of Whitham. Item I bequeth to Agnes my wief my Manors of Whitham & Sewecourt in ye said County of Berks for her Lief. rem^r to Robert Harecourt my Son & his Heires &c. rem^r to Margret Harecourt my Daugh. &c. with my Manor of La Myll & my Manor of Corffe Molen & Corffe Hubert in ye County of Dorsett &c. A Marriage to be had betweene Robert Harcourt son of the test. & Jane Palmer Da. of John Palmer.—Elizabeth Anne & Margaret are the Testat. Daughters, Robert & Symon are ye Test. sonnes and Under age. probat. 16 Aug. 1539. ▬ Ib. f. 234 b. (E. Registro Alynger.) Ultimo Martij 1540. I Edmund Fetyplace of Beselly in ye County of Berks Esqr. bequeth my Body to be buryed in ye Parish Church of Marcham in ye said County of Berks. Item I give to my 4 Dau. vizt. Eliz. Anne, Jane, & Dorothe each 40^l. Item to my youngest sonnes Edw. Georg, W^m, Tho. ech vi^l. xiij^s. iiij^d. Item I make Margaret Fetyplace my wief Execut. & my L^d. Mordaunt my wief's Father & Sr Ant. Hungerford my Father in Law Overseers. probat. 8 Maij. 1540. ▬ Ib. f. 235 b.—Oct. 5. 1538. I William Hare of Beeston St. Lawrence will y^t my wief's (Alice Wayte) Lands in Farryngton in Berkshire shall be sold & the Money wth 600 Marks of my owne to be payd to ech of my son Thomas Daughters (if he have any) 400 Marks.—probat. 2 May 1540. ▬

Remember to tell Dr. Hudson y^t in vol. i. p. 61, of Dionysius Hal. for Titus Manlius is to be read M. Manlius from Livy, l. v. c. 31, as Pighius has observ'd in his Annals, Tom. i. p. 222. ▬ Mr. Cæsar last Week presented to ye Queen ye Address of ye Town of Hertford; but her Majesty was pleas'd to refuse it from his Hands. ▬ Last Sunday (June 30) M^r. Tyler Dean of Hereford was Consecrated B^p. of Landaff at Lambeth. ▬ A Report was spread in several Parts in London y^t Mr. Savage of X^t Church being wth Dean Aldrich, ye Dean should take his Glass, and propose a Health of farther success to ye Duke of Marlborough; upon wch reply'd Mr. Savage, *Hold Mr. Dean, not so fast; ye farther success the Duke has the lower ye Church is.* This story was groundless, M^r. Savage being out of town when the words were said to be spoken, & ye Dean in a place of some considerable Distance from Mr. Savage.

July 4 (Th.). . . . Mr. Milles now acknowledges himself plainly to be Author of ye Book printing at ye Theat. ag^t M^r. Dodwell, and has given in a title wth his name Subjoyn'd, to be put in ye Catalogue of Books now in ye Theatre Press. Before M^r. Perks's Death he would not own it.

July 5. Baron Spanheim has sent to ye Publ. Library a Copy of ye 1st Vol. of his New Edit. of his Book *de usu & Præst. Num.* neatly bound in Turkey Leather, with the following Inscription in a spare Leaf at ye Beginning, under his own Hand.

Inclytæ toto orbe Academiæ Oxoniensis Bibliothecæ | hunc renovatum in Anglia Dissertationum | de nummis Antiquis fœtum, | in grati animi, ob novissime delatum sibi absenti | ab eadem illustrissima Academia | Doctoris juris Civilis titulum | L.M.Q. offert | Ezechiel Spanhemius | Londini III Non. Jul. MDCCVI. | ▬

In Bib. Bod. amongst the Baroccian MS^{ts}. are Scholia upon Oppian in Greek (num. 38), wch M^r. Barnes (Jos.) of Cambridge is now using, with a design to put out y^t Author as he tells me. When Mr. Barnes presented his Edw. 3^d (wch cost him above 600 libs. in all) to King

James (to whom he Dedicated it) his Majesty was pleas'd to talk very freely and kindly to him, & there is no doubt had given him preferment if the Troubles had not follow'd immediately, or if my Ld Sunderland had acted fairly.

July 7 (Sun.). In Salmasius's Epistles p. 276. is a large Disquisition ab^t Livy's and others Expression, *ante diem tertium kalendas,* &c. ▬ Mr. Barnes is now looking over ye Collection of Greek Epigramms, MS^t, in ye Publick Library of Oxon. He tells ye B^p of Norwich lately sent to him desiring he would send to him his conjectures upon some of y^e
10 Epigrams of Brodæus's Edition; wch accordingly he did, and his L^dship has transmitted them to Monsr Le Clerk. ▬ This day being Act Sunday in the Afternoon preach'd at St. Marie's before ye university M^r. Hen. Felton of Queen's Coll. upon these words (Psal. 84), I had rather be a door keeper in the House of the Lord than to dwell in ye Tents of wickedness. 'Twas a neat, well penn'd Discourse, and the Design of it was to set forth ye Nature of Praise and Thanksgiving. Whence he took occasion to shew w^t little Reason the Fanaticks & others have to separate from the Establish'd Church of England. This Mr. Felton was first Commoner of S^t. Edm. Hall, where he tooke his A.M's Degree, &
20 afterwards went into Holy Orders, left ye university and became an Eminent Preacher in and ab^t London. He was always Noted for a very ingenious, sociable and honest Man; but D^r. Mill being always very rough towards him (wch he discovered the more because M^r. Felton's Father, a very severe Person, gave him particular liberty to shew Authority over him, as also did M^r. Goodwin (commonly call'd D^r. Goodwin), something related to him, and who had an Eye over M^r. Felton while of the Hall), I say D^r. Mill being not very kind to him, when he came now to Oxon Mr. Felton immediately enter'd of Queen's College; and Dr. Mill upon this occasion shew'd his venome so much
30 y^t he would not appear at Church, and will not vouchsafe to give him a good Word: a thing much taken Notice of in ye university, and for wch he is by no means to be vindicated. But ye Writer of these Matters knows too well that he seldom speaks kindly of any who have been bred up at his own House, M^r. Worth being the only person that he mentions altogether with Civility; the reason whereof is, because being void of Parts, and having very little learning he was entirely addicted to ye Doctor's Humour, and would never thwart him in w^t he said. Mr. Felton lately put out a six penny Pamphlett against ye Presbyterians of Colebrooke, wch has ye Character of one of ye best
40 Pamphletts y^t have been written.

July 6. Dr. T. Smith to H. Josephus and Livy. Sends for H. Selden *de Dis Syris,* Almeloveen's *Fasti,* Bœclerus *de Scriptoribus Graecis et Latinis,* and Lister's *Apicius* for Bodley; also a specimen for Williams the amanuensis, with instructions. Suggestions concerning Culham (see Camden, *Brit,* vv. in window in S^t. Helen's, Abingdon). Too much incense offered to Spanheim's book; Hardouin could criticise it if he would. Sir Ant. Cope's collections out of Livy very trivial. What does Alypius Antiochenus (? in Gothofredus' *Libanius,* Geneva, 1631) say of Byzantium? Some one should collate the Savilian MS. of Agathemerus' Ὑποτυπώσεις with Tennulius' edition of 1671.

July 8 (Mon.).   Dodesw. vol. 22, f. 252. (E Registro Pynnyng).

Ultimo Aug. 1543. I Dame Eliz. Englefelde Widdow bequeth my body to be byried in ye parish Church of Englefelde in y^o Chapell ther by my Husband. Item I give to Fraunces Engleby my son, Tho. White my Nephew & John Yate all my Manors & Landes, viz. my Manor of Patteshall cum prato yn Ayscotte, Darlescott, Avescote Preston Gayton &c. in Com. Northampton, my Maner of Lillebroks alias Lodbroks in Com. Berks wth Lands in Bray, Cookham & Maydenhed in ye s^d County of Berks. John Englefeld ye test. son hath lands bought by ye test. lately of Tho. Toonye in Beneham in com. Berks. Item I will y^t my Executors take ye Profits of my Manors of Brownseoner & 10 Brincklow in ye County of Warwick untill my son John Englefeld come to ye age of 26 years according to y^o Intent of Sir Tho. Englefeld my late Husband & Father to ye s^d John & if ye s^d Maners be redemed by a Tender of a sum of Money late made to ye s^d Dame Eliz. by Edw. Browghton son and Heire of W^m. Browghton then my Mind is that ye s^d Money be bestow'd in Land for ye use of my s^d son John & ye Heirs of His Body, Sir Georg Throkmorton K^t. ye Testat. Brother offcred ye Testat. Lands to sell &c. Item I give to my Daugh. Susan Englefeld to her Marriage the Profit of my Ward Edward Ferrys wch I would have sold to y^t purpose, & 400^{lib}. besides of her Father Sir Thomas Englefeld's Gyft &c. rem^r to my Husband's suster's children & my 20 syster's children. Item I will y^t my s^d Daugh. Susan be brought up wth M^{rs}. Moumpesson Wief to Edmond Moumpesson Esqr. Item I will y^t my Niece Elianor Burdett be brought up wth M^{rs}. Denton late wief to M^r. Edmund Fetyplace Esqr. Item I ye s^d Dame Eliz. give unto my son in Law Edw. Saunders to ye use & behofe of my Cozen Eliz. Caune his Wive's Daughter 20 lib. Item I give to my Cozen Mary Sanders towards her Marriage xx lib. probat. 10 Feb. 1543.

July 9 (Tu.).   M^r. Cherry of Shottesbrook tells me y^t he met lately with a Pamphlett printed ab^t ye year 1641, conc. Church Discipline &c. written by way of Dialogue. The Author (a Fanatick as appears 30 throughout) he would fain know. I suppose it to have been Hen. Burton, & y^t 'tis ye same Book wth that I have seen among B^p. Barlow's Books in ye Publick Library call'd Conformities Deformity, in a Dialogue between Conformity and Conscience. Lond. 1646. 4°. Burton's Name is to it, both in ye Title Page & at ye End of ye Dedication, wch is to ye R^t. Honble. ye L^d. Major & City of London. — M^r. Topping of X^t. Church tells me y^t he has made some Inquiry ab^t ye Abbey of Culham or Culhham, when he was at Culham near Abingdon about a Week since; but y^t he cannot learn any thing y^t there was an Abbey at y^t place. I think M^r. Leland has mentioned it in his Itinerary. Quære. 40 He also tells me y^t Salmanezzer, the famous Formosan, when he left X^t. Church (where he resided while in Oxoñ) left behind him a Book in MS^t. wherein a distinct Acc^t was given of ye Consular & Imperial Coyns, by himself. — M^r. Cherry has an Apollonius Dyscolus with Is. Casaubon's notes in MS^t at ye Margin. The Binder has some^{wt} prejudic'd them, but yet they may be of great use to any one y^t shall publish him hereafter. Quære whether it be his Book de Constructione seu syntaxi verborum, or his Historiæ mirabiles, publish'd by Meursius? — This Day being Act Tuesday, M^r. Jos. Barnes of Cambridge was

July 9. **Kent to H.** Asks for news, 'especially such as relate to my function.' Has read Smalridge's speeches. Is the Jno. Pennyman mentioned in advts. in *Postman* July (June) 27–29, of University College?

incorporated B. of Divinity of our university, being presented to yᵉ Vice-Chancellor by Dʳ. Hudson, who gave this just Encomium of him, *quo neminem Græcia unquam tulit* Ἑλληνικώτερον. — Mʳ. Cherry tells me yᵗ two Sermons have been preach'd before yᵉ Queen in opposition to Mʳ. Dodwell's Book abᵗ yᵉ Soul, & yᵗ yᵉ Author's link'd him and Dʳ. Tyndall together.

July 10 (Wed.). A Monument of L. Plautius in fig. 33 of Lorenzo Phil. di Rossi's Sepulchr. Antich. Livy perhaps may be illustrated from it.—'Tis too late for it. Monumᵗˢ of the Pompeys ib. num. 39.—of T. Livius, ib. f. 40.

July 11 (Th.). Last night Mʳ. Francis Cherry of Shottesbrook made a visit to Dʳ. Mill, who immediately fell very barbarously upon Mʳ. Dodwell, using such expressions as are not fit to be named. Mʳ. Cherry, a Gentlemen of Eminent Virtues, and singular Learning, and who has upon Account of his great Prudence, Affability and wonderfull Humanity the good word of all acquainted with him, endur'd all with Patience, only when the Dʳ. in his Passion and according to his usual Civility call'd Mʳ. Dodwell (whose humility, Piety and uncommon Learning nobody knows better than Mʳ. Cherry) the proudest man living he made this modest Reply, *not yᵉ proudest Man living, Mʳ. Principal; for he would not have said so of any Man.* The Dʳ. took great notice of yᵉ Expression, & I do not question but will repent at one time or other for this Incivility offer'd both to Mʳ. Dodwell & Mʳ. Cherry who is so intimate a Friend of Mʳ. Dodwell's. But this Rudeness was no more than wᵗ was expected, it being well known yᵗ Dʳ. Mill was always of this Censorious Temper, & for wᶜʰ he stands justly branded in Mʳ. Boyle's Book against Dʳ. Bentley. The best Apology I ever heard made for him is yᵗ he is craz'd & peevish wᶜʰ latter expression is frequently made use of by the Society of Queen's College, & I have heard it offer'd as a reason why he should not be provost there. I am sorry I should have occasion to mention these faylings; but they are so well known, that the world crys out shame upon him for them, & they cannot be past by in silence. — Presently after Mr. Barnes was incorporated Bach. of Divinity in our university he made yᵉ following Extempore verses upon yᵗ occasion [eight Greek hexameters]. . . .

Mʳ. Barnes's Letter of thanks to yᵉ Vice-Chancellor &c. for yᵉ Honour Done him in admitting him B.D. of this University. [72–74]. . .

July 15 (Mon.). A Poem newly publish'd upon yᵉ Success of yᵉ Duke of Marlborough. The Author order'd by yᵉ Queen 500 Guineas.

July 16 (Tu.). Dodesworth vol. 22. f. 254. (E Registro Pynnyng).

23 May 1543. I James Yate of Bucklands in yᵉ County of Berks Gent. bequeth my Body to be buryed in yᵉ Church of Buckland aforesᵈ &c. probat. 16 Jul. 1544.

July 13. Dodwell to H. Has mislaid letters from Grabe and Stephens. Has no notes on Mela, only collations. Sends gossip and thanks for 'literary informations.' Sends copy of letter containing Philopatris. Particulars of some inscriptions in his possession. Mr. Cherry has Robortellus' transcript of the *Fasti Capitolini*, which is worth collating.

July 17 (Wed.). Mr. Wood made a compleat Index to His History
& Antiq. but ye Book being in hast to be publish'd Bp. Fell would not
have it printed to ye great Regret of ye Author. — Mr. Barnes's Verses
made Extempore upon his Entertainment at Oxon when incorporated
[21 Greek hexameters]. . .

Mr. Barnes's verses to two Ladys when he lay sick at London, Oct. 4. 1705.
[English: 9 triplets.] . . Other extempore Verses by Mr. Barnes. Imita-
tion & Contradiction of Flatman's *Like a Dog with a Bottle* [English.] . . Be-
fore his Almanack. Presented to ye Countess of Sandwich [English.] . . On
Anastasia Capt. Charles Eden's Sister [English.] . . On 3 Ladys [English.] 10
On ye Czar of Muscovy's overthrow by ye King of Sweden [English.] On
Judith Minikin in Bury Jayle [English, 1692.] . . Auctoris ignoti [English.]
In *Guilielm. Rogerium* qui *Jacobi* II. statuam posuit Coll. *Universitat.* [Greek
hexameters.] . .

July 18 (Th.). Out of another Book of Mr. Barnes's. Dr. *Cranen*
Physick Professor of *Leyden* writ a little book thirty years ago, wch he
calleth *Oeconomia animalis*, in wch he hath as many chapters as Dr.
Bently has Sermons; and their Titles are also ye same. — *Eman.* Coll.
Treasury. Wills p. 87. Box 30. B.   Dr. *Bradish* of *Piddleton* his will,
wherein he bequeaths 200lib to purchase a Rent-charge for 3 *Greek* 20
Scholarships, after ye Death of his wife. The Scholars to declaim in
Greek twice *per an.* & every one of ye Foundation Fellows then present
to have a pair of Gloves of 2s. 6d.   1638.—Mr. *Browne's* Will, giveing
ye Nags-Head in *Islington*, rated at 60l. *per an.* towards ye Maintenance
of 6 Scholars, to be taken out of *Christ's Hospital*, then at ye University,
3 whereof to be of *Eman.* Coll. 10l. a peice. — *Memorandum Martij*
23. 170⁹⁄₁₀. Mr. *Welbore*, a sensible Gentleman, formerly of *Trinity*
Coll., dining with me, and others, at Dr. *Gower's*, declar'd, and brought
good Authority, yt a poor person far gone with a *Rheumatism, &c.* was
cured only by ye frequent use of this Medicine: *A Spoonfull of Mustard* 30
in a pint of Ale every Morn. for a Week, or so.

[Lines on Marriage] Some Libertine, I knô not whether T. Brown
[Barnes].—Mr. Barnes [a reply].—Acrostich by Mr. Barnes [on Dorothea
Ashfield].—Anacreon 57. v. 915. By ye Same.—Od. 20. v. 303.—On St. *Dunstan's* Bells in ye East, by ye Same. . .—1703. The sd verses were afterwards
hung up in the Belfry.—Mr. *Michael Bold's* Verse 1697.—Mythologia Deorum
ex vet. MS. [Lat. elegiacs.]—Epigrams [one Latin, three English.]—[Ana-
creon] Od. 43. v. 690. OD. 30. v. 471.—Epithalm. Mr. *Clutterbuch*, Lady
Sudbury, 1696. —

To ye Tune of *Since Cælia's my Foe* &c. 1672.   40

1.
Since *Ale* is my Foe,
To ye *Dolphin* I'll goe,
  Where some Brimmer,
  And Swimmer,
Wth Nectar shall flow.

2.
Wine's Lees will appear
Far above yr Dull *Beer,*
  Ordinary
  Canary
Doth *Ale* Conquer clear.

3.
For *Canary* we call,
And our thirst ner doth pall :
  Dutch *Flaggin*
  Will lagg in
The first bout of all.

4.
'Tis ye *Grape's* lively Juice,
Doth rare humor produce;
  But ye *Barly*   50
  Is surly,
And fit for no Use.

5.

While *Ale* & *fair-Water*
Do but Dulness create here,
Witty *Bacchus*
Will crack-us,
At his Fancy's wi' Laughter.

6.

Then let Fools pay Excise,
For Damn'd *Ale*, We'll be wise,
And we'll spare it
For *Claret*;
That will Dash in our Eyes.

7.

Ale & *Beer*'s fit for swine,
But no *Beast will drink Wine*;
So that Reason,
Each season,
Upholds yᵉ Rich *Vine*.

8.

Nay, a *Tapster* once fell
On a *Drawer*, pell mell:
But yᵉ *Tapster*
Got a Rap, Sir,
And yᵉ *Drawer* was *well*.

This is Mʳ. Barnes's own Hand-Writing. ▬

The Muses *Hue and Cry*. Aug. 30. 1694... On Madam Elizabeth Dowsing... Two Epigrams... *Mary Norbournes* Anagr. My Arbour runne. 1703... ▬

Mʳ. *Barnes* stood first for *Greek* Professor of *Cambridge* in yᵉ year 1686, when he mist it, meerly by the Falling off of some, who had promis'd fairly; tho' at yᵉ same time they could not but acknowledge he was far better qualify'd than Mʳ. *Michael Payne*, who carry'd it, & held it nine years. ▬

Out of Mʳ. *Barnes*'s Book, under his own Hand-Writing :

Mʳ. *Piers* of *Eman*. Coll. under a Cloak of Simplicity and Friendship has prov'd a Snake and a Viper. Not to speak of his manifold Espials, Circumventions, Treacherys, &c. *Crimine ab uno disce omnia*. Him I have encourag'd and us'd kindly, ever since his first Admission, being recommended by Letter to my favour & acquaintance from my old Master, Dʳ. *Goad*. When a Fellowship was void, and he absent, I gave him notice and Encouragement; & he thereupon obtain'd it. When *Epictetus* was printed, being myself call'd on for Verses, I put him on some, and caused them to be printed wᵗʰ my own. When *Euripides* came out, *Green* yᵉ Bookseller was to gratify him, I pitching on him to transcribe in order yᵉ Fragments I had collected. I told him, what notes he could produce, should bear his name, as they do. He privately insinuated among my Acquaintance his great Merit in yᵗ Matter, so yᵗ our Society approv'd them so far, as to prefer them to my Performance. I ask'd [him] before them his own Opinion : He impudently own'd his great Deserts in yᵉ Case, and then I told the secret, yᵗ of yᵉ Notes under his Name to *Euripides*, not one word was his own; 'tis all stolne from Tho. *Gataker's M. Antoninus*. I got him, at yᵉ same time, for his Encouragement to prefix a Copy of Gr. Verses to my *Euripides*; toward wᶜʰ Work I lent him my own *Greek* Poëtical Lexicon MS. yet for all yᵗ he made such Verses, yᵗ 'till I had corrected them were defective in *Sense*, true *Greek, Quantity* & *Accent*. Which I have still by me, under his own Hand.

In his Verses on yᵉ D. of *Gloucester*, he made *Ro*. in *Robora* and *Vi*. in *Viribus* short, and so they were at first printed; 'till a B.A. of *Queen's* found out yᵉ Faults, & so yᵉ Sheet was reprinted, he to be at the Charge, tho' not in 2 years paid, as Mʳ. *Crownfeild* knows and tells me. When I was at *London*, about *Paul's* school 1697, he borrowed and had all yᵉ while by him for above 24 Weeks my own *Euripides*, with Corrections, Various Readings, and other Additions, Notes &c. wᶜʰ having compil'd, he has by my own Paines prepar'd a more full *Life* &c. wᶜʰ with some select Playes he is now publishing for *Smith* & *Walford*, whom by his sly Insinuations he has made his, & stole their Regard from me, as he serv'd me with *Rich. Green* before.

If all this be just, or civil, or fair, or tolerable, & yᵗ it is equal, or kind for my Booksellers, for whom I undertook *Homer*, to let another publish any Part of my Works, for wch I am not fully paid yet, *Green* owing me ten Pounds for ye Life of *Euripides,* and five Pounds for ye two Treatises of *Tragedy* and *Theater &c.* without asking me leave, or giveing me Notice, or whether it may be for ye Honour of ye university to discern so ill, or to bestow their Favours so unequally, as all along to discourage and slight a Man, y^t notoriously understands *Greek,* & to cherish and magnify one, y^t never yet was able to give one true specimen of any tolerable Ability in y^t kind, I appeal to y^m y^t know sense & have *Skill* or *Justice,* only begging y^t for y^eir own Credit, they will not suffer *Euripides* to be profan'd by a Person, wholly compos'd of Ill-Nature & Ignorance. —   10

On Major *Phil. Prime's* Sister, 1703. . . .—Not by M^r. Barnes. . . .—
To M^r. *Barnes* upon his expected children.

> HUMANO generi faustissima quaeque precamur;
>   Doctrina tibi sint ingenioque pares.
>   ¹ J. DAVIES.

K. CHARLES II^d's Riddle. . . . — An Acrostich on ye Name MARY NORBOVRN. *Octob.* 12. 1703. . . — [Lines on a noble youth]. *Extemp.* 1 *Novemb.* 1703. . . — Upon M^r. *Fane* the Earle of *Westmorland's* Brother, 1704. . . — M^rs. *Anne Pierrepont.* . ,

July 21 (Sun.). Out of another Book of M^r. *Barnes.*   20
A true Copy of ye Form in wch M^rs. *Dickons* askt Forgiveness of M^r. *Reynolds* before the Chancellor of *Ely,* and in Presence of several Gentlemen, *Nov.* 15. 1699.

I do ask forgiveness of M^r. *Reynolds* for any injurious Words I have spoken of him: particularly for Spreading and Reporting a Story concerning a Letter writ by him to me (as I said) to tempt me to Lewdness. And likewise for making a rash & unadvised Affidavit, before a Master in Chancery. —

> SI facili vena versus mihi Musa dedisset
>   Scribere; scripsissem carmina multa Tibi
> Πολυμαθέστατε vir: sed cum hoc mihi Musa negarit   30
>   Hos quaeso tenues accipe versiculos.

Hanc amicitiae tessaram αὐτοσχεδιασθεῖσαν Viro doctissimo & celeberrimo D. *Barnesio* reliquit

> *Ludolphus Neocorus*
>   d. vi. *Febr.* ¹⁷⁰⁰⁄₁₆₉₉.

July 20. H. to Dr. T. Smith. Williams is transcribing Dr. Bernard's letters. Hudson is resolved upon Josephus. Notes on Culnham, Smalridge, Grabe. Death (on the 25th ult.) of M^r. Edm. Perkes, M. A. Fellow of C.C.C. aged 31; author of a book (Oxford, 4to) against the Protestant Dissenters with Preface by Sacheverell, and of an unpublished work against Barclay the Quaker; joint-author with Milles of an answer to Dodwell. Milles' Cyril (the burden of collating and the 3 Indexes lay upon H., somewhat with prejudice of his health); his *Remarks upon the Occasional Paper Num. VIII,* in vindication of Dodwell's principles about the Schism, he is now ashamed of. His action attributed to self-interest. . . . . ' M^r. Joshua Barnes, ye famous Greek Professor of Cambridge, is now in Towne. He has been incorporated Bach. of Div. immediately after wch he made an extempore Copy of Greek Verses upon y^t occasion. He has look'd over ye MS^t Greek Anthologia of Epigramms wch came into ye Publick Library amongst D^r. Bernard's MSS^ts, with a Design to send w^t are proper to Monsr Le Clerck to be inserted in ye Work he has undertaken. He has printed a specimen of a new Edition of Homer he designs, if y^ere be Incouragement. He designs also an Edition of Oppian, & has examin'd a MS^t Scholiast amongst ye Baroccian MS^t for y^t Intent.'

---

¹ The same *Davies* who has lately set out a new edition of *Caesar's* Comm. in 4to.

E veteris Orbis Descriptione, per Anonymum Graecum Scriptorem à Jac. Gothofredo edita, *Genevae* 1628, p. 28 [134-5.] ... ― Continuation of M*r*. Barnes's Verses,—*Mary Westrow* ... SARAH EVANCE. ... *Cleander's* Epitaph. ... The Canary-Bird's Song. *Sept.* 18. 1697. ... A Dialogue between two young Black-Birds, at S*r John Cotton*'s Baronett, Stratton, *Bedfordshire*. *Aug.* 13. 1700. ... I call'd *Autumn Lovely*, M*rs*. *Mary Honywood Cotton* objected, My Defence. ... On Bitch *Towzer* & her Rival Fairmaid.

July 24 (Wed.).   On the 22*d* Instant was admitted into y*e* Publick Library D*r*. *Hen. Sike* (*L.L.D.*) Professor of y*e Hebrew* Tongue in
10 *Cambridge*. He has publish'd a Book call'd *Evangelium Infantiæ* in *Arabick*, to w*ch* he has added a *Latin* Translation and Notes.   Tis in 8º. For w*ch* he bears a great Character amongst some Men, particularly D*r*. *Mill*, & D*r*. *Bentley*, who know nothing of that language ; tho' I have heard one of his Country-Men, who understands *Arabick*, & is a very good Scholar, speak but slightingly of it.   He is come to *Oxon* with a Design to consult our MSS*ts*. in y*e* Publick Library, in order to publish *Abulfeda's* Geography, w*ch* will be a worthy Work, and will require his utmost care & diligence. ―

Out of M*r*. Barnes's Book [151-153]. . .
20 Baron SPANHEIM'S Answer to D*r*. *Hudson's* Letter writ to him upon Receipt of his Book for y*e* Publick Library. [Dated Londini xvi *Julij* MDCCVI (154-6)]. . . .
Out of M*r*. Barnes's Book.—Νουθετητικόν to young *John Cotton* y*e* Learned Grandson. ... On S*r John Cotton*'s Hunting, at 80 Years of Age. *Aug.* 26. 1700. ... On y*e Greek* Professor's Arms of *Cambridge. Aug.* 28. 1700. ... Ex Anthologia inedita *Meleagri* [six Greek elegiacs].   Communicated to M*r*. *Barnes* by *Neocorus*. ... These following made by M*r*. *Barnes extempore July* 21. when he was at my L*d Salisbury's* Lodgings at X*t* Church [eight Greek hexameters]. . .

_____

30   De Nomine & Familia *Barnes*.

Cambri hodienum Regem vocant *Brennin*, teste *Cambdeno* ; sane apud *Britannos, Gallos*, Barner Judicem sonat & *Barn* Judicare.   Accedit *Syrum* פֿרנס, *Parnes, Pascere* ; unde *Pirnus*, Pascuum, ut *Bochart* : Vide *Lloydij* Lexic. Poëtic. in v. *Parnes*.

Berne, Barne, Barnes, Barns, Barons, but *Bernes* quite another Name. *Siwardus Barnes* ante tempora *Guliel. Conquestoris* floruit, cujus Originem [1] Historiæ *Danicæ, Suevicæ, Gothicæque* hanc referunt.   Vide etiam *Henrici Huntington* Historiar. l. 6. fol. 366. An. XII. *Edvardi Confessoris*, item *Joannis Brompton* Chronicon fol. 945.   *Henric. Knighton*, & ex eo *Guil. Dugdale*,
40 Baronag. 1 Vol.   Denique *Time's Storehouse*, 1 Vol. l. 8. c. 40.   Hic *Siward* dictus est Vir Giganteæ molis & *Malcolmum* R. *Scotiæ* in regnum suum reduxit, & occiso *Macbeth* stabilivit, in Tracœgdia *Mackbeth* per errorem dictus est Steward pro Siward. Illius f. *Osbern Pullax* in *Scotia* occisus *Gloverniam* versus vehebatur, ad sepulturam ; cum Pater *Siward*, præmissis aliquot, qui de vulneribus illius inquirerent, & num in tergo vulnera passus esset, qui cum omnia vulnera illius anteriora retulisset, ipse demum in occursum Pater venit, filium honorifice sepelivit.   Hic VI° ante Conquestum anno defunctus, *Vespasiani* more, erectus, armatus, & stans moritur.   Illius arma cæruleus Leo, Aurea *corona* redimitus, erectus & gressans in *Argenteo* Campo.
50   Illius alter f. *Waltheof* uxorem duxit *Juditham*, Conquestoris neptim, ab eodem avunculo mox decollatus.   Idem *Siward* erat Dux *Northumbriæ*, Comes *Huntingtoniæ, Ecclesiam* Cathedralem *Gloverniæ* fundavit.   Uberes habuit pro-

_____

[1] *Saxo Grammaticus* Dan. Histor. l. 10.   *Joannes Saxonicus, Joannes Magnus* Bp. of *Upsalia* in *Sweedland*, & Archbp. *Olaus*.

ventus in *Vervico* Comitatu, de qua re Sr *W.*^{m} *Dugdale* in *Warwickshire*, fol. 793. a.

Talmud in Tract. *Rosh. Hashanna,* seu *de anni Principio,* c. 3. p. 26, &c. Dixit *Raba de Barnes R. Ase,* si perfecta est hæc Interpretatio &c.   Vid. *Jo. Morini Blesensis* Exercitationes Biblicas, lit. Exercit. vi. c. iv. p. 228.

1324.—M^r. *Richard Barnes,* Vice-President of *Magd.* College in *Oxford* made 1 Master of S^t. *Mary*-Hall in ye said university founded by K. *Edw.* II.   Vid. *Barnes's* Hist. K. *Edw.* III. fol. 22.   1330.—D^r. *Ralph Barnes,* Abbot of S^t. *Austen's* in *Canterbury.* 1 b. fol. 55.

1371.—*John Barnes,* Lord Mayor of *Lond.* An. 45. Ed. 3.   A Great Builder 10 of S^t. *Thomas* the *Apostle's* Church, as appears by his Arms in ye Windows. *Howel's London.* p. 105.

Sr *John Barnes,* a Valiant & Loyal Man, Captaine of *Calais* for K. *Rich.* II. of whom *Froissard* l. 4. c. 161. fol. 169.   *English* in *Emanuel Biblioth.*

Sr *James Barnes, An^o.* xi. *Rich.* II, *An. Domini* 1388.   *John Speed's Chron.* fol. 604. § 77 & 78.   As a Loyal Friend to ye King, Executed by ye Rebell-Lords, together wth Sr *Nic. Dagworth,* Sr *Simon Burley, &c.*

Lord *Barnes, Vid. Winstanley's* Lives, p. 127. in ye Life of *Rich. Nevile* Earle of *Warwick,* sub *Hen.* VI.

Lord *Barnes,* slaine at S^t. *Albans. Ed.* 4. *An.* xi. *vid. Daniel's* History con- 20 tinu'd.

Thomas Ld *Barnes, sub Hen.* VII. An. X^{ti}. 1496.

Juliana Barnes, a Learned Lady, y^t wrote about ye Art of Cookery, also of *Hunting & Fishing. vid. Pitseus* p. 649.   *Wase* on *Grotius* p. 66 & 73.   I have seen Dame *Juliana Barnes* her Doctrine in her Book of Hunting ; & I myself, *Joshua Barnes,* have seen that & other of her Writings, by the kind procurement of my Lo. Friend D^r. *Thomas Browne M.D.* Grandson to Sr *Tho. Browne,* the famous Author of *Religio Med.* & *Vulgar Errors,* & only Son to D^r. *Edw. Browne &c.*   One Passage I myself then noted for ye Quaintness thereof, *viz.* The xv. Properties of a Good Horse, wch the Lady *Juliana Barnes* requires, 30 first iii Qualitys of a *Man,* secondly iii of a *Woman,* Thirdly iii of a *Fox.* Fourthly iii of an *Hare.* Fifthly iii of an *Asse.*   The iii of a *Man,* to be *Bold, Proud,* and *Hardy.*   The iii of a *Woman,* to be *fair-Breasted, Fair-Hair'd,* & *easy to be leap'd on.*   The iii of a *Fox, Fair-Tayle, Short-Ears, a Good-Trot.*   iii of an *Hare,* A *Great Eye,* A *Dry-Head,* a *well Running.*   iii of an *Asse,* a *Big-chine,* a *Flat-leg* and a *good-Hoof.*—Sr *Rich. Baker,* in his Catalogue of Authors, mistakes this *Lady* for a *Man,* & names her *Julian Barnes* ; but he never un-derstood *half* what he wrote, nor saw a *Quarter* of the Authors he mentions.

Barnes we find, ab^t ye Reigne of *Henry* VIII to be ye Name of a *Pursuivant* as *Richard Ratcliffe* Barnes. vid. *Weaver's* Fun. Monuments p. 680.   40

Barnes, a Messenger, was sent from *Henry* VIII into *Germany* for *Philip Melancthon.* Ib. fol. 89. no doubt so call'd from some great Lord, whose Pur-suivant he was, as ye Heralds, Chandois, Lancaster, *Pembroke* &c.

D^r. *Robert Barnes,* a Learned Divine, a good Author & a constant Martyr under H. VIII.   A Loyal Man.   Many of his Family dy'd fighting for ye King fol. 218.   His works with *Will. Tyndal* & *John Frith* martyrs.   His Life. dy'd 1541.

Barnes, a famous Monk of the Order of S^t. *Benedict, Wadesworth's Spanish Pilgrim,* p. 27 & 71.   Another Example of that *Spanish* Tyranny was Father *Barnes,* a *Benedictine* Fryer, late Chaplain to ye Prince of *Portugal,* at *Paris* ; 50 who wrote a Book ag^t y^e *Pope's Supremacy,* & for y^e *Allegiance,* y^t Subjects owe unto y^{eir} Sovereigne, & makeing for *England* to print it, was ye night be-fore his Intended Voyage, upon some Notice given unto y^e *Jesuits* surprised at ye Prince's House, by a Warrant from the chief Secretary of State, & so put to Death in Prison.   He wrote also a Book against Æquivocation.   See more in Vol. 1 of *Athen.* Ox. 1577.

D^r. *Rich. Barnes.* B^p. of *Durham. Godwin's* Cat. of B^{pps}. p. 671.

Wm. Barnes, Couzin to *Wm. Willington* Esquire, to whom ye s^d *Willington* left 5 Messuages, & 260 Acres of Land, by bequest, to him & His Heirs for ever. *Dudg. Warw.* p. 428. 8. in *Chelmescote.*

Bartholomew Barnes. His Quality, Burial, & Epitaph, Stow's Survey of *Lond.* p. 242.

Sr *George Barnes* Ld Mayor of *London.* Stow's Survey &c.

Sr *Cuthbert Barnes* K^t. *Stow's* Survey &c. p. 393.

Rich. Barnes, buried in S^t.*Michael-Basing* Church *Lond. Stow's* Survey, fol.299.

Robert Barnes de Vitis Pontificum Romanorum, laudat. Hist. *K. Ed.* 3. fol. 89. Vid. D^r. *Robt. Barnes.*

10 *Robert Barnes,* buried *S^t. Michael Cornhill, Lond.* with this Epitaph

> Here under was buried *Robert Barnes* by Name,
> Citizen of *London* & Mercer of ye same :
> And this is written, y^t others might remember,
> How Godly he departed ye twentyth on *November.*

Weaver's Fun. Mon. p. 416.

Sr *George Barnes,* uncle to one *Barnes,* lately of *Milnell* in *Suffolk.*

John Barnes, who gave vi Tenemts. to *Emanuell* College.

Barnabie Barnes dedicates a notable Work of his to K. *James* I. *An°.* 1606. Quarto, Engl. call'd *Four Books of Offices.*

20 Several *Barnes's* in *Anthony à Wood's Ath. Oxon.* M^r. *Barnes* living at *Woollwich. Hollingshead,* 2 vol. fol. 1866.

M^r. *Anthony Barnes* M.A. Chaplain to ye Earle of *Lindsey.*

D^r. *Miles Barne,* once Fellow of *Peter-House* in *Cambridge,* Chaplain in ordinary to K. *Charles* II. marryed Madam *Hammond,* at ye Brew-House.

Tho. Barnes fined Alderman of *Lond.* late living in *Coleman*-Street, who dy'd in 1667 & buried at * * * *. He put *Josh. Barnes* into *Xt's* Hospital, promising to take care of him, as he improv'd in learning & had in several Wills left him 400*l. per an.,* but in ye last, one *Benjamin Needham,* who married his Mayd, run away with all, but what he left to *Xt's* Hospital.

30 *Will Barnes* of *Bishops Stortford,* Plummer & Glazier, of Estate above 80^l. *per an.* had many Sons & Daughters, The Eldest *John Barnes,* Father of *William* & *John,* wch latter left *Will.* now living at *Bp.* Stortford, a younger

Edward Barnes, who marry'd first wife *Anne Cock,* by whom he had 8 children, *Eliz.* & *John* &c. both who dy'd of ye Great Plague 1664. wth all their children. His second wife *Mary Mills,* Daughter of [1] *John Mills* Atturney of ye City of *Salisbury,* whose Brother was Mayor of *Salisbury.* Of her he had 13 children, *Mary,* now living, marryed to William *Meredith,* a *Cheshire* man, a Baker, *Jacob,* now living in *Virginia,* &c. *Martha,* Wife of *Felix Rhymes* an *Oxford* Man, by whome one Daughter *Mary,* marryed to *Richard Millard,* who 40 has two Sons, *Rob.* & *Rich.* both living, & a Daughter dead. Another Daughter *Martha,* born 1705. *Nov.*

Joshua Barnes I, who dyed at 7 *ætat. Abrahams,* two, both dead, *Isaac, Daniel, Sarah,* & *Joshua* II. now 50 years old, 1704.

M^r. *William Barnes,* born at * * * 1640, Captain of the 1 Troop of Guards to K. *Charles* II. K. *James* II. & K. *Wm.* III. Queen *Anne,* met him at y^e *Rose* at *Cambridge, April* 21. 1705. Din'd with him at ye same place, the next day, at his Invitation, 65 years old. A Son *John Barnes.*

John Barnes Bookseller at ye Crown in ye Pall-Mall, now living 1706.

July 25. E. Smith to H. Sends passages from the *Liber Niger Scaccarii* (Somers MS.). News of Collier, Flamstead, a new mode of taking the Longitude by Sea, Duke of Buckingham (History of Charles II's reign), Sherlock, Atterbury, Caroll, the Earl of Shaftesbury (who confessed to imbibing Arianism and Socinianism from Locke), Wallis' English Grammar, Crawford's *Memoirs*

---

[1] *John Mills,* dy'd wⁿ his Daughter my Mother, 4 years old, left her 27^l. *per an.*

July 27 (Mon.).   Out of *Is. Casaubon*'s Papers, in *Bib. Bodl.*

Patavij in aede D. *Francisci.*

Christophoro Longolio.

Belgae Romanam civitatem propter eximiam in studijs literarum praestantiam adepto, summo ingenio, incredibili industria, omnibus bonis artibus praedito supra juventae annos, in qua extinctus est magno cum *Italiae* dolore, cui ingentem spem sui nominis excitaverat, *Petrus Bembus* amico atque hospiti posuit.

> Te juvenem rapuere Deae fatalia Dentes
> Stamina, cum scirent moriturum tempore nullo,
> *Longoli,* tibi si canos seniumque dedissent.   10

P. Bembus Cardinalis obijt anno D. 1547. 15 Kal. *Febr.* Vixit ann. 75. m. 7. d. 29.

Lazarus Bonamicus Bassanensis obijt Patavij IV id. Februa. anno CIƆ. D. LII. Vixit ann. LXXIV. Docuit humaniores litteras *Patavij* per annos XXI. Sepultus est in aede D. *Joannis* in Viridario.

Laelius Capilupus auctor Centonum *Virgilianorum* obijt anno D. CIƆ. D. LX. III *Januar.* vixit annos LXII. d. XV.   Sepultus est in aede *Franciscanorum Mantuanorum.*

Hieronymus Cagnolus Vercellensis I. c. clarissimus obijt *Patav.* Kal. *Febr.* 1551. vixit ann. 59.   Sepultus est in aede D. Francisci.

Gabriel Fallopius Mutinensis medicus praestantissimus obijt *Patavij* VII. Id. 20 *Octob.* CIƆ. D. LXII.   Vixit annos XXXIX. m. XI. d. XVIII.   Sepultus est in aede D. *Antonij.*

D. O. M.   *Bartholomaeo Cavalcanti* patr. Flor. qui optimarum artium egregia cognitione instruct. consilio & eloquentia maximis in reb. praeclaram operam | *Paulo* III. P.M. Henrico II. *Francorum* Regi, & *Octavio Farnesio* | *Parmae Placentiaeque* duci varijs belli pacisque temporibus | navavit singularibusque ab ijs honorib. ornat. fuit, ac demum | *Patavium* secedens cum morbo senioque affectus ingenij tamen | monumenta litteris mandaret, magno bonorum omnium dolore | qui illius doctrinam animique magnitudinem admirabantur | è vita decessit.   30

Joannes Cavalcantes patri optimo moerens pos. | vixit ann. 59. m. 10. d. 25. obijt 5 id. *Dec.* 1562. | *Patavij* in aede D. Francisci.

Out of M^r. *Barnes*'s Apendix to *Anacreon Xtianus....* Latine.   In Regiam Quercum [with notes, 185–187.] ...

Out of *Casaubon's Adversaria.*

Narrabat hodie mihi gravis matrona, in nostra religione zelo flagrantissima ; quondam uxor D. *Violetarij,* Medici celeberrimi, nunc vidua : se olim quantum tenera aetas ferebat assidue versatam cum J. *Calvino,* quicum pater ipsius pene convixit *Genevae.* ab hoc igitur narrabat illa audivisse, dolere sibi vehementissime, quod usus exhibendae eucharistiae morientibus esset sublatus. Et affir- 40 mabat lectissima matrona, semel audivisse *Calvinum* orto super ea re sermone, dicentem, optare se ut sibi unus è manu digitus esset praecisus, & ille usus esset restitutus. Sed se reverentia earum Ecclesiarum quae usum hunc damnant impediri, quominus de eo restituendo cogitaret.   Confer aliud simile huic votum *Bezae* in Quaestt. & Respons. p. 161. —

Remember to add to my Notes upon *Livy* ad cap. 18. lib. 4. *quod ubi conspexit, Quod simul ubi conspexit* L. 2. B. N. C. ut & Pall. Rhen. Voss. uterque, atque Rottendorff. teste Jac. Gron.

---

of Scotland.   The Union with Scotland: particulars.   Tom Tuddall, organist of [Pembrook Hall] Cambridge, like to be ruined for a silly pun.   The Life of Boyle, etc.

July 27. Mat. Gibson to H.   Apologises for not visiting him in Oxford. Asks for literary gossip.

July 28. H. to E. Smith (Chaplain to the Countess Dowager of Denbigh).   Will send Dodwell on Lucian : acknowledges Fabrettus. *Lib.*

July 31 (Wed.). Remember to tell D͏ͬ. *Hudson* that the ɪɪɪ⁴ Vol. of *Rhymer*'s Collection from the Tower is out, and that it must be quickly secur'd for yᵉ Publick Library. ▬

¹ Out of *Casaubon*'s Papers.

Inveni in Codice R. B. MS. qui *Origenis* quædam et multa alia continet Epistolam *Joh*. Papæ ad *Photium* Virum famosissimum, qui fuit Adversarius *Ignatij* Patr. *Constant.* &c. de quorum causa Synodus Œcum. VIII. est habita. Ibi leges damnatum ab omnibus Papis R. *Photium* ; præter hunc *Johannem*, qui fuit *Johannes* VIII *Hadriani* Successor, circa annum Domini 872.—Ea Epistola 10 ita habet [200-208.]...

Aug. 1 (Th.). *Charles Seymour* Esqͬ. son to Sir *Edw. Seymour*, remov'd from being Gentleman of yᵉ Bed-Chamber to yᵉ Prince of *Denmark*. ▬ By yᵉ Death of Mͬ. *Methwyn*, Embassador to yᵉ King of *Portugal*, one of yᵉ Places of Master of yᵉ Chancery is become vacant, & 'tis said Mr. *Laune*, the Lawyer, will have it, tho' not without yᵉ usual consideration of 1500 Guineas to yᵉ Lord Keeper. ▬ A vast number of Declarations are printed at her Majesty's Press in order to be distributed upon yᵉ Descent.

Aug. 2 (Fri.). Three Volumes of *English* Historians in *folio* just 20 publish'd, *viz. Milton*, Mͬ. *Daniel*, &c. The 3ᵈ Volume contains yᵉ Lives of K. *Ch.* I. K. *Ch.* II. King *James* II. K. *Will.* & Q. *Mary* : done as said there by a Learned & Impartiall Hand. *Quære.* The Work done merely for Gain. Mͬ. *Strype* (whose Abilities in History may bee seen in one of yᵉ Letters I recᵈ. from D͏ͬ. *Tho. Smith*, and of whom some Mention in these Volumes of Remarks) has had a considerable Hand in writing Notes at yᵉ bottome of yᵉ Page.

Nig. Scac. known to Selden. Would like to see Berger's edition of L. Florus. Remarks on Smith's gossip. False about Mr. Tyrrell absconding, though he has suffered much by Printing ; pity he is not more accurate. Vast industry required for historical work. Perkes, Mill, and Dodwell. 'We have had lately given to yᵉ Publick Library the original MSᵗ. of *The Decay of Christian Piety* written by yᵉ Author of yᵉ Whole Duty of Man. Bᴾ. Fell's hand appears in several Places, and D͏ͬ. Aldrich thinks yᵗ yᵉ rest is not yᵉ Author's own Hand, but a disguis'd one, & yᵗ yᵉ whole is yᵉ Transcript of yᵉ Bᴾ. So yᵗ from it we cannot guess at yᵉ Author.'

July 30. F. Fox to H. 'Reports' a copy of Gruterus' Livy (Frankfort, 1609).

July 31. Hudson to H. Borrow from the Taberders' Library Majoragius upon Artes Rhet. 'Pray lay down a Crown for me to be drunk in yᵉ Common Room, as a Stirrup cup.' What news stirring ?

Aug. 1. The same to the same. Intends to make a new version of Majoragius.

Aug. [ ]. The same to the same. Gruter's Livy to be bought as cheap as possible.

Aug. 3. Dr. T. Smith to H. Instructions and suggestions for Williams. Smalridge's Oration sold out. Knows not how the clergy 'can stave off the reproaches of De Foe in his preface to his virulent Satyre, and such like villainous Fanaticks.' Hopes Dodwell will suppress Part II of his *Case in View*. Remarks on Milles. Thinks Barnes a much better Greek poet than critic, though even here inferior to D͏ͬ. Duport, for whom, as for Dr. Ralph Winterton, judicious scholars have little reverence.

[¹ pp. 190-199 missed by Hearne.]

Aug. 4 (Sun.). L^d. Peterborough being made her Majestie's Ambassador Extraordinary to his Cath. Majestie 'tis said my L^d. Galloway is made Governor of her Majesties Forces in y^t Kingdom. Tis now said Coll. Marsham succeeds M^r. Seymour in place of a Gent. of ye Bed-Chamber to ye Prince.

Aug. 5 (Mon.). Quædam ex Is. Casauboni pugillaribus, quos D^s. *Winton* habebat.

Narrabat mihi affinis meus Vir Honestiss. *Petrus Cabanaeus* Kal. Oct. 1604 cum ante triennium *Rubio* fluvius hujus oppiduli (*Bourdeaulx* vocant, vulgo superioris aetatis notarij cum *Latine* acta conciperent *Bourdelis* :) suburbium 10 totum inundavit, & cubicula inferiora omnium domorum complevit, tum inquam saeviente fluvio, ingentia saxa ab eo delata quae inter se collisa ignem ederent qui super aquas late stagnantes cernebatur. Addebat *Gillerius* Min : verbi divini visum alicubi fluvium velut contectum ignibus. Omnia miracula superat quod ipsi vidimus saxa ingentia non volvisse fluvium, sed in hortos muris clausos attollendo intulisse. Similiter & parietum dejectorum partes.

Narrabant ijdem in hoc eodem *Rubione* cum late stagnaret auditas voces ἀπὸ τῶν παραποταμίων quasi pereuntium in aquis ejulatus, quibus lamentis cum exciti essent qui audiebant, & ad ferendam opem accurrissent, repente planctus in risum est mutatus. Existimabant illi Satanae & malorum Spirituum esse 20 lusus.

Ea tempestas inundationibus aquarum fuit saeviss. & in *Delphinatu* & in alijs provincijs. De *Aleto,* quod oppidum non procul ab *Vicetia* (*Viez*) narrabant ijdem hoc. Alluit muros oppidi, fluviolus   is cum praeter modum intumuisset agebat ferebatque omnia obvia, quae utrinque ad ripas. Erant jumenta, erant homines, erat supellex varia, item lignum, & quicquid ad praediorum instrumenta pertinet. Oppidani cum ferre opem non possent, stabant in ea parte moenium quam praeterlabitur amnis, et erat corona frequens è murorum pinnis spectaculo miserrimo anxia, cum ecce repente aquarum vi subruta moenia collabuntur, & una secum omnes qui superstabant ruina trahit. 30 Deinde per urbem ipsam late vagari aquae, & partem magnam civium interimere. Exstat de hac re libellus tunc editus.

Ossa Gigantis omni fide majora, καὶ ὑπὲρ πᾶσαν ἱστορίαν. Non longe ab oppido cui nomen *Montelimar* ante paucos menses reperta sunt ossa nimia vetustate cariosa, sed tamen ferme integra cujusdam Gigantis, cui simile nihil legi, nil audivi. Modus erat hic. Des^t caetera. —

There is come into ye Publick Library, the Original MS^t of *The Causes of y^t Decay of Christian Piety,* written by ye Author of *The Whole Duty of Man.* The Donor M^r. *Keble,* A Bookseller in *London,* near *Temple-Bar.* D^r. *Aldrich,* Dean of *X^t.* Church has been shew'd 40 the Book, to know whether he could tell the Hand. He reply'd, that he was of opinion that 'twas not ye Author's own Hand, but copy'd by B^p. *Fell* wth a disguis'd Hand. I have carefully examin'd it, & find B^p. *Fell's* Hand in several places ; wch I know to be his from its being exactly ye same wth what I have seen of his Hand before. Particularly in the Title Page, *The Causes of the Decay of Xtian Piety* is added by him in room of *Duty lost in Disobedience* wch is struck out. There is also there struck out *A Practical treatise written by the Author* & for it only added *written by ye Author.* Indeed by comparing these Hands together they will appear to be ye same by the turn of the Letters : tho' we 50 cannot from hence gather y^t B^p. *Fell* was Author. Nor indeed do I think he was, it seeming rather to have been a Club of learned and pious Persons, such as ye B^p., D^r. *Hammond,* ye Lady *Packington* &c. —

In my Notes to *Livy* ad l. iv. c. 23, at yᵉ Word *Voltumnæ* remember to add, *Videndum an legendum potius* Vertunæ. See *Gyraldus's Syntagm. Deor.* ult. Ed. p. 52.

Aug. 7 (Wed.). Mʳ. Barnes tells me yᵗ in yᵉ 8ᵒ. Edition of *Homer's Odysses*, wᶜʰ was printed last Year at yᵉ *Theatre* for a New Year's Gift, are abundance of material Faults, and yᵗ some Words are quite left out. — Happening to shew Mʳ. *Barnes* the MSᵗ. Copy above mention'd of yᵉ *Decay of Xtian Piety*, he presently told me he had a Paper written wᵗʰ Archbᵖ. *Sancroft's* own Hand, wᶜʰ he thought resembled very much
10 the Hand of yᵉ sᵈ Book. This he brought yᵉ next day, and comparing it with yᵉ Book we found several Letters written yᵉ same way, the same Distance as to lines &c. And accordingly we concluded that they were done by yᵉ same Person; & wᵗ confirms this is yᵗ Mʳ. Barnes says yᵗ formerly talking with Dʳ. Holbeach Master of *Eman.* Coll. (of wᶜʰ Archbᵖ. *Sancroft* had been Fellow and afterwards Master) the Dr. told him yᵗ making a visit once to Dʳ. *Sancroft* (he thinks) before yᵉ Restauration he happen'd to see some Papers written by Dʳ. *Sancroft* wᶜʰ he would take his oath were part of wᵗ was afterwards printed under yᵉ Title of the *Whole Duty of Man*. Nothing can be objected agᵗ his being
20 Author, if his Extraordinary Piety, Learning, Eloquence & Modesty be consider'd, &c. — Out of *Casaubon's* Preface to *Polybius*. — Magnus, Deus bone, auctor *T. Livius*, lactea quadam ubertate dictionis divinitus facundus; amans virtutum, osor vitiorum, rectus judicij, rerum togæ, rerum sagi, etsi non ex usu neque experientia, egregie tamen peritus &c. wᵗʰ other things, wᶜʰ consult especially abᵗ the loss of *Livy's* Works.

Aug. 8 (Th.). Mʳ. *Ursinus*, Chaplain to yᵉ Prince of *Denmark* came on this Day to the Publick Library. He hath printed a Book abᵗ yᵉ Antiquities of the *Jews*. — Dʳ. *Woodroof* has just publish'd a Sermon preach'd at *Woodstock* the thanksgiving-Day for yᵉ Success under yᵉ
30 Duke of *Marlborough*, to whom 'tis Dedicated. — Mʳ. *Wilder* also of *Pembrooke* has printed one preach'd upon yᵉ same occasion, Dedicated to yᵉ Bᵖ. of *Bristol*. — Mʳ. *Geree* of *Corpus* has printed one also preach'd at yᵉ *Assize* at *Winchester*. This is a good Discourse, the others Rhapsodical, injudicious, Grub-street stuff. — This Day was a meeting of Heads of Houses in yᵉ *Apodyterium* to examine a sermon preach'd lately at Sᵗ. *Marie's* before yᵉ University by Mʳ. *Hart* of *Magdal.* Coll. wᶜʰ had been represented to yᵉ Court as containing some Reflecting things on some Great Persons. But it appear'd otherwise when sifted, & he is come of to his Credit & like an Honest Man, as 'tis certain he
40 is. — We have an Accᵗ. from *Whitchurch* in *Shropshire* yᵗ yᵉ Dissenters there having prepared a great Quantity of Bricks to Erect a Capacious Conventicle a Destroying Angel came by Night and spoyled yᵐ all & confounded yᵉⁱʳ Babel in yᵉ Beginning to yᵉⁱʳ great Mortification. — One of yᵉ Canons of *Sarum* being lately deceased, the Bᵖ. laboured Tooth & Nayle to have brought in to have succeeded him a certain Haughty Dʳ. (Dʳ. *Kennett*) famous for Arraigning the Blessed Martyr K. *Charles* Iˢᵗ in a 30 of *January* Sermon as also for a late History published by him, wᶜʰ is full of Whiggism, Trifling, Grub-street Matter, & base Reflections out of his Way, but he lost his Aime, & yᵉ Dean

& Chaplaine [*sic*] chose the Reverend D^r. *Wyatt.* The said History is ye 3^d Volume of the *English* Historians ; & is done wth D^r. *Kennett's* usual unaccuracy, Pride, Injudiciousness & Knavery. The said D^r. *Wyatt* was formerly Proctor of ye University of *Oxon* & Tutor to the Eminent D^r. *Bernard.* — Memorandum y^t M^r. *Barnes* has made divers Corrections (wch had Escaped M^r. *Aldrich*) in ye Copy of *Homer's Odysses* (presented him by ye Dean of *Xt. Ch.*) wch was printed at y^e *Theatre.* — D^r. *Hudson* in ye year 1704 very zealous ab^t Sir *Thomas Cook's* Gift of 1000^l. to the University, in order to build a College where *Glouc.* Hall stands. Ask ye D^r. about it. He writ to M^r. *Wilmot* an agent in ye 10 Matter, & had several Directions from M^r. *Ja. Ince* of one of y^e *Inns of Court.* — D^r. *Hudson* has a fair transcript wth a *Scholiast* of some Fragments of *Andromachus* ; a Physitian often mention'd by *Galen.* He was Physitian to *Nero.* He has also in MS^t. *Lucæ Holstenij* Notæ & Correctiones in *P. Gyllij* de Bosporo Thracio lib. 3.—Also Collations on *Tully's* Offices from the first Edition in ye Publick Library. — Also an *Index* of all ye Greek words in *Nicander* done Alphabetically by M^r. *Alex. Rinman.* — Also Collations of a MS^t. wth the *Greek* Orations printed at *Venice* an. 1513. As they are put down in ye Margin of a Copy of y^t Edition in ye Publick Library. — A Catalogue of MSS^ts. in 20 *Gudius's* Library. — *Sextus Rufus* an Epitome of *Roman* History to ye time of *Valentinian.* — Some Grammatical Things in *Greek.* — D^r. *Atterbury* had most of ye Materials for writing his Book ab^t *Convocations* of D^r. *Hutten.* He has acknowledg'd D^r. *Wake* to be in ye right (I am told) and begg'd his Pardon for being so far ingag'd ag^t him. — Over M^r. *Camden's* Picture on the Wall in the History Schole. schola historica / institvta / anno / HIstorIæ VItaM sIqVIs DonaVerIt hIC est. / — In St *Peter's Church in ye East Oxon,* on the North Wall is painted Queen *Eliz.* lying at full length in her Royal Robes wth a Crown on her Head &c. I suppose done ab^t ye year 1603 when she dy'd & was buried at *West-* 30 *minster.* — M^r. *Tudwell* Organist of *King's* Coll. & *Pembroke* Hall in *Cambridge* is expell'd. The reason see in one of my Letters dated *Jul.* 25. 1706. . . .

[**Aug. 15 (Th.).—Sept. 5 (Th.).**] On ye 15th of this Month *Thursday* ab^t 10 'Clock dyed D^r. *Bayley,* President of *Magd.* Coll. He has left ye Character of an Honest Man behind him. He was Elected upon the Death of D^r. *Rogers,* 'till wch time he refus'd the Oath of Allegiance, wch made some Reflect upon him as tho' he conform'd only out of Interest. — The L^d. *Barrimore* is lately married privately to ye L^d. *River's* Daughter. — At the Assizes at *Coventry* ye Church & Whigg Party that 40 there Indicted each other for a Riott at ye last Election for Members of Parliament accommodated ye Matter among themselves. — L^d. Wharton made Justice in Eyre of ye Forests, Parks, Chaces, *&c.* on this side *Trent,* of wch he had been depriv'd upon ye Death of K. *W^m.* and M^r. *Alex. Denton* (formerly of *Edm.* Hall & one of ye Councellors to y^e *Aylesbury* Men conc. ye Election there) is made his under secretary,

---

Aug. 14. H. to F. Cherry. Mela, Shottesbrooke, Philopatris &c. Glad that D^r. Kennett miscarried in the business of Sarum ; characterises that author. Notes on Mr. Hart (Magd.)'s Sermon ; *Decay of Christian Piety,* &c.

purely to encourage him to go on in Councelling the *W—ggs*, at wch he is forward enough. This M^r. *Denton* was a hard student when of ye Hall, and so he has been noted since; but whereas D^r. *Hicks* says he is one who understands ye Saxon Language well, it must be noted y^t 'tis a mistake, he not knowing I think one word of y^t Language. — *Bisse* Fellow of *New* Coll. marry'd to the Countess of *Plymouth*, to whom he was Chaplain. — Executors to D^r. *Bayley* are M^r. *Goodwin* and M^r. *Kenton* Fellows of the Coll. and upon their Absence D^r. *Gregory* of *Glouc.*shire and M^r. *Smallbrooke.* — A 2^d Edition
10 come out of D^r. *Tyndal's Rts. of ye Xtian Church asserted.* — *Quære* who is ye Publisher of a Book come out this year at *Lond.* 8°. call'd, *The Origine & Antiquity of our English Weights & Measures discover'd by their near Agreement wth such Standards that are now found in one of ye Egyptian Pyramids, together with the Explanation of divers Lines therein, heretofore measur'd by M^r. John Greaves* &c. — President of *Magd.* D^r. *Bayly* buried on *Sunday* night ab^t 9 clock, the 18th of *Aug.* He has left a Legacy of 5 *lib^s.* to D^r. *Crosthwait*, & as much to D^r. *Wynne.*
10 lib^s. to D^r. *Tho. Smith*, and 5 lib^s. to M^r. *Gandy.* He also left for ye Publick Library Cardinal *Hoard's* Picture. — Arch. C. 56. A Fragment
20 in Greek, remember to tell D^r. Hudson of it. 'Tis Geographical. A Paper in ye Place where. In the same Book a Greek tract de Paschate. Perhaps Petrus Alexandrinus's. — In the 4th Box amongst Casaubon's Papers is a thin fol. MS^t wherein are Notæ Gratiosi Epidauritæ explaining the Contractions of Words. Also Glossæ veteres variorum non editæ.—Notæ Geographicæ in the same Box. —

D^r. *Hutton* of *Aynhoe* amongst other things has made a great number of collections in order to continue the History of Bp^s as done by *Godwin*; wch he would willingly do if there were any Encouragement for him. — On ye 31st *Aug.* M^r. *Hart* of *Magd.* Coll. was call'd before
30 ye Heads of Houses in y^e *Apodyterium*, there being another order from Court for y^t purpose, they being not satisfied with w^t ye university had done before in reference to his Sermon. The Letter order'd them to give him an Oath, but they did not find themselves oblig'd by statute to do y^t, and so he was dismiss'd. M^r. *Hart* I am told since has taken more time to consider, before ye university send their Answer. D^r. *Mill* was concern'd in informing, as 'tis said, tho' he denys it. On the 3^d of *Sept.* M^r. *Hart* appear'd again before ye Heads of Houses, and gave in his Answer that he did not think himself bound to answer ye Interrogatories upon Oath, (1) Because it was a Criminal Cause. (2) Be-
40 cause he conceiv'd ye university Statute did not oblige him. On *Saturday Sept.* 7th. M^r. *Hart* was call'd again before y^e *Delegates*, when his Answer was agreed to be sent up to Court: and 'twas so accordingly, & ye university clear'd themselves; so y^t now ye Business must fall upon ye Court wholly. — ...

THE RESOLUTIONS OF ye PARLIAM^t OF GOTHAM ASSEMBLED THE 6th OF DECEMBER 1641.

1. Res. That ye Maxims and Politicks of ye most renowned Province of *Gotham* are and shall be contrary to all other wise Governments whatsoever.

2. That if any Counsellor of State w^thin this Province shall presume to offer

any Advice that looks like yᵉ Wisdom and Precautions of other Nations, He shall for so doing be deem'd an Enemy to yᵉ Publick & an Adherer to Forreign Interest.

3. That if any Motion be made by any Member of this House who is the least suspected of Common Sense or Honesty, it shall for yᵗ very reason be rejected.

4. That no Bill be at any time hereafter brought into this House to prevent Occasional Conformity, because this State has in former times succeeded so ill in endeavouring to hedge in yᵉ Cuckow.

5. That all due encouragement be given to Hypocrites, and that they be 10 upon all occasions employ'd by yᵉ State ; because all other Countries are so cruel as not to trust them.

6. That Popish Principles transplanted into a Protestant Climate are peculiarly wholesome and savoury to yᵉ state wherein they grow.

7. That 'tis Expedient yᵗ yᵉ Protestants of *Gotham* as well yᵉ Clergy as yᵉ Laity be implicit Believers.

8. That if any subject of *Gotham* shall henceforth pretend to give credit to his senses, he shall for yᵗ reason be reckon'd out of Senses, and shall be dealt wᵗʰ all accordingly.

9. That it is dangerous to yᵉ State to apprehend Danger too soone or to go 20 about to prevent it, e're it be too late.

10. That yᵉ furiousest Presbyterians beyond yᵉ River *Tweed* are yᵉ properest Guardians of moderate Episcopacy about *Trent*.

11. That yᵉ Bishops of *Gotham* be commission'd to treat with *the Utra-Twedan* Presbyters concerning an Union as well Ecclesiastical as Civil.

12. That an unlimited Toleration in yᵉ Province of *Gotham*, and an unrestrain'd Persecution of yᵉ Episcopal Party *ultra Tweedam* is yᵉ Foundation of Union betwixt yᵉ two Provinces.

13. That if any Subject of *Gotham* in order to obstruct yᵉ said Union, shall complain of yᵉ said Persecution, he's an Enemy to Moderation, and to yᵉ Peace 30 and Welfare of both Provinces.

14. That for yᵉ universal encouragement of Loyalty to yᵉ State all Remembrances of past Services and Disservices be for ever blotted out, and yᵉ standing Rule for yᵉ future be *Tros Tyriusve fuat nullo discrimine habetur.*

15. That yᵉ State cannot be safe from a Forreign Power without destroying it's own Constitution.

16. Finally, that there be Conservators of yᵉ Publick who upon any Extraordinary Emergency shall be empower'd to destroy yᵉ Constitution in order to preserve it & make it prosperous.

> *Tim. Thoughtless Cler.* 40
> *Par. in Prov. Gotham.*

NB. If there is anything in these Resolves that may seem to runne counter to yᵉ General Notions of Mankind, it must be observ'd the *Gothamites* have Customs and Practises vastly different from all other People and perhaps hardly consistent with yᵐselves.

Aug. 17. H. to Dr. T. Smith. 11 Sheets of Livy printed, Dodwell urged by the Bishop of Norwich not to print Part II of *The Case in View.* Death of Bayley, President of Magdalen. Mr. Hart has escaped the fate of Tudwell. Dr. Kennett mightily mortified. ? Author of *Origin and Antiquity of English Weights and Measures* and *Antiquities of Middlesex.* MS. of *the Decay of Christian Piety* ; traces Sancroft's hand. ' It may be 'tis not fair to be inquisitive.'

Aug. 19. Hudson to H. Has dined with Dr. Hutton [of Aynhoe] who would digest some of his papers and prepare them for the press if he were but encouraged with a dignity in the Church... ' Tis certain he's not for Clodpates turn, for yᵒ acctˢ of his assisting Atterbury.' Hutton has received from

Sept. 6 (Fri.). The Chancellor sent on Friday last another very pressing Letter to the Vice-Chanc. to have Mr. Hart examin'd upon Oath. The Vice-Chancellor at a Meeting of Heads yᵉ day following had yᵉ Matter again debated. Dʳ. Bourchier who was then present shew'd both from Common and Civil Law yᵗ yᵉ Vice-Chancellor was not oblig'd to tender an Oath when no body accus'd, nor Mʳ. Hart to answer upon oath, when no particular Allegations were brought against Him. After this Mʳ. Hart was call'd into yᵉ Apodyterium where he deliver'd yᵉ Vicechancellor a paper wᵗʰ a Request yᵗ it might be trans-
10 mitted to yᵉ Chancellor. The substance of it was that he was advis'd by the learn'd in yᵉ Law not to answer upon Oath to any thing, 'till his Accusers should appear, & give in their exceptions against his Sermon. And particularly own'd, yᵗ he had no manner of Reflection upon yᵉ Union, nor any thing in his Sermon yᵗ insinuated yᵉ Church was in any Danger from yᵉ Government; but only yᵗ some Danger seem'd to threaten it from yᵉ Growth of Atheism & Prophaneness & yᵉ Pre-

---

Kennett a printed list of the dignitaries of Norwich since Henry VIII's time. **Pet. Needham to H.** Asks urgently for a collation of the fragments of Hierocles preserved by Stobaeus with a MS. of that Author in New College Library, No. 250. ' I heartily wish you life, & health, & a good stomach still to yᵗ sort of work [Livy], wᶜʰ I must confess has almost jaded Your affectionate Friend.'
Aug. 24. H. to F. Cherry. Remarks on Mela, Robortellus, Browne Willis, Hutton. **Smith to H.** Asks for news of candidates at Magdalen, and of Dr. Bayley's will. Sends a mem. for Dr. Sike of a transcript of Abulfeda by Dr. Gise in All Souls' Library. Congratulates Mr. Hart on his escape from the London Inquisitors. Condemns Kennett and his Life of Charles I. Criticises unfavourably the *Origin and Antiquity of English Weights and Measures. Antiquities of Middlesex* a booksellers' compilation from Weaver &c.; hopes well of Collier's *Ecclesiastical History.* The proposed Life of Charles II. *Rights of the Christian Church* ought to be answered by one of the Bishops or their dependents. Wotton's Life of Boyle should have been in Latin. 'What you conjecture about the *Author of the Whole Duty of Man* I meddle not with at present. I will only acquaint you with a discourse I had with Bᵖ. Fell in his lodgings at Christ Church (about yᵉ yeare 1682) . . . in wᶜʰ hee told me most solemnly, that *hee beleived, that he was the only man* (then alive) *in England, who* knew who *was the Author of the Whole Duty of Man.*' The new edition of Ennius and the *Onomasticon.*
Aug. 30. F. Cherry to T. Cherry. I see no inconvenience in your staying at Oxford till you can procure your orders. Be as frugal as you can. Better wait for new clothes till you come to London.
Aug. 31. H. to Dr. T. Smith. Another letter from Court about Mr. Hart. Dr. Bayley's will; legacies to Non-jurors. 'Mr. Tyrrell says Mʳ. Basil Kennett, was Author of yᵉ new Lives in yᵉ Collection of English Historians, & yᵗ his Brother Dʳ. Kennett was only concern'd in some of yᵉ Additional Notes.' Lhuyd, Maddox. ' A great many in yᵉ University seem sorry for yᵉ Death of Mr. Bennett, as if there were no Bookseller of yᵉ same Public Spirit, & who would be so serviceable as he to yᵉ university.' Notes on MS. NE. D. 2. 19 ; greatest part perhaps written by St. Dunstan. Notes from Dods-worth's MSS. 55 fol. 8 a. to the effect that Pym suborned a man to swear falsely at the Earl of Strafford's trial.
Sept. 3. Professor Joshua Barnes to H. Messages to friends at Oxford, and about various things left behind. The Stonehouse-Dashwood Epithalamium.

vailing of Faction & Schism in yᵉ Nation. — In *Andr. Thevet's Vies des Hommes Illustres* is the Picture of Livy, also of Pliny yᵉ younger, and *Edward the Black Prince.* — Mʳ. *Madox* upon a Work, wᶜʰ is extracted from Records in the Exchequer &c. 'Twill be larger than his *Formulare,* & he has taken a great deal more pains in it, having been upon it about 9 years. The nature of it I know not; but 'twill be put into yᵉ Press very speedily. He tells me yᵗ he will have 3 or four Borders, but knows not whom to imploy for inventing them, unless he can procure yᵉ Dean of Xᵗ. Ch. The Work will be brought down to yᵉ End of Edw. IIᵈˢ Reign. He would give the Habits of yᵉ several Ages, as near as he 10 can from MSSᵗˢ &c. if he were not afraid twould give offence. — Upon yᵉ Turning out from Court of yᵉ Earl of *Abbingdon,* the Earl remov'd yᵉ Horse-Race, wᶜʰ us'd to be yearly, for a Plate wᶜʰ he gave, at Woodstock, to *Port-Meadow* by *Oxford.* Upon wᶜʰ the Dutchess of *Marlborough* continu'd it, beginning last year, when only a parcel of Whiggish, Mobbish People appear'd. And this Year, a Plate being given by her of 50 ˡⁱᵇˢ, 'twas run for on yᵉ Eleventh of *Sept.* when but one Horse run viz. yᵗ of yᵉ Lᵈ. *Kingston*: so yᵗ there was no manner of sport, & 'tis thought yᵉ Dutchess of *Marlborough,* an insatiable covetous proud Woman will have yᵉ Plate again as a present from yᵗ Lord, who 20 is a most Rank Whig. Very few Gentry were at this Appearance, & of yᵉ Nobility only Lᵈ. *Wharton,* Duke of *Richmond,* and one or two more of yᵗ Party: & to grace all yᵉ Bᵖ. of *Sarum* wᵗʰ his Lady, waited upon yᵉ Dutchess. Next day was a Race at Oxon in yᵉ said Meadow, where was a great Appearance of Nobility &c. — Mʳ. *Maddox's* Work is yᵉ Antiquities of the Exchequer. — A Folio Book in University Coll. Library, in the Beginning whereof an Acct of yᵉ Family of yᵉ *Darceys.* — Mʳ. *Timothy Nourse* (of whom there has been mention before) upon his Death gave all or most of his Books yᵗ were wanting to the Library of university College. A better Acct. of yᵗ Benefaction to be expected 30 from their Library Register, when they shall think fit to enter him.

Sept. 16 (Mon.). One Mʳ *Arrowsmith* a Minister of *Norfolk* has been taken into Custody, but is again admitted to bayle. He is accused of having spoken dangerous Words in *November* last relating to yᵉ Queen

---

Sept. 7. Dr. T. Smith to H. Had heard of Dr. Bayley's legacy; will lay aside all resentment &c. Sorry to hear that Mr. Hart is to be farther troubled; the oath *ex officio* obsolete. Will read Kennett's Lives. Mr. Bennett, the bookseller, said to have died worth above £10,000; 'Dr. Fr. Atterbury, who preached the Sermon in the Quire of St: Paul's Cathedral, ... flourished very highly in his commendation.' What is Mr. Madocs engaged upon? Was that entire book written by St. Dunstan? Remarks on the story of Pym *re* the Earl of Strafford's trial.

Sept. 10. Dodwell to H. Enclosure for a friend of H. at B.N.C. Certain information may be shown to Dr. Milles.

Sept. 14. H. to Dr. T. Smith. Hart has declined to answer upon oath, so the matter rests at present. Dr. Mill or Dr. Royse supposed to be the informer. Madox has been near 9 years at work at his book on the Exchequer; he sets less store by Dodsworth's collections than H. Mode of publication as yet uncertain. He designs a border or two, and has been recommended to apply to the Dean of Christ Church.

and Government of wch ye Person y^t ye same was spoke to made no
Deposition 'till *Aug.* last. — A new Book is come out intit. *The History of
ye Church* in respect both to it's antient & present Condition &c.
written by one called a High Church-Man.   It's something in ye strain
of ye Memorial, & if it offends not ye Government, it's certain 'twill
make ye Whig Pamphlettiers yelp.   A Book is published ag^t ye Union
in Scotland supposed to be written by M^r. *Fletcher.* — On Friday the
13th of this Instant *Sept.* died M^r. *William Joyner* who had been twice
Fellow of *Magd.* College.   He turned *Roman* Catholick after his being
10 turned out in *Oliver's* time.   After y^t he went beyond Sea, was entertain'd and patroniz'd by several Great Persons, & lived a Papist to his
dying day, being always chearfull & continually speaking well of y^e
true Protestants; but he could not endure ye Presbyterians, or any of y^t
side, whom he commonly call'd *Puritans.*   Upon King *James's* turning
out ye Fellows of *Magd.* he was restored, but quickly outed again.
After wch he lived in a retired Condition partly near *Brill* in *Oxonshire*
& partly in a House adjoyning to ye North Part of *Holywell* Church in
Oxon, in ye last of wch places he died & was buried in ye Church yard
of y^t Place.   He died pretty wealthy.   There were besides the Minister
20 onely two Scholars at his Funeral viz. D^r. *Hudson* and M^r. *Jo. Caswell,*
the former of wch was his Intimate Friend & Acquaintance. — D^r. *Atterbury's* Sermon preach'd upon the Funeral of M^r. *Tho. Bennett* ye Bookseller in S^t. *Paul's* Church at *Lond.* is printed : He extolls him mightily
for his Industry, Prudence, Skill in his Profession, Integrity, Piety &c. —
In pag. 118. of *Wendelin's* Book *de legibus salicis* mention made of a
MS^t of *Livy* in *Chifletius's* Library.   A. 1. 7. Med. *Seld.* — D^r. *Hough,*
B^p. of *Lichf.* & *Cov.* was Fellow originally of *Magdalen* Coll. afterwards
he was Chaplain to ye Old Duke of *Ormond*, Chanc. of ye Univers. of
Oxon. & upon ye Death of D^r. *Clerk* President of y^t Coll. he succeeded
30 him as President, & a little after was made B^p of *Oxon* wch he held w^th
his Presidentship.   Being weary of y^t Place, by the Whiggish Interest,
wch he devoted himself to, was promoted to ye See of *Lichf.* & *Cov.* &
then (for most of our B^ps have married after they were made B^ps some of
'em once, & some twice, to ye Great Prejudice of ye Church.) according
to ye Custom of ye Age married a swinging fat Wife.   He is not famed
for doing much Good, & the best thing I ever heard of him was his
bestowing a Prebend of *Lichf.* upon M^r. *Collins*: wch M^r. *Collins* was
originally of *Ball.* or *Trinity* College (for he was of them both) & afterwards was made Vice-Principal of *Glouc.* Hall & then School-Master of
40 *Magdalen's.*   Whilst B^p. *Parker* was President of y^t College he was his
Chaplain: that B^p. as well as he of *Lichfield* being taken wth his facetious
Conversation.   Perhaps more of him hereafter. — *Mills* of X^t *Church* so
far from understanding ye Fathers y^t in the Book he is now ab^t ag^t his
Friend M^r. *Dodwell* he always makes use of *Scultetus's Medulla Theologiæ
Patrum*, & being in great perplexity how to get it finish'd often runs to
D^r. *Cudworth's Intellectual System.* — D^r. *Hudson* has often inquir'd of
M^r. Joyner who was intimately acquainted with M^r. Milton whether y^e
said M^r. Milton dyed a Papist or No?   To wch Mr. Joyner constantly
reply'd y^t he was sure he did not.   Yet for all this 'tis credibly reported
50 y^t Sir Xtopher Milton his Brother made a Judge in K. James's Reign

declar'd publickly in Company that his Brother died a Papist & had liv'd in yᵗ Communion for above ten years. For further satisfaction abᵗ this consult a sermon printed by Dʳ. Binks now Dean of Lichfield, wᶜʰ was preach'd at yᵉ Assize at Warwick. — Dʳ. Hudson saw a Letter this Day under Baron Spanheim's own Hand, wᶜʰ assures us yᵗ he has full Liberty from yᵉ King of Prussia to spend. yᵉ remainder of his Days in England or any other Place, & yᵗ yᵉ King has given him a Pension of 4000 Crowns per annum. Baron Spanheim has a great many things wᶜʰ will be serviceable in a new Edition of Josephus, wᶜʰ as soon as he has a little leisure to digest he has promis'd to communicate yᵐ. — Dʳ. 10 *Moreton* formerly of Xᵗ Church & Amanuensis to yᵉ famous Dʳ. Hammond succeeded Dʳ. [1] Sherringham who was Deprived for refusing yᵉ Oaths to K. W. & Q. M. in yᵉ Bᵖᵖrick of Kildare in Ireland. — Memorandum to inquire about one Slatter a Lawyer?

VOL. XII.

Sept. 23 (Mon.), 1706. Memorandum yᵗ Mʳ. *Worth* has omitted a very Material Testimony of *Tatian* in pag. 261 of yᵉ Paschal Chronicle, & yet he has taken one from yᵉ Page just before. . . .

Sept. 25 (Wed.). Out of Luitprandus's Adversaria, pp. 490, 497, 510. Edit. Antv. 1640. fol. . . . — About Zoroaster in Justin, see Kircher's 20 Obeliscus Pamphilius, p. 12. . . . — H. 1. 17. *Art. Seld.* A Book of French Coyns of all yᵉ Kings of France &c. Mʳ. Tyrrel should consult it, & Sʳ. Andrew Fountaine. Title, Figures des Monnoyes de France. —1619. — H. 1. 5. Art. Seld. Paul Lomatius's Treatise of Painting, Carving & Building translated out of Italian into English by Rich. Haydocke (an Oxford Man) who has dedicated it to Sʳ. Thomas Bodley, then building the Publick Library, whose Picture to yᵉ Middle is put in yᵉ Frontispiece. Pᵗ. at Oxoñ 1598. fol. by Joseph Barnes the university Printer, in wᶜʰ Profession he was eminent.

Sept. 27 (Fri.). Remember in yᶜ Preface to *Livy* to consult pag. 198. 30 of Chevillier's Accᵗ of Printing, . . where is something of Andreas & Campanus who Published Livy.

Sept. 28 (Sat.). Dʳ. *Mill* has given 10 libˢ. worth of Books to yᵉ Publick Library : for wᶜʰ he ought to be commended. & indeed to speak yᵉ Truth he is a Person not only of Great Learning, but a great Patron

---

Sept. 21. Dr. T. Smith to H. An attack on the Whigs, sectaries, Scotch Presbyterians &c. *à propos* of Mr. Hart. Condemns Madox' censure of Dodsworth (see *Hist. of Cott. Lib.*, p. xxxvii) ; and commends Rymer's ability and modesty. Asks for news of Passioneo. Has seen Fontaninus' *Vindiciae Diplomatum.* Wants the transcriber to hasten. Sends copy of a letter of introduction written for Mr. James Anderson, author of the *Independency of Crown and Kingdom of Scotland.*

Sept. 28. H. to Barnes. Asks for verses on nuptials of Sir J. Stonehouse and Mrs. Pen. Dashwood: also for notes on Livy. The persecution of Mr. Hart ; 'you see we have Plum-Trees [? informers] in Oxon as well as Cam-

---

[1] Q. an Sherrington.

of it, when the humour takes. — Books sent by Passioneo to Dr. Hudson [5–6]. . . . Mr. Nic. Stampeel of Hamburg entered Student in ye Public Library the 12 of this Month. A Studious, civil Gentleman. He look'd over Junius's MSS. & some others. If he had an opportunity he would publish Tatian's Harmonia Evang. — Ask Dr. Smith abt one Slatter. He transcrib'd lately a Piece of Sr. Robt. Cotton out of Dodesworth's Papers vol. 140. — There is just now come out a Book in 8vo. agt Mr. Dodwell's Book agt ye Soul, by Mr. Edm. Chishull, who took his Master of Arts Degree in ye year 1693, a little after wch he was Repeater of ye Easter Sermons at St. Marie's whereby he shew'd himself to be a man 10 of good Memory, & much abt yt time he went Chaplain to ye Factory at Smyrna, at wch time he collected some Inscriptions wch it may be are valuable. He was esteem'd once a man of Modesty amongst novices, but never as I can hear amongst men of Judgmt and Learning, wch latter opinion of him he has sufficiently made good by his new Book (wch is only the first Part) in wch he has very impudently rank'd Mr. Dodwell amongst ye Meaner Sort of Writers, detracted from his Character, and as much as possible endeavour'd to blast ye Reputation he had deservedly obtain'd of being a most Profound Scholar, a most Pious man, and one of ye Greatest Integrity; wch shews he had nothing else to say agt his 20 Book: & therefore when Mr. Chishull comes to be consider'd in ye Continuation of Athenæ Oxoñ he must be mention'd as a Confident, Opiniative, little Writer, & must be reckon'd as one of little sense for pretending to speak so scurvily of one who has establish'd so good a Character all over ye Learned World. This Mr. Chishull's way of Preaching is by heart, & he appears plausible enough; but there is little Judgmt in wt he says, as appears from wt he has publish'd of yt nature in a certain Sermon preach'd when he went Chaplain to ye Factory. The Society of Corpus take him to be an affected person &c. — As for Mr. Dodwell (I speak wt I have certain knowledge of by being in ye House) he is so constant 30 in his Devotions yt a very great part of his time is taken up in ym, wch is perform'd wth ye Greatest Fervency, & he always appears a Zealous Friend to ye Church of England, & his Failings should not be spoken so abusively against, but he ought rather to be pitied.

---

bridge.' Will send Tatian, Lomatius' Treatise of Painting, &c., translated by Rich. Haydocke, and dedicated to Sir T. Bodley (Oxford: Joseph Barnes, 1598). Mr. Collins made Preb. of Lichfield—'one of ye best things Dr. Hough ever did.' H. to Dr. T. Smith. Mr. Anderson engaged upon a Scotch *Res Diplomatica*; materials scanty. Mr. Maddox thinks little of Rymer's judgment. List of books presented by Abbot Passioneo, chiefly printed at Rome 1700–5, and including *Sacra Exsequialia in funere Jacobi II. Mag. Brit. Regis descripta à Carolo de Aquino* (Romæ, 1702 fol.). 'A great curiosity. Three guineas were offer'd for this Book when 'twas brought over, by a Curious Gentleman.' Dr. Mill has presented £10 worth of Books to the Library, including F. Pagi's work on Baronius' Annals. Unfavourable opinion of Mr. Chishull and his answer to Dodwell. Death of Joyner (13th inst.); in spite of his denial 'tis credibly reported that Sir C. Milton publicly declared that his brother died a Papist, and had been so for ten years before. Has reason to believe Dr. Hudson author of the Censure of Burnet. Among recent visitors to the Library are Slatter a lawyer, and Stampeel a Hamburger; the latter wished he had an opportunity of publishing Tatian's *Harmonia Evangelica*.

Oct. 1 (Tu.). I have inquir'd into M^r. *Chishull's* Character, & can get no other answer y^n that he was always a Rangling Fellow, & better at Raillery & banter y^n Argum^t or Learning, wch he has abundantly made good by his new Book, wch is stuff'd wth y^t Billingsgate, unchristian Language, as makes it laid aside by all Readers in Oxoñ who desire to be inform'd in ye Subject; & blame him mightily for medling wth M^r. Dodwell's Person, when he is well known never to use y^t method himself. — M^r. *Fletcher* M. of Arts and Fellow lately of New-College, when Bach. of Arts or Under-Graduate (Quære) publish'd a Book of Poëms. He was afterwards preferr'd to be under-schoolemaster of 10 *Winchester*. He married a Daughter in Law of M^r. *Masters* who was formerly Fellow of *New*-College and afterwards Parson of *Holton* near *Oxoñ*. W^ch M^r. *Masters* died of ye Small-Pox in ye Parsonage House where he constantly resided & kept Hospitality. After him D^r. *Dunster* Warden of *Wadham* (who had ye Great Living of *Marsh* in *Bucks*) was either because he was a Whig or gave Money as twas suspected preferr'd to ye said Living by M^r. *Whorwood* a Fanatical Bastard son of ye old Rogue *Brome Whorwood* by ye famous Strumpet *Kate Allen*. This *Dunster* one of ye Violentest Whiggs & most Rascally Low-Church Men of ye Age never goes near either of these Parsonages, unless it be to 20 receive his Money, to ye great Scandal of ye Church & prejudice of Religion : & it has been observ'd of him y^t for all his Preferment he is very poor, being much given to Luxury & like his Crony *Royce* to spend all upon his Gutt. — D^r. *Code* originally commoner of *Queen's* College afterwards when Bach. of Arts made Fellow of *All-Souls*. Before or a little after his taking his Master's Degree he had ye Good Luck to have an Estate fall to him. Which made him richer but no better; for being oblig'd to go out Grand Compounder for ye Degree of Bach. of Physick he could for ye filthy Lucre of a little Money swear he could not spend 40 lib^s. per annum. He practises Physick, & pretends to be a very high 30 Church Man, but is never for promoting any thing in ye University y^t tends to ye Interest of Learning, or ye Honour of y^t Place.

Oct. 2 (Wed.). In a Chamber on the West side of Oriel College in ye Window is the Picture of S^r. *Thomas Bodley*, done at the charge of M^r. *Rouse* the Public Library Keeper, who was once in this Chamber. There are also ye Pictures of Queen *Mary* I. D^r. *Blincoe* Provost formerly &c. wth Coats of Arms.

Oct. 3 (Th.). In p. 684. Vol. I. of Livy Jac. Gronovius calls his Father a Lyer. — *Kuster* ab^t a new Edition of Iamblichus's Life of *Pythagoras*, wch he has corrected from MSS. & intends to illustrate wth 40 a new & Elegant *Latin* Translation by *Obrechtus*. After y^t he designs an Edition of *Aristophanes*. — *Strabo* finish'd at *Amsterdam*. Ask D^r. *Smith* ab^t it. — The last time I was with M^r. *Joyner* he talk'd much about Mathematical Learning, & upon y^t occasion run out against M^r. *Hobbes* whom he acknowledg'd to be a Man of Parts, & to have considerable

---

Oct. 3. Kent (Whitchurch) to H. Thinks of returning to Edmund Hall; his house is unhealthy, and has distempered his mind and body. Any hopes of Mr. V. Principal's going off? Would like at least to be a tutor, and regrets leaving the University.

Knowledge in *Mathematicks*, but he profess'd y^t he had a much greater Esteem for D^r. *Hudson's* Knowledge y^t way, & thought y^t the D^r. as he was well vers'd in *Greek* Authors so was more to be valu'd upon y^t score y^n most that have appear'd of late years in *Oxon*: & upon parting promis'd to give me a History of some things not commonly known of curious & Learned men, but I had not an opportunity afterwards of putting him in mind of his Promise. — Memorandum y^t D^r. *Code* very lately defended ye Professors for not reading in ye Schools, as also did D^r. *Crosthwait*, then in company : tho' they could not but know y^t
10 this neglect is much to ye Disgrace of ye University, Forreigners generally asking, when they come to Town, after the Publick Professors, and w^t a Character they bare, & frequently go to ye Schools to hear Lectures, when they are deceiv'd, we having since the time of King James but very poor Lectureres excepting two or three viz. M^r. *Halley* (a great ornam^t to us) &c. — In *Pagi's* Crit. upon *Baronius*, T. 1. p. 74. is an illustration of *Eutropius*. In pag. 223 ibid. some Remark upon M^r. Dodwell's Assertion in Diss. Cypr. xi. that *Balbinus & Pupienus* were kill'd *an. X^{ii}* 238. before ye Month of June. *Pagi* thinks they liv'd longer.

Oct. 5 (Sat.). D. 5. 1. *Linc.* is *Hen. Stephens's* Edition of the *Anthologia*
20 *Epigram.* in which are divers things in MS^t, especially verses at ye Beginning in *Greek*. — In the Italian Edition of *Augustinus's* Dialogues *de Nummis* D. 5. 5. Linc. are some MSS^t Notes relating to Coyns by *Joseph Scaliger*, whose Hand they are writt by. — In pag. 40. Of *Meibomius's Mæcenas* the Heads of Mecænas & *Virgil* from a valuable Coyn.

Oct. 6 (Sun.). The Rude Draught of a Speech design'd to have been spoke by D^r. *Hudson* before the Queen if she had come to ye Publick Library when she was in *Oxon* ab^t 3 years since.

The Zeal your Majesty has been pleas'd to express for ye Interest & Honour of Religion, makes us hope y^t Learning (wch is so necessary for ye Support of
30 it) will not want your Majesty's Patronage & Protection. It has always been ye Glory of Princes to encourage the Promoters of such Arts & Sciences as encrease the Powers of Mankind & free them from ye Bondage of Errours; nor has it been thought unbecoming their Majesty to rescue their Labours & Inventions from ye Injury of time & ye Fate of Mortality. Ptolemy & Attalus

---

Oct. 4. **Barnes to H.** Deprecates Hudson's anger at his silence. Encourages ' this confessor Mr. Hart.' Hopes to finish 50 Psalms (Anacreontick Version) by Xmas. ' In *Plutarch* you 'll find among his Parallels & Apophthegms, many Roman Thefts ; ' he sends three other instances. Messages to Hudson, &c.

Oct. 5. **Dr. T. Smith to H.** Mr. Anderson has returned to Scotland ; Mr. Atwood has written another large book against him. A little Society of Antiquaries in Edinburgh are collecting all parchments and papers which might illustrate Scottish history and antiquities ; but most must come from England, especially from the Archives of Durham. Madox' censure of Rymer very silly and unjust. Will borrow Fontaninus of Dr. Hickes. Query about Pagi's *Critica Historico-chronologica in Annales Baronii* (Paris 1689). Remarks on Dodwell and his opponents. ' That the great villayne, John Milton, dyed a Papist, was wholly unknown to mee before.' Hears that Mr. Slatter is very studious, and a great buyer of books, and far enough at present from designing to be an author. Asks for a copy of Hyde's inscription in *Charta authentica Roberti Seneschalli Scotiae*, presented by Smith.

Kings of Egypt & Pergamus are yᵉ first upon Record yᵗ collected yᵉ Writings of yᵉ Ancients & Establish'd yᵉ way to preserve them intire to future Ages: which has reflected as great a Lustre on their Memorys, as if they had enlarged their Empires and laid Chains on yᵉ Necks of Conquer'd Nations. 'Twas a Prince of your Majesty's Royal Family that gave yᵉ First Rise and Original to this famous Seat of Learning, which now we see so gloriously advanc'd by a Person in high Esteem wᵗʰ that Excellᵗ Princess Q *Eliz.* & 'tis from yᵉ Happy Influence of your Majesty's Governmᵗ. yᵗ we Presage it's future Greatness & promise ourselves yᵉ flourishing of Arts as well as Arms, & that our Age shall then be most renown'd for Learning, when it shall be in the Height of Glory for Victory & Conquest: as yᵉ *Greeks & Romans,* were most fam'd for yᵉⁱʳ Arts & Civility, when they subdu'd & gave Laws to yᵉ World. —

N. B. *Du Vall* made a Map for *Cæsar's* Commentaries.

Oct. 7 (Mon.). Abᵗ 8 years since Dʳ. *Smith* gave to yᵉ Publick Library in *Oxon Roberti Seneschalli Scotiæ charta Authentica* neatly bound in vellam, at yᵉ Beginning of wᶜʰ Dʳ. *Hyde,* then Library-Keeper writt as an acknowledgment, *Bibliothecæ Publicæ dono dedit D. Tho. Smith S. T. D. olim. coll. Magd. in Oxonio Socius Mense Majo—*1697. wᶜʰ he afterwards (for wᵗ reason I know not) struck out again.

Oct. 9 (Wed.). The Queen has created his Highness *George* Augustus[1], Electoral Prince of *Hanover,* a Peer of this Kingdom by yᵉ Stile & Titles of Baron of *Tewkesbury,* Viscount *Northallerton,* Earl of *Milford*-Haven, Marquess & Duke of *Cambridge.* — This Day at two Clock Afternoon was a Convocation, for Chusing a Vice-Chancellor for yᵉ Year ensueing, when the Chancellor's Letter being read wherein Dʳ. *Lancaster* Provost of *Queen's* was Nominated, he was accordingly approv'd by yᵉ whole Body *nemine contrad.* After wᶜʰ Dʳ. *De Laune,* upon laying down his Office (which he had born four years) made a speech as usuall, giving a laudable character of his Successor, for his Parts, Learning, Piety, Integrity & Zeal both to yᵉ Church & university; wᶜʰ consider'd the Members thereof need not fear to receive all yᵉ Benefit & Advantages from him wᶜʰ could be expected from a Vice-Chancellor, & they might hope to have an End put to those Schisms & Confusions wᶜʰ now disturb the whole Kingdom, provided a like Assistance were given by others. When he had Ended Dʳ. *Lancaster* being first sworn stood up and made a Speech, wᶜʰ was neatly penn'd. In it he shew'd how difficult a post he was Enter'd upon & how unfit he was to manage it, especially since his Predecessor (as he said) so much exceeded him in all Qualifications necessary to it, & wᵗʰall he had a Large Cure of Souls wᶜʰ would take up a good part of his time. However he assur'd them yᵗ since yᵉ Chancellor had been pleas'd to nominate, & yᵉ Convocation to confirm him, he would take as much Care aš possible, & endeavour all he could to manage the trust committed to him to yᵉ Honour & Credit of yᵉ university; & for yᵗ End he hop'd the Seniors of yᵉ university, especially those who had yᵉ more immediate Care of Youth, would joyn wᵗʰ him in stiffling the Mischiefs of ill & pernicious Books, written on purpose to ruin both yᵉ Church & university, & bring a Disgrace upon Learning & Religion, among wᶜʰ he nam'd Dʳ. *Tyndale's* Book of yᵉ Rᵗˢ of yᵉ Church, in wᶜʰ are publish'd new Forms of

---

[1] N.B. That he is a Papist.

Ecclesiástical & Civil Governm^t. & M^r. *Lock*'s Humane understanding, written to advance new Schemes of Philosophy & bring an *odium* upon Ancient Learning. This D^r. *Lancaster* has publish'd some Sermons, & is reckon'd a good natur'd[1] man, tho' he formerly gave an Instance to ye contrary, being one of those who turn'd by D^r. *Hudson* from a Fellowship in *Queen*'s. — Provice-Chancellors are D^r. *Paynter*, D^r. *Charlett*, D^r. De *Laune* & D^r. *Gardiner*. — M^r. *Baxter* an Eminent School-Master (who put out *Horace* & *Anacreon*, & was the chief Mourner at ye famous M^r. *Rich. Baxter*'s Funeral, who was his Near Relation) did
10 assure M^r. *Halley* that old *Baxter*, when he was open'd after his Death had a Gaul in him as large as that of an Horse. . . . — M^r. *Flamstead* the *Queen*'s Professor of Astronomy at *Greenwich*, (whether he was originally of any university or no I cannot yet tell, tho' I believe he had an Honorary Degree of Master of Arts conferr'd upon him at *Cambridge*) is now publishing his Astronomical observations at ye Expence of ye Prince of *Denmark*: & 'tis said he would have been a better Astronomer if he had understood a little more of Geometry (in wch science ye Great *Hevelius* was remarkably defective). He is a narrow spirited Fellow, has been barbarous to ye Memory of King *Charles* II who preferr'd him:
20 & whether he has been ever gratefull or no to ye Lord Keeper *North* who gave him a good Living I want to be inform'd. However this is certain that whilst he gazes at ye Heavens he neglects to conduct ye Souls of his Parishioners thither. — 'Twas a memorable saying of my L^d. *Bacon* that a Little Learning made men Atheists, but a great deal reduces them to a better sense of things : so it may be said y^t a smattering in Learning makes men ungratefull to y^eir Mother ye university, when as those who have a better stock of it are always willing to shew their Gratitude, witness S^r. Thomas Bodley, Archb^p. Laud, M^r. Selden, B^p. Barlow, B^p. Fell, D^r. Marshall, &c.

30 **Oct. 13 (Sun.).** This Morning preach'd at *X^t-Church* M^r. *Adams* Student of that Place, upon *Luke* 7. 33, 34, 35.

'Twas ye 2^d Part of a former Discourse preach'd Ap^r. 28 last, & now he endeavour'd to prove, that notw^thstanding good & honest Men meet wth Affronts & Abuses from the world yet they ought to persevere in their Integrity, & undauntedly to go on in their Practise of Virtue : wch he did from these considerations, 1st ye shame that attends ye Desertion of good Principles, 2. that tho' there may be far ye greatest part of Men who traduce Virtue & encourage Vice, yet the wisest Part of Mankind will always honour & reverence the virtuous. 3. That tho' there should be a universal Conspiracy ag^t

---

Oct. 12. H. to Dr. T. Smith. Mention of a Society of Antiquaries at Edinburgh. Dr. Hudson has sent a box of books to Rome. Cancelled Inscription in *Charta Authentica Roberti Seneschalli Scotiae*, presented by Smith; will see justice done him. Dr. De Laune succeeded as V. C. by Dr. Lancaster; the latter in his speech condemned Tindal, and Locke's *Human Understanding*. Doubtful how Dr. Wynne, who abridged the latter, relished it. Dr. Wynne upholds his principles about Government at the Coffee House. Vol I. of Livy will be printed off next week.

---

[1] That is he will turn, & wind & do every thing for Interest. Since experienc'd. (Apr. 16. 1708.)

men of Honesty & Integrity yet the Satisfaction of a good conscience is sufficient to overballance their Spight and Malice. 4. That God will reward them at last, & bring shame and confusion on their Enemies. . . .

Oct. 14 (Mon.). Quære? I think M^r. *Andr. Allam*'s Tutor was M^r. *Edwards* Vice-Principal of *Edm.* Hall, a *Welsh*-Man & of a very crazed, whimsical Temper, & void of Parts or Learning. — About ye Age of *Pindar* see . . *Raderus*. pag. 396. upon y^e *Chron. Paschale.* — D^r. *Bathurst* by his will left w^t Coyns he had y^t were wanting to ye Publick Library. Upon comparing y^m wth ye Catalogue it appear'd that we wanted 15, viz. 7 Silver & 8 Brass. 10

Oct. 15 (Tu.). Out of D^r. *Bathurst*'s Will. [31–34]. . . . M^r. *Hinton*, Chaplain of *Corpus X^ti* College, told me last Night y^t when M^r. *Chishull* was in *Holland*, a certain Professor of those Parts came to him & ask'd him w^t news from *England*. To wch M^r. *Chishull* reply'd y^t he had not heard any of late; upon wch says the Professor, *Decessit Hydius stupor mundi*, D^r. *Hyde* being dead a little before, & of wch he had rec^d a Letter. This shews the Great Respect & veneration they had for ye Doctor upon Account of his wonderfull skill in the oriental Tongues: but as for M^r. *Chishull* he told this about on purpose to ridicule the *Germans*, thinking they had not much Judgment in thinking so honourably of 20 ye Doctor. Which is an argument of his Arrogance & Pride, as likewise is his preaching about two years since at S^t. *Peter*'s in ye East, wherein he abus'd in a most impudent, scandalous Manner the present Lord B^p. of *Worcester*. These things might have been well enough past by in silence, were it not for his greater Abuse of y^t Good & Learned Man M^r. *Dodwell*, at wch ye World even M^r. *Dodwell*'s greatest Enemies crie out shame, and even M^r. *Hinton* blames him for it to the highest Degree.

Oct. 17 (Th.). M^r. *Basil Kennett* has just publish'd a thin Book in 8vo. containing a Paraphrase in Verse on some parts of ye Bible. — 30 [1]One *Old-Field* has published a Book against M^r. *Dodwell*. Quære whether he be not a Presbyterian. — D^r. *Hammond* in some Part of his Works has an Account of y^e *Image of Both Churches*, written by Father *Paterson* as he says. 'Tis a very shrewd Book, and a certaine D^r. of ye Civil Law in this university has once or twice told me y^t M^r. *William Rogers* of *Gloucestershire* (the same *Rogers* who put up ye Statue of King *James* over the Gate of University College, which they neglect at present, the Inscription under being worn almost out) some years since in Discourse about Matters of Religion, recommended it to him for satisfying him in Objections against y^e *Roman* Catholick 40 Religion. — *Memorandum* that y^t Part of D^r. Bathurst's Funeral relating to his Request y^t a Sear-Cloath should be put over his face when dead (to prevent his coming to life again) is printed in the yearly Account of English Affairs for y^t year wherein he died. — M^r. *Hinton* of *Corpus X^ti* tells me y^t when he was in ye Country S^r. *Andrew Fountaine* told

---

[1] *Old-Field* above mention'd, who stiles himself *F. à veteri campo,* wth an *id est, old-Field*, was the Presbyterian Preacher formerly in Oxoñ, & his whimsical, odd, title of his Book shews him to be a Fellow of no Brains or Learning. But look into ye Book itself.

him of a great Curiosity lately discovered, *viz.* a Study of Books, mostly MSS^{ts}, besides divers ancient Rolls. It has continued several Years, the Persons concerned having neglected to break it open, & S^r. *Andrew* has been desired to look them over. Remember to inquire into this Matter, & what ye Books may be. The Gentleman to whom they formerly belong'd being a Lawyer 'tis probable there may be some relating to y^e *English* History, especially our Religious Houses. M^r. *Rymer* should be inform'd of this.

Oct. 19 (Sat.). M^r. *Baxter* (*W^m.*) the Schoolmaster has ready, or
10 very near ready, for ye Press, *Glossarium Britannicum,* a Specimen whereof may be seen in a Part of y^e *Philosophical Transactions* just come out. It seems by y^t to be a very curious Work, & ye Author shews himself to be a scholar and a good Antiquary, as M^r. *Llhuyd* has also told me he is, who further added to me y^t he is tho' related yet of quite different Principles from the noted *Rich. Baxter.* — There is just come downe in 8vo. an Answer of 6^d. Price to D^r. *Wells*'s Pieces against M^r. *Dowley.* The Author's Name, I think, not added. — Just printed in 8°. in one Sheet the Articles agreed upon by the *English* and *Scotch* Commissioners for an Union w^{th} *Scotland.* They are strangely in favour
20 of & for ye Advantage of y^e *Scotch* Nation, & if they should be consented to by ye Parliam^{ts} of both Kingdoms they would as some judge ruine our Nation. But we must leave y^t to time. — D^r. *Wynne* tells me y^t he some years since compar'd B^p. *Burnett*'s Abridgm^t of y^e *History of ye Reformation* wth the *History it self,* and put down the differences, and made divers observations upon the Particulars; which he shew'd to D^r. *Maurice* y^e *Margaret* Professor of Divinity, who was very urgent to have him print them : but he refus'd. — Remember to look over M^r. *Leland*'s Papers whether he makes mention of any *MSS.* of *Livy,* as also to inquire about *Boston* of *Bury,* whether he has any good Account of y^e
30 *MSS.* in *England* in his Time of this Author. — M^r. *Llhuyd* has just Printed in his first Volume (almost ready for Publication) a Catalogue in *Latin* of y^e *Welsh* or *British* Writers, wch he drew up some years since at ye Request of M^r. *Tanner* who promis'd him to bring it into his Edition of *Leland de scriptoribus.* M^r. *Llhuyd* would not have printed it now, only he dreads somew^t ye Miscarriage of y^t Design.

Oct. 19. E. Smith to H. Sends a string of literary queries on behalf of a friend. ' I'm informed here y^t ye prophecy " When ye Church and ye Hill to ye Danube advances &c." was really in ye Hands of M^r. Hall of Queens ye Winter before ye Battle of Blenheim was fought.' ' A most extraordinary Oration providentially discovered in ye Paper Office ag^t making peace with France,' *anno* 1 Henry VIII. Toland is editing it. He is making collections for his Brutus and Life of Socrates. Literary gossip. Brockelsby's Christian Deism—' the prodigiousest Mass of Learning y^t was ever printed in English Tongue.' **Dr. T. Smith to H.** Remarks on the new and the late V. C. Will send news about Anderson and the Society of Antiquaries. Wishes for a correspondent in Scotland, but cannot give himself leave to have anything to do, in the way of familiar writing, with a Presbyterian, though in a matter of mere curiosity and learning. Remarks on Pagi and Montfaucon. Can't understand Dr. Hyde's cancelling the acknowledgment ; Mabillon has reprinted the piece in the Supplement to *de Re diplomatica.* Remarks on the V. C., Dr. Wynne, and Livy.

Oct. 20 (Sun.). Remember in yͤ Preface to *Livy* when yͤ MSᵗ wᶜʰ I have noted all along by yͤ Letter *B.* is mentioned to note yᵗ 'tis a very good one & agrees for yͤ most part with yͤ Emendations made by *Sigonius* from his Books. ― I am told by one who has had occasion to examin yᵗ Mʳ. *Eachard*'s little Book of Geography is stolen from a certain *French* Book, which has been translated into *English*. The Name of yͤ Author I forget. *Quære?* This Mʳ. *Eachard* also stole his *Roman* History from Dʳ. *Howell*'s History, wᵗʰout so much as making acknowledgment, as he has not done of any Authors he made use of. ― He that shall put out a new Edition of *Tacitus* must remember to 10 look over Mʳ. *Rich. James*'s Account of yͤ Isle of *Wight* in MSᵗ in yͤ *Bodleian* Library. Also Mʳ. *Leland*'s *Glossary* or Explication of Names at yͤ End of his *Cygnea Cantio.* as likewise Mʳ. *Leland*'s MSSᵗ Papers relating to some Geographical things of *Britain.* ― A great number of Coyns, of yͤ lesser sort, found lately near *Abbingdon*. Enquire about them.

Oct. 21 (Mon.). Remember to ask Dʳ. *Smith* who first publish'd *Charta Authentica Roberti Seneschalli Scotiæ*, &c. lately Reprinted at yͤ End of *Mabillon*'s Supplemᵗ to his Book *de re diplomatica.* ― Dʳ. *Mill* is of opinion yᵗ the Specimens of Hands in *Mabillon*'s Book *de re diplo-* 20 *matica*, are all wrong, and yᵗ they are not to be depended upon, not yᵗ he thinks *Mabillon* is to be blamed, but yͤ Ingraver, who was imploy'd, who might err for want of *Mabillon*'s being ready always to direct. or it may be yͤ Ingraver might not take them immediately from the originals but from some transcripts. ― Dʳ. *Mill* is of opinion yᵗ there cannot be any great matter considerable in the *Collectio nova Patrum & Scriptorum Græcorum Eusebij Cæsariensis, S. Athanasij, & Cosmæ Ægyptij*, just now publish'd in two Vols in *fol.* by the Learned *Benedictine Montfaucon*. But I am apt to think yͤ contrary. Ask Dʳ. Smith about it. ― Mʳ. Parker (George) the Almanack Maker was ·fin'd last sessions at yͤ *Old* 30 *Bailey* 20 Markes, & to find security for his good Behaviour for 6 Months for Inserting in yͤ Genealogy of yͤ Kings & Princes in his last Almanack yͤ Pr. of *Wales* and his Sister. ― *Friday* last yͤ Printer of yͤ *Review* was carryed by yͤ Messenger of yͤ Press before my Lᵈ. C. Justice & bound wᵗʰ two good sureties to appear yͤ 1ˢᵗ day of yͤ next Terme in yͤ Court of *Queen*'s *Bench Westm.* to answer to wᵗ shall be objected against him by yͤ Queen's Attorney General.—Mʳ. Foe author of yᵗ Paper is also sought for upon yͤ same Account. Tis for his *Review* of yͤ 1ˢᵗ Instant in wᶜʰ he scurrilously & Impudently treats the Lᵈ. Chief Justice *Holt*, on Account of his Speech last Assizes as if his Lᵈship had 40 reflected on yͤ *Scotl.* union. ― Memorandum That when Mʳ. *Tho. Lydiatt* was in Prison, occasion'd by his being bound for some Relations, where he lay a long time, Bᵖ. *Usher*, who was his great Friend, paid 300 libˢ. or more for him, as I have heard it said. *Quære* in Mʳ. *Lydiatt*'s Letters *MSS.* in the *Publick Library*, also in Archbᵖ. *Usher*'s Life, & Mʳ. *Wood*'s Account of Mʳ. *Lydiatt.* ― Dʳ. *Mill* tells me yᵗ Dʳ. *Potter* has *Clemens Alexandrinus* ready for yͤ Press, but yᵗ he cannot get any Book-seller to undertake it. And yᵗ Dʳ. *Potter* has made very curious Emendations. But I am apt to think he has not consulted Books enough upon this occasion.   50

Oct. 23 (Wed.). I am told y^t in one of ye Windows of ye Church of *Wanfield* in *Berks* is the Effigies of K. *Hen.* VI by wch it should seem, that he painted part of ye Windows, or else y^t he was a Benefactor to y^t in some other Respect. *Quære* in M^r. *Ashmole's* Inscriptions &c. in this County, amongst his Books in the *Museum.* — Newly come out *An Explication of ye Gospel-Theism*, &c. by *Rich. Brocklesby*, a Xtian Trinitarian. *fol.* printed for ye Author. I am told 'tis a very learned Work. Quære. — An Account of ye Breeding of Worms in Humane Bodies: Their Nature & several sorts: Their Effects, Symptoms, & Prognosticks:
10 wth ye true means to avoid them, & medicines to cure y^m. By *Nich. Andry, M.D.* translated from y^e *French.* Pr. 5s.

Oct. 25 (Fri.). Lately dead M^r. *Stephen Penton* Bach of Div. formerly Fellow of *New*-Coll. afterw^ds Principal of S^t. *Edm.* Hall & Rector of *Glympton* near *Oxon.*, & at length Prebendary of Rippon in Yorksh. in wch County he had a Living. He might have had other Preferm^t if he had pleas'd; but he always declin'd Greatness, being a truly Honest, good Man, & an Excell^t Scholar, & of so good & facetious a temper (w^thout Reserve) y^t he was belov'd by all that knew him. He has written *Apparatus ad Theologiam. Lond.* 1688. 8°. and two little things in 8°
20 about y^e *Guardian's Duty.* — ... This being the Day on wch the Fellows of *Magd.* Coll. were restored after their being turn'd out by King *James* II. 'twas observ'd wth great Rejoycing *&c.* as it has been ever since that time. — Yesterday died Charles Finch, D^r. of Civil Law, & Fellow of *All Souls.* He was a younger son of *Heneage Finch* Earl of *Nottingham*, & was because of his Birth, more than Parts, he being but a degree from a Natural, & upon y^t Account by some stiled *the Plant Animal*, made Secretary to ye Plantations. — The Dean of *X^t Church* has a MS^t written in ye time of K. *Edw.* III. *Quære* w^t it is? — D^r. *Finch* left above 10000 *lib^s.* to my L^d. *Nottingham*, 300 *lib^s.* to his Sister, and nothing to
30 ye College. or any one else. — At ye End of *Homer's Iliads* pr. in *Greek* by *Asulanus* 1524. 8°, this *Memorandum. Homerus ille, quem Aldus hac eadem forma domi suæ edidit, longe est emendatior. Hæc vero editio mendis scatet.* — D^r. *Bentley* in his New *Horace* has a remark ab^t *rectis oculis. Quære* whether it agrees w^th *rectis oculis* in *Suetonius's* Life of *Augustus.* — M^r. *Stebbing Somerset*-Herald has continued *Fr. Sandford's Genealogical History of ye Kings and Queens of England.* 'Twill be speedily publish'd. — In *Bulifon's Ragionamento Intorno ad un Antico Marmo nella città di Pozzuoli* .... a Curious Marble, (wth an Inscription,) representing Cities destroy'd in the time of *Tiberius.* — *Camillus Peregrinus's Dissertt.*
40 *de Capua* wanting in ye Publick Library. Inquire after it. — M^r. *Mich. Mattaire* M. of Arts, & some time since student of *X^t Church*, & now one of ye School Masters of *Westminster*, has just publish'd a Book *de Dialectis Græcorum*, in a thick 8vo. before wch is D^r. *Knipe's* Recommendation, in wch he says the Author has shew'd much Judgm^t & great

---

Oct. 22. **Pat. Gordon to H.** Hopes to see Henry VIII's Psalter when he comes to Oxford. **Dodwell to H.** Chishull's attack and his answer. 'I find it far easyer to answer his Arguments than to do it consistently with the Duty of a Christian. He knows no more than one degree of Comparison, the Superlative.' More answers forthcoming, from Dr. Whitby and another. Mr. Fox full of prejudice. Remarks on Livian chronology.

Industry. 'Tis 7 shillings Price. — The Book above mention'd of the Dean of *X^t Church*'s was written by *Walter de Millemet Clericus*, in the year 1326, *viz.* the 1st of the Reign of *Edw.* 3. It beginns thus—

Hic incipiunt Rubricæ capitulorum hujus libri de Nobilitatibus, Sapiencijs & Pruden-cijs Regum, editi ad honorem illustris domini Edwardi dei gracia Regis Angliæ in-cipientis regnare, anno Domini ab incarnacione milesimo, trecentesimo, vicesimo sexto.
Tis in quarto & most curiously illuminated, containing some of the chief Courtiers, *&c.* of that time, Arms, Birds, Beasts, &c. The Author I do not find mention'd in *Leland, Bale,* or *Pits.* The Shoes then wthout Heels as appears from the Pictures. At the End of the *Rubricks.* 10 The Pictures of King *Edw.* III. & Queen *Philippa.* The Book itself beginns thus, *De Invocatione dei nominis in principio cujuslibet operis.—In nomine patris & filij & spiritus sancti amen. In principio cujuslibet operis est nomen sanctæ & individuæ &c.* In the 2^d page the Arms of the King of *England.* After that follow the Arms of the Prince of *Wales,* the Pictures of *Courtney,* & *Wake,* The Arms of *Thomas Brotherton* Earl of Norfolk, *viz.* Gules, 3 Lyons *pas. or,* a file of five. 2. of *Edmund de Wood-stock, viz. Gules* 3 Lyons *passant or,* wthin a Border *Arg.* wth other Arms of y^t Nature. The II^d chapter is Epistola Allectiva [ad] Dominum Re-gem ad sciencia: Regalis cognitionem. Just above ye Beginning of this 20 chapter King *Edward* III is painted, *&c.* as also he is in several places. Presently after the Beginning of this chapter is the Author's Name *viz. Walterus de Millemete.* At the bottom of one Page of this Chapter, are ye Arms of *Henry Earl of Lancaster viz. Gules* 3 *Lyons pass. guardant,* or, a *Bendlet Azure.* (2) of *Edm. Earl of Lancaster, viz. Gules,* 3 *Lyons Pass^t. guard.* over all a file of five *Azure* each charg'd wth 3 *flower de Luces or.* From this chapter it appears y^t this Author transcrib'd *Aristotle*'s Book intitled *de secretis secretorum* (wch Aristotle had presented to *Alexander the Great*) for ye use of K. *Edw.* & y^t w^t he has writ in this Book was only by way of Supplem^t & Explication. This to be 30 taken Notice of hereafter by ye Editor of *Aristotle*'s Works. The Author very free in telling the King to preserve the Rights and Liberties of the Church. The Gloves much then as the tip'd Gloves now. The Arms of *John de Eltham* Earl of *Cornwall, viz. Gules,* 3 *Lyons, pass. guard.* wthin a *Bordure arg.* charg'd wth 12 *Flower de Luces.* No Sleeves to y^{eir} Coats. —I take this to have been ye very copy that was presented to King *Edw.* by ye Author. — M^r. *Wotton* has a sermon preach'd at ye Primary Visitation of ye B^p. of *Lincoln,* (against D^r. *Tyndale*'s *Rights of ye Church,*) whereof there is come out a 2^d Edition. — There is an *Answer* to or else *Reflections* come out *upon* D^r. *Atterbury*'s Sermon 40 at M^r. *Bennett*'s Funeral.

Oct. 27 (Sun.). D^r. *Finch* above mention'd, some years agoe being at *Dick Clarks* at *Iffley,* where there was a Merry Meeting, ab^t 9 or 10 at night, after a great many things pass'd between him & M^{rs}. *Colebury Crooke,* sister to Col. *Crooke* of *Studley,* was, as 'tis said, married to her, by M^r. *Rich. Houghton,* A.M. and chaplain of *Queen*'s Coll. & D^r. Halton's Curate at *Iffley* . . . When this matter began to be discours'd of in *Oxon,* and nois'd abroad, D^r. *Finche*'s Friends made him utterly disown ye Marriage, as some think, contrary to his own Inclinations. Upon this the matter was brought into ye Vice-Chancellor's Court : M^r. Houghton, 50 partly out of fear of incurring D^r. Halton's Displeasure, & partly for some other Reasons, best known to himself, shuffled in ye Court, & would not own y^t D^r. *Finch* repeated the words after him; and D^r. Bourchier, the Judge of ye Court, being influenc'd by My L^d. *Nottingham*, &, as some think, some Guineas, the power whereof he is not proof against, adjudg'd the matter in favour of D^r. Finch, & so the matter was drop't, tho' wth this *Proviso* that D^r. Finch should allow her some consideration, wch accordingly, as I am told, he did. — ... The *History of Imbalming* done by M^r. *Tho. Greenhill*, Surgeon, is a very trite Book, not done with any Judgm^t or Learning, & the Author does not seem to have understood *Latin*. He makes *Judæus Apella* an author. — Remember y^t *Sil. Gyraldus* in his Life of *Ovid*, in his Book *de Poëtis* has something ab^t ye Death of *Livy* observing y^t *Ovid* and he died ye same day. — D^r. *Kennett* in his Life of M^r. *Somner* observes y^t himself was ye first who took notice y^t *Cooper's Lexicon* was taken from y^e *French* one of *Charles Stevens*. But D^r. *Mill* tells me that this thought D^r. *Kennett* had from him.

Nov. 1 (Fri.). *Vossius de Mathesi* l. 3. c. 56. § 4. has a laudable Account of *Will. Grisaunt* of *Merton* Coll. He writ *de quadratura circuli*. Ib. l. 3. cap. 52. § 7. *Simon Bredon* or *Biridon*, of *Merton* Coll. He writ *Arithmetice Theorica*. Ib. § 4. *John Killingworth Anglus*. Ib. § 3. S^t. *Aldhelm*. He writ of *Arithmetick*. — The Epitome of *Livy* wanting in ye MSS. of *Oxon.* all but in *New* Col. — Of *Osbern* Monck of *Durham* see *Voss. de Natura Artium sive Mathesi* cap. 59. lib. 3. §. 8. *Robertus* sive *Rupertus Holketh Anglus* born at *Northampton* and professor of Div. at Oxon. see in ye same work. *Nic. Linnensis* see *ibidem.* — The Master of *University* College's whole Income when D^r. *Hudson* was *Burser* in the year 1699 of ye College was 110-10-4, not reckoning his Lodgings, a Load of Hay & other Perquisites. — Ask M^r. *Dodwell* whether he rec^d any Letter from M^r. *Clarke* in Answer to his of the 22^d of *May* last.

Oct. 28. H. to Dr. T. Smith. Anxious to see Montfaucon, and Mabillon's Supplement. Dr. Bathurst's coins included only fifteen not already in the Library. Queries about Wm. Baxter, *Charta Authentica*, and Brocklesby (see *Postman* &c.). Dr. Potter cannot find a publisher for Clemens Alex. Mr. Penton, sometime Principal, lately dead in Yorkshire; also Dr. Ch. Finch, Fellow of All Souls. Notes on Walter de Millemet Clericus' *Liber de Nobilitatibus*, &c., a MS. in the hands of the Dean of Christ Church. Have the two vols. of Inscriptions yet come out ? Literary notes.

Nov. 2. Wm. Offley (The Star and Garter near Bocardo), **to H.** Sends presentation copies of Anacreon from Mr. Barnes, and will take back any books to him. **Dr. T. Smith to H.** Condemns premature criticisms on Montfaucon and Mabillon, 'as if France were now become another Galilee, out of which no good thing could come.' Wishes that some one would publish a commentary &c. on coins in Bodley. 'Monsr Leibnits, in his last letter to mee, writes that the late Andreas Morellus, a Swisse of Berne, a man famous for this sort of study, had before hee dyed, collected in ichthyococea or such like usual matter the icons of above 24,000 medalls, wch hee had lookt over in France, Holland, & Germany : a good part of wch are now engraving by the noble munificence of the Count of Schwarzenburg, who entertained him in his Court as Keeper of his Rarities.' Sends a list of 20–30 copper coins which he is willing to present to Bodley. Wishes that Mr. Baxter could be enabled to print his Glossary (see *Phil. Trans.*) entire. Mr. Burton's MSS. are in Viscount

Nov. 3 (Sun.). *Ebodus Anglus,* familiaris *Augustino* 1°. *Cantuar.* Episc. See Voss. *de Nat. Artium. Finnanus Lindisfarnensis.* ibid. *Aldhelmus Anglus* ib. *S. Wilfridus Ripponensis.* ib. — This day was chosen Fellow of *All Soul's* Coll. M[r]. *Harrison* A.M. of *Glouc.* Hall in room of D[r]. *Finch.* This M[r]. *Harrison* is a very good Scholar, as is generally said; but tho' he had stood several times before yet he could not get the Warden to admitt him, he being more regardfull of Interest & good Eating & Drinking than scholarship. Nor had Mr. *H.* come in now, had not the matter been cry'd out about, much to ye Disgrace of ye Warden, who thereupon began to have some sense. — *Rob. Brograve* A.M. of *Magd.* Hall has publish'd one or more Sermons. I think he was Chaplain to K. *W[m]*. (*Quære*). — M[r]. *Bromley* (*W[m]*) M.A. of *X[t] Church* now one of the Burgesses in Parl. for ye university of *Oxon* (wch office he has perform'd several times, much to ye Content of ye University) is an Honest worthy Gentleman, & has some travells going under his Name printed twice, the last Impression done knavishly as I have before told you. — *Tho. Brooke* A.M. of *Magd.* Hall, was *Terræ filius,* and came off wth pretty good Applause. He was a great Fat, corpulent Fellow. — *Edw. Brown* of *Merton* Coll. D.M. He has writ Travells, a Book wch bears a good character. — *Guil. Bottoner* sive *Buttoner.* see *Voss. de Nat. Art.* Rich. *Lavingham* another Ancient *English* writer. see *ib.* *Hemoaldus* cognomento *Providus,* another. see *ib.* *John Estwoode* of *Ashenden,* near *Oxon.* see *ibid.* — *Rob. Burscough* A.M. of *Queen's* now Archdeacon of *Tottnes,* succeeding D[r]. *Atterbury,* has publish'd some Discourses ag[t] y[e] Dissenters. — *Bury Arth.* of *Exeter* Coll. where he was Rector. I have mention'd him before. He was ejected, & why see the Controversy as printed by *James Harrington* of *X[t] Church.* Besides his *Naked Gospel* he has printed several other Books, as *Latitudinarius orthodoxus, The constant communicant,* pr. at *Oxon. &c.* He is still living, & one of y[e] *Portionists* of *Bampton in the Bush* near *Oxon.* — D[r]. *Rich. Busby* of *X[t] Church,* Head Master of *Westminster* schoole. He was the best y[t] ever was in y[t] place, & great was y[e] Number of Scholars bred up by him. As he was a most Excell[t] scholar, so he was a very [1] good

---

Weymouth's Library. The publisher of the *Charta Authentica* is Mr. Innes, Rector or Praepositus of the Scotch College of Secular Priests in Paris, to which it was presented by Archbishop James Beaton, nephew of Cardinal B. Lord Cromarty printed it in his *Vindication of Robert III* (Edinb. 4to, 1695), and dedicated it to the King, which he explained to mean, 'which you please.' Dr. Potter's Clemens Alex. should be printed by the University, or by the Churchills. Dr. Finch. Mr. Brocklesby in his *Explication of the Gospel Theism* discovers himself a downright Socinian. Was More the author of the Latin oration? Does not believe it is so very Ciceronian. Suggests that Dodwell should write a book of *Retractations.* Glad to hear that the Bishop of Worcester has written a defence of the *jus divinum* of Episcopacy. The two volumes of Inscriptions have been delayed by the want of a qualified person to adjust the several Indices, which cost Jos. Scaliger ten months of hard labour, &c.; the person engaged complaining that Halma did not allow him enough to keep him in tobacco.

---

[1] Yet a Complyer & a time server, & a great Humourist & not very good at Composition, & of much less Judgment than M[r]. Camden.

man. He is buried in *Westminster Abbey*, and he has a noble Epitaph upon him. See some things of him in D^{r}. *Kennett*'s Book ab^{t} *Augmentation of Poor Vicaridges*. He has two *Greek Grammars*, one in Prose & another in verse, the latter suppos'd to be made by his scholars & revis'd by him. — D^{r}. *Seth Bushell* (D. of Div.) has a sermon or more out. *Quære*. — . . D^{r}. *Carsewell* of *Exeter* Coll. now vicar of *Bray*, an old rich, stingy, turn-coat D^{r}. & hated in his parish, has printed two sermons, one whereof contradicts the other. I have mention'd him before, & you may see something of him in reference to his character in *Tho. Brown*'s Dialogue between *David Jones, Edw. Hickeringhall* & *Will. Prynne*'s *Ghost*. — *Tho. Cartwright* D.D. of *Queen*'s Coll. afterwards Dean of *Rippon*, then by ye Favour of K. *James* II. made B^{p}. of *Chester*, & one of the Commissioners, & one who came down to turn out the Fellows of *Magd.* Coll. He has publish'd some Sermons.

Nov. 4 (Mon.). When M^{r}. *Chishull* at S^{t}. *Peter*'s Church reflected upon the B^{p}. of *Worcester* it was observ'd that he said (among other things) that some men's Learning in Chronology dwindled into Prophesy.

Nov. 5 (Tu.). D^{r}. *Mill* tells me y^{t} when the Revolution began he frequently talk'd with M^{r}. *Dodwell* about the Oath of Allegiance, & y^{t} M^{r}. *Dodwell* said he would take the oath & submitt to the Governm^{t} if K. *James* should die before him; wch the D^{r}. thinks he would have done, had it not been for D^{r}. *Hickes &c.* But this I believe to be nothing but talk,[1] & of y^{e} D$^{r's}$ own raising. But *quære?*

Nov. 6 (Wed.). A good *Testimonium* of *Livy* in the *Prolegomena* of *Goclenius*'s *Problemata Grammatica*. . . . *Eutropius* lib. 9. voc. *bacchandi* Voss. de Vitijs Sermonis (pag. 58. l. 1. c. 3. Ed. Fol.).

Nov. 7 (Th.). *John Caswell*, [2] *Quære* whether not originally of *Trinity*-Coll. He was of *Wadham* Coll. where he took his Deg. of *A.M.* & afterwards became Vice-Principal of *Hart*-Hall, wch place he left & afterwards taught *Mathematicks* in the Town privately to Young Gentlemen, & at length was made *Superior* Beadle of Divinity in room of M^{r}. *Violet*, who was formerly of S^{t}. *John*'s, & had a son Fellow of y^{e}

Nov. 4. Dodwell to H. *Preliminary Defence* in the press. Dr. Whitby might have waited for it. Good wishes and advice for Livy. 'My angry Adversary James Gronovius's Epistles relate, as I remember to matters Geographical.' Would be glad if Dr. Hudson could retrieve any of that most learned work against Apion, which is not extant in Greek.

Nov. 5. E. Smith to H. Sends information concerning Begerus' edition of L. Florus, gathered from Mr. Mortier 'ye Topping For. Bookseller,' and Sloane 'a very man in editions;' Begerus was a dully heavy person, and is now dead, leaving only one vol. published out of four. Message from Dr. Thomas Smith about Burton's *Brit. Rom.* Promises to get subscriptions and some notes for Livy. Dr. Kennett's performance. Hymn to the Tack. The Duke of Ormond supported Dr. Lancaster as V. C. against a person of contrary principles, to which the Queen answered that 'she might expect to be trusted with a V. C. since she trusted him with a Kingdom.'

---

[1] Tis certainly false. [2] No.

same College, & a Daughter who by chance snap'd a Gentleman Commoner of ye same College (I think his Name was *Curwin quære?*) of a considerable Estate. The said Mr. *Caswell* has published a short Discourse of *Trigonometry* in Dr. *Wallis's* Works, & some things in ye *Philosophical Transactions.* He is an Hippish Man, & of Low Church as to Principles. — One of ye *Caves* of *Lincoln* Coll. publish'd some Sermons. See in the *Term Catalogues.* — *John Cawley* D.D. of *All-Souls* now Minister of *Henley,* & *Archdeacon* of Lincoln. He married when old a Woman out of ye Exchange. He has published a Discourse in ye Civil Law, the Title whereof see in *Bodley's* Catalogue, & is reckon'd, deservedly, 10 a man of Principles. — *Tho. Clerke* of *Queen's* Schoole-Master of *Widehope* or *Withope* near *Cockermouth* in *Cumberland.* He taught Dr. *Hudson* his *Abcedarium.* He was afterwards of *Queen's* Coll. where he became Fellow, & then Parson of *Sparshalt* in *Berks,* where he died.

Nov. 8 (Fri.). This being the 8th of *November,* was a Visitation, as usual, of the Publick Library. No new orders made at this time either for printing the *Appendix* to ye Catalogue, augmenting the 2d Library-Keeper's Salary, or Visitation of ye Coyns, only something propos'd towards Visiting the Bp. of *Lincoln's,* Dr. *Marshal's* & some other Books, wch were never yet visited. The speech was made by Mr. *Rich.* 20 *Newton* Student of Xt *Church.* 'Twas long & particular in the History of Sr. *Thomas Bodley.* No one else mentioned in it but Dr. *Morrice,* (who was Donor of the Money for the Speech), Dr. *Altham* the *Regis* Professor of *Hebrew* (who it seems had desir'd Mr. *Newton* not to speak any thing in his Speech of him, & therefore wt he said was extremely modest) & Dr. *Hudson* the present Library Keeper: of all whom he spoke very decently; wthout so much as the least mention of Archbp. *Laud,* Mr. *Selden,* Bp. *Barlow,* Dr. *Marshall* or other Benefactors. Not any Accession made to the Register for ye whole last year.

Nov. 9 (Sat.). Dr. *Hudson* tells me yt *Victorius's* Edition of *Tully* in 30 *Fol.* (wch is very scarce, & hardly to be met wth) was printed in two Vols. at *Florence,* & yt *Robt.* or else *Charles Stephens's* Edition was printed from it. *Quære.* I think *Victorius* rather came out at *Venice* in 4 vols. — *Edw. Clarke* M.A. of *University* Coll. afterwards Schoole Master of *Wakefield* in *Yorkeshire,* wch place he discharg'd much to his Reputation, and bred several good scholars, such as Dr. *Potter,* Mr. *Ibbetson,* & others, who were sent thence to *University* Coll. some of wch became Pupills to Dr. *Hudson.* He was afterwards (or at ye same time. *Quære,*) Lecturer of ye Church at *Wakefield,* and by ye Interest of Dr. *Sharpe,* Archbp of *Yorke,* he was made Minister of ye Great Church of St. *Marie's* in *Not-* 40

Nov. 9. H. to Dr. T. Smith. Will be glad to receive his gift of coins for the Library. Col. Codrington will probably give his study, about 12,000 vols., 'of wch some scarce, but ye greatest part Riff-Raff;' Dr. Mill is the same way inclined. No prospect of printing a Catalogue of our coins, or the Appendix to Hyde's Catalogue, in which Dr. Hudson proposes to involve it and have the whole printed over. Yesterday was the Visitation: speech by Mr. Rich. Newton, Ch. Ch., in praise of Bodley, Morris, Altham, and Hudson (last year's man by Mr. Foulkes). Wishes to collect and publish Inscriptions of Berks; also that Dodwell would write a book of Retractations. Chishull on D. and the Bp. of Worcester; when his Sermon on the latter was preached H. was sick of a fever, but he said that 'some men's learning dwindles into

tingham, where he is now.   He has printed one Sermon on yᵉ Death of
K. *Wᵐ.* as I take it.   *Quære?* — *John Cocke* A.M. of *Queen's* (whereof
he was Fellow) one of those who honestly and conscientiously voted for
Dʳ. *Hudson* to be Fellow of yᵗ House.   He was a very good, popular
Preacher, & supply'd the Cure at *Newbury* for some time: by wᶜʰ means
he got the Living of *Thatcham* near *Newbury,* where he now lives wᵗʰ
very good Reputation, discharging yᵉ Duty of a faithfull Pastor.   Upon
his Promotion to this Living *Tim. Halton* & his Gang of Fellows were so
unkind to him as to deny him some common Privileges, wᶜʰ were never
10 deny'd to those who went off to College Livings : but most of those
barbarous Fellows are gone to answer for it in another World, wᶜʰ they
had little regard to in this. — *Rob. Cocks* A.M. of *Bras. Nose* Coll. &
Fellow, afterwards D. Div. & preferr'd to a good College Living not
far from *Chippingnorton* (quaere).   He was always a lewd impudent
Fellow . . . Yet for all this, old *Fulks* yᵉ Apothecary let him have one of
his Daughters, an handsome, virtuous Woman.   Add to this, that he was
one of those Rascally People in *Oxon* who were for discarding King
James and receiving *Dutch William.* — *Wᵐ. Cole* D.M. of *Gloucester* Hall.
Quære whether yᵉ same wᵗʰ him who has publish'd several Books in his
20 Faculty. — Dʳ. *Hen. Compton* first Bᴾ. of *Oxon,* afterwards Bᴾ. of *London.*
Quære whether not Canon & Dean of Xᵗ Church.   He was originally
Noble-Man of *Queen's* Coll.   He liv'd in great Credit & Esteem both
wᵗʰ yᵉ Citizens of *London,* & yᵉ Clergy of yᵗ Diocess 'till yᵉ *Revolution.*
Just upon this he pretended to conduct yᵉ Princess *Ann,* afterwards
Queen of *England,* & to secure her, as was falsly given out, from being
trapann'd by King *James.*   He came into *Oxon* with her with a great
Number of Attendants, he riding at yᵉ Head of them in a blew Cloak,
wᵗʰ a naked Sword.   For this Treachery to King *James,* to whom and
his Brother he ow'd many Obligations, he was afterwards justly requited
30 by yᵉ *Williamites,* who turn'd him by from being Archbᴾ. of *Canterb.*
the desire of wᶜʰ tis thought might make him renounce his Principles of
Loyalty.   This Defeat so disgusted him that he chang'd sides again, &
would passe now for a zealous Asserter of yᵉ Rᵗˢ of the Church &
Crown.   It has been observ'd of him yᵗ he took more care to prefer
French and *Scotch* Men than yᵉ Honest Clergy of yᵉ Church of *England,*
and moreover that he never did any thing towards the Promoting of
Learning or any other Good Work in yᵉ University of *Oxon.*   He has
printed some small things of wᶜʰ hereafter. — *Wᵐ. Coward* D. of *Phys.*

---

prophecy and chronology.' Milles accused of plagiarism. Williams' transcripts
unsatisfactory; he has been paid 13/6 for + 13 sheets, but expects more.
E. Smith to H. Sends a copy of Lat. verses made in Germany upon the
old woman in London that bequeathed £200 to Prince Eugene. Hopes to
get 10 or 12 subscribers to Livy.   **Barnes to H.** Literary and University gossip. ' Our Men want Courage, & suffer yᵐselves to be banter'd of both
Worlds by too much regard of yˢ, thô yʳ Declining renders yᵐ useless to yʳ
Friends & ridiculous to yʳ Enemys. . .' ' I hope [Dr. Hudson] forgets not his
own Proposal of *Lyra Davidica.* I have set my heart upon it, have done many
Psalms & find I have a *Genius* for it. . . . Mrs. Barnes I left in Health, but a
perfect *Oxonian,* as indeed she was before she knew me. *She never before
believ'd any excell. but in* Oxf. : & now she is more confirm'd yⁿ ever.'

and Fellow of *Merton* Coll. (*Quære* whether originally of this Coll. ?) When he was Batch. Fellow he was reckon'd a good Scholar, & translated M^r. *Dryden's Absalom & Achitophel* into *Latin* Verse : some part of wch was likewise translated by D^r. *Francis Atterbury* when he was a young Student of *X^t Church.* Afterwards this *Coward*, upon (or before) being made D^r. of Phys. writ some tract in Physick, I think in 8v^o. *Quære.* At his leaving ye University I think he began to practise Physick at *Northampton*, wch place he was oblig'd to leave upon Acc^t of some Criminal Commerce wth some Woman. He lives now somewhere in the Diocesse of *Norwich* & has writ some Heterodox Books, about the 10 Nature of ye Soul, one of wch against M^r. *Dodwell*, as I have before told you. — *Tho. Creech* of *Wadham* Coll. afterwards Fellow of *All Souls.* When he was of *Wadham*, being chamber Fellow of *Hump. Hody*, he was an extreme Hard Student. When Bach. of Arts he was Collector, & making a Speech as is usuall for ye Collectors to do he came off wth great Applause, wch gain'd him great Reputation : wch was shortly after highly rais'd by his incomparable translation into English Verse of *Lucretius.* (But *Quære* whether this Translation was not before his being Bach. of Arts.) Afterwards he translated into *English Theocritus*, & as tis said was put upon translating *Horace* by M^r. *Dryden*, wch last 20 did not answer the expectation the world had of him. He has also translated some Lives of *Plutarch*, & something of *Virgil* in the collection of Miscellany Poëms. He was an Excell^t scholar in all parts of Learning, especially in Divinity, & was for his Merits made Fellow of *All-Souls.* He put out an Edition of *Lucretius* in *Latin* wth very good Notes and a Paraphrase, wch he dedicated to his good Friend *Christoph. Coddrington* then of *All-Souls*, of whom hereafter. For all these his Deserts he was not regarded by ye Publick, & those who have ye Disposal of Preferm^t : wch wrought very much upon his Natural melancholly, &, as those who knew him most intimately believ'd, heighten'd it to y^t 30 degree, as to make him put an End to his own Life, wch was a great Prejudice to ye Common-Wealth of Learning, he being then upon an Edition of *Justin Martyr*, wch no doubt he would have done admirably well, & the world might have had a great many more excellent things from him if it had been worthy of them. — *Nath. Crew* of *Linc.* College, Nobleman, afterwards Fellow & Rector, B^p. of *Oxon*, & then preferr'd to ye rich B^pprick of *Durham* : wch he has enjoy'd a great many years, together (for some time) wth a temporal Estate left him by ye Lord *Crew.* In King *James's* Reign he was one of y^e *Ecclesiastical Commissioners*, wch was an Office y^t was very invidious, tho' perhaps the 40 Commissioners went no farther than ye Laws of ye Land, & yeir Duty to ye King would justify. Upon ye Revolution he was threaten'd by King *W^m.* & his Rascally Adherents, & to gratify 'em was oblig'd to dispose of his Preferm^ts to such as they recommended. When he was under a Cloud & in some Disgrace D^r. *Hudson*, that he might do the B^p. some Honour as well as gratefully commemorate B^p. *Shirlaw* the Founder of ye D^r's Fellowship, dedicated the first Volume of his *Gr. Geographers* to him : for wch he was no more consider'd by y^t B^p. than by ye others that he has dedicated to. I can say no more of this B^p. than y^t in complyance wth ye Fashion of ye Age he is a *digamist.* — 50

Tho. Crosthwait Fellow of *Queen*'s Coll. & Proctor of yᵉ University, was yᵉ Person to whom Dʳ. *Hudson* was recommended; but he then just leaving off taking Pupils, put him to Mʳ. *Wᵐ. Rooke* then Senior Taberder & afterwards Fellow of yᵉ said College, who was a good Mathematician & an acute Disputant & well vers'd in humane Literature: whose care and kindness yᵉ Doctor has always very gratefully acknowledg'd. The said Dʳ. *Crosthwait*, when Senior Fellow, had yᵉ Principality of *Edm.* Hall conferr'd on him upon Mʳ. *Penton*'s leaving it, wᶜʰ he would have held wᵗʰ his Fellowship; but *Tim. Halton*, taking the advantage
10 of his not subscribing in such time as yᵉ Law requir'd, he lost this Place: yet was reelected by a majority of yᵉ Fellows: but yᵉ sᵈ *Halton* having an Interest wᵗʰ yᵉ Vice-Chancellor he was never admitted again; but Dʳ. *Mill* put into his Place. Dʳ. *Crosthwait* being a sound Divine & a man of good Principles would not comply with yᵉ Government upon yᵉ Revolution, & so was turn'd out of his Fellowship by Dʳ. *Halton*: after wᶜʰ the Dʳ. liv'd (as he does now) very contentedly in a small Hereditary Estate yᵗ he has in yᵉ North. He was always a very good Friend of Dʳ. *Hudson*'s and was a main Instrument in bringing him in Fellow of *University* College, wᶜʰ he effected chiefly by yᵉ Interest yᵗ one Mʳ. *John*
20 *Crosse* had wᵗʰ Mʳ. *Ob. Walker.* Wᶜʰ Mʳ. *Crosse* was originally an Apothecary in *Oxon*, a man of good Principles & great Loyalty, as is evident from the Honest Church of *England* Men's meeting in his House for yᵉ sake of performing Religious offices before yᵉ Restauration. This Mʳ. *Crosse* was one of Bᵖ. *Fell*'s executors, and upon his Death he left an hundred libˢ. for an Anniversary Speech in praise of yᵉ said Bᵖ, & converted all his Estate wᶜʰ lay in *Bedfordshire* into an *Hospital.* — *Quære* whether Dʳ. *Wake* in his Answer to the Bᵖ. of *Meaux*, printed Sᵗ. *Xtome*'s Epistle *ad Cæsarium Monachum juxta Exemplar Bigotianum?*

Nov. 11 (Mon.). In *Le Clerck*'s *Bibliothèque Choisie* Vol. 9. p. 187.
30 is a Letter in *Latin*, the Author whereof calls himself *C. Veratius Philellen.* 'Tis chiefly against *Gronovius* (*Jac.*) whose ignorance & Impudence he has neatly expos'd. 'Tis dated from *Oxon. Idib. Jan.* 1706. I have look'd it over, & it seems to be *Le Clerck*'s own, both by yᵉ style, & yᵉ Vindication of a Passage of his in his *Ars Critica* from the Insults of *Gronovius.*

Nov. 12 (Tu.).... Recueil des Antiquitez et singularitez de la ville de Rouen. par F. N. Taillepied. In it several things relating to *English* History.

Nov. 13 (Wed.). In cap. 9. of *Dickenson*'s *Delphi Phœn.* are two or three pretty stories, worth notice of *Ventriloqui*, or *those that speak in their bellies &c.* & put cheats upon the world, particularly of one at *Oxon an.*
40 1643, commonly call'd *the King's Whisperer*, & of one who got by that means a pretty woman to be his wife, who had been at yᵉ same time married to another, & her Husband then living. — On *Satturday last* (*Nov.* 9.) died Dʳ. *Pet. Mews*, Bᵖ. of *Winchester*, an old Honest Cavalier, & formerly Head of Sᵗ. *John*'s in *Oxon*, & Vice-chancellor of that University. He married his Predecessor's (of Sᵗ. *John*'s) Daughter, &

Nov. 11. Mary Cherry to H. Her brother is very ill, 'but we have yᵉ best advice, wᶜʰ wᵗʰ gods blessing I hope he will survive.' He gives his best service to his namesake and chum.

was afterwards B^p. of *Bath & Wells*, whence translated to *Winchester*. Of him more hereafter.

Nov. 14 (Th.). In *Sheringham's* Discourse *de orig. Anglor.* p. 54 *Festus* and *Plutarch* illustrated. This Book to be nicely look'd over by the Editor of *Tacitus*. Also Verstegan's *Restitution of decay'd Intelligence*, whom *Sheringham* often confutes. — M^r. *Rich. Smallbrooke* of *Magd. Coll.* has just printed his Sermon ag^t M^r. *Dodwell*, to wch he has prefix'd a Preface of two Pages. He uses Mr. *Dodwell* with great Civility: & he has ye Character in ye University of a man of Parts, tho' some in ye college say he is but a Block-head.

Nov. 16 (Sat.). There is come out a Letter to M^r. *Dodwell* vindicating him from the Attacks of M^r. *Clerk* about ye Soul. (The Author M^r. Collins [1], who has since writ 2 others.) — Also, a Book call'd *Chronicon pretiosum*, giving an Account of our *English* Coyns as to their value in several Ages, the Design of wch is to keep M^r. *Worth* in his Fellowship of *All-Souls*, wch in justice and according to ye Letter of the Statutes he ought to leave on Account of the Archdeaconry of *Worcester* conferr'd on him which is rated more in the Queen's Books than is consistent wth his Oath, tho' to avoid this the Author (whoever he be, some say D^r. *Fleetwood* [2]) has endeavoured to shew (but as far as I can yet perceive very knavishly and weakly) that he ought to keep both because his Archdeaconry is not so much as requir'd by ye Statute, provided the value of money be conferr'd as 'twas at y^t time when ye Statutes were made : But of this Book more hereafter, & it may be of the Author, & ye Issue of the Matter. D^r. *Mill* of opinion that M^r. *Worth* ought to keep his Fellowship being mov'd to think so from the weak fallacious reasons here offer'd. The Author in ye Preface shews himself to be ignorant of our Coyns in several Respects, & not to know y^t formerly Payments were made in kine not *specie*.

Nov. 17 (Sun.). About King *Alfred's* translating into y^e *Saxon* Language the *Molmutian* & *Martian* Laws, see *Sheringham de Anglor. orig.* p. 125. — *Lycophron* illustrated there, pag. 163. *Quære* whether D^r. *Potter* ever consulted the Place? — Remember to ask *Jos. Barnes* about M^r. *Goad*, & his character, upon whom he made an elegy, & whether w^t *Ant. à Wood* has said of him be in every respect true? — Quaere ab^t .. verses said to be made upon the L^d. Windsor.... —

Nov. 16. Dr. T. Smith to H. Dissatisfied with the transcripts, which he has been accustomed to get done in London for 12^d. a sheet by a person with a knowledge of Latin. Unwilling to send the coins by carrier. The Lives printed in Holland [Amsterdam]. Dissatisfied with Dutch printing—chiefly for their mangling and leaving out paragraphs unagreeable and distasteful to the goust and palate of the Dutch and French Presbyterians there; partly because of the horrible and scandalous misprints, of which he will compile a list. Remarks on Gudius' sale; Hearne's Appendix to the Catalogue; Dr. Morris and his benefaction; inscriptions of Berks; the vacant bishopric of Winchester (hopes G. B. will not be the man); Mr. Milles.

---

[1] This Collins the Person who was chief Author of y^t most notorious vile Book call'd *The R^{ts} of the Christian Church*. M^r. *Dodwell* has declined all conversation with him.

[2] He is really Author.

King *Charles* II, Duke of *York*, Duke of *Monmouth*, Earl of *Roch.* *Laurendine*[1] & *Frazier* (the King's Physitian) being in company my L[d]. *Rochester* upon the King's Request made y[e] following verses.

Here's [2]*Monmouth* the witty,   But as for y[o] rest,
[3]*Laurendine* the Pritty,   [5]Take *York* for a jest,
And [4]*Frazier* the great Physitian.   [6]And your self for a great Politician.

The L[d]. *Rochester*'s verses upon the King on occasion of His Majesty's saying he would leave everyone to his Liberty in talking when Himself was in company, & would not take w[t] was said, at all amiss, viz.

10   We have a pritty witty King,   He never said a foolish thing,
      And whose word no man relies on: And never did a wise one.

☞ These verses were put in one of the windows of the Room. (*Quære.*) . . .

Nov. 19 (Tu.). In *Queen*'s College Library is an old *Greek* MS[t]. (as D[r]. *Hudson* tells me) containing the *Psalms*, given by D[r]. *Todd*. At y[e] beginning a *memorandum* by some one y[t] he thought it to be transcr[i]bed from the *Alexandrian* Copy; w[ch] D[r]. *Hudson* much doubts. — *Quære* about B[p]. *Fell*'s Brothers? I am told y[t] a younger Brother of his died of a Consumption in X[t] *Church*, & y[t] he was found dead in his Study 20 upon his Knees in a Praying Posture. — D[r]. *Browne* order'd to stand in ye Pillory for his Letter to Secretary *Harley*[7]; & M[r]. *Ward* for some Reflections on y[e] Queen in *Hudibras Redivivus*. . . .

Nov. 20 (Wed.). On *Sunday* last (17th Inst.) about 3 clock in y[e] Afternoon died my very dear Friend M[r]. *Thomas Cherry*, A.M. of *Edm.* Hall, to y[e] Great Grief of all y[t] knew him, being a Gentleman of great Beauty, singular Modesty, of wonderfull good Nature & most Excellent Principles. He was also studious, a lover of Learning, & Learned Men, & had he lived some years longer (he being now little above 23 Years of Age) he would, in all probability, have proved a considerable En- 30 courager of them, an ornam[t] to y[e] Church, (he being newly enter'd into Holy Orders,) &, as he always was, been a farther Comfort to y[e] writer of these Matters, with whom his Memory will be ever precious, he being one of the very best Friends he had in y[e] World.

Nov. 22 (Fri.). 8[o]. F. *Linc.* 42. p. 55. a Piece of *Crenius* in w[ch] some things ab[t] Languages that will be of use to M[r]. *Llhuyd*, also pag.

Nov. 19. F. Cherry to H. Announces the death of his cousin T. Cherry on Sunday last at 3 p.m. **E. Smith to H.** Presses for letter, specimens of Livy, &c. M. Du Soul and his Lucian; his remarks on Dod- well's letter on *Philopatris*. A son of Brigadier Hastings is publishing Mar- cel's Chronological Tables, and desires to have Dodwell's corrections, and name on the title-page.
Nov. 21. R. Trumbull (Witney) **to H.** There is no need for any of Mr. T. Cherry's friends to provide a substitute.

---

[1] Quere.   [2] *Monmouth*, a half witted man.   [3] He was a deformed person.
[4] A mean Empty Physitian.   [5] He would not take a jest.
[6] This well said of the King who was negligent & careless, tho' otherwise a Man of very strong Parts.   [7] Quære.

225. an Epistle of *Boxhornius*. *Pliny*'s Epistles corrected there pag. 188. & 205 & 147. — *Quære* whether W^m. *Lamplugh*, of whom see *Linc.* 8°. F. 42. p. 70, was an *Oxon* man? He is not I think mention'd by *Ant. à Wood*. The person who mentions him, one *Hayne*, was an *Oxon* man. — Remember to tell M^r. *Dodwell* of this passage in Joan. *Sperlingen's Dissertatio de principijs nobiscum natis*, (printed at *Witteb*. 1657. 8°) pag. 48. . . The said Book of *Kesler's* I never yet saw. — On *Wednesday* (20th Inst.) died of an Apoplexy S^r. W^m. *Cowper* Father to ye present Lord Keeper.

Nov. 23 (Sat.). D^r.*Mill* tells me he has Information y^t the B^p. of *London* and B^p. of *Exeter* decline ye B^{pp}rick of *Winch*. & y^t ye B^p. of 10 *Sarum* does not appear at Court, y^t it may not be said he makes Interest for it : by wch it should seem he stands fairest. — . . . Ask *Jos. Barnes* whether he has look'd over *Casp. Bartholinus de Pygmæis. Hufniæ*. 1628. 8°. . . .

Nov. 26 (Tu.). A *Poëm* in *English* come out call'd *Oxon.* being in praise of ye University. The Author M^r. *Tickle*, A.B. and Taberder of *Queen's*. — I have seen in D^r.*Hudson's* Study a quarto Book in *MS^t.* writ by M^r. *Meurer*, formerly a student in ye Publick Library, but expell'd for Knavery. In this Book several things about Libraries, but he speaks very dishonourably of the *English* Libraries, & says that ye 20 *English* are very industrious in magnifying their own Excellencies. He also there insinuates that D^r.*Hyde's* Catalogue is full of Faults, & y^t 'twas drawn up by another Person, as it certainly was, viz. by M^r. Emanuel Prichard. — *Aristides's* Epistle to *Marcus Antoninus* in MS. Baroc. 68. This M^r. *Ibbetson* should have printed or at lea[s]t collated in his Edition of *Antoninus*. *Quære*.

Nov. 28 (Th.). *Memorand.* the Warden of *All-Souls* when D^r. *Hicks's Thesaurus* was brought to him for ye Coll. sent only 3 Guineas, whereas other Colleges gave 5 for them, to ye D^r. & the Provost of *Oriel* refus'd y^t sent to him for ye Coll. quite. Such Encouragers are 30 these two Brothers (in Eating & Drinking) of Learning.

Nov. 29 (Fri.). [Notes from Pighius' Eutropius and Voss. *de Vitiis Serm.*]

Dec. 1 (Sun.). S^r. W^m. *Cowper* did not die 'till last *Tuesday* 26 *Nov.*

Nov. 23. H. to F. Cherry. Condolences on the death of T. Cherry. Has secured what he left in Oxford, including ' a new Pudding-sleeve Crape Gown.' His debts amount to £15 8*s*. 11*d*. and his substitute should be paid 10*s*. a Sunday. **H. to Dr. T. Smith.** Death of T. Cherry. Disappointment with Williams. The *Chronicon Pretiosum* (? by Fleetwood). Other Oxford notes and news.

Nov. 24. R. Trumbull to H. Arrangements for a new curate. His agreement with Mr. Cherry was for £20 *per annum* and his board.

Nov. 26. Dodwell to H. Sends four copies of his new book. ' Since Mr. Chishull's volley of ill words and ill nature, God has been pleased to raise up the zeal of unknown Friends in my defense.' Expects the publication of H.'s Livy will raise him new storms from Gronovius.

Nov. 30. Dr. T. Smith to H. Condolence on death of T. Cherry. God has a controversy with this Church and nation for their horrible defections. Mr. Smalbroke's sermon : Dodwell's book to be censured by Convocation, and burnt. Dr. Fleetwood a better Antiquary and Historian than Casuist. The *Lives* at the binder's ; has been busy with errata &c.

Dec. 1. Trumbull to H. Satisfied with Mr. Nicholson as a Curate, if

His Estate of 2000 *libs. per an.* fallen to his son L^d. Keeper. His Father was a true Friend of ye Church of *England* & was at ye charge of a monument for the Excell^t M^r. *Hooker* Author of *Eccl. Polity.* This S^r. *W^m.* Buried *Saturday* last (30 *Nov.*) in S^t. Peter's *Cornhill* Church. — M^r. *X^oph. Wase* when of *Cambridge* was characteriz'd by M^r. *Pearson* afterwards B^p., to be ye best scholar in y^t university. His schoolmaster also at *Eaton* put him upon a speech when y^e *Spanish* Ambassadour came thither, wch being done admirably well, the Embassadour went away very much pleased, & ye Master told him y^t he was the best

10 scholar of his Age in *Europe.* Had he been kept at *Cambridge* he would have prov'd a Prodigy; but they neglecting him he retir'd into ye Country & afterwards he became a great Drinker, & growing idle, shorten'd his Dayes.

Dec. 4 (Wed.). M^r. *Thomas Cherry* (mention'd above pag. 96) was buried on *Wednesday* the 20th of *Nov.* at S^t. *Andrew*'s Church in *Holborn,* in a vault y^t runs under ye Church, tho' the Entrance be in ye Church-Yard. He was very decently interr'd, being carried in a Hearse, & the Company in Mourning Coaches. The Rooms were very handsomely set out wth black sconces *&c.* proper for such occasions. The Pall was 20 bore up by six Divines, four of wch had been Members formerly of *Edm.* Hall.

Dec. 5 (Th.). The Earl of *Sunderland* is made one of ye Principal Secretaries of State in room of S^r. *Charles Hedges* remov'd. — In pag. 64 of *Haymo*'s Ecclesiastical History a large Quotation out of *Ignatius*'s *Epp. to ye Romans,* which considerably differs from *Vossius*'s Edition. — I hear D^r. *Potter* is to answer *The Rts. of ye Xtian Church,* said to be done by D^r. *Tyndale. Quære?* — *White Kennett,* son of *Basil Kennett,*

---

the difficulty of residence can be arranged. Thanks for loan of Dodwell. Business matters.

Dec. 2. E. Gardner to H. T. Cherry insisted on preaching at St. Clement Danes the day after he was fallen ill, and was thrown into a fever by a ride to Uxbridge. He was buried at St. Andrew's, Holborn; particulars of the funeral. Note on *Chron. Pretiosum.* Enquiries about Mr. Kent. **Dodwell to H.** 'I am sorry the designed edition of Lucian is in no greater forwardness. And more that the Authority of a buffoon (if *Philopatris* had really been Lucian's) should be reckoned on for an Argument by any Divine. But it is the peculiar unhappiness of our Age, that jeasts are taken for Arguments in affairs of the most serious importance.' The Chronological Tables may be sent. Remarks on the Bishop of Worcester, to be communicated to him. **H. to Barnes.** Thanks for presentation copies of *Anacreon Christianus.* Suspects that Veratius Philellen is Le Clerc himself. *Tittle* [Tickell] has written a poem in English called *Oxford.* Asks for an account of Mr. John Goad.

Dec. 4. H. to F. Cherry. Mr. Hayes has entered his son at C. C. C., 'than w^ch, I think, he could not have pick'd out a better in ye whole University.' Has engaged Mr. Trumbull to send 26s. 'I am sorry to hear that [Mr. Dodwell's] *Epist. Discourse* is like to have so severe a sentence pass'd on it by ye Approaching Convocation, & y^t (as I am made believe) 'twill be burnt publickly.'

Dec. 5. Kent to H. Regret at Cherry's death. Sends one subscription, and hopes to get others. **Dr. T. Smith to H.** Has given [Matthews] the carrier a presentation copy of the Lives for Hearne.

a *Kentish* Divine, was enter'd of *Edm.* Hall, & sometimes waited on Dr. *Wallis* to Church with his skarlett, & wt other offices of a menial servt he might do for him I cannot tell. (*Quære.*) When Back. of Arts, (I think) he translated *Pliny's* Panegyrick, to wch he prefix'd a high flown Preface agreeable to ye Loyalty of yt time. When Master of Arts he was preferr'd to *Amersden* by Sr. Wm. *Glyn,* who patroniz'd the said first Performance of his. He became Vice-Principal of *Edm.* Hall, & all ye while he continu'd there pass'd for a High-Church-Man : Otherwise he had not had ye Rectory of *Shottesbrooke* in Berks conferr'd on him by Mr. *Cherry.* A year or two after ye Revolution he went to London, & by ye Interest of Mr. *Brewster* he became Minister of *Aldgate* in ye *Minories.* Here by Degrees he chang'd his old Principles, wch he first discover'd by his writing a Book about *Convocations* against Dr. *Atterbury* whom 'tis said he would have defended if ye Dr. had not put some little slight upon him. He was furnish'd with ye chief Materials for this Book by Dr. *Hutten* of *Aynhoe* in *Northamptonshire,* from whom he has likewise had abundance of other things relating to ye *English* Antiquities, Dr. *Hutten* communicating to him all his *collections.* For this Book of *Convocations* 'tis suppos'd he was preferr'd to ye Archdeaconry of *Huntingdon* : wch so encourag'd him in his *Renegadoe* Actions yt he preach'd a most virulent sermon against ye Blessed Martyr King *Charles* 1st on ye xxxth of *Jan.* wch he printed. And to compleat ye character he has since yt writ a folio volume of the History of *England,* wch is a continuation of the Collection lately publish'd, containing *Milton, Daniel &c.* as I have hinted before. And it may be here observ'd yt *Milton's* History being ye first & Dr. *Kennett's* the last in this work, Dr. *Kennett* seems to have *Milton's* very Principles transfus'd into him, he being as barbarous to ye Memories of King *Charles* II & King *James* as *Milton* was to K. *Charles* Ist. He makes ye world believe yt he will do great Matters in ye Antient church History of *England* ; but wtsoever he knows of these Matters is onely ye Gleanings of Dr. *Hutten.* Dr. *Kennett* has writ some other Books besides these mention'd as ye Life of Mr. *Somner,* the *Parochial Antiquities of Amersden,* & some other Sermons. He was when of *Oxon.* one of the Pro-Proctors, in wch office I do not remember anything very remarkable of him. — *Basil Kennett* his Brother originally likewise of *Edm.* Hall, & from thence elected scholar of *Corpus Xti,* where he studied hard & improved himself by his great Industry. He translated several Books, as ye greatest part of *Puffendorf of yt Law of Nature,* & others ; & writ the *Roman* Antiquities, &c. He is Fellow of his College, & this year went as Chaplain to ye Merchants trading at *Legherne.* Just upon his going thither he printed a Book of Divine Poëms. — Dr. *Hilliard* Fellow of *Corpus Xti* printed a sermon about ye obligation of Oaths in King *James's* Time, & afterwards in ye Reign of King Wm. printed a Pamphlett about Schism. We might have expected other things from him, had he not put an end to his own Life. — Mr. *Tilly* originally of *Wadham* & afterwards of *Corpus,* where he is now Fellow. He has printed two or three Sermons. — Mr. *Mather* of the same College, Fellow, a *Northumberland*[1] man, I think. He has a sermon in print preach'd before ye

---

[1] He was born at Manchester.

university of *Oxon.* at S^t. *Marye's*. — M^r. *Chishull* another Author & lately Fellow of ye same College. He printed a sermon preach'd when he was a Candidate for ye chaplainship to ye Factory at *Smyrna:* wch Factory he attended for about 5 years, & then return'd into *England.* A little after this by ye Interest of some Merchants he got to be Lecturer of the Church in *Crutched Fryers, London;* & then betaking himself to a wife quitted his Fellowship. A little after this he writ & printed a Book against M^r. *Dodwell,* as I have told you above.

Dec. 9 (Mon.). The Salary to ye Officers of the Publick Library not
10 paid this year 'till to-day, tho' S^r. *Tho. Bodley* expresses that 'tis to be paid at farthest 33 days after *Lady Day* and *Michaelmass.* — The Donor of D^r. *Wallis's* Picture in the Gallery of the Publick Library not yet enter'd into ye Benefactor's Book, nor Cardinal *Howard's,* Lord *Abbingdon's,* Duke of *Ormond's, Butler's* (Author of *Hudibras*) & some others. — The Lower House of Convocation have presented a Congratulatory Address to her Majesty, in wch they declare to her Majesty y^t they do not think ye Church in *Danger;* to wch Passage all agreed but two. — L^d. *Godolphin* made an Earl by ye Title of *Oxford.*

Dec. 12 (Th.). Yesterday S^r. *John Walters* chosen Burgess in Par-
20 liam^t for ye City of *Oxon.* in room of M^r. *Norris* deceas'd. Oppos'd by one *Carter* a Brewer's son, & a Councellor, a man of half wit, & a conceited Whigg. None appear'd for him, but some poor sculking Fellows. — Just publish'd M^r. *Dodwell's Preliminary Defence* of his *Epistolary Discourse* about ye Distinction of Soul & Spirit.

Dec. 13 (Fri.). [Scandalous anecdote of Sir *Edw. Hungerford.*] . . . *Fregenae* to be read for Tregellae in l. 2. c. 6. of *Vell. Paterculus.* Not taken nótice of by D^r. *Hudson.* See *Sigonius's* Notes upon *Epit.* 19. of *Livy.*

Dec. 14 (Sat.). D^r. Smith in his Life of Archb^p. *Usher* p. 82. says y^t
30 he some years since Epitomis'd the Archb^p's *Disq. de Lydiana sive Proconsulari Asia,* wch is involv'd in the Archb^p's Life in *English* by *Par,* & here inserted in *Latin.*

Dec. 15 (Sun.). The Preface to *Ant. à Wood's Hist. & Antiq. Univers.*

Dec. 7. H. to Dr. T. Smith. Sends a different reading of the inscription in *Phil. Trans.* 302. Llhuyd's book goes on slowly. Tickell's *Oxford.* Asks for an opinion on the extract from Ignatius *Ad Romanos* in Haymo's *Eccl. Hist.* (ed. Boxhornius). Meurer (in MS.) on English libraries; attributes Hyde's Catalogue to another person [Prichard]. Was Wm. Lamplugh an Oxford Man? Potter is to answer Tindal.

Dec. 9. Dr. T. Smith to H. Sends a presentation copy of the *Lives* for the Bishop of Worcester.

Dec. 14. Dr. T. Smith to H. The Hetruscan inscription. Since the examination (three or four years since) of the Abbate Fabretti's papers, nothing has been done, and he fears 'the old Thuscan language [is] utterly lost and irretrievable. But perchance posterity may be more lucky than the present age.' Haymo's *Hist. Eccles. Breviarium,* and the citation from St. Ignatius' Epistle to the Romans; Haymo unknown to Usher and Pearson. Proposes to edit the *Acts of the Martyrdom of St. Ignatius.* Meurer an ill man. What is the opinion in Oxford of Hadrianus Relandus' *Dissert. Miscellaneae*?

Dec. 15. Trumbull to H. Glad the coin was acceptable; sends 8 more

Oxon. was penn'd by M^r. *Fulman* of *Corpus X^{ti} Coll.* — In *Capellus's Historia Sacra & Profana.* p. 279. is a *memorand.* that 10 is to be read for 20 in 4 cap. l. 20. of *Justin,* in ye story of *Pythagoras.* This to be added to ye Note there out of *Simpson's* Chron. — M^r. *Smalbroke* preach'd on *Saturday* last *Dec.* 14. a Sermon in *Latin* at S^t. *Marie's* for his Bach. of Divinity's Degree ag^t M^r. *Dodwell's* Account of *Episcopacy* as laid down in his *Parænesis.*

Dec. 18 (Wed.). *Petrarch* writ ye Life of *Scipio Africanus.* To be consulted for *Livy.* A large Extract out of *Justin* in *Hendreich's Carthag. Resp.* p. 14. — M^r. *Ralph Trumbull* Rector of *Witney* near *Oxon* sent me 10 a Coyn of *Julia Mammæa,* of Silver, the Description whereof follows, viz. IVLIA MAMAEA AVG. Juliæ Mammææ Caput. Rev. VENVS VICTRIX. Venus stans dextra pomum, sin. hastam, ad pedes scutum. This was found in ye Ruins of an old House in ye Town, where I have been told others have been found: wch shews that this Place was of Note in ye time of y^e *Romans,* a thing not taken notice of by M^r. *Camden* or D^r. *Plot,* who tells us nothing else of it's Antiquity but y^t 'twas of some Account before ye Conquest, being given to *Winchester* by one of ye B^ps. of that See. — Testamentum *Joh. Dee* Philosophi summi ad Joh. Gwyn. 1568. See *Bartholin.* de Medicis Poëtis. — 20

The Present Lord *Wharton's* Grace, whilst his Father was living.

I prithee good Lord take old *Wharton* away,
That y° young Lord *Wharton* may come in his Place:

To drink & to whore & play a 100 tricks more,
With a damn'd Fanatical Face.

Dec. 22 (Sun.). Last Week the Censors of *Christ Church* going out of their Office, as usual, treated the Students and others in the Common room; at wch time M^r. *Adams* & some of the rest happening, as is common amongst Friends, to talk of the Whiggs, & Dissenters, M^r. *Marshall* related to ye B^p. of *Worcester* by his Ladie's side, & *Ben.* 30 *Woodroff,* & perhaps one or two more interposed in behalf of the Whiggs, wch so exasperated M^r. *Adams,* who is an Honest, ingenious, man, y^t he gave some unbecoming Language in respect of ye B^p. of *Worcester,* & with some others voted *Marshall* out of ye common-room. The next

---

dug up at Sennington (Glo.). Wishes to borrow Lesley's *Short Method with the Jews.* Sends 26*s.*

Dec. 17. **E. Smith to H.** Lord Somers is searching for the Begerus. Asks for specimens of Livy for self and Dr. Welwood. Literary gossip. ' Sir Joh. Floyer [is printing] an Invention of a Pulse-Watch wch being nicely set and adjusted to a Man's Constitution tels him when his Blood & that is out of order.' Gifts to the Duke of Marlborough. Sends a copy of a paper which came over lately from Flanders; it was found in a coffin dug up just as they were going to bury an Officer & stuck in ye Hand of ye deceasd, (a document in French, dated Gent, May 29, 1650, promising on behalf of the Society of Jesus to protect Maistre Hyppolite Beam from the infernal Powers, &c.).

Dec. 19. **F. Cherry to H.** Depends on seeing H. in the holidays.

Dec. 21. **H. to Dr. T. Smith.** Mightily satisfied with the Lives. Wishes he may see Smith's edition of the Acts of Ignatius. Mentions the coin of Julia Mammaea discovered at Witney, and those from Sevenhampton or Sennington. Possibly a Roman Fort at the latter.

day this was carried to his Lordship, who desired satisfaction, & would have prosecuted the matter so far as to have obtain'd a Visitation, had not *Adams* begg'd his L^dship's Pardon : wch it seems was easily granted, & so ye thing was dropp'd. . .

Dec. 23 (Mon.). Happening to talk with *Milles* of *X^t Ch.* this morning, he rail'd mightily ag^t M^r. *Dodwell,* & was very confident y^t there was no such Distinction in the Fathers as M^r. *Dodwell* has given about ye Soul's being a Principle *Naturally* mortal but *actually* immortaliz'd by ye Divine Spirit, & said y^t 'twas foolish and ridiculous for
10 M^r. *Dodwell* to give such a one. He withall positively said y^t M^r. *Dodwell* was all along mistaken. Such is the Vanity of this poor Pretender to Learning. — . . See in *Gutherius de vet. Jure Pontificio* next leaf to ye Title Page a Curious Figure of *Rome.* See also pag. 12. *Instrumenta Pontificalia* &c. P. 38. *Typus Simpuli.* p. 41. *Lituus* &c. p. 45. *Sella Curulis.* Look over ye whole Booke.

Dec. 24 (Tu.). The secret Causes of Abundance of Particulars in History are not known to the World ; for Instance in S^r. *Walter Rawleigh,* who was put to Death for things done 20 Years before. 'Tis said the true Reason thereof was his putting a Cast-off Mistress to the Earl
20 of *Salisbury,* & then bragging of it. This comes from D^r. *Eaton,* who had it from one *Bond,* who was a Dependent on the Ld Chancellor *Egerton.*

Dec. 25 (Wed.). On *Thursday* last the Lord Mayor of London's Feast was kept, at wch were present divers Great Persons, & 'twas manag'd with an Exact Regularity. The D. of *Marlborough* sate on the right hand of ye Lord Mayor in the Middle of an Oval Table, & the L^d. High-Treasurer on his Left & ye rest of the Great Men according to their Degrees & Places. The Queen, Prince, Emperour, Duke of *Savoy,* & the other Princes Allyes Healths were drank, & when the Lord Mayor offer'd to begin that of the Duke of *Marl-*
30 *borough,* his Grace rose up twice at table, & would not permitt it 'till that of Prince *Eugene* was drank. His Grace, & the rest of the Great Men as soon as dinner was over (which was about 8 aClock) took Coach & return'd to Court. The Claret that was drank cost 1s. 6d. per Bottle, & the Musick cost 50 libs.

— M^r. *Evans (John)* of S^t. *John's* (the same whome I have taken notice of before in one of these Volumes for his Thanksgiving Sermon at S^t. *Marie's*) having lately very scurvily abus'd the President of S^t. *John's* & the rest of the Society in a speech he made, as usual, upon quitting his Deanery in the College, they have turn'd him out of his Chaplainship in the College on that Account, & will proceed to other
40 Punishment, if he does not behave himself more circumspectly for the future.

Dec. 24. H. to F. Cherry. Is detained by his book in the press; 'besides the Waters are out here and the Ways so bad that I cannot think the Journey would be very pleasant to one who is so bad a Horseman as I am.' Mr. Dodwell's reply seems to him to be 'clearly managed,' but Mr. Milles is confident that he is in an egregious error. Sends a list of T. Cherry's books [44] left in Oxford. The Witney coin. Compliments of the season.
[N. d. (but about Christmas).] **Joshua Barnes to H.** Which Dr. Bayly is dead? Madam Pen. Dashwood's verses. Sorry for loss of Mr. Cherry. Wishes to have Homer printed at Oxford. Livy. *Chron. Pret.* 'Dr. *John Goad, of John Baptist, Oxf.* a Loyal Good Churchman, in

Dec. 27 (Fri.). 'Tis said y^t *Trelawny*, B^p. of *Exeter*, who puts in for ye B^{pp}rick of *Winch.* is an illiterate, mean, silly, trifling, & impertinent Fellow. — When D^r. *Maunder* went out of his Vice-Chancellor's office, 'tis certain he left six hundred & odd pounds in the university chest at *Corpus Christi* : & 'tis observable, that D^r. *de Laune*, who was Vice-Chancellor for four years successively after him, (who at his Entrance upon that office took out all that money) put in only three hundred & odd pounds at the End of his fourth year : which to all the university seems very strange. For he had near so much paid to him, being an old Arrear from the Crowne : wch D^r. *Hudson* first discover'd & put him 10 in a way how to get it. 'Tis likewise very remarkable that the said D^r. *De Laune*, (who was term'd *Gallio*, because he car'd for nothing that made for the Interest of the university,) never gave up any Accounts about the Press, the Incomes of which must have been considerable by reason of my Lord *Clarendon's* Book, the two Hundred Pounds annual Rent paid by the Stationers, Archb^p. *Sheldon's* Settlement upon the Press and Theatre & other Things. And our Curators, of whom 'tis observ'd that *nihil curant præter cutem,* are so mealy mouth'd as to say nothing about it. *Oh tempora ! oh mores !*

Dec. 28 (Sat.). M^r. *Steph. Penton* was buried in his Parsonage Church 20 of *Wath* in *Yorkshire* just under one of ye Walls. I am told y^t he made an Inscription himself to be put on the Wall, much to this purpose : Here lyeth *Stephen Penton*, Rector of this Parish, who tho' dead, yet liveth : And that he order'd some Sentences out of Scripture (which he pitch'd upon) to be put under. He is succeeded in his Prebend of *Rippon* by *Cuthbert Chambers*, originally Commoner of *Edm.* Hall, of which House he became *A.M.* and from thence he was elected Fellow of *Magd.* Coll. where he now is, & perhaps for his Honesty may deserve it : tho' as to his Learning I cannot say much. — I have been told that M^r. *Philip Ayres* of S^t. *John's*, whom I have mention'd before, 30 was a Traveller with M^r. *Drake* a Gentleman of large Estate, but a debauch'd, loose Person, & that M^r. *Ayres* was not much better, in his Younger Dayes (whatever he may be now). When M^r. *Drake* died M^r. *Ayres* became Governour to his Son, who is now a Gentleman Commoner of S^t. *John's*, & has a good Estate notwithstanding the Extravagance of his Father. This *Ayres* (who in company appears a most civil, courteous Person) has publish'd a Book of Verses, & calls himself Esqr. *Quære ?*

Dec. 30 (Mon.). 4°. *Jur. Seld.* is *Articles du Traicte faict en l'annee mil six cens quatre, entre Henri le Grand Roy de France, & de Navarre, et* 40

Oliver's Dayes had a place near *Oxf.* where he read *Common Prayer* constantly all ye time of ye Rebellion, except once, or it may be twice, when his Friends begd, in a manner forced him, to be absent. Turn'd out of *Merchant-Taylors'* by Whigs in K. *Ch* : 2 dayes, under pretence of [Popery] ; suppos^d of ye Greek Church. A very Charitable Man, sending in his Prosperity to all Prisoners &c. wch made him so low, when turn'd out. A great *Grammarian,* Divine, Astronomer, and Judicial *Astrologer.* Mrs. *Barnes* has long since given me leave to see y^t *my University,* next summer, nay, while she lives &c.' Messages. Adds Greek verses, 'Extempore 1704, when I had no prospect for Anacreon, . . . but met with envy &c.'

Sultan Amat Empereur des Turcs. Par. 1615. Two or three Pages
from the beginning is a MS*t*. Letter pasted in of M*r*. *Greaves's* in *English*
to some learned Person who desir'd his Opinion about a Passage in this
Book. I suppose to M*r*. *Selden.* There is also inserted M*r*. *Greaves's*
Resolution, being his Translation, verbatim of the Passage.

Dec. 31 (Tu.). This day being a General Thanksgiving for the last
years success M*r*. *Pearson* of *Queen's* preach'd before the University at
S*t*. *Marie's* upon *Exod.* xviii. 8, 9, 10, 11. In it he extoll'd the Duke
of *Marlborough*, upon which some D*rs*. smil'd, particularly D*r*. *Charlett.*
10 Which D*r*. *Mill* took notice of, & mention'd it afterwards with some
indignation, not knowing that his Friend the B*p*. of *Worcester* did the
like. — D*r*. *Mill* tells me y*t* when B*p*. *Fell* was about publishing *Origen's*
Discourse of *Prayer*, he advis'd his Lordship to put a *Latin* Translation
to it : which His Lordship confess'd would be proper, but said he could
not tell who to imploy in it. The D*r*. offer'd him his service, & advis'd
him to imploy D*r*. *Aldrich*, D*r*. *Isham* & one or two more. Which
accordingly the B*p*. did, & so the Translation was finish'd by them. —
M*r*. *Selden* in his Discourse *de Successionibus in bona defuncti* &c.
c. xxiii has some things relating to the *Testamenta of the xii Patriarchs*;
20 which D*r*. *Grabe* seems not to have knowne, when he publish'd them in
his *Spic. Patrum.* — . . . Temple of Solomon to be look'd over by
D*r*. *Hudson.* The Author *Sam. Lee.* — Pag. 107. of *Boecler's* Diss. Acad.
an Elogium of *Livy.* — M*r*. *Tho : Hind* A.M. of *Linc.* College has just
publish'd in 8*vo*. The 1*st* Vol. of *The History of Greece.* He designs
another Vol. — M*r*. *Jer. Collier* has publish'd Proposals for an *Ecclesiastical History of England*, from the first Plantation of the Gospel in
these Parts to the Present time. He is *impar negotio*, being not a person
of Diligence, or Genius to search Records, *&c.* & so y*e* World must
expect nothing curious from him ; but what will please Novices, they
30 may look for an affected stile, & things put into a formal Dress [1].

Jan. 6 (Mon.), 1707. A letter of *Ludolph Kuster's* to D*r*. Hudson [dated
Amstelodami, d. 17. *Decemb.* St. N. 1706. (pp. 143–161.) — *Memorandum.* That
in the next Years *Mercurius Oxoniensis* the noted men of Oxford who have
died lately be given an account of. — *Vossius* in voc. *cataphractus* . . . About
y*e* Virgin brought to *Scipio* see *Aul. Gellius* l. 6. c. 8.

Jan. 9 (Th.). On *Tuesday* 7 Instant M*r*. *Worth's* Fellowship of *AllSoul's* was declar'd void by the Warden, (his year of Grace being up)

Jan. 2, 1707. Dr. T. Smith to H. Censures Dodwell's book. Hopes
Dr. Potter is qualified to answer *Rights of the Christian Church.* The Life of
Laud should be written in Latin. P.S. Jan. 4. Directions about the
copper coins, which he has handed in a purse to the V.C.

Jan. 6. H. to Dr. T. Smith. Wishes with all his heart that Dodwell
had employed his pen upon another subject. Does not expect any encouragement in his way of study. Great feud lately in Ch. Ch. upon the last year's
Censors relinquishing their office. Notes and Queries. Extract from Lat.
letter to Dr. Hudson from Kuster, acknowledging some transcriptions by H.
for his new ed. of Iamblichus' Life of Pythagoras. K. will next give us a noble
ed. of Aristophanes, having been prevented some years ago by Milles.

---

[1] The work is since published, & is good.

upon Account of his Archdeaconry of *Worcester*. He designs to go tomorrow Morning to *London* to appeal to the Archbishop.

[Note on Livy from *Aul. Gellius* l. vii. c. 18.]

Some coyns [5] found at Cirencester. ...

Jan. 11 (Sat.). *Joan. Fabricius,* Amoenitat. Theol. pag. 668. in Notis ad Orationem de Utilitate Itineris Italiæ [on the tomb of Livy at Padua]. ... — In cod. Bar. 87. containing amongst other things of that kind *Aristotle's* Organon is the Picture of *Joan. Argyropylus,* who after yᵉ taking of *Constantinople* by the *Turks,* went into *Italy,* where he was entertain'd by *Cosmus Mediceus,* and afterwards he taught *Greek* at *Rome.* He is pictur'd here sitting in a teaching posture, with a Book before him, pointing at yᵉ words with his Left-Hand. Dʳ. *Humph. Hody* has caus'd *Burghers* to draw it, with a design to have it ingrav'd, to be inserted in his *History of the Greek Tongue,* now, it seems, almost ready for the Press. — In the Preface to Bᵖ. *Stillingfleet's Discourse concerning the Idolatry practised in the church of Rome,* are these words—*And his* (i. e. Bᵖ. *Jewell's*) *Works ought to be looked on with a higher Esteem than any other private person being commanded to be placed in Churches to be read by the People. Quære* what Authority Bᵖ. *Stillingfleet* had to say this?

Jan. 14 (Tu.). When Mʳ. *Berger,* the Professor of *Wittemberg,* was in Town, of whom mention before, he apply'd himself for a MSᵗ. of *Aristides* in *New-College* to Mʳ. *Ayliffe,* who offer'd him the Use of his chamber, with a Key to go in & out when he pleas'd; but told him he could not, by reason of his oath & the Statutes of yᵉ College let him have it out, & that by lending formerly a curious *Tully* in MSᵗ. it was irrecoverably lost. Mʳ. *Berger* seem'd concern'd at this, and amongst other words said he never met with so much Rudeness and Incivility in any Place as at *Oxon. Quære* whether really any *Tully* was lost out of the Library, & if so whether *Gronovius* had not the use of it?

Jan. 15 (Wed.). Mʳ. *Milles* of *Xᵗ Church* according to his usual Impudence, has abus'd the Dean by calling him an *Haughty, insolent, Ecclesiastick.* —

[Notes on Livy from *Joan. Albertus Faber* in Decade Decadum, *Rapini* Comparatio Homeri & Virgilij, and *Vell. Paterculus.*]

Jan. 18 (Sat.). The following Coyns [27 in Number] given to the Publick Library by Dʳ. *Thomas Smith,* formerly Fellow of *Magd.* Coll. [175–187.] ...

The Bᵖ. of *Sarum* in his Vindication pag. 57. 58. — I can assure the World, that in the List of the Divines who were represented as wishing that the (then) Prince (of Orange) would engage in our Defence, the late Dean of Worcester (Dʳ. *Hickes*) was named for one, how truly, he

---

Jan. 13. Pat. Gordon to H. Hopes to take his degree before Michaelmas. Why publish Livy in 8vo. instead of folio? Asks for address of Mr. Joseph Smith, late Proctor, &c.

Jan. 18. H. to Dr. T. Smith. Thanks for the 27 coins and the guinea; will enter all Dr. Smith's donations in the Great Register. Particulars of five coins dug up lately at Cirencester, shown him by Mr. Wase, Fellow of C.C.C.; 'Mr. Wase the Father has been propos'd by several as extraordinary well qualify'd for translating the Earl of Clarendon's *History of the Rebellion* into Latin, if he were living.' Dr. Hody is printing his collections towards a *History*

best knows. Pag. **91**. ibid.—He (id est D^r. *Hicks*) makes him to be a Venter of Lies and false Stories. He may as well say he was a *Low, Lean, Black Man, that he had a sour Frowardness in his Look, and an Air of Malice spread over his whole Countenance, and look'd like Envy itself*; as we know some (amongst which he means D^r. *Hicks*) do.

[Books to be consulted for emendations of Authors]. . . .

Jan. 19 (Sun.). *Posterius volumen* . . read for *liber II^{dus}*, out of ye MS^t, at ye Beginning of the second Book of *Vellejus Paterculus*. See the Various Readings in the *Oxon* Edition. This may serve to explain
10 *Livy's volumen.* — Ad Plin. l. iv. ep. xi. consider the Note upon *nocens ducta est.*—Look into Heraldus, 4to. T. 4. Th. There are several things about *Livy.*

Jan. 20 (Mon.). Talking this night with D^r. *Mill* about D^r. *Todd's* Design of Printing the Antiquities of *Cumberland*, in *Latin*, he seem'd to slight the whole Design, & spoke but very indifferently of the Inscriptions which D^r. *Todd* has collected in a great number. Which I do not much wonder at, D^r. *Mill* being but a very indifferent Judge in this Part of Learning (however considerable in what he professes) & I formerly heard him rail much against *Inscriptions & Coyns* in general,
20 tho' at the same time he could not but acknowledge several of them to be of great use.

Jan. 21 (Tu.). This Morning died D^r. *Humph. Hody* Greek Professor & Archdeacon of *Oxon*. D^r. *Mill* immediately writ that M^r. *Goodwin* (commonly call'd D^r. *Goodwin*, he is a quack D^r.) might be made Archdeacon, for which he is unqualify'd as being much such another as *Tho. Milles*, having no manner of Learning, & being a confident, vain Fellow. *Humphry Hody* was a Man of great Industry, good natural Parts, and a great Memory: but had but little Judgment: however he was very usefull, and generally was for carrying on things of Learning. Under
30 his Picture was formerly put—*sed carmin major imago*; upon Account he never made but one Distich of Verses, printed in the Oxon verses on King *William's* Victories in *Ireland*, which are very intricate & dull.

---

of the Greek Tongue. Dr. Charlett transmits enclosed list of learned men for Smith to select from for writing their Lives. **Dr. T. Smith to H.** 'I earnestly entreat you to consult your owne convenience in all *time coming*, in the Scotch phrase to wch wee must learne to accoustome ourselves against the time of the compleated union' (which he denounces). Urges H. to devote himself to Roman antiquities; 'for I am satisfied that you have a powerful genius for these studies, which I would have you pursue and cultivate at your leisure hours.' Dr. Woodward's shield was bought of a brasier for £7 or £8. Dissatisfied with the specimen of Collier's *Eccl. Hist.* Kennett well qualified to write *Fasti Britannici.* Küster an extraordinarily learned man. The publisher of Sandford 'an able herald.' Was your Mr. Perkes author of 'A New Quadratrix to the Hyperbola ' in *Phil. Trans.* 306 ?
Jan. 21. H. to Barnes. Hody is dead ; wishes that Barnes might succeed him and carry on his book. Asks for a bibliography of B., towards a 3rd vol. of the *Athenae.* Repeats his opinion of Milles. The MS. of Walter de Millemet. Asks for notice of any discovery of coins, towards an Appendix to Camden's *Britannia.*

Jan. 22 (Wed.). *Fl. Sheppard's* Epitaph upon himself.

O vos, qui de salute vestra securi estis, | Orate pro anima | Miserrimi Pecca-
toris *Fleet: Sheppard* | Etiamnum viventis, & ubicunque est peccantis, | Qui fide
exigua, & tamen spe impudentissima | Optat & exspectat, quam non meruit |
Felicem Resurrectionem. | Anno religionis & libertatis nostræ restitutæ tertio |
Rerum potientibus | Fortissimo *Wilhelmo,* & formosissima *Maria.* |

Tho. Brown's Epitaph on him occasion'd by's Reading the former. . . .
Lord *Dorset* to his Mistress on the Countess of Manchester. . . .

Jan. 24 (Fri.). Last night, (*Thursday*) between 9 and 10 of the Clock,
Dr. *Hody* was buried in the Chapell of *Wadham* College, to which Place 10
he has given all he had (he dying very rich) upon the Decease (as 'tis sd)
of his Widow Mrs. *Edith Daniell.* He had a Design of Altering his Will,
and when his Physitians had declar'd that they thought he could not
recover, he sent Mr. *Dodwell* the Lawyer in all hast to *Monks-Risborough*
in *Bucks*, of which place he was Rector, to bring it up to *Oxon,* & pray'd
heartily that he might live 'till his Return : but he died before Mr. *Dodwell* could come back. Besides the Rectory he was Archdeacon of *Oxon,*
& had a good Estate.   But inquire more about this. — I have been told
since the writing of what goes before that what is there said about Dr.
Hody's altering his *Will* is false : That the *Will* was wholly written by 20
his own Hand, That by it he has left all the Books to the *Bodlejan*
Library there wanting which are in his Study, that he has left an hundred
Pounds to the Parish of Odcomb in *Somerset*-Shire where he was born,
100 Pounds to *Monks-Risborough,* and 100 *libs.* more to the Parish he
had before.   That his widow is to have 100 *libs. per an.* during Life, &
afterwards to Revert to *Wadham*-College, to which Place he has given the
Remaining Part of his Books with what he had else (except 10 libs. apiece
to two Brothers, one whereof was A. M. of *Wadham* College, of which
House also the other was, who it seems by this are both Living) for 10
Exhibitioners who are to study the *Hebrew* and *Greek* Tongues, and are to 30
be examin'd & nominated by the two Professors of each in the University :
which Professors are to have a reasonable Gratuity for their Pains.
Memorandum.   That Wadham Coll. has refus'd this Benefaction for this
reason, that they find they shall be loosers by it, upon account of trouble,
&c. — . . . *John Cudworth* A.M. & Bach. of Div. & Fellow of *Trinity* Coll.
printed a Sermon preach'd at St. *Marie's* in *Latin.* (*Quære* whether he
did not print something else ?) He was suspected as inclining to Popery
in the Time of K. *James* : but most People believ'd 'twas a Calumny
thrown upon him by some of the Fellows of the same college, such as
Arthur Charlett, &c.   He left the College, & had a Living given him at 40

Jan. 23. Kent to H. Has bought books recommended by Hearne.
E. Smith to H. Sends Dr. Sloane's copy of Begerus. Enclosed is Toland's
Essay proving that Livy was not superstitious. ' I firmly believe him [Toland]
to be a man of Rel. & of ye Faith of ye church of Engd. He intends to expose
ye Presbyterians if they will not send in their answr abt Toleration.' He is
to be made Keeper of the Paper Office at £400 a year. ' As to his Principles of
State (wch are truly wiggish) no body here makes distinction in general conversation.'   Hickes and Potter are preparing answers to *The Rights of the Church.*
' Ye Bp of Kilmore was saying at Table yesterday yt we are like to have a great
convert come over to ye Ch. ye E. of Cardigan.'

[1] *Kiddlington* (I think, *Quære?*) where he taught a private Schoole, &
afterwards was prevail'd with to accept the Free Schoole of *Warwick*,
which he left in a little time, & return'd to his old Place & Imployment
where he now lives. — *Will. Davenant* of S[t]. *Mary*-Hall[2] translated a
Book out of *French* call'd *Reflections on Historians*. — S[r]. *Jon. Dawes*
originally Fellow of S[t]. *John*'s Coll. in *Oxon,* which he left upon Account
of an Estate & *Baronett*'s Title devolving upon him. After which he was
chosen Master of *Catherine* Hall in *Cambridge*, & made Dean of *Bocking*
in *Essex.* He is reckon'd a plausible Preacher & has some Sermons in
10 print. — *William De Laune* first Fellow of S[t]. *John*'s coll. then made
Chaplain to *Mews* Bishop of *Winchester,* who gave him a good Living in
Hampshire, which he quitted upon his being Elected President of S[t].*John*'s :
which place he did not obtain without great opposition from his competitor D[r]. *Torriano.* He has printed a Sermon preach'd on the 30th of
January before the House of Commons. He was four years Vice-Chancellor during which time, (being term'd by Honest men *Gallio*) he let all
the discipline of the university go down, and imbezzel'd all the Treasury
of the university, there being a thousand Pounds left in the Chest by his
Predecessor D[r]. *Mander,* which he took out a little after his Entrance
20 upon his Office, and when he left it only put in three hundred and odd
Pounds : which sum was paid him by the Treasurer of *England,* being
an old Arrear to the University, which was first discover'd to him by D[r].
Hudson, who at the same time had a promise from him (which he never
regarded) that it should be apply'd to the Publick Library. It is to be
observ'd that in His Vice-chancellorship, there were a great many Impressions of *Clarendon,* which should have brought good Sums of Money
to the University : so that one should have thought, that with this extraordinary Income, the common Revenus of the university, two Hundred
pounds *per annum* from the Stationers, & a hundred or two Hundred a
30 year belonging to the Theatre, there should have been a considerable
Sum of Money in the Treasury of the University. Moreover it is to be
observ'd, That whereas the Stationers were oblig'd by their lease to take
off 200 Copies of any Book printed at the university's Expense, when
they renew'd their Lease he let them alter that clause, making it run thus,
That they should take off 200 Copies provided they (viz. *Stationers*)
approved of it before it went to the Press. — . . *Jonathan Edwards* of
Jesus College, Fellow and afterwards Principal. A man of good Note for
Honesty, Integrity and Learning. He has writ *A Preservative against
Socinianism* in four Parts, a Pamphlett against D[r]. *Sherlock* about the
40 Trinity, another against B[p]. *Burnet* about an Article in his *Exposition of
the Articles of the church of England.* — *Nath. Ellyson* Fellow of *Corpus
X[ti]* College. Born at *New-Castle,* or thereabouts. He is D[r]. of Divinity.
His first Preferment out of the university was an Archdeaconry. (*Quære?*)
Afterwards he was made Vicar of *New-Castle,* and sometime after had a
good Living given him by the Bishop of .*Durham,* from whom he expects
a Prebend. He has printed a Sermon preach'd at *New-Castle.* Perhaps
he has printed more? *Quære? — Quære* whether M[r]. *Sampson Estwick* of

---

[1] It was Kiddlington by Woodstock, as M[r]. Wood tells us in the 2[d] Ed., but 'tis a
Mistake in Wood for Kiddington.
[2] [*Magdalen hall, P. B.*]

Xt. ch. and . . . . *Entwickle* of *Brasen-nose* have printed any thing? — *Robert Eyre* of *New*-coll. afterwards made Fellow of *Winchester*, has printed a Sermon preach'd at the *Assizes* held there. — *Leopold William Finch* Dᵣ. of Divinity, a younger Son to the Earl of *Winchelsea*. *Quære* whether I have not mention'd him before? — *Joseph Fisher* A.M. and Fellow of *Queen*'s Coll. was from his first Entrance a very severe Student, & was afterwards taken notice of for his being a good Divine, well skill'd in the *Oriental Languages*, and if Bᵖ. *Fell* had liv'd, who had a great Kindness for him, had been set upon some considerable Work, for which he was well qualify'd. This Bishop dying, & none regarding him, or hardly any one else for their Learning afterwards, upon this Account he accepted of a Colledge Living at *Brough under Stainmore* in Westmorland, which was given the college by their Founder *Robert Egglesfield*, where betaking himself to a Wife, who prov'd none of the best, he pin'd away in Grief and Melancholly, & was mightily lamented by all that knew him, particularly by Dᵣ. *Hudson*, who had his Vote when he was turn'd by a Fellowship of *Queen*'s. He has printed a Sermon, preach'd at the wedding of one of his Pupils. — *Quære* whether Dᵣ. *Fitz Williams* of *Magd.* college has printed anything? — Sᵣ. *John Floyer* Dᵣ. of Physick of *Queen*'s College has written several Books in his Faculty, which he practises at *Lichfield*. — *Edw. Fowler* of *Corpus* Xᵗⁱ College, now Bᵖ. of *Gloucester.* See *Ant. à Wood.* He has printed among other Things a Discourse or two upon our Saviour's *Ascension.* — *Austin Freazer* of *Edm. Hall* has printed a Sermon. — *Francis Gastrell* of Xᵗ church, D. of Div. He was first of all made Preacher to the Society of *Lincoln*'s *Inn*, afterwards chaplain to *Harley* Speaker of the House of Commons, & was upon petition of the House to the Queen made Canon of *Christ church.* He has printed divers things. . . — *Mich. Geddes* has printed several Books. *Quære?* — *John Glanvill* A.M. of *Trinity* coll. has printed several Things in *Poëtry.* — *Edm. Halley* of *Queen*'s College, A.M. wᶜʰ Degree was conferr'd upon him by virtue of a Letter of K. *Charles* IIᵈ at his Return from the Isle of Sᵗ. *Hellen*'s, & for his curious Astronomical observations made there. He has publish'd Abundance of Things in the *Philosophical Transactions.* He was made *Savilian* Professor of *Geometry*, upon the Death of Dᵣ. *Wallis*, and a little after translated a Piece of *Apollonius Pergæus* out of *Arabick*, and from him we expect several other things. He has made curious observations about the Tyde in our Channell, and about the variation of the Needle, for which he went as near the Southern Pole as ever any man yet did. He has been in various Parts of the ocean, & would willingly hazzard his Life once more to perfect his observations if he could obtain a Ship from our Government, which never had any Regard for Learning. He has publish'd a Map shewing the Variation of the Needle in the several Parts where he has been. *Quære* whether he did not give Materials to a Discourse prefix'd to the IV volumes of *Travells* in *folio* lately printed at *London?* — *William Hallifax* (D.D.) of *Corpus* Xᵗⁱ Coll. translated *De Chales Euclid* into *English*. Afterwards he went Chaplain to the Factory at *Smyrna.* Upon his Return he was made Chaplain to Foley Speaker of the House of Commons. But never got anything from the Crown as is usual; whereas several other Logger-Heads had been well preferr'd for that poor piece of Merit. Yet he was

consider'd by M^r. *Foley*, who gave him a good Living. — *Will. Hayley*
D.D. of *All Souls*, of which House he was Fellow.   He went away with
Sir *Will. Trumbull* when Envoy to *Constantinople* and *Paris.*   Afterwards
made minister of S^t. *Giles's* in the Fields, & Dean of *Chichester.* He has
printed some Sermons in *English*, and one in *Latin* preach'd before the
Convocation, which the School-Boys find fault with. — *George Hickes*
(D.D.) first of all of *Magd.* Hall, afterwards of *Magd.* Coll. in both which
Places he liv'd in mean Circumstances, & not taken notice of. Afterwards
he remov'd to *Lincoln* Colledge, & became Fellow there.   Then made
10 Chaplain to the Duke of *Lautherdale* & preferr'd by Archb^p. *Sancroft* to
All-Hallows Barking in *London.*   Upon the Death of D^r. *Marshall,*
Bishop *Fell*, who knew D^r. *Hicks's* worth, and had a true value for Men
of Learning, labour'd all he could to have had him Rector of *Lincoln;*
but the Fellows, who knew he would have been for keeping up Discipline,
preferr'd a Person of a quite Different Temper.   Upon the writing of his
Answer to the *Life of Julian the Apostate*, done by *Sam. Johnson*, he was
advanc'd to the Deanery of *Worcester*, which Preferment he lost for not
taking the Oaths to the Prince and Princess of *Orange.*   Of other things
hereafter. — D^r. *Charles Hickman* of X^t *Church.*   He went Chaplain to
20 the Earl of *Rochester* when he was Deputy of *Ireland.* He had had some
Preferment in *London*, and was afterwards made a Bishop in *Ireland.*
He has publish'd a Volume of Sermons. — D^r. *Hinton* now Minister of
Newbury.   *Quære* whether he has not a Sermon or two in print. —
Humph. Hody was Fellow of *Wadham*, Chaplain first of all to B^p. *Stillingfleet*, afterwards Chaplain to Archb^p. *Tillotson* & then to Archb^p. *Tennison.*
— *Matthew Hole* of *Exeter* College. *Quære* whether he has not publish'd
some Books? — *Tho. Hoy* Doctor of Physick of *S^t. John's Coll.*   He has
translated something of *Plutarch's Morals* & publish'd an odd Poëm
call'd *Agathocles.*   He practis'd Physick in *Warwickshire.*   Afterwards by
30 the Interest which D^r. *Gibbons* his Tutor had with the L^d. Chancellor
Somers he the little Insect was recommended to King *William* to succeed
D^r. *Luff* as *Regis* Professor of Physick, which Place he has most scandalously neglected.   He is a ranck, low church whigg, & a mighty Pro-
jector for making Salts.   He is very good at getting Children, but nothing
else that I know of. — *Matth. Hutten*, D.D. of *Brazen-nose* Coll.   He
has a noble Collection of Antiquities made by himself. — *Will. Jane*
D.D. and *Regis* Professor of Divinity in *Oxon.*   He has besides a great
many more Preferments.   But more hereafter. — *James Jeffreys* (D^r. of
Div.) of *Jesus* Coll.   *Quære* whether he was not Prebendary of *Norwich*
40 and Author of some Sermons. — *Inett* (*John*) A.M. of University Coll.
where he was Scholar of the Earl of *Leycester's* Foundation.   He took
his Degree of D^r. of Div. at *Cambridge.*   He was Chaplain to S^r. *Rich.
Newdigate* in *Warwickshire* from whom he had some Preferment.   Afterwards by S^r. *Richard's* Interest with B^p. *Barlow* he got to be Precentor
of *Lincoln.*   He has publish'd a Book of *Devotions*, and a Continuation
of B^p. *Stillingfleet's* Church History of *Britain.*   *Quære* whether anything
else? — Ask some body whether one *Jones* of *Jesus* Coll. did not
write a Book about *Opium?* — *Zach. Isham* of *Christ Church* became
Chaplain to the Bishop of *London*, who gave him some Preferment
50 in *London*, which he left for a Noble Living in *Northamptonsh.* given

him by S^r. *Justinian Isham.* He has publish'd Sermons, & some other Things.

Jan. 26 (Sun.). D^r. *Hody's* Exhibitioners, besides their being nominated by the two Professors of *Hebrew* and *Greek*, are also to be examin'd yearly by them, to see what Progress they make, & to be turn'd out if found negligent: For which the Professors, besides a Dinner at that time with the Exhibitioners, are to have 10 Shillings a piece every time. He died in the fourty fifth year of his Age.

Jan. 27 (Mon.). *Tim. Goodwin* Chaplain to the B^p. of *Oxon* is made Archdeacon of *Oxon.* in the room of D^r. *Hody.* Which *Goodwin* in the year 1696, was made M. of Arts as a Member of S^t. *Edm. Hall,* producing Testimoniall Letters (which some say were forg'd) of his being D^r. of *Physick* of *Leyden,* in which Faculty he understands as little as he does of Divinity. But he is a great Pretender, & a bold, confident man, & will do anything for Preferment which is all he aims at. When he was of *Edm.* Hall he was a stingy, niggardly Fellow, & I do not remember he did any good there, whatever D^r. *Mill* may say. (He hath since publish'd the Life of the B^p. of Salisbury's wife. 'Tis prefix'd to her Devotions. Apr. 20. 1712.)

Jan 31 (Fri.). The following [12] Coyns, found at *Cirencester* in *Glouc*.sh, shew'd me by M^r. *Wase* of *Corpus.* [227–231.] . . .

Feb. 6 (Th.). M^r. *Will. Rogers,* formerly Commoner of *University* College, afterwards a zealous *Roman* Catholick, tells me that M^r. *Woodhead* writ a great many other things besides those mention'd by *Ant. à Wood,* particularly one about *Opticks,* which he says was printed at *Oxon*

Jan. 25. Dr. T. Smith to H. Asks him not to enter his trifling benefactions in the Register. Mentions a rumour of an intended visitation of All Souls' to ferret Tindal out of his burrow. Hopes that Hody had finish'd his *Collections about the History of the Greek Tongue.* The icons of the nine famous Greeks who brought Greek learning &c. into Italy are in T. vi of Lambecij *De Bibliotheca Caesarea Vindobonensi,* App. p. 274. Relates an anecdote of an extraordinary visitation of Bodley to which Marshall, Walker, and himself were invited by B^p. Lloyd. When it was over Walker told S. that notwithstanding all that they had proposed, nothing would be done. 'And Obadiah the Conjurer, as Archb^p. Sheldon used merrily to call him, in this proved a true Prophet.' Wonders at Charlett's proposal that he should undertake certain Lives. He has endeavoured to pursue B^p. Fell's excellent design, and if the Heads of Houses &c. think fit to receive it, he hopes they will find several judicious men capable of bringing it to perfection, and is satisfied that nothing can be more for the credit of the Nation, Church, and University.

Jan. 28. Barnes to H. Would be glad to succeed Hody, and to continue his work. Anxious to hear from Hudson about Homer.

Feb. 1. H. to Dr. T. Smith. Dr. Woodward has sent him a copy of the engraving of the Votive Shield. Cannot learn whether Kennett is engaged on *Fasti Britannici.* Death of Hody on Tuesday the 21st ult., aged 45. His bequests, and desire to alter his will. Succeeded in the Archdeaconry by Mr. Tim Goodwin. Milles puts in for Greek Prof. Lambecius' Catalogue of the Imperial Library presented by the B^p. of Worcester. He was at first amazed at this impertinence of Dr. Charlett's.

Feb. 4. Trumbull to H. Asks for remarks on coins. Returns Dodwell's book, with remarks. What good end did he propose to himself? Asks for a loan of Milles' answer.

by Mʳ. Walker, under whose name it went. 'Tis a small thing, & rare. He likewise tells me that he really believes Mʳ. *Woodhead* to be Author of *the Whole Duty of Man,* & the other Pieces which goes under the name of that Author. But this is hardly credible. . . .

Feb. 7 (Fri.). Mʳ. *Dodwell* tells me his Letter to Dʳ. *Tillotson* to prevent the schism is printed with Bᴾ. *Kenn's* Letter to Dʳ. *Tennison* conc. the Death of the Princess of *Orange.* — In a Book call'd *Mille Testes,* wherein some things are inserted against Mr. *Dodwell's Ep. Discourse,* the Author, Mʳ. *Oldfield,* a Lawyer, says with some confidence
10 that Mʳ. *Fulman* was Author of *The Whole Duty of Man.* — Mʳ. *Cherry* has a Coyn of *Constantius* (the *younger,* I suppose) found at *Thistleworth* in *Middlesex.* — When the Bill for Security of the Church of *England* was read, a Clause was in it to take off the *Sacramental Test,* which was assented to by eleven of the Bishops that were in the House, such as *Tennison, More, Trelawny* (who has chang'd his Principles in hopes of being translated to *Winchester,*) &c. & dissented from by six, *viz.* the Archbᴾ. of *York,* Bᴾ. of *Chester,* the Bᴾ. of *London,* the Bᴾ. of *Rochester,* the Bᴾ. of Sᵗ. *Asaph,* & the Bᴾ. of Durham. Dʳ. *Bull* sate in the Lobby of the House of Lords all the while smoking his Pipe. The Bᴾ. of *Bath*
20 and *Wells* with some others were not in Town. 'Tis said the Duke of *Marlborough* made a speech for taking off the *Test.*

Feb. 10 (Mon.). This Day was a Convocation at two a Clock about the University's Answer to the *Geneva* Letter. The Answer was drawn up and read by Dʳ. Smalrich, signifying that the Aspersions cast upon the Church of *Geneva* was by some private Persons, & such as were Enemies to the Church of *England,* as he shew'd from our *Articles* and *Canons.* They say at *Christ-Church* that in Mʳ. *Milles's* Rhapsody, newly published against Mʳ. *Dodwell,* besides affected Language, there is false Doctrine, illogical Conclusions, & I know not what. — . . .

30 Pag. 19 of Mʳ. *Milles's* Book against Mʳ. *Dodwell.* If this Doctrine should

---

Feb. 8. Dr. T. Smith to H. Remarks on the coins. Gives an account of a Mr. Thomas Perkes, of Mangorsfield, and his conversation with Spirits, from a letter printed at Bristol 1704 and directed to Bᴾ. Fowler. Hopes that Hudson will succeed Hody ; Dr. Potter would be a fit person. Almeloveen writes that when Strabo is published he will begin the Lives of the two Casaubons, for which he has been furnished with materials by Drs. Bernard, Smith, and Batteley. **Feb. [Mar.] 8. Smith to H.** The riot in All Souls' Buttery. Dr. Jane's will. Vol. II. of the *Imitation of Christ* collected and published by Mr. Lee, late fellow of St. John's Coll., Oxon, who afterwards married the daughter of Mrs. Joane Lead, famous for her pretended visions and revelations, and one of the first beginners of the enthusiastic Sect of the Philadelphians, and is said to have joined them, though Smith hopes that he has long since given up those extravagant religious whimsies and fooleries. Fears that he retains too much inclination to the practices of a 'contemplative life.' Condemns devotional books of this character and thinks that Dr. H. [Hickes] has bestowed excessive praise on Thomas a Kempis in his Ep. Ded. Does not believe that a Kempis, or Walter Hilton an English Carthusian Friar (according to O. Walker, from whom Mr. Hatton borrowed his account) was the author of the *Imitatio.* Asks H. to read Leland on Hilton in *De Scriptoribus illustribus*; also Theod. Petreius' *Biblioth. Cartusiana* (Cologne, 8°, 1609), who assigns the *Musica Ecclesiastica* to Hilton chiefly on Possevin's authority (*Mus. Eccles.* being practically identical with the *Imitatio*).

take & be receiv'd in the world, that none but such as had heard (and profess'd the Gospel, & been Baptized) need to fear a future Account &c. These words he quotes as M^r. *Dodwell's* whereas those in hooks are his own. Ibid. pag. 108. a Passage out of *Justin*, wch M^r. *Milles* has corrupted, & pointed falsly, so that 'tis not *Greek*, nor does his Translation answer the Original. M^r. *Chishull* also has mistaken the Place. Ibid. pag. 140. He runns out about a Typographical Mistake of *Austin* for *Justin*, M^r. *Dodwell* joyning *Justin* and *Irenæus* together. M^r. *Milles* might have easily discover'd the Errour by what goes before & what follows after. At the latter End of the Chapter he has 6 or 7 Pages to shew that S^t. *Augustin* (so he writes, whereas the Print is *Austin*, onely one Letter in 10 the Difference) could not be of opinion that the Soul is *naturally mortal*. M^r. *Chishull* guilty of the same mistake, tho' he does not run out to shew S^t. *Augustin's* opinions. D^r. *Turner* & M^r. *Clark* perceiv'd the Mistake, & did not insist upon it. Ibid. pag. 439. He pretends that M^r. *Dodwell* has a great number of manifest Absurdities as well as Inconsistences & Self Contradictions, (with some other Expressions of that nature,) for which he says he has compassion to M^r. *Dodwell*, & out of Respect to his Person & character he will cast a veil over that Place rather than expose it to that scorn and Ridicule of the world, wch if it were open'd & set in its proper Light, it must needs occasion. Yet he does not so much as intimate what these contradictions &c. 20 are nor give reasons to prove them so as well as himself. Ibid. p. 494.—From all which, I cannot but with sorrow reflect upon your unhappy Fate, in undertaking to maintain an opinion, which has driven you into such a method of Arguing, as is as difficult to make consistent with common Honesty, as to reconcile with the Principles of sound Reason.—Yet he has not shew'd this, & 'tis purely Abuse, & quite contrary to that Respect which he says he has for M^r. *Dodwell's* character. 'Tis much the same Abuse with M^r. *Chishull's*. Ibid. p. 492. He has another Abuse of him, making him guilty of the most notorious Falsification upon Account of a Passage in S^t. *Athanasius*, which M^r. *Dodwell* understood otherwise than M^r. *Milles* & for which M^r. *Milles* might 30 be term'd guilty of the same Knavery, were it consistent with the Rules of Christianity. ━

Selden de Success. in Pontific. Hebræor. lib. 1. c. 2 makes mention of a MS^t. of *Nicephorus Patriarch.* in *Sion* College Library: The MSS^ts. in this Library not in the printed catalogue of MSS. of *Engl.* and *Irel.*

Feb. 11 (Tu.). M^r. *Proast* read over a sheet or two of M^r. *Milles's* Rhapsody against M^r. *Dodwell* at the beginning; and he is the Person (of Judgment) whom *Milles* hints at in the Preface: but because M^r. *Milles* would not alter things which appear'd to be wrong, but in every particular was confident, he would read over no more. ━ 40 Several Coyns for Illustrating *Livy* to be taken out of *Landi Numismata.* ━ D^r. *Humphreys* B^p. of *Hereford* writ a Discourse concerning the Antiquities of S^t. *Winifrid's* well. *Quære* where 'tis now? ━ D^r. *Lloyd* B^p. of *Worcester* born August the 27th in the year 1627. *Quære?* (It must be a little before, he being baptized Aug. 26. 1627. See Ath. Oxon. Ed. II. vol. II. col. 1088.) ━ To be printed of *Ptolemy*, His Προκ. Κανόνες, with *Theon* upon it. Some parts of it are printed, but unknown to be of that work, *viz.* The *Canon* by M^r. *Dodwell*, and before by D^r. *Bainbridge* & by *Petavius* in his *Rationarium temporum*: 2. *De*

Feb. 11. Barnes to Hudson. Thinks Hudson will in the end approve of his *Psalmodia.* Is engaged for the Iliad. ' Get me a Bookseller at Oxford & a μισθάριον & I'll begin Pindar within ye Month.' The Odyssey may be for Oxford. Messages, remarks on Livy, &c. Ἔρρωσο.

Apparentijs Stellarum, in Petavius's *Ouranolog.* 3. The *Fasti* of *Theon*
(being part of his com.) pr. at the End of the *Oxon* Edition of St. *Cyprian.*
— Mʳ. *Dodwell* is inclin'd to think that the Inscription explain'd by
Sirmund relating to Scipio *Barbatus* is elder than that of *Duilius*, the
letters of *Duilius* being better cut & the termination *imus* for *umus*
shewing that of *Duilius* to be after *Julius Cæsar.* Consult *Ciacconius*
upon *col. Rostrata.* This of *Duilius* elder than *Pliny*, who mentions it.
Duilius's Inscr. always has *C.* for *G. G.* was invented by *Servilius
Carbo* after the year *ab U.C.* 500. See *Plutarch.* The *Bacchanalia*
10 publish'd by *Gronovius* has always at least often *G.* for *C. Quære.* In
Barbatus note the word *Optume. Scipio Nasica* is, as seems, the first
that had the Title of *Optimus.* — *Reinesius* in his Inscriptions or in his
variæ Lectiones has the *Stemmata* of the *Scipios.* See there whether
some light may be had of *Barbatus. Reinesius's* Defence of himself in
Mʳ. *Charles Bernard's* Hands.

Feb. 15 (Sat.). The Letter above mention'd of Bᵖ. *Kenn*, conc. the
Death of the Princess of *Orange*, is thus intitled, *A Dutifull Letter from
a Prelate to a Prelate, relating to matters of grand concern.* Printed at
London 1703. 8°. Mʳ. *Dodwell's* follows, & is thus intit. *A Letter* from
20 Mʳ. *D——el* to Dʳ. *Tillotson* to prove *Non-Jurors no Schismaticks.* Bᵖ.
Kenn's. Dated *March* 29. 1695.

[List of books by Collier, Hickes, Lesley and Wm. Straghan.]

Mʳ. *Dodwell* is inform'd by one who would not be quoted first that
Mʳ. *Hoadley* assisted Mʳ. *Chishull* in his Answer to the *Epistolary Discourse conc. the natural Immortality of the Soul.*

Feb. 17 (Mon.). Dʳ. *John Potter* is made Rector of *Monks Risborough*
in room of Dʳ. *Hody*, & Mʳ. *Milles* (the *Rhapsodist*) *Greek* Professor in
the university of *Oxford.* The Court could not have put a greater
Affront upon us than pitching upon a Person void of Integrity, Parts or
30 Learning, especially that part of Learning he is to profess, he not understanding the Rudiments of the *Greek* Tongue, as is plain from his
Performance against Mʳ. *Dodwell.* The Arguments made use of to get
him this Place we hear were, (1) That he is a Person of great Eminence.
(2) That he was sent for to *Christ-Church* from another House, because
no one in *Christ-Church* was so able as he to do the Duty of chaplain.
(3) That he was Deputy to Dʳ. *Hody*, & read *Greek* Lectures to the
Admiration and great satisfaction of all the University. Which is
all banter, & just as true as the reasons given by him in his Preface
why his Book did not appear sooner, *viz.* because he was attendant upon
40 the Earl of *Pembroke's* Son (who was absent all the time he was about

---

Feb. 15. H. to Dr. T. Smith. Prof. Milles will not find one friend in
the whole University; he seems not to know the very rudiments of the
Greek tongue. What order was there for placing Jewel's works in churches
to be read by the people? Has Hickes cleared himself from the charge in
Burnet's *Vindication*? Complains of Mill's criticism on Dr. Hugh Todd's proposal for printing the Antiquities of Cumberland. Pretexts for Milles' appointment, criticized.
Feb. 17. Thoresby to H. Desires continuance of correspondence and
autographs.

it) & because he was taken up with the Business of his Place as Chaplain (which he was so far from being diligent in that the Dean scons'd him for scandalous Neglect.) — *Quære* about — *Jones* an *Irish* Dean, whose Son is now Fellow of *All-Souls?* Also about M^r. *Charles Lesley's* Son. . . .

Feb. 18 (Tu.). One *Phineas Bury*, Fellow of *Wadham*-College, a Gentleman of good Parts, help'd D^r. *Bernard* to some Emendations of his own Conjecture upon *Josephus*, which the D^r. I think faithfully quotes as *Bury's* as he had occasion. — *Monfoucault* in his Athanasius, in the II^d. Tom. of his *collectio nova*. p. 18. out of *Athanasius* οὐχ αἷμα τοῦ κυρίου 10 ἐστὶν ὁ οἶνος, ἀλλὰ τῆς ἀμπέλου. This Passage is conc. the *Eucharistical* Wine & is express against Transubstantiation, wch he has not observ'd. In the same place pag. 28. is a passage against the harsh notion of original Sin. pag. . . . is a passage making for M^r. *Dodwell's* opinion conc. the distinction of ψυχή and πνεῦμα. — . . .

Memorandum for the Continuer of Athenæ Oxon. or A Catalogue of M^r. Tho. Milles's works.

1. An Anatomical Description of Man & Woman, in a Sermon at S^t. Marie's. Taken mostly from Gibson's Anatomy. 'Twas the first he preach'd before the university. MS. 4°.   20

2. Remarks upon the *Occasional Paper num. viii.* in Defence of M^r. Dodwell and his Principles about the schism. Printed in a sheet and a half in 4to, in the year 97 or 98. 'Twas Reflected on, with other things, by D^r. Hody, I think, & thereupon M^r. Milles writ,

3. A Defence of the said Remarks. Which is pretty large, & not yet printed. 4to.

4. A Discourse about the Law of Nature. not finish'd.

5. The 2 first comedies of Aristophanes collated with an old edition 4°. M^r. Milles had a design of putting it out, but being of an unsettled temper, & not understanding Greek, he grew weary of it by that time he came to ye 3^d 30 Comedie.

A Sermon upon the 30th of Jan. at S^t. Marie's Oxon 4°.

6. A Letter to M^rs. *Brace-Girdle*, disswading her from the Play-House, Written in the year 1703, at ye time of the Oxon Act.

7. Variæ Lectiones & Annott. in Cyrilli catecheses, Pr. at Oxon. in fol. The Annotations were in a great measure taken from Suicerus's Lexicon, & the Index's & some of the collating part done by another hand.

8. Answer to M^r. Dodwell's *Epistolary Discourse.*

In this Book, which some call Milles's *Rhapsody*, (besides his calling M^r. Dodwell downright knave, (see p. 494.) his insisting, for about 10 40 pages together on a typographical Error of Austin for Justin (See p. 140.) several impertinent Digressions &c. he shews himself to be ignorant in the Rudiments of the Greek Tongue, & to be very meanly skill'd in the Fathers, whom he has quoted at 2^d Hand, having made great use of Scultetus's Medulla Patrum, D^r. Cudworth's Intell. System & other Books of that kind.

Feb. 18. Barnes to Hudson. 'I knô not, but y^t *Mills* may be a Brother, or Kinsman of mine, for my Mother was a *Mills* of *Salisbury*.' Wants to hear finally about Homer and Pindar. An Antichrist has appeared in Babylonia. Has finished the first Book of Psalms, and wishes to print it at Oxford.

VOL. XIII.

Feb. 19 (Wed.).   M^r. *Dodwell's* Letter to M^r. *Rich. King*, about ye Age of *Philopatris* commonly ascrib'd to *Lucian.* [Dated Shottesbrooke, Dec. 4. 1705. (1–54.)]

Out of *Is. Casaubon's* Papers.

Quum essem *Dononchtoni* & *Wisbicci* atque nullus alius fere liber ad manus esset, legi obiter quaedam in *Eunapio Gr.* cujus versionem *Junianam* non habebam.   Itaque nescio an illi vertenti, aut postea *Commelino* observata sint, quæ hic adnotamus. [55–67.] . .

Feb. 20 (Th.).   More things out of *Casaubon's* Papers.

10   Die *Martis* 6. *Aug.* (ye year not added) Stylo veteri, *Dunamia* profecti venimus ad ædes olim Episcopales, nunc D. *Peithou, Dodinchtoni,* sane elegantes, & pretiose instructas.

7. *Witsbicum* appulimus. Fuit autem totum iter à *Dunamia* per loca palustria, quæ nunc q. magna ex parte sicca erant.   Sed hieme alta aqua conteguntur. Est vero pars *Eliæ* propior multo melior, quam pars ad *Wisbicum* quæ per plura milliaria plane deserta est et perpetuum est arundinetum.   Sane si siccaretur hæc plaga pars vel optima certe inter optima *Angliæ* videtur futura.   Nam apud D: *Peithou* qui amœnissimum tractum colit & admodum κατάδενδρον nascuntur cum alij fructus, tum præcocia (Apricocks) quibus meliora *Lutetiæ* edisse 20 non meminimus.

6 *Aug.* Quum jam non multis M.P. distaremus à *Dodinchtono,* occurrit nobis rusticus, qui equo nudo vehebatur, non divaricatis ut fit cruribus, sed rectus stans & dorso insistens equi. qui adeo firmus stabat, ut non dubitaret currere quanta maxima velocitate. Ego simile spectaculum antea non videram. *Witsbicum* porrigitur secundum fluviolum   unde nomen quasi d. fluminis *Wiscæ* ostium (inde beccum apud vulg.) & sunt ædificia humilia, neque continua, nisi ad illam partem, ubi est Arx Episcopalis.   Ea pars & proximæ urbis speciem aliquam refert : reliquæ domus sunt παραποτάμιοι ad milliare unum extensæ.

30   *Dodinchtono* profectis ad milliare 3 aut circiter occurrit in vasta solitudine tuguriolum luteum ταπεινόν. quod vocant *Ophous* sive *Oppenhous,* domus Op. ibi solent haustu cerevisiæ recreari viatores : sed τῇ λιτότητι τοῦ τόπου ἀνάλογός ἐστιν ἡ ποιότης τοῦ πόματος. Magna ἐρημία, raro homines occurrunt. Et inter *Dunamiam* ac *Dodinchtonum* per campos virentes iter fecimus nullo viæ vestigio apparente.

Kal. *Aug.* Narrabat hodie mihi rem miram Reverendiss. Præsul D. *Ep. Eliensis,* quam ille acceptam auribus suis à teste oculato & auctore credebat esse verissimam.   Est vicus in urbe *Londino* qui dicitur vicus *Longobardore.* in eo vico παροικία est & ædes parœcialis, in qua fuit presbyter, homo summæ fidei 40 & notæ pietatis   anno 1563. quo anno, si unquam alias, pestis grassata est per hanc urbem *Lond.*   Narravit igitur hic parochus & passim alijs, & ipsi quoque D. Episcopo, sibi hoc accidisse. Erat illi amicus in sua parœcia insignis vir ut omnes existimabant probus & pius.   Hic peste correptus advocavit presbyterum illum suum amicum, qui & ægrotanti affuit & vidit morientem, nec deseruit nisi mortuum. ita demum repetijt domum suam.   Post horas satis multas à morte hujus quum ipse pro mortuo esset relictus in cubiculo, uxor illius idem cubiculum est ingressa, ut ex arca promeret lodicem sive linteamen ad ipsum ἐντυλίσσειν, ut est moris.   Ingressa audit hanc vocem operi intenta. *Quis hic est ?* terreri illa, & velle egredi.   Sed auditur iterum vox illa, *Quis hic* 50 *est ?* at tandem comperto esse mariti vocem accedit ad illum, *quid,* ait, *marite, tu igitur mortuus non es ?* at nos te pro mortuo compositum deserueramus.   *Ego vero,* respondit ille, *vere mortuus fui : sed ita Deo visum ut anima mea rediret ad corpus. Sed tu, uxor,* ait, *si quid habes tibi parati, da mihi. esurio enim.* Dixit illa, *Verveinam habere se, pullum gallinaceum,* & nescio quid aliud. Sed omnia invecta: quæ brevi esset paratura. *Ego,* ait ille, *moram non fero, panem habes,* & *caseum?* quum annuisset, atque ipse petijsset afferri, comedit spectante uxore. deinde advocato presbytero & jussis exire è cubiculo omnibus qui aderant, narrat illi hæc. *Ego,* ait, *vere mortuus fui : sed jussa est anima redire ad suum corpus, ut scelus aperirem ore meo manibus meis admissum, de quo nulla unquam cuiquam est suspicio. Priorem namque uxorem meam ipse occidi manibus meis, tanta vafritie, ut omnes res lateret.* Deinde modum perpetrati sceleris exposuit. Nec ita multo post exspiravit ac vere tum mortuus est.   10

Generatio in anno ætatis LXXX°. Heri mihi narrabat hic *Londini* filia *Fontani,* dum vixit Ministri in hac Ecclesia *Gallicana,* loquens de suo marito, genero *Fontani,* qui maritus ipsius natus annos supra 70, ante dies xx obijt, mensibus sex post socerum : sæpe illum sibi dixisse, patrem habuisse admodum longævum, qui natus annos octoginta se generarit. Neque erat tamen hic maritus narrantis infirmo corpore, sed staturæ commodæ, & firmæ sanitatis. quod mirum erat in eo qui fuisset generatus à decrepito.

Feb. 21 (Fri.). Books written by M^r. *Dodwell* y^t are printed. [78–95.]

Feb. 22 (Sat.). Out of *Is. Casaubon's* Papers.

Arausione multa videntur rudera magnorum operum, in quibus etiam hodie 20 mirandam se exhibet *Romanorum* industria.

Extra urbem sat [*sic*] balneæ, opus semidirutum. Speciem præbet turris rotundæ, in ambitu sunt quatuor fornices sic positi ut bini binis è diametro respondeant. Apparent cellarum fornices intra parietes hinc & inde. item tubi per quos aqua fluebat.

Arcus qui dicitur *Marij,* opus est plane stupendum, & antiquitatis monumentum nulli alij secundum. Figura operis quadrata est. Constat fornicibus tribus: medius arcus & major cæteris & magnificentior. In operis lateribus quatuor sculptæ sunt res gestæ illius cujus honoris sacratur id monumentum. Habentur in ijs sculpturis effigies plurimæ armaturæ *Romanorum.* Ibi clypeo- 30 rum formam didicimus hoc fere modo ... magnitudinem quoque eorundem ex illo monumento colligere possumus.

In urbe est ædificium illud ingens & nunquam satis celebratum sed non satis hodie cognitum, quod *Sirc* vocant : Circus fuit... gradus & sedes sed hodie dirutae, fornices tamen supersunt : nam fornicibus constabat opus graduum. suntque interibi cellæ in q. alebantur belluæ.

Of a Body being strangely preserv'd.

Romæ hoc ipso anno, quo *Innoc.* octavus summus Pontif. factus est, Via *Latina* repertum est in arca marmorea muliebre cadaver antiquissimum, venenis oblitum, colore corporeque tam integro, & tractabili ut recentiss. 40. videretur. Caro digito percussa resurgebat, ligno educta retrahebatur, artus flectebantur, & nullum gravem odorem nisi medicamentorum emittebat, nihilque ei ne capilli q. præter cerebrum & intestina deerant. Sed quum magna frequentia gregatim ab omnibus ad superstitionem usque quotidie in Capitolio viseretur, maximi Pontif. jussu inde asportatum. Ubi sit abditum ignoratur.

Feb. 23 (Sun.). Out of *Dodsworth* Vol. 61. pag. 64. Epitaphs found in S^t. *Warbert's* Church of *Chester.* [100–118.]

Feb. 22. Dr. T. Smith to H. Hody and his affairs. Surprise at Milles' appointment. Copies of Jewel and Fox placed in Churches by order of Council. Explains Hickes' conduct at the Revolution. Has high expectations of Todd's History &c. of the Church and Diocese of Carlisle. Hopes the All Souls' rioters have been punished. When may he expect payment of Dr. Bailey's legacy of £10?

Feb. 24 (Mon.).   Ibid. fol. 76. a.

Querela Ecclesiæ de *Penwortham* in Com. *Lancastriæ* per *Johannem* [1]*Richardson Oxoniensem* in Artibus Magistrum facta 23 *No.* 1634.

Heu pereo, specie, [2]LATRONEM nacta, patroni ;
   Ah, quam deplumor ! quam mihi sicca cutis !
BARBARVS has segetes decimabit ? Laicus arva ?
   Hæccine Relligio est expoliare Deos ?
Evome frusta miser templi : nec Struthyo [3]Sacrum
   Digerere argentum ventre potente potest.
Redde [4]*Tolosanas* merces ; Descende caballo
   [5]*Sejano* : Dominos dejicit ille suos.
Innocuos cessa manes temerare [6]piorum,
   Hæc messis non est laica ; Tolle manus.
Propria dona Deus repetit : Repetente negabis
   Numine ? num sacrum debuit esse Macrum ?
Anne animæ prodest animarum sanguine crudo
   Ditari ? et totos dilaniare Greges ?
Communes merito jugulant [7]suspendia fures ?
   An qui prædatur Numina liber erit ?
Sic Aquilam vidi proprium comburere nidum,
   Ex ARA prunam dum levat illa levem.
Letali [8]corvum sic scorpius enecat ictu,
   Dum lætus, letum devorat ipse suum.
Ergo age, crudivorum tollas ex vulnere [9]telum.
   Cœlestis clamat [10]Cæsar, habeto tuum,
Redde meum [11]*Simon*, animas mihi redde ruentes.
   Jam (MAGE) redde mihi prædia, templa, lares.

An Account of yᵉ Contents of a very Ancient Vellam MSᵗ. in yᵉ *Bodlejan* Library mark'd NE. D. 2. 19 [since Auctarium F. iv. 32]. It belong'd formerly to Mʳ. *Tho. Allen* of *Glouc.* Hall. [121-131.]

Feb. 25 (Tu.).   Another Copy of Verses call'd *Querela Ecclesiæ de Penworth.*, &c. by Mʳ. *Richardson* : See pag. 119.

Ecce redivivum genuit *Lancastria* [12]*Micham*.
   Hunc pietas (Mirum!) sacra vorare jubet.
[13]Hujus Templa sacer bona . . digerit, Aras
   Atque Erebum, atque animas, Luciferumque ferum.
Obtigit huic monstro (si fas) Ecclesia [14], pestem
   Agnoscit : Decimis nil minus ille tumet.
Conducit *Macrum*, frugalior ille Levitam
   Ære levi, ut melius possit obesse gregi.
Atque duos tribuit, [15]*Mica* prudentior ipso,
   Siclos, ne luxu diffluat, inde [16]cavet.

---

[1] See pag. 132. Memorand. that this Mʳ. *Richardson* is not so much as mention'd by Mʳ. *Wood* in *Athen. Oxon.*, at least not put down as a writer.
[2] Latronem specie patroni.   [3] Struthio ferrum concoquit.
[4] Aurum *Tolosanum* à *Cæpione Romano* direptum è Templ[o] *Tolosæ* fuit exitiale suis possessoribus.
[5] Equus *Sej.* fuit talis, ut qui eum haberet nunquam esset felix.
[6] Pinguissima in veteri lege Deo devovebantur.
[7] Suspendia est casus Nominativus.
[8] Corvus arripiens scorpium ut comedat, ab eo necatur.
[9] Telum sacrilegij.   [10] Deus.
[11] *Simon Magus* casus vocativus.   [12] *Micah. Judges* 17. ver. 10.
[13] Hujus sacer stomachus.   [14] Ecclesia pestem agnoscit.
[15] *Micah* tribuit 10 Siclos.   [16] Ne minister luxuriet det per annum 40s.

Pascitur ille fame plebis, miserique Ministri,
[1] Alterutro pascit carius, [2] ille sues.
Concio nulla placet pretium quæ postulat ; omnes,
Ni gratis veniant, ablegat ille preces.
Non [3] tanti constat pietas ut munera poscat,
Ille Deum, & cœlum non, nisi gratis, amat.
Quam durus sermo [4] mercede rependere cœlum;
Non tanti Christus, nec Paradisus erit.
Ergo Capellanus, qui vili prædicet, illi
Quæritur ex hara, si petat ille nihil.   10
Servus, adulator, Coridon huic sufficit hero
Dummodo nil poscat Barbarus ille placet.
Fungitur officio jam carpentarius ipse
Pastoris satis est si numerare potest.
Et numerat certe stipendia lauta per annum.
Non aliter Templi proditor esse potest.
Clericus in numero est nullo, sed prædia cleri
In summo. Anne hoc est Relligione frui !
Quin potius viduo reddas patrimonia Templo :
Vel modice clerum nutriat Ara suum.   20
Fundator Christus contractus damnat iniquos.
Quam male præscribunt Laica pacta Deo?
Si [5] Sacras Templi vendas, sine jure, columbas
Exspecta à Christo verbera, lora, plagas.
Anne in vendentes sanctas clamare columnas
Nescis ? quæ, [6] mysta [7] balbutiente, stupent.
Sed dices partem cantus mihi jure reservo;
Perfide . . . . proderis ore tuo.
Pars tamen illa quota est ! Totum superare videtur,
Quod retines. Solvis siccine vota Deo?   30
Cortice sic pastus quondam [8] Cyllenius Hermes
Spernitur, et nucleos turba profana vocat.
Cortice presbyteri viles saturantur inani
Pastorem pascens cortice, perdis oves.
Saxea corda geris [9] *Fluidæ* sub nomine Sylvæ.
Conveniet præco ligneus ergo tibi.
At patrijs [10] hæres (fateor) virtutibus [11] hæres
[12] Si pecco patres æmulor esse meos.
Illi vendiderant orbati prædia Templi
Nonne licet parili vendere jure mihi?   40
[13] Sed me quid moveant aliena gravamina ? quæres,
[14] Nonne agerem caussas ordinis ipse mei?
Ipse quoque expertus damnum, me vindico læsum.
Sensit avaritiam concio nostra tuam.
[15] Intercepta silet, Sermones quærit inemptos
Clausa manus. [16] Sordent auribus empta Midæ.
Perge fame verbi miserum damnare popellum.
Perge sacerdotes extenuare tuos.

---

[1] Plebs vel minister.   [2] Ille patronus.   [3] Illius opinione.
[4] Dare aliquid pro coelo.   [5] Matt. 11. 15.
[6] Sacerdos.   [7] Minister hodiernus balbutit.
[8] Impij in fabella offerebant cortices nucum, ipsi edebant nucleos.
[9] Nomen ejus *Johannes Fletewode.*   [10] *Hæres* est verbum, Hæreo, *to stick to.*
[11] *Hæres* est nomen, *Heyre.*   [12] vox patroni.
[13] Vox Patroni ad auctorem.   Quid pro quære.   [14] vox presbyterorum.
[15] Concio intercepta per servum prohibentem.
[16] Empta sordent, i. e. displicent auribus asininis.

[1] Perge Capellanos famulorum addicere mensis.
  Perge etiam spolijs luxuriare Dei.
  Exuvijs *Christi* luxum satiare memento.
[2] Afflictis *Christi* claudere perge sinum.
  Perge suo magnum depellere jure Tonantem.
[3] Cocyti solum pascua jure tene.
  Aut Deus [4] æterno firmat mendacia verbo,
  Aut [5] sacri fures Tartara nigra petent.

FINIS.

10   **Feb. 26 (Wed.).**   An Abstract of S[r]. *Anthony Bend* K[t] his will Recorder of *London.* — See *Dodsworth.* vol. 32. f. 5. a.   Dat. 26. *April.* 1618. probat. 28. *Octob.* A°. eodem. . . .

[6]**Aug. 29, 1706.**   In the morning about 11 Clock was Elected President of *Magd.* Coll. M[r]. *Harwar* Fellow of y[t] House: He was originally commoner of *Edm.* Hall.   He came in President w[th]out any opposition.[7] — M[rs]. *Goffe*, who brought in a Mask to M[r]. *Edwards* the Printer y[e] woman to whom was committed *the Memorial of the Church of Eng.* is apprehended, & order'd to be prosecuted by y[e] Attorney General. — The following Coyns in Brass, shew'd me
20 by M[r]. *Pridie* Bach. of Div. & Fellow of S[t]. *John's* College.   I. IMP. NERO CAESAR AVG. P. MAX. TR. P.P.P. *Neronis* Cap. Rev. ARA PACIS S.C. Ara.   Coyn'd in y[e] 3[d] Consulship of Nero, *An. X[ti]* 58. at wch time *Corbulo* subdu'd *Armenia* & compell'd *Tiridates*, to receive the Kingdom of *Armenia* from *Nero.*   This caused the temple of *Janus* to be shut.—II. One of *Claudius Cæsar.*   The Inscription on the Head imperfect.   On y[e] Reverse a military Figure with a Buckler, & the Letters S.C.—III. One of *Constantine ye Great.*   The Inscriptions on both sides defaced.   On ye Reverse a Military Figure, & behind him a Captive.—IV. IMP. C. ALLECTVS. P. F. AVG.   *Allecti.* Cap. radiat. VIRTVS
30 AVG. Q. C.   Triremis prætoria.   Coyn'd when Allectus was overcome & slain by *Constantius* Cæsar, & *Britain* recover'd. — M[r]. *Tyrrel* says that the last volume of the *English* Historians was not done by D[r]. but his Brother *Basil, Kennet,* & y[t] the D[r]. had only a Hand in the Additional P[t] to ye two first.   *Quære?*   NB. I have been told since for certain that the D[r]. was Author. — *Dodesworth* vol. 32. f. 26. a.   The superscription about ye Monument of S[r]. *John Hastings* K[t]. buried in a chapel on y[e] South side and upper Part of y[e] Church of *Gressenhall* in *Norfolk* next y[e] Chancel there. . . . —

Dodesworth vol. 55. f. 8. a.

40   It hath been credibly reported that the man w[ch] kill'd M[r]. *Shirley* (Servant to y[e] L[d]. *Digby* in y[e] *Isle of Man,* when my L[d]. was there in his Passage from *England* to *Ireland*) did at his Execution confesse that M[r]. *Pym* suborn'd him to swear falsly upon y[e] Earl of *Strafford's* Tryal, & furnish'd him with a cloake lyned with Plush & other cloathes suitable, whereas he knew nothing thereof further than M[r]. *Pym* instructed him. . . .

---

[1] Quia Minister sedet in mensa cum servis, non cum patrono.
[2] Sinum, i. e. benevolentiam.
[3] *Cocytus* est fluvius Infernalis.   Sumitur hic pro Inferno.
[4] Scriptura.   [5] Church-Robers.
[6] [This is so displaced in Hearne's MS.—C. E. D.]
[7] He is an Hypochondriacal easy Person, and good for little or nothing.

Feb. 27 (Th.). Out of *Is. Casaubon's* Papers.—Ex libro *P. Pithaei*, qui inscribitur *P. P. de SS. Bibliorum Latinis Interpretibus.* [150–161.] . . . In *Casaubon's Adversaria* Tom. 3 in yᵉ last Box is something about Ἰνδικοπλεῦσται. —

Miscellaneous notes on coins and gems, and various classical authors, from the same volume. [162–177.] . . . —

Mʳ. *Dodwell's* Letter occasioned by one from an unknown Hand.

Shottesbrook, Sept. 10. 1706.

Unknown Sir, This is to let you know that I have received your Letter. I am sorry to find by it that you run into the same mistake with my other 10 published Adversaryes, in taking my opinion, not from my Book, nor even from my whole Title-Page, but that part of it onely which Dʳ. *Turner* is pleased to separate from the rest by his *etc.* I am sure you could not in my Book have found any milder or less lasting punishment for the now living Atheists or Epicureans, who are likely to see my Book than by the commonly received opinion. Dʳ. *Coward* himself has publickly cleared me from the Slander of being of his own opinion, concerning the Exstinction of yᵉ Soul upon it's dissolution from the Body. And I have been as plain in asserting that all who hear of the Gospell are obliged to accept of Eternal Rewards under payn of incurring Eternal punishment in case of their not complying with the terms of 20 it. Nor did I ever make that inference from *Tertullian* you impute to me, that his Doctrine concerning the Originall of yᵉ Soul *ex traduce* obliged him to own yᵉ Actual Mortality of yᵉ Soul but only it's natural Mortality. By this you will easily understand how little I am concerned in what you have produced from him to shew that he believed the Actual Immortality of yᵉ Soul, which I never denyed. I shall therefore intreat you to make use yourself of yᵉ Advice of Monsieur *le Blanc*, so much commended by you, not to charge me with this consequence of yᵉ Epicurean Mortality of yᵉ Soul, which I utterly deny, and I am very confident that neither you, nor any Epicurean living will ever be able to prove fairly from any Principle admitted by me. By this you 30 will not only do me Justice, but secure the Publick (as much as lyes in you) from the ill consequences in Practice which those impious Infidels draw, not from any opinion truly owned by me, but from one that is falsely imputed to me. In truth the false imputers of such opinions to me must answer, before God, for the Consequences of their own Slanders, not I who am slandered with the Imputation of that opinion which is so far from my real sentiments. They therefore ought to retract their charging me with that opinion which allows any of your present Epicureans the benefit of actual mortality, not I who never maintained it. In doing so, they might more contribute to stop the mischief occasioned by their own mistaken Representation of my sense 40 than I can who never granted Premises to ground those mischievous inferences of yᵉ Unbelievers. I hope ere long to publish a Preliminary Defense as to this charge of Impiety. Then I shall be less concerned for yᵉ Dispute relating to yᵉ natural Mortality of the Soul when those pious Readers, whose Judgements I most revere, shall have devested themselves of the Prejudices unhappily conceived, and shall be willing to give an equal hearing to me as well as to my Adversaryes. This I hope you will be pleased to accept at present. When that is published, and you have throughly informed yourself of my Principles, not from rumours, but from my Book itself ; I may hope for more usefull objections from a Person of your abilityes, if you shall think it worth 50 your time. In the mean time I am ready to joyn with you in all good designs for Religion as yourself can wish, and am

Your unfeigned well-wisher

HENRY DODWELL.

Casaub. Adversar. Tom. 3. p. 374. b. [184–187.]. ... 188. .... *Is.*
Casauboni Notae in Themistij Orat. a Pantino editas, è schedis MSS.
in *Bibl. Bod.* [188–197.] ... Out of another Paper of *Is. Casaubon.*
[198–200.] ... Ex altera scheda soluta *Is. Casauboni.* [200–203.] —
The Etruscan Inscription on one of yᵉ Legs of yᵉ Statue, mention'd in
one of yᵉ former Volumes to have been sent to Dʳ. *Hudson* from a
German & wᶜʰ Dʳ. *Hickes* has attempted to interpret in a Letter to
Dʳ. *Sloane* in yᵉ *Philosophical Transactions* I read thus; MVI : GLEDEM :
STVLPOE : ADIFIMVI GASII : DIRI. XDCECLES : CETA. Beginning from yᵉ
10 Rt. Hand according to yᵉ Hebrews, as *Bernardinus Baldus* has ad-
monish'd in his *Divinatio in Tabulam Eugubinam, Lingua Hetrusca veteri
perscriptam, Aug. Vind.* 1613. 4°. The Original Copy whereof is in MSᵗ.
amongst *Is. Casaubon's* Papers.

Feb. 21 (Fri.). A 2ᵈ Vol. of *Tho. à Kempis's* works is come
out in *English* with a Recommendatory Epistle by Dʳ. *Hicks,* who gives
a fair Account of the Translater, & of the work. To it is prefix'd a
large Account of the Author's Life, & of his Book *de Imitatione Christi,*
in reference to which Book there is part of a Letter added sent from
Oxon. concerning the MSS. in the Publick Library, which I suppose
20 was sent by Mʳ. *Heywood* of Sᵗ. *John's,* who took some pains lately in
looking the *MSS.* over.

Feb. 23 (Sun.). Yesterday about 3 in the Afternoon died Dʳ. *Will.
Jane* Canon of Christ-Church, Dean of *Gloucester,* & her Majesty's Professor of Divinity in *Oxon.* & Rector of *Ewelme.* He died very rich,
which he has left to Mʳ. *Peter Foulke* Student of *Christ-Church* his
Relation.

Feb. 24 (Mon.). A Description of Killingworth-Castle in Warwickshire, in a Book amongst *Selden's* in Bib. Bodl. 8°. Z. 8. *Jur. Seld.* wherein
is a Relation of Queen *Elizabeth's* Entertainment there, *an.* 1575. In pag.
30 16 of the same Book, an Account of Musick and Dancing, on the Sunday, after Divine Service, perform'd in a very extraordinary manner, with
other Diversions. Pag. 26. Another Account of Sports on the Sabbath,
amongst which the *Quintine.* Account of Hock-Tuesday at Coventry
p. 34. — 8°. Z. 32. *Th. Seld.* A Book taken out of *Nic. Sanders* de
Schismate Anglic. call'd *Justitia Britannica,* giving an Account of the
Persons depriv'd of their Places by *Hen.* VIII. at the beginning of the
Reformation. — 8°. Z. 31. *Th. Seld. Hieron. Megiserus's* Specimen of
fifty Tongues, in which he has represented the Lord's Prayer. —
Menckenius of *Leipsick,* lately dead. He was the Publisher of *Acta
40 Eruditorum Leipsic.* — *Janus Lascarus* has writ the best about Greek
Ligatures. The Title of his Book, *De veris Literarum Græcarum apud
Antiquos formis.* — *Livy* l. 24. c. 10. ... Which shews the Prodigies he
relates were not all believ'd by himself, but that he related them as he
found them in Annals, into which they were inserted by those who had
believ'd them real. — We are told Dʳ. Jane has left 500 *libᵉ.* to *Christ-
Church* to purchase a Parsonage with, an Annuity of 25 *libᵉ. per an.* to
a Sister, and the rest to his Cousin Mʳ. *Peter Foulks,* to the value of
above twenty thousand Pounds. —

A Lesson for the *Greek* Professor or A Dialogue between *Timothy* and *Tell-Troth*, in Answer to M[r]. [1]*M*——s Book ag[t] M[r]. *D*——*ll*.

Tim. What have you there? *Tell-Tr.* M[r]. *M*——*s* Answer to M[r]. *D*——*ll*. *Tim.* 'Tis a bulky one; surely 'tis not all to the purpose. *Tell-Tr.* Yes 'tis to M[r]. *M*——s purpose. *Tim.* Pray what was that? *Tell-Tr.* To get Preferment. *Tim.* No, this can't be. I fancy he is a Man of greater Simplicity than to write with such a Design. *Tell-Tr.* You'll be easily undeceiv'd, when you hear, that he is made Professor of the *Greek* Tongue, in the University of *Oxon.* for this doughty Performance. *Tim.* 'Tis impossible. How should an *English* Book recommend a Man to the Q——s Favour for such a Place? 10 *Tell-Tr.* Just as a slight Tincture of Poëtry did *V*——*g* for a Place in the Heralds-Office; or &c. *Tim.* I can't allow your Comparison. For you may easily perceive that M[r]. *M*——*s* is no Dabler in *Greek*, by the Learned Quotations at the Bottom of the Page. *Tell-Tr.* Quotations may be had at second hand. But what will you say if these shew him to be a meer *ignoramus* in *Greek*, & one that has not learn'd the first Rudiments of the Tongue. *Tim.* This is all spight & malice. Surely you were a Competitor for the Place. *Tell-Tr.* Not I. For I don't pretend to be qualify'd for it. *Tim.* I'll never believe you, unless you'll prove what you say. *Tell-Tr.* To satisfie you, I'll give you instances enough of his Ignorance in a few Lines. *Tim.* 'Tis ex- 20 ceeding strange, but if you do convince me, I'll quite desert the Party, who would make us believe they have ingross'd all the wit and Learning in the Nation. *Tell-Tr.* To do you so great a kindness, I'll play the Critick for once. Turn to page the 11th line the 1st of the Quotation at y[e] Bottom of the Page, and there you will find ὅ for ὁ twice, a fault that a novice would hardly be guilty of. *Tim.* That's only an Error of the Press, or want of *Accuracy* in correcting. *Tell-Tr.* I am afraid 'tis want of his *Accuracy* in the Language; for the Book is full of false Accents, as pag. 31st lin. 2. τοὺς τε for τούς τε. pag. 37. lin. 4. πρῶτον γε. for πρῶτόν γε. lin. 8. ἦ δε for ἡ δὲ. lin. 14. ἅδην for ᾅδην. lin. antepenult. ὠ for ὦ. p. 38. lin. 3. ἕν for ἐν. l. 4. ἁρπὰζ' for ἅρπαζ'. l. 6. πάν- 30 τῶν for πάντων. l. penult. ποδώκες for ποδῶκες. & I dare swear a 100 more of y[e] same nature. *Tim.* But these are little matters not worthy to be regarded by a Professor. *Tell-Tr.* That's st[r]ange, at this time of day, when little men are so much regarded. *Tim.* But I think there's no need of niceness in such *Punctilios.* *Tell-Tr.* The Learned world has been of another opinion. However I'll say no more of *Accents.* Turn back again to the 31[st] Page line the 3[d]. and there you have false *Concord*, τοὺς τηλευτήσαντες for τοὺς τελευτήσαντας. Pag. 37th l. 14 & 15. you have false verse, and false concord too. *Tim.* 'Tis all Errour of the Press, & could never flow from the Pen of a Learn'd Professor. *Tell-Tr.* 'Tis not to be imagin'd that a Compositor should committ 40 the faults in the last Page and Lines I mention'd for how should he read?

καὶ γὰρ καθ' ἅδην δύο τρίβους νομίζομεν,
Μίαν δικαίων, χ' ἀτέραν τῶν ἀδίκων.

Tim. Why? where's the fault? the sense is plain, and neither the Author nor Compositor to be blam'd as far as I can see. *Tell-Tr.* 'Tis unreasonable to exspect that I should both find faults & Eyes to see 'em. Pray how does μίαν agree with τρίβους, and what sort of verse is the latter? *Tim.* Pray gratify my Curiosity for once and inform me. *Tell-Tr.* That's an easy matter. The Author has made μίαν to agree with τρίβους, whereas if you read the verse thus, as it should be, 50

Μίαν δικαίων, χ' ἀτέραν, ἀδίκων ὁδὸν,

the Concord will be visible, & the difficulty solv'd. *Tim.* This is not ignorance but a plain Blunder. *Tell-Tr.* You may call what you please a Blunder, as I suppose you will the word ἀμβλήματα in pag. 38. lin. ult. *Tim.* No, I'll

---

[1] Id est Thomas Milles.

call that an Error of the Press, & must acknowledge the Book to be full of them : Yet for all that yᵉ Author knows better things. *Tell-Tr.* That may be; but I am sure he does not understand how to print or Correct *Greek.* For I do not doubt but that upon the Review of his Book to find the *Errata,* he us'd the best of his Skill: because he could not but be sensible the Criticks would fall upon him. Yet for all this out of an hundred, at least, he has found but one. *Tim.* Now 'tis plain you are malicious. For I can see two he has taken notice of in the very first Line of the *Errata.* *Tell-Tr.* Now you are out on't. For the first μέν ἐσται is so far from being a Correction of a gross Error,
10 that he doubles it: for you must know that ἔσται is no enclytick, as he would have it. *Tim.* I am entirely of opinion that all these faults are nothing else but little Inadvertencies. *Tell-Tr.* I find you have a perfect command over your own thoughts. But 'tis matter of wonder to me, that he should committ more faults in a few Lines than others do in a whole Book. *Tim.* I don't doubt but you have shewn 'em all. For Malice is quick-sighted, and very exact in enumerating all little Slips of an Adversary. *Tell-Tr.* No such thing. I'm as favourable to him as 'tis possible. Pray consult pag. 107. where, not to take notice of the Errors in the three first Lines, &ᶜ. you have one notable Blunder, I might say two, in the fourth line, couch'd in the words ἐν ἀνθρώπου
20 εἴδη for ἐν ἀνθρώπου εἴδει. And if you turn over to the next Page, you will find in the 3ᵈ Line κρείττονί πο χορῳ for κρείττονί ποι χώρῳ. And I might likewise refer you to pag. 109, 111, 113, 115, 116, 117, 121, 125, 126, 128, 129, &ᶜ. But, least you should likewise say these are Errours of the Press, I'll not insist upon 'em. *Tim.* I'm glad to find you so mercifull. But I fancy you would shew your Teeth if you could bite. *Tell-Tr.* Seeing you provoke me, I'll do your Business. *Tim.* I despise your Threatenings. *Tell-Tr.* And so do I your little men : silly Pretenders to Criticism, without Sense or Learning. *Tim.* Hei! day! What in the High-Rope! A high-Flyer & a Tantivi! *Tell-Tr.* I ner'e regard your Names, but am content to be an humble observer. *Tim.*
30 Of what? *Tell-Tr.* Of false Criticisms, and nonsensical Corrections of an Author when he needs none. *Tim.* What do you mean ? *Tell-Tr.* I find that in pag. 108. your assuming Professor, to amuse the ignorant, dealing worse with *Justin Martyr* than *Trypho* the *Jew* would have done. *Tim.* Pray how? *Tell-Tr.* By mangling his words so, by his Corrections and Interpunctions, as to make them neither Sense nor *Greek.* *Tim.* If you make this Charge good you'll bring me down a peg lower in my Conceit of him. *Tell-Tr.* Turn then to pag. 108. lin. 5. where you have αἱ δε κολάζονται· ἐς, ἂν αὐτοὺς καὶ εἶναι καὶ κολάζεσθαι ὁ Θεὸς θέλῃ. Now (to pass by his making κολάζονται to be the future tense in his translation, and his false concord of αὐτοὺς for αὐτὰς) I
40 would gladly know what that ἐς, ἂν &ᶜ. means. For I'm sure neither *Justin* M. nor Sᵗ. *Austin,* whom elsewhere (p. 140, 176.) he ignorantly takes for *Justin,* would have writ so. *Tim.* Now I must own you kill two Birds with one Stone. And I wonder how you came to be so good a Mark's-man. *Tell-Tr.* You should rather wonder how such an *insolent Ecclesiastick* should be made Professor. *Tim.* I am apt to believe his Arguments against Mʳ. *Dodwell,* & his other Performances, were cast into the Balance against the Merits of others. *Tell-Tr.* And something else too. For to say nothing of *Cyrill,* for the sake of honest *Dick Sart,* I do assure you that there is nothing material in his Book against Mʳ. *Dodwell* but what was started by Mʳ. *Clarke* or Mʳ. *Chishull.* *Tim.*
50 Who tells you so? *Tell-Tr.* Even Mʳ. *D——ll* himself, whom I take to be a competent Judge in this matter. *Tim.* 'Tis strange the world should be so easily impos'd upon. *Tell-Tr.* 'Tis not more strange than true. But *si mundus vult decipi, decipiatur. . . .* [220–230 blank.]

Feb. 27 (Th.). Last week Sʳ. *Christoph. Hales* going to Coventry to stand in the Election for Parliament-Man for that Place, he was, in his Journey, most unmercifully set upon by the Whiggish, Fanatical Party, and arrested, & carried to Goal, where they kept him so close that he could not speak to those that pass'd by & were inclin'd to vote for him. The Debt was about 100 *libs.* & this Act was done meerly to hinder an honest Gentleman from doing Service to his Country, in this time of Danger, when these crop ear'd whelps make it their business to undermine the Church, & once more ruine us. — ... For an Emendation of Livy see an Epistle of *Rubenius* to *Wendelin.* at the End of his Book de Natali Augusti.

Feb. 28 (Fri.). Some Coyns [7] sent me by M[r]. *Ralph Trumbull* of *Witney.* . . . .

March 1 (Sat.). D[r]. *Jane* was buried at *Christ-Church* on *Thursday*, 10 about 4 in the Afternoon. The Funeral was very mean. He has a Relation, a Servitour of *Exeter* Coll., his Sister's Son, who was neither invited, nor had any Legacy left him. D[r]. *Code* also of *All-Souls* Coll. (a Physitian) is related, but not invited. — On the 30th of *January* last was an abominable Riot committed in *All-Souls* College. M[r]. *Dalton* A.M. & M[r]. *Talbot*, son to the B[p]. of *Oxon*, A.B. both Fellows, had a Dinner drest, at 12 Clock, part of which was woodcocks, whose Heads they cut off, in contempt of the memory of the B. Martyr. At this Dinner were present two of the Pro-Proctors, of *Oriel* Coll. M[r]. *Ibbetson*[1] and M[r]. *Rogers* to their shame be it spoken, both low church Men. 'Tis 20 to be noted that this *Dalton*, an Empty Fellow, is one of those whom the Archb[p]. of *Cant.* D[r]. *Tennison*, put into the Society upon the Devolution to him of that Power when D[r]. *Finch* the late Warden died. He was for having *Calves-Heads*, but the Cook refus'd to dress them. — When King *William* was in Oxon in 1695, *Ant. à Wood* who saw him in the Theatre resembled him to one *Hen. Earle*, a poor, thin, meagre, hawk-nos'd Fellow in S[t]. *Clements* Parish, who was indeed exactly like him. — M[r]. *Higgons* Archdeacon of Meath in Ireland is taken into Custody for Preaching for the Security of ye Church of Eng. in this time of Danger. 'Tis said D[r]. Tennison sent for him before, & threaten'd 30 him; but M[r]. Higgons defi'd him. Quære? — *Hen. Cuffe* assisted in the first Edition of *Longus's Pastorals* printed at *Florence* in 1598. 4[o]. Not taken notice of by *Ant. à Wood.* — A Great Number of Roman Brass Coyns found at *Garsford* near *Abbingdon.* — M[r]. *Higgons* when before D[r]. *Tennison* told the D[r]. that his Sermon was as good as his Grace could make himself, & that the Clergy were afraid of speaking their Minds, whereas on the Contrary he was resolv'd undauntedly to declare his mind, & to do what he could to prevent the Danger approaching. — ... D[r]. *Code* of *All-Souls* who was as nearly related to

---

March 1. H. to Dr. T. Smith. Milles is to edit Hody's History of the Greek Tongue. The riot in All Souls' Buttery. Death of Dr. Jane; his legacies. Who is author of the English Translation of Tho. à Kempis (2 vols., with recommendation by Mr. Hickes)? Mr. Heywood (St. John's) has lately made much use of the MSS. of à Kempis in Bodley. Dodwell commends the part of Mill's Prolegomena already printed.

---

[1] M[r]. *Ibbetson* has since told me several times that he is heartily sorry for this thing, & that he was ignorant of the whole Matter, & had not ye least hand in carrying it on: wch perhaps may be true, he being a Man of very good sense, tho' it must be allow'd that he is a Whig.

Dr. *Jane* as Mr. *Foulkes*, & had good reason to expect a considerable Legacy from ye Doctor, was not so much as mention'd in his will; at which Dr. *Code* was extremely surpriz'd, seeing Dr. *Jane* often gave him to understand that he would amply reward him for his pains in attending upon him in several Journeys to *Gloucester* and *Exeter* : And ye said Dr. *Code*, (who has reason to believe that he was once in Dr. *Jane's* Will) is fully perswaded that this last will of Dr. *Jane* was made at the Instigation of Mr *Foulkes*, and by the contrivance of *Brookes* the Attorney, when Dr. *Jane* hardly knew what he did, having in a manner quite lost
10 his Memory. After Dr. *Jane* was dead Mr. *Foulkes* sent for Dr. *Code*, & when he came to him told him that it was to undeceive him, seeing there was nothing left him in the will. He gave him mourning &c. which is all perhaps he must expect, tho 'tis said Dr. *Code* intends to come upon him for the Loss of his Business in attending Dr. *Jane*, & for Fees as a Physitian in many Journeys made with the Dr. — When the Corps of the Bp. of *Chester*[1] was carry'd from *London* to that place to be buried, 'twas met by five Hundred Horse, & 25 Coaches, at some Distance from ye City of *Chester*, & when near the Boundaries of the City was met by the Mayor & Aldermen in their Formalities : all which
20 is a Demonstration of their Love and Affection they had to their late Bishop. He was a Man of a good Temper and Disposition, and had the Reputation of a good Scholar. He was Fellow of Trinity Coll. in Oxon. afterwards got a Welch Deanery and some other Preferments, and a little after the Revolution was made Bp. of Chester upon the Death of Dr. Cartwright. He has printed a Disswasive from Revenge, something about the Council of Trent in answer to a part of the Guide in Controversies, some sermons & perhaps some other things.

March 8 (Sat.). One Freke, of *Wadham* College, (I think he took no degree) has writ a Book, call'd *Essays about Learning*. He was
30 a whimsical Man. — Mr. *Leigh* of St. *John's* (commonly call'd *Rabbi Leigh*) of whom the Town's People of *Oxon* had a mighty opinion, has writ a Book call'd *Horologium Christianum*. He also made Additions to *Prideaux's Introduction to History*, which Additions I have by me in an interleav'd Book that I obtain'd from *Lichfield* the Printer. — Mr. *Thorpe* of University College is the Person who takes care of the Printing of *Iter Alpinum*, in which there are to be several Plates, which are to be done by Subscription, to which Dr. *Hudson*, Dr. *Woodward*, Dr. *Sloane*, Sir *Isaac Newton* (who has given 8 libr.) & others are contributors. — Mr. *Babington* was enter'd Gentleman Commoner of
40 University Coll. (under the tuition of Dr. *Hudson*) on *Thursday* last. His Grandfather *Zach. Babington* has publish'd a Discourse in the Law. The Master of University college (Dr. *Charlett*) knew him, & may give some Account of him. — The Dean of Xt *Church*, Dr. *Aldrich*, at the Request of Dr. *Hudson* (who is never backward in forwarding anything

---

March 6. H. to F. Cherry. Milles and his professorship. Thanks for Robortellus, which he has bound up ; proposes to transcribe it, and collate it with Sigonius', Pighius', & Gruter's copies. Asks for a sight of various coins.

---

[1] Dr. Stratford.

for the Publick) has invented & caus'd to be drawn Borders for M^r. Madox's Book about the *Exchequer Court* now ready for the Press.

March 9 (Sun.). S^r. *Andrew Fountaine's* Father is dead, & was buried the 20th of last Month. — Remember to look into *Beaumont's* book about Spirits conc. a Relation of *Thomas Perkes* of *Mangorsfield's* conversing with them. The Relation is also printed by itself, the Author M^r. *Bedford* a Divine. This *Perkes* died above a year since, & was very ingenious, as I have been told by some *Bristol* men, who knew him, who also say that he was not melancholy, but always of a chearfull Disposition. — I have heard it said by some of *Christ-* 10 *Church* that D^r. *Jane* did not die worth above 10 or 12 thousand *libs*. But this is a particular unknown, M^r. *Foulkes* keeping it intire to himself.

March 13 (Th.). Amongst *Junius's* Books num. 31. & Archb^p. *Laud's* num. E. 65. two Books printed at *Harlem*. They contain Extracts out of the *Apocalyps*, & have wooden cuts to explain & illustrate them. They answer in a great measure to a MS^t in a thin fol. in Bibl. Bodl. B. 86. Arch. & are the first Specimens of printing at *Harlem*. The MS^t hath blank leaves all along & I suppose were put for a Comment as there is a *German* one in that of *Laud's*. Both the printed ones are in colours 20 (as the MS^t is) and I believe were done in imitation of some MS^t from whence without doubt they were taken. In archbp. *Laud's* a little after the beginning is a leaf which has Pictures on both sides, different from the rest (which are only on one side) & seem to have been done with a Pen. They have a date at the bottom, viz. 1495, & 1496. At the End of *Laud's* there is writ 1529. at which time it seems that the MS^t Comment was writ by the Possessor of the Book. The Leaves are pasted together with a green Paint. The Signatures (there being no pages) are towards the top of the Leaf. — Among D^r. *Hody's* Books there are 9 Volumes in fol. of his own Collecting, in MS^t and 8 Vols. 30 in 4to. — The Printed Book of *Junius* above mention'd is not out of the Revelations, but out of several Places in Scripture, mostly Historical.

March 15 (Sat.). *Francis Prasalendius*, a *Græcian* of the Isle of *Corcyra*, lately a student in the Publick Library, & of *Gloucester* Hall, has printed a Book in the *Greek* Language (writ very well as I am inform'd by one of the Græcians of *Glouc.* Hall,) against *Traditions*, in which he falls upon D^r. *Woodroffe* very smartly. He printed another Book before this upon the same subject. . . .

March 15. H. to Dr. T. Smith. Mr. Dodwell tried to prevent Mr. Lee from becoming Philadelphian; with what effect H. cannot tell. Will be glad to see Smith's Discourse on Walt. Hilton; sends account of him from *Bibliotheca Cartusiana* by Theod. Petreius (Cologne, 1609, 8vo.). Hen. Cuffe assisted in ed. 1 of Longus' *Pastorals*, (Flor. 1598, 4to.). Not noticed by Wood. Mr. Bedford's story about Thos. Perkes of Mangorsfield confirmed (cf. Beaumont on *Genii*). He was in his senses to his dying day, and seemed penitent for having concerned himself in these matters. Bagford and his History of Printing; he might find several things for his purpose in the School-Tower, particularly among Mr. Twyne's notes. Remarks on various early books.

March 16 (Sun.). D^r. *Charlett* show'd me a Letter from M^r. *Bromley* wherein he intimates that in the Bill for printing sufficient care is taken of the Universitys, and that the Publick Libraries of each are to have copies of Books printed and reprinted by y^e *London* Booksellers. — Ponticus Varennius in Epist. Ded. ad Hist. Brit. I. [conc. Livy]. . . .

March 19 (Wed.). The following Letter sent to D^r. *Wells* from an unknown Hand in *Oxford* as appears from the Post Mark. . .

Reu^d. Doctor,—I pray leaue of your writeing as you doe, that all Dissentors are Guilty of a Damnable Sin In not hereing at the Church of England, I have
10 heard seuerall of the Uniuerssitly say yow haue done more hurt then good, and I think yow are very uncharitable In Condemning all those that Doe not Conforme, I hope It Is not from malice that makes yow soe furious, Consider them words he that hateth his brother Is a murderor, I pray god to give yow Right Understanding In all things that yow may preach and write the truth as It Is In Jesus. |

Superscrib'd,   Sr Yours
To the Reuerend Doctor Wells
    at Cotesbach neer Lutterworth, In
        Leistershire.

20 — M^r. *Obadiah Walker* Master of *University* College borne at *Dartfield* in *Yorkshire.* The Rector of this Place is M^r. *William Greenwood,* A.M. of *University*-College, in which House he had a Fellowship which he resign'd yesterday. *Quære* about *Sam. Crooke* Vicar of *Darfield?* He is a *Cambridge* Man, & in full orders, but a very novice as appears from a Letter I have seen to M^r. *Greenwood,* which ends thus,—*For I have read & experienc'd too, that that (Love) keeps the Parson from Parochial Duty, For who can at once court Religion and Beauty.* and superscrib'd, *To the Reverend M^r. William Greenwood | Fellow of University Coll. in Oxford. | Let this go by London. Perhaps he's there. |* — M^r. Wood in
30 Athen. Oxon. Ed. II. Vol. II. col. 933. tells us M^r. Ob. Walker was born at Worsperdate near Barnesley in Yorkshire.

NOTES AND ILLUSTRATIONS.

VOL. I.

Page 1, line 1. **Hearne's Catalogue** was printed in *The Monthly Miscellany*; *or, Memoirs for the Curious*, Dec. 1708 and Jan. 1709 (Hope Collection 72). It forms No. XII in *Catalogus Operum Thomae Hearnii.* See Thoresby's *Correspondence*, ii. 138, 146.

1. 2. The Bodleian MS. of the *Anthologia astrologica* of **Vettius Valens** (now Arch. Seld. B. 19) is described in Mr. Coxe's Catalogue as ' Codex chartaceus, in folio, ff. 1⌊8⌋6, sec. xvii., sumptibus Christophori Longolii descriptus, postea Johannis Dee.' Dr. Edward Bernard (1638-1697), whose Life was written by Dr. Thos. Smith, made the acquaintance of Huet, the learned Bishop of Avranches (1630-1721), at Paris in 1676. In a letter dated Jan. 29, 1704, Hearne enquires of Dr. Smith whether Huet ever edited Vettius Valens, ' as Sʳ. Edw. Sherburn tells us (in the Appendix to his translation of Manilius) he designed.' Part of Vettius Valens is printed at p. 332 of Lydi *de Mensibus* ed. Roether (Lips. 1827), 'ex Jacobi Gronovii apographo, quod Creuzerus a Wyttenbachio dono acceperat.' Roether refers to Fabric. *Biblioth. Graec.* ii. 510, and iv. pp. 144, 162, 219, ed. Harles. See Dodwell's *Epistolary Discourse*, pp. 245 *sqq.*; Dr. Bliss's note, *Reliq. Hearn.* I. 1 (1869); and Index to this vol.

1. 6. **William Joyner** (1622-1706), Fellow of Magdalen, resigned his fellowship and became a Roman Catholic during the Civil War, was restored by James II in 1687 and deprived in the following year. See Wood's *Athenae* (iv. 587 ed. Bliss). According to Macaulay (*History*, i. 368) it is doubtful whether even Christopher Milton was ever formally received into the Church of Rome; but see Foss, *Biographia Juridica, art.* Milton.

1. 9. The characters of **Godolphin** (1645-1712) and **Wharton** (*c.* 1640-1715) have been sketched by Macaulay (i. 125 and ii. 462). A very high (probably exaggerated) estimate of the former as a financier will be found in Dr. J. H. Burton's *Reign of Queen Anne* (i. 35); but for those who care little for politics his memory will be ever fresh as the husband of the Margaret Blagge whose Life was written by Evelyn and first published by Bishop Wilberforce in 1847. See also Burnet, ii. 239 *sq.*

1. 21. **Claude Saumaise** (*c.* 1593-1653) is perhaps now best remembered by his *Defensio Regia pro Carolo I.* Dr. Johnson's remarks on him in the Life of Milton, and his quotation from Hobbes, are to somewhat the same effect. Hearne just below expresses a decided preference for Milton's Latinity over that of Salmasius.

1. 27. **Edmund Scarborough**, M.A., Prebendary of Sarum, published at Oxford from his father's MS. in 1705 *The English Euclide.* For Sir Charles (*c.* 1616— *c.* 1695) see *Fasti Oxon.* ii. 97. He left another son Charles (D.C.L. 1702), who seems to be confused with Edmund by the Dictionaries.

1. 29. The Greek Testament as edited by **Dr. John Mill** (*c.* 1645-1707), at this time Principal of Edmund Hall, was published after thirty years' labour, only fourteen days before Mill's death. The controversy which raged over this work is well known; but what is popularly but incorrectly known as Mill's text is still in great repute, and is continually reprinted. For its relation to later editions one can scarcely do better than refer to Prof. Jebb's Chapter (X.) on Bentley's proposed edition of the New Testament in his Life of the great scholar.

2. 5. Sir Geo. Mackenzie (1636-1691), founder of the Advocates' Library, published his *Jus Regium* in 1684. See a full account of him in *Fasti Oxon.* ii. 411. The earliest edition of Buchanan's *De Jure Regni* in the Bodleian is dated 1580; ed. 3, 1581.

2. 10. Dr. Jonathan Edwards (1629-1712; V. C. 1689-91) published his *Preservative* in four Parts, 1693-1703, and the Index was compiled by Hearne himself. **Dr. John Edwards** (1637-1716), sometime fellow of St. John's, Cambridge, published Part I of *The Preacher* in 1705, and Part II 1706.

2. 14 *sqq.* I can find no *separate* edition of the *Fragmenta Sallustii* by **Popma**; but see his *Fragmenta veterum historicorum Latinorum* (1620). Nor was a second edition of **Dodwell** on Occasional Communion ever published, if we may accept as complete the bibliography prefixed by Hearne to Dodwelli *De Parma Equestri Woodwardiana Dissertatio* (1713).

2. 19. Selden xi. 2 is thus described in Mr. Coxe's Catalogue: 'Philonis Judaei de specialibus legibus, quae referuntur ad tria Decalogi capita, octavum, nonum et decimum, ac de furto non faciendo, de falso testimonio non dicendo, ac de non concupiscendo, tum de iis, quae ad haec singula referuntur; denique de justitia praeceptis decem universis congruente.' The whole MS. is of the 11th century.

2. 24. This MS. is now catalogued Cod. Barocc. 38. **J. W. Berger** (d. 1751) does not appear to have ever carried out the intention here attributed to him, but the Scholia were printed in Jebb's edition of Aristides (Oxford: 1722-30).

2. 29. Hearne's edition of **Livy**, with which he was at this time engrossed, was published at Oxford in 1708 in 6 vols. 8vo.

2. 36. D. G. Morhof published ed. 1 of his *Polyhistor* at Lübeck in 1688, and his *De Patavinitate Liviana Liber* in 1685. The late Mr. Mark Pattison (*utinam abesset infaustum illud nuper!*) says of Salmasius' Latin that it 'was all the more readable because it was not classical or idiomatic' (*Milton*, p. 106).

2. 38. Sir James Astry, of Woodend, Harlington, Beds. (B.C.L. 1677), one of the Masters in Chancery, corrected ed. 3 of Spelman's *Glossarium Archaiologicum* (1687), and prefixed a Memoir of the author. He likewise published (1700) a translation of Faxardo's *Royal Politician represented in Emblems*. **Isaac Vossius** (b. 1618), son of Gerard, was appointed Canon of Windsor 1673, and died at his lodgings in the Castle in 1688, 'leaving then behind him,' says Evelyn in his letter to Pepys of Aug. 12, 1689, 'the best private library, as it was then supposed, in the whole world,' which was purchased and carried away by the University of Leiden. Bentley likewise negotiated for its purchase on behalf of the University of Oxford: see Monk's *Life of Bentley*, i. 21 *sq.*, Jebb's *Bentley*, 8.

3. 2. The *Memorial of the Church of England*, which had the honour of being denounced in a message from the Queen, and which recurs so often in these Collections, was written by **Dr. James Drake** and H. Pooley, M.P. for Ipswich, whose names are mentioned as joint authors in the Preface to the edition of 1711. See Boyer, *Reign of Queen Anne*, 178 *sqq.*, 210; *Life of Calamy*, ii. 35; and Dr. Bliss's note, *Reliq. Hearn.* i. pp. 2 *sqq.* Some particulars of the life of Drake will be found in D'Israeli's *Calamities of Authors*. The great Minister of State was of course Godolphin, who is alluded to in the *Memorial* as Volpone.

3. 14. William Dugard (1605-1662), M.A. Camb. 1630, printer, and head-master of Merchant Taylors' School (1644), secured a measure of immortality by his connexion with the printing and publication of the *Eikon Basilike* (see Wagstaffe's Vindication, ed. 3, p. 107). The productions of his press are noticeable for their comparative accuracy and somewhat pedantic spelling. His *Lexicon Graeci Testamenti Alphabeticum* was published in 1660. He was a Latin poet of some pretensions.

3. 16. The first complete version of the Bible in Spanish, by **Cassiodoro Reyna**, was published in 4to. in 1569. It is commonly called *The Bear's Bible* from the printer's device on the title-page. See Ebert, i. 180.

3. 22. Dr. Benj. Woodroffe, Canon of Christ Church, whose eccentricities will be familiar to the readers of Prideaux' *Letters to Ellis*, was Principal of Gloucester Hall 1692-1711. He 'had the care of the Greek youths. He published a Greek pamphlet, like Greek funeral inscriptions. In 1703, *The Case of Gloucester-hall, in Oxford, rectifying the false stating thereof*, without title or date.' [This was really by

John *Baron* but anonymous.] Noble's *Continuation of Granger*, i. 97. For further particulars of Dr. Woodroffe and his ' Greek youths,' the reader may be referred to Wordsworth, *Social Life at the English Universities*, pp. 324 *sq.*; G. Williams, *Orthodox Church in the 18th Century*, pp. xviii. *sqq.*; the Rev. E. S. Ffoulkes in *Union Review*, 1863 (no. xvii. of ' Fragmenta Varia ' and Article xxxiii); Pearson, *Chaplains to the Levant Company*, 43 *sq.*; *Fifth Report of Hist. MSS. Comm.* 377; Wood's *Life* 283, &c.

3. 33. **Timothy Nourse,** Fellow of University from 1658 till his secession to the Church of Rome in 1673 (*Athenae Oxon.* iv. 448). See Wood's story of his reconversion and relapse, *Life*, p. 198.

3. 45. Wood has a very laudatory notice of **Andrew Allam** (1655-1685) in *Athenae Oxon.* iv. 174, culminating in the remark that ' nothing but Years and Experience were wanting, to make him a compleat walking Library.' Dr. Kennett never published his collections on the subject here referred to, which are preserved in vol. 935 of the Lansdown Collection in the British Museum, under the title of ' Diptycha Ecclesiae Anglicanae: sive Tabulae Sacrae,' &c.

4. 2. **Peter King,** afterwards Lord King and Chancellor of England (1669-1733), published his *History of the Apostles' Creed* in 1702. He had previously written (1691-2) *An Enquiry into the Constitution, Discipline, Unity, and Worship of the Primitive Church* (answered by Sclater the non-juror); but the book here alluded to, if projected, never saw the light. See Foss, *Biographia Juridica, art.* King. For some interesting particulars of King's earlier life, the reader may be referred to Mr. Fox Bourne's Life of his kinsman John Locke, *passim.*

4. 5. **Sir John Osborn,** Bart., of Chicksand, Beds. (1659-1720).

4. 34. The story of **Jonas Proast** (or Provast), M.A. 1666, Chaplain of All Souls, and his ten years' struggle with the Warden, Dr. Leopold Finch, on his wrongful dismissal, ending in Proast's final victory, is told in Prof. Burrows' *Worthies of All Souls*, pp. 308 *sqq.* He was Archdeacon of Berks 1698-1710.

4. 50. *The Dyet of Poland* (Pamph. 260), Dantzick (= London), 4to., is attributed in the Bodleian Catalogue to Defoe; while a reply, *The Dyet of Poland, a satyr, consider'd paragraph by paragraph,* is bound up with Dunton's tracts.

5. 1. **William Wotton** (1666-1726) was, according to Chalmers, ' admitted of Catharine Hall, Cambridge, in April 1676, some months before he was ten years old; and upon his admission Dr. John Eachard, then Master of the College, gave him this remarkable testimony: *Gulielmus Wottonus infra decem annos nec Hammondo nec Grotio secundus.*' His part in the Phalaris controversy is well known: see Monk's *Life of Bentley*, i. 9; Swift's *Battle of the Books*, &c.

5. 6. **George Keith,** a voluminous writer himself and the cause of voluminous writing in others, the friend of Fox (see the Diary *passim*) and Penn, and tutor of Barclay, left the Quakers in 1694, and was in 1702 presented to the living of Edburton, near Shoreham. See Bickley's *George Fox and the Early Quakers*, pp. 351 *sqq.*; Sewel, *History of the .. Quakers*, ii. 493 &c.; Burton, *Book-Hunter* (1885), 189; *infra* pp. 15 *sq.*

5. 26. **William Stratford,** d. 1729, was likewise Archdeacon of Richmond. He was a benefactor to the Library of Ch. Ch. His monument, together with that of **Dr. Antony Radcliffe,** Canon 1681-1705, and founder of Peckwater Quadrangle, is in the Cathedral. See Wood-Gutch, *Colleges and Halls*, 495, 499. There is an error in Le Neve-Hardy, ii. 531, where the date of Radcliffe's death is given as 1703.

5. 53. The writer of the article ' St. Anthony,' in the *Dictionary of Christian Biography*, holds that the Life is by St. Athanasius, but is probably interpolated.

6. 10. For leather money see *Notes and Queries*, 1st Ser., vol. vii. 137 (quoting Camden's *Remaines, art.* Money), 366.

6. 32. **Sir Andrew Fountaine,** of Narford, Norfolk, contributed an article entitled ' Numismata Anglo-Saxonica et Anglo-Danica' to Hickes' *Thesaurus.* Hearne dedicated to him his edition of Justin (1705). In the course of his travels he amassed large collections of articles of *virtù,* which were dispersed so recently as June 1884 at Messrs. Christie's. He is repeatedly mentioned by Swift in the *Journal to Stella.* In 1727 he was appointed Warden of the Mint, and retained that office till his death in 1753. See Nichols' *Bowyer*, p. 110. He is often mentioned in these Collections. For a letter from him to Hearne, see *Academy,* June 21, 1884, p. 439.

6. 35. J. Burman (M.A. 1704), afterwards Vicar of Newington, Kent, was *stepson* of Dr. Plot (1640–1696), who married his mother Rebecca, widow of Henry Burman, in 1690.

6. 48. See *Chronicque de la Traïson et Mort de Richart deux Roy dengleterre*, ed. Benj. Williams (London: 1846), and Preface. Cf. Nicolson, *English Historical Library*, p. 81; Hardy's *Descriptive Catalogue of Materials*, i. 871. The British Museum MS. was edited with translation by J. Webb, M.A., in 1819.

7. 13. Samuel Parker, eldest son of the Bishop of Oxford of the same name, author of the *Bibliotheca Biblica*, and editor of various ecclesiastical historians, died in 1733. Some account of him will be found in Lathbury's *History of the Nonjurors*, 374.

7. 17. Various memoranda of Hearne's relating to **Antony Wood** are brought together at the end of Wood's *Life* (ed. 1848). Wood was constantly during life suspected of an inclination to the doctrines and practices of the Roman Church. So in 1674 Humphrey Prideaux wrote to Ellis (*Corresp.*, Camden Soc. p. 15): 'Tony Wood, our antiquary, having pored so long on old monkish storys, at last dotes on them and is turned Papist.' See also Wood's own remarks in the *Life*, 178, 207, &c.

7. 36. Evelyn, Earl of Kingston, created Marquis of Dorchester 1706, Duke of Kingston 1715, held various high offices of state under George I. Henry **Earl of Kent** became Lord Chamberlain April 23, 1704; Marquis of Kent 1706; and Duke of Kent 1710.

8. 1. See the *Ox. . . d Dialogue*. Between a Master of Arts and a Stranger. London, 1705 (Gough, Oxf. 113).

8. 10. The reference is to Clarendon, Book IV, § 44.

8. 12. For particulars of Dr. **Radcliffe's** favours to Obadiah Walker, of which Hearne will tell us more hereafter, see Pittis' racy Life of the great physician. Walker was indebted to Dr. Radcliffe for his tombstone in St. Pancras Churchyard, which bore the touching inscription, PER BONAM FAMAM ET PER INFAMIAM.

8. 14. Jas. Badger (New Coll., M.A. 1686) was master of New College School. See Wood's *Life*, p. 302.

8. 20. If infamy could kill—Oates is justly characterised by Hume as 'the most infamous of mankind'—the inventor of the Popish Plot would scarcely have survived to the ripe age of 85. Probably his last public appearance was at Westminster Hall in 1702 for scandalising and assaulting Mrs. Eleanor James (*Selections from the Sommers Tracts*, 606 sqq.).

8. 34. Luttrell (*Brief Relation*, July 19, 1705) writes:—'The close of last week Monsieur **Hugueton**, the French banker, who came lately from Paris, was examined at Guildhall upon a writ of enquiry for the queen, and deposed, that since the war he had remitted to the French army in Flanders and Italy the sum of 4,210,520*l.*; and further deposed, that since November last he had given out bills to several bankers of Paris in his own hand for 4 millions of livres for the use above; half of which was paid, and the other half in safe hands here, which her majestie may have when she pleases, and amounts to 105,263*l.*' For the cause of his flight see *ib.* vol. v. pp. 513, 569.

8. 38. Sam. Swynfen, Pemb., B.A. 1699; New Inn Hall, M.A. 1702; B.M. 1706; Pemb. D.M. 1712.

9. 1. For **Richard James** (1592–1638), nephew of Thomas James, the first Librarian of the Bodleian, see the amusing Life in *Athenae Oxon.* ii. 629. He had the honour to be described by Selden in the Preface to *Marmora Arundeliana* as 'vir multijugae doctrinae studiique indefatigabilis;' and to be the friend and librarian of Sir Robert Cotton, with whom he was a fellow-prisoner in the Tower (1629) when these verses were written, under circumstances described in Mr. S. R. Gardiner's *History of England*, vii. pp. 139 *sqq.* His MSS. passed into the hands of Greaves, and from him into the Bodleian (Macray, *Annals*, 103). The Rev. A. B. Grosart has edited part of his works.

9. 15. This allusion to **Calanus** is explained by Dr. Bliss *ad loc.*, who quotes Arrian, vii. 2.

9. 26. For an account of this action see Stanhope's *Reign of Queen Anne*, i. 203, and Boyer, pp. 196 *sqq.*; and for the proceedings in the Parliament at Edinburgh, Stanhope, i. 224; Boyer, 184.

9. 37. This book is described in Ballard's *Memoirs*, pp. 14 *sqq.*

9. 43. The *Antiquities of Middlesex*, by **John Bownack**, never got beyond the second Number, the public agreeing with Charlett's and Hearne's opinion of its merits. A copy in the Bodleian has MS. notes by Dr. Rawlinson.

9. 46. Abednego Seller's Life is in the *Athenæ*, iv. 563. He is now best remembered as the author of *The Devout Communicant.*

10. 20 *sqq.* Thomas Bisse, M.A. 1698, afterwards Chancellor and Prebendary of Hereford, *ob.* 1731; **William Tilly**, M.A. 1697, and Rector of Albury, near Rycot. Tilly's Sermon was quoted by Bp. Burnet in the 'Church in danger' debate; Boyer, 217.

10. 46. A copy of the inscription on **Dr. Busby's** monument is appended to Wood's biography of him in Dr. Bliss's edition of the *Athenae.* Mr. **Lewis Southcombe**, Rector of Rose-Ash, Devon, is described as a '*Penitent*' in Appendix VI to the Life of Kettlewell.

11. 2. Joseph Woodward, D.C.L. 1687.

11. 5. Abraham Woodhead (1608-1678), one of the most estimable of the converts of that period to Roman Catholicism, was somewhat absurdly put forward as the author of *The Whole Duty of Man.* (See *Athenae*, iii. 1157.) His controversial works were, for the most part, printed posthumously by Obadiah Walker at his private Press in University College. The books so produced generally bear the head of King Alfred on the title-page.

11. 18. Edmund Perkes of C.C.C., M.A. 1697; he is described as 'of Cambridge' in the Bodleian Printed Catalogue. Hearne records his death in 1706. **Wm. Buckeridge**, mentioned just below, was M.A. in 1688.

11. 35. Particulars of **Bodley's** Agreement with the Stationers' Company are given at pp. 30 *sqq.* of Macray's *Annals of the Bodleian.*

11. 40. Samuel Wesley (*c.* 1666-1735) was the father of two more famous sons. He was presented to the living of Epworth, Linc., *c.* 1693; and in 1705 printed a poem on the Battle of Blenheim, as a reward for which he was appointed by the Duke of Marlborough chaplain of Col. Lepelle's regiment. This preferment he lost for the reasons here stated; and by two incendiary fires he was reduced to poverty, and was thrown into a debtors' prison, from which he was delivered by a public subscription. *The Life of Christ: an Heroic Poem*, was first published in folio in 1693; reprinted with additions, &c., 1697. See Nichols' *Lit. Anec.* v. 212 *sqq.*; Southey's *Life of Wesley*, i. 6 *sqq.*; Stevens' *History of the Life and Times of John Wesley*, chap. ii.; Index to Rawlinson MSS.

11. 47. 'Perconite' is, I suppose, equivalent to Perkinite, Perkin being an uncomplimentary nickname for the Pretender, containing a delicate allusion to Perkin Warbeck. See *e. g.* a quotation from a tract of 1690 in Abbey and Overton's *English Church in the 18th Century*, i. 53; *ib.* p. 77, a quotation from Leslie *an.* 1710, 'All the last reign they gave the Pretender no other name than Perkin and Impostor.'

12. 4. *The Memorial ... answered Paragraph by Paragraph* is attributed in a MS. note in the Bodleian copy to 'Dr. Pittis's son.' For other replies, see Bodleian Catalogue.

12. 6. James Perizonius (Voorbroek), 1651-1715, was Professor at Franeker and at Leiden, editor of Q. Curtius and Ælian, and author of various works on classical literature, history, and chronology, &c.

12. 48. Humphrey Hody (1659-1706), Regius Professor of Greek, and benefactor of Wadham, published his work, *De bibliorum textibus originalibus, versionibus graecis et Latina vulgata*, in 1705. He was distinguished as a scholar at an early age; so that Isaac Vossius characterised him as 'juvenis Oxoniensis' in criticising his dissertation *Contra historiam Aristeae*, published in 1684.

13. 4. Of **Thomas Milles**, who is frequently confounded by Hearne's correspondents with Dr. Mill, we shall hear a good deal in the sequel. He was M.A. 1695, succeeded Hody as Professor of Greek in 1706, was consecrated Bishop of Waterford 1708, died 1740. His edition of St. Cyril was published at Oxford in folio 1703.

13. 25. Dr. Henry James, M.A. 1667, President of Queens' Coll., Cam., Bentley's immediate predecessor in the Regius Chair of Divinity, Prebendary of Canterbury

1705, d. 1717.—Zaccheus Isham, M.A. 1674, chaplain to Compton, Bishop of London, Rector of St. Botolph's Bishopsgate, and Canon of Canterbury 1691, published some Sermons and a Treatise on the Catechism (*Athen. Oxon.* iv. 654).

13. 32. Patrick Young (1584–1652) was library-keeper to James I and Charles I, and the friend of Selden and of all the scholars of his time. Dr. T. Smith published his biography in his *Vitae quorundam eruditissimorum et illustrium virorum* (1707).

13. 44. Halley (1656–1742) had succeeded Dr. Wallis as Savilian Professor of Geometry in 1703. **David Gregory** (1661–1708) was elected Savilian Professor of Astronomy in 1691. An uncomplimentary remark by Roger Cotes will be found at vol. i. p. 259 of Rigaud's *Correspondence of Scientific Men*; and particulars of Gregory's death in *Letters from the Bodleian*, vol. i. pp. 176 *sqq.*, together with Sir Isaac Newton's testimonial in his favour on his candidature for the Savilian Professorship.

14. 22. Dr. John Earle (1601–1665), after the Restoration successively Dean of Westminster and Bishop of Worcester and Salisbury, was the author of the well-known *Microcosmographie*, which was edited with notes by Dr. Bliss in 1811, and has recently been reprinted by Mr. Arber. He was likewise the author of the Latin translation of the *Eikon Basilike*, published at the Hague 1649 (12mo.). See Walton's *Lives*, 'Hooker' (vol. i. pp. 326–7, ed. 1805).

14. 30. For the *Friendly Debate between a Conformist and a Nonconformist* (1668), see Patrick's Autobiography (1839), pp. 59 *sqq.*

14. 31. The proposed Latin translation of **Greaves'** two treatises was, I believe, never executed. See Ward's *Lives of the Gresham Professors*, 146 *sq.* There was a French translation in 1663.

14. 34. It was, according to Walton (*Lives*, vol. ii. p. 204), the *Eikon Basilike* that **Sanderson** designed to translate; 'but when he had done half of it most excellently, his friend Dr. Earle prevented him, by appearing to have done the whole very well before him.'

14. 41. The full title of this book, together with a third memorandum by Hearne himself, dated Aug. 22, 1707, is given by Dr. Bliss in *Reliq. Hearn.* i. 14.

VOL. II.

Page 15, line 30. For the day of thanksgiving, see Boyer, p. 198; and for the debate in the Scottish Parliament, *ib.* 184 *sqq.*

15. 36. W. Marten, M.A. 1630.

16. 23. For a Catalogue of **Dr. Dee's** MSS., see his *Private Diary* (Camden Soc.), pp. 65 *sqq.*; and for his life and works, the biography in Smith's *Vitae*.

16. 25. This is now included in Cod. Barocc. xv (f. 22). It is printed in the Works of St. Chrysostom, v. 539.

17. 2. John Thorpe (1682–1750), B.A. 1701, F.R.S. 1705, published a volume of Scheuchzer's *Itinera Alpina* in 1708. He practised as a physician at Rochester, and devoted his leisure hours to the study of the antiquities of that city and of the county of Kent. His *Registrum Roffense* was published by his son of the same name in 1769.

17. 6. The book referred to is entitled, *Some remarkable passages in the holy Life and Death of the Rev. E. T., most of them drawn out of his own Diary*, by Joseph Boyse. There is an analysis of it in Calamy-Palmer, *Nonconformist's Memorial*, ii. 449 *sqq.* Boyse will be familiar to all readers of Thoresby's Diary and Correspondence.

17. 11. J. W. de Berger, d. 1751, was Professor of Eloquence at Wittemberg; and his brother, **J. G. de Berger**, d. 1736, an eminent physician and author of *Physiologia Medica*, &c. A third brother, **J. H. de Berger**, was Professor of Law at Wittemberg. J. A. Fabricius published his *Bibliotheca Graeca* at Hamburg in 14 vols. 1705–1728; ed. 2 of his *Bibliotheca Latina* in 1708: his projected ed. of Eunapius does not appear to have ever seen the light.

17. 37. The reference is to *The Ladies' Calling*, part ii. sect. i. par. 3. The fact that Woodhead was a Roman Catholic is, as Ballard remarks, almost sufficient of itself to put him out of court as the author of a series of works so obviously Anglican as those of the writer of *The Whole Duty of Man*.

17. 39. A full account of the extraordinary impostor George Psalmanaazaar (d. 1763, *aetat*. 83), taken from his own Memoirs, will be found in the Dictionaries. He is said to have been convinced of the error of his ways by reading Law's *Serious Call*. Dr. Johnson had a very great liking for his society, and used to 'sit with him at an alehouse in the city;' he 'reverenced him for his piety, and would as soon have thought of contradicting a Bishop.' See also Napier's *Johnsoniana*, p. 72; Mrs. Piozzi had heard Johnson say that 'his piety, penitence, and virtue exceeded almost what we read as wonderful even in the lives of saints.'

17. 43. Cf. Luttrell, v. 576: 'Tuesday last died the Right Hon. Phillip, Earl of Leicester, at his seat of Penchurch, in Kent, aged about 27, and succeeded in honour and estate by his brother, John Sydney, Esq., M.P. for Brackley.' Tilney was twice returned for Whitchurch, and twice unseated on petition, in 1708.

18. 16. The reference is to Hearne's ed. of Livy, vol. vi. p. 259. For 'promis'd' (line 11) *read* 'procur'd.'

18. 38. Apollonii *De sectione Rationis libri duo ex Arabico MS., Lat. versi; accedunt ejusdem de sectione Spatii libri duo Lat. restituti . . .* opera Edm. Halleii was published at the Sheldonian Theatre in 1706.

18. 41. The exact title of Prideaux' great work was to be *The History of the Ruin of the Eastern Church*. His subsequent publications were of minor importance till the appearance of Part I of his *Connection* in 1715. See *Life of Prideaux*, 98 *sqq*.

19. 3. For a short account of Guiscard's previous career, see Boyer, pp. 244 *sq.*, and Burnet's *Own Time*, vi. 37 *sqq*. He afterwards attained greater notoriety by his attempt on Harley's life. See references in Index to Scott's ed. of Swift.

19. 10. Tanner was at work on Leland so early as 1695 (see Thoresby's *Correspondence*, i. 211, 238 and Index to Tanner MSS.), but part of the work ultimately fell into the hands of the 'all-editing Hearne,' as he is styled by Prof. Burrows, while the *de Scriptoribus* was edited by Ant. Hall in 1709, who published Boston in 1722. Charlett's pathetic account of Wood's dying gift of these materials to Tanner is printed in the *Life*, p. 321. Tanner's edition (the second or 'spurious' one of the *Athenae*) was published in 1721.

19. 17. Dr. Thomas Wood, New Coll., D.C.L. 1703, was the eldest son of Wood's third brother, Robert, by his wife, Mary Drope. For particulars of the *Vindication* (which is prefixed to ed. 2 of the *Athenae*), and of the Appendix to Pope's Life of Bp. Seth Ward, see Wood's *Life*, p. 293 and *n*. Frequent mention will be found of James Tyrrell, grandson of Archbp. Ussher, in Fox Bourne's *Life of Locke*.

19. 37. Dorothy Lady Pakington's claim to the authorship of *The Whole Duty of Man* is best stated by Ballard, *Memoirs of Learned Ladies*, pp. 316 *sqq*.; but her case is a very weak one. The best *résumé* of the whole controversy is that contributed by Mr. Solly to the *Bibliographer* for August, 1882; and perhaps I may be permitted to refer to my articles in the *Academy*, vol. xxii. pp. 348, 364, 382, where I have advocated the Allestree-Fell authorship.

19. 39. Francis Willoughby's (1635–1672) *Ornithologia* was published posthumously by Ray in 1676, and in English in 1678.

19. 41. Mr. Ellis, of Isleworth, reckoned among his pupils Theobald, the Shakespearean Commentator, and both the sons of Archbishop Sharp. The Archbishop, however, withdrew his son 'who then only remained with him,' 'as soon as he was informed that Mr. Ellis had refused to take the oath' (*Life of Sharp*, i. 269). Cf. Boyer, 217.

20. 1 *sqq*. For these events, cf. Luttrell, v. 577 *sqq*.

20. 12. See Dr. Bliss's note on this Bible, *Reliq. Hearn*. i. 11 *sq*.

20. 44. Ridley was consecrated Sept. 25, 1547 (Stubbs, *Registr. Sacr. Angl*.).

21. 9. Sir Edmund Warcupp, nephew of Speaker Lenthall, was a Captain in the Parliamentary Army; D.C.L. 1670; knighted in 1684. This narrative was finally bequeathed to the Bodleian by Ballard (Macray's *Annals*, p. 187 and *n*.). Sir Edward Walker's *Historical Collections* appeared in folio, London, 1705.

21. 24. The present press-mark of this MS. is ' Bodley 956.'

21. 48. **Read**, the oculist, is mentioned in the *Spectator*, Nos. 472, 547. See Swift's *Journal to Stella*, April 11, 1711; Noble's *Continuation of Granger*, ii. 231; and *Tatler* (Nichols' ed.), vi. 60 *sqq*. His knighthood was conferred upon him ' in consideration of his good services done by restoring to sight gratis great numbers of seamen and soldiers.' **Edward Hannes** (*Athenae*, iv. 667), Ch. Ch., D.M. 1695, succeeded Dr. Plot as Reader in Chemistry in 1690, and died 1710. See an account of a stratagem of his to get into practice in London in the Life of Radcliffe, p. 37 (ed. 1715). He was a contributor to the *Musae Anglicanae*, and a benefactor to Westminster School.

22. 5. Cf. Luttrell, v. 561, 577, 582. The soldier was named Joseph Dalton, and Major Winsley was accused of abetting him to murder McLennan, who was supporting Sir John Jennings against Col. Crawford, a ' Tacker,' as candidate for Queenborough.

22. 28. **J. G. Pritz** (1662–1732) wrote an Introduction to the Reading of the N. T. and a work *De Immortalitate Animae*, and published editions of the Greek Testament, of St. Macarius, and of the letters of Milton. The term ' Superintendent ' (or ' Senior '), almost = bishop, is explained in the *Life of Sharp*, i. 404.

23. 12. For Dodwell's refusal to take holy orders and consequent resignation of his fellowship at Trinity Coll., Dublin, see the Life by Brokesby, pp. 23–25. We are told that Jeremy Taylor offered to procure him a dispensation to continue him in his fellowship, which Dodwell declined.

23. 22. **Dr. Wake**, Dean of Exeter 1702, afterwards Archbp. of Canterbury, was consecrated Bishop of Lincoln, October 21, 1705. **Dr. Launcelot Blackburn** was installed Dean of Exeter, Nov. 3, 1705, and promoted to the Bishopric in 1717. Sir Jonathan Trelawny was the occupant of the See at this time.

24. 40. The date of the Bodleian copy of this fraudulent edition of Alex. **Sardus'** *Liber de Nummis* is 1685. The genuine work was originally published at Mainz, 1579.

25. 4. Cf. Marshall, *Early History of Woodstock Manor*, p. 259.

25. 14. The author of *An Essay towards a Proposal for Catholic Communion* was **Dr. Joshua Bassett**, Caius, M.A. 1665, Master of Sidney-Sussex, 1686–1688. He was deprived in the latter year as a Roman Catholic. There is a brief summary of this controversy in the *Life of Sharp*, i. 61 *sq*. See Index to Tanner MSS.

25. 15. Of **Edward Stephens**, a very interesting character among the early nonjurors, we shall hear much in the sequel. See *note* on p..95, l. 33.

25. 41. For an exposition of **Grabe's** views with regard to the expediency of prayers for the dead, &c., the reader may be referred to Lathbury's *Nonjurors*, pp. 301–2. See also Secretan's *Life of Nelson*, 220 *sqq*.

26. 10. **Bonaventure Giffard** was elected by King James's fellows President of Magdalen, March 1688, and removed in the October following. He was arrested after the Revolution, but released on condition of transporting himself beyond sea. He published one or two Sermons. He is mentioned, *Life of Frampton*, 157.

26. 13. For this fire in St. Clement's Lane, see Luttrell v. 580.

27. 6. **Richard Tenison**, Bp. of Killala 1681, Clogher 1691, Meath 1697 (see Cotton, *Fasti Eccl. Hib.* iii. 120 *sq*.).

27. 10. This letter is No. XXXV in Hearne's Catalogue of Dodwell's works.

27. 18. **Hans Sloane's** *Voyage to the Islands Madera, Barbados, Nieves, St. Christopher's, and Jamaica, with the Natural History*, was published in 2 vols. folio; Vol. i. 1707, Vol. ii. 1725,

27. 22. **Drusius** (John Driessche, 1550–1616) was professor of Oriental languages successively at Oxford, Leiden and Franeker. He published a large number of treatises, chiefly on points of Hebrew scholarship, most of which are included in the *Critici Sacri*. His correspondence was very voluminous. See *Athenae*, ii. 159; *Fasti*, i. 188. He was B.A. (Merton) 1572, M.A. 1573. For his son (Ch. Ch., B.A. 1605), see *Fasti*, i. 304. Sir Thomas Bodley resided at the Hague except for one or two brief intervals from 1588–1597. There is a Latin letter from Drusius to Bodley among the Harleian MSS.

Page 27, line 31. **Dr. Peter Allix** (1641-1717), who settled in England on the Revocation of the Edict of Nantes, never published his projected History of the Councils, which was to occupy seven volumes. Full particulars of his life and writings will be found in the article devoted to him in the *Dictionary of National Biography*, i. 334.

27. 36. **Nathaniel Spinckes** (d. 1727, aged 73) was one of Collier's chief opponents on the subject of the 'Usages' (see Lathbury's *Nonjurors*, p. 365). His life was written by John Blackbourne. He was a friend of Nelson, and was entrusted with the management of the fund raised by the deprived Bishops (Secretan, 68 *sq.*). Beside this answer to Bassett, he wrote against the 'new prophets;' and his *Sick Man Visited* was long held in high repute.

28. 9. Under Sept. 12, 1699, Luttrell records : 'Norton Pawlet, esq., a gentleman of 2000*l.* per annum, is married to a daughter of Sir Charles Morley;' and he mentions a report of his death June 12, 1705.

28. 14. **Neville** was Recorder of Bath, knighted 1681, Baron of the Exchequer 1685; dismissed, 1686; re-appointed, 1689; Justice of the Common Pleas, 1691. 'He seems to have acted an honest and independent part on the Bench:' *Biographia Juridica*, 479.

28. 32. **Capt. Charles Hatton** will be familiar as the brother of Lord Hatton, and son-in-law of Chief-Justice Scroggs, to readers of the Hatton Correspondence, edited by Mr. E. Maunde Thompson for the Camden Society. He was a friend of Fell, Pepys, Evelyn, &c., and a strong Jacobite. He was sent to the Tower in 1690 (Clarendon's *Diary* 252). See Index to Tanner MSS.

28. 39. William the Third's unsuccessful attempt to confer on **Portland** Crown lands in Denbighshire of the value of over 100,000*l.* is mentioned by Macaulay (ii. 555) ; who remarks of *Gloria Cambriae ; or Speech of a Bold Briton against a Dutch Prince of Wales* (1702) that this speech of Price, 'the bold Briton,' was probably never spoken, and that [Curll's] *Life of the late Hon. Robert Price* (1734) is 'a miserable performance, full of blunders and anachronisms.' An analysis of this Life will be found in Chalmers, and full particulars of Price's honourable and consistent career in Foss, *Biographia Juridica*, 538-9. He died in 1732, aged 78.

29. 6. An abstract of **Dr. Ralph Bathurst's** will (proved June 16, 1704) is given by Warton in his *Life of Bathurst*, 191 *sqq.* Bathurst left to the Bodleian the portraits of South and Allestree, and such medals as were wanting in the collection.

29. 29. **William Beveridge** (1637-1708), Prebendary of Canterbury 1684, and Bishop of St. Asaph 1704, had refused to accept the bishopric of Bath and Wells in succession to Ken on the deprivation of the latter in 1691 (*Life of Ken*, by a *Layman*, p. 386). As to his life there was, *pace* Dr. Mill, only one opinion ; but an unfavourable view of his works and of their tendency was put forth in a pamphlet (1711) entitled *A Short View of Dr. Beveridge's Writings*. See Baker-Mayor, *History of St. John's*, 703 *sqq.*

29. 46. Nicolson has some remarks on the *Chronicon Lichfeldense* in his *Eng. Hist. Lib.* 132.

30. 3. **Dr. Edward Young**, Dean of Salisbury 1702-1705, died Aug. 9 in the latter year, and was succeeded by Dr. John Younger.

30. 5. Mr. Fox Bourne points out in the Preface to his *Life of Locke* (p. v), that Le Clerc's *Éloge de M. Locke* was itself little more than a translation of two letters addressed to him by Lord Shaftesbury (author of the *Characteristics*) and Lady Masham. The English translation was first issued in 1706, and afterwards, with corrections, by Curll in 1713 (8vo).

30. 6. **Thomas Rymer**, historiographer royal, published Vol. I of the *Foedera* in 1704, and 15 volumes had appeared at the time of his death in 1713. He began his literary career as a poet ; and his *View of the Tragedies of the Last Age* drew upon him general derision, Macaulay going so far as to characterise him as 'the worst critic that ever lived.' His view of the Phalaris controversy is given in Jebb's *Bentley*, 63.

30. 16. Thomas Wagstaffe (1645-1712), Chancellor of Lichfield 1684, and consecrated suffragan Bishop of Ipswich by the non-juring Bishops in the presence of Henry Earl of Clarendon, is now probably best remembered as the defender of the authenticity of *Eikon Basilike*. See some particulars concerning him in Lathbury's *Nonjurors*, pp. 228 *sq*. A letter from Dr. Radcliffe to Bp. Lloyd of Norwich, covering bills for 500*l*. for the use of 'the poor suffering clergy,' is printed at p. 48 of the Life of Radcliffe. Some of the Royalist clergy under the Commonwealth, e.g. Bathurst, had similarly taken to the practice of medicine.

30. 24. Cherry did not long survive Dodwell, and the Life of the latter was written by Francis Brokesby, with a Dedication to Nelson, and published in 1715.

30. 43. Benjamin Cole, bookbinder and engraver, had been familiar with Antony Wood : see extract from Hearne in Wood's *Life*, 338.

31. 5. Francis Godwin (1561-1633), Bishop of Llandaff and Hereford, author of *Rerum Anglicanarum Annales, Henrico VIII, Edv. VI et Maria regnantibus*, and of the well-known *Catalogue of all the Bishops of England*, &c. His *Man in the Moon*, to which Swift was indebted, was published posthumously in 1638 ; and his *Nuncius Inanimatus* appeared with the imprint 'In Utopia' in 1629, and confessedly suggested Bp. Wilkins' *Mercury* (see 'To the Reader,' ed. 1802, II. xi). Dr. Thos. Smith published his translation of the *Nuncius*, together with *The Man in the Moon*, in 1657.

31. 8. These poems are not now ascribed to Matthew Prior, if it is he who is intended here. They are generally attributed to William Shippen (1672-1743): see Noble, iii. 243 *sqq*.

31. 13. William Lloyd (1627-1717), Bishop of St. Asaph 1680, of Lichfield 1692, and of Worcester 1699, had long devoted his attention to the interpretation of prophecy: see Evelyn's *Diary*, April 26, 1689, and May 18, 1690 (where we read of his dealings with two fugitive ministers of the Vaudois, *cf. infra*) ; and that he continued to take a keen interest in the subject is proved by Swift's reference to him in the *Journal to Stella*, July 1, 1712. His works were mainly chronological. His *Exposition of the Prophecy of Seventy Weeks* remained imperfect. See letters in *Life of Prideaux*, 238 *sqq*. The Terrae-Filius of 1703 styles him ' pseudopropheta canus.'

31. 28. Boyer records (p. 198): 'It was even whisper'd at Court, That the Thanksgiving Day would not have been solemnized, but for the good News, which, at this very Juncture, was brought from Prince *Eugene's* Army, and for which the Guns of the Tower were fired.'

32. 4. With this compare Wood's own story in the *Life*, p. 182, how ' Dr. Bathurst told me that he was told that I was used to listen at the common chamber [of Trinity], and elsewhere, and that I never spoke well of any man.'

33. 16. Thomas Gylby, St. John's, B.A. 1696; All Souls, B.C.L. 1703.—**William Hayley** was Dean of Chichester 1699-1715 ; and **Thomas Hayley** held the same Deanery 1735-9.

33. 26. For the Battle of **Cassano**, see *Life of Prince Eugene* (1741), pp. 195 *sq*.

33. 41. Abel Evans, M.A. 1699.

34. 4. Henry Wharton (1664-1695) published his *Enthusiasm of the Church of Rome demonstrated in some Observations on the Life of Ignatius Loyola* anonymously in 1688.

34. 12. Francis Fox was Prebendary of Salisbury 1713-1738. He published two sermons—one on the lawfulness of oaths in 1710.

35. 23. Dr. Welbore Ellis was translated to Meath 1731 and died 1733. Dr. Moreton was his predecessor in the see of Kildare (Cotton's *Fasti*, ii. 45).

35. 30. The *Rehearsal* (extending to 398 Nos. in all) was by Charles Leslie, and was written 'to combat the principles of Tutchin, Defoe, and the rest of "the Scandalous Club," as they were not ashamed to call themselves.' No. 1 appeared Aug. 5, 1704. *Catalogue of the Hope Collection*, p. 13. (Some extracts from it are given in the *Life and Writings of Charles Leslie*, by the Rev. R. J. Leslie, 377 *sqq*., &c.) I do not find a paper called *The Review of the Rehearsal* either in this Catalogue or in Nichols' *Lit. Anecd.*

35. 34. *A Cat may look on a Queen* was by **John Dunton** (1659-1733): see *Lit. Anecd.* v. 76. His *Life and Errors* was edited by Nichols in 1818, and an analysis is given in the *Lit. Anecd.* v. 59-83.

35. 39. John Rogers succeeded Bp. Hough as President of Magdalen. He died Feb. 10, 1703, and was succeeded by Dr. Thomas Bayley.

36. 4. Charles Leslie (1650–1722), the well-known author of *The Snake in the Grass*, the *Easy Methods*, and numerous other controversial works, put forth the tract here referred to in 1702. In the same year he published, as an appendage to a sermon of his own on the same subject, Dodwell's *Discourse concerning the Obligation to marry within the true Communion, following from their Style of being called a Holy Seed*. See Macaulay, ii. 107; Brokesby's *Life of Dodwell*, 370 *sqq*. It need hardly be said that Leslie adhered to the party among the Nonjurors which maintained the schism after the return of Dodwell, Nelson, and Brokesby to the National Church. A Life of him has just (1885) appeared, by the Rev. R. J. Leslie; but for most purposes sufficient particulars of him will be found in Lathbury's *Nonjurors*, 366, &c. It may be added that Mrs. Lucy Hutchinson takes a somewhat similar view of the ill effects of Charles I's marriage in her Memoirs of her husband (p. 89, Bohn's ed.).

36. 4. This tract of Leslie's is printed in Vol. i. (pp. 431 *sqq*.) of the Clarendon Press (1832) ed. of his Theological Works. Spelman's *History and Fate of Sacrilege* was published in 1698.

36. 20. A good many particulars of the printing and publication of the **Polyglott Bible**, edited by Brian Walton (4 vols. 1657), are brought together in *Lit. Anecd.* iv. 7 *sqq*.

36. 23. Lady Elizabeth Churchill, third daughter and co-heir of John Duke of Marlborough, married Scroop Egerton, fourth Earl and first Duke of **Bridgwater;** died 1714. The Dowager Countess was Jane, eldest daughter of Charles Duke of Bolton; died 1716. Her two eldest sons lost their lives in the fire at Bridgwater House, Barbican, April 11, 1687.

36. 28. Jacobus Merlo Horstius published 'Analecta quaedam ex Bernardo' in his *Septem Tubae Orbis Christianae ad reformationem ecclesiasticae disciplinae* (Cologne, 1635). His *Paradise for the Christian Soul* was translated &c. by Dr. Pusey in 1845–7.

37. 7. J. Scheffer's edition of Justin (Hamburg and Amsterdam, 1678) is characterised by Ebert, ii. 872, as 'equally bold and unhappy in conjecture.' His *Lectionum academicarum liber* appeared at Hamburg in 1675.

37. 11. John Holland, M.A. 1691, D.D. 1707; Prebendary of Salisbury 1716.

37. 21. This extract from Gascoigne is printed at pp. 227 *sq*. of Mr. Thorold Rogers' *Loci e Libro Veritatum* (Oxford, 1881).

37. 33. The battle of **Stratton** was fought May 16, 1642; see Clarendon, ii. 270 (ed. 1720). The fertility of the soil after the fight is noticed by Hals, as quoted in Davies Gilbert's *History of Cornwall*, iv. 14.

37. 39. For some account of **Malalas** (John of Antioch) and his chronicle, and the importance of Hody's edition (1691) in Bentley's literary history, see Jebb's *Bentley*, pp. 9 *sqq*. Prideaux had been entrusted with an edition of Malalas by Fell in 1674, and gives a half-humorous, half-despairing account of his author in the *Letters to Ellis*, p. 22; cf. the *Life*, p. 3.

37. 44. William Smith, M.A. 1674, 'above twelve years senior Fellow of University,' was afterwards rector of Melsonby, co. York. His *Annals of University College; proving William of Durham the true founder: and answering all their Arguments who ascribe it to King Alfred*, was published in 1728 (aetat. 76), and *Literae de re nummaria* in 1729, both at Newcastle-upon-Tyne. Mr. Allan presented to the Society of Antiquaries twenty-six 4to. volumes of MSS. relating chiefly to Oxford, extracted by Smith from the public libraries there, *Lit. Anecd.* vi. 126. In 1726 Smith presented to the Bodleian a collection of tracts (in twenty-five vols.) on the Roman Catholic controversy of 1680–90 (Macray, *Annals*, p. 150). Some idea of Smith's character may be gathered from the Preface and Supplement to the Preface to his *Annals of University College*, and a good many personal details of himself and his contemporaries from the latter portion of the book.

38. 11. Jeremy Collier (1650–1726) published *The great historical, geographical, genealogical, and poetical Dictionary; being a curious Miscellany of sacred and prophane History collected from the best Historians, Chronologers, and Lexicographers, but more especially out of Lewis Morery*, in 2 vols., 1701. A Supplement appeared in 1705, and an Appendix in 1721.

38. 26. For **Mrs. Esther Inglis** (b. *c.* 1584), see Ballard's *British Ladies*, where particulars of her skill in caligraphy are given ; also Macray's *Annals of the Bodleian*, pp. 48 *sq.*, and a notice by David Laing in the *Proceedings* of the Soc. of Antiquaries of Scotland.

39. 2. **John Stearne** the elder died 1669, aged 46. A work of his, *De Obstinatione*, was published posthumously (1672) by Dodwell, his pupil, with *Prolegomena Apologetica*, which formed Dodwell's first printed work (Brokesby's *Life*, 26 *sqq.*). His son of the same name became Preb. of St. Patrick's 1679, Chancellor 1702, Dean 1704, Bishop of Dromore 1713, and of Clogher 1717; died 1745. Swift corresponded with him for many years. See Index to Scott's Swift ; and Cotton, *Fasti Eccl. Hib.* ii. 104 ; iii. 80 *sq.*

39. 23. **William Lloyd**, son of the Bishop, was implicated with his father in some election proceedings in Worcestershire, which brought on both the displeasure of the House of Commons. He was prebendary of Worcester and rector of Fladbury, and died 1718. For **Ray** and his coins, see Macray's *Annals of the Bodleian*, pp. 124–5.

40. 3. The terms of this presentment are given by Boyer, p. 179.

40. 16. Some particulars of **Grabe** (1666-1712) and his circumstances are given in *Lit. Anecd.* iv. 197 *sqq.* Vol. i. of his edition of the LXX appeared in 1707, and the work was only completed in 1720, when he had been long dead. See Nelson's *Life of Bull*, pp. 402 *sqq.*, and references in note on p. 25, l. 41.

40. 30. This letter, describing the death by a carriage accident of Mr. Wm. Cherry, is in the Rawlinson Correspondence, vii. 53 (dated April 6, 1705).

41. 7. See **Burnet's** *History of the Reformation* (ed. Pococke), vol. ii. p. 252.

41. 27. For a list of **Parsons'** writings, see de Backer, *Écrivains de la Compagnie de Jésus*, 3° Série, pp. 561 *sqq.*

41. 43. The edition of the *Sphaerica* by Joseph **Hunt** (M.A. 1703) was published in 1707.

41. 50. Dr. **Wm. Binckes**, Dean of Lichfield 1703-1712, was at this time Prolocutor of the Lower House. For a history of the whole dispute, see Lathbury's *History of Convocation*, pp. 363 *sqq.*

42. 7. A summary view of Oxford contributions to the knowledge of the Coptic language and literature will be found in Mr. A. J. Butler's *Ancient Coptic Churches of Egypt*, vol. ii. pp. 257 *sq.*

42. 19. This design was finally carried out by Edward Thwaites, whose edition of **Ephraem Syrus** in Greek was published at Oxford in 1709.

42. 48. Dr. **Hickes** published in 1701 *Devotions in the ancient Way of Offices . . reformed by a Person of Quality* [Susanna Hopton]. This Manual was originally compiled from Roman Catholic sources, and published under the title of *Reform'd Devotions*, by the Rev. **Theophilus Dorrington**, rector of Witresham, Kent.

43. 1. **James Bonnell** (1653-1699) was Accountant-General of Ireland 1684-1693. His 'Exemplary Life and Character' formed the subject of a work by Wm. Hamilton, Archdeacon of Armagh, published in 1707.

43. 10. Dr. **Peter Barwick** wrote a very curious and interesting Life of his brother Dr. John Barwick (1612-1664), Dean of St. Paul's after the Restoration, which was published in Latin 1721, and in an English translation by Dr. Hilkiah Bedford in 1724. Peter Barwick was born in 1619, and was blind for the last ten years of his long life. A sketch of his own career is prefixed to the Life of his brother.

43. 25. Dr. Bull's tract on 'The Corruptions of the Church of Rome,' is printed, together with other pieces, in *Several Letters which passed between Dr. G. Hickes and a Popish Priest*, 1705. See Secretan's *Life of Nelson*, 25, 37.

43. 31. The Rev. **John Morton**, Rector of Oxendon, published *The Natural History of Northamptonshire* in 1712.

43. 32. Francis Hargrave published an *Essay on the Antient and Present State of Stamford* in 1726, which was followed the year after by *Academia tertia Anglicana: or, the Antiquarian Annals of Stamford*, by **Francis Peck** (1682-1743). See *Lit. Anecd.* i. 507 *sqq.*

44. 7. Sir Robert Clayton survived till July 16, 1707. He had moved the Exclusion Bill in 1681. See the sketch of him in Macaulay, i. 633.

44. 38. A note of Dr. Rawlinson's, quoted in an Appendix to the *Life of Wood* (p. 344), records that 'Mr. **Sheldon** died May 30, 1710, and left to Christ Church quadrangle 1000ᵇ. he was a non-juror, and nephew to Archbishop Sheldon.' We read of a *Roger* Sheldon of Christ Church in the same work, p. 177, *sub anno* 1671.— I do not find in the *Catalogue of Graduates* any Sheldon of about this period except Richard Sheldon of Christ Church, B.A. 1710, who of course cannot be the person here intended. Ralph Sheldon, nephew of Wood's patron of the same name. and a connexion of the Archbishop, appears in Cosin's list of those who refused to take the oaths to George I, under the counties of Oxford and Warwick.

45. 3. For *The Secret History of Queen Zarah* and its bibliography, see Mr. Solly's article in the *Bibliographer*, Dec. 1881, pp. 21 *sqq.*

45. 11. No. 1 of *The Whipping Post, or, a new Session of Oyer and Terminer for the Scribblers*, was published June 9, 1705.

45. 16. For Tanner's projected edition of Leland (already referred to), see also *Lives of the Antiquaries*, i. p. 51 *n.* Wanley never realised his design of publishing the Bible in Saxon.

VOL. IV.

Page 45, line 29. **Robert Pearse**, of Lincoln, B.A. 1701.

46. 5. Madox published his *Formulare Anglicanum* in 1702, and his *History and Antiquities of the Exchequer* in 1711 (see his letter to Dr. Charlett in *Letters of Eminent Persons*, i. 214 *sq.*). The *Firma Burgi* (1726) was the last work which he lived to complete, but his *Baronia Anglica* was posthumously published in 1741. **Dr. Nathaniel Johnston**, of Pontefract, 1627-1705, figures frequently in Ralph Thoresby's *Diary* and *Correspondence*, and particulars of his life are given at vol. i. pp. 39 *sqq.* of the former book. Madox' criticism on him was perfectly just. **Sir John Fortescue's** *Difference between an Absolute and Limited Monarchy* was first published in 1714 from the MS. in the Bodleian by his descendant John **Fortescue Aland**, F.R.S. (1670-1746), afterwards Solicitor-General, Baron of the Exchequer, and a Peer of Ireland. For Fortescue's works, see Stubbs' *Constitutional History*, iii. 257 *sqq.*, and for his editor, Foss, *Biographia Juridica*, 5.

46. 21. The Bishop of Carlisle was of course Dr. William **Nicolson**, author of *The Historical Library*, whose correspondence was published by Nichols in 1809. Particulars of the collections of **Roger Dodsworth** (1585-1654), often referred to hereafter, are given by Mr. Macray, *Annals*, pp. 96 *sq.*

47. 10. This inscription is printed in Leland's *Itinerary*, vol. ii. 71 *sqq.* Some account of Ela, daughter and heiress of William, Earl of Salisbury, d. 1261, and her husband, William Longespée, natural son of Henry II, d. 1226, is given in Marshall's *Early History of Woodstock Manor*, 51 *sq.*

47. 40. This is the earliest mention in these Collections of **Thomas Baker** (1656-1740), afterwards the famous *Socius Ejectus* of St. John's College, Cambridge, and its historian. He did not as yet reckon Hearne among his correspondents. See *Life of Ambrose Bonwicke*, ed. Mayor, 208 *sqq.*; Masters' *Memoirs of Baker*, 43 *sqq.*

48. 15. Charles, Duke of Shrewsbury (Birch's *Life of Tillotson*, 55 *sqq.*, Ballard MSS. x. 103), married at Rome Adelleida, d. of the Marquis Palliotti of Bologna, maternally descended from the Earl of Leicester, Q. Elizabeth's favourite. She was Lady of the Bedchamber to Caroline, afterwards Princess of Wales, and a relation of the Marquis Palliotti, who was executed at Tyburn for killing his servant (Noble, i. 51 *sq.*).

50. 10. The first eight verses of this poem, a corrected copy of which is given on p. 54, are printed in Noble's *Granger*, ii. 232, where they are attributed to Mr. Gwinnett.

50. 23. Dr. **William Talbot** was Bishop of Oxford from 1699 to 1715. There is a full account of him in Noble's *Granger*, iii. 72 *sq.* Mr. Marshall dismisses him briefly in his *Diocesan History of Oxford*, pp. 164 *sq.* He was succeeded in the Bishopric by Dr. **John Potter** (*c.* 1674-1747), mentioned below, afterwards Archbishop of Canterbury.

51. 6. Sir Stephen Fox married in 1703, as his second wife, Christian, youngest d. of the Rev. Charles Hope, of Naseby (d. 1719), by whom he had four children—Stephen, created Lord Ilchester; Henry, Lord Holland; and two daughters. He died in 1716, aged upwards of 90. A popular account of his life will be found in the Princess Marie Liechtenstein's *Holland House*, i. pp. 32 *sqq.*

51. 15. George Royse, D.D., Provost of Oriel 1691, Dean of Bristol 1693, d. 1708. He printed three sermons, including that here referred to, which was on Proverbs xvi. 32. Some account of him is given by Dr. Birch in his *Life of Tillotson*, 376 *sq.*

51. 20. Joseph Abell, originally of Lincoln, M.A. 1702.—**Dr. George Ryves,** Warden of New College 1599-1613, was V. C. in 1601.—For **Dr. Richard Lydall,** see Wood's *Life*, pp. 297 *sq.*

51. 36. Sir John Walter was elected M.P. for the City of Oxford Dec. 11, 1706.—Sir Simon Harcourt (1660-1727) became Attorney-General in 1707, Lord Keeper 1710, and Lord Chancellor in 1713, having been created a Baron in 1711. After the accession of George I he was characterised by Swift as a Trimmer. See Foss, *Biographia Juridica*, 326 *sq.*

52. 12. Thomas Dalton, B.A. (Queen's) 1702; M.A. (All Souls) 1706. **Dr. Finch** died Nov. 14, 1702. Tanner dedicated his *Notitia Monastica* to him in 1695.

52. 26. Nicholas Martin, C.C.C., M.A. 1683, attended Wood in his last illness and attested his will. He was likewise Vicar of Witham.

53. 3. For these political changes, see Boyer, 208; Burnet, v. 219 *sq.* According to Burnet there was in **Sir Nathan Wright** 'nothing equal to the post; much less to him who had lately filled it' [Somers], whom he succeeded in 1700. See also Duchess of Marlborough's *Vindication*, 147 *sq.* If we may believe Speaker Onslow (*ap.* Burnet) Wright was certainly 'no looser' by his tenure of office. Montague, second Earl of **Abingdon**, mentioned below, was restored to favour on the change of Ministry in 1710. He died in 1743.

53. 12. Uffenbach, on the contrary, had heard a good account of **Dr. J. Laughton's** 'great learning and courtesy,' and exclaims *Rara avis in his terris* (Wordsworth, *Schol. Acad.* 6). Laughton was Public Librarian 1686-1712.

53. 48. Dr. Wm. De Laune, President of St. John's 1698-1728, is unhappily familiar to us in the pages of Amherst's *Terrae Filius.* See also *Life of A. Bonwicke*, ed. Mayor, 151, and Index to this vol.

54. 33. A good account of the history and significance of 'the **Tack**' will be found in Burton's *Reign of Q. Anne*, i. pp. 90 *sq.* It had a special literature of its own, including *A brief Account of the Tack*, and *The Character of a Tacker.* Calamy's view of the Tack naturally differed from Hearne's, see *Life*, ii. p. 28; cf. Burnet, v. 176 *sqq.*

55. 17. Dr. Freind (1675-1728) was at this time physician to the army in Spain under the Earl of Peterborough, of whose conduct he published a *Defence* which ran through three editions. See *Life of the Earl of Peterborough* (1853), ii. 204.

56. 4. A copy of the Oxford Almanack of 1706 is preserved in Alderman Fletcher's volume in the Bodleian. Facing it is an explanation (London: Printed and Sold by *Benj. Bragge*, in Avey Lane. 1706. Price 6d.) in double cols., that on the left in the form of Tory queries, and that on the right a Whig rendering.

56. 15. Dr. John Harris, F.R.S., author of *Lexicon Technicum* and other scientific works, d. 1719.

56. 12. Earl Cowper died October 10, 1723. In Noble's *Granger*, ii. 18, it is mentioned that a pamphlet in defence of bigamy has been attributed to his pen. The Editor of the Life of Calamy quotes (ii. 474) a passage from *Questions sur l'Encyclopédie* in which Voltaire remarks:—'Il est public en Angleterre, et on voudrait le nier en vain, que le Chancelier Cowper épousa deux femmes qui vécurent ensemble dans sa maison avec une concorde singulière qui fit honneur à tous trois. Plusieurs curieux ont encore le petit livre que ce Chancelier composa en faveur de la polygamie.'

56. 24. Particulars of this gift of **James Tyrrell** will be found in Macray's *Annals of the Bodleian*, p. 125, *anno* 1707.

57. 2. Antony Alsop, M.A. 1696, Preb. of Winchester 1715, d. 1726. He lives in literary history by his edition of Æsop, in the Preface to which Bentley is described as 'Richardum quendam Bentleium, volvendis lexicis satis diligentem;' see Monk's *Bentley*, i. 96. Sir Francis Bernard published a quarto volume of his Latin Poems in 1752. See *art.* in *Dict. of Nat. Biog.* i. 345.

57. 21. Dr. William King (1650–1729), Chancellor of St. Patrick's 1679, Dean 1689, Bp. of Derry 1691, Archbp. of Dublin 1703. See Cotton, *Fast. Eccl. Hib.* ii. 23. His best-known work, *De Origine Mali*, was published in 1702. He was a frequent correspondent of Swift ; see Index to Scott's edition.

57. 45. Luttrell records (v. 600), ' *Mr. Pettis* is committed for writing a half-sheet call'd Fire and Faggot, being a reflection upon burning the Memorial.' He was like-wise the author of *The Memorial answered Paragraph by Paragraph*, and of the Life of Dr. Radcliffe.

58. 36. The **Fountain Tavern** afterwards 'gave its name to the Fountain Club, a political association opposed to Sir Robert Walpole.' See Cunningham's *Hand-Book of London*, p. 191.

58. 40. This great feat of arms is familiar to most from the graphic description in the *Memoirs of Captain Carleton*, long attributed to Defoe, but now generally admitted to be authentic. See *e.g.* Burton, *Reign of Queen Anne*, vol. ii. p. 171 *sqq.*

59. 3. This Sermon, on 1 Tim. iii. 1, was duly printed.

59. 17. For the authorship and bibliography of *Leycester's Commonwealth*, see Appendix III to *Reliquiae Hearnianae*. Cf. also D'Israeli's *Calamities of Authors*, ' Authors by Profession;' de Backer, *art.* Parsons ; and Lingard, vi. 254.

59. 21. Mr. John Smith, M.P. for Andover, had been Commissioner of the Treasury and Chancellor of the Exchequer under William III. He resigned the Chair in favour of Sir Richard Onslow in 1708. For particulars of him and his unsuccessful opponent, see Manning's *Lives of the Speakers*, pp. 408 *sqq.*, 416 *sqq.* One of the very last entries in Evelyn's *Diary* relates to this election :—' The Parliament chose one Mr. Smith Speaker. There had never been so great an assembly of members on the first day of sitting, being more than 450. The votes both of the old, as well as the new, fell to those call'd Low Churchmen, contrary to all expectation.' On Feb. 27 following this accomplished English gentleman closed his life, full of years and of honour.

59. 31. Hearne's information here is curiously incorrect ; **Dr. Binckes** had a majority of 14.

59. 32. Wm. Randall, M.A. 1681.

59. 34. The **Mitre Tavern** appears in literature at least as early as 1611. But it owes its fame chiefly to Dr. Johnson and his contemporaries.

59. 45. The Queen's speech on this occasion is given in full in Boyer, p. 209.

60. 17. This Index, whether or not it was authentic, has remained a standard speci-men of absurdity in indexing. See *e.g.* Mr. H. B. Wheatley's *What is an Index ?* p. 17 ; *Bibliotheca Parriana*, p. 702.

60. 21. Dr. George Clarke, ' Judge Advocate General to Charles II and his three successors ; Secretary of War to William III ; Secretary to Prince George of Denmark ; one of the Lords of the Admiralty in the reign of Queen Anne ; and in five Parliaments Burgess of the University.' He was fellow of All Souls for 56 years, and was a bene-factor to Worcester and Brasenose Colleges. He died in 1736. See *Worthies of All Souls, passim*, esp. pp. 314 *sqq.* ; and Luttrell, v. 605.

60. 24. Besides his *Natural History of Lancashire* (1700), **Dr. Charles Leigh** (F.R.S. 1685) published one or two medical works, and a *History of Virginia* (1705). There is an amusing criticism of the *Lancashire* in Nicolson's *English Historical Library*, p. 17.

60. 35. There is a story in the *Secret History of the Calves-Head Club* (p. 101) of ' a Company of four Whigs . . together a tipling ' one Jan. 30, one of whom ' shrugg'd up his Shoulders, and with a Fanatical Grin . . said, with a *Gusto*, The Q——n has a fine white Neck,—.'

61. 28. For a popular account of **Florence of Worcester**, see Gairdner's *England* (' Early Chroniclers of Europe ' Series), 63 *sq.* ; Nicolson, 56.

61. 32. John Forbes, of Corse (1593–1648), was expelled from his chair at Aberdeen in 1640 for refusing to subscribe to the Covenant. This edition of his complete works was published at Amsterdam 1702–3, with a Life by George Gardens of Aberdeen.

61. 32. John Urry, of Ch. Ch., B.A. 1686, d. 1714. His edition of Chaucer was published in 1721. See Noble's *Granger*, ii. 294. For the **Lady Margaret**, see *Memoir of Margaret Countess of Richmond and Derby*, by the late C. H. Cooper, F.S.A. (Cambridge, 1874); Baker-Mayor, *History of St. John's College*, 55; Mullinger's *University of Cambridge*, i. 434 *sqq.* Bishop Fisher's Funeral Sermon on this great patroness of learning was reprinted with a Preface by Thos. Baker in 1708.

61. 40. A letter of **Archbishop Marsh** (1638-1713) to Dr. Thomas Smith, explaining his intention of founding a Public Library at Dublin, is printed at vol. i. pp. 103 *sqq.* of *Letters from the Bodleian*, and particulars of his life are given in a note; cf. Cotton *Fasti, Eccl. Hib.* i. 16, &c. See Edwards' *Memoirs of Libraries*, ii. p. 63 ; and for the library of Trin. Coll., Dublin, *ib.* ii. 45.

VOL. V.

Page 63, line 3. Joshua Barnes (1654-1712) was appointed Professor of Greek at Cambridge in 1695. Despite his many works, he is probably now best remembered by Bentley's remark that he understood as much Greek as a Greek cobbler. For Prof. Jebb's opinion of him, see his *Life of Bentley*, p. 72 ; cf. Monk, i. 52 *sqq.* We shall hear much of him in the sequel. The book here referred to is characteristically entitled, 'Αὐλικοκάτοπτρον; sive Estherae Historia, Poetica Paraphrasi, idque Graeco carmine, cui versio Latina opponitur, exornata ; una cum Scholiis, seu Annotationibus Graecis; in quibus (ad sacri Textus dilucidationem) praeter alia non pauca, Gentium Orientalium Antiquitates, Moresque reconditiores proferuntur. Additur Parodia Homerica de eadem hac Historia. Accessit Index Rerum ac verborum copiosissimus' (London, 8vo. 1679).

63. 12. Dr. Arbuthnot (d. 1735), afterwards so famous as a wit and the companion of wits, succeeded Sir E. Hannes as physician in ordinary to the Queen. Up to the present time his publications had been confined to scientific subjects.

63. 28. The most popular account of **Dee** is probably that in D'Israeli's *Amenities of Literature* ('The Occult Philosopher, Dr. Dee').

64. 26. An excellent account of **Dr. Moore**, Bishop of Norwich 1691-1707, translated to Ely, and d. 1714, has been contributed to the *Bibliographer*, Nos. 33, 34, and *Book-Lore*, No. 3, by the Rev. Cecil Moore, who promises a Life of that learned Prelate and famous collector.

64. 50. Zacagni published at Rome in 1698 *Collectanea monumentorum veterum ecclesiae Graecae ac Latinae quae hactenus in Vaticana bibliotheca delituerunt* (4to).

65. 40. James Crosse, M.A. 1702.—**Dr. Charles Trimnell**, chiefly known at this time as an opponent of Atterbury in the Convocation controversy, was consoled for his defeat by being made Bishop of Norwich in 1708, whence he was translated to Winchester 1721. He died in 1723. See *Life of Prideaux*, 111.

66. 11. The expulsion of **John Ayliffe** (M.A. 1703, B. and D.C.L. 1710), on account of certain passages in his *Antient and Present State of the University of Oxford*, is mentioned in *Oxoniana*, iv. 227, and Burrows' *Worthies of All Souls*, 368 (see Ballard MSS. i. 121-132). For the life of **Alciati** (1492-1550), whose fame does not now rest on his attainments as a jurisconsult, see Green, *Andrea Alciati and his Books of Emblems*, 1-96.

66. 16. Jacob Bobart the younger published Part III of Robert Morison's *Plantarum Historia Universalis Oxoniensis* in 1699.—Wm. Dale, Queen's, M.A. 1690.

66. 31. The gallant **Rouvigny**, Earl of Galway, lost his right arm at the siege of Badajoz : Boyer, p. 201 ; Luttrell, v. 608. Macaulay (ii. 82, &c.) gives some account of the family.

67. 8. Particulars of **Charles Bernard**, serjeant-surgeon to Queen Anne 1702, d. 1710, and of the sale of his library, are given in *Lit. Anecd.* iv. 104 *sq.* The edition of *Caesar* by John Davies, President of Queens' Coll., Cam., was published in 1706.

68. 10. Details of the life and death of Mr. **Joseph Crabb**, Hearne's predecessor as Under-Keeper (1674-1712), will be found in Macray's *Annals of the Bodleian*, pp. 129 *sqq.*

68. 26. Peter Foulkes, M.A. 1701 ; see Index.

68. 43. Stephen Blackhead has come down to posterity through the great literary merits of Sprat's *Relation* ; and the *Life of William Fuller, the late pretended Evidence, now a Prisoner in the King's Bench, who was declared by the Honourable House of Commons,* Nemine contradicente, *to be a Notorious Impostor, a Cheat, and a False Accuser of Persons of Honour and Quality. With all his Pranks and Villanies, &c. to this Present First of March* (1692) is not unworthy to be bound up (as in a volume now before me) with that graphic story. See Macaulay, ii. 361 *sqq.*; and ii. 327. Macaulay remarks of Sprat's *Relation* that 'there are very few better narratives in the language.'

69. 12. By a majority of sixteen over Sir Gilbert Dolben (Luttrell, v. 609).

69. 15. James Tyrrell's *General History of England* extends only to the reign of Richard II.—**Laurence Echard** (*c.* 1671–1730), a kinsman of the ingenious author of *Grounds and Occasions of the Contempt of the Clergy,* published vol. i. of his *History of England* (in the Preface to which he acknowledges obligations to Tyrrell) in 1707, and vols. ii. and iii. in 1718 ; a supplementary volume, entitled *The History of the Revolution and the Establishment of England in the year* 1688, appeared in 1725. For both writers see Nicolson's *English Historical Library,* p. 74.

69. 22. Lathbury gives an analysis of Dodwell's *Case in View* (1705) in his *History of the Nonjurors,* pp. 194–8. See also Brokesby's *Life,* 453 *sqq.*

69. 49. Richard Willis, S.T.P., Prebendary of Westminster (*vice* Busby) 1695; Dean of Lincoln 1701 ; '16th Jan. 1714–15 he was consecrated bishop of Gloucester, with leave to hold this dignity in commendam, which he did till Oct. 1721, when he was translated to Salisbury.' Le Neve-Hardy, ii. 36. He was translated to Winchester 1723, and died 1734.

70. 20. Blakewell, or **Bakewell Hall,** in Basinghall Street, 'a weekly market-place for woollen cloths,' derived its name from Thomas Bakewell, who was living in it in the 36th of Edward III. 'The profits or fees paid on pitchings were given by the City to Christ's Hospital, and in 1708 were reckoned at 1100*l.*' (Cunningham's *London, s. v.*)

71. 34. Dr. **Fiddes** (1671–1725) published his well-known *Life of Wolsey* in 1724.

71. 44. This work (Hearne has mis-spelt ' Diaetetical') is included in the second edition of the *Athenae* (ii. 388). In 1660 Gayton published a trifle under the name of 'Asdryasdust Tossoffacan'—an anticipation of a far greater author.

72. 4 *sqq.* For Father Matthew **Patenson,** Pattenson, or Patison, as the name is variously spelt, see *Athenae,* ii. 744.—**Jeremiah Stephens,** Prebendary of Lincoln 1639, died 1664.—**John Sudbury** was Dean of Durham 1661–1684.

72. 21. See Masson's *Life of Milton,* ii. 219 *sqq.,* where Smectymnuus is very fully treated. The authorship was apparently an open secret from the first.

72. 36. Antony Wood briefly characterises **Henry Care** at the end of his article on Marchmont Needham. He wrote on the Roman Catholic side after the accession of James II, and died 1688. *Athenae,* iii. 1189; iv. 368.

73. 3. George Acworth, LL.D. and sometime Orator of Cambridge, incorporated D.C.L. at Oxford 1566. He likewise published (1562) *Oratio in Restitutione Buceri et Fagii* ; Wood, *Fasti,* i. 175. See Strype's *Life of Parker,* i. 250, &c., and art. 'Acworth' in *Dict. of Nat. Biography,* i. 69.

73. 6. On Bishop **Barlow's** bequest, see Macray's *Annals of the Bodleian,* p. 111. The controversy with regard to the date of this book is well known; see a summary of it to the year 1817 in *Letters from the Bodleian,* i. 160 *sqq.* Until the appearance of Mr. Madan's work on the subject, the reader may be referred for a few facts relating to the early history of printing in Oxford to Cotton's *Typographical Gazetteer,* First Series, pp. 207 *sqq.*; Second Series, pp. 165 *sqq.*

73. 20. For John **Corbet** (1620–1680), see Wood, *Athenae,* iii. 1264; Calamy-Palmer, *Nonconformist's Memorial,* ii. 259 *sqq.*; Calamy, *Account,* ii. 133. His Funeral Sermon was preached by Richard Baxter.

73. 22. *The Catholique Apology,* 'by a Person of Quality,' was by **Roger Palmer,** Earl of Castlemaine. Lloyd's reply, *The late Apology in behalf of the Papists, reprinted and answered in behalf of the Royallists,* provoked a counter-reply ; and another pamphlet of Lloyd's, *A seasonable Discourse shewing the Necessity of maintaining the Established Religion in Opposition to Popery,* called forth 'a full answer and confutation' from Palmer.—**Robert Pugh,** once an officer in the Royal Army, wrote an answer to Bate's *Elenchus Motuum Nuperorum,* entitled *Elenchus Elenchi,* and seems afterwards, from his *Bathoniensium et Aquisgranensium Thermarum Comparatio,* to have become, as here mentioned, a physician.

73. 35. **Edward Worsley,** S.J., was likewise the author of rejoinders to Jeremy Taylor and Stillingfleet.

73. 35. **F. Carswell** (Exeter, B.A. 1660), Chaplain in Ordinary to Charles II, published *The State-informer enquired into* (1683), and *England's Restoration parallel'd in Judah's* (1689). *Fasti,* ii. 223, 381; *Notes and Queries,* 6th S., xi. 167.

73. 42. **Joseph Cannell,** M.A. 1705, published in 1708 *The Case of the Pretender Stated.*—Donne's Βιαθάνατος was published posthumously by his son in 1648.

73. 50. The lamentable end of **Thomas Creech** (1659–1700), Fellow of All Souls, the translator of Lucretius, Horace, &c., is well known (see Col. Codrington's statement in *Letters from the Bodleian,* i. 128 *sqq.*). There is some account of him in *Worthies of All Souls,* 318 *sq.* His insanity is mentioned by Charlett (Tanner xxii. 54) so early as 1698.—Dr. **John Adams,** of King's Coll., Cam., M.A. 1686, Provost 1712, Preb. of Canterbury and Canon of Windsor, died 1749, published *An Essay concerning Self-Murther* in 1700.

74. 38. For the parish and church of **Warfield,** about *eight* miles S.W. of Windsor, see Lysons' *Berkshire,* 410.

75. 19. For **John Goodwin** (1593–1665), Vicar of Coleman Street, see Neal's *History of the Puritans,* ii. 437 (ed. 1837), Calamy-Palmer, *Nonconformist's Memorial,* i. 196 *sqq.* His *Redemption Redeemed* was published in 1651 fol. The text of Barlow's letter, and some account of Barlow's Remains (1693), will be found in Appendix II to *Reliq. Hearn.* iii. 199. Dr. Bliss there notes that almost every volume which once formed part of Bishop Barlow's library 'contains some valuable MS. remark in his own hand.'

76. 46. Burnet states (*Life of Hale,* pp. 36 *sqq.,* ed. 1856) that the Lord Chief Baron drafted a bill for a comprehension of the more moderate Dissenters, embodying the results of conferences between the Lord Keeper Bridgeman, Dr. Wilkins, and 'two of the eminentest of the Presbyterian divines.'

77. 2. **Dr. Perrinchief** was the writer of the Life of Charles I prefixed to the folio ed. of the *Works,* 1662, but he was largely indebted to Fulman's collections.

77. 6. On the *Petition for Peace,* see Calamy's *Abridgment of Baxter's Life,* pp. 160, 414.

77. 8. **Valentine Greatrakes** and his miraculous power of curing diseases by 'stroking' are familiar to most who have dabbled in seventeenth-century literature. Among his supporters were many men of distinction, including Stubbe, Boyle, Henry More, Patrick, Wilkins and Cudworth. See *Athenae Oxon.* iii. 1077 *sqq.*: Birch's *Life of Boyle,* 151 *sqq.,* and entries in Bodleian Catalogue.

77. 11. An account of the chequered career of **Payne Fisher** (*Paganus Piscator*), 1616–1693, who fought on the King's side at Marston Moor, and was afterwards Poet Laureate to the Protector, is given in the *Athenae* (iv. 377). *His Catalogue of most of the Memorable Tombs, Gravestones, Plates, Escocheons, or Atchievements in the demolish'd or yet extant Churches of London* (1668), is said by Wood to be mostly taken from Stow's *Surrey;* and *The Tombes, Monuments, and Sepulchral Inscriptions lately visible in S. Paul's Cathedral, and S. Faith's under it* (*n. d.*), from Dugdale's *S. Paul's.*

77. 20. **Timothy Halton,** Provost of Queen's 1677–1704, was likewise Archdeacon of Brecknock and of Oxford, and Canon of St. David's. The library was built in great part at his expense; and he bequeathed £1200 towards the new buildings of the College.

77. 43. Cf. Luttrell, v. 611. The 'two chosen members' were Sir Christopher Hales and Mr. Gery.

78. 2. Wood gives a very unfavourable account of **Francis Rouse** (b. 1579) and his works in the *Athenae,* iii. 466. He was Provost of Eton from 1643–1658, and was likewise a member of the Assembly of Divines, of the Long and Little Parliaments, and of Cromwell's House of Lords. See Lyte's *History of Eton College,* 241 *sqq.*

78. 8. **Peter Needham,** of St. John's, Cambridge, published his ed. of the *Geoponica* in 1704.—**Marchmont Needham** (1620–1678) was of course the turn-coat

author of *Mercurius Britannicus, Pragmaticus,* and *Politicus*—'the great patriarch of newspaper writers,' as he is styled by D'Israeli. His dispraise is in the *Athenae,* iii. 1180.

78. 21. I do not know where this MS. is to be found; but Coke's opinion on the subject is well known; see *e.g.* Lathbury's *History of Convocation,* p. 230.

78. 32. **Anderton** likewise published, in 1671, a *History of the Iconoclasts.*

78. 40. Aubrey's Life of **Sir Wm. Petty** (1623–1687) will be found at vol. ii. p. 481 of *Letters from the Bodleian;* and further particulars, with references, in the *Register of the Visitors of the University of Oxford,* ed. Burrows, pp. 227, 335. His grave at Rumsey, Hants, was marked only by the following inscription:—HERE LAYES | SIR WILLIAM | PETTY.

79. 9. For the controversy aroused by Hody's publication in 1691 on the subject of this Baroccian MS., see Lathbury's *Nonjurors,* pp. 137 *sqq.,* and 182; Brokesby's *Life of Dodwell,* 235 *sqq.* Hody was bluntly accused of 'shamming the world with part of the MS. for the whole.'

79. 15. **Parsons'** *Conference about the next succession to the Crowne of Ingland* was published in 1594.

79. 19. The editor of this book was the Rev. **Edw. Symmons,** author of the *Vindication of King Charles* (1648), to the very great importance of which in the *Eikon* controversy I have called attention (*Academy,* May 26, 1883). For the incident here referred to, see S. R. Gardiner, *History of England,* x. 142.

79. 21. **Henry Walker** was the acknowledged author of *The Churches Purity, Corda Angliae,* and a sermon on Luke xiii. 24; a pamphlet satirising him (1642) is likewise mentioned in Cat. Bod., wherein he is described as 'a most judicious quondam iron-monger, a late pamphleteer,' &c.

79. 35. **Dodwell's** new book was of course *A Case in View consider'd:* see Brokesby's *Life,* 435 *sqq.,* Lathbury's *Nonjurors,* 194 *sqq.*

79. 40. Luttrell writes on Nov. 10, 'Dr. Sherlock, minister of the Temple, worth 300*l.* per ann., has resigned the same, and the queen has given it to his son' (v. 610). Dr. William Sherlock, Dean of St. Paul's, d. 1707. His eldest son, Thomas Sherlock (b. 1678), became in succession Bishop of Bangor, Salisbury and London, and d. 1761. He held the mastership of the Temple till 1753.

80. 1. **Edw. Boughen,** Ch. Ch., Chaplain to Dr. Howson, Bishop of Oxford, Rector of Woodchurch, Kent, ejected, and restored 1660, published other controversial pamphlets (*Athenae,* iii. 388). He died soon after the Restoration, aged about 74.

80. 7. **John Sheffield,** Earl of Mulgrave, Marquis of Normanby, and Duke of Buckinghamshire (1649–1721), was praised as an author by Roscommon, Dryden and Pope, and less favourably criticised by Walpole (*Noble Authors*), Johnson (*Lives of the Poets*), and Macaulay (*History,* i. 465). I do not find any sufficient ground for the statement of his disgrace in 1682.

81. 38. For **John Gilbert,** M.A. 1680, see *Athenae,* iv. 794.

81. 44. According to Aubrey, in *Letters from the Bodleian,* ii. 628, there was a close friendship between **Hobbes** and **Selden** after the publication of *Leviathan* till Hobbes' dying day. Selden left Hobbes a legacy of 10*l.* A summary account of Hobbes' 'Mathematical War' with Dr. Wallis, which lasted for twenty years, is given in D'Israeli's *Quarrels of Authors.*

81. 50. Cf. Luttrell, v. 611.

82. 4. **Lord Haversham's** speech on this occasion is given by Boyer, pp. 211 *sqq.,* and in *Memoirs of Lord Haversham* (1711), 12 *sqq.* Cf. *Life of Sharp,* i. 269 *sqq.,* 307 *sqq.*

82. 14. **Barzillai Jones,** Dean of Lismore 1683, Treasurer of Waterford 1684, and Chancellor 1686, attainted by James II 1689. See Cotton's *Fasti Eccl. Hib.* i. 169.

82. 18. **Leoline Jenkins** was Principal of Jesus 1661–1673; afterwards Ambassador at Cologne and Nimeguen, Burgess for the University, Judge of the High Court of Admiralty, and Secretary of State; knighted by Charles II. He died 1685. His Life of his predecessor as Principal of Jesus, Dr. F. Mansell, was published in 1854.

Many of his letters and despatches are printed in various Reports of the Historical MSS. Commission.

82. 32. **Tho. Goddard**, Magd., M.A. 1695; Canon of Windsor 1707, d. 1731.

82. 40. For some particulars of the **Crokes**, see *Life of Wood*, pp. 82, and 83*n.* Unton Croke, *sen.*, d. 1671; Sir Richard Croke, Recorder of Oxford, d. 1683. See also *Fasti Oxon.* ii. 129 &c.; Index to Rawlinson MSS.; and Sir A. Croke's *Genealogical History of the Croke Family* (1823).

83. 4. **Dr. Wm. Beaw** (New Coll., D.D. 1666) was consecrated Bishop of Llandaff June 22, 1679, and died Feb. 10, 1706.

83. 18. This portrait was painted in 1701-2. See Dr. Wallis' and Sir Godfrey's letters to Pepys on the subject in the Pepys Correspondence (pp. 734 *sqq.*, Warne's ed.).

83. 34. Wood's complaints of **Bishop Fell** and his notions of editing are well known to all readers of the *Life* (see e.g. p. 173). Cf. also Aubrey in *Letters from the Bodleian*, ii. 615 *sqq.*, and *Thomae Hobbes Angli Vita* (1681), 199 *sqq.*

83. 39. **Thomas Bennett** (M.A. 1680), B.D., Master of University 1690-1692.

83. 41. **William Oldys**, New Coll., D.C.L. 1667, was Advocate for the Office of Lord High Admiral of England, and to the Lords of the Prizes, the King's Advocate in the Court Martial, and Chancellor of the Diocese of Lincoln [?]; Wood's *Fasti*, ii. 54.—Dr. **Clarke** was first elected Burgess in 1685, in place of Sir Leoline Jenkins deceased.

84. 31. Copies of similar documents are printed in Gutch's *Collectanea Curiosa*, i. 287 *sqq.*

85. 15. **Hudson** was elected Librarian in 1701 by 194 votes, his opponent, J. Wallis, mentioned in the next note, mustering 173 (Macray, *Annals*, 123). Cf. Charlett in Pepys Corresp., Feb. 18, 1701. Hudson's Life is in *Athenae*, i. 457.

85. 25 *sqq.* **Edm. Marten**, M.D., Warden of Merton 1704-1709.—**John Bateman**, M.A. 1667, B. and D.M. 1682, a nonjuror.—Prof. Burrows' estimate of **Dr. Gardiner** (Warden of All Souls 1702-1728) is a good deal more favourable than Hearne's (*Worthies*, pp. 349 *sqq.*).—**John Walrond**, M.A. 1680, figures in the *Athenae*, iv. 583, as the author of a copy of verses on *Death.*—Dr. **Jas. Fayrer** was at this time Professor of Natural Philosophy, and **John Wallis**, M.A., of Magd., was Laudian Professor of Arabic 1703-1738.

85. 39. **John Hickes**, B.A. 1675, D.D. 1701.—**James Parkinson**, M.A. 1675, Head Master of K. Edward's School at Birmingham 1694 (d. 1722), was the author of the second work printed at Birmingham (Matthew Unwin, 1717)—*A Loyal Oration, giving a short Account of several Plots, some purely Popish, others mixt.* See *Book-lore*, vol. i. pp. 41 *sqq.*; Cotton's *Typ. Gaz.*, Ser. 2, p. 22.

85. 46. **John Naylor**, M.D. 1678.

86. 8. A summary account of these proceedings is given in Lathbury's *History of Convocation*, pp. 397 *sq.*

86. 15. Dr. J. **Covel** (1638-1722) succeeded Cudworth as Master of *Christ's* in 1688. He was from 1670 to 1677 chaplain to the English ambassadors to the Porte, and published *Some Account of the present Greek Church* just before his death. See Williams' *The Orthodox and the Nonjurors*, xii.; Pearson, *Chaplains to the Levant Company*, 16 *sq.* Part of his collection of MSS. of the N. T. is in the Brit. Mus.

86. 25. This 'Profession' is printed in Appendix XIII to the *Life of Kettlewell*. See Lathbury's *Nonjurors*, 48 *sq.* Jenkin was afterwards Master of St. John's, Camb. (1711 -1727). See Baker-Mayor's *History of St. John's College* 1005 *sqq.*

86. 29. There are MS. Scholia to the *Lysistrata* in Barocc. MS. 38 (pr. Amsterdam 1710), and Miscell. Greek 101.

86. 32. **Nicholas Lockyer** (d. 1685) also published various sermons. He succeeded Francis Rouse as Provost of Eton in 1658. See *Athenae*, iv. 162; Lyte's *History of Eton*, 252 *sqq.*

86. 39. **Sir John Monson**, of South Carleton, Linc., d. 1684. See *Fasti Oxon.* ii. 40.

86. 42. See Luttrell, v. 613.

87. 4 *sqq.* **E. Bagshaw**, d. 1662, *Athenae*, iii. 618; **F. Vernon**, 'hack'd to pieces in

Persia' 1677, *Athenae*, iii. 1133; **Simon Ford**, *Athenae*, iv. 756; **Edw. Palmer**, *Fasti*, ii. 301 ; **John Maxwell**, Bp. of Ross 1633, of Killala 1640, Archbp. of Tuam 1645 (Cotton, *Reg. Eccl. Hib.* iv. 68 *sq.*), likewise wrote *The Burthen of Issachar* and *Sacrosancta Regum Majestas*, which latter drew forth the famous treatise of Samuel Rutherford entitled *Lex Rex*, see Dr. Thomson's Life of Rutherford (1884), 117 *sqq.*; **John Ley**, *Athenae*, iii. 569; **Thomas Browne**, *Athenae*, iii. 1003 ; **Dudley Digges**, *Athenae*, iii. 63. For **Joseph Wasse**, see Wordsworth's *Scholae Academicae*, p. 97. *The Character of a London Diurnal* is printed at p. 83 of **Cleveland's** *Works* (ed. 1687). **E. Walsingham**, *Fasti*, ii. 60 ; **T. Tully**, *Athenae*, iii. 1055. For the answer to **William Prynne** referred to, see *Athenae*, iii. 1271 ; **Henry Marten**, *Athenae*, iii. 1237.

87. 53. The majority in favour of the petitioner was 72 ; Luttrell, v. 613.

88. 18. Raphael Fabretti, of Urbino (1619–1700), was the author of the well-known works *De Aquis et Aquaeductibus veteris Romae* and *De Columna Trajana Syntagma*. The works here mentioned were never published.

88. 30. This project was never fulfilled. **White Kennett's** MS. collections passed by purchase to Mr. West, to the Earl of Shelburne, and finally to the British Museum, where they are now deposited.

91. 19. For ' Aguileja ' read ' Aquileja.'

91. 48. Edward Fowler (1632–1714), C.C.C., D.D. 1681, Bishop of Gloucester 1691, in the room of Dr. Robert Frampton deprived.

92. 4. Dr. Murray has favoured me with his four earliest instances of the use of **Latitudinarian** as a substantive. The first, curiously enough, is from Pepys' *Diary*, March 16, 1669 ; and the three following are from Wycherley's *Plain-Dealer*, Butler's *Remains*, and Goodman's *Old Religion* respectively.

92. 16. Henry, seventh **Duke of Norfolk**, m. 1677 Lady Mary, d. and sole heir of Henry Mordaunt Earl of Peterborough, but the marriage was dissolved by Act of Parliament in 1700. She married secondly Sir John Germain (described by Evelyn, April 1700, as a ' Dutch gamester of mean extraction who had got much by gaming'), and died Nov. 16, 1705.—John, **Duke of Argyle**, was created in 1705 Baron of Chatham and Earl of Greenwich.

92. 23. See Boyer, p. 213. The address of the Upper House of Convocation is given by him, pp. 225 *sq.*

92. 25. See Archbp. Sharp's remarks on the Bill for the security of the succession, *Life*, i. 310.

92. 40. Sir Henry Spelman (1562–1643) left this work in MS. The Rev. Jeremiah Stevens began to print it in 1663, but the sheets were destroyed in the Fire of London. Gibson published the Posthumous Works of Sir Henry Spelman under the title of *Reliquiae Spelmannianae* in 1698.

93. 5. Dr. **John Goodman**, Rector of Hadham, Chaplain in Ordinary to Charles II, Archdeacon of Middlesex 1686.

93. 18. Dr. Geo. Hall, Archdeacon of Canterbury 1660, was Bishop of Chester 1662-1668.

93. 30. More correctly *John* **Sergeant**, of St. John's Coll., Camb. (see *Athenae*. iii. 496). He engaged in controversy with Hammond, Tillotson, and Stillingfleet.—**Dr. Thos. Morton** was translated from Lichfield to Durham 1632, d. 1659.

93. 34. The treatise here referred to is No. 21 in **Ochino's** *Thirty Dialogues*, published in Latin at Basel, 1563. See the English trans. of Dr. Benrath's *Bernardino Ochino of Siena*, pp. 265 *sqq.*— **Johannes Lyserus** *d.* 1684. He was devoted to the practice of chess and the doctrine of polygamy ; though, according to Bayle, he had been much embarrassed by one wife. He published his *Polygamia triumphatrix* in 1682.

93. 46 *sqq.* Henry Hickman, *Fasti Oxon.* ii. 122 ; *Anthony* **Horneck**, *Athenae*, iv. 529; **John Wilson**, B.N.C., sometime Vicar of Backford, Calamy-Palmer, i. 325 *sq.*; **Peter Walsh**, a Minorite, engaged in controversy with Stillingfleet and Barlow ; **Henry Thurman**, *Athenae*, iii. 922 ; **Samuel Rolls**, sometime Fellow of Trin. Coll. Camb., Calamy-Palmer, i. 298 ; **C. M. Du Veil** (or Viel), a native of Metz, see Chalmers' Biographical Dictionary, and Birch s *Life of Tillotson*, pp. 75 *sq.* For the quotation in ll. 23 *sqq.* see *Joannis Rossi Historia Regum Angliae*, p. 131 (ed. 1745). —The Life of Bishop Bedell (1570–1641), by his son, has since been published by Professor Mayor (Cambridge, 1871). For **John Doughtie**, see *Athenae*, iii. 976.— H. **Turberville** provoked rejoinders from Tombes and W. Thomas, Bp. of Worcester. Dr. **Lucy** was Bishop of St. David's 1660–1678. **Samuel Thomas** (*Athenae*, iv. 390) was Prebendary of Wells and Vicar of Chard, and a nonjuror.

95. 10. **Mrs. Bracegirdle's** character and style of acting have been sketched for us by Colley Cibber in his *Apology*, pp. 140 *sqq.* (cf. Macaulay's *History*, ii. 390). The same work contains some remarks on theatrical performances at the Act at Oxford (pp. 382 *sqq.*). Cf. also Wordsworth's *Social Life at the English Universities*, pp. 193 *sqq.*

95. 20. For a brief account of **Addison's** *Travels*, see chap. ii. of Mr. Courthope's Life in the 'English Men of Letters' Series; cf. Boswell's *Journal of a Tour to the Hebrides* (ed. 3), 320.

95. 30. A list of **Peter du Moulin's** works is given by Wood, *Fasti*, ii. 195 *sq.*

95. 33. A Catalogue of **Stephens'** writings will be found at vol. i. pp. 63 *sqq.* of the *Reliquiae*. We shall hear more of the author hereafter. Meanwhile the reader may be referred to an article by the Rev. E. S. Ffoulkes in the *Union Review*, i. pp. 553– 570; Williams' *The Orthodox and the Nonjurors*, xxiv. *sqq.*; Wordsworth, *Scholae Academicae*, 325; and Leslie's Works, i. 513 *sqq.*

95. 38. **John Vincent Cane**, 'a learned Franciscan friar,' d. 1672; *Athenae*, iv. 107.

96. 32. For coins in Bodley the reader must be referred to Wise's *Nummorum-antiquorum Scriniis Bodleianis reconditorum Catalogus* (1750). In addition to its numismatic interest, this volume is illustrated with copper-plates, among others, re-presenting Wise's house and grounds at Elsfield.

97. 3. **Herbert Thorndike**, Fellow of Trinity Coll., Cambridge, Proctor 1638, Prebendary of Lincoln 1636, of Westminster 1661, d. 1672. He contributed to the Polyglott Bible, and published *A Discourse of Religious Assemblies* and various other works.

97. 17. **C. Fontana's** work here referred to, *L'anfiteatro Flavio descritto e delineato*, was not published till 1725. Oddy's edition of **Dio Cassius** was never completed.

97. 25 *sqq.* **Dr. Thomas Jeames** died in 1685. Prof. Burrows, in commenting on this passage (*Worthies of All Souls*, p. 291), speaks of the delightful author of the *Natural History of Oxfordshire* as 'a Papist.' He was undoubtedly high in the favour of James II. The royal mandate for the election of **Finch** is printed in Gutch, *Coll. Cur.* ii. 282, and Finch's apology for accepting it, addressed to Sancroft, in the same vol., pp. 49 *sqq.*—Sir **Edward Hales**, the first champion of the dispensing power, Constable of the Tower and gaoler of the Seven Bishops, is familiar to all readers of Macaulay. His son and heir, **Edward Hales**, gentleman commoner of University, who delivered two orations before the King on his visit to Oxford in 1687, was killed at the Battle of the Boyne.—Dr. **Gilbert Ironside**, Warden of Wadham, V.C. 1687–8, became Bishop of Bristol in 1689. 'After he was settled there,' says Wood (*Athenae*, iv. 895), 'being then about sixty Years of Age, he took to him a fair and comely Widow to be his Wife, being the Daughter of one *Robinson* of *Bristol*.' He became Bishop of Hereford 1691, and died ten years later.—**Bingham**, author of *Origines Ecclesiasticae*, took his M.A. degree Dec. 17, 1688.—The history of **Jonas Proast** and his relations to Warden Finch is given in *Worthies of All Souls*, pp. 308 *sqq.*

98. 1. An account of the sudden death of Dr. **Levinz** (in 1697) is given in *Letters from the Bodleian*, i. 88, where the candidature of Hudson and Creech is mentioned.

98. 19. **Jas. Harrington**, Ch. Ch., M.A. 1690.—**Thomas Wood** was Bishop of Lichfield 1671–1692.

98. 29 *sqq.* **John Bennett**, M.A. 1683; **Edmund Entwistle**, M.A. 1682.

98. 38. **Jas. Buerdsell**, M A. 1692.

98. 45. **John Willes**, M.A. 1669. See for his works *Athenae*, iv. 681. This ser-mon was preached at the Warwick Assizes 1690 on Amos iii. 6.

98. 49. The Mayor of Oxford has for centuries had the right of attending the Coro-nation banquet of the Sovereign, as assistant (with certain burgesses of Oxford) to

the Lord Mayor of London (who is in turn assistant to the Duke of Norfolk). He presents wine to the Sovereign in a gilt cup covered, and receives as a fee three maple cups, and often, *de gratia Regis*, the gilt cup itself. See Paper of the late Gibbes Rigaud, read before the *Oxf. Arch. Society*, Mar. 3, 1885.

99. 9. See Boyer, pp. 213 *sq.*

99. 13. A letter by the Rev. Tho. Tomkins (see *Athenae*, iii. 1046) was published in the *Bibliographer*, No. 29, p. 150.—Joseph Trueman, Calamy-Palmer, iii. 93.

99. 30. J. C., *i. e.* John Cheney or Cheny. This work was in answer to Baxter.

99. 37. Dr. John Hall, Master of Pembroke 1664, Professor of Divinity 1676, Bishop of Bristol 1691; Dr. Henry Maurice, of Jesus, only held the professorship from July 18 to Oct. 30, 1691, and was succeeded by Dr. Thomas Sykes, afterward President of Trinity, d. 1705.

100. 10. Dr. De Laune is one of the chief butts of Amherst in his *Terrae Filius*. See p. 3 of that work for the *jacta est alea* incident; also pp. 16-20. The charge of 'shaking the elbow' occurs *totidem verbis* at p. 2. The *Terrae Filii* in 1703 were Hen. Roberts, Magd. Hall, and Rob. Turner, Wadham. The speech is printed in the *University Miscellany* (ed. 2, London, 1713).

100. 27. Mary, eldest daughter of Sir Matthew Hale, married secondly 'Edward Stephens, Esq., son to Edward Stephens, Esq., of Cherrington in Gloucestershire,' Burnet's *Life of Hale, ad fin.* Baxter wrote 'Additional Notes to Burnet's *Life of Hale* in a letter to E. Stephens.'

100. 32. For Nathaniel Homes, see *Athenae*, iii. 1065; and for George Bate (1608-1668), principal physician successively to Charles I, Oliver Cromwell and Charles II, *ib.* iii. 827.

100. 35. The writer of *An Account of Mr. Firmin's Religion* (1698) states, p. 52, that Mr. Firmin 'caused to be written *a brief History of the Unitarians*, and *brief Notes on the Creed of Athanasius*, in the years 1689 and 1690.' This produced a rejoinder from Sherlock, which in its turn gave rise to a heated controversy.

100. 40. Derodon or Rodon was Professor of Philosophy at Nîmes and other places. He was banished from France on account of this work, and took refuge at Geneva, where he died in 1664.

100. 47. This is of course Robert Fergusson, the 'Judas' of Part II of *Absalom and Achitophel*. See Macaulay's *History*, i. 259 *sq.*, with the references there given.

100. 52 *sqq.* For Dr. Thomas Pittis, see *Athenae*, iv. 220; John Humphrey, *ib.* iv. 743. E. Sheldon's translation of the *Rule of Faith* is mentioned in Wood's *Life*, p. 179. 'Mr. Rimer' is of course the editor of the *Foedera*.

101. 31. Samuel Johnson, rector of Corringham, Essex, and chaplain to Lord Russell, published his *Julian the Apostate* in 1682 for the purpose of exposing the doctrine of passive obedience as laid down by Dr. Hickes in a sermon preached before the Lord Mayor in 1681. Some particulars of Johnson's troubled and eventful career are prefixed to the folio edition of his ' Works;' but Macaulay has drawn a portrait of him (i. 378 *sqq.*) by which he is popularly known.

101. 47 *sqq.* Montrose's best-known literary effort is the lines ' Upon the Death of King Charles the First, written with the point of his sword,' which are commonly printed at the end of the King's ' Works.' and which were set to music by Pepys. There is some account of him in Lloyd's *Memoirs*, pp. 638 *sqq.*—Denis Petau (1583-1652) is characterised in Mark Pattison's *Memoirs*, 322 *sq.*—For Francis Osborn (c. 1589-1659), see *Athenae*, iv. 560, &c.—Dr. George Bright, Eman. Coll., Camb., Dean of St. Asaph 1689-1696, edited vol. i. of the Works of Dr. John Lightfoot (London, 1684).

102. 5. An interesting Life of the charitable Thomas Firmin (1632-1677), by ' one of his most intimate acquaintance,' was published in 1698, and reprinted 1791. For his relations to Tillotson and others, see Birch's Life of that prelate, pp. 292 *sqq.*; *Life of Sharp*, ii. 10, *Life of Frampton*, 187, and his own biography.

102. 10. This address is printed in full in Boyer, p. 226.

102. 25. Wood says (*Athenae*, ii. 297) that the *Display* was ' written mostly (especially the Scholastical part)' by Barcham.

102. 31. Dr. T. Brown, Canon of Windsor 1639-1673.

102. 34. For a list of **Burton** or **Crouch's** books, see *Reliquiae Hearnianae*, Appendix VIII (iii. 234 *sqq*.). See also Dr. Bliss's note at i. 291, Lowndes' *Manual*, *art.* Burton; and *Book-Lore* i. 129 *sqq*.

102. 42. **Thomas Jones**, *Athenae*, iv. 51.

103. 13 *sqq*. **Scioppius** (*c.* 1576–1649), styled by D'Israeli (*Curiosities of Literature*) 'the Attila of authors,' and by Mark Pattison 'the most telling and feared libeller of the day,' wrote an immense number of treatises, chiefly polemical, which have now fallen into oblivion. Cf. Pattison's *Life of Casaubon*, 443 *sq*. For **John Spenser**, S. J. (1601–1671), see de Backer, v. 700.—**Robert Wild**, *Fasti Oxon*. i. 512; **Joseph Glanvill**, *Athenae*, iii. 1244; **Walter Charleton**, *Athenae*, iv. 752.

103. 28. **Dr. Richard Baylie**, President of St. John's 1632 (Dean of Salisbury 1635), ejected 1648, restored 1660, and died 1667, was V. C. 1636, 1637 and 1661; but **Dr. Blandford**, Warden of Wadham, was V. C. in 1662, 1663, so that with him must rest the responsibility for this curiosity of licensing. No licenser's name appears; another ed. was published at Oxford 1668. Some MS. works of Bussières (1607–1678) are preserved in the Library of Lyons: de Backer, i. 157. See also *Life of Bonwicke* (ed. Mayor), 167.

103. 44. This work is generally attributed to Daniel Heinsius, and satirises the life, origin, and character of Scioppius. For **William White** (Gulielmus Phalerius), see *Athenae*, iii. 1167.

103. 51. **Dr. Burges** (*Athenae*, iii. 681) was a bitter opponent of Gauden, who directed against him his *Anti-Baal-Berith* (a most offensive and scurrilous work) in 1661. He died at Watford in 1665. A more favourable account of him, with references, appears in Neal's *Puritans*, iii. 146 *sq*. and *n*.

104. 12. This anecdote is related of **South** in all the biographies; see *e. g.* *Athenae*, iv. 631, and for his benefactions to Christ Church Wood-Gutch, *Colleges and Halls*, 454. The reason of Wood's rancour against South is explained in the former's *Life*, p. 355.

104. 22. Particulars of the reception of the **Declaration of Indulgence** throughout the country are given by Macaulay, i. 502 *sqq*. It was read by only three clergymen in Herts (Ballard MSS. xii. 21). There is an interesting account of Prideaux' action on the occasion in his *Life*, pp. 41 *sqq*. **Thomas Deane**, of Univ. Coll., was M.A. 1676; **Francis Nicholson**, M.A. 1673.

104. 33. Alderman **William Wright** was M.P. for the City of Oxford in the Parliaments of 167⅝, 1679, and 16⁸⁹⁄₉₀. See *Life of Wood*, 211, 216, 223, 238. His son was afterwards Recorder of Oxford, *ib*. 310; Luttrell, i. 471. The Terrae Filius of 1693 indulged in some delicate *badinage* at the expense of the Alderman and his daughters.

105. 17. The Queen's Speech of Nov. 27 is printed in Boyer, p. 214.

105. 28. **T. Snelling**, *Athenae*, iii. 275; **T. Gilbert**, *ib.* iv. 406; **Edmund Elys** *ib.* iv. 470, Rector of East Allington, Devon, a nonjuror, and an opponent of cock-fighting (*Harleian Miscell.* vii. 66); **R. Sharrock**, *Athenae*, iv. 147 ('learned in Divinity, in the Civ. and Com. Law, and very knowing in Vegetables and all pertaining thereunto'). **Dr. Lowth** was nominated Dean of Rochester by James II (Luttrell, i. 472), but the appointment was rendered futile by the Revolution. He was Vicar of Cosmus Blene in the diocese of Canterbury, and a nonjuror (*Life of Kettlewell*, Appendix, p. xiv).

106. 6. Cf. Luttrell, v. 565, 614.

106. 34. **Dr. Peter Birch**, Preb. of Westminster 1689, d. 1710. There is an interesting life of this *protégé* of Fell's, 'who always shew'd himself forward in gaining Proselites,' in *Athenae*, iv. 659. He published several sermons, one of which provoked an answer entitled *A birchen Rod for Dr. Birch*.

106. 40. The **Astrop Wells**, the virtues of which were discovered by Lower and Willis about 1664, were the occasion of Locke's friendship with Shaftesbury: see Christie's *Life* of the Earl, i. 295; Fox Bourne's *Life of Locke*, i. 139.

106. 48. **Timothy Goodwyn**, D.D. of Utrecht, cr. M.A. Jan. 22, 1696; Archdeacon of Oxford 1707; Bishop of Kilmore 1715, and Archbishop of Cashel 1727; d. 1729.

106. 44. The Bishop m. 'a daughter of Mr. Crispe, an eminent attorney of Chipping Norton, who died without issue; and secondly, Catherine, d. of Alderman King of London; by whom he left a very numerous family. Charles Talbot, his eldest son, was appointed chancellor of Great Britain . . 1733.' Noble, iii. 72 *sq.*

107. 2. **William Elstob,** 'the famous Saxonist,' better known perhaps as the brother of Elizabeth Elstob, was born 1673, and studied at Cambridge and afterwards at Oxford, becoming Fellow of Univ. in 1696. He was appointed Rector of St. Swithin and Mary Bothaw 1702, and d. 1714. Among the works published by him were two Anglo-Saxon homilies, and an ed. of Ascham's Latin Letters (Oxford, 1703). See Nichols' *Anecdotes of Bowyer,* 11 *n.,* and Index to Tanner MSS.

110. 4. I would gladly, out of respect for our antiquary, have suppressed this paragraph; but I have thought it necessary to retain it as an instance of the lengths to which men of high character could suffer themselves to go in traducing a political opponent. Bp. **Burn**et married as his third wife Elizabeth, widow of Robert Berkeley, of Spetchley, in 1698. Her two children by the Bishop died in infancy, and she only survived till 1709. Her *Method of Devotion,* with an account of her Life, was reprinted by Archdeacon Goodwyn (106, 48 *n.*) in 1713. See Ballard's *Memoirs,* 398; Burnet, vi. 309.

VOL. VI.

Page 110, line 13. A full account of the 'Proceedings against Anthony à Wood,' and of all the circumstances of the case, is given in an Appendix to the *Life,* pp. 350, *sqq.* The amount of the fine was 34*l.,* and it was laid out on *two* statues—those of Charles I and the Earl of Danby. See Wood's own comments, *Life,* pp. 290 *sqq.*

110. 31. **Marcus Meibomius** (1611-*c.* 1710) published *Antiquae Musicae Auctores septem Graece et Latine* in 1652.

110. 36. There does not seem to have been any London edition of *Photius' Lexicon* before that of Porson, published by Mawman under the superintendence of Dobree in 1822. (Ebert, *Bibliograph. Dict., s.v.* Zonaras.)

111. 7. **Edmund Hickeringill,** of St. John's and Caius, Cam., and Rector of All Saints, Colchester. See *Athenae,* iv. 314.

111. 13. For a defence of himself by **Cave** against a similar charge of appropriating other men's labours, see Chalmers' *Biograph. Dict., art.* Wharton.

111. 16. **Richard Aungervyle,** commonly called **Richard de Bury,** was Bishop of Durham 1333-1345, and the well-known author of *Philobiblon.* For some remarks on him and his book, see Macray's *Annals,* pp. 4 *sq.*; Edwards' *Memoirs of Libraries,* i. 377 *sqq.* The *editio princeps* was printed at Cologne 1473, but the best-known edition is that edited by Thomas James, and printed at Oxford 1598-9. The first English trans. was that of John B. Inglis, 1832; a French trans. appeared in 1856, and the first American ed. 1861. See also Burton, *The Book-Hunter,* 199 *sqq.*

111. 40. For Nicolson's view of the relation between Marianus Scotus and Florence of Worcester, see *English Historical Library,* 56, 57. He knows not whether to call Florence 'An Epitomizer, or Transcriber of *Marianus.*' See also Gairdner, *Early Chroniclers of England,* p. 64. The trans. of Boethius is attributed to Alfred in the last authoritative utterance on the subject. See Prof. Freeman's article 'Ælfred' in the *Dictionary of National Biography,* i. 133 *sqq.*

112. 25. This memorandum is printed in Wood's *Life,* p. 339; and that at page 113, l. 17, *ib.* p. 340.

112. 40. For a summary of this debate see Boyer, pp. 215 *sqq.*

113. 2. **John Dyer** died intestate Sept. 6, 1713, leaving an only son. His grandson, Robert Dyer (d. 1748), bequeathed 20,000*l.* to Christ's Hospital. His newsletter, which was discontinued on his death, was printed in a type resembling writing; *Lit. Anecd.* i. 3. 71 *sq.* He is styled by 'Abraham Froth' (*Spectator,* No. 43) 'our Authentick Intelligence, our *Aristotle* in politics.'

113. 44. **Samuel Hill,** St. Mary Hall, B.A. 1666, Prebendary of Wells 1688, Archdeacon 1705, d. 1716.

114. 6. Sir W. Blackett is described by Luttrell (v. 619) as 'M.P. for Newcastle-on-Tyne, one of our richest commoners.' In 1699 he mentions a rumour that he was to be created a peer.—**Robert Clavering**, Linc., M.A. 1696; Canon of Ch. Ch. and Regius Professor of Hebrew 1715; Bishop of Llandaff 1725, and of Peterborough 1729; d. 1747.

114. 20. The passages thus characterised occur at pp. 238 and 275 of Strype's *Life of Chcke*, ed. 1705.

114. 25 *sqq*. Miles Stapylton, M.A. 1683; D.D. 1700.—**R. Grey**, M.A. 1686.—**John Beauchamp**, M.A. 1683.—An interesting article on **Joseph Bingham** (1668–1723), based on materials supplied by his great-grandson, will be found in Chalmers. The writer mentions that the MS. of this unfortunate sermon (Tanner MSS. xxiv. 90) was then in his own possession. See Perry, *Hist. of the Ch. of England*, iii. 240 *sq*.—**H. Bird**, M.A. 1700.

115. 7. Wasse published an ed. of Sallust (1707) and left materials for an ed. of Thucydides (which appeared in 1732); but he does not appear to have carried out either of the projects here mentioned. See Wordsworth, *Scholae Academicae*, p. 97.

115. 16 *sqq*. Robert Wyntle, B.A. 1702.—**John Tanner**, B.A. 1704.

115. 26. Dr. William Aglionby is frequently mentioned in Luttrell. He had previously been envoy to Spain. He was a good linguist, and a wit, and his *Painting illustrated, in three Dialogues*, was published in 1685. Swift notes that he had been a Papist (*Characters of the Court of Q. Anne*).

115. 27. Of **Browne Willis** (1682–1760), later on a constant friend and patron of Hearne's, we shall hear much in the sequel. He had as yet published nothing, but had certainly shown indications of 'thinking fit to be generous.' He is said to have spent 1200*l*. in 'adorning and repairing' Bletchley Church.

115. 47. John Dormer, S. J., Rector of the English College at Liége, d. 1700. See de Backer, iv. 183.

116. 34. William Denison, M.A. 1700; **Charles Usher**, B.A. 1696, author of a pamphlet entitled *A Letter to a Member of the Convocation of the University of Oxford, containing the Case of a late Fellow Elect of University College* (1699).

116. 50. The **Kit-Cat Club**, the name of which at a later date was connected with art rather than with politics or letters, was founded by Tonson, and originally met at a Mutton-pie House in the Strand. See *Spectator*, ed. Morley, No. 9 *n*; Ashton, *Social Life in the Reign of Q. Anne*, 182 *sqq*.; *Lit. Anecd.*, Index.

117. 3. Claymond's MSS. are numbered 178–181 in Mr. Coxe's Catalogue, and are entitled 'Glossae sive Commentarii in C. Plinii Historiae Naturalis libros iv-xxvii (inc.).' Claymond was the first President of C.C.C. (1517-1537).

117. 7. It was this son John who was the occasion of Sir Thomas' oft-quoted remark to his wife, 'Thou hast prayed so long for a boy that thou hast one now who will be a boy as long as he lives.' Erasmus addressed him in a letter as *optimae spei adolescens*, and dedicated to him *In nucem Ovidii commentarius*, and his Account of the Works of Aristotle.

117. 10. E. Wells, Ch. Ch., M.A. 1693, D.D. 1704, published in 1706 *A Letter from a Minister of the Church of England to Mr. Peter Dowley, a Dissenting Teacher of the Presbyterian or else Independent Perswasion*, which led to some controversy; but he was best known for his *Help for the understanding of the Scriptures* and *Geography of the Old and New Testament*.

117. 14. Dr. Thomas Bayley was President of Magd. 1703-6. See *Life of Frampton*, 158.

117. 31 *sqq*. Geo. Paul, M.A. 1706. Dr. **James Talbot**, of Trinity, Professor of Hebrew, published his ed. of Horace in 1699. Bentley's *Horace* was not published till the close of 1711 (see Jebb's *Life*, pp. 126 *sqq*.).

118. 2 *sqq*. 'Good fellowship' appears to have hindered the accomplishment of this design. The work mentioned a few lines below was only a reprint of Cavendish's well-known narrative.

118. 6. Neocorus, i.e. Ludolph Küster, afterwards Professor of Greek at Berlin, published his *Suidas* in 1705.

118. 12. Edward Acton, of Aldenham, Salop, was created a Baronet by Charles I,

Jan. 17, 1643. See Kimber and Johnson's *Baronetage*, i. 572 *sqq.* Several members of the family figure in the *Dict. Nat. Biog.* vol. i.

118. 26 *sqq.* **R. Adams** of B.N.C., *Athenae*, iv. 603.—R. Adams, M.D., Principal of Magd. Hall 1694, nominated by the Chancellor, to whom the right of nomination was confirmed in a suit arising out of this appointment (Wood's *Life*, 301 *sq.*; Wood-Gutch, *Colleges and Halls*, 687 *sq.*; Munk's *Roll of the R. Coll. of Physicians*, i. 512); d. 1716.—**F. Adams**, b. 1651, Rector of Linc. 1685-1718, Preb. of Durham 1685, 'laid out [1500*l.*] in beautifying the Chapel and Rector's Lodgings. He was also a contributor to the building of All Saints' Church, bequeathed 200*l.* to purchase houses for enlarging the site of the College; and a large collection of Books for the Library' (Wood-Gutch, *Colleges and Halls*, App., p. 264).

119. 4 *sqq.* **S. Adams**, Sen. Proc. 1705, Reader in Moral Philosophy 1703, M.D. 1706, d. 1711.—**W. Adams** was the author of *Fifteen Sermons before the University of Oxford*, published by Sacheverell 1716.—For **John Adams**, author of the *Index Villaris* (1680), see *Dict. Nat. Biogr.* i. 97 *sq.*

119. 26. **Nathaniel Bacon**, incorporated M.A. 1672, author of *An historical Discourse of the Uniformity of the Government of England till the Reigne of Edw. III* (1647).

119. 28. **Lancelot Addison** was appointed Dean of Lichfield 1683, and Archdeacon of Coventry 1684. He died April 20, 1703, aged 71. Hearne's bibliography is by no means complete: see *e.g.* Courthope's *Addison*, p. 23; *Dict. of Nat. Biog.* i. 131 *sqq.* —Lancelot Addison the younger was afterwards (1706) Fellow of Magd. Another son, Gulston, was so named after his maternal uncle, Dr. W. Gulston, Bishop of Bristol 1679-1683. Addison's contributions to the *Musarum Anglicanarum Analecta* are printed vol. ii. (ed. 1699), pp. 3, 44, 56, 157, 187, 199, 243, 284. See Courthope, p. 38 *sq.*

120. 8. Was he of the same family as the well-known politician and antiquary [Governor] Thomas Pownall (1722-1805), sometime M.P. for Minehead, Somerset?

120. 16. Cf. Boyer, p. 218; *Life of Sharp*, 363 *sqq.*

120. 36. **Robert Parsons**, Univ. Coll., M.A. 1670, published this sermon at Oxford 1680 (Sir T. Browne, in writing to his son, *Works*, iii. 470, remarks that it 'is like to sell well'). Parsons was installed Archdeacon of Gloucester 1703 in succession to Hyde the orientalist, and d. 1714. See *Fasti*, ii. 319; Marshall's *Woodstock* (with Supplement), Index.

120. 40. **Wm. Pindar**, M.A. 1670, published a sermon on Prov. xvii. 27.

121. 3. The speech of **Lancelot Addison** as 'Terrae Filius' gave such offence that 'he was forced to recant in the Convocation on his knees, and glad he was that he could escape with no greater punishment.' *Oxoniana*, iv. 215; see also i. 107. After the Restoration he was appointed chaplain to the garrison of Dunkirk, and, two years later, to that of Tangier.

121. 18. For the presentation copy of the Works of James I see Macray, *Annals*, 47 *sq.*—**George Calvert** (c. 1582-1632) was appointed Secretary of State 1619; but resigned in 1624, professing himself a Roman Catholic; he was created Lord Baltimore 1625. He is now best remembered by his connexion with Newfoundland, Virginia, and Maryland. See Lloyd's *State Worthies*, p. 750 (ed. 2).

121. 38. **Hugh Broughton** (1549-1613) was one of the most famous Hebraists of his day. See Strype's *Life of Whitgift*, ii. 527 and *passim*. His Works were published in 1662, and entitled *The Works of the great Albionean Divine, renowned in many Nations for rare skill in Salems and Athens tongues, and familiar acquaintance with all Rabbinical Learning, Mr. Hugh Broughton.* Many of his MSS. are preserved in the British Museum. See also Index to Tanner MSS.—**John Speed** (c. 1555-1629), the well-known historian, published in 1616 *A Clowd of Witnesses; and they the Holy Genealogies of the Sacred Scriptures.* James I gave him a patent securing the property of the Genealogy printed before the Bible to himself and his heirs. I do not find the 'two owls' in any of Mr. Fry's facsimiles.

122. 19. For **Hare** and his collections, see Nicolson's *Eng. Hist. Lib.* 150; Fuller's *History of the University of Cambridge*, 35 (ed. 1840).

122. 32. For the debate in the Commons on this subject, see Boyer, 219.

122. 41. See Macray's *Annals*, p. 324.

122. 43. There is mention of **Archibald Pitcarne's** book *de Inventoribus* in a letter from A. Verwer to Gregory in Rigaud's *Letters of Scientific Men,* i. 252. It is said that David Gregory found in the papers of his uncle James Gregory some hints concerning Newton's method. The latter was an intimate friend of Sir Isaac, and was entrusted by him with a MS. copy of the *Principia* for the purpose of contributing observations thereon, which were incorporated in the second edition. For the reception of the *Principia* at Oxford, see Wordsworth, *Scholae Academicae,* pp. 71, 245 *sq.*

123. 11. **Robert Dobyns,** M.A. 1695.—Prince George's incapacity is familiar to us from Macaulay (i. 582); but cf. Burnet's *Own Time,* v. 380.

123. 19. **T. Guidott,** Wadham, B.M. 1666. See a full bibliography of his works, *Athenae,* iv. 733. Wood is even less complimentary than Hearne in his remarks on Guidott's personal character.

123. 26. The honoured names of **Aldrich** and **Fell** need no comment. There is a too brief account of the former in the *Dict. of Nat. Biog.* i. 251. An adequate Life of the latter is one of the great *desiderata* in Oxford History, but see the extremely valuable references brought together by Prof. Mayor, *Notes and Queries,* 4th S. iv. 313. **J. Massey,** Fellow of Merton, M.A. 1675, Proctor 1684; installed Dean of Ch. Ch. Dec. 29, 1686, and fled from Oxford Nov. 30, 1688. He died in Paris 1715. Wood-Gutch, *Colleges and Halls,* 441. For Fell's New Year's gifts, which were continued under his successor and imitated by Dr. Charlett, see *Athenae,* iv. 198.

124. 2. **Geo. Darrell,** All Souls, Canon of Westminster 1607, and Lincoln 1618, d. 1631.

124. 39. Addison did not marry the **Countess of Warwick** till Aug. 3, 1716; see Mr. Leslie Stephen's article in the *Dictionary of Nat. Biography,* i. 129.

124. 45. **Charles, Earl of Orrery** (1676-1731), was of course the hero of the Phalaris controversy. By this marriage with the daughter of the Earl of Exeter he was the father of John, Earl of Cork and Orrery (1707-1762), the friend of Swift, Pope and Johnson.

125. 3. Particulars of this **Sir John Pakington** (d. 1727), and his feud with the Bishop of Worcester, are given in Kimber's *Baronetage,* i. 189. He was the grandson of the Lady Pakington to whom the authorship of *The Whole Duty of Man* has been attributed.

126. 10. For the arms and motto of the University, see Macray, *Annals of the Bodleian,* 15, and the same author's letter in *Notes and Queries,* 6th S. vol. vi. p. 194. His conclusion is, that 'four mottoes, or at any rate three, stand upon an equal footing of prescriptive authority, and that custom alone has regulated their use.'

126. 27. **T. Wise,** M.A. 1694, D.D. 1708, Prebendary of Lincoln 1720, d. 1726. (Boase's *Register,* 84.)

127. 1. **Henry Howard** second son of the poet Earl of Surrey, b. *c.* 1539, created Earl of Northampton March 1604, d. 1619. He was deeply implicated in the murder of Overbury. His principal work was *A Defensative against the Poison of supposed Prophecies* (1583). See Lloyd, *State-Worthies,* 780. He is repeatedly mentioned in Goodman's *Court of King James I.*

127. 8. For **S. Slade,** M.A. 1593, see *Fasti,* i. 262.

127. 21. **J. Gagnier,** a convert from Roman Catholicism, was appointed to act as substitute for Prof. Wallis in the absence of the latter in 1717. Besides the work here mentioned he published *Vindiciae Kircherianae,* Abulfeda's *Life of Mohammed,* &c. He died 1740.

127. 28. **Johnson's** (C.C.C., M.A. 1683) ed. of the *Antigone and Trachiniae* appeared in 1708, and his Sophocles complete in 1746. This was republished in 1758 by Bowyer (*Lit. Anecd.* ii. 312 *sqq.*), who likewise issued in 1761 a new ed. of Johnson's *Epigrammatum Delectus* (1699).

127. 47. **Denzil Holles,** created Baron Holles 1661; d. 1680.

128. 16. Thomas Osborne, Earl of Danby, Marquis of Caermarthen, and **Duke of Leeds,** whose career is part of the national history, died July 26, 1712, at the age of 80. Some years after our present date he greatly distinguished himself at the trial of Sacheverell.

128. 37. An account of the consecration of Trinity College Chapel is given at p. 302

of Wood's *Life*. It is amusingly free from technicalities. Wood bestows one of his warmest eulogies on Dr. H. **Maurice** (*Athenae*, iv. 326), whose tenure of the professorship was so brief. His most successful work was an answer to Baxter's *Church History of Bishops* (1682).

128. 47. For remarks on **Trussell** and his works, see Nicolson, *Eng. Hist. Lib.* 14, 72, 134.—**Walter Curll** was consecrated Bishop of Winchester 1632 ; d. 1647.

129. 26. See Rogers, *Protests of the Lords*, i. 177 *sqq.*

129. 32. For **Ewelme** Church and its monuments, see Skelton's *Antiquities of Oxfordshire, Ewelme Hundred* (with illustrations) ; and for the question as to the connexion of Sir Thomas **Chaucer** with the Poet, Marshall's *Early History of Woodstock Manor*, 107 *sqq.*

130. 1 *sqq.* **Dr. Sykes'** will was proved April 16, 1706.—**Roger Almont**, M.A. 1666.—**Dr. John Baron**, Master of Balliol 1705-1722.—**Edw. Chamberlayne** (1616-1703) lived to bring out twenty editions of his *Angliae Notitia*, and continuations were published by his son (d. 1723).—**Andrew Allam** was, like Chamberlayne, of Edmund Hall (1655-1685) ; see Wood's story to the same effect, *Athenae*, iv. 175; *Dict. of Nat. Biog.* i. 293.

130. 36. A summary of the little that is known of the early history of **Winchester** will be found in Benham's *Diocesan History of Winchester*, 2 *sqq.* Cf. *Ductor Historicus*, ii. 309 ; Tanner's *Notitia Monastica* (ed. 1), 75.

131. 21. Hearne's own account of his visit to **Silchester**, the ancient Calleva, has been printed in *Letters from the Bodleian*, ii. 184 *sqq.* Cf. Murray's *Surrey, Hants, &c.* (1865) 292 *sq.*

131. 31. **Sigebert** is very briefly dismissed by Mr. J. B. Mullinger in *The University of Cambridge from the Earliest Times*, vol. i. p. 66. See *Ductor Historicus*, ii. 290 *sqq.*

131. 33. **W. Worth**, Edm. Hall, B.A. 1695, M.A. 1698; All Souls, B.D. 1705, D.D. 1719 ; Archdeacon of Worc. 1705, and Prebendary 1716; d. 1742. He was the occasion of Fleetwood's publishing ed. 1 of his *Chronicon Preciosum* ; see chap. i. of that work.

132. 32. Particulars of this book and its author will be found in Blades' *Biography and Typography of William Caxton* (ed. 2), p. 220. Dr. Cotton has an interesting description with references, of the Würzburg Missal of 1481 in his *Typographical Gazetteer*, Series I, p. 120.

133. 4. **William Watson**, a secular priest, and bitter opponent of the Jesuits, published his *Decachordon of ten quodlibeticall Questions concerning Religion and State* in 1602. He was executed in 1603 for his share in the ' Bye ' or ' surprising treason ' (see Lingard, ed. 6, vii. 8 *sqq.*). He is mentioned in F. Morris's *Life of Father John Gerard,—passim.*

133. 9 *sqq.* **C. Wase** was Fellow of King's Coll., Cam., and afterwards superior Bedel of Law in Oxon. His son of the same name, of C.C.C., was M.A. 1684, Proctor 1691 ; d. 1711.—**R. White** (Vitus), Canon of Douai ; see Nicolson, *Eng. Hist. Lib.* 72.—**T. Hasker**, M.A. 1694.—**T. Winder**, M.A. 1704.

134. 3. For this and other Block-books in the Bodleian, see Macray, *Annals*, 321, and on the subject generally, De Vinne, *Invention of Printing*, 193 *sqq.*

134. 15. **John Wynne**, M.A. 1688, D.D. 1705, Principal of Jesus 1712, Bishop of St. Asaph 1714, and of Bath 1727 ; d. 1742.

134. 44. For a memoir of **Sir Thos. Hanmer** (1677-1746), of Shakespearean fame, see that somewhat miscellaneous book, *The Correspondence of Sir Thomas Hanmer, Bart.*, edited by Sir H. Bunbury, Bart. (Moxon, 1838), and Manning's *Lives of the Speakers*, 423 *sqq.* He had entered Parliament in 1702.

VOL. VII.

Page 138, line 31. See Luttrell v. 627; 'Tis said the Lord Treasurer has explained correspondence with France, charged on him by Mr. Cæsar, to be only this, that the late queen Mary, at St. Germains, sent to him for a jewell she had left behind her; upon which, he shewed King William the letter, and his majestie ordered it to be transmitted to her; and accordingly she received the same, and returned a letter of thanks, which his lordship also shewed the King.' There is of course no doubt whatever of Godolphin's guilt; see Burnet's *Own Time*, iii. 8 *n.*; Macaulay, ii. 267 *sq.*; 430, 589 *sqq.*

138. 53. **H. Sacheverell**, M.A. 1696, was not as yet much known outside University circles. He was a friend of Addison, who dedicated to him in 1693 his *Account of the Greatest English Poets.*

139. 26. **Samuel Wesley** was the father of no less than nineteen children, of whom only three sons and three daughters grew up (Southey's *Wesley*, i. 10).

139. 36. For the motto of the East India Company, see *Notes and Queries*, 3rd S. ix. 43, quoting Burke's *Armory*. Hearne seems to have been misinformed.—'Et uterque Poenus Serviat uni,' Hor. *Od.* II. ii. 11 *sq.*; 'Credat Judaeus Apella,' Hor. *Sat.* I. v. 100.

140. 10. Some particulars of Mr. **Bromley's** ancestry are given in Manning's *Lives of the Speakers*, 416 *sqq.*

140. 40. In a similar spirit Ken remarked of this work of Dodwell's that ' he built high on feeble foundations, and would not have many proselytes to his hypotheses ' (Abbey and Overton, i. 117). Some letters of Nelson to Charlett are printed in Secretan's *Life* of the former, 225 *sqq.*

140. 41. For **Edmund Chishull**, C.C.C., M.A. 1693, Chaplain to the English Factory at Smyrna 1698–1702, Chaplain to the Queen 1711, d. 1733, see *Lit. Anecd.* i. 270 *sqq.*; Pearson, *Chaplains to the Levant Company*, 34 *sq.* His *Antiquitates Asiaticae Christianam Aeram antecedentes* was published by Bowyer in 1728, and his *Travels in Turkey and Back to England* appeared under the auspices of Dr. Mead in 1747.

140. 49. **John Allibond**, Magd., D.D. 1643, Master of Magd. Coll. School, d. 1658. *Fasti*, ii. 69.

141. 13. Ebert (ii. 814) mentions an ed. of the *Illustrium Imagines* published at Rome 1517, 8vo. Jacobus Sadoletus is said to have been the editor.

141. 34 *sqq.* **Rob. Pearse**, B.A. 1701; **John Musson**, B.A. 1701; **John Grandorge**, M.A. 1693, D.D. 1708, Preb. of Canterbury 1713; **Abraham Kent**, M.A. 1705. The last-named was a frequent correspondent of Hearne's.

142. 3 *sqq.* For Paulerspury, see Murray's *Northamptonshire* (1878) 128.—**Sir B. Bathurst's** eldest son, by his wife Frances, d. of Sir Allen Apsley, was Allen, afterwards Lord Bathurst.

142. 10. **Sir Wm. Fermor**, Bart. created Baron Lempster 1692; d. 1711. According to Collins he ' erected, from the very foundation at Easton-Neston .'., the ancient seat of his family, a regular and fair pile of building of free-stone; added pleasant gardens and plantations; and adorned the whole with a magnificent and costly collection of ancient Greek, Roman, and Egyptian statues.' See Murray's *Northamptonshire*, 125 *sq.*; *Lit. Anecd.* ii. 4. Lady Sophia, sixth daughter of the Duke of Leeds, and relict of Donatus Lord O'Brien, was his *third* wife. For ' bonds of resignation,' cf. *Life of Frampton*, 141.

142. 27. A good deal of correspondence has appeared in *Notes and Queries* on the subject of **Arabic Numerals**; but little of much value has been added to the statement quoted in Vol. i. p. 230 from the *Archæological Journal*, vi. 291, that the earliest date of their occurrence in any work connected with building is 1445, though they were common in MSS. after 1320, and in astronomical tracts as early as 1290.

142. 29. **Laurence Nowell**, younger brother of the better-known Dean of St. Paul's, Dean of Lichfield 1559, d. 1576, is described by Wood (*Athenae*, i. 425) as ' a most diligent searcher into venerable antiquity, a most learned Clerk also in the *Saxon* Language, and . . . one of the first that recalled the study thereof.' Lambard the Kentish antiquary was his pupil. A MS. of his writing entitled *Polychronicon* was in the possession of Ralph Thoresby; and a Saxon vocabulary compiled by him passed through the hands of Lambard, &c., into the Bodleian Library, where a transcript of it by Junius is likewise preserved.

142. 31. For this inscription, and references to authorities, see Davies Gilbert's

Parochial History of Cornwall, i. 178 *sqq*. A popular history of the Parish of St. Neot was published by the editor's grandfather, in 1833 (Bodmin : Liddell & Son).

142. 44. The MS. now known as Cod E. (ed. Hearne 1715). See Tischendorf's *Monumenta Sacra*, Nova Collectio, tom. ix, Scrivener's *Introduction, &c.* ; Macray's *Annals*, 64.

145. 27 *sqq*. **Nicholas Trivet's** *Annales sex Regum Angliae* was published by Antony Hall, Oxford 1719, and Adam Murimuth's Continuation in 1722. See Nicolson's *Eng. Hist. Lib.* 64; Gairdner's *Early Chroniclers*, 223 *sq.*—For **Peter Ickham,** see Nicolson 63.—Johannis Rossi, Antiquarii Warwicensis, *Historia Regum Angliae* was published by Hearne at Oxford in 1716, the ed. consisting of only 60 copies. A second ed. was published in 1745. Nicolson 69.—For **St. Swithun** and **St. Edmund,** see *ib.*, 106, 104.—**T.** Otterbourne and **Wethamstede's** Annals were published by Hearne in two vols., Oxford, 1732. Nicolson 67.—**Walter,** Canon of **Gisburn,** is better known as Walter Hemingford. See note on p. 162, l. 7.—**John Merylynch,** monk of Glastonbury, wrote additions to Martinus Polonus, &c. Hearne borrowed his chronicle, with that of Bever, &c. in 1734, from the Harleian Library, where they formed No. 641. See Catalogue of Rawlinson MSS. B. 185. Fuller information concerning all the authors mentioned in this paragraph will be found in Sir T. Duffus Hardy's *Descriptive Catalogue*.

145. 39. Cf. Rogers' *Protests of the Lords*, i. 174 *sq*.

146. 14. For Hallam's final opinion on this subject, see *Middle Ages* (ed. 11), iii. 420 *sq*. Cf. Wood-Gutch, *Annals*, i. 23. Hearne gave considerable attention to the subject in later years ; and it is dealt with exhaustively by Mr. Parker in his *Early History of Oxford* (1885), pp. 40 and foll.

147. 32. Full particulars of the life and works of **Isaac Barrow** (1630–1677) are given in Ward's *Lives of the Gresham Professors*, 157 *sqq*. His *Euclidis Elementa* was published at Cambridge 1655, and *Euclidis Data* in 1657.

147. 50. **Dr. Thomas Comber** (1644–1699), author of the *Companion to the Temple*, Preb. of York 1677 and Precentor 1683, was promoted to the Deanery of Durham 1691. For a criticism on his doctrine of the divine right of Tithes, see *Life of Sharp*, ii. 12 *sqq*.

153. 27. **W. Dobson,** M.A. 1672, D.D. 1705, continued President of Trinity till his death in 1731, at the age of 81.

153. 38. This edition of Pindar was published at the Sheldonian Theatre in 1697. Ebert (iii. 1379) remarks that its ' real intrinsic value . . is very little : yet it is greatly sought after by collectors.'

154. 9. **Roger Almont** d. Aug. 31, 1710, aged 67 (Wood-Gutch, *Colleges and Halls,* 533).

154. 15. The reference is to *Marmora Oxon.* No. cxlii. pp. 276 *sq.* ; Hearne's *Livy,* vi. 247.

154. 26. Perhaps it may be mentioned without indiscretion that an elaborate edition of Fortescue on Monarchy may be expected at no very long interval from the Oxford University Press. The ed. referred to by Hearne was published in 1714.

154. 31. **F. Robortello,** 1516–1567 ; **C. Sigonius,** 1524–1585.

155. 18. **John Bale** (1495–1563), Bishop of Ossory. See his biography at end of the Life of Leland in *Lives of the Antiquaries* (1772) ; Tanner's *Eng. Hist. Lib.* 155 *sq.*; Fuller's *Worthies*, iii. 160 ; *Athenae*, Index.

155. 20. For this book, see Ebert *Bibliographical Dictionary*, ii. 809 (No. 10414).

158. 4. **Wm. Colnett,** New Coll., B.A. 1689 ; All Souls, M.A. 1693, D.D. 1704.

158. 50. **Sir E. Sherburne** (1618–1702), of the ancient stock of the Sherburnes of Stonyhurst, is best remembered by his English verse translations from Seneca and Manilius, and by his remote connexion with the Phalaris controversy. See an account of this circumstance in Jebb's *Bentley*, 33. There is a very interesting account of his career in the *Fasti*, ii. 30. He was commissary general of the artillery under Charles I and his sons, but refused to take the oaths to William III.

159. 19. The Archbishop of York was of course **John Sharp,** d. 1714. An account of his position, political and ecclesiastical, will be found in Abbey and Overton, i. 127 *sqq*. The Life by his son is a highly interesting record of his career, and throws much light on the general history of his time.

159. 24. James Ford, M.A. 1693. I do not find the name of Loggan on the list of Chancellors of Salisbury. **John Loggin,** New Coll., was M.A. 1688.

159. 34. Richard of Canterbury was consecrated April 7, 1174; and **Richard Grant,** of Wethershed, June 10, 1229 (Stubbs' *Reg. Sacr. Angl.*).

160. 3. Printed in Hearne's *Livy,* vi. 259.

160. 34. Matthew Griffith, d. Rector of Bladon 1661, suffered under the Commonwealth as a Royalist and Episcopalian, *Athenae,* ii. 711 ; Lloyd's *Memoirs,* 521 ; Marshall's *Woodstock,* 299 *sq.* His daughter was killed at the sack of Basing House.

160. 37. Plot, *Nat. Hist. Oxfordshire,* 349 ; Marshall's *Woodstock,* 12.

161. 6. Dr. W. Lloyd married the daughter of Philippa, sister of John Fell and wife of Dr. Walter Jones, Preb. of Westminster.—The Rev. **Henry Jones,** Ch. Ch., M.A. 1675, Bp. Fell's nephew (see Fell's will in Seventh Report of Hist. MSS. Comm. p. 691), and Bp. Lloyd's brother-in-law, was Rector of Sunningwell, and through him some of Fell's MSS. passed into the Bodleian. We shall hear more of him hereafter. He appears in the list in the *Life of Kettlewell* among the nonjurors in the diocese of Salisbury. See Macray's *Annals of the Bodleian,* 109, 120.

161. 25. Sir Geo. Wheler, Preb. of Durham, published *A Journey into Greece, in company of Dr. Spon of Lyons,* in 1682. The genuineness of the Codex Traguriensis of the Coena Trimalchionis has been generally admitted since 1669, when the MS. was despatched from the library of the proprietor Nicolaus Cippius, at Trau, to Rome, where it was finally pronounced to be at least 300 years old : see Smith's *Dict. of Biog. art.* Petronius. The *Coena* was first published at Padua by Martinus Statilius (Petrus Petitus), 1664. See full bibliographical particulars, with references, in Ebert, iii. 1340 *sq.*

161. 48. Richard Ibbetson, M.A. 1701. He was afterwards one of the heroes of the 'riot in All Souls buttery.'

162. 7. Walter Hemingford's *Historia de rebus gestis Edvardi I. Edv. II. & E. III.* was published by Hearne in two vols. 1731. Cf. Nicolson, 79. The MS. referred to is Magd. liii. 20 (Coxe). Gale had previously edited the same author's *De gestis regum Angliae ab a.* 1066 *ad a.* 1300 in his *XV Scriptores.* For **Walter Coventry,** see Nicolson, 61.

163. 2. Some remarks on **Sir Simonds D'Ewes** (1602-1650), the well-known legal antiquary, and editor of *The Journals of all the Parliaments during the Reign of Q. Elizabeth,* will be found in Mr. S. R. Gardiner's *History,* vii. 222 *sq.* His Autobiography was published in 1845 under the editorship of Mr. J. O. Halliwell (London ; 2 vols. 8vo.). A catalogue of his MSS. is given in Harleian MSS., No. 775. Particulars of Wanley's librarianship will be found in *Lit. Anecd.* i. 85 *sqq.*

163. 10. For the dates, &c., of the Copyright Acts, as affecting the Bodleian Library, see Dr. Griffiths' *Enactments in Parliament specially concerning the Universities,* p. 187 *n.*

164. 17. The **Rev. W. Stephens,** B.D., rector of Sutton, Surrey, published a Sermon on the failure of the Assassination Plot in 1696. That here referred to was preached before the House of Commons, Jan. 30, 1700, and provoked adverse *Reflections.* Cf. Luttrell, vi. 7.

164. 34. Hearne should have written *Dionysiacs.*

165. 48. Dr. John Bramhall was Archbishop of Armagh 1661-1663. A sermon of **Richard Bancroft** (Archbishop of Canterbury 1604-1609) was reprinted in Gandy's *Bibliotheca Scriptorum Ecclesiae Anglicanae* (1709).

166. 5. Dr. E. Fowler (1632-1714), Vicar of St. Giles's, Cripplegate 1681, Bishop of Gloucester 1691. His first work, curiously enough, was *The Principles and Practices of certain Moderate Divines of the Church of England (greatly misunderstood) truly represented and defended.* Cf. Thoresby's, *Diary,* ii. 102 *sq.* For his relations to his parishioners, see his Life in Chalmers' *Biograph. Dict.*

166. 19. See **Barnes'** *Anacreon Christianus,* together with explanatory note, at pp. 384 *sqq.* of his ed. of Anacreon (1705).

166. 23. See the account of the whole matter in Boyer, *Reign of Queen Anne,* 221.

167. 1. This work is not generally attributed to **Grosseteste** (Bp. of Linc. 1235-1254). See *e.g.* Perry's *Life and Times of Grosseteste,* p. 8. Pegge, *Life and Times* *of Grossteste*, 270, quotes Hearne, *Annal. Dunstap.* 299, where our author ascribes it to Grosstesle, appealing to Leland and MSS.

167. 15. The 'Difference and Disparity' is stated to be 'Written by the *Earl of Clarendon* in his younger dayes' at p. 184 of the 1685 ed. of the *Reliquiae Wottonianae*.

167. 20. Luttrell's entry (vi. 9) is: 'Queen dowager dyed at Lisbon the 31st past, by which the nation will save 40,000*l*. per ann.' She had returned to Portugal in 1692. See Miss Strickland's *Lives of the Queens*, viii. 466 *sqq*.

167. 27. This ed. of the *Onomasticon* was published by Wetstein, 1706, in 2 vols. folio, under the editorship of Lederlin and Hemsterhuis.

167. 29. Dr. Dunster was Warden of Wadham 1689-1719; Dr. Royse, Provost of Oriel 1691-1708; Dr. John Irish, All Souls, D.C.L. 1677; W. Worth, All Souls, B.D. 1705.

167. 48. Lord George Hamilton was created Earl of Orkney, in the Peerage of Scotland, in 1696, on his marriage with Elizabeth Villiers; d. 1736. See Noble, i, 70 *sq*.

168. 8. 'The Byble, which is all the holy Scripture; in which are contayned the olde and newe Testament truly and purely translated into Englysh by Tho. Matthew.' *n.p.* 1537. fol.

168. 17. Stevens is of course a slip of the pen for *Edwards*; see p. 166, l. 24.

169. 8. The only T. Spencer of this date known in literature appears to be the author of *England's Warning-peece, or, the History of the Gun-powder Treason* (London : 1659).

169. 8. Sir Jeffrey Jeffreys was Sheriff of London 1699, and was knighted in the same year; candidate for Brecknock 1700; Alderman of London 1701, d. 1709.

169. 19. This was no doubt George Strahan : see *Lit. Anecd.* i. 62, &c. He was again in trouble in 1709; see Luttrell, vi. 423.

169. 28. For the familiar expression 'to dine with Duke Humphrey,' see *Notes and Queries*, 4th S., iv. 3, 13.

VOL. VIII.

Page 170, line 28. Theobald Churchill, M.A. 1683, seventh son of Sir Winston Churchill, d. 1685, and was buried in St. Martin's in the Fields.

171. 1. Grabe was in favour of the 'Usages,' as sanctioned by the First Prayer Book of Edward VI (cf. Walton and Medd's ed., xxii *sq*.), which afterwards (1717) led to a schism among the Nonjurors. See Campbell's *Middle State*, 79 (*ap.* Lathbury, *Nonjurors*, 278). The Usages were of course the mixed chalice, prayers for the dead, the prayer for the descent of the Holy Ghost upon the Elements, and the Oblatory Prayer. They were all introduced in the New Communion Office put forth by Collier, Brett, and Campbell in 1718. See Abbey and Overton, i. 151 *sqq*.

171. 38. Byrom Eaton, D.D., Fellow of B.N.C., Principal of Gloucester Hall 1662-1692, Archdeacon of Stow 1677, and of Leicester 1683, d. 1703, and was buried at Nuneham Courtney (Wood-Gutch, *Colleges and Halls*, 636).

172. 1. Dr. Edward Fowler survived till 1714.

172. 10. Sebastian Edzard published several theological works in Latin, chiefly against the Calvinists; his first work was entitled *Jacobi patriarchae de Shiloh vaticinium a depravatione Johannis Clerici assertum* (London, 1698).

172. 23. This ed. is characterised by Ebert as 'of value.' Edw. Dechair, M.A. 1701; John Potter, M.A. 1694, D.D. 1706, and afterwards Regius Professor of Divinity, Bishop of Oxford, and Archbishop of Canterbury.

173. 15. Moses Wiles, M.A. 1696, D.D. 1711.

174. 9. Sir George Rooke (1650-1709), the hero of Vigo and captor of Gibraltar, m., as his third wife, Catherine Knatchbull, of Mersham Hatch, Kent, Jan. 16.

174. 12 *sqq*. Luttrell, vi. 7 : 'Last night dyed capt. Hill, a commissioner of the

navy, and father in law to sir Clowdesly Shovell, to whom it's said he has left near 100,000*l.*' Charles Sackville, D. of Dorset, whose Life Johnson wrote, d. Jan. 29, aged 68.—Henry, Duke of Beaufort, m., as his second wife, Lady Rachel Noel, d. of the Earl of Gainsborough.—Charles, Lord Bruce, m. Lady Anne Savile, eldest d. of William, Marquis of Halifax.—Lord Scudamore (says Luttrell) 'is married to Mrs. Digby, daughter to the last lord Digby ; his fortune 10,000*l.*'

174. 43. For **Adam Littleton**, see *Athenae*, iv. 403 ; *Fasti*, ii. 320. Bp. Barlow attributed this pamphlet to John Carrick, student of Ch. Ch.

175. 1. See Ballard's *Memoirs*, 268 *sqq.* ; Macray's *Annals of the Bodleian*, 48 *sq.*

175. 27. This sermon was on Genesis xlii. 21. Kennett's former sermon here alluded to was preached in 1704, and called forth at least four replies.

175. 32. **Matthew Woodford**, M.A. 1698, afterwards sub-dean of Chichester. **Samuel Woodford** (p. 179, l. 9), Wadham Coll., was B.A. 1656, Preb. of Chichester 1676, of Winchester 1680 (*Athenae*, iv. 730 ; Wood's *Life*, 91). For **Denham's** version of the Psalms, see *Athenae*, iii. 826. Wood only knew of it by Woodford's mention in his *Occasional Compositions in English Rhimes*.

175. 50. **Otho Nicholson**, Ch. Ch., an Examiner in Chancery, was a younger son of Thomas Nicholson of the county of Lancaster. See his epitaph in Wood-Gutch, *Colleges and Halls*, 459. Carfax Conduit was erected at his expense in 1610 ; see *Gentleman's Magazine*, Dec. 1771.

176. 15. The Archduke Charles, titular King of Spain, arrived at Windsor Dec. 29, 1703. Full particulars of the visit are given in Miss Strickland's *Lives of the Queens*, xii. 98 *sqq.* (ed. 1848).

176. 23. For the character of Sir **Joseph Williamson** (d. 1701), see Mr. Christie's Introduction to his Letters (Camden Soc. 1874) ; *Athenae*, Index ; Noble, i. 155 *sqq.* ; Lonsdale's *Worthies of Cumberland*, vi. 217 *sqq.* P[ayne] F[isher] wrote a *Carmen Heroicum* in his honour (ed. 2, 1675).

176. 35. The inscription to Julius Vitalis is printed in Spelman's *Life of Alfred the Great* (ed. Hearne), 226 *sqq.* Dodwell wrote critical notes upon it, which were published by Musgrave, 1711.

176. 37. The Life of **Dr. Tobie Venner** (1577-1660) is in the *Athenae* (iii. 491). Wood remarks that this book 'was written in condescension to mean capacities.'

176. 41. He is described by Luttrell (vi. 12) as ' one Dr. Brown, who formerly wrote a tract against the circulation of the blood,' i. e. **Joseph Browne**, M.D., author of *The modern Practice Vindicated* and a *Treatise on the Blood*, editor of Sir Theodore Mayern's Works, and continuer of the *Examiner* (Noble, ii. 232).

176. 46. The *Expositio sancti Jeronimi in Simbolum Apostolorum*, Oxon. 1468, has caused much controversy. See S. W. Singer's *Account of the Expositio*, Lond. 1812, supporting the genuineness of the date, and W. Blades in the *Antiquary*, vol. iii. No. 13 (Jan. 1881), taking the general view that the date is an error for 1478. The question has been complicated by a forgery in R. Atkyns' *Original of Printing*, Lond. 1664, p. 4. Rufinus was the author of the *Expositio*, not St. Jerome.

177. 10. The first book printed by **Caxton** in England was probably *The Dictes and Sayings of the Philosophers*, 1477. See Blades' *Biography and Typography of William Caxton* (ed. 2), 188 *sqq.*, &c. In l. 19 Hearne has written ' Octavos ' for ' Quartos ;' and in l. 35 ' Wod ' for ' Rood.' Cf. Wood-Gutch, *Annals*, i. 623 *sqq.*

177. 31. The *Expositio Alexandri super tres* [*Aristotelis*] *libros de Anima*, Oxon. 1481, is the first folio produced by the Oxford Press, and the copy at Brasenose is the only known one on vellum. Some copies exhibit a woodcut border on the first leaf, the first engraved border found in English printing. The author is supposed to be Alexander ab Ales or Hales.

177. 44. For **Thomas Bennet** (d. Aug. 26, 1706, aged 41), ' a first-rate Bookseller in St. Paul's Church-yard, particularly noticed by the Established Clergy of that period, and by the leading men at Oxford, as appears by the controversy of Mr. Boyle with Dr. Bentley,' see *Lit. Anecd.* iii. 709 *sqq.* His funeral sermon was preached by Atterbury, and roused some controversy.

177. 48. For the history of this question under Q. Elizabeth, see Kennett's *Case of Impropriations*, pp. 153 *sqq.*, with the references there given; cf. Spelman, *De non temerandis Ecclesiis* (ed. 5, 1676), *passim.*

178. 12. See Boyer, 227 *sq.* **Dr. John Cawley** was Archdeacon of Lincoln, 1667–1709.

179. 5 *sqq.* For **Miles Stapylton**, see *Worthies of All Souls*, 290 *sq.* He belonged to a Roman Catholic family. He was B.A. (Univ.) 1679, M.A. (All Souls) 1683, B. and D.D. 1700, in which year he became Preb. of Worcester. He died 1731.—**Richard Simon** (1638-1712), priest of the Oratory, the learned author of the *Histoire critique du Vieux Testament* and many other works.—**Jean Hardouin**, S. J. (1646-1729), published his ed. of Pliny 1685, and his *Chronologiae ex nummis antiquis restitutae prolusio, de nummis Herodiadum*, in which this and other minor paradoxes were maintained, in 1693. He formally recanted his errors in 1708. See *Lit. Anecd.* Index; de Backer, i. 372 *sqq.*—**Christopher Wase's** trans. of Vitruvius never saw the light.

179. 49. Edward Ward (*c.* 1667-1731) is best known as the author of *The London Spy.* He kept a public house in Moorfields, which was frequented by members of the High Church party (Jacob). He is mentioned in the *Dunciad*, i. 233. See Noble, ii. 262.

180. 31. Was this **John Powell**, a lawyer of Gloucester, to whom Bp. Frampton addressed a letter preserved in Tanner MSS. xxxii?

180. 42. Henry Gandy, M.A. 1674, was Senior Proctor 1683. He was a Bishop among the nonjurors, and a vigorous opponent of the 'Usages.' He died in 1733. Noble has fallen into an extraordinary error with regard to him (iii. 173).

181. 12. The Proctors in 1706 were Brune Bickley, New Coll., M.A. 1696, B. and D.M. 1710; and **Peter Foulkes**, Ch. Ch., M.A. 1701, B. and D.D. 1710, afterwards Preb., sub-dean and Chancellor of Exeter.—**Thomas Bickley** was Bishop of Chichester 1586–1596.

181. 45. D. Passionei (1682-1761) was raised to the Cardinalate in 1738, and in 1755 became librarian of the Vatican, the treasures of which he liberally opened to Dr. Kennicott. He was an enthusiastic collector of books and works of art.

182. 6 *sqq.* **Tho. Husbands**, All Souls, B.A. 1697; New Coll., M.A. 1700.—**John Maximilian De L'Angle**, M.A. 1694.

182. 19. For **Robert Dormer** (1649-1726), see Foss, *Biographia Juridica*, 224; and for the **Leicester** election (ll. 36 *sqq.*) Luttrell, vi. 6, 11, 14.

183. 6 *sqq.* **Almeloveen's** ed. of Strabo appeared at Amsterdam 1707.—**Gronovius** did not publish an ed. of Josephus, but his notes, as well as those of Cocceius, were incorporated in the Dutch ed. of 1726.—**Verwey** never brought out his edition of Hesychius.—There is mention of Peter van der Aa the bookseller in *Athenae*, iv. 463.

183. 36. One is irresistibly reminded of Radcliffe's quotation from Sir Roger L'Estrange's version of Æsop's Fables, applied to William III, regarding the man who felt himself '*so well, that I am e'en ready to die of I know not how many* good signs *and Tokens*' (*Life of Radcliffe*, p. 40, ed. 1715).

184. 9. For **St. Scholastica's** day, see *Oxoniana*, i. 119 *sqq.*, and cf. Wood's *Life*, 224 *sq.*

184. 30. Ralph Emmerson, M.A. 1700.

184. 34. For the history of the Abbey of North Osney or **Rewley**, see Leonard Hutten's 'Antiquities of Oxford,' printed at the end of the *Textus Roffensis*, ed. Hearne, 1720. Cf. Dugdale, *Monast. Angl.* (1846), v. 697, *sqq.*; Skelton's *Oxonia Antiqua Restaurata*, Plate 113 and letterpress; Tanner's *Notitia Monastica* (ed. 1), 183.

185. 12. Dr. Hudson was born near Cockermouth, and according to the *Biographia Britannica* was educated under *Jerome* Hechstetter. The latter's nephew, here spoken of, was perhaps Leonard Fell, Queen's, B.A. 1684. See p. 186, ll. 42 *sqq.*

185. 16 *sqq.* This insinuation against **Bryan Twyne** (1579-1644) had already been noticed and not too vigorously refuted by Wood (*Athenae*, iii. 108 *sqq.*).—For **Thomas Allen** (1542-1632) see *Athenae*, ii. 541; Fuller's *Worthies*, iii. 137; *Letters from the Bodleian*, ii. 201, *Dictionary of National Biography*, i. 312 *sq.*; and for **Miles Windsore** (c. 1541-1624), *Athenae*, ii. 358. There is no reason to believe that Twyne made an unfair use of other men's labours. See *Letters from the Bodleian*, i. 148 *sqq.* It will be remembered that William Smith, in his *Annals of University College* (1728), refuted Twyne's arguments in favour of the mythical (Brutus-Alfred) antiquity of the University of Oxford (153 *sqq.*).

186. 17. The first book printed in Virginia was produced at **Williamsburg** about 1682. A charter was granted to the College by William and Mary 1691 ; see ' *The present State of Virginia and the College*, by Messieurs Hartwell, Blair and Chilton. To which is added, The Charter for Erecting the said College, granted by their late Majesties King William and Queen Mary of Ever Glorious and Pious Memory, (London, 1727),' pp. 67 *sqq.*

186. 24. **George Carter**, Univ., B.A. 1693 ; Oriel, M.A. 1696; D.D. 1708; Provost of Oriel 1708-1727, Preb. of Rochester, Peterborough, and St. Paul's.

187. 4 *sqq.* For the MSS. presented by **Oliver Cromwell** to the Bodleian, see Macray's *Annals*, 55 ; on the purchase of Ussher's library for Trinity Coll., Dublin, Edwards' *Memoirs of Libraries*, ii. 47 *sqq.*; and for Ussher's funeral, Parr's *Life*, 78 *sq.*

187. 14. *Some Passages of the Life and Death of the Rt. Hon. John Wilmot Earl of Rochester, who died 26 July, 1680, written by his Lordship's Direction on his Death-bed*, by Burnet, was published in 8vo, 1680. Some particulars of Wilmot's career will be found in Marshall's *Early History of Woodstock Manor*, 235 *sqq.*, and Supplement, 20 *sqq.*

187. 22. **Dr. Thomas Lyndesay**, Fellow of Wadham, Dean of St. Patrick's 1693, Bishop of Killaloe 1695, of Raphoe 1713, Archbp. of Armagh 1714, d. 1724 (Cotton, *Fast. Eccl. Hib.* ii. 102 *sq.*). He was a correspondent of Charlett.

187. 26. **William Nicolson**, Bp. of Carlisle 1702, Derry 1718, Archbp. of Cashel 1727 ; d. 1727 (Cotton, i. 17). Some interesting letters from him to Archbp. Wake, referring to the rebellion of 1715, are printed in Ellis' *Original Letters*, series I. vol. iii. 360 *sqq.* His correspondence, edited by Nichols, is well known ; and there is an amusing account of his difficulties with regard to giving Atterbury institution as Dean of Carlisle in the *Life of Archbp. Sharp*, 235 *sqq.* **Edward Rainbow** was Bishop of Carlisle 1664-1684.

187. 34. **Dr. Hough** was consecrated Bp. of Oxford 1690, and held the Presidentship *in commendam* till 1701 ; Bp. of Lichfield 1699, Worcester 1717 ; d. 1743.— Thomas Goodwin, M.A. 1683, D.D. 1706.

187. 43. **W. Beaw**, New Coll., M.A. 1644, D.D. 1666, Vicar of Adderbury, Oxon ; Bp. of Llandaff 1679. See Index to *Fasti*; Burrows' *Register of the Visitors*, 527, &c.

188. 11. **James Fayrer**, D.D. 1704. He seems to have published nothing to justify his election to the Professorship of Natural Philosophy.

188. 20. The **Terrae Filii** for 1693 were Henry Alworth, Ch. Ch., M.A. 1692, and H. Smith, Ch. Ch. A manuscript copy of this speech is in the possession of Mr. Madan, a collation of which renders Hearne's version more intelligible, if not more edifying. *E.g.*, at p. 189, l. 1, Hearne has wrongly transcribed ' curculiunculus ;' l. 30, read ' Ubi Promus sit, quaero, ubi Coquus, ubi Mancipalis, ubi Lixa ?' and 'Respondit' should be 'Respondet ;' p. 190, l. 18, 'Coslæo' is clearly a mistake for ' Crosleijo,' l. 29, ' periculosus ' for ' feroculus,' and ' Politica ' for ' Poetica.' For the first two lines of the translation of Hody, Mr. Madan's MS. reads : 'Let now sad Ireland no more cry Heigh-ho ; | Lions do things would make a harp sing Jö.'

188. 35. **Dr. Arthur Bury**, Preb. of Exeter 1661, Rector of Exeter Coll. 1666, ejected by the Visitor 1690. His *Naked Gospel*, 'by a true son of the Church of England,' was almost avowedly Socinian (Abbey and Overton, i. 488). See an account of the whole affair in *Athenae*, iv. 482, and references in *Fifth Report of the Hist. MSS. Comm.* 376, 377, 380. Considerable litigation ensued ; but the House of Lords finally gave judgment in favour of the Visitor Dec. 10. 1694. See Wood's *Life*, 294, 308 ; Boase, *Register of the Rectors &c. of Exeter College*, xxxiii *sqq.*, 68. 'He was living at Bampton in Oxon about 1714 (?).'

189. 11 *sqq.* The 'nick-nackatory' is mentioned in *Terrae Filius* No. xliv.—Cf. letter of Lhwyd in MS. Aubrey 12 (240); ' The generality of the people at Oxford doe not yet know what yᵉ Musaeum is ; for they call yᵉ whole Buylding yᵉ Labradory or Knackatory, and distinguish no farther.' **Dr. Ludwell** reappears in the Terrae Filius speech for 1703 as being for some cause discommonsed.

190. 5. The relations between **Dr. Hyde** and his wife had long been a subject of gossip in Oxford : cf. Prideaux' *Letters to Ellis*, p. 46 ; *Life of Radcliffe*, ed. 3.

191. 23. **George Sawbridge** (*Lit. Anecd.* iii. 597), was fined 200*l.*: Luttrell, vi. 41.

191. 40. For this letter of the **Princess Sophia**, see Stanhope's *Reign of Q. Anne,* i. 233, and reference. An abstract of Sir Rowland Gwynne's letter to the Earl of Stamford (dated Hanover, Jan. 1, 1706) is given in Boyer, 224 *sq.* It was handed to the press by Mr. Charles Gildon.

192. 13. **John Disney, b.** 1677, took orders when about forty years of age, and was Vicar of St. Mary's, Nottingham, from 1722 till his death in 1730. He planned a great work, to be entitled *Corpus Legum de Moribus Reformandis,* and published several essays relating to the Laws against Immorality and Profaneness, as well as a *View of Ancient Laws* on the same subject (Cambridge, 1729, fol.). In connexion with the subject mentioned by Hearne, he published in 1714 *The Genealogy of the most Serene and most Illustrious House of Brunswick-Lunenburgh,* .. *drawn up from the best Historical and Genealogical writers.* His Life in the *Biog. Brit.* was written by his grandson of the same name, the biographer of Dr. Jebb, Jortin, Brand Hollis, &c.

192. 41. **John Mayow,** D.C.L. 1670, d. 1679; see *Athenae,* iii. 1199.—**Tho. Mayow,** M.A. 1669, D.M. 1678.

193. 2. This account of the early career of **Matthew Tindal,** the Deist, seems to be correct. He was afterwards of Exeter, and finally, till his death in 1733, Fellow of All Souls. His father was John Tindal, incumbent of Beer-Ferres, Devon. His earliest works were *An Essay concerning the Laws of Nations and the Rights of Sovereigns,* and *An Essay concerning Obedience to the Supreme Powers* (1694). Dr. Hickes published at least two answers to his *Rights of the Christian Church asserted.* See *Athenae,* iv. 584; Burrows' *Worthies of All Souls,* 381, &c.; Noble, iii. 323.

193. 28. This Sermon, on Matt. xxvii. 25, was preached Jan. 30, 1703.

193. 32. **Wm. Lowth** (1661-1732), father of the learned Bishop of London, Preb. of Winchester 1696, published his *Vindication of the Divine Authority and Inspiration of the Old and New Testament,* in answer to Le Clerc's *Five Letters,* in 1692.

193. 39. **Thomas Wood,** nephew of Antony (see note on p. 19, l. 17), was rector of Hardwick, Bucks. His subsequent publications were on legal subjects.

193. 49. **Sanchoniathon's** History is now generally admitted to be a forgery of Philon Byblius, who possibly invented even the name. Dodwell first attacked its genuineness in 1681, his attention having been called to it by Dr. Thomas Smith; Brokesby's *Life of Dodwell,* 84 *sqq.*

194. 19. The reference is to **Dr. Thos. Gibson's** *Anatomy of Human Bodies anatomized* (1684).

195. 7. **Edward Cranke,** M.A. 1698.

195. 33 *sqq.* **Hugh Hutchin,** M.A. 1701.—**Robt. Cock,** Ch. Ch., M.A. 1692.

195. 50. The *Poetical Courant* (Jan. 26—June 29, 1706) is No. 68 in the Catalogue of the Hope Collection. It was edited by Samuel Philips, Gent., late of St. John's Coll., Oxford.

196. 6. The same use of *infucata* occurs in the inscription in Shottesbrooke Church to Anne Cherry; see *Thomae de Elmham Vita Henrici Quinti,* ed. Hearne, p. 388. This is the only instance in Ducange, but the word seems to occur in both senses in classical Latin.

196. 10. Some details of the position of the Episcopal clergy in Scotland at this time are given in Lathbury's *Nonjurors,* 442 *sqq.* Cf. also the *Life of Archbp. Sharp,* i. 383 *sqq.*

196. 30. **Thomas Collins,** Gloucester Hall, M.A. 1667, became Master of Magd. Coll. School 1673 (Wood's *Life,* 190).—For **Ch. Allestree,** see *Athenae,* iv. 656.

197. 9. **Henry Nicholson's** *Conference between the Soul and Body concerning the present and future State* appeared in 1705. It was afterwards printed with a recommendation by Dodwell, together with Ken's Morning and Evening Prayers.

197. 18. **Thomas Goddard,** Canon of Windsor 1705; d. 1731.

197. 19. For **Thomas Lydiat** (1572-1646) see Fuller's *Worthies,* iii. 21 (ed. Nuttall) and *Athenae,* iii. 185, which confirms this account of his poverty, and where some particulars of his controversy with Scaliger are given. Dr. Johnson introduces him in his *Vanity of Human Wishes.*—The account of the extreme distress of the 'ever

memorable' **John Hales** (*Athenae*, iii. 409 ; *Letters from the Bodleian*, ii. 362) is probably exaggerated ; see the article in Chalmers' *Biographical Dictionary.*—For **Fuller** it is only necessary to refer to Mr. J. E. Bailey's exhaustive *Life*.

198. 15. See ' Dr. Wallis's *Account of some Passages of his own Life*,' printed by Hearne in his ed. of *Peter Langtoft's Chronicle*, and an extract from a letter to Dr. Fell, in which Dr. Wallis remarks : ' Of those letters and papers (whatever they were) I never saw any one of them, but in print : nor did those papers, as I have been told, need any deciphering at all, either by me, or anybody else : being taken in words at length, just as they were printed.' See various particulars of **Wallis's** Life (1616–1703) in *Athenae, passim* ; and for **Dr. Richard Zouch** (*c.* 1590–1661), Principal of St. Alban's Hall 1625, *ib.* iii. 510. The portrait here mentioned was painted by Sir Godfrey Kneller at the expense of Pepys, and correspondence relating to it is printed at the end of the Diary in the ordinary editions. Dr. Wallis's books are preserved in the Savile Library (Macray's *Annals*, 251).

199. 10. See p. 3, ll. 33 *sqq.*

199. 12. There is an interesting account of **Michael Hudson** in *Athenae*, iii. 233. He accompanied Charles I on his flight from Oxford in 1646 ; see Gutch, *Coll. Cur.* ii. 452 *sqq.*, and Lloyd's *Memoirs*, 624 *sq.*

199. 23. Luttrell adds (vi. 22) that ' several speeches were made that 'twas too severe, being to take away the estates of such who, at the age of 18, did not turn to the Church of England, and given to the next protestant heir ; that it would disoblige our allies, and look like persecution.'

200. 10. **Wasse's** ed. of *Sallust* appeared in 1710 ; **J. Davies'** ed. of *Caesar* 1706 ; **P. Needham's** *Hierocles* 1709 (see *Life of A. Bonwicke*, ed. Mayor, 170, and for **W. Piers**, *ib.* 188 *sq.*).

200. 23. **Bp. Tanner's** first wife was Rose, eldest d. of Dr. Moore, Bishop of Ely : she died March 15, 1706, aged 25. Of **Dr. Finch** full details are given in *Worthies of All Souls*, 291–314, &c. His one publication was *A thanksgiving Sermon on the Restoration*, on Is. i. 26. On the regiment of foot and troop of horse raised by the University at the time of Monmouth's rebellion, see Wood's *Life*, 265 *sqq.*

VOL. IX.

Page 201, line 10. **Cuthbert Ellison, B.A.** 1704.—**John Hodgson, B.A.** 1699.— Sir **William Glynne** (d. 1721) was a burgess for the University in 1698, and M.P. for Woodstock in the Parliament of 1702. His only son William, of All Souls, cr. M.A. 1713, died before him.—For **Roger Dodsworth** (1585–1654), see Index to *Athenae ; Life of Wood*, 192, 329, and Macray's *Annals of the Bodleian*, 96 *sq.* Hearne's praise is by no means exaggerated.

201. 42. For the Royal Palace, &c., it is only necessary to refer to Marshall's *Early History of Woodstock Manor*. The passage from Brompton is quoted at p. 50. The hint as to the demolition of churches for the construction of the park wall is taken from J. Rossi, *Hist. Regum Angliae*, afterwards edited by Hearne (p. 138, ed. 1745) ; Mr. Marshall points out that there is no ground whatever for such a suggestion, p. 21. For the 'strange passages' that befell the Parliamentary Commissioners at Woodstock in 1649, see Plot's *Nat. Hist. Oxfordshire*, 206 *sqq.* ; Marshall, 204 *sq.* and Supplt.

202. 24. **Dr. Tho. Tully** was Principal of Edmund Hall 1658–1676 ; see *Athenae*, iv. 1055 ; *Life of Bull*, 212 *sqq.*

203. 5. **William Wall** (1646–1728) was Vicar of Shoreham for fifty-two years (Perry, *History of the Church of England*, iii. 240). He was a warm admirer of Atterbury, *Lit. Anecd.* i. 114 *sq.* The reference is to vol. i. 659 (ed. Cotton, 1862) of his *Infant Baptism*, ed. 1 of which appeared in 1705.

203. 30. **Ménage** (1613–1692) does not seem to have published a book on this subject.

203. 33. This announcement of the death of **Mr. H. Pooley** was premature. He was counsel for the Earl of Oxford on his trial, and was elected M.P. for Ipswich May 11, 1705. His successor was elected Nov. 21, 1708. In this year Dr. Radcliffe placed 50 guineas in his hands, for Dr. Drake's defence (*Life*, 46).

204. 10. Wm. Brome, Ch. Ch., B.A. 1687. He was Urry's executor, and edited Somner's *Treatise of the Roman Ports and Forts in Kent.* He corresponded with Charlett, Rawlinson, &c. See Index to Ballard MSS., and to Nichols' *Lit. Anecd.*

204. 13. Cf. Luttrell, vi. 24; Bancroft's *History of the United States,* iii. 18 *sq.*— **John Granville,** cr. Baron Granville 1702, d. 1707.

204. 35. Col. [Robert ?] Finch had been a prominent Jacobite in 1690; see Luttrell, ii. 38, &c. The love of antiquities appears to have been characteristic of the family: cf. *Lit. Anecd.,* Index.

205. 9. George Smith published his trans. of Pliny's *Panegyric* at London, 1702, 8vo.

206. 10. Olaus Wormius (1588–1654), the learned author of many works on Scandinavian literature, history, and antiquities, was thrice married, and had sixteen children. His son William (1633–1704) published *De corruptis antiquitatum Hebraearum apud Tacitum et Martialem vestigiis libri duo* (1693). His grandson, Christian, published *Historia Sabelliana* (1696), and *De variis causis cur delectatos humanis carnibus et promiscuo concubitu Christianos calumniati sunt Ethnici* (1695).— **Thermodus Torfaeus** (d. *c.* 1720) published the three works here mentioned at Copenhagen in 1697, 1702 and 1706 respectively.

206. 21. J. Caswell, Wadh., M.A. 1677; Savilian Professor of Astronomy 1709–1713, published *A brief (but full) Account of the Doctrine of Trigonometry both plain and spherical* (Oxford, 1685, fol.). See Wordsworth, *Scholae Academicae,* 71, 246.— **Joshua Reynolds,** M.A. 1697.

206. 42. Sir W. Glynne was Kennett's first patron, and presented him in 1684 to the vicarage of Ambrosden. Kennett was presented to the rectory of Shottesbrooke in 1693, Nichols' *Lit. Anecd.* i. 394 *sqq.*

207. 9. John Sheffield, Duke of Buckinghamshire, m. thirdly, Lady Catherine Darnley, d. of James II by Catherine [Sedley] Countess of Dorchester. She m. 1699 James, third Earl of Anglesey, and was divorced from him 1701.

207. 19. Edw. Hinton, M.A. 1694.

207. 34. Hearne seems to have overlooked Wood's statement (*Athenae,* iii. 623, 627) that the King's translation was that published in 1655.

208. 21. On Feb. 16 Luttrell writes (vi. 17): 'On Thursday Mr. Nevill . . was married to Mr. Butler's sister of Hartfordshire, her fortune 8000*l.*' **Grey Nevill,** Esq., was M.P. for Abingdon in the Parliament of 1705.

208. 39. See Lathbury, *History of Convocation,* 402 and ref.

209. 3. For the **Chetham** Library, Manchester, see Edwards' *Memoirs of Libraries,* i. 635.

210. 1. Dr. Allix (1641–1717) published this work in 1699. It gave rise to some controversy, and was reprinted in 1821.

210. 8. There is a long memoir of **Mary Astell** (c. 1668–1731) in Ballard's *Memoirs,* pp. 445 *sqq.* See esp. the testimonies of Hickes, Dodwell, Evelyn, and Atterbury concerning her, pp. 452 *sqq.* On Dodwell's Preface to this ed. of Francis de Sales (Dublin, 1673) see Brokesby's *Life,* 36 *sq.*; and on his *Two Letters of Advice* mentioned below, *ib.* 33 *sqq.*

211. 8. The genuineness of **Philostratus'** *Life of Apollonius Tyanaeus* is now generally admitted: see *Dictionary of Greek and Roman Biography,* art. Apollonius.

211. 11. John Gilbert, Hart Hall, M.A. 1680.—**Francis Brokesby** was rector of Rowley, near Hull; see Secretan's *Life of Robert Nelson,* 72 *sq.* and refs.

211. 21. Kennett's trans. of Pliny's *Panegyric* was published in 1686, under the title *An Address of Thanks to a good Prince, presented in the Panegyric of Pliny upon Trajan, the best of the Roman Emperors.*

211. 23. Two editions of **Dr. Hickes'** *Jovian; or an Answer to Julian the Apostate* appeared in 1683, and he was installed Dean of Worcester Oct. 13 in the same year; so that Hearne's statement is inaccurate.

211. 40. Dodwell's views are set forth in his *Dissertationes Cyprianicae* (1682), No. xi. See Hearne's Bibliography of Dodwell (No. viii); Brokesby's *Life,* 102 *sq.*

Ruinart's reply appeared in the Preface to his *Acta primorum Martyrum* (1689). Dodwell's Dissertation was undertaken at the instance of Bp. Lloyd.—**Dr. Tho. Turner** was President of C.C.C. 1688-1714.

211. 50. **Humphrey Wanley** was the son of Nathaniel Wanley, vicar of Holy Trinity, Coventry, and author of *The Wonders of the little World.* He was brought up to the trade of a draper. See *Lit. Anecd.* i. 84 *sqq.*, and Index, and *Library Chron.* June and July 1884; and for his work in the Bodleian Macray's *Annals*, 116 *sqq.* Some interesting letters of Pepys to him are printed in *Life, Journal, and Correspondence of* Pepys, ii. 261, &c.

212. 20. With Bp. Lloyd's view of **Sir Matthew Hale's** character, cf. that of Roger North, *Life of the late Lord Keeper Guilford*, pp. 61 *sqq.* (ed. 1744).

212. 30. For a list of **Francis Bugg's** numerous works against the Quakers, see the Bodleian Catalogue. The work here referred to is *Quakerism struck speechless; or, a farther Discovery of the great Mystery of the little Whore.* Bugg is described by Sewel, *History of the . . People called Quakers*, ii. 509, as 'an envious apostate,' who 'charged the Quakers with some Socinian notions; and being set on by some churchmen, endeavoured also to render them odious with the government.' He is mentioned in an amusing letter in Tanner MSS. (xxi. 39).

212. 43. **Joseph Trapp** (1679-1747), Professor of Poetry 1708, published his *Abra-Mule; or Love and Empire* in 1703. See *Lit. Anecd.* i. 40, Index to Scott's ed. of Swift, and *Mus. Angl. Analecta*, ii. 255.

213. 1 *sqq.* **W. Denison**, M.A. 1700; **S. Jemmat**, M.A. 1661; **Nicholas Ridgway**, M.A. 1699. For 'Repetitions,' see *Life of Ambrose Bonwicke* (ed. Mayor), 68 and 202 *sq.*, and cf. *infra* p. 290, l. 9.

213. 30. **Edw. Thwaites** was Regius Professor of Greek 1707-11, and died in the latter year, aged 44. There is an account of his courage under the operator's hands in *Letters from the Bodleian*, ii. 118 *sq.*, and a Memoir in *Lit. Anecd.* iv. 141 *sqq.*

214. 16 *sqq.* **George, Earl of Berkeley**, d. 1698.—**Dr. Richard Thompson**, Dean of Bristol, died 1685, and was succeeded by Dr. W. Levett, who died 1694, and was in turn succeeded by Dr. Royse.—**Dr. Robert Say** was Provost of Oriel 1653-1691. See Burrows' *Register of the Visitors*, lxx, &c.—**James Davenant**, M.A. 1664.—**Dr. Wm. Dobson** was President of Trinity 1705-1731.—**Dr. Charlett** was Procter 1683, and Master of Univ. 1692-1722.

214. 6. There is a Life of **Griffenfeld** (1635-1699) in the Bodleian (Douce 97), entitled *Mémoires du ci-devant Grand-chancelier de Dannemark*, etc. Imprimé l'An MDCCXLVI. [by Tycho Hofman, F.R.S.] Cf. *Biog. Univ.* xviii. 476.

215. 22. An official account of this celebration was printed in *Secularia sacra Academiae regiae Viadrinae* (Frankfurt 1706). Sufficient details will be found in Wordsworth's *Scholae Academicae*, 98 *sq.*; Monk's *Life of Bentley*, i. 190 *sq.*

215. 37. **W. Percivall**, Ch. Ch., M.A. 1695, contributed a poem on the Battle of the Boyne to *Mus. Angl. Analecta*, and published an elegy on the death of Dean Aldrich (1710). He was afterwards Archdeacon of Cashel.

216. 7 *sqq.* **George Carter**, Provost of Oriel 1708.—**Dr. Wm. Lancaster**, Provost of Queen's 1704-1716, the 'Sly-boots' of *Spectator* 43.—**John Waugh**, Proctor 1695, Preb. of Lincoln 1718, Dean of Gloucester 1720, Bp. of Carlisle 1723, d. 1734, *actat.* 78, and was buried at St. Peter's, Cornhill.—**Tho. Staynoe**, M.A. 1666, Archdeacon of Caermarthen 1677, d. 1708.—**Edmund Gibson**, Precentor of Chichester 1703, Archdeacon of Surrey 1710, Bishop of Lincoln 1716, of London 1723, d. 1748, aged 79. He published the *Chronicon Saxonicum* in 1692. Many letters from him relating to the new ed. of the *Britannia* are printed in Thoresby's Correspondence.—**Dr. Tho. Green**. Master of C.C.C. Camb. 1698, resigned 1716, Preb. of Canterbury 1701 and Archdeacon 1708, Bp. of Norwich 1721, of Ely 1723, d. 1738; Jessopp's *Diocesan Hist. of Norwich*, 219.—For **Sir W. Trumbull**, see *Worthies of All Souls*, 195, &c.

218. 11. **Samuel Clarke** (1675-1729) was Bishop Moore's chaplain and executor, the author of the *Scripture Doctrine of the Trinity* (1712), &c., and editor of Homer. He was one of the chief of the Arian divines of the last century, and his Life was written by Whiston and by Bp. Hoadly. See *Lit. Anecd.*, Index.

218. 15 *sqq.* **W. Hayley**, M.A. 1680, Dean of Chichester 1699, d. 1715. See Pearson's *Biographical Sketch of the Chaplains to the Levant Company*, 17.—**Richard**

Willis, M.A. 1694, Dean of Lincoln 1701, Bp. of Gloucester 1715, of Salisbury 1721, of Winchester 1723, d. 1734, aged 71. See *Q. Anne's Son*, ed. Loftie, 124.—**Charles Trimnel**, M.A. 1688, Preb. of Norwich 1691, Archdeacon of Norfolk 1698, Bp. of Norwich 1708, of Winchester 1721. d. 1723; *Life of Prideaux*, 111.—**Henry Downes**, M.A. 1693.—**Rich. Traffles**, D.C.L., Warden of New College 1701-1703.

219. 34. **Sir Walter Clarges** (son of Sir Thomas Clarges, one of the chief agents in the Restoration, father of Anne Duchess of Albemarle, and Burgess for the University 1688-1695), was M.P. for Westminster. He was the defendant in the famous action by which it was sought to establish the illegitimacy of the second Duke of Albemarle; see Luttrell, v. 708. He was a great ally of Henry second Earl of Clarendon, in whose Diary his name constantly recurs.

219. 45. For ' vectibus ' read ' vestibus.'

220. 1. The reference is to the well-known story (*Antiquities*, XI. viii. 4) of the meeting between Alexander the Great and Jaddua the High Priest. Bp. Lloyd published a vindication of this passage 1691.

220. 9. **John Gardiner**, M.D. 1706.

220. 13. **Dr. Rich. Crakanthorp** published his *Defensio Ecclesiae Anglicanae, contra M. Ant. de Dominis* in 1625. Marco Antonio de Dominis (*c.* 1561-1625), Archbp. of Spalatro (1602), author of *De Republica Ecclesiastica*, came to England with Bedell, and was made by James I Dean of Windsor (1618) and Master of the Savoy, but was reconciled to the Roman Church and returned to Rome in 1622. A careful sketch of his career, position, and character will be found in Mr. S. R. Gardiner's *History*, iv. 282-289.

220. 22. **Robert Loggan**, B.C.L. 1684.

220. 34. **Dr. John Hall**, Bp. of Bristol 1691-1710.

220. 45. For **Henry Stubbe** and his attacks on the Royal Society, see *Athenae*, iii. 1071 ; Birch's *Life of Boyle*, 188 *sqq.*

221. 19 *sqq.* **Samuel Barton**, M.A. 1672, Preb. of Westminster 1696; d. 1715.—**Wm. Halifax**, M.A. 1678. There were editions of De Challes' *Euclid* in 1685, 1704, &c.—**Wm. Gallaway**, M.A. 1681, Preb. of Worcester 1700, d. 1716.—**Paul Foley** was Speaker 1695-1698 (Manning, *Lives of the Speakers*, 399 *sqq.*).

221. 43. The book referred to is ' *Notae in Elegias et Fragmenta C. Pedonis*, a Theodoro Gorallo.'

221. 49. **Dr. Milles** afterwards, as we shall find, fully admitted the authorship of this criticism of Dodwell.

222. 48. This proposed edition of *Dion Cassius* was, I believe, never published.

223. 7. **Dr. J. Turner** had previously entered into controversy with Dr. Wm. Coward on the subject of the immortality of the soul. He preached the Boyle Lecture in 1708, ' On the Wisdom of God in the Redemption of Man.' The pamphlet here mentioned is not in the Bodleian.

223. 13. **Thomas White**, M.A. 1699.

224. 8. The printed fragment of **Abdollatiph's** compendium of the History of Egypt, edited by Pococke and Hyde, ends at p. 96. The Arabic text was first published by Joseph White, Laudian Professor of Arabic, at Tübingen 1789, and the complete work (Arabic and Latin) at Oxford in 1800.

224. 18. This MS. is numbered CCLXXX, fo. 146 in Mr. Coxe's Catalogue of New Coll. MSS.—**John Reynolds**, B.A. 1699. His ed. of Pomponius Mela was published at Exeter 1711, 4to., with 27 maps, and reprinted 1719, 1739.

224. 29. For a memoir of **Wm. Lloyd**, the deprived Bishop of Norwich, see Baker-Mayor's *History of St. John's Coll.*, Cam., 679-80 ; *Life of Prideaux*, 32 *sqq.* ; Jessopp's *Norwich*, 210 *sqq.* Several letters from him are printed in [Anderdon's] *Life of Ken*. His death on Jan. 1, 1710, was a most important event in the history of the Nonjurors, as it was the occasion of the return of Dodwell, Nelson, and Brokesby to the National Church.—**Dr. Humfrey Humphries**, Bp. of Bangor 1689, of Hereford 1701, d. 1712.

225. 2. **Henry Stephens**, M.A. 1697.

225. 33 *sqq.* **Gronovius'** ed. of the *Apotelesmatica* was published in 1698.—**James Owen**, of Salop, wrote *A Plea for Scripture Ordination, Moderation a Virtue* and

Moderation still a Virtue (both 1704), and a *History of Images and of Image-Worship.*

225. 44. **Roger Griffith**, Archdeacon of Brecknock 1704, d. 1708.

227. 4. **Thomas, third Earl of Berkshire**, left no male issue, and was succeeded by his grand-nephew Henry Bowes Howard, fourth Earl of Berkshire and Suffolk (1688-1757), of Elford near Lichfield.

227. 9. **George Hudson**, M.A. 1703; **Joseph Todhunter**, M.A. 1702. **Anthony Hall**, M.A. 1704, editor of Leland *de Scriptoribus*, N. Triveti *Annales*, &c. He married Dr. Hudson's widow, and d. 1723. One at least of his MSS. passed into Hearne's possession.

227. 46. **W. Shippen** was Proctor 1664. His degree of D.D. was by diploma from Archbp. Sancroft; *Fasti*, ii. 219.

227. 50. An estimate of the character of this distinguished Orientalist (1678-1720) may be formed from Ellis' *Letters of Eminent Literary Men*, 350 *sqq.*, where the editor remarks that he 'was one of those persons who are so unfortunate as to neglect economy.' See *Lit. Anecd.* ii. 519 *sqq.*

228. 2. **Charles Aldworth**, M.A. 1672, held this professorship till 1720. He published nothing, so far as I can discover.

228. 12. **Dr. Altham**, sen., M.A. 1675, Proctor 1682, was Regius Professor of Hebrew 1691-1697 and 1703-1714. Dr. Hyde was appointed 'per incapacitat. R. Altham' (Le Neve-Hardy).

229. 10. **Dr. Wm. Piers**, Bp. of Bath and Wells 1632, d. 1670.—Wm. Piers, b. 1661, M.A. 1688, published the *Medea* and *Phoenissae* in 1703 : Wordsworth, *Scholae Academicae*, 383. See Robinson, *Merchant Taylors' School Register*, i. 275.

229. 18. **Dr. Bull** was Bp. of St. David's 1705-1710; **Dr. Beveridge** of St. Asaph 1704-1708.

229. 37. A 'chronological and distinct account of the Works' of Bp. Burnet is given at the end of the *History of his Own Time* (vol. vi. pp. 329 *sqq.*, ed. 1823).

230. 1 *sqq.* **Francis Godwin**, Bp. of Hereford 1617-1633.—**Rich. Coleire**, M.A. 1693, Proctor 1701.—**Thos. Collins**, M.A. 1667.—**Thos. Hoy**, M.A. 1683, Regius Prof. of Medicine 1698-1718.—**Edw. Wells**, D.D. 1704. He was rector of Bletchley, and of Cottesbach, co. Leicester. See *Lit. Anecd.* vi. 187, &c.; *Bodleian Catalogue.* —**R. Altham**, jun., M.A. 1684, Proctor 1693, Preb. of St. Paul's 1695, Archdeacon of Middlesex 1717, d. 1730.—**H. Bagshaw**, M.A. 1692.—**J. Barnard**, M.A. 1683.—**J. Bateman**, M.A. 1667.—**Dr. Lydall** d. 1704; **Dr. Marten** d. 1709.—**T. Bateman**, M.A. 1680.—**Dr. Bathurst's** 'Literary Remains' are printed at the end of Warton's Life. He was V.C. 1673.—**L. Beaulieu**, Ch. Ch., B.D. 1685. Preb. of Gloucester 1687, d. 1723.—**T. Beconsall**, M.A. 1686.—**Dr. H. Beeston**, Warden of New Coll. 1679-1701; **Dr. R. Traffles** 1701-1703; **Dr. T. Brathwait** 1703-1712, Warden of Winchester 1712-1720.—**Peter Birch**, M.A. 1674.—**R. Blackmore**, M.A. 1676; M.D. of Padua; knighted 1697; d. 1729. See in Johnson's *Lives of the Poets.*—**R. Brograve**, M.A. 1679.

232. 15. For **Gevartius'** notes on Manilius, communicated to Bentley by Sir Edw. Sherburne, and by Bentley to Graevius, see Monk's *Life of Bentley*, i. 49 *sqq.* Bentley's ed. of Manilius was not published till 1739 (*ib.* ii. 397). Gevartius' view of the age of Manilius has met with no acceptance. See Jebb's *Bentley*, 142 *sqq.*: 'there is no reason . . for doubting that the whole poem was composed, or took its present shape, between A.D. 9 and A.D. 14.' Among English translators of Manilius were Sherburne and Creech.

232. 16. **Peireskius** made the acquaintance of Camden, Cotton, Savile, and other scholars on his visit to England in 1606 (Gassendi's *Life*, trans. Rand, 100).

232. 32. **Fronto Ducaeus**, S. J. (Fronton Le Duc), 1558-1624, published at Paris (1624) *Bibliothecae veterum Patrum, seu Scriptorum ecclesiasticorum, tomi duo Graecolatini*. He is mentioned by T. Smith in the *Vitae* in the Life of Patrick Young; cf. *Life of Peireskius*, 184, &c. See de Backer, iv. 188 *sqq.*

232. 41. **Orlando Gibbons**, Mus. Bac. 1606; *Fasti*, i. 406.

233. 37. **Dr. Potter** succeeded Dr. Jane as Regius Prof. of Divinity in 1707. See Duchess of Marlborough's *Vindication*, 175.

233. 40. Cf. Macray's *Annals of the Bodleian*, 325 and *n.*

233. 48. Nic. Battely (not to be confounded with John B., author of *Antiquitates Rutupinae*) published ed. 2 of Somner's *Antiquities of Canterbury* in 1703.

234. 10. The book referred to is *Alcinoi philosophi in doctrinam Platonis Introductio, Gr. Lat. cum syllabo Scriptorum Platonicorum qui supersunt*, per Joh. Fell (Oxon. 1667); and the Cambridge book *De rebus divinis dialogi selecti, Gr et Lat.* (1673 and 1683). Cf. Wordsworth, *Scholae Academicae*, 115 and *n.*

234. 27. Andreas Arnoldus, C. F., Norimbergensis, published this work at Paris, with ded. to Sancroft. Cf. p. 14, l. 39.

234. 42. The bulk of Foxe's MSS. are among the Harleian MSS. in the Brit. Mus.

235. 6. This book, originally printed in 1700, was reprinted in 1760. The highest price recorded by Lowndes is 4*l.* 10*s.*

236. 5. Geo. Smalridge, M.A. 1689, Preb. of Lichfield 1693, was at this time supplying the place of the Regius Professor, Dr. Jane. He was made Canon of Ch. Ch. and Dean of Carlisle 1711, Dean of Ch. Ch. 1713, and Bp. of Bristol 1714, d. 1719.

236. 11 *sqq.* **John Pridie**, M.A. 1694; **Moses Hodges**, M.A. 1685.

237. 1 *sqq.* **Tho. Yalden** (1671–1736), M.A. 1694, figures, it may be necessary to mention, in Johnson's *Lives of the Poets.*—**Dr. Jane** had held this professorship since 1680; he became Dean of Gloucester 1685.—**John Matthews**, M.A. 1673.

238. 6. For an analysis of *The Shortest Way with the Dissenters*, its aim and its effects, see Minto's *Daniel Defoe* (in 'English Men of Letters'), 34 *sqq.* The author was pilloried July 29–31, 1703. See also Burton, *Reign of Q. Anne*, i. 92.

239. 1 *sqq.* **Joseph Abell**, M.A. 1702.

239. 4. There is a copy of an ed. of the following year in Bodley (Douce BB. 28): 'Prymer of Salysbury vse. Par. Thylman Karuer, at the expenses of Johan growte, bokeseller in London. 1534. 8°. min.'

239. 9. Some of **John Owen's** (d. 1622) Epigrams were translated by John Vicars 1619, Robt. Hayman 1628, and others.—**Joshua Sylvester** (1563–1618) is now chiefly remembered as the translator of Du Bartas. He was likewise the author of *Tobacco battered, and the Pipes shattered*, &c.

239. 23. Wotton's collections for a Life of Boyle afterwards passed into the hands of Dr. Birch: *Lit. Anecd.* iv. 369, 454.

239. 42. The Oxford *Sallust* of 1701 purports to be edited by W. Ayerst, afterwards chaplain to Lord Raby, when ambassador at Berlin (*Life of Sharp*, 410 *sqq.*). Some of his letters are preserved among the Wake MSS. in Christ Church Library. He published a Sermon preached before Her Majesty's plenipotentiaries at the Congress of Utrecht, 1712.—**R. Ibbetson**, Oriel, M.A. 1701, published his ed. of Marcus Antoninus 1704. The three following works were of course edited by Hearne.—**Wm. Wyatt** was Public Orator 1679–1712.

240. 11. The author of the *Account of the growth of Deism* was William Stephens, Rector of Sutton (Halkett and Lang).

240. 25. There is a copy of the *History of the Revolution* in the Bodleian, Pamph. 267, but I do not find the author's name.

240. 29. Benj. Marshall, M.A. 1703, author of *Tabulae Chronologicae* and a defence of Bp. Lloyd's interpretation of Daniel.

240. 44. Dr. Hugh Wynne, B.C.L. 1667, Fellow of All Souls, Chancellor of St. Asaph, d. 1720.—**Benj. Cooper**, Registrar 1659-1701.—Wood states in his autobiography (p. 34) that he was postmaster to Mr. Edw. Copley, Fellow of Merton.

241. 3. Proast's name does not appear in Professor Masson's list of the Assembly of Divines (*Life of Milton*, ii. 521).

241. 5. This work of Dodwell's was published in 1698; Brokesby's *Life*, 311.

242. 3. James Colmer, M.A. 1689, twice expelled by Dr. Bury and restored by Bp. Trelawny; vacated his fellowship 1695. See Boase's *Register of Rectors, &c. of Exeter*, xxxii, &c.

243. 7. The first dated ed. of this book was printed by Valdarfer at Milan 1474, 8vo. (Ebert *s. v.*).

243. 17. The reason for the adoption by Leslie of this title is given by Macaulay, ii. 343, where other authorities are quoted. See also *Life of Charles Leslie,* 137 *sqq.*

244. 19. **Edward Lhwyd** (*c.* 1670-1709) published his *Lithophylacii Britannici Ichnographia* in 1699, and vol. i (on Glossography) of his *Archaeologia Britannica* in 1707. He was elected esquire beadle of divinity a few months before his death in 1709. See Nicolson's *Eng. Hist. Lib.* (ed. 2), 24.

245. 2. Dr. Cotton gives 1489 as the date of the first book printed at **Hagenau,** but adds no further particulars. John Siberch, the friend of Erasmus, printed seven books in 1521, and two more in 1522, after which he is lost sight of (Mullinger, *Univ. of Cambridge,* i. 625; Wordsworth, *Scholae Academicae,* 378).

VOL. X.

Page 246, line 13 *sqq.* For these appointments, cf. Luttrell, vi. 46. Francis, second Ld. Carington, 'a Papist,' was the son of Charles Smith, cr. Ld. Carrington 1643.

246. 25. Selden's father was 'a sufficient Plebeian, and delighted much in Music, by the exercising of which he obtained (as 'tis said) his Wife' (*Athenae,* iii. 367). For Henry Jacob, Fellow of Merton, d. 1652, see *ib.* (iii. 329). Hearne alludes to Cowley's *Preface,* p. v, where he expresses his vehement desire to 'retire himself to some of our *American Plantations.*' See Sprat's remarks in his well-known Life, and Johnson's Life of Cowley, *ad init.*

246. 47. I am informed that the MS. of Zouch's *Academiae Oxon Privilegia* is in the British Museum, 'MS. Sloane 749.' It does not appear to have been ever printed.

247. 34. This letter, with others of Briggs and Lydiat, is printed in *Letters illustrative of the Progress of Science in England,* ed. J. O. Halliwell, 1841. See Briggs' Life in Ward's *Lives of the Gresham Professors,* 120 *sqq.*

248. 14 *sqq.* Dr. W. Coward, author of *Second Thoughts concerning the Human Soul,* &c. was likewise a physician of some celebrity in his day. He died *c.* 1724. His uncle, Dr. John Lamphire, was Principal of Hart Hall 1663-1688, and Camden Professor 1660-1688.—Whiston's *Essay on the Revelation of St. John* was published in this year. In MSS. Rawl. D. 377 fol. 80 is the title, and one page of *Thesaurus Linguae Anglo-Saxonicae dictionario Gul. Somneri quoad numerum vocum auctior cura Thomae Benson* (Oxford: 1690, 4°), with a MS. note, 'The first attempt upon the epitome of Somner with additions.' 'But, when the work appeared in 1701, it had another title, and was printed in octavo ;' *Lit. Anecd.* iv. 141.—Thos. Benson was made Preb. of Carlisle 1716.—James Thwaites, M.A. 1707.

250. 14. Dodwell's opinion of his learned correspondent **Mary Astell** is quoted in Ballard's *Memoirs of Several Ladies of Great Britain* 452.

252. 13. **Gudius** had died in 1689. The Duke of Wolfenbüttel purchased his MSS. through the agency of Leibnitz (Edwards' *Memoirs of Libraries,* ii. 425). A Catalogue of his books was printed at Hamburg under the title of *Bibliotheca exquisitissimis libris in theologia, jure, medicina, historia literaria, omnique alio studiorum genere instructissima.* Gudius detected the error regarding the supposed discovery of the tomb of Livy at Padua (*Lit. Anecd.* iii. 299).—Emeric Bigot (1626-1689) inherited the nucleus of his library from his father, and entailed the collection on his family.

252. 39. For **Hadrian Beverland,** see *Fasti,* ii. 334. He was befriended by Vossius, who procured him a pension on his arrival in England. After Vossius' death he fell into extreme poverty, and his reason gave way. He seems to have died *c.* 1712. There is a portrait of him by Kneller in the Bodleian Gallery. See Hearne's ed. of Peter Langtoft, clxxii., Indexes to Rawlinson and Tanner MSS., and *Cat. Bod.* (where the latest entry is dated 1710). The ed. of Catullus here referred to was published in 1684, four years before Vossius' death.

253. 16. These are not the initials of any of Boyle's Lecturers between 1699 and 1706, if we may rely on the list in *Lit. Anecd.* vi. 453.

253. 20. **Blondel** on Baronius does not appear to have been printed. It need hardly be said that the *locus classicus* on Baronius for English students is to be found in Pattison's *Life of Casaubon,* 362 *sqq.*

253. 22. See **Cave's** letter to Archbp. Tenison (Oct. 1697) in the *General Biographical Dictionary*, ed. Chalmers, xxxi. 343 *sqq. (art.* ' Wharton ').

253. 27. **G. C. Goetzius** published (1726) *De vestium nigrarum usu commentatio philologico-antiquaria.*

253. 39. **Richard Monnox, M.A.** 1698.

253. 42. ' *Historia vitae et regni Richardi II. Angliae Regis, a Monacho quodam de Evesham consignata,*' was edited by Hearne. A letter concerning the author from Llwyd to Dr. Smith was printed with it.

254. 29. Mr. James Gairdner, of the Public Record Office, has kindly examined this letter, and informs me that it was undoubtedly addressed to *Wolsey* and not to *Pole.* Wolsey was Mary's *compater*: see account of her christening in Calendar of S.P., Hen. VIII., ii. No. 1573. Mr. Gairdner is disposed to date it between October 1526 and August 1527, but more probably about October 1526. Mary at that date was under ten years of age! This letter was printed by Hearne in Titi Livii Forojuliensis *Vita Henrici Quinti,* pp. 122 *sq.*

255. 9. **Dr. John Nicholas,** Warden of New Coll. 1675, Warden of Winchester 1679, Preb. of Winchester 1684, d. 1712.

256. 11. **Edw. Strong, M.A.** 1698.

256. 21. **John Claymond,** President of C.C.C. 1517-1537. For the connexion of the bees with Corpus, see Plot, *Nat. History of Oxfordshire,* 180 *sqq.*

256. 22. **Vaccaria** is explained in Ducange (ed. 1846) as ' Ager vel praedium vaccarum numerum colendo idoneum.'

256. 31. Cf. Macray's *Annals of the Bodleian,* 52 and *n.* ; Marshall, *Early History of Woodstock Manor,* 158. **Elizabeth** was a prisoner at Woodstock 1554-5, and it may be noticed that two sets of verses written by her during this period are signed ' Elizabeth, Prisoner.' See Warton, *Life of Sir T. Pope,* 64 *sqq.*

257. 4. For full particulars of this book and inscription, see Macray's *Annals of the Bodleian,* 42 *sqq.*

257. 20. For the library of the **Escurial,** see Edwards' *Memoirs of Libraries* ii. 550 *sq.* It contained 567 Greek MSS., a catalogue of which, by Miller, was printed at the expense of the French Government in 1848.

259. 7. **Dr. Tyson's** (1649-1708 ; Magd. Hall, M.A. 1673) principal works are *Phocaena, or the Anatomy of a Porpess, dissected at Gresham Colledge* (1680) ; *Carigueya, seu marsupiale Americanum ; or, the Anatomy of an Opossum* (1698); and *Orang-Outang, sive homo sylvestris ; or the Anatomy of a Pygmie* (1699). He was at this time physician to Bethlem and Bridewell Hospitals.

259. 14. **Richard Smalbroke, M.A.** 1694; Preb. of Hereford 1710, Bp. of St. David's 1724, of Lichfield and Coventry 1731, d. 1749.

260. 10. For **Sir Owen Buckingham,** see Index to Luttrell. He was Lord Mayor 1704-5.

260. 16. Of the Societies for Reformation of Manners, which were so vigorously supported and equally vigorously opposed in the early part of the eighteenth century, see Secretan's *Life of Nelson,* 96 *sqq., Life of Sharp,* i. 170 *sqq.* The 14th ed. of an *Account of the Progress of the Reformation of Manners* was published in 1706. They were at first so successful that ' our constables sometimes of late have found it difficult to take up a swearer in divers of our streets.' They continued active for about forty years.

260. 26. **Philip Ayres** was the translator of *Pax redux, or the Christian Reconciler ; a short account of the Life and Death of Pope Alexander VII*; and De Salas' *Fortunate Fool*; see Dict. of Nat. Biogr. ii. 292.

261. 15. The account of the banishment of **Thomas de Mowbray,** Duke of Norfolk, is borrowed by Shakespeare from Holinshed, i. 493 *sqq.* His duchess was Elizabeth daughter and co-heir of Richard Fitz-Alan, Earl of Arundel. He died at Venice 1413.

261. 26. **W. Perriam, M.A.** 1704; Preb. of Salisbury 1738, d. 1743.

261. 41. For the Barkers, see *Lit. Anec.* i. 72. This family held the patent of Royal printers from at least 1555 to 1665.

262. 11. This MS. is No. CCII. in the Catalogue of Queen's College MSS. Mr. Coxe refers to Bentley's Preface to his *Horace,* ed. 1728.

262. 13. An adequate account of the misunderstanding with regard to the MS. of the Letters of Phalaris. and Bentley's triumphant refutation of the charge of discourtesy, is given in Monk's *Life of Bentley,* i. 66 *sqq.,* 84, 98, &c.; Jebb, 49 *sqq.*

263. 17. Stephen Penton was Principal of Edmund Hall 1675–1684.

264. 35. William, third **Lord Stawel,** d. 1742.

264. 37. Dr. Bingham m. Dorothea, d. of the Rev. R. Pocock, rector of Colmer, Hants.

264. 39. Dr. Samuel Mews was succeeded by Dr. Ch. Woodroff, St. John's, D.C.L. 1704.

265. 10. Robert Johnston's *Historie of Scotland during the Minority of King James* was published in Latin at Amsterdam 1642, and in English at London 1646.

265. 15. Ulric Obrecht (1646 1701) was made 'praetor royal' of Strassburg after its occupation by Louis XIV. His notes on Quintilian were added to Burman's ed. of 1720.

265. 26. Robert Whitehall, M.A. 1684.—**John Glanvill,** M.A. 1685.—**Trapp** and **Yalden** have been already mentioned. There is a full catalogue of the works of the former in Chalmers.

VOL. XI.

Page 266, line 18. **Ralph Grey** succeeded his too notorious brother, Forde Baron Grey of Werke and Earl of Tankerville, in 1701.

266. 24. W. Musgrave, New Coll., M.D. 1689, F.R.S., settled in Exeter in 1689, where he published several medical and antiquarian works, the best-known of which is his *Belgium Britannicum.* He died in 1721. His grandson was Samuel Musgrave, the editor of Euripides. See Index to *Lit. Anecd.*

267. 4. Barten Holyday, Ch. Ch., M.A. 1615, Archdeacon of Oxford, the translator of Juvenal and Persius, &c., d. 1661. See *Athenae,* iii. 520; Wood's *Life,* 128.

267. 48. John Walrond, M.A. 1680; Tho. Crosthwait, D.D. 1684, Principal of Edmund Hall 1684–5.

268. 50. Hickes became Lauderdale's chaplain in 1676. Burnet, i. 173, says that the latter 'was very learned, not only in Latin, in which he was a master, but in Greek and Hebrew. He had read a great deal of divinity, and almost all the historians ancient and modern.' Specimens of his correspondence will be found in the two vols. of the *Lauderdale Papers* recently edited by Mr. Osmund Airy for the Camden Society.

269. 24. Cf. Luttrell, vi. 62.

269. 27 *sqq.* **John Tyler,** Magd., M.A. 1686; Preb. of Hereford 1688, Dean 1692; Bp. of Llandaff 1706, d. 1724.—**John Savage,** of Eman. Coll., Cam., B. and D.D. 1707.—**Barnes'** *History of that most victorious Monarch Edward III* was published in 1688.

270. 10. J. Brodeau (1500–1563) published Annotations on Oppian in 1552. *Epigrammata Graeca cum Annotationibus Brodaei et H. Stephani* was published at Frankfurt in 1600.

270. 13. H. Felton, M.A. 1702, Principal of Edmund Hall 1722, chaplain to the Duke of Rutland and Rector of Whitwell, Derbyshire; d. 1740.

271. 33. This book of Burton's was published in 1646.

273. 15. The origin and progress of the feud between **Barnes** and **Bentley** is narrated in Monk's *Life of Bentley,* i. 52 *sqq.,* 291 *sqq.*

274. 17. M. Payne, Fellow of Trin. Coll., Cam., d. 1695.

274. 28. Barnes was on the foundation of Christ's Hospital. **John Goad,** on whose death he wrote an elegy, succeeded Dugard as Head Master of Merchant

Taylors' School 1661–1681, and afterwards kept a private school in Piccadilly. See *Athenae*, iv. 267; Robinson, *Merchant Taylors' School Register*, i. xiv.—Cornelius Crownfield was Printer to the Univ. of Cambridge 1696–1742 (Wordsworth's *Scholae Acad.* 393, &c.).

275. 33. For Ludolph Küster (1670–1716), see Monk's *Life of Bentley*, i. 154 *sq.*, &c., 404. He had adopted the *nom de guerre* of Neocorus (=sexton = Küster) in his earliest work *Historia critica Homeri*, Frankfurt 1696.

275. 52. The Scholia on Oppian here referred to are contained in Barocci MS. 38, fol. 85 *sqq.* (printed in Cramer's *Anecdota Graeca*, iv. 269).

276. 9. Dr. Henry Sike, formerly of Utrecht, is again familiar to us from Monk's *Life of Bentley*, i. 185 *sq.* Bentley had secured his election in 1705. He committed suicide in 1712. A letter from Adrian Reland (*ib.* i. 329) mentions his promise of some excerpts from Abulfeda. The MS. referred to at p. 286, l. 26, is now No. 287 in the All Souls collection of MSS, and is in the handwriting of W. Guise, M.A., formerly fellow, whose widow bequeathed it to the College. It is thus described: 'Canon seu rectificatio Terrarum regis fortis principis τῆς Hamath; est scilicet geographia, auctore Abul Pheda Ismaela filii τοῦ Almelec Al Naser.' See Pearson, *Chaplains to the Levant Company*, 23.

279. 1 *sqq.* Sixty-one volumes of Casaubon's MSS. were bequeathed to the Bodleian in 1671 by his son Meric (Macray, *Annals*, 95). They are catalogued in *Codices Gracci*, Part I, 825–850. Some remarks on the general character of these *Adversaria* will be found in Mark Pattison's *Life*, 481 *sqq.*

280. 11. Sir Edward Seymour had been dismissed from the Comptrollership of the Household in 1704. Charles was his third son by his second wife.

280. 13. John Methuen died in Portugal July 2. He was the hero of the Methuen Treaty: see *Spectator* No. 43, Burton's *Reign of Q. Anne*, ii. 69 *sqq.* He was succeeded as ambassador by his son.

280. 23. A juster estimate of Strype's merits as an ecclesiastical historian is given by Sir H. Ellis in his *Letters of Eminent Literary Men*, p. 176.

280. 50. For James Duport, see Mullinger, *Cambridge Characteristics in the Seventeenth Century*, 181 *sqq.*

281. 4. Samuel (afterwards Lord) Masham, b. 1680, was the youngest son by his first wife of Sir Francis Masham, who is known to us from the Life of Locke. For an account of the circumstances of his marriage to Abigail Hill, see the Duchess of Marlborough's *Vindication*, 177 *sq.*

281. 37. I have not yet been able to satisfy myself with regard to the handwriting of this book. I incline to think that the alterations on the title-page &c. are in Fell's hand, and that the remainder of the MS. is from the pen of an amanuensis. The alleged resemblance to Sancroft's very characteristic hand is purely imaginary. Samuel Keble, of Fleet Street, was a high-church bookseller, having relations with the nonjurors. See *Lit. Anecd.* i. 702, where Dunton's character of him is quoted; and Index to Rawlinson MSS. He compiled the very unsatisfactory list of the editions of *Eikon Basilike* printed at the end of Wagstaffe's *Vindication.*

282. 14. Sancroft was Master of Emanuel 1662–5, and Thos. Holbeche 1676–1680. Sancroft published remarkably little considering his extensive collections and great learning.

282. 26. G. Ursinus published at Copenhagen in 1697 *Antiquitates Hebraicae scholastico-academicae.* He is not of course the same Dr. Ursinus whose name is so frequently mentioned in the account of the negociations for the introduction of the Liturgy of the Church of England into Prussia at the beginning of the 18th century (*Life of Sharp*, i. 403 *sqq.*).

282. 30 *sqq.* John Wilder, M.A. 1703.—John Geree, M.A. 1697, Preb. of Hereford 1734.

282. 36. On Mr. Hart's sermon, see Luttrell, vi. 83.

283. 1. Thos. Wyatt, St. John's. Jun. Proc. 1659.—Hearne is in error here; the new Prebendary was Rice Adams, Hart Hall, B.A. 1678.

283. 8. For Sir Thomas Cookes (d. 1701) and his benefaction of 10,000*l.*, see Wood-Gutch, *Colleges and Halls*, 630 *sq.*; Nash, *Hist. of Worcestershire*, ii. 408.

283. 31. For **Dr. Tudway**, Professor of Music and organist of St. Mary's, and his deprivation, see Monk's *Bentley*, i. 261 *n.*, Luttrell, vi. 77. He subsequently signed a humble apology, and his suspension was taken off March 10, 1707.

283. 35. There is an anecdote of **Dr. Bayley** in the *Life of Frampton* 158.

283. 37. Dr. John Rogers was President 1701-3.—James, fourth Earl of **Barrimore**, m. as his second wife, Elizabeth, daughter and heir of Richard Savage, Earl Rivers. See Luttrell, vi. 76, &c. He commanded a regiment under Lord Galway, and was taken prisoner at the Battle of Almanza.

283. 42. Lord Wharton was originally appointed Chief Justice in Eyre 1697 (see Macaulay, ii. 618, &c.).—Alex. **Denton**, M.P. for Buckingham 1708 and 1714, Judge of the Common Pleas 1722, d 1740. Foss, *Biog. Jurid.* 220.

284. 6. Philip Bisse, M.A. 1693, Bishop of St. David's 1710, of Hereford 1713 ; d. 1721. Ursula, Dowager Countess of Plymouth, second wife of Thomas Windsor-Hickman, Earl of Plymouth, (d. 1717 aged 70), is wrongly described by Luttrell as 'daughter to the Duke of Leeds.' (His mistake is explained by a reference to *Lit. Anecd.* vi. 225, as compared with i. 703.) Noble, on the other hand, marries the Bishop to the Dowager Duchess of Northumberland. But he is unfortunate with the Bisses ; under T. Bisse (iii. 100) he hopelessly confuses HEARNE and Wood.

284. 26. Matthew Hutton, B.N.C., M.A. 1661. See Index to Tanner and Rawlinson MSS.

287. 10. An advertisement of races at **Woodstock** in 1688 is printed in Marshall's *Early History of Woodstock Manor*, 246.—Evelyn Pierrepoint, Earl of **Kingston**, was created Marquis of Dorchester Dec. 23, 1706.

288. 22. Thos. Bennet was 'the prime mover of the famous dispute upon Phalaris.' (See Boyle, *Bentley's Dissertations examined*, 2 *sqq.*) For some remarks on Atterbury's sermon, which provoked a protest from Hoadly, see Monk's *Life of Bentley*, i. 182 ; also *Lit. Anecd.* iii. 709 *sqq.*

288. 26. John Hough, M.A. 1676, D.D. and Pres. of Magd. 1687, Bp. of Oxford 1690, of Lichfield 1699, of Worcester 1717, d. 1743, *aetat.* 93. His wife was Lettice, d. of Thomas Fisher, of Walsall, and widow of Sir Charles Lee.—Samuel **Collins**, B.A. 1671, Preb. of Lichfield 1705, d. 1710.—**Bp. Parker** was installed President by proxy Oct. 25, 1687, and d. March 20, 1688.

289. 8. Baron Spanheim died at London Oct. 28, 1710, aged 81, and was buried in Westminster Abbey Nov. 18 (Chester's *Registers*, 270).

289. 11. Wm. Moreton, M.A. 1666, chaplain to the Duke of Ormond, Dean of Ch. Ch. Dublin, 1677, Bp. of Kildare 1681, of Meath 1705 (*Athenae*, iv. 891 ; Cotton, *Reg. Eccl. Hib.* ii. 45). Dr. Wm. Sherendon (or **Sheridan**), Dean of Down 1669, Bp. of Kilmore 1682, deprived 1692 (*Fasti*, ii. 199, Cotton, *op. cit.* iii. 226). Dr. Robert **Huntingdon** (Prov. of Trin. Coll. Dublin, Bp. of Raphoe 1701, Cotton, *op. cit.* iii. 353) was offered, but refused to accept, his see. Dr. T. Smith published his *Life and Letters* in 1704. Dr. Hammond's best-known amanuensis was Wm. Fulman, and Moreton must have been, one would think, too young at Hammond's death, in 1660, to occupy that position. It is Fulman who is described in Fell's *Life of Hammond*, 90, as 'a very dextrous person.'

VOL. XII.

Page 289, Line 25. **R. Haydocke**, Fellow of New Coll., was for many years a physician at Salisbury. See *Athenae*, i. 678, and references.

289. 28. Joseph Barnes was the sole printer in Oxford between 1585, when with the help of the University and the Earl of Leicester he re-established printing there, and 1617, when he died. See *Athenae*, i. 687, &c., *Fasti*, i. 339, and Wood-Gutch, *Annals*, i. 625, ii. 223 ; and for portraits of Bodley, Granger, i. 322 *sqq.*

290. 8. Edm. Chishull, M.A. 1693, published in this year *A Charge of Heresy maintained against Mr. Dodwell's late Epistolary Discourse*. After exposing the

French prophets (Calamy, ii. 71 &c.), he to a great extent deserted the field of theology for that of antiquities. See Index to *Lit. Anecd.*; and for **Dodwell's** piety, Brokesby's *Life*, 542 *sq.*

291. 8 *sqq.* **Tho. Fletcher, M.A.** 1692, published in the same year *Poems on several Occasions.*—**Edw. Master**, D.C.L. 1663.—**Brome Whorwood** was M.P. for Oxford in the two Parliaments of 1680, and in that of 1681. His son of the same name was drowned in his passage from Hampshire to the Isle of Wight in 1657. His wife is described by Wood (*Life*, p. 72) as 'the most loyal person to K. Ch. I in his miseries, of any woman in England.' He died 1684, and was buried in the church of Halton (*al.* Holton) near the grave of his father Sir Thomas Whorwood. (*Fasti*, ii. 43.) For Holton, see Skelton's *Antiquities of Oxfordshire*, Bullingdon H., p. 7; the manor-house remained in the possession of the Whorwoods till 1801.—**Philip Code**, B.A. 1694, M.A. 1698.

291. 36. **Anthony Blencow** was Provost of Oriel 1572–1617; and **John Rouse** Bodley's Librarian 1620–1653 (Macray's *Annals*, 44 *sq.*).

291. 39. For Küster's editions of Iamblichus (1707) and of Aristophanes (1712), see Monk's *Life of Bentley*, i. 192 *sqq.*

292. 8. On the scarcity of Professors' Lectures at this time, see Wordsworth, *Scholae Academicae*, 10 *sqq.*, &c., with Uffenbach's remarks, and *Terrae Filius*, No. 10; for 'Wall Lectures' Wordsworth, *op. cit.* 220. Wood in his Life of Fell (in *Oxoniana*, i. 62) speaks of 'Ordinaries (commonly called *Wall Lectures*), from the paucity of Auditors.' **Halley** was Savilian Professor of Astronomy 1704–1742.

292. 27. There was a **Public Act** on the Queen's visit to the University August 27, 1702, an account of which is given in Boyer's *Reign of Q. Anne*, 33.

293. 24. Under the date of Aug. 1, Luttrell has an entry (vi. 72) which is scarcely marked by his usual accuracy:—'There is a dispute between the queen and the duke of Ormond .. about chusing a vice chancellor in the room of Dr. Wm. Delaune, deceased, both claiming it as their right.' But cf. *infra* p. 302, l. 15 *sqq.*

294. 9. **Richard Baxter** d. Dec. 8, 1691.—**Wm. Baxter**, his nephew (1650–1723), master of a private boarding-school at Tottenham High Cross, and afterwards of the Mercers' School, published his *Anacreon* 1695, and his *Horace* 1701. His *Glossarium Antiquitatum Britannicarum* (p. 296) appeared in 1719. See *Anecdotes of Bowyer*, 49. —**John Flamsteed** (1646–1719) was of Jesus Coll., Cam. He was appointed Astronomer Royal 1675, and was presented to the living of Burstow, Surrey, about 1684. Evelyn thought more highly of him: see *Diary*, Sept. 10, 1676. Many of his letters are printed in Rigaud's *Letters of Scientific Men*, and some uncomplimentary remarks of his on Hevelius of Danzig (1611–1687) at pp. 109, &c. of vol. ii. For his relations to North, see *Life of the late Lord Keeper Guilford*, 286 (ed. 1742).

294. 24. The reference is to Bacon's Essay 'Of Atheisme,' (1598); 'Lastly, this I dare affirme in knowledge of nature, that a little naturall philosophie: and the first entrance into it doth dispose the opinion to Atheisme: But on the other side much naturall philosophie, and wading deepe into it, will bring about mens mindes to religion: Wherefore Atheisme every way seems to be ioined and combined with folly and ignorance, s[o]e that nothing can be more iustly allotted to be the saying of fooles then this, *there is no God.*'

295. 4. Cf. the remark on **Allam's** tutor in *Athenae*, iv. 174; it was 'his misfortune to fall under the Tuition of a careless and crazed Person.'

295. 11. A sufficient analysis of **Bathurst's** will is given in Warton's *Life*, 191 *sqq.* It was proved June 16, 1704.

295. 29. This book was *An Essay towards a paraphrase on the Psalms in English Verse, with a Paraphrase on Proverbs xxxi and Revelations iii.*

295. 33. The *Image of both Churches*, by P. D. M. (Tornay 1623), is attributed by Halkett and Lang to Matthew Pattenson, or Patison, Doct. Med. According to Wood (*Athenae*, iv. 139), he 'mostly collected it from the Answers of *Anti-Cotton* and Joh. *Brierley* Priest.'

295. 36. **William Rogers** is repeatedly mentioned in Wood's *Life*, where he is generally described as a barrister 'of Lincoln's Inn.' See *ib.* 273 for the erection of this statue (1686).

296. 17. The pamphlet referred to is probably *Remarks on Dr. Wells his Letter to Mr. Peter Dowley.* The names of all the publications (half-a-dozen or more) in this controversy will be found in the *Bodleian Catalogue.*

296. 29. For **John Boston** of St. Edmundsbury, see Nicolson's *English Hist. Lib.* 155, and the references there. His *Speculum Coenobitarum* was edited by Antony Hall in 1722 : but the loss of his account of English writers (now known only by extracts in the Preface to Tanner's *Bibliotheca Britannico-Hibernica*) is most serious.

297. 5. Laurence Echard (*c.* 1671–1730), the author of the well-known History of England to the Revolution, published *A Most compleat Compendium of Geography, General and Special* in 1691, and *The Roman History* in 4 vols. 1699–1706. Both met with considerable success at the time. Dr. **William Howell's** (d. 1683) *Institution of General History* appeared in 1661, in a Latin trans. 1671, and in two folio vols. in 1680. Three remaining parts were published in 1685–6. Gibbon speaks of him (ii. 321, ed. Smith) as ' that learned historian, who is not sufficiently known.' See *Fasti,* ii. 355.

297. 11. See Nicolson's *Eng. Hist. Lib.* 14 ; 'There is also a Fragment (of Seventeen *Quarto* Pages) Entitul'd, *Antiquitates Insulae Vectae,* in *Bodley's* Library, among the MSS. of *Richard* James.' For James' MSS. in Bodley see Macray's *Annals,* 103 *sq.*

297. 30 *sqq.* For **Parker** 'the astrologer' and **Defoe's** *Review,* cf. Luttrell, vi. 98. There is an account of the Almanacs of the period in Ashton, *Social Life in the Reign of Q. Anne,* 308 *sqq.*—Lord Chief Justice **Holt** d. March 5, 1710. See Foss, 351 *sqq.*—**Lydiat** is said to have been released from prison by the contributions of Sir W. Boswell, Ussher, Laud and others (Aikin's *Lives of Selden and Ussher,* 405). Wood adds Dr. Robert Pink, Warden of New Coll., to the list of his benefactors (*Athenae,* iii. 186).—**Potter's** ed. of Clemens Alexandrinus did not appear till 1715.

298. 2 *sqq.* There is some account of **Warfield** in Lysons' *Berkshire,* 410.—**Dr. Brocklesby's** book is now in the Bodleian (5. A. 101).—For **Stephen Penton,** see *Athenae,* iv. 550.

298. 20. October 25 was likewise the anniversary of the installation of the Bishop of Oxford as President of Magd. and of the deprivation of the twenty-five fellows (see *Diary of Bishop Cartwright,* 92).

298. 23. Charles Finch, Ch. Ch., B.A. 1678; All Souls, B.C.L. 1683, D.C.L. 1688, was the fourth son of the Earl of Nottingham.

298. 33. On Aug. 16 **Bentley** had written to Prof. Sike, who was then at Oxford examining Oriental MSS., ' I do not wonder that some of the Oxford men do talk so wildly about my Horace; but their tongues are better than their pens; and I am assured none of them will write against my notes' (Monk's *Bentley,* i. 189). For this emendation (accepted by Porson), see Jebb's *Life,* 131.

298. 40. M. **Maittaire** (1668–1747) had retired from the second mastership of Westminster in 1699, and was now devoting himself to literary work, and especially to bibliography. See Index to *Lit. Anecd.*—Dr. **Thomas Knipe** was second master of Westminster under Dr. Busby, and succeeded him as head master; d. 1711 (Noble, ii. 119); Welch, *List of Scholars of Westminster School,* 44.

299. 2. This MS. of **Walter de Milemete** is No. 92 in Dean Kitchin's Catalogue of the Ch. Ch. MSS. It was presented by ' Guil. Carpender, olim Alumnus,' in 1707.

300. 22. The MSS. of **Livy** referred to are 277–9 in New Coll. MSS. (Coxe).

300. 27. According to Dr. Rawlinson (*Letters from the Bodleian,* i. 31) Charlett had till June 1707 'no more than 8l. to support his headship.' The postage of his letters is said to have cost him more than his official income.

301. 4—303. 11. Sedgwicke Harrison, M.A. 1705.—R. **Brograve,** M.A. 1679.— T. **Brooke,** M.A. 1683. Cf. Wood's *Life,* 255 (July 1683), 'Tho. Brookes of Mag. hall, a fat fellow, on Saturday *optime.*—Edward **Browne** (*c.* 1642–1708), D.M. 1667, only son of the author of the *Religio Medici,* published his *Travels,* Parts I and II in 1673 and 1677, and a new ed. of the whole in 1685. *Fasti,* ii. 299; Luttrell, vi. 609. His only son Thomas (mentioned p. 277, l. 27) d. 1710.—R. **Burscough,** M.A. 1682, Preb. of Exeter 1701, Archdeacon of *Barnstaple* 1703; d. 1709. He published *A*

Treatise of Church Government, A Discourse of Schism, &c.—For the bibliography of the **Bury** controversy, see Boase and Courtney's *Bibliotheca Cornubiensis,* ii. 772 *sq.*—**Busby** (1606-1695) published (*inter alia*) *Graecae Grammaticae Rudimenta* (1663) and *Rudimentum Grammaticae Graeco-Latinae metricum* (1689). See *Athenae,* iv. 417. His epitaph is given *ib.* 419. Cf. Stanley, *Memorials of Westminster Abbey,* 292, 446-8; Chester's *Registers,* 236.—Seth **Bushell,** St. Mary Hall, D.D. 1672, was author of *A Warning Piece for the Unruly.*—Bp. **Cartwright** has left us a too faithful picture of himself in his *Diary,* edited by the Rev. Joseph Hunter for the Camden Society in 1843. He died at Dublin 1689. See *Athenae,* iv. 252, where there is a list of his works.—Edmund **Vilett,** M.A. 1672; Tho. **Vilett,** M.A. 1685.— John **Cave,** M.A. 1661, published sermons in 1679 and 1682.—John **Cawley,** D.D. 1666, Archdeacon of Linc. 1667, d. 1709, *aetat.* 77. He published in 1689 *The Nature and Kinds of Simony discussed; Athenae,* iv. 580, Burrows' *Register,* 299, &c.—Tho. **Clerke,** M.A. 1681.

303. 21. **Richard Newton,** M.A. 1701, Principal of Hart Hall 1710 and of Hertford College 1740, Canon of Ch. Ch. 1753, and died the same year, *aetat.* 77. He is known as a would-be reformer of the University, born before his time, and well deserves a biography. See the remarks on his *University Education* in the Appendix to *Terrae Filius.*—For Dr. **Morris's** bequest, and lists of the speakers since 1682, see Macray's *Annals of the Bodleian,* 105 *sqq.* The remark in l. 48 (see also p. 68, l. 26) enables us to add another name to the list, viz. that of Peter Foulkes (Ch. Ch., M.A. 1701) for 1705.

303. 30. According to Ebert (i. 321), **Victorius'** ed. of **Livy** (which came out at Venice in 4 vols., 1537-4-5-6) is 'fine and sought after, but not scarce.' Robert Stephens' ed. of 1538-9 is a reprint of it.

303. 42. Hearne's estimate of **Codrington's** books was scarcely a just one. See Burrows' *Worthies of All Souls,* 329, 337; *Letters from the Bodleian,* i. 133. Codrington d. in Barbadoes April 7, 1710.

303. 34. **E. Clarke,** M.A. 1681. Wakefield School likewise reckoned among its *alumni* Richard Bentley and John Radcliffe.—J. **Cocke,** M.A. 1680.—R. **Cocks,** M.A. 1681.—Wm. **Cole,** B.M. 1660; author of *De Secretione animali Cogitata* (Oxf. 1674), *A physico-medical Essay concerning the late Frequency of Apoplexies* (Oxf. 1689), *Purpura Anglicana* (1689), &c.—Compton (1632-1713), Canon of Ch. Ch. 1669 (not Dean), Bp. of Oxford 1674, of London 1675. For his conduct at the time of the Revolution, see Macaulay, i. 583 and refs., and for his character, Burnet, ii. 88 *sq.* A list of his publications is given in Chalmers' *Biographical Dictionary.*

305. 14. For the duties of 'Collectors' see Wordsworth, *Scholae Academicae,* 220, 232 *n.*—**Creech** took his B.A. degree in 1680, and his trans. of Lucretius was published 1682. Col. Codrington's letter on the subject of his death (*Letters from the Bodleian,* i. 128 *sqq.*) has been already referred to.

305. 35. **Nathaniel Crewe** (1633-1721). Rector of Linc. 1668-1672, Dean of Chichester 1669, Bp. of Oxford 1671-1674, and of Durham 1674 1721, became Lord Crewe in 1691. He left no issue. He was a great benefactor to the University and to Lincoln and other colleges. See *Athenae,* iv. 886, Burnet, ii. 88 (a very unfavourable estimate), Macaulay, i. 374.—**Skirlaw** was Bp. of Coventry 1385, Bath 1386, Durham 1388, d. 1405.

306. 1 *sqq.* T. **Crosthwaite,** M.A. 1664, Proctor 1672, Preb. of Exeter 1678, Princ. of Edmund Hall 1684-1685.—W. **Rooke,** M.A. 1677.—Robt. Boyle lodged with **Crosse** during his residence in Oxford; see Birch's *Life,* 110, where Crosse's hospital near Ampthill is mentioned. Lysons' *Beds.* 39; *Life of Wood,* 135, 306. He does not seem to have been one of Fell's executors: see *Seventh Report of Hist. MSS. Comm.* 692.

306. 30. Hearne was right in his conjecture as to the identity of **C. Veratius Philellen:** see Monk's *Life of Bentley,* i. 273. Bentley borrowed from this *nom de guerre* the idea of that of 'Phileleutherus Lipsiensis,' under which his *Emendationes in Menandri et Philemonis Reliquias* was published.

306. 43. **Peter Mews** or Meaux succeeded Dr. Baylie as President of St. John's 1667, and resigned 1673; Dean of Rochester 1670, Bp. of Bath and Wells 1673, of Winchester 1684. See *Athenae,* iv. 887. He had fought at Naseby.

807. 12. **Anthony Collins** (1676–1729), the Deist, published several pamphlets on this subject between 1707 and 1711. His *Discourse of Freethinking* came out in 1713, and among its answerers were Bentley, Swift and Hoadly.

807. 12. **Dr. Wm. Fleetwood, Bp.** of St. Asaph 1708, of Ely 1714, d. 1723, published a second and improved ed. of his *Chronicon Preciosum* in 1726. The book is criticised in *Terrae Filius*, No. 3.

308. 14. This is now No. 208 in the Queen's Coll. MSS. (Coxe).

308. 18. **Robert Fell**, B.A. 1663, M.A. 1666, Student of Ch. Ch., was buried in the Cathedral Jan. 20, 1667 (Wood-Gutch, *Colleges and Halls*, 572).

308. 24. **Tho. Cherry**, M.A. June 28, 1706, was curate of Witney at the time of his death. He was a nephew of William, father of Thomas Cherry, Hearne's patron and friend. Some amusing letters from him to his ' chum ' will be found in the earlier portion of the Hearne Correspondence.

308. 38 *sqq.* **Moses du Soul** edited Plutarch (1719–1724) ; *Lit. Anecd.* iv. 286.— **Ralph Trumbull**, vicar of Witney, was brother of Sir William Trumbull : *Diary of Henry Earl of Clarendon*, 181-2, &c.

309. 16. **Tho. Tickell** (1686–1740), B.A. 1705, is now best known by Johnson's *Life*, as the friend and literary executor of Addison, and author of the famous elegy on the great essayist.

309. 24. Full particulars of **Hyde's** *Catalogue* (1674), and of the suspicions regarding its authorship, will be found in Macray's *Annals of the Bodleian*, 97 *sqq.*, together with some account of Emmanuel Prichard, janitor, of Hart Hall.

309. 33. **Sir W. Cowper** was M.P. for Hertford in several Parliaments, and a supporter of the Exclusion Bill. His father was William, Knt. and Bart. (1582–1664), collector of the imposts on strangers in the Port of London ; and was imprisoned in Ely House for his loyalty in the time of Charles I. At the end of Walton's *Life of Hooker* is printed the epitaph 'long since presented to the world, in memory of Mr. Hooker, by Sir William Cooper, who also built him a fair monument in Borne Church, and acknowledges him to have been his spiritual father.'

310. 22. **Sir Charles Hedges** had been Secretary of State since Nov. 5, 1700. He afterwards became Judge of the Prerogative Court, and d. 1714.—**Lord Sunderland** was son-in-law of the Duke of Marlborough, who had long urged his appointment on the Queen. See Duchess of Marlborough's *Vindication*, 160 *sqq.*

311. 13. Particulars of the controversy on the rights of Convocation, and of Kennett's part in it, will be found in Lathbury's *Hist. of Convocation*, 359 *sqq.* Kennett became Archdeacon of Huntingdon in 1701.

311. 40. **Basil Kennett**, M.A. 1696, was, for some time after his arrival at Leghorn, in considerable danger from the Inquisition. He died very shortly after his return to England, Jan. 31, 1715, having been elected President of C.C.C. in the May previous. His *Romae Antiquae Notitia* appeared in 1696, and *An Essay towards a Paraphrase on the Psalms, in Verse*, in 1706.

311. 42 *sqq.* **Henry Hellier**, M.A. 1682, D.D. 1695, published the two works mentioned in 1688 and 1697 respectively.—**Wm. Tilly**, M.A. 1697.—**John Mather**, M.A. 1699, published a sermon on John v. 14 in 1705. He was President of C.C.C. 1715–1748.

313. 28 *sqq.* **Wm. Adams**, M.A. 1698 (?).—**Benj. Marshall**, M.A. 1706.

314. 23. This banquet took place at Vintners' Hall, after the standards and colours taken at the Battle of Ramillies had been carried in state from St. James's to Guild Hall ; Luttrell, vi. 119, Boyer, 274.

315. 3 *sqq.* **Dr. Mander** was V. C. 1701-2, and Dr. De Laune 1702-6. The amount of the latter's defalcations is said to have been upwards of 3000*l.*; see *Terrae Filius*, No. 4, and Ayliffe's *Antient and present State of the University of Oxford*, i. 216. The latter remarks : ' There were some laudable efforts made to recover part of this sum in the Vice-Chancellorship of Dr. *Lancaster* by Vertue of a Sequestration ; but his honest endeavours have since been rendered vain and fruitless, by the base Spirit of one of his Successors.' Dr. De Laune paid ' near 300*l.* in full discharge of all demands ' in 1719.

315. 26. **Cuthbert Chambers**, M.A. 1702.

316. 7 *sqq.* **Tho. Pearson,** M.A. 1695, Principal of Edmund Hall 1707-1722.—
Tho. Hind or **Hine,** M.A. 1703. He likewise published a sermon in 1717.

317. 8. Argyropylus, Rector of the University of Padua 1442; Prof. of Greek at
Florence *c.* 1456, and 15 years later at Rome, where he died after 1489. He translated
various works of Aristotle, and published an *Expositio Ethicorum Aristotelis.*
(*Encycl. Brit. art.* ' Argyropylus.') See also Greswell, *Memoirs of Angelus Politianus
&c.,* ii. pp. 81 *sq.* Some Greek epigrams addressed to him by Politian were printed
in Hody's *De Graecis illustribus Linguae graecae literarumque humaniorum in-
stauratoribus.*

317. 40. The best answer to this accusation is contained in a letter among the
Ballard MSS. (xii. 23). Hickes writes to Charlett, October 17, 1688 : ' I hope by
this time the danger of the invasion is over, especially if our fleet be gon out, as I
hear it is. This place [Worcester] affords no newes, but that there is some danger
of being distinguished by names, and parties again, wch God prevent, and give us all
one heart to do our duty, and stick to our principles of loyalty in the strictest
manner, as I hope, we of the ch. of Eng. shall. . . Pray let me know, if the London-
Clergy do not in this juncture unanimously preach up Loyalty.'

318. 13. Dr. Hugh Todd (1658-1728), Preb. of Carlisle 1685, whose dispute with
Bp. Nicolson is set forth in the Letters of that prelate, left in MS. *Notitia Ecclesiae
Cathedralis Carliolensis,* now in the Lambeth Library, and a *History of the Diocese of
Carlisle.* See *Athenae,* iv. 535.

318. 22. Hody, whose premature death was a loss to scholarship, was only 47 years
of age, and had been professor of Greek since 1699. Like Bentley, he was for some
time Stillingfleet's chaplain. His controversy with Dodwell, and his share in the
Convocation dispute, are well known. He became Archdeacon of Oxford in 1704.
His work *De Graecis illustribus* was published posthumously in 1742. See Jebb's
Bentley, 11 *sqq.* ; Lathbury's *Nonjurors,* 138 *sqq.* ; Birch's *Life of Tillotson,* 375 *sq.* ;
Wood-Gutch, *Colleges and Halls,* 595. Noble (ii. 117) gives the following verses
written on Hody as a poet : ' Of old, we read, there was nobody | Made verses
like to Humphry Hody ; | But now, each chandler knows full well | That Lloyd
and Gardiner bear the bell.'—Hearne has written *carmina* ; but ? *carmine.*

319. 1. On **Fleetwood Sheppard,** see *Athenae,* iv. 67 ; Index to Luttrell ; Tanner
MSS. 466. 62. He was one of Charles II's boon companions, but was unacceptable
to his successor. William III appointed him Gentleman Usher and afterwards Black
Rod, and he was knighted *c.* 1694. He died Aug. 24, 1698, and was buried at
Rollright.

319. 11. Edith, widow of Dr. Hody, d. Nov. 28, 1736 ; Wood-Gutch, *Colleges and
Halls,* 608.

319. 34. Jno. Cudworth, M.A. 1670, published in 1688 *Fides Ecclesiae Anglicanae
vindicata ab incertitudine ; sive concio coram Acad. Oxon. habita in Matth.* vi. 23.
' Many years before his death, he kept a school in the parsonage-house, where he
educated with great reputation the youth of the best families of the neighbourhood.'
He died Dec. 10, 1729. See Warton's *Kiddington* (ed. 2.), 12, 13 ; *Fasti,* ii. 393.

320. 4. Wm. Davenant, M.A. 1680. See *Fasti,* ii. 372. He was fourth son of
Sir Wm. Davenant, and trans. into English Franc. La Mothe Le Vayer's *Notitia
Historicorum selectorum.*

320. 5. Sir Wm. Dawes (1671-1724), Master of Cath. Hall 1696, Preb. of
Worcester and Dean of Bocking 1698, Bp. of Chester 1708, Archbp. of York 1714, in
succession to Sharp. His *Whole Works* were published in 3 vols. 8vo., 1733. See
Noble, ii. 76 *sqq.* ; *Life of Sharp,* i. 332 *sq.*

320. 10. For **Dr. De Laune's** election, see *Letters from the Bodleian,* i. 88.

320. 36. Jonathan Edwards, Princ. of Jesus 1686, Treasurer of Llandaff 1687,
d. 1712. He was at one time Rector of Kiddington ; Warton's *Kiddington,* p. 12.

320. 41. N. Ellison, Edm. Hall, B.A. 1675 ; C.C.C., M.A. 1678 ; Preb. of Durham 1712 ; d. 1720, being Archdeacon of Stafford (Hardy-Le Neve, iii. 313).

320. 47—322. 48. S. Estwicke, M.A. 1680, published 1724 *Concio habita in S.
Alphegi Ecclesia de temporis redemptione.*—**Edm. Entwistle,** M.A. 1682, Archdeacon
of Chester 1695, d. 1707.—**J. Fisher,** M.A. 1682, published 1695 a sermon entitled *The*

Honour of Marriage (*Athenae*, iv. 539).—John Fitz-William, D.D. 1677, published a sermon on the Rye House Plot 1683.—Sir John Floyer published various works on Baths and Bathing, &c. He sent young Sam. Johnson to be 'touched' by Q. Anne, and Johnson long after pronounced his learning and piety to deserve permanent record : Boswell's *Life*, i. 18, iv. 272 ; *Lit. Anecd.* v. 19.—Bp. Fowler's sermon here referred to was published in 1706.—Augustine Freezer, M.A. 1679.—F. Gastrell, Canon of Ch. Ch. 1703, Bp. of Chester 1714, d. 1725.—Michael Geddes, Ball., M.A. Edinb., incorp. 1671, Chancellor of Salisbury 1691, d. 1713. He published *The History of the Church of Malabar, Church History of Ethiopia, The Council of Trent no free Assembly, &c.*—J. Glanvill, M.A. 1685. His Poems were published 1725. —Wm. Hallifax, M.A. 1678, was Chaplain to the English Factory at *Aleppo* 1688-1695 : d. 1722. See Pearson, *Chaplains to the Levant Company*, 24, 58.—Wm. Hayley, M.A. 1680, Dean of Chichester 1699, d. 1715, Pearson, *op. cit.* 17.—A sketch of Lincoln Coll. in Hickes' time will be found in the *Life of Kettlewell*. Dr. Marshall, who died a little over a year before Bp. Fell, was succeeded by Dr. Fitzherbert Adams.—Dr. Ch. Hickman, Bp. of Derry 1702, d. 1713, published. in 1706, 14 sermons preached in St. James', Westminster ; Pearson 17.—(?) John Hinton, Preb. of Salisbury 1683, d. 1720.—Matth. Hole, M.A. 1664, Preb. of Wells 1688, Rector of Exeter Coll. 1715, d. 1730, aged 90. He published several sermons: see Boase, *Register*, 75, 90, who refers to *Terrae Filius*, Nos. 29, 30, where Hole figures as Dr. Drybones. He left 100*l.* to the College.—T. Hoy, D.M. 1689, published his *Agathocles* 1683 ; Reg. Prof. Med. 1698–1718.—James Jeffreys, M.A. 1672, Preb. of Canterbury 1682, d. 1689.—John Inett, M.A. 1699, published *Origines Anglicanae* 1704-10. Precentor of Lincoln 1682, resigned 1687, d. 1718.—John Jones, D.M., published in 1700 *The Mysteries of Opium revealed.*—Zaccheus Isham, M.A. 1674, Preb. of Canterbury 1691, d. 1705.

323. 23. For Abraham Woodhead, see *Athenae*, iii. 1157.

324. 9. For Francis Lee, D.M., author of the *Life of Kettlewell, Apoleipomena*, &c., see Secretan's *Life of Nelson*, 69–71, where there is a mention of Mrs. Lead. Lee recanted his errors in his *History of Montanism* (1709). I did not notice in time that this letter by a slip of the pen was wrongly dated, and is consequently misplaced.

324. 10. W. Fulman (1632-1688 ; *Athenae*, iv. 239) was an antiquary of some distinction, and his collections are now in the Library of C.C.C. He was Hammond's amanuensis and the editor of his Works, and a suspicion that he may have been the author of the *Whole Duty* has probably occurred to every one who has made a careful study of the subject. There is, however, no evidence whatever to connect him with it.

324. 12. As to the Bill for the further Security of the Church of England upon the Union with Scotland, cf. Boyer, 277 *sq.*; Luttrell, vi. 133 *sqq., Life of Archbp. Sharp*, i. 390 *sqq.*; a proposal to expressly insert the Test Act as well as the Act of Uniformity was rejected in the Lords by some 30 votes, and in the Commons by 48.

325. 7. Milles's work, especially his insistence upon the misprint of 'Austin' for 'Justin,' is unfavourably criticised in Brokesby's *Life of Dodwell*, 529.

325. 42. Dr. Humfrey Humphries was Bp. of Hereford 1701-1710 : *Athenae*, iv. 896. There are several publications on the subject of St. Winifred's Well, at Holywell, Flintshire. Bp. Fleetwood published *The Life and Miracles of St. Wenefrede*, 1713 ; and I have seen a notice of a broadsheet, containing a Historical Description of the well. James II was surprised that Dr. Plot had never visited it (*Life of Wood*, 281).

326. 16. Anderdon, in his *Life of Ken* (p. 418, ed. 1 ; ii. 656 *sqq.*, ed. 2), denies that the *Letter to the author of a sermon entitled, 'a Sermon preached at the Funeral of her late Majesty, Q. Mary,'* afterwards reprinted under the title of *A Letter from a Prelate to a Prelate,* is justly attributed to Bp. Ken. The evidence of Dodwell, however (cf. p. 324, l. 5), seems to be conclusive as to Ken's authorship. See *Academy*, March 14, 1885.

327. 6. Phineas Bury was Proctor 1665.

Page 328, Line 5 *sqq.* A slightly varied account of the incidents related in the first few paragraphs is given in Isaaci Casauboni *Ephemerides*, 864 *sqq., s. a.* 1611.

329. 18. A complete list of Dodwell's publications is given by Hearne in the Introduction to *Henrici Dodwelli de Parma Equestri Dissertatio*, xiii–xxvii. It extends to 57 numbers. An abstract of the more important of them is given by Brokesby in his *Life of Dodwell*, to which it may be suspected that most readers at the present day are indebted for their knowledge of Dodwell's views.

330. 2. **John Richardson** does not appear in the list of incumbents of **Penwortham** (Baines' *History of the County . . of Lancaster*, 1870, ii. 151 *sqq.*). John Fleetwood, by a will made in 1657, left an endowment of 40*l. per annum* for 'a good, able, and sufficient preacher.'

330. 28. Hearne's remarks on this MS. are superseded by Mr. Macray's description with references, in *Annals of the Bodleian*, 20.

332. 14. **Joseph Harwar**, M.A. 1680, d. July 15, 1722.

334. 20. **Tho. Haywood**, M.A. 1702.

334. 23. **Wm. Jane**, Canon of Ch. Ch. 1680, Dean of Gloucester 1685, Preb. of Exeter 1703, Precentor and Treasurer 1704. His will was proved Nov. 10, 1707.— **Peter Foulkes**, Preb. of Exeter 1704; Canon of Ch. Ch. 1724, d. 1747.

334. 33. Dr. Plot gives an interesting description of the **Quintain** as practised in his time, and particulars of the observance of **Hook-day**, in his *Natural History of Oxfordshire*, 200 *sqq.*

334. 39. **Otto Mencke** (1644-1707) published Vol. i. of the *Acta eruditorum* at Leipzig in 1682.

336. 54. **Sir Chr. Hales** was returned for Coventry, but was unseated on petition Feb. 6, 1707, and was not re-elected. He had sat for Coventry in the Parliament of 1702.

337. 13. **Philip Code** (or Coode), M.A. 1698.

337. 15. **Tho. Dalton**, Queen's, B.A. 1702; All Souls, M.A. 1706.—**Charles Talbot** became Lord Chancellor and Baron Talbot of Hensol in 1733; d. 1737, aged 53. See Foss, *Biographia Juridica*, 646 *sqq.*

337. 25. There is an account of K. William's visit to Oxford in 1695 in a letter from Gibson to Charlett, Ballard MSS. v. 53.

337. 28. Cf. Luttrell, vi. 145, &c. **Francis Higgins**, Preb. of Ch. Ch. Dublin, 1705, Archdeacon of *Cashel* 1725, d. 1728 ; see Cotton, *Fasti Eccl. Hib.* ii. 66 *sqq.* ; Noble, ii. 115. He published a thanksgiving sermon 'for the success in forcing the enemies' lines in the Spanish Netherlands, under the command of the Duke of Marlborough,' and one on Rev. iii. 2, 3, suggesting that the Church was in danger, &c. He was again prosecuted in 1712 as ' a disloyal subject and a disturber of the public peace.'

337. 31. For **Cuffe** see Warton's *Life of Sir T. Pope*, 404 *sq.*

338. 16. **Nicholas Stratford**, D.D. 1673; Preb. of Lincoln 1670, Dean of St. Asaph 1674, Bp. of Chester 1689. For his works, chiefly polemical and directed against the Church of Rome, see *Athenae*, iv. 670.

338. 35. **John Thorpe**, M.A. 1704, father of the antiquary of the same name, published a volume of Scheuchzer's *Itinera Alpina tria* in 1708. Hearne has mentioned him and his work before.—**Zach. Babington**, Ch. Ch., M.A. 1669, published (1677) *Advice to grand jurors in Cases of Blood.*

339. 4. John Beaumont's *Historical, physiological, and theological Treatise of Spirits and Apparitions* appeared in 1705.

339. 14. Particulars of the block-books in the Bodleian are given in Macray's *Annals*, 321. Cf. *Caxton Celebration Catalogue*, 45 *sqq.* Hody's MS. *Collectanea* are contained in twenty-three volumes.

340. 21 *sqq.* **Wm. Greenwood**, M.A. 1701.—**Samuel Crooke**, St. John's, Cambridge, M.A. 1702.

INDEX.

END OF VOL. I.

www.ingramcontent.com/pod-product-compliance
Lightning Source LLC
Chambersburg PA
CBHW032338280326
41935CB00008B/370